The Quality Yearbook

1994

The Quality Yearbook

1994

James W. Cortada
John A. Woods

McGraw-Hill, Inc.
New York   San Francisco   Washington, D.C.   Auckland   Bogotá
Caracas   Lisbon   London   Madrid   Mexico City   Milan
Montreal   New Delhi   Paris   San Juan   Singapore
Sydney   Tokyo   Toronto

1 2 3 4 5 6 7 8 9 0   DOH/DOH   0 9 8 7 6 5 4 3

ISBN 0-07-024013-2

ISSN 1072-9135

The sponsoring editor for this book was James H. Bessent, Jr., and the production supervisor was Claire Huismann. It was composed by Impressions, a division of Edwards Brothers, Inc.

Printed and bound by R. R. Donnelley & Sons Company.

 This book is printed on recycled, acid-free paper containing a minimum of 50% recycled de-inked fiber.

Contents

PART THREE Implementing Quality

Preface

This is your annual review of quality management. Its purpose is to provide you with a single source of the current thinking on quality management principles and practices. Each year will bring a new edition with mostly new material, but that builds on previous years. Over time, we expect the subsequent editions to form a growing encyclopedia of quality management. Each year's edition will be fresh and current, but without dating previous volumes.

The need for such a book is great. Hundreds (if not thousands) of articles and books now appear each year on business practices. Yet none of us has time to read the best ones, let alone all of them. One goal for the yearbook is to gather the best articles and chapters in a single volume, while providing a detailed bibliography where you can find additional items to read.

The book is not intended just for use by TQM experts or quality assurance managers, though they will find it a valuable reference. Rather, we have targeted all managers and employees in all industries. The kinds of activities quality management concerns itself with are emerging as the best practices for all work activities. Therefore, we all can benefit by having a source that keeps us current on these practices. *The Quality Yearbook* succeeds or fails largely on whether it provides us all with an accurate reflection of our understandings of how organizations can best function.

The Quality Yearbook has two purposes:

1. To provide an *annual documentation* of the most useful ideas, tools, and articles in quality.
2. To serve as an *annual comprehensive reference* for finding information on activities, publications, awards, and organizations dealing with quality management.

Our Goals

Clearinghouse. Because there is so much coming out about quality, McGraw-Hill and the Editors of this book perceived a need for a kind of "clearinghouse" to which people from all different organizations might turn as a starting place to learn about current thinking in quality. *The Quality Yearbook* includes the best and most useful selection of information available. Its utility is founded on this premise, and its success will be a testament to how well we fill this need.

Lasting Value. Because it will be revised annually, *The Quality Yearbook* will focus on information that has come out in the period immediately preceding its publication. While currency is one of its strengths in this fast-changing field, each edition also is intended to have lasting value. Managers will find articles throughout the book that will continue to be applicable for several years as they go about implementing quality in their organizations. However, for all those actively engaged in the quality revolution, each year's edition will give them updates on all the book's content areas plus selected new topics that reflect the latest developments in the field.

Authoritative Review.   Yet another goal for *The Quality Yearbook* is to help develop clearer thinking about and implementation of quality principles. By providing managers and others interested in quality with an authoritative review of the latest discussions about the applications and extensions of these principles, each edition can help to standardize the categories into which we place our understandings.

Organization

We have divided *The Quality Yearbook* into four logical parts:

Part One, Background for Quality, provides a section on classics in quality to help you gain a sense of the roots of this approach to management. Included is an article on quality as a paradigm, followed by four classic excerpts from the works of Feigenbaum, Ishikawa, Juran, and Deming, the theorists most responsible for raising people's consciousness about quality.

Part Two, Quality by Industry, includes an anthology of articles and cases selected from a wide variety of current books, magazines, and journals that profile what is going on in quality in major industrial sectors that are pioneers in TQM: Manufacturing, Services, and the Public Sector.

Part Three, Implementing Quality, presents the best articles and ideas from the past year on the theory and techniques of quality management. We have broken the readings into four categories:

1.   Quality Transformation
2.   Quality Tools and Techniques
3.   Functional Processes
4.   Standards and Assessments

Part Three provides a wide spectrum of articles that explain the whys and hows of implementing quality, including many different examples from different industries.

Part Four, Quality References, provides additional information on the quality management movement in reference format:

■   A comprehensive annotated bibliography of books and articles, organized in the same way as *The Quality Yearbook*, current through late 1993.
■   An annotated directory of U.S. and international quality organizations, including addresses and phone numbers for getting more information.
■   A directory of quality awards that lists award categories, criteria, and how to apply.

- An annotated guide and rating of journals and magazines that regularly cover quality topics, including addresses and information on subscriptions.
- A guide to making training decisions for your organization.
- A special section on "quality quotes" for use in writing and speaking about quality management.
- A glossary of quality terms so complete that, by itself, it forms a small textbook on what quality management covers.
- A special section at the end of the book includes profiles of the 1993 Baldrige Award winners and the 1994 Baldrige Award criteria.

Criteria for Selection of Articles

We applied three prime criteria in choosing material for inclusion in *The Quality Yearbook*:

1. **Articles must be current**. Because this is an annual publication, part of its value comes from the timeliness of its content. Therefore, with few exceptions, the articles on industries, on management, and on quality techniques were published in 1993.
2. **Articles must be practical and help managers to solve problems and do their work more efficiently and effectively**. Articles selected represent the best thinking about how to implement quality solutions to the problems of managing the organization as a system designed to delight its customers. The principles of quality are not difficult to grasp. However, actually executing these principles is demanding and complex. The articles in this book are designed to ease that process. With that stated, it should be noted that this is not a book aimed at statisticians or engineers involved in the technical side of quality management.
3. **Articles must be authoritative.** There is a great deal to choose from in putting this type of book together. The articles and other materials that made the cut are ones that represent the best of their class, providing readers with a standard for reading and judging other materials.

Who Should Use This Book?

The Quality Yearbook will be very useful for quality professionals within businesses, government, and education, as well as for consultants assisting organizations in adapting quality principles. However, because it provides such a strong base for building one's understanding of quality principles, its value extends to people at all levels in all types of organizations. It will be a reliable source to consult to understand basic issues in quality and to find out from its various reference lists where to look next.

Using *The Quality Yearbook*

This book is not meant to be read cover-to-cover. We suggest that you peruse and read those parts of most interest and relevance to the situation and fields in which you are involved. Here are some examples of how various individuals might use it:

- An internal quality consultant will find the coverage on functional processes to be especially valuable in advising and helping others in the organization implement quality principles in their areas.
- A company CEO seeking to assist in creating a quality culture will find Part Three valuable in defining and implementing techniques to succeed in this undertaking.
- A private consultant will find the book useful in keeping up with and reviewing the latest understandings and ideas in quality.
- Any manager attempting to improve or reengineer processes will find specific information on how to undertake this task.
- A manager who is a novice to quality will find the broad coverage, bibliographies, and other reference material to be very useful in learning about and implementing this approach to organizations.

The Vision for This Book

This book is an evolving documentation of the quality revolution. We designed it to help people take part in this revolution. It will be improving continuously. We are including reply cards with each edition, and we seek suggestions, criticisms, reactions—feedback of all types—from users to help us make this ever more useful from year-to-year.

The principles and insights of quality are here to stay. This new understanding of management is already finding a place in all organizations. The vision of this annual publication is to help spread the word and ease its adaptation by every kind of organization.

*   *   *

A Note on Production

Nearly all the articles in this book and all the items listed in the bibliography were published in 1993. We have also included an overview of the 1994 Baldrige Award criteria and the 1993 Baldrige Award winners, which were not announced until late October 1993. We were able to do this in a 800 page book published in January 1994 by applying quality principles in its preparation.

We have worked as a team with McGraw-Hill to reduce cycle time substantially in production. Normally, to get a book out in January of any year would require that we finish the manuscript by June to get into the publisher's queue for its six-month production process. Instead, the editors, with the agreement of the publisher, worked with Impressions, a book production company in Madison, Wisconsin, to edit, design, compose, and prepare the final pages for printing simultaneously with the final writing and selection of materials. By doing this, we were able to reduce cycle time for all production work to two months.

Once we completed this process, we did a check and review on the whole production process, which will result in improvements and more efficiencies in the production of *The Quality Yearbook's* future editions.

Feedback from You

Besides doing a check and review of the production process, we also plan to regularly review the book's overall quality, that is, its value to you in learning about and implementing quality management in your organization.

You have a role to play in this. We have included feedback forms at the end of this book that ask you what you thought of it, what was of most value to you, and what you would like to see improved. Please fill out these forms, and let us know how our team can make this a more useful book to you. In next year's edition, we'll report on what we found out, and you'll see the improvements implemented.

Acknowledgments

This book was a big undertaking for us, and we are indebted to many people who have played a role in its coming together. First, we want to acknowledge Phil Ruppel and Jim Bessent at McGraw-Hill for suggesting we prepare this book and working with us in its development. Jim Bessent, our sponsoring editor, was especially helpful throughout in facilitating our relationship with McGraw-Hill.

We want to thank the editors and publishers of the several magazines, journals, and books from which we drew the articles that make up the heart of this book. All were very forthcoming in supplying the permissions that allowed us to reprint the pieces you see here. This group represents a wide spectrum of opinions and the leading publishers on quality topics today.

Curt Reimann and Harry Hertz of the National Institute of Standards and Technology (NIST) went out of their way to get us a copy of their article on the Baldrige award and ISO-9000 standards. We also want to thank Bob Chapman, senior economist at the NIST for rushing us the information on the 1994 Baldrige criteria and 1993 award winners we've profiled in the book.

In selecting articles for the K-12 education section, we want to thank David Bayless, Gabriel Massaro, and Nancy Roche for suggesting several articles to include in this section. They are consultants working with several school districts in implementing quality management. They can be reached through Bayless & Associates at P.O. Box 14389, Research Park Triangle, NC 27709.

Ron Heilman, head of the Center for Quality and Production at the University of Wisconsin, Milwaukee, and a founder of First in Quality, Milwaukee's quality initiative (one of the best in the United States) supplied us with a summary of where quality management is going in higher education. Ron has been helpful in many other ways throughout the project.

At Impressions, we were fortunate to work with Cynthia Horton and Joyce Jackson, and to have Claire Huismann as the production manager for our book. Turning a manuscript into a book involves a mass of details, and she kept track of these in a way that allowed us to successfully meet our goal for reducing the cycle time for production. She was a pleasure to work with.

We would like to acknowledge Brian Joiner, Peter Scholtes, Lynda Finn, and others at Joiner Associates from whom we have upgraded our understanding of quality principles. Surinder Batra, at the IBM Baldrige-winning plant in Rochester, Minnesota, helped us with ISO-9000 issues. We learned a great deal about process reengineering from three IBMers: Robin Lehnert, Kris Hafner, and Jim Purtell. Tom Jenks, of the IBM Consulting Group, taught us about effective measurements. Valerie A. Zeithaml further impressed us with what "voice of the customer" means.

Finally, we want to thank our wives and children for their encouragement while making it possible for us to spend many weekends and evenings together working on this book. Their contribution is as important as any we have had.

James W. Cortada
John A. Woods

PART ONE

Background for Quality

Quality management has gained more and more prominence over the past decade and for good reason: It is a more realistic approach to efficiently delivering products and services that people value. And it does this by empowering employees, emphasizing teamwork, and using a sound scientific approach to continuously improve how work gets done. One purpose of this book is to provide up-to-date documentation of the many ways managers of all kinds of organizations are applying TQM principles and tools to all facets of work.

To provide a foundation for the many articles that follow in this edition of *The Quality Yearbook*, you'll first find what we hope is a thought-provoking essay on what TQM is all about and why this approach to management is often misunderstood. This is followed by a special collection of what we call "Classics in Quality," excerpts from the books of some of quality management's leading thinkers.

The Classics

We decided to include these excerpts from some of the classics in quality because we feel it's important, interesting, and vital to learn about and read the work of the pioneers in total quality management. We selected the pieces that follow to give you just a taste of what these writers have had to say about fundamental principles of quality, principles on which everything else in this book is based.

W. Edwards Deming, Joseph M. Juran, Armand V. Feigenbaum, and Kaoru Ishikawa, the authors of the works selected, are all of equal stature (if not renown) in developing the theory and practices that make up the heart of quality management. They have long understood the value of the insights this approach to understanding organizations provides. Each has dedicated his career to studying and communicating the ideas of quality management. Their goal in doing this has been to help all organizations continuously improve their ability to serve customers. They know that quality management practices are the best way to create the mutually beneficial alliance between customers and companies that allows organizations to survive and grow in an unforgiving competitive environment.

Each writer has his own slant on things. We think you will find this material fascinating reading and very up to date. And while the copyrights of the books from which these excerpts come are all reasonably current (except 1964 for the Juran excerpt), remember that each of these writers actually began articulating these ideas in the forties and early fifties. It has just taken us until the nineties to start hearing them in earnest.

TQM: What's It Really All About?

John A. Woods

His answer was an old one belonging to a philosophic school that called itself *realism*. "A thing exists," he said, "if a world without it can't function normally. If we can show that a world without Quality functions abnormally, then we have shown that Quality exists whether it's defined or not."

— Robert Pirsig
Zen and the Art of Motorcycle Maintenance

There are any number of articles about Total Quality Management (TQM) not being all it's cracked up to be. Companies try it, and things are no better than they were before. It's just another gimmick, a quick fix that doesn't fix anything. People implement process analysis and teams; they try listening to their customers; they start statistically measuring everything to better control activities; they look for benchmarks; they empower people; they try to reduce cycle time; they try to practice Plan, Do, Check, Act (PDCA), and the results don't seem to be there. So what's going on?

What's going on is this. There is a profound misunderstanding of Total Quality Management by both practitioners and its critics. On the surface, this approach to management seems like it is about *doing* the things listed above. In fact, that is not what it is about. TQM is about understanding the nature of organizations and their role in the larger society in which they exist. Let me reiterate that: TQM is about *understanding the nature of organizations and their work.*

Paradigms

You will often hear the word *paradigm* used when describing Total Quality Management. Advocates for TQM say it is a new paradigm managers must adopt. That is true as far as it goes. What is unspoken is that you somehow have a choice about whether you will adopt this paradigm. You can continue to do what you already do or you can adopt the new way, the quality way, to manage your organization. This is where the misunderstanding starts.

Paradigms do not describe options. They explain things. They provide ways to order and make sense of our experience. They provide a context for understanding phenomena. Every discipline incorporates a model or paradigm for interpreting data. These models are revised, thrown out, or accepted based on how well they explain what we observe. In the early twentieth century, modern physics emerged as a better way to explain physical observations than

Paradigms do not describe options.

Newtonian physics. In psychology, understanding the brain, its chemistry, and the complex biology of this organ is replacing Freudian and other psychoanalytic models for understanding and dealing with psychotic (as well as normal) behavior. Would you think that today's physicists have an option about whether to adopt the modern physics paradigm?

A good paradigm, regardless of the discipline, often does not just replace another paradigm, it *subsumes* it. This means the new paradigm is more complete, takes in more possibilities, and explains observations better. Finally, it allows us to act in ways that are more likely to achieve the results we want and expect. This is the real power of a paradigm. *It affects how we behave, and it helps explain the results we get.* The point is that if you aren't aware of the new paradigm or don't understand it, you will be using some other one that explains things less effectively. Therefore, you will act in ways consistent with this less effective paradigm, and your results are likely to be less satisfactory than the results of those who are aware of the new more complete model and make the appropriate changes in their behavior. W. Edwards Deming, in his inimitable style, says simply, "Theory [he uses the word "theory" for the idea of paradigm] is a window into the world. Theory leads to prediction. Without theory, experience and examples teach us nothing."[1]

Better paradigms help us understand and deal with the world more accurately, realistically, and effectively.

Thomas Kuhn, the author most often credited with the exploration of the importance of paradigms in science, illustrates a change toward a more effective paradigm in this way: "Looking at the moon, the convert to Copernicanism does not say, 'I used to see a planet, but now I see a satellite.' That locution would imply a sense in which the Ptolemaic system had once been correct. Instead, a convert to the new astronomy says, 'I once took the moon to be a planet, but I was mistaken.' "[2] That's a somewhat esoteric quote, but it is from an authority, and it illustrates the point I wish to make here. Better paradigms help us understand and deal with the world more accurately, realistically, and effectively.

Let's take an example from sports. Many golfers have a problem with slicing the ball when they drive off the tee (for non-golfers, that's having the ball curve off to the right and into the rough rather than the fairway). This is frustrating to say the least. But there is a truism about golf: "The ball goes where you hit it." Metaphorically, this statement is a paradigm for understanding why a ball goes straight or curves. If players want to stop slicing and start hitting straight, this paradigm tells them they have to change the way they address the ball and swing the club. This will alter the club's angle of impact with the ball, and when done right, cause the ball to fly straight. If players who slice do not understand this "paradigm" and incorrectly think that the direction of the ball is the result, for example, of how they turn their bodies during the swing, they will continue to have problems. Now this

---

1. W. Edwards Deming, *The New Economics For Industry, Government, Education,* Cambridge, MA: MIT Center for Advanced Engineering Study, 1993, p. 106.

2. Thomas S. Kuhn, *The Structure of Scientific Revolutions, Second Edition, Enlarged,* Chicago: University of Chicago Press, 1970, p. 115.

doesn't mean they can't play, but it does mean that they won't score as well as those who can hit straight. If a golfer, through instruction and experience, comes to understand the golf paradigm and learns to make adjustments to hit the ball straight, he or she will become a better player.

The Organization as a System

What's the relation of these ideas to TQM? In terms of organizations and their management, those who understand the TQM paradigm grasp the insight it provides into *organizations as systems.* Further, they understand that what systems do is *transform and add value to inputs to create outputs that solve the problems of some group of customers.* You can misunderstand and act as if an organization were not a system, but that does not change the fact that this concept is a very powerful metaphor for *defining* what an organization is and does.

In less competitive markets and times, managers could ignore the insight that organizations are systems and do OK, but this affects an organization's efficiency and ability to deliver products and services that delight customers. And it makes organizations vulnerable to others that are more efficient and effective at determining customer needs and then meeting them. Recent history validates how vulnerable many companies have become. In terms of our golf analogy, you might do fine against your opponents when everyone else also slices. However, when you encounter a golfer who really understands that the ball just goes where you hit it and has adjusted his or her swing and is now a straight hitter, you're going to have a problem competing.

Managers may believe that the hierarchical model with a focus on holding individuals accountable for accomplishing organizational goals is the best way to keep things together and get results. However, this does not change the fact that this is *not* the best way if the quality paradigm is accurate. In other words, if the organization *really is a system, whether managers realize this or not,* then the hierarchical model is not the best way to get the most out of organizational resources, that is, to profitably delight customers so the organization will continue into the future.

This is an important point. If the quality paradigm has value, it is not just in telling what you should do, but also in helping you grasp what you are already doing. In other words, quality is not a set of procedures but a way to understand procedures and which ones work well and which ones work poorly and why. It provides a context for making sense of the behavior and existence of all organizations. Paraphrasing Thomas Kuhn, the convert to the TQM paradigm does not say, "I used to see an organization as a hierarchy, but now I see it as a system." Instead, the convert to quality says, "I once took an organization to be a hierarchy, but I was mistaken."

From this perspective, all organizations are "quality" organizations. The only item at issue is whether managers realize this or not and, therefore, how well managers perform. For example, the Chrysler Corporation has always been a system that takes inputs and transforms and adds value to them to serve the transportation needs of customers. That is what it was in the late seventies when it almost died, and that it is what it is today as it successfully launches the new LH car line. The difference is that back in the seventies, the system was working very poorly, and now it's working a lot better. Back then, Chrysler managers did not understand that their company was a system whose purpose is solving personal transportation problems, and today it appears they do.

What I have just suggested is that all organizations are systems, whether their managers and employees understand that or not. So what is a system? In his book *System Requirements Analysis*, Jeffrey Grady describes a system in this way: "In the broadest sense any two or more objects interacting cooperatively to achieve some goal or purpose constitute a system." He goes on to say, "The key to system existence, and the superior performance of a system over an unorganized collection of independent objects, is the cooperative interaction among the multiple system resources [to attain a goal]."[3] Let's use that as our starting point.

Few people would argue that the idea of an organization, at its heart, implies this notion of cooperative interaction among members to attain some goal. After all, if there is no cooperation, little of value will get done. So it seems reasonable to suggest that defining an organization as a system is accurate. And this is one of the characteristics of an organization that the Total Quality Management paradigm helps us to recognize. Organizations are not systems because TQM says they are. Rather, *the TQM paradigm simply points this out.* Given this system view of organizations, the next issue is to determine how a system works to achieve its purpose.

> Organizations are not systems because TQM says they are. Rather, *the TQM paradigm simply points this out.*

The System and Its Purpose

But before looking at how a system works, let's first reflect on what an organization's *purpose* is. The following may seem like Commonsense 101, but it is useful to review anyway. Edward O. Wilson, in his Pulitzer Prize-winning book, *On Human Nature*, states that "Reciprocation among distantly related or unrelated individuals is the key to human society."[4]

Without getting too academic, Wilson's point is that reciprocation or *exchange and specialization* are the foundation of our society and civilization. By organizing ourselves, we can use our individual and complementary skills and resources to create things to exchange with others in our society (and, today, around the world). This specialization allows us to make much better use of resources and time to the mutual benefit of us all—customers and organizations.

Of course, central to making this work is that to bring about exchanges, we have to deliver something that others will value, want, and have the funds to buy. It's useful here to remember what constitutes value. Ted Levitt reminds us that people "do not choose to buy a particular product; they choose

---

3. Jeffrey O. Grady, *System Requirement Analysis*, New York: McGraw-Hill, Inc., 1993, p. 2.
4. Edward O. Wilson, *On Human Nature*, New York: Bantam Books, 1979, p. 163.

to buy the functional expectations they attach to it, and they buy these expectations as 'tools' to help them solve the problems of life."[5] The point is that organizations survive, prosper, or die depending on how well they create products and services others will value as "tools to help them solve the problems of life."

If that sounds like the TQM idea that "quality is defined by the customer," it is. But in actuality, this is not a TQM idea. It is a recognition of the way things work by those who have articulated the TQM paradigm. Remember, if TQM is a valid and useful way to make sense of organizations, it will give us insight into what actually is going on. Quality has always been defined by the customer, but in less demanding times, we did not need to know that to succeed. Now success requires that we understand this, and the quality paradigm merely recognizes this point.

Processes

Now that we've seen how organizations are systems, let's look in more detail at what characterizes a system and how to make it work well. I have said already that in a system there is cooperative interaction to attain a goal. What illustrates this interaction? The usual way of describing it is as a *process*. A process is the steps that depict how the system achieves its objective. McDonald's and Burger King are systems for creating good, but generally unhealthy, food using highly refined production processes that guarantee speed and consistency of output. The central part of their processes has to do with how the meat is cooked, how the sandwich is constructed, how it is packaged, how it is kept hot, and numerous other steps. The people responsible for executing these steps become expert at them.

Quality has always been defined by the customer, but in less demanding times, we did not need to know that to succeed.

To illustrate processes or the steps in accomplishing a task, people often use flow charts with each box representing a step in the process. Instead of using a flow chart, we could simply list the steps. However, we don't have to do either; charts and lists are simply useful to better understand how to accomplish some task. Charts are especially beneficial when a process has many steps. W. Edwards Deming talks about charts and processes in this way: "Every activity, every job is a part of a process. A flow diagram of any process will divide the work into stages. The stages as a whole form a process." He then states, "Each stage works with the next stage and with the preceding stage toward optimum accommodation, all stages working together toward quality that the ultimate customer will boast about."[6] But, again, though such charts are useful and convenient, they are not necessary for there to be a process. The point to remember is that without a process, efficient or inefficient, nothing gets accomplished.

---

5. Theodore Levitt, *Marketing for Business Growth*, New York: McGraw-Hill Book Company, 1974, p. 253.
6. W. Edwards Deming, *Out of the Crisis*. Cambridge, MA: Massachusetts Institute of Technology Center for Advanced Engineering Study, 1986, p. 87.

So all organizations have processes, stated or unstated, documented or undocumented, to get work done. They go through a series of steps, taking capital, raw materials, time, and labor and transform these into something of value for customers. A focus on processes is a central notion of TQM. TQM suggests that managers should carefully analyze the processes in their organization to understand how the work gets done.

Since organizations are systems with processes, and TQM is a paradigm for making sense of organizations, we should not be so surprised that a concern with process would be an important aspect of the TQM model. Stated differently, managers should not be interested in processes because TQM says they should. They should be interested in processes because that is necessary to make sense of how work gets done and how to do things better. The TQM paradigm just acknowledges this fact of organizational life and brings it to our attention in no uncertain terms. And if the paradigm is a realistic description of organizations, this is just what we should expect it to do.

In Japan, the concept KAIZEN or *improvement* is at the heart of the way they manage organizations. Masaaki Imai, in his best-selling book on this concept, says, "The implications of [KAIZEN] in Japan have been that this concept has helped Japanese companies generate a *process-oriented* way of thinking and develop strategies that assure continuous improvement involving people at all levels of the organizational hierarchy."[7] In other words, facilitating KAIZEN *requires* that managers consciously be aware of processes if they want to make improvements.

Organizations as Systems: Implications

So let's summarize. *All* organizations are systems (people and resources interacting cooperatively to achieve a goal) with processes (the steps involved in that cooperative interaction) with the purpose of creating products and services that customers will want and pay for. These are the basic insights into organizations that the TQM paradigm articulates. It is from these insights that people like W. Edwards Deming, Joseph Juran, Kaoru Ishikawa, and many others have suggested ways to manage organizations that are consistent with this paradigm. There is little arbitrariness in the procedures and methods they prescribe. They are like a doctor who knows that an antibiotic is the best thing to prescribe for a severe bacterial infection. This is not an arbitrary decision the physician makes. It is consistent with an understanding of how antibiotics interact with the human body to quell infections. Similarly, suggested TQM procedures are consistent with an understanding of how to improve the processes that define how a purposeful organization (i.e., a system) works.

---

7. Masaaki Imai, *KAIZEN: The Key to Japan's Competitive Success,* New York: McGraw-Hill Publishing Company, 1986, p. 4.

Deming, for example, was able to make his contribution not from the experience of being a high-powered business manager, but as a statistician. What he grasped early in his career is the value of *statistics as a tool* for measuring the output of processes within a system. When he looked at systems made up of people, that is, organizations, this led him, step-by-step, into figuring out just what it is that characterizes such systems and how to make them work most efficiently and effectively and improve through time. His ideas, along with those of Juran and others, about how to make the organization continuously work better to meet customer needs have come to be identified as "Total Quality Management."[8] Armand Feigenbaum, another of the founders of the modern quality management movement, defines TQM and its procedures in this way: "The total composite product and service characteristics of marketing, engineering, manufacture, and maintenance through which the product and service in use will meet the expectations of the customer."[9] It is important to appreciate that such definitions and subsequent prescriptions for management simply emerge as the most logical approach to take when you have the systems view of an organization. In other words, what the TQM paradigm provides, beyond its insight into the nature of organizations, is sound direction for determining how to make them work better.

The central focus of that working better is on the processes involved in transforming inputs into outputs that delight customers. Whether it seems immediately apparent or not, everything you read here and in every book on quality (indeed, every book on business), when boiled down to its essence, is about leading, analyzing, measuring, and improving those transformation processes that characterize what organizational work is (even when they never say that in so many words). That idea encompasses all the specific activities and more that are now identified with TQM and that I mentioned at the beginning of this article. These include: statistical process control, cross-functional teamwork, re-engineering, benchmarking, listening to the voice of the customer, driving fear from the workplace, quality function deployment, cycle time reduction, and many others.

Organizations that consciously and intelligently practice Total Quality Management undertake these kinds of activities *not* because it is a good idea to do so nor because some quality expert told them to. They selectively undertake these activities because they *know* that is how to learn about and manage the processes that characterize their work. Further, they know that these are the activities that direct everyone toward the continuous improve-

Everything you read here and in every book on quality (indeed, every book on business), when boiled down to its essence, is about leading, analyzing, measuring, and improving those transformation processes that characterize what organizational work is.

---

8. It is interesting to note that Deming himself does not refer to his ideas as TQM. He finds that to be a restrictive term that pigeonholes his work and prescriptions in an inappropriate manner. The point for this article is that the ideas of Deming and others are identified as TQM, and this article's fundamental premise that TQM is the most realistic approach to take to management is consistent with Deming's view.

9. Armand V. Feigenbaum, *Total Quality Control, Third Edition, Revised.* New York: McGraw-Hill, Inc., 1991, p. 7.

ment of those processes so as to improve productivity and maintain the company's competitive edge.

TQM, Systems, and Traditional Management

Fundamentally, the actions suggested by the TQM paradigm should not be unfamiliar to managers, even those working in the most tradition-bound organizations. I have already pointed out that whether a manager acknowledges it or not, organizations *are* systems with processes for getting work done. If you reflect for a minute, you can see that this is true and that what managers do is manipulate processes, consciously or unconsciously, skillfully or erratically, to get work done. What TQM does is point this out.

The questions for the traditional manager, once exposed to the insights of TQM, are (1) how well am I doing at making my company's processes work well? And (2) how well am I doing at rapidly improving these processes so we can perform and compete better and better? The answer to these questions is usually, "Not very well when one assumes the organization is a hierarchy with little focus on cooperative interaction and heavy emphasis on individual accountability for results." There is a reason for this. The hierarchical results-directed approach to managing a system is not process oriented. If organizations were really hierarchies and individuals really had control over getting things done as independent agents, then the traditional approach would be the best way to manage. However, since this approach limits the productivity of a system, we should not be surprised at the inability of such companies to compete effectively against the Japanese, for example, who are guided by the principles of KAIZEN and TQM.

Before Xerox understood the implications of the TQM paradigm for increasing productivity and delighting its customers, it was considered a well-managed company in the traditional sense. But in the 1970s Japanese companies began to take serious market share from Xerox. David Kearns, the former chairman of Xerox, tells of this in his recent memoirs:

> Whereas most American corporations were advancing 2 or 3 percent a year in productivity, we were achieving gains of 7 or 8 percent. But despite these gains, the Japanese continued to price their products substantially below us. We kept wondering: how were they doing it? Our team went over everything in a thorough manner. It examined all the ingredients of cost: turnover, design time, engineering changes, manufacturing defects, overhead ratios, inventory, how many people worked for a foreman, and so forth. When it got done with its calibrations, we were in quite a shock. Frank Pipp [a Xerox executive] remembers the results as being "absolutely nauseating. It wasn't a case of being out in left field. We weren't even playing the same game."[10]

---

10. David T. Kearns and David A. Nadler, *Prophets in the Dark: How Xerox Reinvented Itself and Beat Back the Japanese*, New York: HarperBusiness, 1992, p. 121.

Xerox finally discovered that its approach to getting things done was simply not the best way to manage a *system*. That's what the Japanese knew as well. They understood the implications of TQM for managing their systems to create products that customers wanted, and that's why they were eating Xerox's lunch in the copier marketplace.

I don't want to belabor this point, but it is at the heart of this article. If organizations are systems, you do not have a choice about whether focusing on process management is what you should do. That is what managers do, whether they are aware of it or not. Remember what I said earlier, *paradigms do not describe options*. Traditional business assumptions and practices with their focus on individuals and arbitrary expected results make for very poor management of processes and therefore, ironically, erratic results and performance in the marketplace. TQM conversely, with its focus on process and delighting customers, suggests ways to maximize system efficiency and effectiveness and therefore success in the marketplace.

> If organizations are systems, you do not have a choice about whether focusing on process management is what you should do.

For managers to implement TQM *procedures* without an understanding of the paradigm that gives meaning to these procedures does not bode well for the success of these efforts. It seems in this country we are constantly looking for the magic answer to all our problems. The latest answer for managing organizations is TQM. But in actuality the TQM paradigm does not give us the answers. What it does do, though, is help managers ask the right questions and therefore begin to figure out in each situation what they should do.

TQM: Getting It

No one can force managers to change their beliefs about whether TQM is the best paradigm and set of procedures to help make an organization more productive and successful in the marketplace. You may or may not believe that the TQM paradigm better explains organizations and their work. However, I hope you will reflect on the ideas presented here and those available from many other sources in light of your own experience. Think deeply about whether the systems and processes explanation of organizations and their purpose helps you gain better insight into your experience. If it does, then you will appreciate the value of the TQM paradigm and its suggested methods and tools for better understanding and managing the processes that make up organizational work.

> The TQM paradigm does not give us the answers. What it does do, though, is help managers ask the right questions.

In his book *The Fifth Discipline*, Peter Senge speaks of metanoia, a profound shift in the way we view and order our lives. In experiencing such a shift, Senge suggests that we learn in the deepest ways to "reperceive the world and our relation to it."[11] I think TQM requires such a metanoia. Without appreciating this shift of view, the methods and procedures of TQM will not work well for you. And with such a shift, literally a metanoia, they cannot fail to begin making things work better for you both personally and

---

11. Peter M. Senge, *The Fifth Discipline: The Art and Practice of the Learning Organization*, New York: Doubleday Currency, 1990, p. 14.

organizationally. That is what the Japanese know, and that is what Baldrige Prize-winning companies like Xerox, Motorola, and Ritz Carlton know.

In the book *Making Quality Work*, we read of a conversation the authors had at the Kansai Electric Company, a Deming Prize-winner in Japan: " 'Some IBM executives were here on a study visit just yesterday,' one Kansai executive noted. 'They told us that, at IBM, total quality management is seventy percent attitude and only thirty percent quality control technique.' He then frowned and silently shook his head. We could guess what he was thinking. Such a 'soft' approach to managing quality might be acceptable but it would never pass muster in Japan. We were wrong. 'In Japan,' the Kansai executive concluded, 'total quality management is *ninety* percent attitude.' "[12]

> 'In Japan,' the Kansai executive concluded, 'total quality management is *ninety* percent attitude.'

Everything that you read about TQM and its effective implementation depends on that attitude. Like everything else, if TQM has utility, if, in the words of Ted Levitt, it helps you solve the problems of life, then you will see its value. Then you will successfully learn and adapt its methods to your work.

* * *

These Ideas and *The Quality Yearbook*

We have designed *The Quality Yearbook* to help you sort through the most current thinking and applications of these principles in all kinds of private and public organizations. The ideas presented are not difficult to understand. They intuitively make sense. However, taking advantage of these insights to improve the practice of management takes great effort, discipline, dedication, and vigilance.

A quality consultant friend to whom I showed this article told me managers at one of her client companies could sit around all day talking about the merits of the systems approach to understanding organizations, but this didn't seem to affect the way they managed. This client was an aluminum smelter, and despite their buying into these ideas, she observed it didn't keep them from

- having various parts of the organization compete for putting out more aluminum than the other parts
- keeping a dirty and disorganized workplace
- not providing adequate work tools to employees
- having unstandardized processes
- having poor relations between management and labor.

The problem was that they could not make the connection between this theory and its application to their work. They failed to understand the importance of optimizing their system and to learn the practical methods and hard work of how to do it. We contend that the basic insights this article

---

12. George Labovitz, Yu Sang Chang, & Victor Rosansky, *Making Quality Work*, New York: HarperBusiness, 1993, pp. 1-2.

describes are vital to really understand the contributions of TQM to effective management practice, and that these managers did not *really* comprehend them. If they had, they wouldn't have behaved as they did. However, after you get these insights in your guts, you've got to work at implementing them every day to see the difference they can make in improving the efficiency of your work and the delight of your customers.

This book can give you some direction for doing this. Our goal is to expose you to a wide array of areas in which TQM is making a positive difference in organizational and individual performance. We hope it will help you learn about some quality tools and the functional areas in which you can use these tools. As a reference and guide to TQM, we think you'll find this book a valuable resource, a book to which you will turn first for a sense of what's going on and where you can get more information.

Feedback

As with any product, in using this book, you'll learn two things about it: One is how helpful it is, and the other is how helpful it isn't. We want to solicit your comments, feedback, criticisms, and suggestions for improving the book. You are our customers, and we know that we succeed as a supplier of TQM information to the degree that we give you the information you need in a format that makes it accessible and easy to use. Please invest the time to fill in the feedback form bound into this book. It's postage paid and will help us both. Thanks for your business and best wishes for the successful implementation in your organization of the insights and methods TQM teaches us.

CLASSICS IN QUALITY

Quality—A Major Business Strategy

Armand V. Feigenbaum

This excerpt from Armand Feigenbaum's definitive textbook on quality control, first published in 1951, provides useful insights into the strategic implications of quality management and its effect on any company's profitability.

Quality—A Major Business Management Strategy

Because quality is a crucial hinge for business success or failure in today's quality-performance-oriented markets, it has become a major business strategic area in itself and a significant factor in what has come to be called "business strategic planning." The key is that quality control must be structured explicitly and measurably so as to contribute to business profitability and positive cash flow.

The principal characteristic of orienting quality as a primary business strategy is that the quality-control program must foster sound business growth strongly and positively. It must provide major competitive advantage to the company.

Quality leadership for a firm means a commitment to the engineering, production, and sale of products which consistently will perform correctly for buyers when first purchased and which, with reasonable maintenance, will continue to perform with very high reliability and safety over the product life. This is a much more basic and much more demanding business goal than

---

traditional policy, termed "customer quality satisfaction," which in some firms has primarily meant that product service and technical assistance will be readily available to customers. The policy that a firm "will always fix the product so that it will work again for the buyer" is honorable and important. However, it represents a policy of customer service to deal with after-sales aspects of product problems; it does not represent modern quality strategic leadership in the marketplaces served by the company.

Two basic general management steps are required to establish quality as the necessarily strong business strategic area it must be in a company today:

- The total-customer-satisfaction-oriented concept of quality, together with reasonable costs of quality, must be established as one of the primary business and product planning and implementation goals and performance measurements of the marketing, engineering, production, industrial relations, and service functions of the company.
- Assuring this customer-satisfaction quality and cost result must be established as a primary business goal of the quality program of the company and of the quality-control function itself—not some narrower technical goal restricted to a limited technical or production-oriented quality result.

A case in point is the development and introduction of new products so as better to serve old and new markets. In the past, quality-control programs usually directed their attention to assuring that unsatisfactory new products would *not* be shipped to customers—even though this meant schedule delays and inability to meet new markets on time and at a given price—and these continue to be vital and necessary quality-control objectives. But quality-control programs now must also be much more effective in assisting the company to assure that these new products *will* be shipped without the likelihood of these delays and costs.

The emphasis of quality-control programs must expand from the concentration upon feedback— to concentration also upon feedforward.

From a technical point of view, this means that the emphasis of quality-control programs must expand from the concentration upon feed*back*—so that unsatisfactory product does not go to market—to concentration also upon feed*forward*—so that both the unsatisfactory product is not likely to proceed very far in the first place and that a *satisfactory* product will be the concentration of product development.

Moreover, while improvements that are directly quality-oriented are the major targets of such strategic planning, many other company activities are favorably impacted by strong quality control because often what improves quality also simultaneously improves many other areas of the company. Indeed, quality-control programs have a positive impact that is very broad and very deep. Quality therefore provides a major "focus" and managerial "handle" for getting at major improvement areas throughout the company.

Major Business Requirements

Profit Strategy	Reduced Cycle Times	Marketplace Response	Resource Utilization	**Planned Business Contributions**
	X	X		Much higher quality levels in new product introduction.
X	X		X	Reduced new product introduction time cycles. Quicker response to market changes.
X		X		Greater effectiveness in meeting increasing quality competition.
X				Substantial improvements in quality costs as an aid to profitability.
X				Indirect labor reductions. Many fewer people can maintain quality.
			X	Much improved opportunities in employee work structuring, self-steering, and motivation.
	X	X		Much better control over product design modifications and performance.
		X		Stronger, more visible posture for meeting regulatory standards, safety and consumerist requirements.
		X		Stronger, more visible quality programs as marketing and technical aids
X			X	Greater opportunities for improved manageability and management control of operations.
	X		X	Even more systematic basis for delegation of authority.
		X		Improved assurance in product service in the dealer situation.
X		X	X	Reduced frequency and expense of field quality problems.

Figure 1. **Business strategic areas of quality programs.**

Figure 1 illustrates the business strategic impact areas of the quality program of a large consumer durable manufacturing corporation with regard to the major business requirements of:

- Profit strategy
- Reduced cycle times
- Marketplace response
- Resource utilization

The quality program is thus specifically established as one of the principal areas in the business strategic planning and policy of the company and a major area in the modern business management concept.

The Place of Total Quality Control in the Modern Business Management Concept: Profitability and Positive Cash Flow

The major new business strategic importance of quality has made it a central area of direct and explicit management attention today. Business managers are aware of the axiom that salability plus producibility plus productivity equals profitability. It takes but a moment's reflection to realize that total quality control contributes substantially to each element in this business formula.

Salability is enhanced through total quality control in that the balancing of various quality levels and the cost of maintaining them are market-planned in an organized manner. The result is that the manufactured product really can meet the customer's wants *both* in the satisfactory function of the product and the price that must be paid for it.

Producibility is improved because quality control offers guidance, based on quality experience, to the designing engineer while new products are being developed and to the manufacturing engineer while their production is being planned. Such guidance takes many forms, for example, consideration of the relationship between new design standards and the quality capabilities of the manufacturing plant.

Productivity is increased by emphasizing the positive control of quality rather than after-the-fact detection and rework of failures. The amount of salable production that comes off the assembly line becomes much higher than it would otherwise be, without increasing a penny in the cost of production or increasing a single unit in the rate of production. Furthermore, positive action taken in the incoming-materials area frequently increases the production rate of the manufacturing equipment itself because defective purchased material is prevented from reaching the assembly line, where it will waste the efforts of skilled workers and expensive machines.

Thus, note that total quality control has a vigorous impact upon each of the three factors which influence profitability. Through careful analysis of customer wants and needs, the product can be provided with those qualities which motivate purchase by the customer and thus increase *salability*. When the quality of the product design and production process is established with *producibility* in mind, manufacturing costs can be substantially reduced and the possibility minimized of negative cost offsets such as costly product-recall action or very expensive product-liability suits. With the balanced manufacturing capability for quality production in place, *productivity* rises as costs per unit decrease. Thus, the industrial manager finds in total quality control a powerful new tool to increase the *profitability* and the positive cash flow of the business.

Business managers are aware of the axiom that salability plus producibility plus productivity equals profitability.

The Pareto Principle

J. M. Juran

Besides Deming, Joseph Juran is the most influential U.S. threoretician in quality management. This excerpt is from Managerial Breakthrough, *a book first published in 1964 that is as relevant and vital today as when it was published, probably more so. The book provides a down-to-earth review of the breakthroughs a manager must make to deal effectively with organizational systems. This piece describes the important analytical concept of the Pareto Principle, which he did so much to popularize.*

Vital Few and Trivial Many

A manager has an idea for Breakthrough: "Our inventory of finished goods is too big. Let's cut it." His staff meeting agrees—the attitude hurdle is cleared. So far, so good. We have moved from *whether* to cut inventories to *how* to cut inventories. Soon the question is asked, "What does our inventory consist of?" The Controller is given the job of answering this. He comes back with a table of figures, of which Table 1 is an extract.

We see from the Controller's figures:

1. Of the 500 catalogue items, the top 25, or 5 per cent of the *items*, account for 72 per cent of the *dollars*. We will call these 25 items the *vital few*.
2. The bottom 395, or 79 per cent of the items, account for only 5 per cent of the dollars. We will call these 395 items the *trivial many*.

The implications are profound. If, by magic, we could wipe out the last 79 per cent of the items completely, we would cut the total inventory by only 5 per cent. In contrast, if we could reduce the inventory level of the vital few, by just one-third, the result would be a rousing 24 per cent cut in the total inventory!

In other words, any real cut in inventory can come only out of the vital few.

To summarize what we just went through:

We started with 500 problems of reducing inventory—too many to get our arms around, so we listed these problems in their order of importance.

This listing showed that *as a practical matter*, we have only 25 problems, a number we *can* get our arms around.

If we could reduce the inventory level of the vital few, by just one-third, the result would be a rousing 24 per cent cut in the total inventory!

Table 1. **How Much Inventory**

Catalogue description	Dollars of inventory for this item	Numerical rank of this item	Cumulative percentage of items	Dollars, cumulative, for all items	Per cent of dollars, cumulative
A1 generators	$90,000	1	0.2	$ 90,000	9.0
A4 generators	60,000	2	0.4	150,000	15.0
QK motors	52,000	3	0.6	202,000	20.2
4F valves	7,400	25	5.0	720,000	72.0
K9 caps	27	105	21.0	950,000	95.0
MT sleeves	1	500	100.0	1,000,000	100.0

The generalization of the foregoing is what the author has called the Pareto principle. What we did was to:

1. Make a *written* list of all that stands "between us and making this change."
2. Arrange this list in *order of importance.*
3. Identify the *vital few* as projects to be dealt with individually.
4. Identify the *trivial many* as things to be dealt with as a class.

Universal Assortment; Universal Sorter

In the case just recited, a problem in inventory reduction exhibited a complex appearance—a wide assortment of obstacles to Breakthrough. The role of the Pareto principle was to sort these many obstacles into two piles, the vital few and the trivial many. (Once sorted, the two piles can be dealt with by means we will examine later.)

The role of the Pareto principle was to sort these many obstacles into two piles, the vital few and the trivial many.

The stunning thing is that *all* management attempts at Breakthrough face a wide assortment of obstacles, and that, on application of the Pareto principle, *all* these assortments exhibit the properties of the vital few and trivial many. The fact that these managerial problems exhibit this universal property makes the Pareto principle a universal tool for analysis. Like the Training Within Industry universal on How to Instruct, the Pareto principle is a universal for sorting any conglomerate mixture into two neat piles, the vital few and the trivial many.

Let's examine some cases in various management situations.

In the marketing function, any sales manager knows that customers are a mixture; a few per cent of them contribute most of the sales. In the sales manager's dialect, these vital few customers are "key accounts." For example,[1] a company with 389 customers found that:

1. Blecke, Curtis J., *National Association of Cost Accountants, N.A.C.A. Bulletin,* The Small Order Problem in Distribution Cost Control, Sec. 1, pp. 1279–1284, June, 1957.

The top 10 per cent of the customers accounted for 60 per cent of the total dollar sales.

The bottom 80 per cent of the customers accounted for 24.8 per cent of the dollar sales.

Customer orders also exhibit the principle of the vital few and trivial many. The same study showed that of a total of 2,753 orders:

The top 13 per cent of the orders resulted in 66 per cent of the sales dollars.

The bottom 68 per cent of the orders resulted in only 7.1 per cent of the sales dollars.

Figure 1 is an analysis of sales volume by product, and shows graphically the relationship of the vital few and trivial many. There are 39 products in the line. The top 6 products account for 72 per cent of the sales; the bottom 18 products account for less than 3 per cent of the sales.

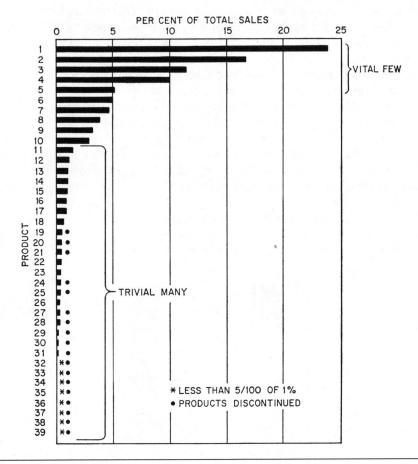

Figure 1. **Vital few and trivial many in the product line.**

The vital few (by other names) show up in other aspects of marketing. Analysis of sales volume of individual salesmen discloses who are the "star salesmen." Analysis of credit losses discloses who are the "deadbeats." Analyses of sales by territory, by marketing channel, and in still other ways, all exhibit the phenomenon.

One manager has a very simple way of dramatizing the Pareto principle. He draws the diagram of Fig. 2. He explains it as follows:

> The column on the left represents our total number of dealers, and the column on the right our total volume of business. The diagonal indicates that about 80 per cent of our customers give us less than 15 per cent of our volume.

The *manufacturing function* is well supplied with activities which exhibit a mixture of vital few and trivial many. One of the most exhaustively studied has been in connection with quality control. The "diseases" of the product, like the diseases of man, are highly concentrated as to their incidence. This is so whether the diseases are classified by product, by process, by cause, by defect name, by department, by operation, by operator, or by part number. To illustrate:

To production control the "vital few" are the "bottlenecks."

In an instrument company, of 85 product diseases in one department, the worst 3 accounted for 71 per cent of the losses due to defects. In a machine tool company, 2 of the 15 departments contributed over half the scrap and rework; one intricate part was the cause of 50 per cent of the loss.

In meeting delivery schedules, the Pareto principle is out in full force, although the dialect is again local. To production control men, the "vital few" are the "bottlenecks." A formalized approach (PERT) for predicting bottlenecks in complex system planning has coined the term "critical path" as a label for the vital few.

Cost of manufacture likewise can use the Pareto principle.

In one company, out of 250 catalogue items of expendable tools and supplies, the top 5 items, or 2 per cent, accounted for 64.9 per cent of the dollar

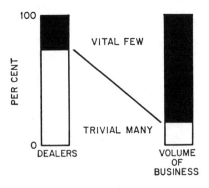

Figure 2. **A simple graph of the Pareto principle.**

cost. The lowest 95 percent of the items accounted for only 17.2 per cent of the dollar cost.

Requisitioning materials from stores is another instance. Analysis of size of requisitions in one company showed that:

> the top 3 per cent of the requisitions accounted for 62 per cent of the value of material requisitioned.
> the lowest 81 per cent of the requisitions accounted for only 5.5 per cent of the material requisitioned.

The same relationship holds for cost of maintenance and repairs. In one company, analysis of cost of maintenance by causes showed that:

> 6 per cent of the causes resulted in 83 per cent of all maintenance and repair charges. (In this company the lingo of the maintenance department referred to these vital few cases as "hospital jobs.")
> 76 per cent of the causes resulted in only 8 per cent of all maintenance and repair charges.

In the *personnel function* it is well known that employees are a mixture exhibiting the vital few and trivial many as to absences, accidents, tardiness, alcoholism, etc.[2]

In the *purchasing function* it is pretty well known that a few per cent of the orders account for the bulk of the money spent. This phenomenon becomes the basis for a graduated table of delegation as to whose signature is final on purchase requisitions.

But the matter does not end there. For example, a company studying some other aspects of purchasing found that:

> the worst 6 per cent of the vendors caused 81 per cent of the late deliveries.
> the worst 5 per cent of the vendors caused 87 per cent of the rejections for quality.

In the *purchasing function* it is pretty well known that a few per cent of the orders account for the bulk of the money spent.

In the *technical function* the universal mixture is likewise present, though not as fully explored as in other functions. The sales potential of new products is an example. The few big projects have more sales potential than a whole host of small ones. Analysis of the work done by service laboratories has often shown that there is a shocking amount of formulation, making of samples, etc., devoted to the trivial many orders.

In new product research and development there are always the vital few problems. The researcher's dialect is "critical" components, or the "state-of-

---

2. Even as to talkativeness. A researcher counted the number of times that people spoke in a 2-hour conference of eight persons. There were a total of 70 remarks. The most talkative man spoke up 41 times, the second 21 times. Together, these "vital few" made 62 of the 70 statements, or about 90 per cent of the total. The remaining six conferees, the trivial many, spoke a total of 8 times, with four of these conferees maintaining silence. (From American Management Association Production Series, No. 187, p. 39, 1949.)

the-art" components. These will take more effort than all the trivial many combined.

In the *financial function*, the assortments susceptible to the Pareto principle are legion, although many are known only to the accounting fraternity. For example:

At B.F. Goodrich Company, a study of vendors' invoices showed that:

(a) The top 11 per cent of the invoices accounted for 68 per cent of the dollars recovered because of vendors' errors.
(b) The lowest 34 per cent of the invoices accounted for only 1 per cent of the dollars recovered because of vendors' errors. This relationship was used in reducing the effort of checking. The vital few invoices continued to be checked in detail. The trivial many were put on a sampling basis.[3]

A similar study, with parallel results, is seen in the problem of aging of the 100,000 accounts receivable of a large department store.[4]

Cutting across all functions is the activity of *organization planning*. A basic concept here is the principle of delegation—that while there are myriads of decisions and actions to be taken, comparatively few of them need to engage the attention of the top men. In the dialect of the managers, these vital few are the basis of the "exception principle."

The principle is very old. An early example is charmingly related in the Old Testament. Following the exodus of the Israelites from Egypt, their leader Moses found himself the sole judge of the disputes which arose among the people. The number of such disputes was enough to make this solitary judge a bottleneck in decision making. In consequence, the people "stood by Moses from the morning into the evening," waiting for Moses to make decisions. Moses' father-in-law, Jethro, saw this spectacle and ventured advice. (For which Jethro has become regarded by some as the first management consultant on record.)

Jethro's advice	*Translated into modern management dialect*
"And thou shalt teach them ordinances and laws, and show them the way wherein they must walk, and the work they must do." (Exodus 18:30)	Establish policies and standard practices, conduct job training, and prepare job descriptions.

---

3. Buhl, William F., Statistical Controls Applied to Clerical and Accounting Procedures, *American Society for Quality Control Transactions*, 1955, pp. 9–26.

4. Trueblood, R. M, and R. M. Cyert, Statistical Sampling Applied to Aging of Accounts Receivable, *Journal of Accountancy*, March, 1954, pp. 293–298.

"Moreover thou shalt provide out of all the people able men, such as fear God, men of truth, hating covetousness, and place such over them, to be rulers of thousands, and rulers of hundreds, rulers of fifties and rulers of tens." (Exodus 18:21)

Set up an organization; first-line supervisors to have 10 subordinates; second-line supervisors to have 5 subordinates, etc.; appoint men who have supervisory ability.

"And let them judge the people at all seasons; and it shall be that every great matter they shall bring unto thee, but every small matter they shall judge; so it shall be easier for thyself, and they shall bear the burden with thee." (Exodus 18:22)

Institute delegation of authority; routine problems to be decided down the line, but exceptional problems to be brought to higher authority.

We can now summarize the foregoing. The vital few are everywhere, but masquerading under a variety of aliases. In their more benevolent forms they are known by such names as key accounts or star salesmen. In their weak moments they are known as the bottlenecks, chronic drinkers, deadbeats, Most Wanted Criminals, critical components.

We could go on and on. In preparing bids, experienced managers know that a few major components are decisive. The rest can be thrown in as a percentage. In valuing a plant, the experienced engineer singles out the major pieces of equipment and values them individually. The rest he figures as a percentage, or by studying a sample and applying the findings to all.

(We probably need a new name for the analysis that separates out the vital few. "Pareto analysis" is not very vivid, and it credits the wrong man anyhow.)

The trivial many are also everywhere. They are the cats and dogs of the product line, the nuts and bolts of the inventory, the small customer orders, the petty cash stuff.

The vital few are everywhere, but masquerading under a variety of aliases.

What Is Quality?

Kaoru Ishikawa

Kaoru Ishikawa is one of the pioneers of quality management and control and one of the most influential thinkers on these principles. This excerpt from his book Introduction to Quality Control *provides a thoughtful review of his definition of quality. Especially useful is his listing of the four aspects of quality.*

What Is Quality?

To understand the philosophy of statistical quality control (SQC), it is probably best to split this term into its component parts and clarify each before putting them together and looking at the term as a whole. I will start by discussing the meaning of the word "quality."

In Japan, "quality" is translated as 'hinshitsu,' a word written with two Chinese characters, one meaning "goods" and one meaning "quality." I think this is an excellent rendering. When I went to the U.S. in 1958 to study quality control, I found that even there the interpretation of the word "quality" differed from company to company. For example, quality control in the Bank of America's QC program meant controlling the quality of branches, borrowers, and policy making; while United Airlines, in a service industry was running an excellent statistical quality-control program based on an interpretation of quality as quality of service. Companies like Bell Systems and General Electric were implementing quality control from the design stage right up to use of the product by the consumer.

Thus, in quality control, the meaning of the word "quality" need not be restricted to quality of product, but can be used for quality in general, including quality of management, and in Japan we are seeing the successful promotion of this wider sense of quality control. However, when starting to promote quality control in Japan, with its scarcity of natural resources and its need to survive through trade, I treated quality as meaning "product quality," and moreover, "the quality that people will buy with satisfaction."

The meaning of quality may also differ from product to product, from general consumer goods and consumer durables to industrial substances and other production materials, but there is in fact very little basic difference, whatever the type of product or industry.

> In Japan, "quality" is translated as 'hinshitsu,' a word written with two Chinese characters, one meaning "goods" and one meaning "quality."

Thus, although the type of quality discussed in this book is mainly that of industrial products ("hard quality"), quality in the service industries ("soft quality") can be regarded as an extension of this. The approaches to quality discussed below can be applied with very little modification to both manufacturing industry and tertiary (i.e., service) industries. At first, the use of the word "hinshitsu" for quality of service as well as for quality of goods seemed strange, but total quality control is now widespread, and many service industries are implementing TQC programs. In Japan today, "hinshitsu kanri" means controlling the quality of both products and services.

Quality to Satisfy the Customer

Talk of making good-quality products is often misunderstood as making products of the best possible quality. However, when we talk about quality in quality control, we are talking about designing, manufacturing, and selling products of a quality that will actually satisfy the consumer in use. In other words, "good quality" means the best quality that a company can produce with its present production technology and process capability, and that will satisfy the consumers' needs, in terms of factors such as cost and intended use.

Example 1: Which would you prefer to buy, a top-of-the-range camera costing $1,000, or an ordinary camera costing $200 which is perfectly adequate for family snapshots?

Example 2: Which would you buy, a newspaper printed on top-quality paper costing $10, or the same newspaper printed on ordinary newsprint priced at 50 cents?

As the above examples suggest, people will not buy products that are out of their price range, no matter how good the quality (in its narrow sense) might be; conversely, they will not buy a product that does not do its job (such as a camera that only takes blurry pictures), no matter how cheap it is. We buy goods fit for our purposes and our incomes. In today's diversifying and polarizing consumer markets, this is a particularly important consideration at the stages of new-product planning, quality design, new-product development and the selection of research topics, since this is when we decide what products to make and at which market sector they will be aimed.

Some manufacturers and trading companies cling to outdated commercialistic attitudes, acting as if they were still operating under the wartime rationing system, when anything made could be sold. Such organizations, which believe they are doing their job if they somehow manage to fool people into buying their products, have been left behind in the march of civilization and are out of tune with the present democratic age. When viewing our enterprises from the long-term perspective and considering their survival and their use to the community, it is clear that the very least they must do is switch from the old "seller's-market" way of looking at things (the "product-out" approach) to a consumer-oriented, buyer's-market philosophy (the "market-in" approach).

The Four Aspects of Quality

We wish to produce good quality for the consumer; we must therefore decide in advance what quality of product to plan, produce, and sell. To do this, we must consider the following four aspects of quality, and plan, design, and control it comprehensively.

1. Q (quality): quality characteristics in their narrow sense.

    Performance, purity, strength, dimensions, tolerances, appearance, reliability, lifetime, fraction defective, rework fraction, non-adjustment ratio, packing method, etc.

2. C (cost): characteristics related to cost and price (i.e., profit); cost control and profit control.

    Yield, unit cost, losses, productivity, raw materials costs, production costs, fraction defective, defects, overfill, cost price, selling price, profit, etc.

3. D (delivery): characteristics related to quantities and lead times (quantity control).

    Production volume, sales volume, changeover losses, inventory, consumption, lead times, changes in production plans, etc. Quality control is impossible without numerical data.

4. S (service): problems arising after products have been shipped; product characteristics requiring follow-up.

    Safety and environmental characteristics, product liability (PL), product liability prevention (PLP), compensation period, warranty period, before-sales and after-sales service, parts interchangeability, spare parts, ease of repair, instruction manuals, inspection and maintenance methods, packing method, etc.

Are you paying too much to your products' visual design and not enough to their real quality?

When products are accompanied by good after-sales service, are of reliable quality, and have good compatibility and long lifetimes with little dispersion, the consumer will probably buy them with confidence. Conversely, the consumer will be unsure about buying products with short lifetimes and poor reliability with which something goes wrong a few days or a few months after purchase. The number of complaints against products is also likely to decrease if instruction manuals are written clearly enough for amateur users or children to understand. Customers will not bother to read instruction manuals that are either boastful or so complex that only specialists can decipher them. Is your company receiving complaints arising from misoperation because customers are using the product incorrectly? Do your instruction manuals contain precautions explaining unsuitable conditions or methods of use? Are your products being broken or damaged, or are their lifetimes shortened because of poor packaging and transportation methods? Packaging is also an important quality, but are you paying too much to your products' visual design and not enough to their real quality?

The Red Beads

W. Edwards Deming

This chapter from Deming's latest work, The New Economics for Industry, Government, Education, *is the author's own description of the famous red beads exercise. This exercise provides participants in Deming's seminars as well as readers with a dramatic understanding of variation, worker performance, and what happens when managers do not understand these ideas. Deming writes this chapter in a style that while terse, also reflects the verbal approach he employs in his seminars. He wastes few words in making his points, and we believe this demonstrates the urgency with which he wants to help people understand these important concepts about work in organizations.*

Aim of This Chapter

The aim of this chapter is to teach by an experiment a number of important principles. A summary of the principles learned appears at the end of this chapter.

The Experiment with the Red Beads

In the experiment in my lectures I play the role of the foreman. "It takes many months to train a foreman for this work, so I'll act as foreman myself." Volunteers from the audience come forth in response to the advertisement that appears further on.

Material Required:

4000 wooden beads, about 3 mm in diameter:
800 red
3200 white

A paddle with 50 holes or depressions that will scoop up 50 beads (the prescribed work load).

Two plastic rectangular vessels, one to fit into the other (to save space). In my equipment, the beads (in a plastic bag) and the paddle fit into the small vessel; the small vessel fits into a larger vessel. Sizes, in my equipment:

Larger vessel—20 cm $\times$ 16 cm $\times$ 8 cm
Smaller vessel—19 cm $\times$ 13½ cm $\times$ 6 cm

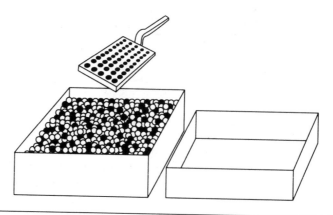

Figure 1. **Beads and paddle.**

The incoming material (mixture of 4000 red and white beads) arrives at the company in the larger vessel.

Procedure

The foreman explains that the company plans expansion to take care of a new customer. The new customer needs white beads; he will not take red beads. Unfortunately, there are red beads in the incoming material (a mixture of white beads and red beads).

Expansion requires that the company hire 10 new employees, so the company advertises:

Vacancies: 10

6 Willing Workers. Must be willing to put forth best efforts. Continuation of jobs is dependent on performance. Educational requirements minimal. Experience in pouring beads is not necessary.

2 Inspectors. Must be able to distinguish red from white; able to count to 20. Experience not necessary.

1 Inspector General. Same qualifications as Inspectors.

1 Recorder. Must write legibly; good in addition and division; must be sharp.

Six Willing Workers come from the audience, step up to the platform, right side.

Volunteers for Inspectors and for the Inspector General come forth. They step up to the platform, stand on the left, the Inspector General between the two Inspectors, No. 1 and No. 2.

A Recorder comes from the audience, steps up on the platform. The foreman explains to her that she is on the payroll, but that there is nothing to do for a while.

The foreman explains that everybody will be on an apprentice program for three days, to learn the job. During apprenticeship they may ask questions.

Once we start production, there will be no questions, no remarks; just do your job.

Our procedures are rigid. There will be no departure from procedures, so that there will be no variation in performance.

The Recorder records the names of the Willing Workers, of the Inspectors, and her own name. Her record shows on a form that is projected on to the screen, visible to everybody in the audience.

The foreman explains to the Willing Workers that their jobs depend on their performance. He explains that our procedures for dismissal are very informal. You just step down and collect your pay. There are several hundred people here ready to take your place. There will be no resignation. (The foreman explains that he made this rule because a Willing Worker, in the Salem Inn near Boston, tried to quit when the experiment was about half finished. She had had enough.)

We have work standards here, the foreman explains, 50 beads per day for each Willing Worker. In fact, the only thing that we do right here, the foreman explains to the audience, is that the two inspectors (too many) are independent; they will count red beads independently. Each inspector will record his count on a piece of paper. Neither inspector will see the other's count.

Step 1. Mix the incoming material. Pour the incoming beads into the smaller vessel. Grasp the larger vessel on the broad side, pour from the corner. Merely tilt the larger vessel; do not turn it nor shake it. Let gravity do the work. Do you understand gravity? Gravity is dependable and is cheap.

> We have work standards here, the foreman explains, 50 beads per day for each Willing Worker.

Next, by the same motions, return the beads from the smaller vessel into the bigger one.

Step 2. Produce beads. Use the paddle, 50 depressions therein. Grasp it on the long side with thumb and finger, insert it into the beads, agitation, no further agitation. Now raise the paddle, axis horizontal, tilt 44°. Every depression will contain a bead.

Step 3. Inspection. Carry your work to Inspector No. 1. He will record on a paper, in silence, his count of the red beads. Then to Inspector No. 2, same for him. The Inspector General compares the counts of the two inspectors. If they disagree, there may be a mistake. If they agree, there may be a mistake. The Inspector General is responsible for the count. He will, when satisfied, announce in a loud voice the count, then the word *Dismissed.*

Step 4. Record results. The Recorder, during apprenticeship, makes no record of the count. Once we go into production, she will show on the screen the count of red beads, work load by work load, as announced by the Inspector General. Everybody in the audience will make his own record, and later, plot his own chart.

The foreman calls the attention of the Willing Workers to our slogans and posters (Fig. 2). They will help the Willing Workers.

Figure 2.   **Posters to help the Willing Workers.**

Results

Day 1. The first day is a disappointment to the foreman (see the chart, Fig. 3).
He reminds the Willing Workers that their job is to make white beads, not
red ones. He thought that he had made this clear at the outset.

We are on the merit system here. We reward good performance. It is obvious that David, with only 4 red beads, deserves a merit increase in pay.
There are the figures right in front of everybody. He is our best worker.

And look at Tim, our worst performer, 14 red beads. We all like him, but
we must put him on probation.

The foreman announces that the management have declared a numerical
goal—not more than three red beads in a work load.

Day 2. The second day is another disappointment, worse than the day
before. The management are watching the figures. Costs are overrunning revenues. I explained at the outset that your jobs are dependent on your own
performance. Your performance has been deplorable. Look at the figures. If
David can make only 4 red beads on Day 1, anybody can.

The foreman is perplexed. Our procedures are rigid. Why should there be
variation?

I explained at the out-
set that your jobs are
dependent on your
own performance.
Your performance
has been deplorable.

Record of the number of defective items (red beads) by Willing Worker, per day. Lot size 50, each Willing Worker per day.

Willing Worker	Day				All 4	5	
	1	2	3	4			
Scott	9	11	7	8	35	16	11
Spencer	6	11	11	9	37	8	10
Larry	12	7	5	5	29	6	9
Seri	11	10	13	9	43		
Tim	14	8	9	11	42		
David	4	11	12	12	39		
All 6	56	58	57	54	225	60	
Cum x̄	9.3	9.5	9.5	9.4	9.4	XXX	

The chart at the left is for Nashville, 14 November 1990. The control limits therefor, extended, predict the range of variation to be expected in the future. The present experiment is an example of the future. For Nashville,

$$\bar{x} = \frac{225}{6 \times 4} = 9.38$$

$$\bar{p} = \frac{225}{6 \times 4 \times 50} = .188$$

$$\begin{matrix} UCL \\ LCL \end{matrix} = \bar{x} \pm 3\sqrt{\bar{x}(1-\bar{p})}$$

$$= 9.38 \pm 3\sqrt{9.38 \times .812}$$

$$= 17.66 \longrightarrow 18$$

$$= 1.10 \longrightarrow 1$$

Wooden beads Census count, one by one
Total 4000
Red 800
White 3200
Paddle No. 4

Interpretation of chart

The process exhibits good statistical control. This conclusion is based on intimate knowledge of the procedures prescribed and followed by the six Willing Workers, as well as on study of the chart. This is an example of a constant-cause system. There is no evidence that one Willing Worker will in the future be better than any other. Differences between Willing Workers and between days are attributable to variation inherent in the system (common causes).

The Willing Workers have put into the job all that they have to offer.

One way to decrease the proportion red in the product is to reduce the proportion of red beads in the incoming material (management's responsibility).

The control limits may be extended into the future as prediction of the limits of variation to expect from continuation of the same process.

Inspectors: Frank, David   Recorder: Mary Di   Inspector General: Mark

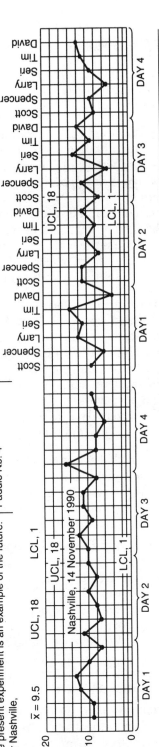

Figure 3. Data produced by the experiment (Quality Enhancement Seminars, Newport Beach, 16 January 1991); calculation of the control limits; results plotted on the chart (right side); interpretation of the chart. Comparison with a previous experiment (left side of chart) in Nashville, 14 November 1990.

Look at David. That merit raise in pay, that raise that we gave him yesterday, obviously went to his head. He became careless, and made 11 red beads the second day.

It is obvious that Larry began to pay attention to business, 7 red beads, down from 12 the first day. He has earned this day a merit increase in pay, our best worker.

Day 3. Posters and bulletins announce that the third day will be a Zero Defect Day. Much fanfare: hire a band, raise the national flag alongside the company's flag; a wine and cheese party the evening before.

The foreman is disappointed and desperate. The Zero Defect Day shows no improvement.

The foreman reminds the Willing Workers that the management are watching the figures, costs are overrunning revenues. The management has served notice: unless the fourth day shows substantial improvement over previous performance, the management will close the place down. Your jobs are your own responsibility, entirely up to you, as I told you at the outset.

Day 4. The fourth day shows no improvement, more disappointment. But the foreman announces good news. Someone in our management—our own management—came forth with a fantastic plan: keep the place open with the best workers. Think of it! Fantastic, and from our own management. A contribution to management the world over, for all time. You are very proud of our management, I am sure; our own management.

The three best workers are obviously Scott, Spencer, Larry. They will work two shifts every day: we must keep up production. The other three may pick up their pay. They did their best. We are all indebted to them.

Day 5. The fifth day begins. The foreman is disappointed with the results. So is the management. The foreman announces that the management have decided to close the place down after all. The wonderful idea to keep the place open with the best workers did not produce the results expected.

Best Workers?

What was wrong with the wonderful idea to keep the place open with the best workers? What the management meant (implicitly) was best in the future.

Three workers (Scott, Spencer, Larry) were the best in the past. They won the game, past tense. When retained on the job, they turned out to be a disappointment, blasted management's hopes. They had no more chance to do better in the future than any other three workers. It was inevitable that three of the six Willing Workers would be the top three. The three best workers in the past had no more chance than any other three to do well in the future.

Management is not playing games; management is prediction (so stated in 1987 by Dr. Michael Tveite).

Thoughts from a Willing Worker Named Ann

A Willing Worker named Ann, after the experiment on the Red Beads came to a close, expressed to me some provocative thoughts. Please put these

The foreman is disappointed and desperate. The Zero Defect Day shows no improvement.

thoughts into writing, I pleaded with her. Please write them just as you told them to me. She did. Here is her letter.

> When I was a Willing Worker on the Red beads, I learned more than statistical theory. I knew that the system would not allow me to meet the goal, but I still felt that I could. I wished to. I tried so hard. I felt responsibility: others dependent on me. My logic and emotions conflicted, and I was frustrated. Logic said that there was no way to succeed. Emotion said that I could by trying.
>
> After it was over, I thought about my own work situation. How often are people in a situation that they can not govern, but wish to do their best? And people do their best. And after a while, what happens to their drive, their care, their desire? For some, they become turned off, tuned out. Fortunately, there are many that only need the opportunity and methods to contribute with.

I knew that the system would not allow me to meet the goal, but I still felt that I could.

What Do You Mean By the Same Conditions?

A good question for advancement of understanding of a process could be this one: What do you mean by continuation of the same process? Answers:

Same beads. Change beads: the results will be different.
Same paddle. Change the paddle: the results will be different.
Same procedures. This could only mean the same foreman. A change
    in foreman could produce vastly different results.

In regard to change of paddle, we may look at the figures. I have used over the years four paddles; call them 1, 2, 3, 4, with results in the table below, $\bar{x}$ being the cumulated average over a long series of experiments. New beads came into use with paddles 2, 3, 4.

Paddle	$\bar{x}$
1	11.3
2	9.6
3	9.2
4	9.4

Paddle No. 1 was made of aluminum in 1942 by a friend in RCA, Camden. I used it in the United States. I taught the Japanese with it. Paddle No. 2 was smaller and easier than No. 1 to carry, made for me by Mr. Bill Boller of Hewlett-Packard. No. 3 was made of apple wood, beautiful, but a bit bulky. No. 4 was made for me of white nylon by AT&T Technologies in Reading.

The differences are large. For example, if anyone were paying for 9.2 per cent ash in his coal, and getting 9.6 per cent, he would wonder what is the trouble with the bottom line.

No one could predict what $\bar{x}$ will cumulate to for any given paddle.

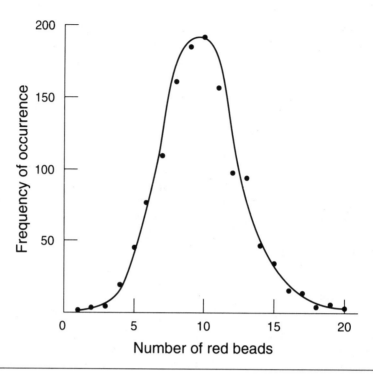

Figure 4.   **Distribution of red beads over 53 experiments, up to 11 June 1992.**

Cumulated Distribution of Red Beads

Figure 4 shows the distribution of red beads over 53 experiments, compiled by my secretary Cecelia S. Kilian, as of 11 June 1992. In one experiment there were 20 red beads, 1 bead beyond the upper control limit in that experiment. In my judgment, based on intimate knowledge of the process, I would say that this event was a false signal, not indication of a special cause.

Another Lesson from the Red Beads

Knowledge of the proportion red in the incoming material is not a basis for prediction of the proportion red in the output. The work loads produced by the Willing Workers were not drawn by random numbers from the supply. They were drawn by mechanical sampling.

Japanese engineers, having taken my eight-day seminar in 1950 and 1951, began to wonder about the prevailing method for getting samples of iron ore from a shipload of iron ore. The samples of iron ore are handed to a chemist who performs an assay to estimate the proportion of iron in the ore. The problem is, how much is the shipload of iron ore worth?

The prevailing method of collecting the primary samples was to scoop up from the top of the load a few shovelfuls of iron ore. A committee of JUSE (Union of Japanese Science and Engineering) on the sampling of bulk materials, Dr. Kaoru Ishikawa, chairman, seeing that the average proportion in the

Yawata Steel Company — 22 December 1955

Ore	Class	Old	New	Difference
Dungan	A	59.95	55.33	4.62
Larap	B	56.60	55.30	1.30
	C	59.25	58.06	1.19
Samar	D	55.55	50.42	5.13

output of red beads was not the proportion red in the incoming material, began to enquire into the sampling of iron ore, coal, copper ore, and other materials imported into Japan. The committee went to work on the problem. The table above shows some results. Note the date, five years after my first teaching of engineers in the summer of 1950.

The Japanese engineers have contrived a new method for collection of the primary samples. Halt at random times during the unloading the conveyer belt that conveys the iron ore from ship to furnace, or to the pile. Every particle of iron ore on board has a chance to be in the sample. By the old method, only the iron ore at the top got in.

The reader may prefer the new method, not because it yields less iron ore than the old method, but on engineering grounds. The new method showed 10 per cent less iron for the Dungan Mine, Class A, and for the Samar Mine, Class D; 2 per cent less for the other two ores (all from India). The difference is worth consideration.

The methods of this committee, continually refined, have become international standards for the sampling of bulk materials.

Summary of Lessons from the Red Beads

1. The system turned out to be stable. The variation and level of output of the Willing Workers, under continuance of the same system, was predictable. Costs were predictable.
2. All the variation—differences between Willing Workers in the production of red beads, and the variation day to day of any Willing Worker—came entirely from the process itself. There was no evidence that any one worker was better than another.
3. The output (white beads) of the Willing Workers showed statistical control, was stable. They had put into the job all that they had to offer. They could, under the circumstances, do no better. (A principle stated by Dr. Joseph M. Juran around 1954.)
4. We learned why it is that the ranking of people, teams, salesmen, plants, divisions, departments, as is done in the merit system or in the appraisal of people, is wrong and demoralizing, as it is actually merely ranking the effect of the process on people.

5. We learned about the futility of pay for performance. The performance of the Willing Workers—so bad it was that they lost their jobs—was governed totally by the process that they worked in.

6. The foreman gave out merit increases in pay, and put people on probation, supposedly as rewards and punishment of performance. Actually, as it turns out, he was rewarding and punishing the performance of the process, not of the Willing Workers.

7. The experiment was a display of bad management. Procedures were rigid. The Willing Workers had no chance to offer suggestions for improvement of output. No wonder the place closed and the Willing Workers lost their jobs.

8. On the job, anyone has an obligation to try to improve the system, and thus to improve his own performance, and everyone else's. The Willing Workers on the Red Beads were victims of the process. They could not, under the rules laid down by the foreman, improve their performance. (Replacement of a red bead with a white one, or a second scoop, was expressly forbidden.)

9. The management fixed in advance, on no basis whatever, the price of white beads.

10. The inspectors were independent of each other. This is the one thing that was right in the experiment. Agreement of the inspectors (with a possible rare exception) indicated that we had a system of inspection, dependable. If the inspectors had come to consensus on the count of red beads, we could not assert that we had a system of inspection. We could only assert that they gave us figures.

11. It would have been good had the management worked with the supplier of beads to try to reduce the proportion of red beads in the incoming material.

12. Knowledge about the proportion of red beads in the incoming material (20 per cent) would not enable anyone to predict the proportion of red beads in the output. The work loads of the Willing Workers were not random drawings. They were an example of mechanical sampling. Mechanical sampling does not tell us the content of the lot that was sampled. (See *Out of the Crisis*, p. 353.) True, the red beads produced, lot after lot, exhibited a random process, only common or chance causes of variation.

13. There was no basis for management's supposition that the three best Willing Workers of the past would be best in the future. Three Willing Workers won the game, past tense, but this was no indication of relative standing in the future. Management is prediction, not playing games.

14. The foreman himself was a product of the system. That is, he was apparently in line with the management's philosophy. Production of white beads only was handed down to him by his management. His rewards were dependent on the product of his workers.

The reader may perceive Red Beads in his own company and in his own work.

PART TWO

Quality by Industry

While quality management principles remain the same for all types of organizations, different industries apply these principles in ways particular to their businesses. Part Two provides a diverse collection of articles on how quality management is making a difference in various industries. We have clustered this collection around *manufacturing, services*, and *the public sector*. In selecting articles for each sector, we sought to have a balance between principles and applications, with an emphasis on the application of these ideas.

Where possible, we have also sought to have quality professionals assist us in understanding what is going on in particular industries. We are fortunate in this edition to have recruited Ron Heilman, head of the Center for Quality and Productivity at the University of Wisconsin, Milwaukee, to work with us. He has prepared an excellent review of the current state of TQM in higher education. Overall, here's what you'll find in Part Two:

Manufacturing

Within manufacturing we focus on automobiles and electronics because they continue to lead most industries in the application of quality practices. The two articles on the automotive industry provide an overview of the industry as a whole and the challenge of building and delivering a car in three days. The electronics articles include one industry overview piece and the intriguing story of how Intel came to implement TQM. You'll also find two other articles that document the quality approach at Allen-Bradley and Whirlpool. We decided to include one article on *agile manufacturing*, applicable across manufacturing sectors, which documents the move toward what some call "mass customization" or the "virtual corporation."

Services

In the past few years, service industries have made enormous progress in using quality principles to maintain their competitive edge, level of growth, and profitability. This is especially evident in the hospitality industry. We include an article profiling the Ritz Carlton Hotel Company, winner of a 1992 Baldrige, and some of the documents they use to track quality. You'll also find an excerpt from the best-selling book *Reengineering the Corporation* on how Taco Bell used reengineering, a quality management tool, to turn itself around.

Banking and insurance are other types of service industries where quality management has had an impact. We include an intriguing selection of articles here on the value of quality principles to better meet customer needs and on how these ideas are working in various organizations, including commercial banks, mortgage banks, and insurance companies. To introduce the services section, we also found an excellent piece from *Business Horizons* on the general application of Deming's 14 points to service industries.

Public Sector

In 1993, the use of quality principles to upgrade efficiency and the value of the work performed for customers is the most important development in the public sector. We have divided this section into four parts: *Health Care, Education (K-12), Higher Education,* and *Government.* Each section includes articles by prominent practitioners and journalists that overview the contribution quality is making to how they manage their organizations and deliver their services. In addition, as mentioned above, you will find the industry reviews by our contributors. This entire section becomes especially timely as President Clinton and Vice-President Gore seek to reinvent government—with quality as the guiding principle.

*   *   *

For additional material on what is going on by industry, please consult the bibliography in Part Four. It includes a detailed, annotated list of materials across several industries, of which the articles in Part Two are only a small sample.

Manufacturing Sector

Agile Manufacturing
Stepping Beyond Lean Production
John H. Sheridan

Agile manufacturing, mass customization, lean production—these are the concepts that describe the wave of the future. But they are not just concepts; they describe the practices of the most astute manufacturers as they move to minimize waste and create nearly custom products that maximize customer satisfaction and value. This article from Industry Week *describes this new approach to manufacturing, applicable regardless of the industry.*

Since the early 1980s, industry analysts concerned about global competitiveness have popularized the terms "world-class manufacturing" and "lean production." Both connote essentially the same things—elimination of inventory and other forms of "waste," greater flexibility in production scheduling, shortened leadtimes, and advanced levels of quality in both products and customer service. Companies that truly understood the concepts, and how to apply them, had a sure-fire recipe for success. Or so it seemed. But as is the case with many recipes—or, in the current vernacular, "paradigms"—there is always a strong temptation to tinker with the ingredients.

So, even as many manufacturing firms still struggle to implement "lean/flexible" production concepts, industry thought leaders have been peering farther into the future, trying to formulate a new—if still somewhat amorphous—paradigm for successful manufacturing enterprises in the next century. The vision is still fuzzy around the edges. And some of the underlying support systems don't yet exist. But a fairly broad consensus has been reached on what to call this new paradigm: It's "agile manufacturing."

At first blush, agile manufacturing may sound like simply another way of describing the lean/flexible approach to running a manufacturing business. But while there are similarities, there are fundamental differences as well.

For one, lean production is regarded by many as simply an enhancement of mass-production methods, whereas *agility* implies breaking out of the mass-production mold and producing much more highly customized products—when and where the customer wants them. In a product-line context, it amounts to striving for economies of scope, rather than economies of scale—ideally serving ever-smaller niche markets, even quantities of one, without the high cost traditionally associated with customization.

Agility implies breaking out of the mass-production mold and producing much more highly customized products.

Moreover, advocates point out, agile manufacturing requires an enterprise-wide view, whereas lean production is typically associated with the factory floor. And agility embodies such concepts as rapid formation of multi-company alliances to introduce new products to the market.

"Not many people really understand the essence of agility," laments Rick Dove, chairman of Paradigm Shift International, an Oakland consulting firm. "It is the ability to thrive in a time of uncertain, unpredictable, and continuous change. On the other hand, the essence of *lean* is the efficient use of resources. You generally need to be lean to be agile, but you don't want *everything* that *lean* brings to the table. If a plant gets as lean as it is possible to be, then it becomes extremely fragile to the impact of change. The ultimately lean organization is optimized for doing what it is doing—and nothing else. It is static," Mr. Dove asserts. "But in the future, the ability to be competitive will be determined by how well you can reconfigure—your software, your equipment, or your organization structure. If you have to change quickly, how do you do that? What obstacles do you have to overcome?"

For example, companies that are implementing work teams may find it difficult to reconfigure team structures, he notes, "because people develop loyalty to the team."

Leading the Way

At the forefront of the movement to shape the new manufacturing paradigm in the U.S. is an organization affiliated with the Iacocca Institute at Lehigh University—the Agile Manufacturing Enterprise Forum (AMEF). An industry-led effort, originally supported with $5 million in Dept. of Defense funding, AMEF was formed to carry on the work of a 1991 Iacocca Institute study in which more than 150 industry executives participated. Their efforts culminated in a two-volume report titled *21st Century Manufacturing Enterprise Strategy*, which described how U.S. industrial competitiveness will—or might—evolve during the next 15 years. Hoping to facilitate the transition, AMEF has sponsored two major conferences and has created 18 ongoing "focus groups" to further explore various aspects of agility and the infrastructure needed to support them.

The Iacocca Institute/AMEF efforts were inspired, at least in part, by a five-year Japanese study known as "Manufacturing 21," which sought to script scenarios for Japanese competitiveness in the next century.

Many American executives are worried, says Robert W. Hall, director of new programs for the Association for Manufacturing Excellence (AME), because, while the U.S. is still in the relatively early stages of trying to grasp the implications of agile manufacturing, "the Japanese have already begun putting small parts of the infrastructure into place."

It is now widely recognized that Japan—which for years put its R&D emphasis on manufacturing processes, while American firms emphasized product research—was far ahead of the U.S. in implementing lean manufacturing. Toyota's Taiichi Ohno "was talking lean production 40 years ago," notes Donald L. Runkle, vice president-engineering support at General Motors Corp. Yet it wasn't until the 1980s that American industry and the universities which train future industry leaders caught on.

"We long ago hitched our wagons to the product path and the now-dated mass-production paradigm, and we followed them to the brink of the current crisis," Mr. Runkle told an AMEF audience in Florida last December.

GM has condensed the "science" of lean manufacturing into a list of 17 principles, he notes. "But the corresponding rules for the agile enterprise have not been written yet. We do not know, for example, what is the agile equivalent of just-in-time inventory. . . . But we do know that it is important for America to invent the rules of agile manufacturing. We missed the last paradigm shift, and we cannot afford to miss the next one."

The shift, however, may take different shapes for different companies and different industries. An AMEF backgrounder points out that there is no universal "prescription" for becoming agile: "Each organization must evaluate agility in light of its goals and objectives and the competitive environment in which it operates. . . . The transition to agility will be different for each organization and represents a set of choices from a menu."

At the moment, AMEF activists and others are pondering a fairly extensive menu which includes:

- **Greater product customization**—manufacturing to order, but at relatively low unit cost.
- **Rapid introduction of new or modified products**—in some cases, through quick formation of temporary strategic partnerships to take advantage of brief windows of opportunity in the marketplace. These alliances would blend together core competencies of the partners, combining pieces of each organization into a new "virtual enterprise" or "virtual corporation."
- **Advanced inter-enterprise networking technology**—which has been dubbed Factory America Net (FAN)—to facilitate the formation of virtual companies and to simplify linkages for conducting "electronic commerce."
- **Upgradable products**—designed for disassembly, recyclability, and reconfigurability.
- **Increased emphasis on knowledgeable, highly trained, and empowered workers**—whose talents, coupled with instant access to

information, will significantly increase an organization's flexibility and responsiveness. In an agile world, proponents contend, workers—rather than equipment—will be treated as a company's primary assets.

- **Interactive customer relationships**—in which the physical product becomes a platform for providing an evolving set of value-adding services.
- **Dynamic reconfiguration of production processes**—to accommodate swift changes in product designs or entire new product lines.

In addition, various agile manufacturing scenarios envision: greater use of flexible production technologies such as rapid prototyping, an open-systems information environment, innovative (nonrigid) management structures, product pricing based on value to the customer, and a commitment to environmentally benign operations and product designs.

"Somebody needs to be the visionary—and we are trying to be that visionary," says W. Scott Wade, a Texas Instruments executive on loan to AMEF. "At the forum, we believe that everything needs to be industry-led. And the more industries that can be brought together and thinking about agility, the quicker things like standardized information technology can be introduced."

Mr. Wade is working with two of AMEF's focus groups—those exploring employee empowerment and environmental issues. Indeed, he asserts, there is a connection between the environment and agility. For example, the Environmental Protection Agency (EPA) and state permit processes can delay the construction or modification of production facilities. "If you are going to be agile and quickly respond to the marketplace, you want to minimize the number of permits you have to obtain and also consolidate those permits and bring people into play as quickly as possible. Our environmental focus group is working with the EPA, exploring ways to consolidate permits so that a company doesn't have to make 25 different applications to get something going.

"Many people think of agility just from a shop-floor standpoint. And we are trying to say, 'No, it's the entire enterprise.' And when you think about the entire enterprise, [agility] does affect many different issues."

Agile Production

Paradigm Shift's Mr. Dove concurs that agility encompasses much more than the production process. But, he adds, manufacturers need to address shop-floor issues as well.

"We are putting more and more programmable stuff into our factories, and much of it needs to be integrated. But one thing we haven't learned well is how to build the equipment so that we can change it later on. In automating a factory, the focus has been on making things work—not on the ability to change," says Mr. Dove, who heads up the AMEF focus group on agile production. His group is developing "tools" to define agility in the factory and to help manufacturing managers to evaluate how agile their organizational structures and machine architectures really are. "For example, you might have a robot arm with 3 degrees of flexibility and, suddenly, something new and more complex is added to your product line which requires 4 degrees of freedom. So yo have to scrap the old robot and buy a new one." However, he points out, if the robot arm had been designed in such a way that its range of flexibility could be increased by simply replacing a joint, that would make it easier—and far less costly—to reconfigure the production process.

"Reconfiguration is the real issue in agility," Mr. Dove stresses. "The essence of an agile corporation is the ability to [assemble] the resources it needs quickly. . . . If, for example, you get a big order that suddenly requires you to devote 60% of your production capacity to handle it, rather than the 20% you normally devote to that product line, then somehow you need the ability to reconfigure the plant facility itself.

"People say that you'll have to pay a price for that. Well, they said that about lean manufacturing—and it turned out not to be true. With lean manufacturing, we discovered that flexibility can actually be cheaper, because you get costs out of the system in places where you traditionally never looked for them. . . . The issue here is how to do those things so that they are affordable."

Increased Customization

As product quality becomes the bare minimum—the price of market entry—customer gratification or "delight" will become a driving force in determining marketplace winners and losers, contend proponents of agility. And, increasingly, products will be configured to the users' requirements at the time of sale or order.

"The notion is that we are now at the point where people's expectations are that someone is going to ship them a custom product—without sacrificing quality, time to market, or cost," says Roy Smith, vice president of the Enterprise Integration Information Systems Div. of Microelectronics & Computer Technology Corp. (MCC), Austin.

"If you are agile," asserts AME's Dr. Hall, "you can give the customer the configuration he wants simply as a part of the production process itself. You don't need independent product development. You build more customer preference into the system that can be accommodated very rapidly." One Japanese firm, he notes, now custom builds bicycles in a matter of four or five hours. "However, it then holds them for a week or two, because most customers don't believe they're getting a quality product if it's ready the next day."

In many minds, the concept that epitomizes agile customization is the "three-day car." An AME research report on Japan's "Manufacturing 21" study observed that long production leadtimes are a major reason why auto dealers stock hundreds of cars on their lots—incurring heavy inventory carrying costs. "If a custom-built car from the factory had a short leadtime and required no dealer stock, the resulting savings would help to offset the higher materials cost of a modular-structure, custom-build car," the AME report noted.

> As product quality becomes the bare minimum—the price of market entry—customer gratification or "delight" will become a driving force in determining marketplace winners and losers, contend proponents of agility.

It described a scenario in which an auto buyer participates in the design of the vehicle, selecting from a range of options on a computer workstation at the dealership. Such features as seat contours, instrument panel layout, and body trim might be custom-designed (within certain limitations). After checking to ensure that the selected configuration is feasible, a distributed CAD/CAM system would then enter the data into the manufacturer's production system—which would subsequently relay the appropriate information to supplier plants. Components would be built to order and shipped to the assembly plant in the proper sequence. Bottom line: a car built to customer specifications and delivered within three days—compared with the six-week leadtime that U.S. automakers typically require to produce a vehicle to order. Elements of such "customer-integrated" systems are being developed by Japanese automakers, who have fine-tuned their just-in-time production systems to the point that they are able, at least in Japan, to build a car to order in five days.

In this country, GM's Saturn Corp. can, too—at least, given the ideal mix of circumstances. "We have some advantages that other manufacturers don't have," says Max Hurst, Saturn's manager of vehicle management in Spring Hill, Tenn. "One of them is that we are a single-source plant. All our cars are built right here. So, to change an order, we have real-time access to the same database that is being used to release orders to production."

In planning production, Saturn "images" orders for its dealers, Mr. Hurst explains. "That means we create the order for the retailer. Then the retailer has an opportunity to say, 'I want more reds or more blues, or more manuals than automatics—or whatever.' They edit the orders, rather than create them." And they do it by accessing the computer database that controls production scheduling. At any given point in time, four days' worth of orders have been released to production—and these cannot be changed. But if a dealer wants to speed a special customer order, he could alter the specifications for a car that is near the point of being scheduled for production. "If that car is among those released to production the next day, then four days later it is built," Mr. Hurst says.

And if the dealer is within a one-day truck trip of the Tennessee plant, conceivably a customer could have his pre-sold car built and delivered within a five-day period. "However, if the customer is on the West Coast, then it goes to two weeks plus four days—because we ship cars to the West Coast by rail. And it takes two weeks to ship by rail."

An issue that often punctuates discussions of product customization is: Will people pay whatever additional cost is involved? "The reason mass production came into vogue," observes Charles Carter, vice president-technology at the Assn. for Manufacturing Technology (AMT), Washington, "is that the customer was willing to buy a fairly standardized product because he could get it at a reasonable price. . . . Even today, if you want to customize a personal computer, you aren't going to get if for $1,600"—at least not if it means creating a unique microprocessor design. What some call customization, Mr.

Carter adds, is really a matter of configuring standardized components—like 386 or 486 microprocessor chips—to the user's requirements.

"All choices have an associated cost," adds Saturn's Mr. Hurst. "There is a price tag to infinite combinations of producing anything. And I'm not sure you do the consumer any favor by giving him a smorgasbord of options, because the people who pay for that are the people who buy the cars."

A current trend in the auto industry is to limit the number of options or combine options into a relatively limited number of packages. Part of the thinking is that most buyers really don't want to be bothered "designing" their own cars, feature by feature. Offering a plethora of choices can be frustrating to consumers, says AME's Dr. Hall. "It's like going into a restaurant where the menu is 27 pages long."

Design for Agility

Those who've pondered agility see a number of implications for product design. One of the more intriguing is "design for upgradability"—which would enable customers to replace components of a product, rather than discarding the whole thing and buying a new version. Using modular configurations, products could be designed to evolve as the needs of users change—extending the useful life of many basic components. "You might call it remanufacturing," says Dr. Hall. "In the case of a car, instead of trading in your old one and buying a new car, you'd take it in for an upgrade. They may do some reconfiguration, perhaps give you some new electronics, then check out the running components and tell you it will last another three years.

"Whether it is automobiles, computers, or refrigerators . . . what you are really putting together is a mechanical framework that can be reused. If components can be reused, that is a very environmentally conscious design. It's even better than recycling, because we don't have to remelt the metal."

A related concept is "design for disassembly"—a subject of growing interest in the auto industry. In Germany, automakers have been told they will be responsible for recycling cars at the end of their useful lives. And, some analysts predict, similar requirements could spread to the U.S.

"So if you are designing a car," says AMEF's Mr. Wade, "you suddenly have to start thinking about how you will disassemble it." Among other things, design for disassembly will facilitate product upgrades, he points out. In the future, auto dealers may undergo a metamorphosis—from simply selling cars out of inventory to reconfiguring them. The trend is already apparent with desktop computers, where users can upgrade them by replacing items like memory boards, Mr. Wade notes. "I think you are going to start to see that more and more in other product lines."

Using modular configurations, products could be designed to evolve as the needs of users change—extending the useful life of many basic components.

The Virtual Company

AMT's Mr. Carter suspects that, to some extent, agile manufacturing is becoming a buzzword that means different things to different people. "What agility is may be in the eye of the beholder," he says. "In my view, the biggest new thing is the so-called virtual company, where people who may consider themselves competitors—people not in the traditional user/supplier relationship—get together to form a consortium."

It's not that strategic alliances are anything new, but in the agile manufacturing vision, they will occur more frequently and more rapidly—aided by advances in computer networking and high-speed communications. And the inter-company relationships will be tighter, as long as antitrust issues can be resolved. One of the things that distinguishes agile manufacturing from lean production, says GM's Mr. Runkle, is that "you can be lean by yourself, but you cannot be agile by yourself. In fact, doing business with companies that are not agile can impede your own agility."

He sees virtual companies as "the epitome of the agile enterprise"—a vehicle to "whisk high-quality, low-cost new products to customers" by tapping the specialized know-how of best-practices units within the participating companies.

The 1991 Iacocca Institute report cited speed to market with complex new products as a major benefit of "virtual" companies. "Often," it stated, "the quickest route to the introduction of a new product is selecting organizational resources from different companies and then synthesizing them into a single, electronic business entity: a virtual company. If the various distributed resources, human and physical, are 'plug-compatible' with one another . . . then a virtual company can behave as if it were a single company dedicated to one particular product. For as long as the opportunity lasts, the virtual company continues in existence. When the opportunity passes, the company dissolves and its personnel turn to other projects. . . . The ability to form virtual companies routinely is a powerful competitive weapon. It exploits a number of distinctive American strengths—notably, world leadership in information science and a vast, diverse supplier base."

> The quickest route to the introduction of a new product is selecting organizational resources from different companies and then synthesizing them into a single, electronic business entity: a virtual company.

Full realization of the vision will depend on the evolution of such support systems as Factory America Net (FAN) and "pre-qualified partnering" services.

FAN would combine a comprehensive on-line industrial database with other services to facilitate the creation of virtual enterprises. One of the building blocks for FAN is the Enterprise Integration Network (EI Net) technology being developed by MCC, itself a consortium of some 80 high-tech U.S. companies.

But while the envisioned FAN database might contain a wealth of information about companies and their products of capabilities—a kind of national "Yellow Pages"—it will provide little insight "into the real-world performance and culture of a company," the Iacocca Institute report acknowledged.

Thus, services such as prequalified partnering—a form of industrial match-making—will be needed. Companies in a hurry to find potential partners or suppliers would rely on these independent services to help them make quick evaluations.

Among the obstacles to rapid formation of virtual companies are some thorny legal issues (including the protection of intellectual property rights), as well as finding ways to determine the value of each stakeholders's contribution, so the accountants will know how to divvy up the profits.

And there are cultural issues, such as the tendency of American companies toward autonomy and a reluctance to share proprietary information. More to the point: a tendency toward distrust. "In order to form a virtual company, you have to have people who are willing to share data and work with someone who has been perceived as a competitor," says AMT's Mr. Carter.

One who is skeptical that this reluctance will soon disappear is Henry Duignan, chief operating officer at Ross Operating Valve Co., Troy, Mich. He contends that ingrained adversarial attitudes in American business "leave trust out of the equation. And without trust, you can't do any of that." U.S. firms cooperate only when they find themselves in "dire straits," he adds. "The only thing that drives American companies together is that they are getting their pants beat off by foreign competition."

AMEF's Mr. Wade, too, acknowledges that "American businesses have not, either from a legal or a marketing standpoint, been big in teaming with other companies to achieve success." But, he argues, that will have to change in order to achieve rapid response to globally competitive markets.

Antitrust and other legal issues will present major challenges, Mr. Wade adds. As an example, he recalls an incident in which Texas Instruments and Westinghouse joined forces to build components for an advanced radar system. "It took the two company presidents just two hours of discussion and a handshake to reach an agreement on what they were going to do. But it took nine months—and 3½ inches of documentation from the lawyers—to make it happen."

An Agile Workforce

Since the agile enterprise will be in a constant state of evolution, its competitive capabilities will rely not so much on equipment, but on the creativity and skills of its workforce. "Just as mass production leveraged people's physical power and dexterity, agile manufacturing will leverage their capabilities to handle information and make decisions," says GM's Mr. Runkle. "Agile manufacturing will increase the competitive impact of a person's intellectual power." Thus, companies striving for agility will need to step up their investment in the training and growth of workers at all levels. Yet, Mr. Runkle notes, the $530 billion a year that U.S. businesses and the federal government invest in new plant and equipment dwarfs the $48 billion devoted to training—which is less than half the per capita investment in training in Japan and Germany. With the initiative of the workforce becoming increasingly important in an agile world, management practices that prevailed in the mass-production paradigm will have to change. And in many companies they *are* changing: Adversarial relationships are giving way to trust and open sharing of information. Cross-functional task forces—sometimes resembling internal "virtual enterprises"—are being created to solve problems and exploit

With the initiative of the workforce becoming increasingly important in an agile world, management practices that prevailed in the mass-production paradigm will have to change.

opportunities. And a growing number of companies are empowering lower-level employees to make the kinds of decisions that must be made quickly in an agile environment. "The only way you are going to make rapid decisions is by giving information to the lowest level in the organization structure that is required to make a decision," asserts AMEF's Mr. Wade. "If you have a hierarchical information chain, you can't be rapid.

"If lower-level people have to make the decisions, you have to empower them—and continue on the training cycle of empowerment. And that is why we believe empowerment is going to be one of the key issues of agility."

Manufacturing Sector

AUTOMOTIVE INDUSTRY

Auto Industry Quality
What Are They Doing?

Jerry Wolak

This article by Jerry Wolak, managing editor of Quality *magazine, provides a brief overview of how American automobile manufacturers are implementing quality techniques to eliminate waste and better meet customer needs.*

In a down economy, in a depressed industry, in a time of political apprehension, the US auto industry faces continued challenges from foreign competition. But during a recent meeting—"Quality Concepts '92 (QC92)" sponsored by the Engineering Society of Detroit (ESD) and the American Society for Quality Control (ASQC) Automotive Div.—the "big three" let it be known that they are still in for the long haul, willing to take on the competition. Representatives from Chrysler, Ford, and General Motors told of each company's plan to survive in a tough worldwide market.

And "survival" requires a "change of paradigm" on behalf of US automakers, according to Harry (Hank) Lenox, chief engineer, engine product and manufacturing engineering engine div., Ford Motor Co. US auto companies have thought about making cars one way and one way only. The industry has been driven by "bottom line" results that, in effect, put blinders on it. The

Reprinted with permission from *Quality*, January 1993, a publication of Hitchcock/Chilton Publishing, a Capital Cities/ABC, Inc., Company.

ELIMINATING REDUNDANT QUALITY AUDITS

In a move proposed by the Automotive Industry Action Group (AIAG) and the American Society for Quality Control (ASQC), Chrysler, Ford, and General Motors have taken a first step toward eliminating redundant quality audits of supplier companies. Automotive suppliers estimate that adoption of a common quality assessment process, including audits, could reduce their combined costs by a half billion dollars annually and improve product quality.

Automakers routinely conduct quality assurance audits of outside suppliers' plants. Until now, Chrysler, Ford, and GM have required their first-tier suppliers to conduct extensive quality audits of their own supplier firms. So, thousands of second- and third-tier supplier companies are subject to multiple audits with one audit often duplicating another, wasting supplier time and money.

Such nonproductive duplication can be eliminated. New, streamlined audit procedures are described in a letter sent to first-tier automotive suppliers by the AIAG and ASQC and signed by the "big three" purchasing chiefs. It says that companies audited by Chrysler, Ford, or GM no longer need to be audited by any other supplier company. Additionally, when a first-tier supplier audits a second- or third-tier supplier, the auditing company can choose Chrysler's "SQA," Ford's "Q101," or GM's "Targets for Excellence" quality assessment processes. A supplier company qualifying under any of these programs will be considered to qualify under all three.

According to the jointly signed letter, "This action will promote more effective use of resources in the supply chain, accelerating quality improvement."

Adoption of standardized quality processes and reporting requirements by the "big three" can "eliminate paperwork and redundancies that have generated excess costs that ultimately show up in the sticker price on the showroom floor," says Harold A. Poling, chairman of Ford.

The mutually acceptable quality assessment process "is certain to make life simpler and easier for suppliers at a time when they are under intense pressure to lower prices while maintaining or improving quality," says F. Larry Rogers, AIAG's executive director.

results have been cars that lack customer appeal with less value for the dollar than that of foreign competitors.

The US auto industry has failed to understand its customers' motivations. During the Carter administration's "gas lines," Detroit continued making cars that used too much gas. The Japanese, having been building cars for a gas-scarce market, found a welcoming market during those days when prices at the pump went from the midtwenty-cent range to over a dollar in several short months.

Admittedly, "customer focus has not been a part of General Motors' mandate for about the past 20 years," says Norbert (Norb) L. Keller, director of quality, mid-size automotive div., General Motors Corp. But a welling up of quality awareness is changing the way Detroit, including GM, views its business. As we have been told, GM recognizes that it has ignored its customers. But now it focuses on the customer. "We use QFD. It's a planning tool to get customer input; a tool for speeding the voice of the customer throughout the organization. We do this because customer satisfaction equals quality focus," says Sam Winegarden, chief engineer, premium V engines, powertrain div., GM.

Customer focus has captured not only GM, but Ford and Chrysler also. Chrysler focuses on customer needs, desires, and wishes, and then applies lessons learned to its products, processes, and technology development to bring the manufacturing cycle full circle. It's a neat package. Chrysler listens to the customer to improve itself, but in turn "Chrysler uses new technology for customers' benefit," says G. Glenn Gardner, general manager, large car platform (LCP) engineering, Chrysler.

What the auto companies said at the QC92 meeting is not out of line with the findings of an Ernst & Young survey, done jointly with the American Quality Foundation—International Quality Study (IQS), *Automotive Industry Report*. That survey found that customer requests are:

- Considered a primary basis for selecting new products more frequently than are internally generated observations of competitors or market analysis.
- In three years, nearly three-quarters of automotive companies in Canada, Germany, Japan, and the US expect that customers will at least "usually" play a prominent role in the identification of new products.
- Feedback from current customers, customer visits, and personal contact through customer surveys are all projected to take on greater importance as methods to generate ideas for new products.

> How else can the entire organization know "what the customer wants" if whole departments are not talking with one another?

Teams

Customer focus, albeit a paradigm shift for the US auto industry, is just one item on the table. Another is that of cross-functional teams. These teams are an outgrowth of customer focus. How else can the entire organization know "what the customer wants" if whole departments are not talking with one another?

The cross-functional team concept is being embraced by the US auto industry, according to the IQS. And Chrysler has raised such teams to a new level at its new technology center in Auburn Hills, MI, site of QC92. The center is designed to physically locate team workers close to one another to facilitate team interaction. "Teams comprise product engineering, manufacturing, engineering, sales, marketing, supply, procurement, etc. Everyone building cars must work together. The technology center 'adjacencies' are designed to energize interaction and facilitate process-driven design," says Melvin T. Young, director of technology center's development program.

A cross-functional team redesigned GM's Northstar engine that is being advertised as "not needing a tuneup until 100,000 miles." In its design effort, the GM team used design for manufacturing (DFM). According to Sam Winegarden, chief engineer for premium V engines, powertrain div., GM, "DFM works best when disciplines are colocated, not spread out, using capable people on functionally diverse teams." Cadillac's Northstar engine typically had 1,700 parts. But the new design reduces the number of parts to under 1,200, he notes. New design features make the engine more user-friendly, such as a water pump that does not bolt to the engine block. It is designed for twist-lock installation. And fewer three-plane joints are used, eliminating many of the joining problems that three-plane joints present. "And many systems and part designs have reduced sensitivity to variation—that is, parts were designed so they cannot be mislocated," Winegarden adds.

Cadillac's Northstar engine typically had 1,700 parts. But the new design reduces the number of parts to under 1,200.

Management

Although much of what was said at QC92 focused on specific instances of quality practices working at their best within the respective automakers, each

---

TOOL FOR PROCESS IMPROVEMENT

Manufacturers are using coordinate measuring machines (CMMs) more often as production improvement tools rather than simply applying them in final inspection applications. When used throughout a manufacturing process, CMMs provide flexibility and enable increased uptime and improved product quality unattainable with hard gaging.

General Motors (GM) powertrain div., Toledo, OH—manufacturer of automotive transmissions—has experienced these benefits first-hand. The company had been using dedicated gages to check machined parts in final inspection. Worn gages or gage modifications drove up cost and consumed time. "Gage modifications had to be scheduled during production downtime. But with a 24-hour-a-day, 7-day-a-week production schedule, it wasn't easy to fit in gage changes," says Dave Walling, technical service coordinator. "Even if we could have gone back to the same gage manufacturer, we realized the need for a more flexible measuring procedure not offered by dedicated gages." In 1988, the company integrated Zeiss USMC CMMs into its transmission case machining lines.

Today, production-floor CMMs are positioned among the machining stations and conveyors that move parts from one station to the next. The CMMs are programmed to accept transmission cases for inspection on a varying inspection cycle and to inspect various machined features and cast details. Each part is transferred automatically into an enclosed room on the manufacturing floor for preprogrammed CMM inspection, then returned to the manufacturing cycle after the inspection is completed.

Continued—

Tools for Process Improvement (continued)

"The ability to study real-time data generated by a high-accuracy CMM allows us to quickly modify process parameters to stay within specification limits," says Walling. "With dedicated gages we couldn't process as much information in real time."

Inspecting parts is only one CMM function. When parts are not being measured, the CMMs most often are used to verify part pallets, ensuring that each pallet is identical because pallet variation can affect part quality.

Production CMMs also validate "upstream" process variables, particularly roughing stations. If the roughing operations are not on location, the downstream finishing operations cannot be completed, even if the finish tools are properly set.

"The CMMs have taken the guesswork out of correcting problems," says Walling. "We can make process improvements more easily based on the data generated by the CMM."

CMMs have played a key role in reducing variation in part manufacturing. Furthermore, the Toledo plant has reduced downtime and scrap as a result of its streamlined production process.

As a CMM measures parts or tooling, the data are used to track the process to catch errors before they become serious. "CMMs provide the ability to statistically predict and project errors for preventive maintenance. It's our road map to knowing when to change tools," says Walling.

Another prerequisite in the Toledo plant's selection of a CMM supplier related to service and maintenance programs. Downtime can mean millions of dollars lost in the automotive industry, so it was critical that the CMMs be reliable. Zeiss agreed to train Toledo workers in CMM maintenance, enabling the company to have its own workers available to respond immediately to problems. "Machines will fail sometime," says Walling. "By putting our workers through the Zeiss service engineer training school, we're able to perform service and maintenance the minute it's required."

The production-floor inspection system is linked together, allowing workers throughout the process to share data. Part inspection data, for example, are sent to a mainframe, making them available to SPC analysts. These specialists program software parameters on shopfloor workstations to look at parts statistically. The statistical data that are gathered provide information on how the process is running. This critical information is used to study manufacturing trends and quality. Part designs, tool changes, preventive maintenance programs, and short- and long-term capability studies are performed based on data generated by the CMMs.

"We have a total of 11 CMMs networked together," explains Walling. "The paperless information-sharing between CMMs increases the flexibility of our manufacturing facility, which in turn increases overall production efficiency."

story did allude to management's involvement in the overall process, implying that management involvement is a given. Nothing can be done without management's knowing and supporting the efforts to redesign engines or build completely new automobiles.

"Management's responsibilities are to create the environment, develop and communicate the strategic direction, and lead implementation teams," says Leon Skudlarek, UAW plant chairman at GM's Livonia engine plant, powertrain div. It is their responsibility to lead—to do whatever it takes to get the job done and done right the first time.

G. Glenn Gardner, general manager of large car platform engineering at Chrysler, says, "Management must plan for success instead of failure." But what does planning for success mean to the auto industry and its management? By definition, cross-functional teams must be a cross section of the work force. Involvement on a team would then mean blurring of the traditional distinctions between management and worker levels. "Barriers between workers and management must be broken down," says Joseph Reilly, administrative assistant, UAW Ford joint programs.

And as those barriers fall, "management will become invisible," says Pete F. Corbett, area manager, Ford's Sterling axle plant.

Here again, the IQS verifies the blurring of worker/management distinctions concluding that: automotive company management maintains control over such quality team activities as the formation of teams and project selection and implementation. However, autonomy of the quality team is likely to increase in the US. Certainly the discussion and encouragement of "employee empowerment" in the US may be driving the move toward greater team autonomy (Figure 1).

> "Management's responsibilities are to create the environment, develop and communicate the strategic direction, and lead implementation teams."

Tools

TQM, customer focus, cross-functional teams, and new management methods open avenues of communication and increase awareness of the tools avail-

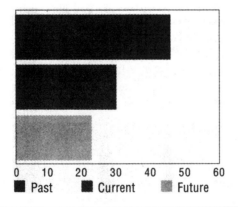

0 10 20 30 40 50 60
■ Past   ■ Current   ▨ Future

Figure 1. **Team autonomy—percent of companies where management "always or almost always" approves the formation of teams.**

able to do a quality job. Here too, the Ernst & Young/American Quality Foundation survey found that US automakers use a variety of quality tools. SPC charting is not often used, followed by Pareto analysis, business process improvement, histograms, QFD, cause-and-effect analysis, brainstorming, design of experiments, failure mode and effect analysis (FMEA), and scatter diagrams (Figure 2).

Without the focus, without the voice of the customer, and without top management support, quality tools would be useless. But at GM's powertrain div., the focus, voice, and support have enabled it to develop a "quality network process model—a tool to analyze, understand, and improve any process," says Leon Skudlarek, UAW plant chairman, at the division's Livonia engine plant. And within the framework of the quality network, the action steps we take are through the use of gage repeatability and reproducibility (GR&R), gage audits, conformance to specifications, and good planning methods," he says.

Because what happens up front in an assembly process is so critical to its success, Ford focuses on several key elements "to design for assembly, such as design verification, training, quality operating systems, continuous improvement, etc.," says Roman J. Krygier Jr., assembly operations manager. "Events or processes before assembly account for 70 percent of quality failures." Such considerations make matching the quality tool to the correct application critical for the success of the entire operation.

And at Chrysler, the application is the criterion for selecting quality tools. Under the umbrella of customer focus, we choose the appropriate quality tool to "identify and resolve [specific] problems . . . and [help with] application of new methods," says Chrysler's general manager, large car platform engineering, Gardner.

Profitability of the whole organization is still the dominant criterion in the industry, according to the IQS. Companies expect profitability to remain

> *Without the focus, without the voice of the customer, and without top management support, quality tools would be useless.*

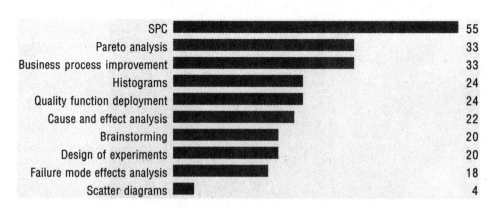

SPC	55
Pareto analysis	33
Business process improvement	33
Histograms	24
Quality function deployment	24
Cause and effect analysis	22
Brainstorming	20
Design of experiments	20
Failure mode effects analysis	18
Scatter diagrams	4

Figure 2. **Future importance of quality tools in the US auto industry. Percent of companies indicating that these tools will be of primary importance in achieving future quality improvements.**

the most important criterion, but overall quality performance and team performance will increase dramatically. Team performance is growing in importance as the concentration on individual performance is beginning to diminish. In the years ahead the balance will have shifted to make team performance overtake individual performance in importance.

The obvious extension of the concept of diminishing individual performance in favor of team performance is a diminishing of differences between auto companies on quality issues. The Automotive Industry Action Group (AIAG) and the American Society for Quality Control (ASQC) are jointly working toward that end by initiating uniform practices for auto industry supplier audits. (See sidebar "Eliminating Redundant Quality Audits.") And late in 1991, the "big three," working under the auspices of the AIAG and ASQC, developed a SPC reference manual, helping suppliers reduce their costs of meeting the car makers' quality requirements.

"We are working toward uniform practices on quality among other joint research projects. But it wasn't very long ago that auto companies didn't talk to one another," says GM's Norb L. Keller.

The Challenges of The Three-Day Car

Robert W. Hall

This article by Robert W. Hall, Director of New Programs for the Association for Manufacturing Excellence, provides a detailed look at agile manufacturing at work in the automobile industry.

Agile manufacturing is a vision. A vision can never be a precise forecast; no two people ever "see" it exactly the same way. But if we consistently evoke the vision for guidance, it becomes the driver of major change.

Agile manufacturing comes in three versions: one from the Agile Manufacturing Enterprise Forum, a U.S. group that coined the term "agile," an earlier version from Japan, and a modified version by the author. Technically, agile manufacturing is more realistic than Star Wars. Behaviorally, it poses even bigger challenges. The most severe of 12 major human challenges recognized here are to our business and organizational thinking.

The three-day car challenges all industry, not just the automotive sector. The surviving enterprises will be totally different in form and practice. Excellence as we know it now is but an entry fee to this new world.

"Agility" is a rigorous interpretation of the term "flexibility" in manufacturing: Deliver what the customer wants, including design changes, when wanted, where wanted, at reasonable cost, with no quality glitches and no environmental degradation. At a ridiculous extreme, agility means meeting any need for change instantly. It's a 21st century ideal for manufacturing excellence—if such a different milieu can still be called "manufacturing."

Scenarios, starting with the Manufacturing 21's "three-day car," bring this vision to life. The three-day car began with the Japanese Manufacturing 21 Project reported in AME's *Manufacturing 21 Report*.[1] The Agile Manufacturing Enterprise Forum embellished the "three-day car" as one of the four scenarios in their 1991 projection of 21st Century manufacturing.[2]

The first Agile Forum scenario is "Ultra-Comm:" multi-media, modularly-designed computers networked like mobile phones and available everywhere. The devices themselves would be built to customer order by a "virtual company"—a networked coalition of about 60 partners. Although it is expensive, equipment much like the electronics that drive this scenario is

> Deliver what the customer wants, including design changes, when wanted, where wanted, at reasonable cost, with no quality glitches and no environmental degradation.

Reprinted from *Target* by permission of the Association for Manufacturing Excellence, 380 W. Palatine Road, Wheeling, IL 60090, (708) 520-3282.

already available. The databases and the human organization to use its full potential will take much longer to develop.

The second scenario is small-scale production of specialty chemicals in a zero discharge environment, with high-yield, computer-controlled processes in small plants positioned close to markets. All chemical businesses will move in this direction, and even big oil refineries will try to be more flexible. The third scenario is the Application Specific Integrated Circuit (ASIC). After a few more generations of development and a thousand or more times improvement over today, the size and speed of integrated circuits will be adequate for most day-dream applications. At some point, further miniaturization will cost more than it is worth; then circuit competition will shift to software that allows customers to design their own application specific circuits, thus changing the character of the industry. It's a stretch, but the industry can see it coming.

But the scenario that captures the most attention is the "three-day car." Automotive technology integrates many technologies, and everyone can relate to cars. The industry is big, old, and traditional, so this scenario starkly contrasts the new with the old. It has sparked elaboration and expansion through successive versions because the three-day car implies a great deal about the direction of all industry.

By 2001, the Japanese auto industry expects to have four major bases of production: Japan, North America, Europe, and the Newly Industrializing Countries (NICs).

Japanese Projections for the Auto Industry

By 2001, the Japanese auto industry expects to have four major bases of production: Japan, North America, Europe, and the Newly Industrializing Countries (NICs). Much auto production will transfer overseas, so over the next decade annual unit production in Japan will decline by 20 percent or more. To offset the loss of volume revenue, higher-priced models must be produced domestically. As the United States experienced, a mature Japan cannot compete against low-cost areas making "econobox" cars. In the 90s, the Japanese domestic industry must learn how to profitably build higher-value, special-niche models selling fewer than 20,000 units over a lifetime. The Mazda Miata is an example of one step in this strategic direction.

Changes in the North American market will drastically affect the nature and speed of changes in the automotive production system in Japan. Overall, the North American market is expected to be nearly flat, growing by one percent per year, assuming that the price of oil stabilizes (but not necessarily at a low level). Japanese, European, and American companies will stage a dog fight for the high end of this market (sports/luxury models which, along with pickup trucks, gained market share in the past decade).

By 2001, electric vehicles will be made commercially, but not for large segments of the market, and solar cars will be about where gasoline-powered ones were a century earlier. Despite the environmental pressure, the internal combustion engine will probably have several more reprieves before disappearing. The potential for more efficient conversion of fuel energy to motion is still considerable, and so is the potential for alternative fuels such as liquid propane gas (LPG). Clean exhaust and vehicular fuel efficiency will remain high on the list of customer demands.

The degree of success of Japanese transplant manufacturing is critical to manufacturing changes in Japan itself. Japanese manufacturers expect to level out production in North America at 2.5–3.0 million vehicles per year in the early 1990s. The plan has long been to add supply plants and link with American suppliers until local content tops 80 percent. That is necessary to both decrease trade deficits and hedge against currency fluctuations. Export volume to North America will drop into the vicinity of 500,000 vehicles per year, a decrease of two million units below the 1986 level. Rather than competing on price, most of these exports will feature high performance, luxury, or unique design.

If the yen exchange rate stays above ¥120 to the dollar, exports to the United States will decrease slowly. If it sinks below ¥100, exports will drop rapidly.

Combining both homeland-built and transplant-built vehicles, the total number of Japanese nameplate cars sold in the United States will remain a nearly constant percent of the market. The new threat to both Americans and Japanese in the North American market could well be imports from NICs, which could rise to between one and two million units by 2001, depending on the trade policies of the U.S. government.

NIC nameplates will take some of the "entry level" market share from both Japanese and Big Three companies. More likely is that a percentage of Japanese transplant production will be sold as American nameplates, and that both Japanese companies and the Big Three will sell NIC entry-level imports under their own labels. One or more Japanese car companies could move their headquarters to the United States. (Honda is the most-rumored possibility.)

Transplants in North America will continue to mass produce mid-scale vehicles. Production strategy will be to implement factory automation along with productivity and quality improvements so that the quality of cars is equal to those built in Japan at a competitive price. The most "advanced" processes will not start in the transplants.

> One or more Japanese car companies could move their headquarters to the United States.

The total European auto market will grow slightly faster—1.5 percent per year. Japanese transplant production will be limited to one million units per year with development of suppliers to meet local content requirements. Production strategy will be similar to that in North America except that when producing smaller standard cars, cost reduction is more important. Protectionist regulations will limit Japanese imports to 200,000 or fewer units per year, mostly car types not made in Europe.

While the auto markets stagnate in the established industrial economies (how many more cars can we use?), they could boom in some of the developing countries. However, for some time rapid growth will be confined to pockets of the People's Republic of China, the former Soviet Union, and Eastern Europe. Most of this developing world market will be for mass-produced econoboxes, but affluent "third-worlders" will be a significant market for upscale cars.

Sometime in the 1990s, South Korea will probably replace Japan as the major exporter (in units) to North America. Taiwan, Malaysia, and other NICs moving into automotive production may also try to establish marketing beachheads in North America. Japanese companies have joint relations with a number of NIC auto companies. These joint ventures will mass produce a limited number of inexpensive basic models exportable to a world-wide market, including Japan. Procurement strategy will again aim for high local content, focusing on the quality of parts.

The Japanese domestic car market will continue to expand by 1.5 percent per year—but might top out due to traffic congestion. If current forces continue, imports from established countries will capture five to ten percent of this market, about one percent from the United States and the rest from Europe. Most of these will be "upscale" cars unique to Japan. The major shift will be in small cars imported from the NICs.

Challenge No. 1 is to break dependence on economy of scale in production.

About half of the Japanese domestic market will fragment into many small niches. The other half will be supplied from domestic production of basic transportation nameplates selling 20,000 to 100,000 units per year, much as now. The fragmented half will consist of numerous different models produced in quantities of less than 10,000 per year. A small, but significant, number of customers will desire cars to be tailored to their individual requirements—extensive customization.

The Japanese auto industry must learn to deal with offshore competition, especially from the NICs. Serving the niche and custom markets is the most difficult challenge. If niche markets can be dominated and a "fair" share of the basic car market retained, the Japanese domestic auto industry will remain healthy.

Flexibility: A First Step for the 90s

An intermediate strategy is vital because we cannot instantly transform to the wild world of the future. Today, not a decade from now, **Challenge No. 1 is to break dependence on economy of scale in production**—big lots and long runs. Production is more likely for a specific market.

Internationally, "economy of scale" is in marketing, common processes, and common systems, and the nature of these functions will begin changing significantly from the way we know them today. World-wide name recognition promotes marketing, but people want what they want. Properly used, a common information system for product and process development in every production base in the world should stop engineers in both product and process development from "reinventing the wheel." Any production base should be able to quickly modify any design for its target customers and start building it—if its personnel, equipment, tooling and processes have been developed for flexibility.[3]

Challenge No. 2 is to create a system to produce vehicles in low volumes at reasonable cost. Manufacturing excellence practices are a great start enabling this, but to take advantage of it, the time and cost of new model development and start up must be drastically cut. This is now the number one priority of the Japanese auto industry. Product and process design must occur in parallel. Tooling and equipment conversion time and expense must be reduced by about an order of magnitude.

In order for this intermediate system to be financially sound, many new models must make a profit on 10–20,000 cars in their lifetime. Development cost can be held down by reusing old ideas and modifying them to new needs. Certification of power plants and tooling for body parts are the most expensive development costs.

Intelligent Body Systems

The Nissan Intelligent Body System, already in use, is an opening move to reduce new body costs. The basic idea is to design flexible body handling and metal fabrication equipment, so that equipment within a given size range needs no modification for new body shapes, and only tooling remains as the major new model expense. In fact, the objective in a stamping shop is die changes in five minutes or less (on monster dies) for small lot sizes. Then flexible equipment in a body shop should weld any sequence of body styles without any time for changeover. That is possible if equipment can accommodate any configuration within its working space.

Other car companies are known to be working on their own version of the Intelligent Body System. Implementation is made easier by the convergence of body shapes. The need for a low coefficient of wind drag restricts the envelope in which all body shapes can be differentiated.

In addition, assembly lines are designed and manned by highly-skilled, adaptable workers who can trade off work among themselves within team-operated line stations. A large number of detailed practices, including ability to re-position equipment and materials, either manually or automatically, allow workers to assemble multiple models intermingled in sequence at varying rates. At the same time, with less focus on rock bottom cost, the Japanese companies are investing in equipment (and kaizen time) to make the work and the working environment physically easier on the workers. More variety equates to high mental alertness, but less physical stress. But this is 1990s intermediate strategy, not a three-day car for the 21st century.

The objective in a stamping shop is die changes in five minutes or less (on monster dies) for small lot sizes.

The Manufacturing 21 "Three-Day Car"

If one wants to offer truly customized cars to a segment of the market, unit body construction has limitations no matter how intelligent the system to design and build it. To break through this, the Japanese Manufacturing 21 team considered many different concepts to achieve several challenging objectives:

Challenge No. 3: Deliver a car with customer features very quickly—within three days after ordering. Today, delivery takes about three days if the order is expedited through the system. (Ten days or so is a more normal Japanese domestic customer leadtime.)

Challenge No. 4: Further downsize the scale of the production operations.
Build clusters of small plants, with suppliers feeding a mini-assembly plant,
all near the customers to cut the transport traffic, expense, and time.

Challenge No. 5: Allow the same components to be configured many different ways.

Challenge No. 6: Create work stimulating to the people doing it.

All of these challenges can be met by a modularly designed car. Fabricate
and assemble each module in a small space compared with today's plants.
Final assembly would also require little space. This cannot be done with unit
body designs because large parts must be fabricated on big machines, welded
together in a large body shop, painted as a unit, and then have hundreds or
thousands of parts attached to a big unit. The space necessary to do this can
only be compressed so far.

Cars designed in structural modules could be subassembled in different
locations, then brought together for final assembly and attachment of the
body panels. The external shape of the completed body is thereby partly independent of the form of the structural framework. (This design concept is
one step beyond that of the Saturn and the Pontiac Fiero, in which body panels
fasten to an underbody framework. The extra step is building the underbody
in modules so a big plant is not required, and is similar to a 28-module production concept once proposed by Chrysler.) A design truly ingenious in dimensional stability and modular interconnects could even be assembled in a
dealer shop.

A design truly ingenious in dimensional stability and modular interconnects could even be assembled in a dealer shop.

Smart designs that enable compensation in assembly for dimensional variation in parts might allow them to still be made of sheet metal. However, if
parts are to be reused or re-manufactured many times, some parts may need
to be made of more durable materials. These problems may require high-tech
materials, but within down-to-earth budgets.

Whatever the final result of technical changes to designs and production
processes, the key factors are the development of suppliers and the acceptance
of customers. If large subassemblies are fabricated and assembled prior to final
assembly, the supply network must change. The modules are either made by
the car company itself or by very capable suppliers working very closely with
the car company. The high-tech demands of the process and the degree of
coordination required suggest that the suppliers need to be "high-tech" partners of each other as well as of the customer company.

This concept also presumes that many features of a car are electronically
achieved. For example, on a few models the ride of a suspension can now be
adjusted by the driver.

Ordering a Three-Day Car

This car would not be ordered off a dealer lot. Instead of taking a spin around
the block, the customer might view displays or demonstrators, then enter a
simulator. Inside this "flight trainer" he can position controls in different
locations and replicate different rides and responses—a form of virtual reality.

The set of preferences checked would be stored and converted to design requirements for the order.

From the simulator, sit down at a design work station, probably with help from an advisor (future speak for a salesperson). The work station would be a CAD-type program linked to the production and design system. Using the station the customer can check the physical appearance of the car inside and out. With a 3-D screen, the visualization may be close to reality. The system will allow the prosumer to select feasible or safe designs and option combinations.

The three-day car will be exclusively made to order—no dealer inventory. By today's system, American Big-3 dealer stocks "normally" range from 60–90 days' of sales, which cover the normal leadtime for a factory order of 6–7 weeks, plus order cycle time. In Japan today, similar leadtimes to receive a factory-ordered car range from 3–21 days, so the average domestic dealer stocks 20–30 days of cars, which covers his leadtime for replenishment (about a week for the sales order cycle plus about 10–20 days from order-to-receipt using a pessimistic forecast).

The three-day car will be exclusively made to order—no dealer inventory.

Cars built in modules would probably require more expensive materials. Initially this concept might appeal only to affluent car buffs, but eventually would be a system for everyone. Customers must learn to trust their own judgment on styling and features. The total design-to-delivery time must be short, though from the customer's viewpoint how short is debatable. However, if custom-built cars need no dealer stock, those savings alone would help offset the higher cost, and for customers of modest means, payments for a long-life vehicle could be spread over a longer period.

Challenge No. 7, crucial to success, is cultivating the automotive "prosumer." A prosumer is a customer that participates in his own service or order fulfillment, especially if done with computer assistance—a high-tech version of a "do-it-yourselfer." In this case, the prosumers participate in the design of their own vehicles.[4]

The car company's prosumer-friendly design software will first be used to select a combination of body structure, drive train components, and suspension components that have been tested for safety and performance. A number of creature-comfort features can be custom-designed, depending on how much the customer wants to pay. The seat contour can be custom-profiled, the car's lighting system designed as the customer likes, the instrument panel layout modified to suit personal preferences (easily done if it just consists of repositioning images on screens). Within limits, prosumers might even modify the shape of body panels (want your monogram stamped in the door?), design their own trim, and "imagineer" sound systems to their own tastes. Of course, features that are electronically controlled can be modified by a different PC board or different software, possibly without visiting the dealer.

Challenge No. 8 is creating an ordering system that will instantly check the combination of requests by the customer for engineering safety and feasibility. As soon as an order is generated and checked, it will be transmitted to the cluster of factories that will build it. Leadtime to delivery: three days. That is where the three-day car got its name.

This story in various forms has circulated in Detroit for some time. A popular version of it has a three-day car achieved if the line-up of vehicles in an assembly plant's schedule is no more than a three-day sequence. That's far short of the idea. Many Japanese assembly plants today have fewer cars than that in the vehicle build sequence.

Engineering, Production, and Delivery

Data requirements are huge. Suppose a custom designed vehicle is damaged. Securing its CAD/CAM record (or escort memory) and transmitting it to the proper plants would be necessary to make the replacement parts.

Challenge No. 9 is managing large masses of data and controlling their flow. It is made easier by the transmission of "macro" commands to the locations where detailed data is kept. For example, your suppliers will maintain on their site the part of your bill of materials representing the parts they make.

Learning the human discipline to operate such a system seems as daunting as generating the data and software. Central control would create a choke point, less likely if distributed control is coordinated throughout the network. (Japanese refer to both the software and "humanware" aspects of this as a "holonic" system.)

After an order is entered, it is transmitted from the dealership to the cluster of plants (car company plus supplier plants) selected to build the order based on distance and backlog. Orders would flow to the plants individually, not in groups as in 1992. One can imagine that some order requests would not automatically process on the design software, or translate into CAM instructions at the plants and kick out for immediate engineering attention. Some questions would have to be referred to the locations where work is done, and one can anticipate that the connoisseurs among auto prosumers would relish that form of "car talk." (Most customers will probably prefer to order something suitable using a minimum of their time to evaluate complex alternatives.)

As soon as the assembly plant has sequenced an incoming order, the sequence and relevant data, including CAM instructions if necessary, is transmitted to all supply plants. (Imagine an elegant database organization for this.) Each plant keeps very little parts inventory that is not designated for an actual order, but fabricating plants might need to have the correct raw material on hand to start an order. All this planning needs to sequence jobs through two or more tiers of suppliers (easier if everyone can work in lot sizes of one in any sequence). With no backlog, fabrication work could begin almost immediately after an order's processing is validated.

Each cluster of plants operates its quick-change, adaptive equipment nearly around the clock. Some equipment self-repairs its own minor faults, so no long daily downtime periods are required. System maintenance downtime takes a few hours once a week, similar to the periods required for large

Each plant keeps very little parts inventory that is not designated for an actual order.

computers. Once activated, many cells can operate "in the dark" for prolonged periods without attention.

An order begun in fabrication passes to module assembly and then to final assembly in Vehicle Identification Number (VIN) sequence. Sequence control moves material where needed when needed. Processes in any plant can check the sequence and status of orders in assembly plants or in other fabrication plants as necessary. From any point in the system news of a "really serious glitch" can be quickly transmitted throughout the system so that orders can be resequenced, if necessary, but that is rarely done. Challenge No. 9 means production control by computer synchronization of the whole system so that material, tools, tests, and data march in unison through the network of supply areas into final assembly. Though similar to the "broadcast" system now used by auto companies to bring such items as seats to assembly in proper sequence, the system is neither MRP nor a pull system. It cannot work by itself, but only if all the items to be marched are "designed for marching."

The production and engineering concepts for the three-day car simply assume that Total Quality and the failsafing of operations are at maturity.

Though some parts for repair and retrofitting may be made by "off-line" facilities, a portion of the main system's production time is regularly set aside to make parts. Many customers of modularly designed cars will surely want to change its features or add "new releases" (like software) to existing cars. They might install the easy ones themselves. Service agreements must contain clauses on retrofitting.

By day three, the order should be ready to ship. Since the order is usually built by a cluster of plants close to the customer, the car should arrive at the dealership within a day. Some customers may come to the plants to pick up the cars themselves, and even to watch it being assembled.

The production and engineering concepts for the three-day car simply assume that Total Quality and the failsafing of operations are at maturity. The system will choke unless defect rates on complex cars and processes are infinitesimal. (Japanese refer to this as "Zero Defects,"—easily confused with an earlier phase of our development in North America.)

The synchronization of a distributed system—assembly, feeders, suppliers, dealers, planning centers, maintenance, service centers, etc.—carries JIT concepts to a new level. Everything—CAD/CAM systems, product specifications, vehicle performance data, customer credit information—must be able to link. Nothing like it exists today, although databases and data communications could grow into this state.

The Agile Manufacturing Version

In the summer of 1991, the Agile Manufacturing Enterprise Forum at the Iacocca Institute, Lehigh University received a grant from the Department of Defense to create an American vision of 21st century manufacturing. They adapted the Japanese scenario of the three-day car to the United States. One modification illustrated the Department of Defense as an institutional prosumer of military vehicles. An enhancement emphasized the modularity and interchangeability of many parts and subassemblies in the basic design. A customer's "pet" features, such as a custom-contoured seat, could simply be retained while much of a vehicle was reconfigured to a different purpose for its owner, as might be desired when going through a life change such as a growing family, retirement, etc.

Another addition considered prosumer maintenance of a complex vehicle. Using one or more special service compartments, they could perform normal oil changes and other fluid additions while "dressed in a suit." Each vehicle's full history would be recorded and updated by an on-board "smart chip." The system would tell the owner when service was needed. Unless a malfunction were disastrous, the "limp in" design should prevent unfortunates from being stranded in some God-forsaken locale.

The agile scenario also projected the future of "roadside service" to include electronic diagnosis. Any apparent malfunction not self-diagnosed by the vehicle itself could be recorded during vehicle operation for later play on a service center's diagnostic computer. Better yet, if digital data can be easily transmitted via Ultra-Comm, a remote car can be diagnosed by the manufacturer's computers while on the road.

A major challenge of bringing such a world to pass was human development: flat organizations, tight links between small operating units, and enterprise integration of relationships between people as well as those between computers.

The Agile Forum scenario also began to bring out environmental implications. A totally-instrumented car should be much less prone to drift out of "environmentally safe" operating condition.

Finally, while the American version concentrated on technical requirements, it noted that a major challenge of bringing such a world to pass was human development: flat organizations, tight links between small operating units, and enterprise integration of relationships between people as well as those between computers. Although the present trends toward team organization will strengthen, the Americans viewed future organizations more as a linking of entrepreneurial operating units.

The Plot Thickens

Both the American and the Japanese versions of the three-day car were devised by people with manufacturing experience. They subjected their dreams to reality checks. While no one can foretell any long-term scenario with precision the concepts are not crackpot. The conclusion: The technology is at hand. The human will to change is more doubtful.

Reflection by the author on the implications leads to other possibilities. Any system resembling the three-day car changes the basic nature of the auto industry.

Challenge No. 10 is recognition by everyone involved that the basic mission of an auto company is to provide transportation service to its customers. Manufacturing, as we have known it, is only part of the means to provide transportation. Since almost everyone who has brainstormed this scenario in depth is committed to strengthening manufacturing, few like to admit that the scenarios do not revitalize rust belt industry according to a conventional economic growth scenario. The 21st century will not be like the 20th, with factories absorbing millions of additional workers.

In fact, the big old mass production companies will probably not live in anything like their present form. For example, sharply reduced tooling costs will drastically change the production economics of General Motors, Toyota, and other behemoths and reduce barriers to entering business. Smaller operating companies hooked to partners may "enter the auto enterprise system." To see why, add a few more twists to the scenario.

The design of the three-day car envisions a mechanical frame that is really a platform for the electronics, software, and cosmetics (more like ships, aircraft, and computer frames). The cars may be equipped for "smart highways"—traffic advisories allowing drivers to avoid jams, and computer-controlled vehicles that allow dense packing in high-traffic flows. In addition, a current planning trend is to improve the connections between cars and other forms of transport—planes, ships, and trains. That will surely become part of the intelligence network available to drivers of 21st century "smartwagons."

Thus equipped, a car can be easily tracked. A car bristling with electronic sensors and transmitters will also deter thieves seeking to practice rapid disassembly on modular equipment. However, one can easily imagine civil libertarians revolting at the thought that police can constantly check their vehicle's whereabouts. Privacy issues will surely arise. (Will parking in lover's lane become a quaint 20th century custom?)

To continue lightening the mechanical platform, components should be made of more durable materials. For instance, precise, long-life bearings might be smaller than today's, but still more reliable. Interchangeable, retrofitable frame parts might have a working life longer than people do. That is not a growth scenario in the historic sense, though the replacement of the current stock of vehicles should provide steady business. The 160 million cars now licensed for American roads will not pass from existence quickly.

In the long-run, we may really have a case for remanufacturing, rather than manufacturing as we have known it. Remanufacturing upgrades a product into a better-than-new condition. Then cars would not be so much bought and sold, as periodically taken to service centers for refurbishment and upgrade.

> Cars would not be so much bought and sold, as periodically taken to service centers for refurbishment and upgrade.

Challenge No. 11 is learning remanufacturing. Ecology could become as big a driver of the scenarios as the desire for ultimate transportation service. A car which can be remanufactured is "greener" than one which requires recycling of its base materials. If the electronic content changes the quickest, the ability to remanufacture or recycle PC boards will become a rising issue.

At the outset, a three-day car might be only for the affluent, but if the scenario becomes ecology-driven, it will evolve into a system for the average driver. If the car or its parts must be disposed of by its manufacturer (or service company), then owning a car begins to be less interesting. Long-term car leasing, already a trend, could avoid complications. On the other hand, long-term ownership combined with service contracts might be a way to make a superior vehicle affordable to the average person. (How about a 20-year mortgage on your car?)

So What?

The advent of a new millennium leads to anticipation of more change than may actually occur, but the shape of changes now beginning casts the shadow of those to come. An assumption of the "three-day car" is that Total Quality, Just-in-Time, Employee Involvement, and other acronyms we now call excellence are but the foundation for a different kind of manufacturing system, and perhaps a modified economic system.

The acronyms themselves should fade as their content becomes mainstream, but they will never be totally natural. Therefore inculcation of the attitudes for them must begin early in life.

Challenge No. 12, and the biggest of all, is a redirection of ourselves and our human institutions. It begins with our approach to education (much belabored by industry leaders). We need a more rigorous approach to career education, and more intense development of people by the enterprises within which they work. We cannot yet recognize that in an information age, the key to the use of all technology and all capital is ourselves—the human element. If that can be accepted, then some of the requirements to bring the vision of a three-day car to reality are:

- **"Visionary" guidance:** The value of a common vision is direction, not precision. It enables diverse people to stumble in roughly the same direction by different paths. For instance, the ideal of designing both products and processes must be "agility," which assumes an understanding of all the underpinnings of that phrase.
- **"Open System" Information:** Of course, computer systems must universally talk to each other. However, despite enthusiasm for enterprise integration, we still have islands of automation. CAD/CAM systems that cannot communicate, and EDI linkages that are really used as fax machines.

The problem is far deeper than computer systems compatibility. Intellectual capital derives its name from the assumption that if we know something unique, the world must come to us to buy it, and we protect that opportunity through non-disclosure. That assumption turns on us when we find that what we do adds value only if it will fit into a universal system. In the 19th century, railroads discovered that none of them added value unless each used the same width track. In this century, we simply expect any telephone to connect to all other telephones. In the 21st century virtually any system must interact with other systems, and that is first a problem of human perception.

- **Decentralized Interactive Organization:** This shift has begun today with emphasis on flat organizations and teams of every kind: functional, cross-functional, and cross-company. If team members are remote and computer connected, they may be termed "virtual companies." We are headed for a radically different form of business. The organization of even an auto business—a big-scale enterprise by any standard—will likely consist of much smaller operating units with tight linkages between entities operationally focused on separate processes from raw material to customer service—and back again. An auto company as we think

An assumption of the "three-day car" is that Total Quality, Just-in-Time, Employee Involvement, and other acronyms we now call excellence are but the foundation for a different kind of manufacturing system, and perhaps a modified economic system.

of it today may become a transportation service network consisting of comparatively small operating units.

- **Common Interactive Human Processes:** The need for this is more subtle. Computer interaction is insufficient. Whether the new human organization is called a network, a holonic system, virtual companies, or buckyballs,[5] it cannot function unless work habits and customs have a common framework, but one that allows individuals to exercise freedom and creativity. Otherwise the "culture clash" will wreck the three-day car.

Human systems include everything from expectations of normal work times to common drawing conventions. They are "the way we learn to get things done." No one unlearns a lifetime of experience quickly. Such basic changes force us to put at risk whatever small career status we may have acquired, learning by doing and discovering anew "what really works."

We have barely begun to use information technology in all its possible forms as an interactive tool. Today we still often work with programmers as an armless carpenter telling someone else exactly how and where to drive each nail. We must learn different concepts by which things get done. (Imagine a three-day house).

Those interacting in the same network must have common visions and strategies, and at least three practices in common:

1. A method to diagnose and solve problems—bedrock TQM;
2. A common concept of good operating performance. ISO 9000 is an early form of common standard, but much tighter, more comprehensive, codes of performance will become necessary;
3. A shared sense of common systems. (For example, common conventions to describe products and more precise concepts to describe products and more precise concepts for how operations should mesh. We now think of meeting shipping dates instead of how our total sequence of work meshes with those of everyone else that we must merge into.)

> Any version of the three-day car leads to the conclusion that achieving prosperity and quality of life in the future depends on us improving ourselves and not hoping for more fortunate circumstances.

Today in the systems business it is commonly said that hardware has outrun software. Beyond that, software is years ahead of the "humanware." The kind of world which is upon us is not beyond imagination, but any version of the three-day car leads to the conclusion that achieving prosperity and quality of life in the future depends on us improving ourselves and not hoping for more fortunate circumstances.

Notes

1. Iwata, Makashima, Otani, et al. *Manufacturing 21 Report.* Research Report of the Association for Manufacturing Excellence, AME, 380 West Palatine Road, Wheeling, IL, 1990.

2. Iacocca Institute. *21st Century Manufacturing Enterprise Strategy,* Lehigh University, Mohler Laboratory #200, Bethlehem, PA, 1991. In two volumes. The scenarios are in Vol. 1. (Also available from AME.)

3. Hall, R. W. and Nakane, J. *Flexibility, Manufacturing Battlefield of the 90s,* Research Report of the Association for Manufacturing Excellence, 380 West Palatine Road, Wheeling, IL, 1990.

4. The term "prosumer" was coined by Alvin Toffler in *The Third Wave,* William Morrow and Co., New York, 1980.

5. Buckyball, the newly-discovered sixty-carbon spherical molecule.

Robert W. Hall is Director of New Programs for the Association for Manufacturing Excellence and is also Editor-in-Chief of Target. *He is a founding member of the Association. Hall was an examiner for the Malcolm Baldrige National Quality Award from 1988–1990 and is on leave from Indiana University. His new book,* The Soul of Enterprise, *will be published by Harper Collins this year.*

ELECTRONICS

Continuous Quality Improvement in the Electronics Industry

Gail Stout

The electronics industry has been a conspicuous leader in the implementation of quality manufacturing principles to better meet the needs of many different customer groups. This article documents the approaches and methods several different electronics firms are implementing in the ninetys. Among the companies this article profiles is Allen-Bradley. For an insider account of this company, see the article by Larry Yost, "The Allen-Bradley Story."

In the scope of history, the electronics industry is in its early stages, yet it has become one of the most important industries of the twentieth century. According to the US Commerce Department, electronics is the largest industrial employer in the US (from 1991 records): electronics, 2.39 million jobs; automotive, 0.8 million jobs; aerospace, also 0.8 million jobs; and steel, 0.4 million jobs. In the present information age, information is transmitted largely through the power of electronics in many formats: cellular telephone, computer, video, television, programmable appliance, automotive circuitry, etc.

Perhaps because the electronics industry is a recent revolutionary invention whose initial semiconductor building blocks required precise measure-

Reprinted with permission from *Quality*, February 1993, a publication of Hitchcock/Chilton Publishing, a Capital Cities/ABC, Inc. Company.

ment, documentation, automated processes, and controls, quality practices developed quickly within the industry. Integrated circuit manufacturing is fundamentally a quality-driven business. Therefore, it's not unusual that since the first Malcolm Baldrige National Quality Award was given in 1988, seven of the seventeen awards have been to electronics firms. In 1991, all three winners—Solectron Corp., Zytec Corp., and Marlow Industries, Inc.— were directly involved in electronics manufacture.

Market Rebounds

Since the first Malcolm Baldrige National Quality Award was given in 1988, seven of the seventeen awards have been to electronics firms.

However, progress within the industry has taken a circuitous route. Throughout the mid- to late-1980's, the US semiconductor industry lost market leadership to Japanese competitors who strictly practiced continuous quality improvement methods. Throughout the 1980's, US semiconductor firms experienced a loss in market share. According to many industry experts, the US is now rebounding.

Dan Hutcheson, a semiconductor industry analyst at VLSI Research, San Jose, CA, reports that in 1992 the US semiconductor industry had 43.8 percent of the market while Japan had 42.1 percent—the first year since 1985 that the US regained leadership.

And it's not just in chips, but also in chip manufacturing equipment that the US is gaining ground. According to Hutcheson, "In 1992, 53.4 percent of the semiconductor equipment market was held by the US compared to 38.3 percent by Japan. In 1991, the US had begun to earn back its leadership position with 46.7 percent vs. Japan's 44.9 percent. The difference, I believe, is that US semiconductor equipment has finally gained quality acceptance. Even the Japanese are buying it, and during a recession like they're presently experiencing, Japanese firms generally close ranks. With the recession in Japan, the market share there is likely to continue a downward path."

Other forecasts are not quite as pronounced, though market growth points toward recovery for the US beginning this year. In 1991, according to Dataquest, a silicon valley market research firm, the leading five companies in the semiconductor industry were: NEC at 8 percent; Toshiba at 7.7 percent; Intel (US) at 6.7 percent; Motorola (US) at 6.4 percent; and Hitachi at 6.4 percent.

Craig Barrett, vice president of Intel, the nation's largest chip maker, reports that Japan's marketshare in 1992 fell to 43.8 percent from 46.5 percent in 1991. On the other hand, the US share rose to 42.5 percent in 1992 from 39.1 percent in 1991.

The electronics industry is made up of many segments that only begin at the chip stage. Other portions include: semiconductor equipment and components, circuit boards, assembled boards, and final products. In such a diverse industry, quality is not a singular vision. Each company in each segment has its own approach to continuous quality improvement, though many similarities can be identified.

One thing is certain: The electronics industry as a whole is now listening to quality experts. It is not sufficient to be on the cutting edge of technology without a balanced view of the marketplace. And the move toward quality improvement is an international one with the ultimate consumer or customer judging what value for cost is best.

In the US, military markets historically determined standards for quality in electronics. Now, since military cutbacks have forced electronics firms to look for alternate markets, many of the same high-tech electronics experts who formerly created products for military use are now entering the sphere of industrial or business products. In any case, divisions between markets are becoming less distinct and what was once done by mainframe computers are now tasks for workstations. Furthermore, high-level communications are used for everyday products rather than being reserved for military purposes.

The following profiles provide insight into the methods and approaches to continuous quality improvement at a few leading electronics firms. Research consortiums such as SEMATECH and MCC are not only having an impact on the electronics industry's advances in solving tough industry problems, but also on advancing the progression of quality improvements within the industry. Therefore, these two consortiums are also profiled.

Continuous Quality Improvements at Motorola

Motorola Inc. is one of the leading suppliers of electronic equipment, components, and services for worldwide markets. Some of its products include pagers, two-way radios, cellular telephones, semiconductors, defense and aerospace electronics, computers, and automotive electronics. Net sales for this large, diverse company totaled $11.34 billion in 1991. The company has successfully become a global company with non-US revenues reaching up to 50 percent of the total in 1992. Motorola has sales of up to $1 billion a year in Japan, a country where excellent quality is essential for a product's success.

In 1988, Motorola won the first Baldrige Award in recognition of its process for managing quality. On September 25, 1992, when former President George Bush visited Motorola's Schaumburg, IL, headquarters, he commented on the company's ability to increase its holding in the Japanese semiconductor market. Bush said, "Your company has led the industry effort in gaining access to this important market. You've done this by designing and producing quality devices and circuits that the Japanese want."

Bill Smith, vice president and senior quality assurance manager at the Land Mobile Products Sector of Motorola, has a history of involvement in the company's continuous quality improvement practices, how they began, and where they're headed. "We don't call the process continuous quality improvement because that implies *Kaizen* (a Japanese term for evolutionary improvement in small steps). Motorola is more aggressive than that."

Emphasis on quality improvement began after a corporate meeting in 1979. Robert W. Galvin, then CEO, chairman of the board, and son of the company's founder, reviewed Motorola's achievements after a particularly good year. After his presentation, one executive stood up and declared that according to his customers, a quality problem existed. From that point on, total customer satisfaction became the fundamental objective and quality improvement became the focus of the company.

> Motorola has sales of up to $1 billion a year in Japan, a country where excellent quality is essential for a product's success.

Six Sigma

Until 1987, Motorola had a "top ten" goals list for quality. But because of the diverse, decentralized nature of the company, different measures of quality were taken. Then, in 1987, the top ten list was discarded and replaced with a unifying plan to measure quality improvements in the common language of six sigma, an equivalent to 3.4 defects per one million opportunities in every operation of the firm, from manufacturing through customer service. The goal was to go from a defect level of 6,000 parts per million (ppm) to 10 times improvement by 1989 and at least 100 times improvement by 1991, achieving six-sigma capability by 1992.

In 1987, Motorola's written pronouncement claimed that the firm would "With a deep sense of urgency, spread dedication to every facet of the corporation and achieve a culture of continual improvement to assure total customer satisfaction. There is only one ultimate goal: zero defects—in everything we do."

In looking at accomplishments so far, Motorola did meet its improvement goals by 1989 and 1991. And by 1991, some plants were pockets of six-sigma excellence, such as the wafer fabrication plant in Toulouse, France. But as a whole, the company's manufacturing operations approached a 5.5-sigma capability, translating into 30 ppm defects, just short of its original goal.

In approaching 5.5-sigma capability, the firm reduced in-process defect levels by 150 times; improved the reliability of products shipped to customers; saved manufacturing costs to the tune of $900 million in 1992 and over $3 billion since the 1987 quality improvement initiative.

Many firms might downgrade expectations if a goal is not met by the targeted date; not Motorola. Reasoning that future products, especially semiconductor chips with billions of devices and trillions of instructions per second, will require quality levels in a parts-per-billion format, George Fisher, Motorola's present CEO and chairman of the board, stated new goals for 1992 and beyond. "The basis for our six-sigma efforts in 1992 and beyond will be to: continue our efforts to achieve six-sigma results—and beyond—in everything we do; change our metrics from parts per million to parts per billion (ppb); and go forward with a goal of 10 times reduction in defects every two years."

The Effects of Baldrige

Winning the Baldrige Award in 1988 has given unmeasurable recognition to Motorola's quality efforts. So far, according to many employees, the only problem is in living up to their reputation. Paul Noakes, vice president and director of external quality programs, gave over 100 talks on Motorola's quality program in 1991. "We're passionate about improvement," he says.

Motorola University, an educational facility at corporate headquarters, is open to the public, as is the associated Motorola Museum, an attached building that tracks the company's product history. Not only has the firm educated its own employees (at least 40 hours of training are required each year at every level), but the company has also become an educator at large.

When Motorola executives insisted that its suppliers also apply for the Baldrige, the firm offered guidance and aid to ensure the supplier's success. A few suppliers balked, but those that became involved also became proponents of quality practices after seeing measurable results. Many suppliers such as Xerox Corp., Business Products and Systems; IBM, Rochester; AT&T, Network Systems Group; Marlow Industries; Zytec Corp., and Federal Express; subsequently won Baldrige Awards, too. Many others have received site visits.

ISO Status

Motorola has 18 sites registered to ISO 9000. Each of these sites is outside the US in locations such as Europe, Hong Kong, and Malaysia. According to Scott Shumway, vice president and director of quality for the semiconductor sector, "We're not pushing ISO 9000 for our US companies because our QSR (quality systems review, an internal system) is much more stringent than 9000."

Changes in Quality Practices

The semiconductor sector of Motorola has experienced a few quality changes in a day-to-day activities. Customers, for instance, would like to discontinue incoming tests altogether and have parts placed directly on the manufacturing line. This places a heavy reliability burden on the semiconductor manufacturer.

At each major customer site, Motorola's semiconductor sector has a resident field quality manager, so that any problem that customers experience related to the company's components is solved on site. "You're never six sigma until you're six sigma in your customer's application. Line fallout of semiconductor products will be the measure of who will survive in this industry. One example is Ford, where zero line fallout is imperative; that places a challenge on us," Shumway says.

Semiconductor manufacturers like Motorola are relying on automated test equipment more than ever. Often test equipment is application specific; handlers are automated robotic equipment; and test sites are built into the product whenever possible. As components become more complex, more measurement and control are done at the wafer level, because at high levels of complexity, repair is not possible. The challenge is to keep the production process in control at low levels of manufacturing. Built-in reliability begins with robustness in the design state of semiconductor manufacture.

"We're not pushing ISO 9000 for our US companies because our QSR (quality systems review, an internal system) is much more stringent than 9000."

SCI's Quality Growth

SCI, headquartered in Huntsville, AL, is the largest contract board assembler in the US. The company has 19 plants around the world, 10,000 employees, and made $1.5 billion in revenues during 1992. The company has been in existence for over 32 years, though initially it began as an aerospace company. Early on, many of the computers in the Saturn program were made by SCI.

During the 1970's when the computer industry started to grow, SCI diversified into contract manufacturing to take advantage of the burgeoning industry.

In July 1991, Jean Sapp, the president and CEO, brought the quality managers together and discussed his plan to have each plant registered to ISO 9002 by June 30, 1993. SCI's plant in County Cork, Ireland, and the plant in Ayrshire, Scotland, have been certified.

"At about $30,000 a plant, it's costly for us, but our customers are insisting on ISO 9002. How you measure the value of ISO, no one really knows. Getting ready for registration has obviously affected our operation, though. There's a higher level of discipline than before. Furthermore, although board designs come to us in finished formats, the customer is relying on us for testing the finished board, for keeping up with new technologies, and for having the latest equipment in board assembly. If the customer feels its important to be ISO-registered, that's our goal," Sapp notes.

Joe Ketner, quality assurance plant manager, felt satisfied with the registration process at his plant in San Jose because it offered continuous assessment and more uniformity within the whole operation than in the past. The quality manual before preparation for ISO was a corrective action plan that cut across all departments. Now there's a management system for each function that is specific to that function. Top management support for process improvement permeates all functions: finance, sales, materials, quality, engineering, manufacturing, and management. People now know what they're doing and how to do their job in detail.

Tests Performed by SCI

SCI is customer-driven to test boards once assembled. After boards are loaded at a rate of 18,000 surface mount components an hour, both sides, in-circuit testing begins. Spring-loaded probes called Pogo contacts touch resistors and record values. Although this type of ATE test has only an 80-percent confidence level, it does check each component.

Functional tests, done less frequently, check to see if the board actually runs in the intended final product. Other tests to weed out early life failures include burn-in, freeze/bake, and stress tests. More often than not, customers want fully tested, warranted boards, although they want it all at a low cost.

Continuous Quality at Solectron

Solectron Corp., Milpitas, CA, is a contract manufacturing company that does surface mount, through-hole, systems assembly remanufacturing, software development, and flexible circuit assembly. It operates at four site locations: Penang, Malaysia; Bordeaux, France; Charlotte, NC: and Milpitas, CA, under the direction of Ko Nishimura, CEO. It employs about 4,000 workers worldwide. Each year, since the company was founded in 1977, sales have increased dramatically. From about $265 million in 1991, sales increased to $407 million in 1992, up 53 percent.

Many of the programs that Solectron follows are remarkably similar to those of Motorola. ("We copy good ideas shamelessly. But don't quote me on that because I think that Bob Galvin said it first," said one amused employee.) Solectron's philosophy of customer satisfaction relates to the primary objective of Motorola's total customer satisfaction primary objective. Solectron also has a six-sigma program. Whereas Motorola established Motorola University for training of employees, Solectron University also trains employees in professional growth. Motorola requires a minimum of 40 training hours of per employee per year while Solectron requires over 95 hours of technical training in a year. And both have won the Baldrige Award. There is, however a fundamental difference in size and diversity. And a few subtle differences are apparent in Solectron's continuous quality improvement practices.

At Solectron, the Baldrige criteria provided the framework for quality improvements during the last four years. But over the last year ISO 9002 has been the company's focus. According to Richard Allen, director of corporate quality, the Baldrige focuses on results and excellence in performance while ISO documents the quality framework.

> Solectron requires over 95 hours of technical training in a year.

So far, quality improvement has taken many paths: inspection, then SPC, quality circles, Baldrige, ISO 9002, and next comes the British Approval Board for Telecommunications product certification planned for early 1993. When it comes to goal-setting, Solectron's ambitious plan has specific achievements designated early-on.

Allen-Bradley's Approach

Allen-Bradley (A-B), a Rockwell International company, produces a broad line of industrial controls and information products for the plant floor: machine vision, drives, computer numerical controls, programmable controllers, application software, industrial computers, sensors, and automatic identification systems to communication networks. All serve the electronics industry.

A-B's quality policy states that the company is "committed to enhancing our customers' success worldwide with products, services and responsiveness that set industry standards for quality and value. We relentlessly strive to be the best in every aspect of our business by fostering a culture of trust, teamwork, responsibility, high expectations, and open communications with employees, customers, and suppliers." And a statement of this policy hangs on the wall in each of the company's 25 plants around the world.

> According to management, on a cumulative basis, TQMS paid back $13 for every dollar A-B invested.

Since the firm began in 1903, the first products were mechanical parts. Initial quality standards were based on inspection-based procedures with good/bad sorting taking place as products rolled off the assembly lines. By the 1970's, when electronic product technology made a quality system based on inspection obsolete, A-B developed a total quality management system (TQMS). This was a defect prevention-based system using process controls and metrics measurements. It emphasized engineering and manufacturing team efforts. TQMS succeeded in increasing quality and product reliability; over $129 million in quality costs were saved over eight years. According to management, on a cumulative basis, TQMS paid back $13 for every dollar A-B invested.

At the beginning of the 1990's, Allen-Bradley reached another landmark in continuous quality improvement methods. Customers in the 90's demand more than defect-free products. They also want defect-free delivery and services. Consequently, A-B realigned its management system to one of total quality for customer satisfaction (TQCS).

The keys to success in TQCS include leadership from senior management to drive the effort; a coordinated process of companywide systems involving employees in all disciplines; continuous improvement and measurement to keep everyone on track; aggressive goals centered on customer satisfaction; and communication to keep every employee informed and involved.

Many of the continuous improvement initiatives sound remarkably like those of other quality leaders in the industry: reduce variation in key processes to six-sigma levels; accelerate improvement in products, service, and customer satisfaction by 20:1 every five years; and achieve continuous cycle time reductions in key business processes. Because many customers are international, Allen-Bradley is working to achieve recognition for its processes by registering facilities to ISO 9000. Over 21 plants are registered to 9001. Customers' needs are paramount.

The Role of Consortiums

Consortiums have provided a catalyst for quality improvements in the electronics industry. SEMATECH (SEmiconductor MAnufacturing TECHnology), for example, is a consortium of US semiconductor manufacturers working with government and academe to sponsor and conduct research aimed at ensuring leadership in semiconductor manufacturing technology. It was proposed by the Departments of Defense and Commerce in 1987 and passed by Congress (Public Law 100-180) in 1988. The consortium's mission is to create a fundamental change in manufacturing technology and to strengthen the domestic infrastructure to provide US companies the continuing capability to be worldclass suppliers. Members include: AMD, AT&T, Digital Equipment, Harris Semiconductor, Hewlett-Packard, IBM, Intel, Motorola, National Semiconductor, Rockwell, Texas Instruments, and DARPA (a Department of Defense unit).

SEMATECH's budget ($200 million) is provided half by the federal government and half by member companies. Semiconductors are vital elements to economic health and national security, therefore, both private and defense industries glean profits from sharing the investment risk.

What has SEMATECH accomplished to spur continuous quality improvements in the semiconductor industry? It has developed a quality improvement program based on Malcolm Baldrige criteria called Partnering for Total Quality. SEMATECH's involvement was to create a consistent partnering approach applicable to all companies within the semiconductor industry when working with their suppliers and to supply industrywide guidelines designed to accelerate implementation of total quality for US semiconductor equipment and materials suppliers.

The criteria for the SEMATECH Partnering for Total Quality recognition include a detailed organizational assessment, development of a list of requirements, a joint assessment with the help of a third-party firm or customer/mentor, and development of an action plan. An overall companywide commitment to the total quality process must be made. So far, results from partnering have been positive. Over 110 equipment and materials companies that might not have applied for the Baldrige have followed SEMATECH's program and improved their product quality while reducing new product release cycle time.

ISO 9000 Task Force

Another committee currently underway at SEMATECH addresses the development of a US approach to the use and implementation of ISO 9000 in the semiconductor industry. Ray Martin, cochairman of the ISO 9000 committee, is organizing the members' experiences with worldwide registrars. He constructs matrices after asking a list of questions to member companies. Many members have some off-site branches registered. By 1994, most SEMATECH member companies plan to be registered. Some of the information developed by the committee revealed that most companies have more stringent internal standards and documentation in place than is required. According to Martin, there is a need for a government/industry recognized registrar accreditation body in the US. A unified approach to keeping ISO registration costs under control should be one outcome of this committee's work.

Partnering

Microelectronics and Computer Technology Corp. (MCC), Austin, TX, a consortium of diverse electronics, computer, aerospace, manufacturing, and other advanced technology organizations, is building enabling technologies to accelerate multichip module (MCM) manufacture. MCMs are made from bare dice connected in one complex layered-module. Multichip modules are predicted to be the next electronics building block to systems requiring over 50 mHz of speed. Rather than the usual practice of mounting a single chip into an individual package and then connecting the package leads to the board as is the practice today, with MCMs, many chips are interconnected directly in one module. Therefore, the number of interconnects is reduced while density and complexity is increased. With the power and speed promised by this new module, what formerly was handled in a mainframe may eventually only be the size of a workstation.

Adding to the problem of building intricate MCMs successfully is one of finding good dice (integrated circuit chips) from which to build these new complex components. This is quickly becoming a bottleneck to advancing the new technology. MCC and SEMATECH are jointly providing guidelines for procurement and use of known-good die (a term for bare die that is warranted as being "good" or defect-free by the semiconductor manufacturer), since this is a joint problem between the semiconductor chip supplier and the user of the die to produce a MCM. The yield of a MCM depends on the quality of the unpackaged die used.

Through the efforts of the two consortiums, die suppliers (DEC, Harris, H-P, Intel, IBM, Micron, Motorola, Rockwell, and TI) and die users (General Electric, Hughes, n-Chip, and others) as well as additional third-party vendors (Chip Supply, Elmo Semiconductor) are working together to solve the known-good die quality issue within the industry. Industry meetings, jointly developed guidelines, and other partnering approaches increase the speed of electronics technology development.

Continuous quality improvement within the electronics industry as a whole takes diverse paths. The approach is often to follow the Baldrige guidelines (Motorola, Solectron, and SEMATECH). Registration to ISO 9000 (offshore Motorola, SCI, Solectron, Allen-Bradley, and SEMATECH members) is quickly taking hold in the US. When a difficult problem stymies the industry, consortiums often create the communication catalyst required to further development of the technology.

Gail Stout is a senior editor of Quality.

Intel's Circuitous Route to Implementing Total Quality

Tom Clark, Larry Walz, George Turner, and Bish Miszuk

As with other companies that have little competition and prosper even when run inefficiently, Intel discovered the value of quality management only when the market changed and competition heated up. This article presents a case study of how the company transformed itself by implementing the principles and procedures of quality.

Intel's computer service division, Deer Valley, AZ, was established in the late 1970's to service highly proprietary Intel systems-level products. As a result, the division enjoyed a growing business with a low volume of service calls, little competition, and high profit margins.

This changed dramatically as the computer industry shifted in emphasis from proprietary products to the PC (personal computer). As Intel designed more and more products for PC platforms, the service division went through a number of changes including: a significantly reduced profit margin; a complex support infrastructure; cost reduction; frequent reorganization; continually changing strategic direction; and routine layoffs, mostly in direct service delivery. By 1988, Intel was managed vertically, with a 4:1 indirect vs. direct employee ratio, and had completely lost sight of the customer. This only made problems worse.

False Starts

Between 1988 and 1990, Intel's computer service division forged ahead, attempting deep changes in business management. A team formed to focus on business process change. Furthermore, an expensive, 18-month customized training program called "managing for value" (M4V) became the impetus for a formal organizational development program. Forty-five managers and supervisors got together for a week in an attempt to redefine all processes within the organization.

Reprinted with permission from *Quality*, February 1993, a publication of Hitchcock/Chilton Publishing, a Capital Cities/ABC, Inc. Company.

Nevertheless, all of these attempts failed to correct the problems because no matter how well everyone worked together in these sessions, they reverted to old ways when back in the work environment. What was learned did not affect daily behavior. Any crisis would redirect attention away from lasting change.

The Turning Point

Meaningful change for the organization began in 1990. Intel made the commitment to apply for the Malcolm Baldrige National Quality Award and established a quality technology group. This group had two basic charters: first, to develop tools for each division to use when implementing the Baldrige management style within Intel; second, to deploy the program within Intel. The computer service division was one of the first divisions to deploy the program.

The quality technology group developed two tools that led to meaningful change. The first, the "quality leadership series," an in-house developed course for senior managers, was given to senior staff early in 1990 and then to middle managers and other employees. This series of proctored self-study courses helped to map the way the company conducted business as compared with Intel's stated values and determine how to best implement process change to meet these values. Key lessons were learned from the series. Surprisingly, some managers stonewalled effective process change while employees in general had a broader understanding of problems than management. Employees found that they were in a better position to affect change.

In November 1990, the quality technology group rolled out a new tool called "management by planning" (MBP). This tool provided a complete roadmap to implement total quality within the organization. Once again, 45 managers and supervisors gathered for a week and created four strategic objectives with 20 strategies, 50 tactics, and 200 projects supporting those four strategic objectives—as though sheer numbers could solve each problem as it became identified and classified. Ignoring virtually all warnings, the group then began working on each objective at once.

45 managers and supervisors created four strategic objectives with 20 strategies, 50 tactics, and 200 projects supporting those four strategic objectives—as though sheer numbers could solve each problem as it became identified and classified.

Another Crisis

By April 1991, it became apparent to Intel services' top management that the quality program was well off track. Not only were the process improvement tactics showing little progress, but many of the teams were not even meeting. The organization was simply pursuing far too many tactics and trying to solve all of its problems at once. Additionally, the commitment to make real changes varied greatly from manager-to-manager and employee-to-employee. Priorities were not apparent and even minor issues, such as the logistics of scheduling project team meetings, bogged down.

To compound the situation, business conditions and profitability were deteriorating. Top management knew that 1991 would have to be the turning point for a return to profitability. Yet poor financial results early in 1991 indicated that profitability by year's end would probably not be possible.

PROCESS CHANGES NECESSARY FOR INTEL'S SUCCESS

Reaching these two main goals of customer satisfaction and customer total outage were only the end results. A multitude of cross-functional process changes had to happen for these goals to be met. These included:

1. A 25-percent reduction in contract processing time.
2. The time and materials billing process reduced throughput by 40 percent.
3. The repair inventory backlog reduced from 5,500 to 0 pieces.
4. Repair throughput increased from 290 to 450 pieces/month.
5. Spare parts purchases were reduced by $250,000/month.
6. Expendable part priority orders were reduced from 30 percent of total priority orders to 8 percent.
7. Overall priority orders were reduced 25 percent.
8. The customer contract database was completely audited and corrected.
9. Nonrevenue generating service calls were reduced by 90 percent.
10. Two new major marketing programs were put in place.
11. Geographic coverage expanded from 41 to 186 cities.
12. A remote support center reduced on-site service calls (phone fixes) by 30 percent for calls that were taken by the center.
13. Reporting of customer service call data was standardized.
14. Spare parts replenishment cycle time was reduced from 131 to 34 days.

With this new crisis point, management's reaction, for the first time, was swift. It had become obvious that certain senior managers were not engaged in process change; therefore, only a small core group of six top managers who bought into the program met several times over the course of a week.

After careful consideration, it became clear that customers' needs were not being met; it was time to start listening again. After review, the original 200 reduced to just two measurements of success. One was customer satisfaction as measured by our independent monthly survey; the other was customer outage time, a measure of the elapsed time from customer phone call to final resolution of the specific equipment problem. All other indicators were merely subsets of customer satisfaction and customer outage time.

After review, the original 200 reduced to just two measurements of success.

The next step seemed to be narrowing down the 50 tactics and 200 projects to a manageable and achievable number. However, the company soon realized that it would really take much more than that. Part of the problem originated with Intel's managers. By November 1990, several senior, long-term managers were not engaged or committed to the new quality focus. While subteams met to work out the tactics, for example, several of these managers frequently stood on the sidelines or did not attend meetings at all. Beyond that, with deteriorating business conditions, Intel was clearly overstaffed at top levels. A reduction in the workforce targeting some upper-level employees and restructuring costs occurred.

To move forward, the general manger insisted on a serious quality and process improvement refocus. The new management team would have to enthusiastically support a total quality focus. Additionally, all employees would have to be engaged in the process. Intel would also focus on a limited number of targets to pursue. Finally, three process improvement managers were chosen from within the management team. These three individuals would be responsible for keeping the organization's process improvement efforts on track.

Some lessons Intel's employees had earlier ignored finally began to be understood. There were also some basic lessons learned by other organizations involved in a successful quality overhaul:

- It takes commitment to total quality by senior management, including a willingness to make hard decisions.
- Heightened importance, such as that caused by crisis situations, is necessary to cause real change.
- Management alone is not fully equipped to develop effective solutions to basic process problems.
- Only a small number of the most important targets can be pursued simultaneously.
- Management must listen to and engage the employees.
- Dedicated and empowered process improvement managers are necessary for success.

It took almost four years before Intel's computer organization learned these lessons.

Regroup and Retrain

The process managers identified four critical business process tactics, thus replacing the original 50 tactics. The four tactics were: to reduce customer outage time; to improve the administrative process and spare parts availability; and to increase support capacity. Using their knowledge of the business, the managers then made a preliminary pass at some supporting projects. Cross departmental teams were chosen to validate the four tactics and refine the supporting projects. It was very important at this stage to end the "top down" nature of handling this second crisis point. The employees had to be engaged immediately. Teams representing each functional group and every level of employee in the organization validated the direction and worked out the details behind the strategic focus on customer satisfaction and customer outage time.

The process managers and their teams took two weeks to make a proposal for the next steps. Each of the four tactics and their 17 supporting projects had clear measurement expectations and time-frames. The process managers acted as facilitators to keep the groups focused. They also played the role of devil's advocates to ensure that the organization focused its limited resources only on the most critical problems. Additionally, they made sure the teams considered all alternatives. "We can't" was unacceptable. Furthermore, the projects that had fallen by the wayside were specifically identified and conscious decisions made as to the rank order of selected projects.

Once consensus was received from the general manager's full staff, the team embarked on implementation. The approach this time was really not fundamentally different from the earlier management by planning (MBP) approach in November 1990. But the quality improvement plan was much more realistically put together and process-oriented, not functionally oriented. Serious thought was put into tactic selection to match efforts to the most critical needs. And, Intel's computer service division began to use the key total quality lessons learned from other companies that had been ignored in the past, such as the empowerment of employees at the lowest level and allowing them to be the experts. This time dedicated process managers were in place to keep the projects on track.

Execute

Each project's owner (not necessarily a manager) pulled together the necessary team with cross-functional members. The 17 project teams began to meet weekly and were asked to find solutions to the root problem causes, not just symptoms. Basic quality tools such as process flow charts, cause/effect diagrams, and Pareto analysis were used. The teams then developed measurable milestones, enlisted ownership of each milestone, and received commitments to their resolution.

Process management roles were important throughout the program. First, process managers received the full support and empowerment from the general manager. Second, process managers attended all the team meetings as facilitators.

This entailed two basic functions. One was to keep the teams on track and the other was to ensure that teams looked at all possible solutions. Additionally, process manager were responsible for working with team members on a one-to-one basis to help the team members understand how to work within the system.

Each of the 17 teams was required to submit a one-page progress update to the general manager containing highlights, lowlights, and progress against milestones. Five teams were selected each week on a rotating basis to present further detail to the general manager and the management team. Teams that were not making any progress were continually scheduled for detailed reviews until they showed progress. Later, reviews were changed to biweekly, but with the same focus on tight scrutiny of results.

This review process was a key to Intel's success. Human nature is such that progress tends to be made when people are held accountable. Teams took the reviews seriously. In fact, project owners were asked to have their entire team in attendance when their project was reviewed. This ensured that all team members were accountable and heard the same message. The general manager maintained a high degree of involvement in these reviews. Process

Human nature is such that progress tends to be made when people are held accountable.

managers kept the sessions on track and did diligent follow-up on action items assigned in the sessions. Rewards in many forms were used to recognize positive results, ranging from group recognition awards to group dinners. Rewards always went to teams, never to individuals.

Eventually, early successes began to produce high enthusiasm. The company was having fun.

By May 1991, it became clear that the process was beginning to work. Problems and issues became visible quickly. Then corrective actions were performed quickly. One functional group accomplished more in two months while the manager was on extended leave than they had over the past two years with the manager present. Several employees who were marginally meeting requirements suddenly became stars because now the team valued their opinions. Employees at relatively low levels made meaningful decisions and executed solutions. As process problems arose, they were fixed within a day or two. The team felt that it worked on the root cause of problems instead of symptoms. Eventually, early successes began to produce high enthusiasm. The company was having fun.

LESSONS FROM INTEL'S EXPERIENCE

The lessons learned from implementing the total quality model in Intel's computer service division have resulted in significant positive change. Through a painful process of false starts and failed attempts, Intel's employees finally found the process that worked. In retrospect, many of these lessons had been outlined many times in different types of training; however, it wasn't until the company faced a severe business crisis with a good set of quality tools that it was able to become successful. Intel's computer service organization learned:

- To be prepared to change the fundamental way it managed business.
- To make changes in management at all levels if and when necessary.
- To demand high-level organization commitment, complete management buy-in, and a high level of enthusiasm throughout the company.
- To encourage and stimulate high organizational visibility, responsibility, and accountability.
- To define tactics down to the basic few indicators that affect a customer's perception of a product.
- To choose dedicated, qualified process managers.
- To empower employees to make process decisions.
- To support and nurture employee enthusiasm throughout the process.
- To direct managers to step back and facilitate for employees.

The key lesson for Intel was the importance of team effort. Everyone involved in the process of implementing a total quality program must continually ask themselves, "What effect will this decision have on other functions within the organization?"

Results

After seven months, the progress, initially measured in small steps, resulted in dramatic improvement in both customer satisfaction and customer total outage. Customer satisfaction had risen from a 70 to 80 percent rating in May 1991, to a 95 percent rating in December 1991. At the same time, customer total outage was significantly reduced from an average of 25 hours in May 1991 to an average of 11 hours in December 1991.

Intel's computer service organization's attempts at implementing a total quality process took several iterations and false starts. Yet, once established, dramatic improvements occurred resulting in high levels of customer satisfaction and significantly reduced time to complete customer service calls. Lessons learned by Intel can be applied to other organizations currently starting down the total quality path.

Tom Clark is district support manager; Larry Walz is divisional controller; George Turner is divisional process manager; and Bish Mizur is divisional quality manager at Network and Services Div., Intel, Inc., Phoenix, AZ.

The Allen-Bradley Story

Larry Yost

The Allen-Bradley Company, a unit of Rockwell International, manufactures electromechanical products like push buttons and other switches. To better meet customer needs and become more productive, the company began implementing a total quality strategy. This article, by an A-B senior vice-president, describes their approach.

In the mid-1980s, Allen-Bradley saw that the requirements for world-class competitiveness in manufacturing were changing. The company's Milwaukee headquarters was manufacturing such basic electro-mechanical products as push buttons, starters, and limit switches. But reaching new levels of competitiveness meant more than starting, stopping, and sensing. Customers were looking for ways to improve productivity and add value to their products, and this required a new generation of microprocessor-based products.

In 1986, solid-state products represented only a fraction of the Milwaukee operation's total sales. Market forecast projections indicated that by 1995, these products would contribute more than one-third of the company's total revenues and would continue to grow. If it was going to bring a new generation of solid-state products to market quickly, Allen-Bradley would have to clear some significant hurdles.

Traditionally, the company had had the luxury of taking years to introduce a new product. High quality was achieved by running multiple pilot orders before releasing the product for sale. Each pilot run ironed out more bugs, and a lot of time passed until the tooling and processes met the company's quality standards. To support such an extended tooling-up time and long product life cycles, the company carried high inventories of components, work-in-progress, and finished products.

But the projected flood of new solid-state products meant the company had to develop a totally new strategy for designing, industrializing, and manufacturing its next generation of industrial control products.

The development of this new vision, however, was not driven by a manufacturing need—the company was making enough product to meet current demand. It was driven by business necessity—a need to build an exceptional product introduction capability, and a requirement to build manufacturing capacity for products that hadn't even been developed yet. If the company

Reprinted with permission from *Journal of Business Strategy*, May/June 1993, Faulkner & Gray, Inc., New York, NY.

didn't move fast, the window of opportunity would slam shut and lock out the future.

Developing a Manufacturing Strategy

One of the most important first steps was to assess solid-state manufacturing capabilities in Milwaukee from all major vantage points—from design cycle to inventory policies.

Once the internal assessment was completed, teams began benchmarking other companies. Small teams toured and interviewed the best-in-class electronic manufactures in North America: AT&T, Digital Equipment Corp., Delco, several Rockwell International plants (Allen-Bradley's parent firm), Northern Telecom, and the company's own plants in Cleveland, OH, and Dublin, GA. Teams also went to Japan and met with counterparts at several Nippondenso and Sony plants.

Following the benchmark process, a interdisciplinary team developed an overall electronic manufacturing strategy (EMS). It included a clearly stated mission, tactics, and objectives designed to implement that strategy. EMS went well beyond simply looking at a manufacturing facility and focused on the needs of the business and the structures required to fulfill those needs. It included such functions as marketing, product design, industrialization, manufacturing, materials, quality assurance, component engineering, and service and support.

EMS1 has the capability to manufacture more than 100 different circuit board types in lot sizes as small as one on a continuous-flow assembly line.

A New Facility Is Born

Since manufacturing advanced solid-state products was the most critical and most complex element of the overall strategy, it was tackled first. The result of this viewing was called EMS1.

Built in phases over a three-year period, the 27,000-square-foot facility on the eighth floor of the Milwaukee headquarters building began with islands of automation—stand-alone machines—and evolved to full-computer integration. Through EMS1, the company reduced work-in-progress to one day and achieved one-day turnaround of pilot products.

EMS1 has the capability to manufacture more than 100 different circuit board types in lot sizes as small as one on a continuous-flow assembly line. Eventually there may be as many as six or more types of circuit boards being produced at any time. All of these different circuit boards travel automatically through EMS1 in the most direct route and in the shortest possible time. This seemless flow-through of circuit boards is unique in the electronics manufacturing industry.

But productivity in assembly and testing is only part of the story. A key competitive issue involved shortening the time it takes to introduce new products into the market. After looking at the process used to develop new products, it became apparent that there needed to be smoother integration between marketing, design, engineering, industrialization, production, and materials.

One of the most important steps used to facilitate these changes was the opportunity for two-way communication between functions. Participants included development engineers, PC board layout personnel, and members of such groups as product industrialization, production control, and quality assurance and quality control.

Participants discussed design for manufacturability guidelines as critical ingredients for faster time to market. Unified design guidelines, which call for components that have been pre-approved for quality, directly affect overall speed, quality, and cost. A tremendous amount of time and money is saved by using a pre-approved component.

A set of approved design guidelines also helps to decrease tool-up time and lessen potential problems associated with introducing untried configurations onto a highly automated line. In addition, significant cost benefits are gained through high inventory turnover, the result of using a minimum number of components.

The company now generates pilot products in weeks, not months.

Integrated Design and Manufacturing

After the first layout of a new design is completed on a computer-aided design (CAD) workstation, it is sent electronically to test engineering, product industrialization, production, and inventory control. This helps eliminate the errors associated with manual systems and shortens development time. The company now generates pilot products in weeks, not months.

Last year, for example, a customer asked for a specific product that Allen-Bradley didn't have. Designers received the request to build a prototype on a Thursday afternoon. By Friday afternoon, "build information" was electronically transmitted to EMS1. By noon Saturday, five completed printed circuit board assemblies were available for test and evaluation. When power was applied, those printed circuit boards performed as designed.

Material Purchasing

Ninety-eight percent of the components used in the company's printed circuit board assemblies are purchased from outside suppliers. Each printed circuit board assembled in EMS1 requires approximately 425 different components. This number of components and the worldwide supplier base presented an enormous set of production, quality, and cost challenges.

The first mandate was to ensure that quality components arrived on the shipping dock. The company spent considerable time choosing suppliers and working with them on quality standards and requirements. When a shipment of components arrives for EMS1, it generally goes directly to the facility; no inspection is required. Another mandate concerned lowering inventory costs. Teams from Allen-Bradley benchmarked a number of companies and found that common practice in the electronics industry is to pick component parts from a stockroom and apply them to a given order. Typically, the order is staged or held until all components for a circuit board have been received. But during that time, customer needs can and do change.

This approach did not meet the EMS guidelines for flexibility, speed, and time-to-market. Planners wanted to be able to change priorities and avoid allocating components until the moment the day's production schedule was developed. The materials management group developed an electronic pull system that electronically tracks the demand for a component and ties that demand to the appropriate area on the manufacturing floor.

By integrating the material procurement system with manufacturing operations and operating under a just-in-time (JIT) strategy, the company was able to greatly reduce its inventory costs. EMS1 achieves 12 inventory turns per year for work in progress, which is significantly above electronic industry averages.

JIT also uncovers operational problems. In this way, JIT has become a quality enhancement program because it helps identify issues before they become costly problems.

Training and Empowerment

Because the company had little experience in solid-state manufacturing, it sought an educational partner and found one in The Milwaukee School of Engineering (MSOE).

MSOE designed a math and electronics curriculum specifically organized for EMS1 production workers. The program is taught in the plant at the company's expense. EMS1 production team members spend 150 hours in the classroom. Allen-Bradley provides the facilities and financial and managerial support; MSOE provides the teachers, texts, and curriculum.

The company drew almost exclusively from its own work force to staff EMS1—people who have been with Allen-Bradley for between 20 and 30 years. Teams of production workers have almost total responsibility for their respective operations. Process technicians act as team leaders. If there is a production problem, each team does whatever it takes to get it fixed. If there is a quality issue, they stop the line and resolve the problem.

The success of Allen-Bradley's EMS program continues to exceed planners' expectations. The company is gaining a competitive edge by replicating systems designed and implemented under its guidelines. EMS1 and the supporting design and materials systems are helping to speed new products to market. As a result, the company has been able to lower total development and manufacturing costs of all its products.

Larry Yost is senior vice president, operations group, at Allen-Bradley Co., a Milwaukee-based unit of Rockwell International Corp.

Manufacturing Sector

OTHER INDUSTRIES

Whirlpool's World-Class Manufacturing

John J. Kendrick

In the heavily competitive home appliance market, Whirlpool is the world's leading manufacturer. This article explains how the company makes quality an attitude by "concentrating on team building, continuous training, and motivation throughout the organization." They know this is absolutely vital for the company to create its world-class products.

Whirlpool Corp. is the world's leading manufacturer of major home appliances. The company manufactures in 11 countries and markets products in more than 90 countries. Its major brand names include Whirlpool, KitchenAid, Roper, Estate, Bauknecht, Ignis, Laden, and Inglis. And Whirlpool supplies Sears, Roebuck and Co. with many home appliances marketed under the Kenmore brand name.

Headquartered in Benton Harbor, MI, Whirlpool understands that it must be able to compete on a world class basis. Its future success depends on a continued commitment to achieving world class excellence, expressed through customer-focused quality. To make quality an attitude, the company is concentrating on team building, continuous training and motivation throughout the organization.

Whirlpool's approach toward management, workers, and the union proves that cooperative effort is the way to earn success. This effort is described by work team development, continuous training, and instilling the need for continued productivity and quality improvement in all workers.

Gainsharing Plan

Whirlpool's gainsharing plan results from cooperation between management, unions, and workers to develop a system that rewards improved performance.

Reprinted with permission from *Quality*, March 1993, a publication of Hitchcock/Chilton Publishing, a Capital Cities/ABC, Inc., Company.

The plan recognizes and rewards improvements as measured by these four factors:

- Producing more parts at a lower equivalent unit labor cost.
- Controlling supplies and tooling costs.
- Reducing rework and scrap costs.
- Developing a quality system that shares rewards fairly.

The gainsharing plan has had a significant effect in increasing a team attitude and total work force cooperation. The progress made in lowering parts per million (ppm) rejects is a good example of the success of the program.

The Benton Harbor, MI, component division's reject rate performance was 7,000 ppm. By 1988, team effort improved that rate to 800 ppm. Further quality improvements lowered it to 113 ppm in 1990. The division's 1991 efforts resulted in a reject rating of 10 ppm, including a 0 ppm rating for 11 of the 12 months. This is clearly world class quality.

The Benton Harbor plant supplies machined components for automatic washers and dryers, factory service parts to the LaPorte, IN, plant, and a part for a gas range manufactured in Oxford, MS. Benton Harbor's gainsharing program has helped to slash rework by 31 percent, scrap by 62 percent, and its reject rate by 99 percent since 1988. The gainsharing plan, called "Commitment to Excellence," rewards workers with cash payouts based on improved productivity and quality and other savings.

"At Whirlpool, we believe that total quality (TQ) means that no matter how good a product is or how reliable a process is, that level of performance is not good enough the next time around," says Al Voorhis, plant manager at Benton Harbor. "Companies that lead their global industries constantly seek to exceed the expectations of their customers and refine the productivity of their operations. To be most successful, continuous quality improvement must become a part of the corporate culture, not just a necessary task."

World-Class Manufacturing

Workers at the Benton Harbor plant make parts used in Whirlpool appliances produced in North America. The plant reviews all of its operations to bring the factory up to world-class standards. In doing so, it launched a project involving the machining of pinion gears used in washing machines. Reviewing the process showed that its 19 steps could be reduced to 13 and, at the same time, make quality and cycle-time improvements.

The Benton Harbor division produces over 2.7 million pinion gears a year. It operates three shifts and runs the equipment 24 hours a day. Maintaining quality and high-volume production requires using statistical process control (SPC).

A DataMyte computerized monitoring program is an integral part of this quality system. A computer is interfaced to production line gages so data can be analyzed in real time. Part measurements, batches, or work shift data can be displayed or printed to determine where they fall in the acceptable tolerance range. Using the DataMyte system enables operators to spot trends, and it prompts corrective action early on.

> We believe that total quality (TQ) means that no matter how good a product is or how reliable a process is, that level of performance is not good enough the next time around.

According to Voorhis, Japanese companies developed quality manufacturing processes after World War II, and the excellent goods produced by these companies presented terrific competition for manufacturers throughout the world. US companies that survived the initial shock of the initial Japanese onslaught are now finding ways to cope and this is where world-class manufacturing comes in. The North American home appliance industry has always been exceedingly competitive. As a result, prices for appliances have remained low while quality improved. These gains in productivity have resulted in a strong appliance industry in North America.

Since 1988, the plant's productivity rose from 92.8 parts per man hour to 110.6—an increase of more than 19 percent. Moreover, rejected parts decreased to 10 per million.

The parts made at Benton Harbor account for only about five percent of a Whirlpool washer—not enough to change its cost. Other Whirlpool plants, though, and some outside suppliers also have raised their productivity and lowered cost. Whirlpool's Columbia, SC, plant, for example, raised its productivity about 20 percent since 1990 and cut cost by about 9 percent.

Worldwide Excellence System

In 1991, Whirlpool introduced its Worldwide Excellence System (WES) that provides a TQ framework to incorporate TQ standards and instill workers with a continuous quality improvement mindset. WES integrates existing Whirlpool quality initiatives with Malcolm Baldrige National Quality Award criteria and ISO 9000 series standards to form a corporate quality management system centerpiece. It guides assessment of customer expectations and Whirlpool's ability to meet or exceed those expectations. WES requires fact-based strategic planning and management, worker development, products and process improvement, and measurement of results.

The Whirlpool business group, for example, raised its quality performance by installing process and cycle-time improvements. It increased the effectiveness of its strategic-planning process as it cut planning time by more than 40 percent. In total, the quality management program reviewed and improved 25 processes during the first year, including production scheduling and compensation claims.

Whirlpool Appliance Group (WAG) reorganized its sales and distribution during the program's first year, combining sales and support offices and opening a telephone-sales facility. The changes are aimed at providing better customer service, reducing costs, and increasing sales. In a sales telemarketing test of 100 accounts, sales rose by nearly one half.

The quality initiative includes concentration on productivity improvements in European operations. At the automatic-washer manufacturing plant in Amiens, France, a work team comprising marketing and manufacturing workers is trimming production cycle time from two weeks to two days. Manufacturing of cooking products at Cassinetta, Italy, now is based on weekly demand—and inventory was cut by 60 percent, following work team effort.

John J. Kendrick is a senior editor of Quality.

Planning Deming Management for Service Organizations

Thomas F. Rienzo

This article from Business Horizons *provides a detailed review of Deming's principles and their application in service organizations. These ideas serve a valuable base for exploring quality management in several different service sectors.*

The word "quality" carries an almost spiritual character in globally focused, highly competitive businesses. Articles extolling the virtues and techniques of quality are *de rigueur* in current American business periodicals. Quality is a universally acknowledged factor in successful businesses. Allen F. Jacobsen, chairman of the board and chief executive officer of 3M Company, says, "I'm convinced that the winners of the '90s will be companies that make quality and customer service an obsession in every single market [in which] they operate."

Corporate America has begun an ambitious effort to improve the quality of goods and services offered by American companies. These efforts, sustained by fierce global competition, will continue. The United States Commerce Department reported a trade deficit of $4.02 billion in June 1991 with an accumulated midyear 1991 merchandise trade deficit of $30.27 billion. That is an improvement over the $48.28 billion deficit measured through the first half of 1990. Currently, negative trade balances with Japan alone exceed $3 billion per month.

Reprinted with permission from *Business Horizons*, May/June 1993, Graduate School of Business Administration, Indiana University.

Because of this, many firms in the United States are attempting to emulate successful Japanese business performances. Japan's economic success is rooted in quality; Japanese quality is rooted in W. Edwards Deming.

Deming: A Biographical Sketch

W. Edwards Deming received his formal academic training in mathematics and physics, earning a Ph.D. from Yale in 1927. After completing his degree, he found employment in the U.S. Department of Agriculture applying statistical techniques to the effects of nitrogen on farm crops. While working there, Deming met Walter Shewhart, a statistician with Bell Telephone Laboratories. Shewhart had created methods of statistically measuring variation in industrial processes, called control charts, that permitted workers to distinguish between random variation and special causes affecting changes in manufacturing processes. Deming was impressed. He traveled regularly to New York to study with Shewhart, whose statistical philosophy and techniques form the heart of Deming's quality seminars today.

During World War II, Deming taught numerous courses in statistical quality control, using Shewhart control charts, to improve the quality of American war production. Though successful during those years, statistical techniques faded in the United States after the war ended. American companies, which operated in a seller's market with virtually no competition, considered Deming's methods of statistical process control time-consuming and unnecessary. By 1949 they were no longer part of corporate America. Deming himself lamented that "there was nothing—not even smoke" (Walton 1986).

Deming first brought his statistical quality control techniques and management philosophy to Japan in 1947. He found the Japanese eager students. By 1951, the Deming Prize, which recognized superlative achievement in quality, was established in Japan. In 1960, Deming became the first American to receive Japan's Second Order of the Sacred Treasure award because of his great impact upon Japanese industry.

Although he was an industrial superstar in Japan, Deming was not well known in the United States. He made a comfortable living as a statistical consultant, but most American business managers were not aware of his management methods, which formed the foundations of Japanese manufacturing excellence. American managers *were* aware, however, of stiff Japanese competition beginning in the 1970s. They realized that Japan was setting world quality standards for many manufactured goods.

One television show changed Deming's status in the United States. On June 24, 1980, NBC broadcast "If Japan Can . . . Why Can't We?" The final quarter hour of the show focused on Deming's contributions to Japan as well as on business improvements documented at Nashua Corporation, a U.S. company following the Deming quality philosophy. About four months before his 80th birthday, W. Edwards Deming became famous in America. Since that time his services and seminars have been in great demand throughout the world.

System of Profound Knowledge

Deming claims that many firms cannot perform well from a long-term perspective because their managers do not know what to do. He is fond of repeating "There is no substitute for knowledge!" vigorously and frequently during his seminars.

American managers cannot provide answers to their problems because they do not know what questions to ask. William Scherkenbach (1990) claims the whole of Deming's management philosophy is directed toward asking the right questions. In Deming's view, insightful management hinges on the application of an awareness process he has labeled "profound knowledge," which consists of four components:

1. Appreciation for a system
2. Theory of variation
3. Theory of knowledge
4. Psychology

These components are interdependent and interactive. Deming created his Fourteen Points for Management to provide a method of developing and implementing profound knowledge in the workplace.

Appreciation for a System

Deming defines a system as a series of functions or activities within an organization that work together for the aim of the organization. A system cannot function effectively without a clear aim, communicated to everyone capable of measurably affecting system operation. Complex systems, like businesses, must have full cooperation among components to accomplish their aims.

Managers are charged with the responsibility of optimizing systems; flow diagrams can help them understand what they are attempting to optimize. **Figure 1** shows Deming's perspective of production viewed as a system. Deming first used this chart in 1950 while explaining his quality management theories to Japanese business leaders. Flow diagrams help clarify relationships between system components, help define connections between processes, and provide insight into interactions. A systems approach to business activities also reveals that all processes have suppliers providing inputs and customers utilizing outputs. Most companies have a large number of processes whose suppliers and customers are internal to the corporation.

Theory of Variation

Systems are most efficiently optimized by concentrating on activities as far upstream as possible. Some understanding of variation is required to accomplish optimization. Variation always exists in any process, whether it involves equipment or people. Deming insists that managers have some means of distinguishing between changes in a process occurring at random, compared with changes resulting from some special cause affecting the process.

Statistical methods can help provide that distinction. Deming says, "Management is prediction!"[1] A process in statistical control is stable; as such, it

> In Deming's view, insightful management hinges on the application of an awareness process he has labeled "profound knowledge.

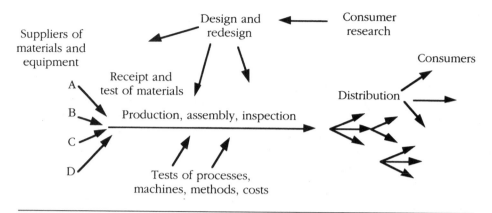

Figure 1.   **Production viewed as a system.**
Source: Deming (1986).

furnishes a rational basis for prediction. Methods used to assess variation in systems are described in literature involving statistical process control.

Theory of Knowledge

Deming is convinced that hard work and best efforts are necessary though not sufficient conditions for achieving quality or satisfying a market. His Second Theorem declares, "We are ruined by best efforts misdirected."

Deming expects managers to realize that they must concern themselves with issues that cannot be objectively measured.

Many shortcomings of American business do not result from a lack of effort, but from a lack of knowledgeable theory concerning subject matter that businesses attempt to manage. Deming believes that theory is essential: "Theory leads to questions. Without questions, experience and examples teach nothing. Without questions, one can only have an example. To copy an example of success, without understanding it with the aid of theory, may lead to disaster." He also claims, "There are no shortcuts to mastery of subject matter; there is no substitute for knowledge."

Deming expects managers to realize that they must concern themselves with issues that cannot be objectively measured. He frequently quotes Lloyd S. Nelson: "The most important figures for management are unknown and unknowable" (Deming 1986). The multiplying effect on sales attributable to happy customers, losses from annual ratings, or losses from inhibitors to pride of workmanship defies objective measurements.

Psychology

Psychology provides insight into human relationships and the ways in which people respond to circumstances in their lives. Deming is concerned about a knowledge of psychology in management because he sees current norms squeezing out workers' self-esteem and self-respect. He recommends eliminating a number of common management techniques that he believes are destructive, and offers suggestions for improvement (see **Figure 2**). Deming believes that managers place too much emphasis on extrinsic motivation,

FAULTY PRACTICE **Skills only required**	BETTER PRACTICE **Theory of Management Required**
Management of outcome with immediate action when figures deviate from expectations or standards	Work on the system to reduce failure at the source. Avoid tampering. Instead, distinguish by appropriate techniques between special causes and common causes.
The so-called merit system—actually a destroyer of people.	Institute leadership. Reward cooperation.
Incentive pay for individuals—pay based on performance. The incentive is numbers, not quality.	Put all people on regular systems of pay. Provide leadership.
Problem report and resolution. This technique often results in tampering, making things worse.	Study the system. Learn methods to minimize net economic loss.
Work standards (quota and time standards) rob people of pride of workmanship and shut off any possibility of obtaining valid data to improve process.	Provide leadership. Everyone is entitled to pride of workmanship.
MBO—Management by Numbers ("Do it. I don't care how, just do it.")	Improve the system to get better results in the future.

Figure 2. **Faulty management practices and suggestions for improvement.**

Source: Deming notes from "Transformation for Management of Quality and Productivity," Seminar, February 19, 1991.

thereby missing opportunities to help people achieve real satisfaction in their work lives.

The Value of Profound Knowledge

Profound knowledge is crucial to the long-term operation of business because each component brings essential insight into optimization of the organization as a holistic entity, and success in business is measured by performance of the entire company. Appreciation for a system minimizes the damaging effects of suboptimization, in which one part of a company performs well at the expense of the business system. Theory of variation provides for recognizing a stable system in statistical control. Management is prediction, and rational prediction is possible *only* with processes in statistical control. Deming flatly rejects the contention that major threats in business result from lack of effort: they result instead from not knowing what to do. Theory of knowledge tells us what to do. Psychology helps get everyone in the organization involved in its improvement.

Profound knowledge is itself a system. Components are interdependent and interactive. The aim of profound knowledge is optimum performance. Although Deming's management methods are presented in a business

Deming flatly rejects the contention that major threats in business result from lack of effort: they result instead from not knowing what to do.

environment, profound knowledge can be applied in any area of human endeavor in which people attempt to achieve a goal through a system.

The Fourteen Points for Management

Deming's Fourteen Points provide a method to develop and implement profound knowledge in business and guide long-term business plans and goals.

Point 1: Create constancy of purpose for improvement of product and service. Continuation of a business requires a core set of values and a purpose that do not change with time. Constancy of purpose means accepting obligations that include innovation, research, education, and continuous improvement of product and service design.

Point 2: Adopt the new philosophy. The new philosophy seeks to optimize holistic systems rather than suboptimize components. It eschews management practices that rob people of their pride of workmanship, and seeks profound knowledge as the basis for plans and decisions.

Point 3: Cease dependence on mass inspection. Inspection to improve quality is too late, ineffective, and costly. Quality does not come from inspection, but rather from improvements in the process. No amount of inspection affects process quality.

The new philosophy seeks to optimize holistic systems rather than suboptimize components.

Point 4: End the practice of awarding business on the basis of price tag alone. Price has no meaning without a measure of the quality being purchased. Reliance on price must be replaced by evaluations of the effects of purchased goods and services on the operation of all processes involved in their use. Purchasers and suppliers should move from adversarial positions to cooperative ones.

Point 5: Improve constantly and forever the system of production and service. Quality should be built in at the design stage, and systems should be redesigned continually for improved quality. Variation should be minimized as systems draw nearer and nearer toward operating at optimum points. Statistical tools and operational definitions (definitions determined by use in practice) can be extremely useful in implementing this point. They can provide the means with which to measure improvement.

Point 6: Institute training. Training should be based on system optimization and customer satisfaction. It should be a springboard from which workers can develop pride of workmanship. Training should provide managers and workers with the tools they will need to evaluate processes and improve systems. Deming recommends at least some training in statistical thinking so workers can appreciate variation.

Point 7: Adopt and institute leadership. Real leadership requires profound knowledge. Deming states that leaders must know the work they supervise. They must be empowered and directed to inform higher-level management about conditions that need correction. Higher-level management must act on that information. Leadership is the engine that drives systems toward optimization.

Point 8: Drive out fear. Deming (1986) claims that "no one can put in his best performance unless he feels secure." Fear begets misinformation, hidden agendas, and padded numbers. It may induce workers to satisfy a rule or a quota at the expense of the best interests of the company. All these consequences make system optimization very difficult.

Point 9: Break down barriers between staff areas. This point is a direct result of an integrated, systemic view of business processes. Optimization of systems is impossible unless all components recognize their systemic function and have some feedback concerning the way their activities are affecting system performance. Interstaff teams provide the best means to break down barriers between staff areas and enhance communication.

Point 10: Eliminate slogans, exhortations, and targets for the work force. Deming claims that posters and exhortations are directed at the wrong people. Posters represent the hope that workers could, by some additional effort, accomplish the goals set by management. Managers must learn that the responsibility for improving the business system is theirs, not the workers'. If posters and exhortations ask people to do what the system will not allow them to do, the only result will be disillusionment and frustration.

Point 11a: Eliminate numerical quotas for the work force. Deming views a quota as "a fortress against improvement of quality and productivity." He continues, "I have yet to see a quota that includes any trace of a system by which to help anyone do a better job" (1986). Quotas do not consider quality. They cannot provide data valuable in improving the system; they destroy pride in workmanship.

Point 11b: Eliminate numerical goals for people in management. Numerical goals are set when managers do not know the capabilities of the systems they are managing. They are generally set in ignorance, or, at best, on the basis of what seems reasonable by experience. Stable systems do not need numerical goals. Output will be determined by system capability. Unstable systems have no capability. There can be no basis for setting a numerical goal in an unpredictable system.

Point 12: Remove barriers that rob people of pride of workmanship. This point recommends that all workers be given the tools and training they need to do a job in which they can take pride. It requires managers to listen to workers and act upon their suggestions and requests. Listening and follow-up action, which are hard work, need to be reinforced by high-level management. Some organizations seem more interested in bureaucratic procedures than their own employees.

Point 13: Encourage education and self-improvement for everyone. Systems will improve as a result of applied knowledge, which is linked to education. Deming writes, "In respect to self-improvement, it is wise for anyone to bear in mind that there is no shortage of good people. Shortage exists at the high levels of knowledge; this is true in every field." Deming recommends life-long learning, whether in formal or informal settings. Committed, knowledgeable people have the best chance of optimizing systems in which they work.

Point 14: Take action to accomplish the transformation. If business systems are to be optimized, everyone must be involved. The leadership for this

> If posters and exhortations ask people to do what the system will not allow them to do, the only result will be disillusionment and frustration.

involvement rests clearly with management. Managers must show the work force that they are serious about adopting a systems view of their business. They must demonstrate their concern for worker interests, provide adequate training to measure system performance, and measure attempts to improve it.

Deming's Fourteen Points as Moral Principles

The Fourteen Points are not a list of action items. They are more similar to a code of conduct or a value system that provides a frame of reference with which to view the world. They are similar to the Ten Commandments—statements of principles that are considerably easier to list than to implement. Implementation requires judgment and guidance. Deming preaches a philosophy of life that is very similar to that of major religions: continuous, lifelong improvement from conversion to new core beliefs. The Deming philosophy really does require a transformation in thinking. Deming is guiding firms on a pilgrimage that takes time and perseverance, and he freely admits that there is no quick fix, no instant pudding. There will be struggle and some degree of pain, but the potential rewards are tremendous.

> Deming preaches a philosophy of life that is very similar to that of major religions: continuous, lifelong improvement from conversion to new core beliefs.

The journey Deming proposes demands faith. He comments on innovation as an obligation of his first point (Deming 1986): "One requirement for innovation is faith that there will be a future." When he writes, "He that would run his company on visible figures alone will in time have neither company nor figures," and tells us that the most important figures for management are unknown and unknowable, he is advocating acting by faith. How else can anyone deal with what is not visible, or what is unknowable, except by faith?

Application of the Fourteen Points in Service Industries

Although quality as preached by Deming and others has been seen as principally applying to the manufacturing sector, there is no question that service businesses also can benefit from adoption Deming's philosophy in their firms. Below are some examples of successful implementations of this philosophy.

Windsor Export Supply

Windsor Export Supply is a division of Ford Motor Company. Its 250 employees take orders for parts from Ford's foreign manufacturing plants, most of which are located in South America. It also fills orders for Ford parts from customers outside the Ford organization.

Once an order is placed with Windsor, it purchases parts from Ford's North American plants, arranges shipment, and collects payment. In the early 1980s, orders began diminishing for the division in the face of stiff Japanese competition. Ford's manufacturing capacity had also grown overseas, and demand was declining for North American parts. Although Windsor was still profitable, Ford executives sought advice from Deming on improving the performance of the Windsor organization.

Windsor was the first service group at Ford to receive training in the Deming management philosophy. Ford's initial efforts with Deming focused on the factory floor. There were many barriers to pride of workmanship at Windsor. Managers were surprised to learn that white-collar service employees felt the same kind of frustrations in their jobs as blue-collar factory workers. Harry Artinian of the Ford statistical methods office noted, "If you took the white shirts and ties off those people and put them in overalls, you'd hear the same words" (Walton 1986).

Deciding what parts of the Windsor process to measure and optimize was a complicated procedure. In manufacturing, the accounting system highlights scrap, rework, and excess inventory. Those kinds of figures do not exist for service functions. The process of targeting significant inhibitors to performance at Windsor depended upon the knowledge and experience of the company's managers. The management team responsible for instituting Deming methods began with training and flow diagrams, hoping to get one good project as a consequence. Worker response was encouraging, and six projects were initiated.

One successful project involved freight auditing. Windsor would receive invoices from freight carriers through a contracted auditor, who completed the company paperwork and issued instructions for payment to the Ford accounts payable office in Oakville, Ontario. The contracted auditor was chosen to take advantage of "state-of-the-art" methods. But late payments and missing information were routine occurrences. Past due bills mounted, occasionally for months. Almost everyone involved in the system was frustrated.

> In manufacturing, the accounting system highlights scrap, rework, and excess inventory. Those kinds of figures do not exist for service functions.

The freight auditing optimization team measured elapsed time between the date Windsor received an invoice and the date Oakville issued a check. Using control charts, the team found that the system was stable with an average response time of 14 days, but as many as 35 days might pass between invoice receipt and issuance of a check. The team used cause-and-effect diagrams to identify reasons for delay. They found keypunch errors, misfiling, missing codes, and misplaced bills. Attempts to resolve those problems with the contracted auditor proved unsuccessful, so Windsor took over the auditing function, making a number of changes to correct problem areas. The final result of these efforts was a drop in average response time to six days and a reduction in the proportion of rejected bills at Oakville from 34 percent to less than 1 percent.

Parkview Episcopal Medical Center

Parkview Episcopal Medical Center is one of two hospitals serving Pueblo, Colorado. Hospital Corporation of America, which manages the facility, designated it as a "role model" hospital for quality improvement. Strict limitations in revenue prompted Parkview to undertake the cultural changes associated with Deming management. Ninety-five percent of its patient base is made up of Medicare and Medicaid beneficiaries, HMO members, and the medically indigent. "With that amount of fixed payment," CEO Michael Pugh says, "it's clear that we have to do something different to survive" (Koska 1990).

Pugh was introduced to the Deming quality management philosophy for the first time in the spring of 1988. By autumn, many Parkview senior managers had received quality training. Pugh established a Quality Improvement Council of senior managers to help guide the implementation of Deming's "new philosophy." The hospital jumped on Deming Point 6, "Institute Training," with a vengeance. Quality improvement teams were formed to address hospital problems under the direction of a group of managers trained specifically to lead them. Almost all department managers attended a week-long course on statistics taught by a consultant. All hospital employees were scheduled to attend a quality awareness course.

Pugh estimates that it takes two to three years to integrate Deming quality methods into organizational culture. He advises managers to expect a steep employee learning curve. As Parkview moves further into its new philosophy, Pugh notes definite improvements in employee morale. The hospital turnover rate was less than 12 percent in 1990, compared with rates of 15 to 18 percent in previous years. Cost savings are more difficult to quantify, but quality improvement teams in operating room (OR) scheduling and food service delivery provided the hospital with more than $10,000 in annual savings in each department during 1990.

It takes two to three years to integrate Deming quality methods into organizational culture.

Parkview's approach to surgery scheduling provides an example of its utilization of the Deming approach to quality. The hospital had a history of not meeting early morning surgery schedules; 48 percent of morning surgical procedures began late, affecting operating times for the remainder of the day. Therefore, an OR quality improvement team was formed that included nurses, technicians, and physicians. The group tracked actual causes for delays, finding two common system causes: either the surgeon was late, or the OR was not ready. The team tried to encourage surgeons to arrive on time by 1) reminding physicians that they were expected to be on time for surgeries; 2) not permitting any surgeon who was late to surgery two times in one month to schedule the first case of the day and 3) posting the names of late doctors in the physician's lounge.

When the team examined instances when the OR was not ready to begin surgery at the scheduled 7:30 a.m. starting time, it discovered that extensive surgeries, such as total knee or hip replacements, were most likely to start late. The OR staff, coming in at 7:00 a.m., was unable to prepare instrumentation for extensive operations in 30 minutes. The team suggested moving starting times for major surgeries to 8:00 a.m. Leann Leuer, R.N., director of surgical services, commented, "By changing the rules a little bit we still start on time. Morale has improved because staff has more time to set up, and the surgeons aren't angry because they don't have to stand around waiting." As a result of the teams' efforts, the number of late surgeries dropped from 48 to 8 percent.

Generic Application of the Deming Management Philosophy

The Fourteen Points must be fully integrated into an entire business to realize the full benefits of Deming's management philosophy. However, Deming does not see this generally being done. He recognizes that statistical quality control has permeated unique processes on the shop floor, but he estimates that only about 3 percent of the benefits of his management transformation lie in this area. The big gains are in overall business strategy and company-wide systems.

Why have firms concentrated on unique shop floor processes and largely ignored company-wide systems, where Deming estimates that 97 percent of the benefits of the "new philosophy" wait to be tapped? Lack of effort is not a satisfactory explanation; in Deming's perspective, it rarely is. Many high-level American managers have not moved beyond unique shop-floor quality control because they have not accepted the Fourteen Points as desirable moral principles, or because they do not know how to bring the Deming philosophy into their company systems. Generic guidelines for implementing the philosophy throughout entire organizations would be helpful for managers who accept Deming's teaching but do not know how to get beyond statistical quality control at the shop floor.

Guidelines for Implementing Deming Management

The Deming quality philosophy requires adopting a corporate culture based on his Fourteen Points for management. Because high-level managers are responsible for corporate culture, they must be the first converts to the new philosophy to provide an environment in which Deming's ideas can have lasting effects. Conversion begins at the top and travels down through the organization. Following adoption of the new philosophy, high-level managers need training in statistical thinking and the Fourteen Points. They should also create flow diagrams for systems under their authority to help them understand what they are charged with optimizing. Declaration of systems aims follows with an attempt to implement the Fourteen Points in the organization. Once aims are declared, training of middle management can begin.

> Many high-level American managers have not moved beyond unique shop-floor quality control because they have not accepted the Fourteen Points as desirable moral principles.

The Shewhart Cycle, also called the PDCA cycle, can be a helpful procedure in implementing the Fourteen Points. In the cycle, changes or experiments are planned and carried out. The effects are studied to determine whether changes have improved the system or offer any insight into prediction. A number of cycle iterations may be necessary before satisfactory results are achieved.

Responsibilities of Management

The Deming philosophy must first transform upper management. Training, system diagrams, and the PDCA cycle are critical in implementing the Fourteen Points. Wherever possible, upper management should take action to improve the business system.

Once systems aims are declared, middle managers can begin learning the new philosophy. They must also be trained in statistical methods and the Fourteen Points. To better understand the systems for which they are responsible, middle managers should create flow diagrams, recognizing the aims that their systems are supposed to serve. Middle managers are close enough to the front lines of their businesses that they can use their training to target the largest system inhibitors to performance facing their sections of the company.

A variety of process tools are available to aid middle managers in bringing attention to large performance inhibitors. Flow diagrams increase understanding of systems. Cause-and-effect diagrams help clarify relationships between business components. Pareto charts and histograms demonstrate frequency of occurrences. Run charts and scatter diagrams show trends in process performance. Control charts allow managers to distinguish between common process variation and special causes that need immediate attention. These tools are discussed in detail in many statistical quality control texts.

Although middle management generally identifies significant system inhibitors to performance, lower management and non-management employees are in the best position to generate recommendations for improvement and deal with special causes that are not part of the system. One highly effective way of approaching inhibitors to performance is through interdisciplinary teams that target specific problems or opportunities.

Training is essential for the teams to function effectively. All employees should be exposed to the Deming philosophy, be informed of system aims, and learn statistical methods of measuring process performance. The PDCA cycle and process tools previously discussed are crucial ingredients for process optimization. Lower-level managers and workers can deal immediately with unique special causes outside their statistically stable systems. After study, they can also recommend ways of improving systems to upper management.

Company-wide implementation of Deming concepts, at all levels, is shown in **Figure 3:**

One highly effective way of approaching inhibitors to performance is through interdisciplinary teams that target specific problems or opportunities.

- Upper management is responsible for creating a corporate culture consistent with Deming's philosophy, instituting the Fourteen Points, understanding business supersystems, and declaring system aims. Upper management also must act to improve corporate business systems, often at the request of lower levels of management.

- Middle managers must adopt the new philosophy, understand systems for which they are responsible, implement the Fourteen Points, and target for attention significant inhibitors to performance. They too must take action to improve their business processes, frequently in response to recommendations from lower levels of management.

- Lower management and non-managerial workers must be instructed in the new philosophy and receive training to measure system performance and recognize special causes of variation. They must seek solutions to significant problems, often through interdisciplinary teams. Lower-level managers can take immediate action on special causes of process variation and recommend system changes to higher management. Deming concepts cannot be successfully applied without open communication among managerial levels.

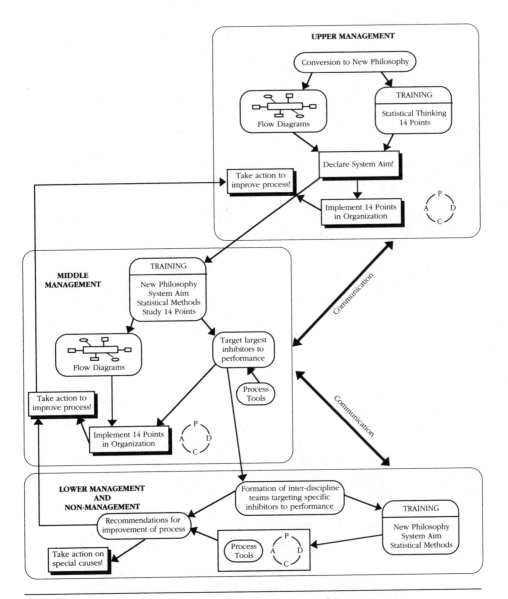

Figure 3. **Implementing Deming concepts company-wide.**

Rules of Implementation

Figure 4 lists key activities involved in instituting Deming management methods on a company-wide basis, with general rules guiding their implementation. Systems are understood beginning with customer needs and desires, but optimized beginning with suppliers. Adoption of the new philosophy is accomplished top-down, as is the identification of significant inhibitors to performance. Solutions to overcoming those inhibitors, however, are

Activity	Rule of Implementation
Understanding systems through flow diagrams	Create flow diagram by beginning with customers and work back to suppliers
Optimizing systems with the aid of flow diagrams	Begin with suppliers and work forward to customers
Adopting the new philosophy	Adopt top-down, beginning with upper management
Identifying significant system problems and opportunities, and setting priorities in seeking solutions	Identify problems and opportunities top-down, frequently starting with middle management
Seeking solutions to problems involving common causes	Solutions emerge bottom-up from teams of workers and first-line supervision
Acting to correct special cause problems	Comes from workers and first-line supervision, unless higher-level management is needed to authorize substantial monetary expenditure
Acting to correct common cause problems	Comes from management at appropriate level, after receiving recommendations from problem-solving team

Figure 4.   **General rules of implementation.**

developed bottom-up. Line workers and first-line management can act on special causes of variation, but management alone can make changes to improve common cause variations inherent in the system.

Cultural change is essential in any organization attempting to adopt Deming management because its major challenge comes not in planning, but in execution. Mary Walton (1990) explains the development of a Deming quality lifestyle as a sequence of five stages:

Stage 1: The Decision to Adopt. Management recognizes that historic ways of doing business no longer produce desired results.

Stage 2: Incubation. The quality message is transmitted throughout the organization, emphasizing that upper management is committed to change. Vision and mission statements are created.

Stage 3: Planning and Promotion. Company quality needs are determined and plans are developed to introduce the quality transformation throughout the company.

Stage 4: Education. Employees are trained in statistical thinking and given tools to evaluate and improve the systems in which they work.

Stage 5: Never-ending Improvement. Quality techniques become enmeshed in every operation of the organization. Quality becomes a part *of* business activities, not apart *from* business activities.

Continuous improvement is a never-ending journey that requires time, effort, and perseverance. Groups not truly converted to Deming's value system may well abandon the Fourteen Points when initial feelings of enthusiasm wane. The Deming philosophy is also paradoxical. Profound knowledge demands tremendous amounts of data and information, yet Deming insists that managers act on faith to manage what is invisible and unknowable.

W. Edwards Deming has preached his gospel of management transformation for more than 44 years. It is time for more American companies to listen to his message.

Notes

1. This and all other non-referenced Deming quotations are from his "Transformation Seminar" given at the Adam's Mark Hotel, Philadelphia, February 19–22, 1991.

References

W. Edwards Deming, *Out of the Crisis* (Cambridge, Mass.: MIT Center for Advanced Engineering Study, 1986).

Lucinda Harper, "Trade Deficit Shrank in June to $4.02 Billion," *Wall Street Journal*, August 19, 1991, p. A2.

A. F. Jacobsen, speech, quoted in *Business America*, March 25, 1991, p. 4.

Mary T. Koska, "Adopting Deming's Quality Improvement Ideas: A Case Study," *Hospitals*, July 5, 1990, pp. 58–64.

William W. Scherkenbach, *The Deming Route to Quality and Productivity: Road Maps and Roadblocks* (Rockville, Md.: Mercury Press, 1990).

Mary Walton, *Deming Management at Work* (New York: Putnam Publishing Group, 1990).

Mary Walton, *The Deming Management Method* (New York: Putnam Publishing Group, 1986).

Thomas F. Rienzo is a research engineer with Hercules Incorporated, Kalamazoo, Michigan.

HOTELS & RESTAURANTS

Putting on the Ritz

Cheri Henderson

The Ritz-Carlton won the 1992 Baldrige Award, the first hotel company to do so. While always being service-oriented, the Ritz-Carlton chain has adopted TQM because they know it enhances productivity, employee satisfaction, and quality of service to customers. This article profiles the company and how it uses quality principles and won its Baldrige.

Mention the Ritz-Carlton hotels, one of the nation's premier luxury hotel chains, and you conjure up dreamy visions of luxury—pampering in a style to which a guest should become accustomed and one that means the guest and his needs are understood. At the essence is customer-sensitive service, a notion that seems so obvious as to be superfluous. However, the meaning is more cryptic than clear, and its implications more tangible than perceived. Managers at The Ritz-Carlton Hotel Company have a passion for service, a passion that begins with understanding what service is and how it can be achieved consistently.

This is passion with an energy. That source of energy is Horst Schulze, a one-time dishwasher apprentice who worked his way by 1988 into the dual chairs of president and chief operating officer, and who considers himself a fanatic about customer satisfaction. Mr. Schulze expresses the company's service philosophy in a statement as deceptively simple as the concept of

---

Reprinted with permission from *The TQM Magazine*, November/December 1992, IFS Publishing, Inc.

service itself: "We are ladies and gentlemen serving ladies and gentlemen." Service, then, begins with people, not servants, responding to the requirements of other people. No one's importance is inherently diminished.

Service Through People

"Service can only be accomplished by people," says Mr. Schulze. The hotel can be breathtakingly beautiful and the food memorable, but a poor employee attitude can quickly sour the experience. Mr. Schulze isn't just concerned with the pleasantness of a guest's stay; he is concerned about something deeper: the very well-being of the guest. He wants his guests to be physically and emotionally comforted—even nurtured—by their Ritz-Carlton experience. In the company's credo, employees are told, "The genuine care and comfort of our guests is our highest mission."

> Service, then, begins with people, not servants, responding to the requirements of other people.

This starts with the company's three steps of service: a warm greeting in which the guest's name should be used, anticipation of and compliance with the guest's needs and a warm farewell, again using the guest's name if possible. All employees, during training, memorize and learn to live the credo, the service philosophy and the three steps of service. They also carry with them laminated cards bearing the essentials of Ritz-Carlton service, including 20 well-defined, employee-empowering 'basics', as they are called.

These basics are not necessarily common sense, nor are they integral to all service philosophies, which is what makes them unique to the Ritz-Carlton. For instance, a Ritz-Carlton employee will not point a guest in the desired direction; rather, he will lead the guest to the destination. "If you're in one of their hotels, and you have to go to the lavatory, and you're four minutes away, they'll take you," says Brian A. Kaznova, an executive consultant who has worked with The Ritz-Carlton Hotel Company for more than two years and has familiarized the company with the Malcolm Baldrige award criteria. Even employees' language is carefully thought out. Employees are directed to speak respectfully and with a definite lack of such colloquialisms as 'OK' or 'folks' or 'hello'. ('Good afternoon' is an acceptable substitute for more casual greetings.)

In attending to guest complaints, employees are required to respond within 10 minutes and follow up with a phone call within 20 minutes to ensure satisfaction. It is the responsibility of the attending employee to solve the problem, and management is generous, to say the least, in granting latitude. For example, the company is pilot-testing a policy of giving authority of up to $2,000 to front-desk employees to ensure total customer satisfaction. Also in the test phase is giving sales managers discretion, up to $5,000, in dealing with group bookings.

The Ritz-Carlton Hotel Company's philosophy goes beyond service itself to what Mr. Kaznova calls relationship quality. "It's the interaction between people. It's a very, very positive thing. It lays the groundwork for everything they do," he says. That groundwork is laid in the hiring of employees, for which the company has a formula that sets an industry standard.

The Seven-Day Countdown

Ritz-Carlton's initial practice was targeted selection, according to Mr. Kaznova, through which 10 people would be interviewed for every job. Managers since have turned to the more efficient and effective method of character trait analysis, through which employees are hired based upon a profile of personality characteristics for each of about 130 jobs. To arrive at that method, Mr. Schulze says managers identified the best five employees in every job category company-wide, based on longevity, working relationships and attitude. The result is impressive: The Ritz-Carlton Hotel Company's turnover is 48% annually, versus more than 100% industry-wide.

What happens after hiring is also unusual. During the week before the opening of every hotel, all 15 members of the Ritz-Carlton's senior staff—Mr. Schulze and 14 people who report to him—train hotel employees in what is called the *seven-day countdown*. "The first three days, we explain to our employees, 'What is our heart? What is our soul? What is the philosophy? What is the credo?'" says Mr. Schulze. The company chief also spends time with members of every department of every new hotel and works with team members on visioning—that is, how they envision their roles. In addition, he makes himself available to answer questions of virtually any nature, further eliminating barriers between line employees and management.

Time with customers and employees accounts for a fully 90% of the schedules of the senior staff members.

Senior managers never miss a day of training, Mr. Kaznova says, and will work alongside employees in preparing the hotel for opening. That means Mr. Schulze himself will make beds and serve and perhaps even wash dishes, as he once did in Europe. This requires an incredible investment of time and dedication on the part of senior managers considering the company has opened 17 hotels since 1988, and has plans for many more hotels worldwide. Time with customers and employees accounts for a fully 90% of the schedules of the senior staff members. "They have tremendous compassion and empathy for the line workers, and they realize that the line worker is the one who directly impacts the customer and, in essence, the company's market share, profit margin and overall success," Mr. Kaznova says.

Members of the Ritz-Carlton staff, beginning with Mr. Schulze, view success as the product of teamwork. Teams are groups of equally empowered people without whose efforts the product would be incomplete. In introducing himself to fellow employees, Mr. Schulze says, "My name is Horst Schulze. I'm president of this company; I'm very important," after which he quickly adds, "but so are you. Absolutely. Equally important."

After training is completed, employees are put to the test. Each year, they must be certified in their positions. To meet standards, they must score 100% on a written test and receive favorable reviews from supervisors. Even senior managers are tested. According to Mr. Kaznova, 75% of all 14,000 Ritz-Carlton employees were certified by 1991. Nearly 100% certification will be completed for 1992. "It's all geared towards caring for customers. All geared towards excellence," Mr. Schulze says. "An employee will really do a good job if he feels he is part of an organization. And we tell all our employees, 'We don't want you to work for this organization. We want you to be part of this organization.' "

Founded on Excellence

A quality approach to service is new only in name to the Ritz-Carlton staff. Since the opening of the Ritz-Carlton Boston in 1927, it has catered to the needs of the prestigious traveler, whether an individual, a meeting planner or a corporate traveler. Its innovative quality approach, a 'born at birth' philosophy, contributes to the Ritz-Carlton mystique in the design, control, assessment and continuous improvement of the company's hotels. According to Mr. Kaznova, company managers weren't always aware of the Ritz-Carlton's own quality practices and were initially fearful of Total Quality Management because they perceived it as too regimented and geared towards manufacturers, rather than service providers.

Through the mid-1980s, the Ritz-Carlton appeared to be doing everything right. Occupancy and rates were higher than the competition, and expansion plans were in the works. As the recession clouded the company's otherwise sunny future, managers began to be concerned about reducing service variability, cost of quality and reducing waste, such as in cycle time. They were made aware of the need for a quality process in developing a customer-driven fast-growing international company, and turned to Mr. Kaznova for direction.

"The company had a superb reputation for service excellence and product and service quality prior to my coming in," Mr. Kaznova says. "Now we are using the Malcolm Baldrige National Quality Award criteria as a business management system for a hotel company, without giving up their basic beliefs, their basic vision, their basic values, and without hindering creativity or adding bureaucracy."

Planning, though informal, had always been a great strength in the company, but managers needed better systems of measurement and documentation, Mr. Kaznova says. For instance, a few years ago comment cards represented the company's only measure of customer satisfaction. That system was faulty because comment cards tend only to be a vent for complaints. Through its total quality process, Ritz-Carlton workers now conduct mail and telephone surveys against best-of-breed competition and collect process-oriented market samples. In keeping with the Malcolm Baldrige criteria, the Ritz-Carlton also benchmarks such competitors as the Four Seasons hotel company.

The company also has an intense interest in its internal customer—the employee. Through causal analysis, managers have established statistically what every supervisor knows logically, and that is: employee satisfaction is directly related to customer satisfaction. An improved understanding of their internal and external customers and their competition helps managers in their strategic quality planning for both the short and the long term.

"Now it flows into the human resource plan, and they kind of caddy-corner each other. Anything that happens to one affects the other," Mr. Kaznova says.

Managers have established statistically what every supervisor knows logically, and that is: employee satisfaction is directly related to customer satisfaction.

Quality with a Mission

Management was initially surprised at how neatly its quality process flowed with existing operations and also at the ease with which they could identify and quantify problems through basic, consistent documentation. The results were also surprising. Managers were able to attach costs of quality to common industry problems such as failure to have a room ready on time. A 'cost of error calculation' form is one way quality leaders measure the price of failure to adhere to guest requirements, which can result in lost repeat customers. Each nonconformance requires additional time, from the housekeeping supervisor to the front office manager. It also requires complimentary cocktails, an amenity sent to the room and a follow-up letter. The total annual cost of error, once all these factors were added up, proved to be exceedingly higher than ever perceived.

Contrary to the logic of quality, however, the answer was not to prepare rooms more quickly. "The more time they spend making up rooms, the more customer retention they'll have, which is paradoxical to the quality approach. That's based on extensive research," Mr. Kaznova says. The answer, then, was to improve efficiency in room turnaround without sacrificing time spent on preparation of the quarters.

> Managers were able to attach costs of quality to common industry problems such as failure to have a room ready on time.

Managers at the Ritz-Carlton, which boasts a 95% customer satisfaction rate, eventually hope to wean the company from its need for advertising and rely upon its established base of travelers. One step towards this goal is the company's computerized guest profiling system, through which are registered the individual preferences of 240,000 guests who have stayed at least three times at any of the hotels. This allows front-desk employees at any of the US properties immediate access to such information as to whether a guest smokes, whether he prefers wine or a rose in the evening, or what kind of pillow he likes, states Mr. Kaznova.

Another product of the Ritz-Carlton's quality process is the ability to resolve tricky conflicts between internal and external customer requirements. For instance, guests—many of whom are on demanding schedules—want breakfast that can be delivered to their rooms within 30 minutes. However, the time required by chefs to create a meal can be difficult to pin down. In conferring with chefs, managers found not all the selections they had wanted to offer on the 30-minute menu were feasible, and that with others, time ranges would work better than specific time requirements for meal preparation, taking into consideration the chef's work style. In this way, chefs are given a loose structure in which to work without inhibiting creativity or independence.

Causal analysis, as a more definitive tool, has allowed employees to detect multilevel problems whose roots, without a formalized system in place, might have gone undetected. At one point, guests were complaining that room service breakfast delivery was slow. A cross-functional team of housekeeping, laundry and room service workers—groups that are the main users of service elevators during peak periods—was put together to determine what was slow-

VISIBLE PROOF OF QUALITY AT WORK

Through its Total Quality Management practices, The Ritz-Carlton Hotel Company has achieved the following goals:

- Increased expenditures for TQM threefold over the past three years.
- 86% of the workforce has attended at least one quality seminar.
- Company-wide staff turnover has been reduced to 48%, versus more than 100% industry-wide.
- Each employee receives more than 100 hours of quality training.
- Employee satisfaction scores improved from 80.3% in 1989 to 85.3% in 1991.
- More than 75% of all employees have been certified in the technical aspects of their jobs.
- Retention of key group accounts reached 100% in 1991.
- Problem-solving teams have been implemented in all 720 work areas of the company.
- All Ritz-Carlton hotels are rated either four or five stars by the Mobile Travel Guide, four or five diamonds by the American Automobile Association and extraordinary-to-perfection by the Zagat organization.
- All employees are being certified as quality engineers.

ing down the elevators. The reason, upon investigation, showed to be linen delivery in the early morning. So the new problem was: Why were linen deliveries requiring so much elevator use? Team members found four causes; not enough stocks of specific linens, a disorganized system of delivery, sporadic delivery and no specified inventory levels on each floor.

The solution was to schedule a linen runner for the overnight shift to stock the required linens on each floor according to a specified inventory level, so that housekeepers could go directly to the floor and begin cleaning guest rooms without unnecessary waiting. As a result, the cost per occupied room in housekeeping has been reduced from $7.90 at the end of 1991 to $7.30 at the beginning of 1992. The average time required to clean a room has decreased from 30 to 28.5 minutes, so that clean rooms are turned over to the front desk 30 minutes earlier each day. Also, the elevator waiting time has been reduced by 33%, from 7.5 minutes to about five minutes during peak hours.

All of this helps keep dirty linens in a continuous flow to the laundry, rather than in several batch deliveries, and provides housekeepers with adequate supplies with which to do their jobs. Tracking in a daily yes-no survey from June showed improvement—from 50 to 60 negative answers a week down to 10 by early July. Morale, though not to be measured until the latter part of the year, has also improved.

Giving Employees a Voice

Each day, quality leaders at every hotel log guest complaints, such as the ones about elevator timeliness, in a quality product report. The form accounts for concerns such as facilities reliability, i.e., whether furniture or equipment is missing, defective or otherwise inappropriate; supplies and food and beverage reliability; employee reliability; services missing; and guest security. It also measures process and internal customer complaints in employee facilities, employee supplies, employee services, employee security and hotel purchasing. Quality leaders record total defects for that day and year-to-date, along with the percentage of complaints resolved successfully. The end result is a total quality production figure that provides a daily gauge of individual hotel processes.

The Ritz-Carlton managers rely heavily on employees to provide feedback about what they see about the company that works and what doesn't. Employees submit about 30 internal customer complaints at each hotel every day, and with full expectation that their complaints will be heard and responded to, according to Mr. Kaznova. The goal is to have two times as many internal complaints as customer complaints, in order to solve problems before they ever get to the external customer. Since February, managers have begun work on 6,000 employee suggestions and have adopted 2,000. "Employees are saying, 'It's incumbent upon me to make this the best place to work, and if I see something wrong, it's my responsibility to report it', and the whole thing is solved within 30 days," says Mr. Kaznova.

> The goal is to have two times as many internal complaints as customer complaints, in order to solve problems before they ever get to the external customer.

Mr. Schulze says all the ideas are, in the end, money-saving suggestions, but some managers may fear the initial investment that may be required. At one meeting, the president was compelled to listen to a room service waiter's suggestion about implementing a recycling program, despite reservations about the program's probable cost. However, out of Mr. Schulze's commitment to employee ideas, he asked the waiter to submit a proposal. The initial cost was $50,000, which included the price of necessary machinery. "We cringed and we did it," says Mr. Schulze. As a result, the company has reduced garbage pickups by two days a week and is able to sell cardboard and paper, resulting in a $80,000 a year savings, or a net profit of $30,000.

It's that spirit of caring, whether about internal or external customers, that makes a service organization, and it's that spirit of caring that makes the Ritz-Carlton the industry standard for quality. The company's small, hands-on, top tier managers fully empower staff members to embrace and act upon service quality principles. "They can do things for customers or employees that normally will require any company 50 times as much time to get implemented and done," Mr. Kaznova remarks. "They could turn around a customer satisfaction survey from inception to completion in six days."

Despite the company's successes, Mr. Schulze categorizes his company as a 5.5 on a 1-to-10 scale, which he says still puts the Ritz-Carlton ahead of the competition. "But, with 14,000 employees putting their minds to it, I know we'll be a nine one day," he says.

"That's why we will absolutely lead this industry—not at all because of what I do and what I believe, but because the passion exists all around. And quality cannot be only following the Malcolm Baldrige example. Quality has to be heart."

Cheri Henderson is a correspondent for The TQM Magazine. *She may be contacted at 1083 Kelly Creek Circle, Oviedo, FL 32765-5704 (Tel: (407) 366-5336.*

Ritz-Carlton Quality Documents

The following documents provide some sense of how the Ritz-Carlton implements total quality in its organization. Included here are (1) The Ritz-Carlton Credo, (2) The Three Steps of Service, (3) The Ritz-Carlton Basics, and (4) The Ritz-Carlton Daily Quality Production Report and accompanying explanation. These can serve as models for other service organizations that want to take quality seriously.

THE RITZ-CARLTON

CREDO

The Ritz-Carlton Hotel is a place where the genuine care and comfort of our guests is our highest mission.

We pledge to provide the finest personal service and facilities for our guests who will always enjoy a warm, relaxed yet refined ambience.

The Ritz-Carlton experience enlivens the senses, instills well-being, and fulfills even the unexpressed wishes and needs of our guests.

"We Are Ladies and Gentlemen Serving Ladies and Gentlemen"

THREE STEPS OF SERVICE

1
A warm and sincere greeting. Use the guest name, if and when possible.

2
Anticipation and compliance with guest needs.

3
Fond farewell. Give them a warm good-bye and use their names, if and when possible.

THE RITZ-CARLTON BASICS

1 The Credo will be known, owned and energized by all employees.

2 Our motto is: "We are Ladies and Gentlemen serving Ladies and Gentlemen". Practice teamwork and "lateral service" to create a positive work environment.

3 The three steps of service shall be practiced by all employees.

4 All employees will successfully complete Training Certification to ensure they understand how to perform to The Ritz-Carlton standards in their position.

5 Each employee will understand their work area and Hotel goals as established in each strategic plan.

6 All employees will know the needs of their internal and external customers (guests and employees) so that we may deliver the products and services they expect. Use guest preference pads to record specific needs.

7 Each employee will continuously identify defects (Mr. BIV) throughout the Hotel.

8 Any employee who receives a customer complaint "owns" the complaint.

9 Instant guest pacification will be ensured by all. React quickly to correct the problem immediately. Follow-up with a telephone call within twenty minutes to verify the problem has been resolved to the customer's satisfaction. Do everything you possibly can to never lose a guest.

10 Guest incident action forms are used to record and communicate every incident of guest dissatisfaction. Every employee is empowered to resolve the problem and to prevent a repeat occurrence.

11 Uncompromising levels of cleanliness are the responsibility of every employee.

12 "Smile – We are on stage." Always maintain positive eye contact. Use the proper vocabulary with our guests. (Use words like – "Good Morning," "Certainly," "I'll be happy to" and "My pleasure").

13 Be an ambassador of your Hotel in and outside of the work place. Always talk positively. No negative comments.

14 Escort guests rather than pointing out directions to another area of the Hotel.

15 Be knowledgeable of Hotel information (hours of operation, etc.) to answer guest

inquiries. Always recommend the Hotel's retail and food and beverage outlets prior to outside facilities.

16 Use proper telephone etiquette. Answer within three rings and with a "smile." When necessary, ask the caller, "May I place you on hold." Do not screen calls. Eliminate call transfers when possible.

17 Uniforms are to be immaculate; Wear proper and safe footwear (clean and polished), and your correct name tag. Take pride and care in your personal appearance (adhering to all grooming standards).

18 Ensure all employees know their roles during emergency situations and are aware of fire and life safety response processes.

19 Notify your supervisor immediately of hazards, injuries, equipment or assistance that you need. Practice energy conservation and proper maintenance and repair of Hotel property and equipment.

20 Protecting the assets of a Ritz-Carlton Hotel is the responsibility of every employee.

Figure 1. **This figure shows the front and back of a trifold card given to all Ritz-Carlton employees to remind them of the company's commitment to quality and continuous improvement.**

The Ritz-Carlton Hotel Daily Quality Production Report

OCCUPIED ROOMS

PLUS COVERS

MINUS FINAL ASSESSMENT AND GUEST COMPLAINTS:

GUEST COMPLAINT CATEGORY	HSK		ENG		RES/COM		CIS		COS		F&B		GSVC		SEC		MISC		TOTALS	
	T	YTD	T	YTD	T	YTD	T	YTD	T	YTD	T	YTD	T	YTD	T	YTD	T	YTD	T	YTD
FACILITIES RELIABILITY																				
Inadequate																				
Missing																				
Worn																				
Inoperable																				
Incorrect																				
SUPPLIES/F&B RELIABILITY																				
Inadequate																				
Missing																				
Unsatisfactory																				
LADY/GENTLEMEN RELIABILITY																				
Attitude																				
Error - Timely																				
Error - Other																				
SERVICES MISSING																				
GUEST SECURITY (i.e. loss)																				

(TOTAL PRODUCTION: GSVC, SEC, MISC, TOTALS)

TOTAL SYSTEMS RELIABILITY & TIMELINESS DEFECTS

MINUS IN PROCESS AND INTERNAL CUSTOMER COMPLAINTS:

EMPLOYEE FACILITIES: Inadequate, Inoperable, or Incorrect
EMPLOYEE SUPPLIES: Wasteful Use, Inadequate, Missing, Unsatisfactory, or Incorrect
EMPLOYEE SERVICES: Work Done Over or Done Poorly
EMPLOYEE SECURITY: Mysterious Disappearance, Accident, Injury, Loss or Safety Hazard
HOTEL PURCHASING: Order, Shipment, or Storage Defects

RESOLVED SUCCESSFULLY %

TOTAL QUALITY DEFECTS

TOTAL QUALITY PRODUCTION

QUALITY PERCENTAGE:

DATE_____

Figure 2. **This is a reproduction of the form the Ritz-Carlton uses to track daily defects in quality for each of its hotels. See the next page for an explanation of how the company uses this report.**

Explanation of Daily Quality Production Report
The Ritz-Carlton Hotel Company

The primary purpose of the Daily Quality Production Report (DQPR) is to aggregate the various sources of customer reaction data from throughout the hotel. Each day, the company collects and reports information from over 15 sources so that they can analyze it on a periodic basis (monthly and quarterly). Management's goal is to determine the areas of greatest concern to eliminate these problems forever.

Most of the sources used have been produced daily over the past ten years. However, until about two years ago, this data was merely recorded without any kind of analysis over time. They merely detected these "opportunities" (guest complaints, accidents, problems), then tried to correct each of them without focusing on those areas that occurred the most or caused the most disruption to the business. The focus was on immediate correction (reaction) versus a more quality approach of root cause analysis (proactive).

Once they began putting this information together and reviewing it on a daily basis with the Executive Committee, they noticed two distinct advantages:

1. Executives took a more active role in the day to day "quality" production, which balanced with the traditional "financial" production.
2. By looking at the pattern problems, they were able to focus their efforts to those ares of greatest concern, instead of chasing every problem with band-aid solutions.

One Company's Experience—Taco Bell

Michael Hammer and James Champy

Fast food is the most prevalent type of service organization most of us are likely to interact with. The principles and practices of quality management are vital to these restaurants' being able to compete in an era when tastes are changing and competition is intense. This article from the best-selling book Reengineering the Corporation *explains how Taco Bell used the technique of process reengineering to revitalize itself during the 1980s to become one of the nation's largest, most popular, and most profitable fast food chains.*

The Taco Bell subsidiary of PepsiCo was sick and getting sicker when John E. Martin was named CEO in 1983. Martin's problem was not convincing people that the company had to reengineer for the long-term future. His problem was getting change that was radical enough and soon enough to save the company. Martin had inherited the leadership of a company that was becoming smaller and less profitable by the day. Here's what John Martin recently had to say about the changes he initiated at Taco Bell.

> For us, the process of reengineering has been like a voyage of discovery—a voyage we have been on now for nearly a decade, and one that we realize will continue as long as Taco Bell is in the business of serving customers.
>
> Throughout the entire process, our greatest insight has been our most basic—namely, that everything begins with a simple decision to listen to our customer.
>
> When I became CEO in 1983, Taco Bell was much like every other quick-service restaurant business. We were a top-down, "command-and-control" organization with multiple layers of management, each concerned primarily with bird-dogging the layers below them. We were also process-driven, in the old sense of the word, with operational handbooks for everything—including, literally, handbooks to interpret other handbooks.
>
> Like our competitors, we were caught up in the process of processing; we were striving for bigger, better, and more complicated in just about everything we did.

If something was simple, we made it complex. If it was hard, we figured out a way to make it impossible.

We operated this way, because with all our layers of management, we needed to make things difficult so we could keep everybody busy. The more commands and controls we had in the system, the more the system justified its own existence.

Unfortunately, in our ever-increasing efforts to micromanage every aspect of restaurant operations, we became so focused on ourselves and our processes that we forgot to ask a basic question: What the heck do our customers think about all this?

If something was simple, we made it complex. If it was hard, we figured out a way to make it impossible.

Did they care that our assistant restaurant managers could assemble and disassemble the twelve parts of a deep fryer with a blindfold on? Did they care that somebody in our industry probably wrote a handbook on it, including recommendations for the type of blindfold to use? Did they care, in the final analysis, that we managed to turn the relatively simple business of fast food into rocket science, all under the presumption that it was good for them?

Even before taking over as chief executive officer, I had a notion that our customers didn't give a hoot about any of our elaborate systems. My appointment as CEO gave me an opportunity to prove it. It's important to remember that back in the early 1980s, Taco Bell was very much a regional Mexican-American restaurant chain that had enjoyed a fair degree of success in a relatively small niche. In 1982, we had fewer than 1,500 restaurants and did $500 million in total sales; our major competitors, mostly in the hamburger business, were light years ahead of us.

The fast-food world was passing Taco Bell by. In fact, our cumulative real growth from 1978, when PepsiCo acquired Taco Bell, to 1982 was a negative 16 percent compared to the total industry's positive 6 percent.

We were going backwards—fast.

The problem was Taco Bell really didn't know what it wanted to be in those days. So our first order of business was to create a vision for the company. Since we had no place to go but up, we decided to think the unthinkable and create a vision of Taco Bell as a giant in the fast-food industry—not just the leader in the Mexican category, but a competitive force with which all restaurant organizations in all categories would have to contend.

A lot of restaurant people, including many in our own organization, thought that our new vision was something more than farsighted. Farfetched was a word we heard often. But Taco Bell was in an "up or out" situation; there was only one thing we knew for sure, and that was we had to change in a very big way.

Nowadays, when I think back to that early vision and to the massive amount of change we've had to create to fulfill it, I'm reminded of something Robert Kennedy once said: "Progress is a nice word. But change is its motivator, and change has its enemies." His point was that you can't get from Point A to Point B without dealing with some problems.

For Taco Bell to progress from a regional Mexican-American restaurant chain to a national force in the industry, we had to accept the fact that our greatest enemies were the tradition-bound ideas to which many of our employees clung.

In those days, traditional thinkers believed they knew what customers wanted without even asking *them*. Fancier decors, bigger kitchens, more sophisticated equipment, larger staffs, broader menus, outdoor playgrounds. Without asking our customers, in other words, we assumed that what they wanted was bigger, better, and more complex. By following through on this tradition-bound thinking, we were providing slower and costlier service.

So we began our voyage by asking our customers what *they* wanted, and what we found out was encouraging. Our customers, it turned out, didn't want any of those bigger, better, fancier things we assumed they did. What they really wanted was very simple: good food, served fast and hot, in a clean environment, at a price they could afford.

That was it. All the rest meant little to them.

The initial research we did at Taco Bell became our declaration of independence. It helped us look at Taco Bell in an entirely different way and allowed us to turn customer value into the key element of our business proposition.

When a customer walks into a quick-service restaurant and gives us a dollar, a large part of what he or she is paying for has nothing to do with what the customer actually receives for the money. Sure, all the cost factors are important from a business point of view. But what's important from the customer's point of view? Is labor important? No. Is rent important? Not unless you're a PepsiCo shareholder.

In the end, the only important category to customers is food and paper, because that's what they get back for the dollar they give us. Amazingly, though, the percentage of his or her dollar the customer pays for food and paper—in other words, the cost of goods sold—is, historically, the one variable chains have tried to reduce. Even today, restaurant people brag about holding food and paper costs down to twenty-five or twenty-six cents, and putting the extra pennies into marketing, which accounts for about eight cents out of every customer dollar.

One of our well-known, fast-food competitors spends about $1 billion a year marketing its business. That's the cost of about eight billion bean burritos, enough to give every person on this planet one and a half burritos free every year.

So we decided to reduce everything but our cost of goods sold, including the cost of marketing. If we created a better deal for the

> What our customers really wanted was very simple: good food, served fast and hot, in a clean environment, at a price they could afford.

consumer, we thought, perhaps we wouldn't have to pay so much to twist people's arms to get them to buy our product.

With that decision, we were creating a true paradigm shift that launched our entire reengineering process.

I cannot tell you how exciting and liberating that shift was for our company. By thinking entirely outside the box, by saying to ourselves that the old methods were the way of the dinosaur, we unleashed a power within our company that has produced enormous success, and, in fact, has enabled us now to think realistically about becoming the dominant force in the convenient food industry within the next ten years. Our initial vision has a good chance of becoming reality. Not bad for a sleepy little Mexican-American restaurant organization.

How was that power manifested in the reengineering process?

It took several forms—including a complete reorganization of our human resources and a dramatic redesign of our operational systems to make them more innovative and customer focused.

By traditional restaurant standards the reengineering of our management processes was radical. We eliminated entire layers of management and, in the process, completely redefined nearly every job in the system.

For example, we did away with the "district manager" supervisory layer, which traditionally oversees the management of five or six restaurants. By eliminating that job category, we dramatically changed the job description of our restaurant managers, who had previously reported to the district managers.

For the first time in the fast-food industry, we told restaurant managers that they were responsible for running their own operations without the help—or the hindrance—of another layer of supervision. "You're in charge now," we told them. "How your unit performs in terms of sales, profitability, and customer satisfaction is in your hands, and we will evaluate your performance and decide your compensation based on those very specific business indicators." That was an unheard of move for the command-and-control, quick-service restaurant industry.

The reorganization proved painful for some managers, especially those who still believed the ultimate test of their abilities was assembling the deep-fryer blindfolded. Many managers, however, adapted easily and immediately to the new approach. In fact, they responded so well that eventually we changed their job title from restaurant manager to restaurant general manager. Since they were each responsible for a $1 million to $2 million a year business, they were clearly operating in a general management capacity.

For several years after this reorganization, we saw an exodus of the traditional thinking managers. Most, in fact, wound up working in management positions with our competition, where the area supervisor who oversees a span of five restaurants is still very much the norm.

By contrast, at the Taco Bell supervisory level, our reorganization produced an entirely new job category that we call "market manager." This position exists nowhere else in the restaurant industry.

In 1988, Taco Bell had about 350 area supervisors controlling about 1,800 restaurants. Today, we have just over 100 market managers responsible for about 2,300 company-owned restaurants. Market managers each oversee at least 20 restaurants. Some are in charge of 40, which if you know the restaurant business, you know is an enormous responsibility.

Successful market managers in the new Taco Bell manage by exception, which means they must work only to solve problems, not create them. Equally important, they have to completely reject the old command-and-control style in favor of a model that promotes flexibility, relies on the most advanced management information systems in the business, encourages innovation, and empowers the people around them to do their jobs.

The new market manager position prompted a shake out, as had the previous change.

Some former area supervisors rose to the new challenge, others switched to restaurant general managers and became very productive, while still others left Taco Bell for the more comfortable confines of our competitors.

Several of those who left, in fact, took me aside and said, in effect, "Hey, John, you're out in left field without a mitt. This new Taco Bell will never work. There are too many changes."

Each time I would listen, smile, shake their hand, and thank them for being an important part of Taco Bell's successful *past*.

After each of those conversations, I was more committed to the reengineering process than ever. Why? Because at Taco Bell, we had accepted that even though change could be painful, it was also an inevitable byproduct of growth and success. It is when people *stop* taking me aside and saying, "John, these changes will never work," that I'm going to start worrying, because that's when Taco Bell is starting to stagnate.

The great American author John Steinbeck once wrote, "It is the nature of man as he grows older to protest against change, particularly change for the better." To understand the truth of that statement, just take a hard look at America's electronics industry, our once great railroad industry, and the struggling steel and auto manufacturers. They all grew comfortable in their old age, resisted the inevitability of change, and are now paying the consequences. Which is precisely why I say the reengineering process at Taco Bell is a never ending process of change and renewal.

> Successful market managers in the new Taco Bell manage by exception, which means they must work only to solve problems, not create them.

Change begets change, and so at the same time we were reorganizing our management resources, we had to rethink everything else we did. Throughout the total reengineering effort, we maintained just one simple rule—enhance those things that bring value to the customers and change or eliminate those that don't.

We have to accept the fact that we are not in the same business we were in during the sixties and seventies. The old ways don't apply, and we must change every aspect of our business accordingly.

Take, for example, our Taco Bell restaurant buildings. To enhance value to our customer, and to eliminate what we didn't need, we had to completely reengineer them. Before 1983, a typical Taco Bell restaurant was comprised of 70 percent kitchen and 30 percent customer area. Like everybody else in the industry, we had complicated our operations to the point where our internal needs were pushing the customer out the door. Today, after eight years of reengineering, we have turned the situation around. Our new restaurants average 30 percent kitchen and 70 percent customer area. We've been able to double the number of seats within the same square footage as our older style building.

Our competitors' units, by the way, have become bigger and bigger, while ours have stayed the same size. A new full-sized Taco Bell restaurant, including seating, could fit into the *kitchen* space of some of our typical fast-food hamburger competitors.

Moreover, our downsizing of the kitchen area hasn't hurt productivity one bit. In fact, it's done just the opposite. In the early 1980s, when our kitchens used to make up 70 percent of the total restaurant space, we considered peak capacity for a top unit to be about $400 per hour. Today, our top restaurants have a peak capacity of $1,500 per hour. Moreover, our average pricing today is about 25 percent lower than it was nine years ago.

What we have achieved through reengineering is a synergy of all our processes. As our value-based marketing strategy drives sales and transactions, our efforts at reengineering make those sales more profitable, and, at the same time, increase the customer satisfaction ratings we track on a continual basis.

Other reengineering success stories for us have been a system we call K-Minus, a program we call TACO, or Total Automation of Company Operations, and some of our latest out of the box thinking in alternative points of distribution and applied technology. Let me explain.

K-Minus, which stands for a kitchenless restaurant, evolved from our belief that we are a customer-driven, retail service company, *not* a manufacturing company. We believe our restaurants should *retail* food, not *manufacture* it.

Today, our meat and beans are cooked outside the restaurant at central commissaries; all we need is hot water to reheat the ingredi-

Throughout the total reengineering effort, we maintained just one simple rule—enhance those things that bring value to the customers and change or eliminate those that don't.

ents for serving. We also K-Minus the preparation of our corn shells and cheese, as well as all the dicing and chopping of lettuce, tomatoes, onions, and olives.

So far, the results from K-Minus have been outstanding. We've already pushed fifteen hours of work per day out of the restaurant, which translates system-wide to about eleven million hours per year.

Taco Bell saved about $7 million from K-Minus just last year. We also benefited from greater quality control, better employee morale (because we eliminated most of the drudgery of food preparation), fewer employee accidents and injuries, big savings in utilities, and, of course, more time to focus on the customer.

The TACO system gives each restaurant a level of MIS sophistication that is unparalleled in the fast-food industry. That system puts the power of computer technology in the hands of our people, promoting self-sufficiency, and eliminating thousands of hours of paperwork and administrative time that are better spent directly serving our customers.

Equally important, programs like K-Minus and TACO serve as agents of change for even more advanced ideas, such as alternative points of distribution and new technology. Here's what I mean:

When people look at a classic, free-standing Taco Bell restaurant, they see something that in the future could just as easily be a McDonald's, a Burger King, or any other competitor. It is a building, comprised of bricks and mortar, glass and assorted restaurant equipment, and for the past thirty or forty years it has both defined and confined who and what we are.

Defined and confined because inside those four walls, our target audience is people who eat at fast-food restaurants. Outside those walls, our target audience is people who eat. Inside the walls, the total market is $78 billion. Outside the walls, the total market is the sum of all meal occasions, or about $600 billion, in the United States alone.

When we started to redefine ourselves in terms of what I like to call the total share of stomach, we began to look at our bricks-and-mortar restaurant as just one point of distribution in a universe of many distribution points.

Moreover, we stopped confining ourselves to the goal of becoming the value leader in the quick-service restaurant industry and set our sights on a new goal: to become the value leader for all foods for all meal occasions.

So we're knocking down those traditional walls, and taking our food to places where people congregate. Right now, these include corporate and industrial dining centers, schools and universities, airports, and stadiums. I'm happy to report that those new distribution points are all doing great, but as far as I'm concerned they're just a start.

The real promise comes from the points of distribution we haven't discovered yet. That's because reengineering brings about change,

change produces new ideas, and new ideas result in growth. For Taco Bell, the growth has been sensational. Since 1989, sales have increased by 22 percent per year. This exceptional sales growth has been driven by increased transactions, the best indicator of our success.

In terms of profit growth, Taco Bell has averaged earnings increases of 31 percent since 1989, which is incredible when you take into account the enormous financial investments we've made in technology, organizational changes, and power building our company. Our huge profit growth is happening at a time when the rest of this industry is struggling to increase profits at all.

And because of our continuing efforts to reengineer our operations and to think of our growth not in terms of four-walled restaurants but in terms of points of distribution, we expect these numbers to sky-rocket in the years ahead. Vending machines, supermarkets, schools, retail outlets, street corners—you name it, we'll be there. In fact, we're confident that in the next decade, Taco Bell will have tens of thousands of points of distribution, which is a long, long way from the current 3,600 restaurants we now operate. We'll get there, because if we don't, somebody else will. That's the reality that drives our business, and constantly pushes us to think of unique opportunities to enhance customer value.

Another of those opportunities involves the application of new technology. Our guiding principle here, as everywhere else, is that every technical innovation we implement must simultaneously enhance service and reduce costs.

> We're confident that in the next decade, Taco Bell will have tens of thousands of points of distribution, which is a long, long way from the current 3,600 restaurants we now operate.

The progress we've made in implementing effective technology has been so outstanding that CBS News did a segment on our advances. Consider, for example, our taco-making machine. It can churn out up to nine hundred tacos an hour, all perfectly proportioned, all served at exactly the right temperature, all individually wrapped and ready to deliver to our customers. It has another plus, too; it shows up for work every day! In a real sense, our new taco-making machine serves as a symbol of the progress we've made through reengineering.

I remember vividly the day the idea was placed on the table just a couple of years ago. Sure, there was some snickering, and sure, there were people who thought the idea would never get off the ground. But that's okay, because the really important thing is that the *new* Taco Bell didn't let the *old* Taco Bell stand in the way of progress.

If we had let traditional thinking guide our actions, that taco-making machine would never exist today.

To sum up, Taco Bell went from being a $500 million regional company in 1982 to a $3 billion national company today all because we listen to our customers and are not afraid to change. I predict that by the year 2000, Taco Bell will be a $20 billion company, again, because we're a company that listens to our customers and is not afraid to change. When someone says to me—and they do—"John, that forecast is completely farfetched," I just keep in mind two things: First, when the traditional thinkers tell you your goal is farfetched, you're probably on to something big. Second, when they stop telling you it's farfetched, you've probably already lost the war.

John Martin's story is inspiring. His reengineering effort paid off magnificently as Taco Bell's sales soared from $500 million to $3 billion in an industry that is declining. Several points are worth underscoring in this case.

The most dramatically drawn lesson is Martin's recognition that the customer must be the starting point for everything in reengineering. In reconceptualizing the company's processes, Martin and his people always began with the customer's needs and worked backwards from there. This perspective stands in sharp contrast to that of the traditional manager who put fryer maintenance skills at the top of the list. Equipment maintenance is important, but it's not what customers are hoping for when they walk through Taco Bell's door. In the standard, bureaucratic company structure, people correlate their personal importance with the number of their direct reports or the value of the assets they control. This is one of the values that reengineering has to change, because it leads to the building of infrastructure—larger and more complicated kitchens—that doesn't serve customers' real needs. Taco Bell's reengineering was unambiguously customer-driven in that every change was tested against a standard: Does this add value for the customer?

> Taco Bell's reengineering was unambiguously customer-driven in that every change was tested against a standard: Does this add value for the customer?

Another lesson to come out of John Martin's experience: Expect resistance and be prepared to deal with it. People with a vested interest in the way things are will be upset when you change them. If some people are upset it's a good sign that you're doing something significant.

The Taco Bell case also illustrates the ripple effect we've discussed. Change a process, and that change ripples into other aspects of the organization. Taco Bell changed the food-assembly process, which precipitated a change in the managerial structure, which meant the company had to change its compensation system. Process change ripples into universal organizational change.

Finally, Taco Bell has made its corporate vision clear with that brilliant phrase, "We want to be number one in share of stomach." That statement tells anyone hearing or reading it that the company's opportunities are far greater than just selling Mexican fast food in sit-down restaurants. Every company that is reengineering should seek a phrase that is as clear, eloquent, and eye-opening as that one.

BANKING

Achieving Quality with Customer in Mind

Diogo Teixeira and Joseph Ziskin

Here you'll find an excellent review of the place of quality principles in enhancing management practices and customer responsiveness in commercial banking. Written by two executives from Ernst & Young's Center for Information Technology and Strategy in Boston, the article takes advantage of information gleaned from that company's International Quality Study.

Banks have traditionally placed a high premium on both customer relationships and financial integrity. A smile, a personal greeting, and accurate processing of customers' records and transactions—these were considered the key elements of superior quality service.

These are still admirable attributes, and always will be. But banks—particularly in today's globalized, deregulated, and competitive arena—have come to realize that quality encompasses much more. Quality must permeate the organization, extending to how banks identify and meet customer expectations, develop and deliver new products, and run their operations.

The Quality Imperative

Quality is not a new word or corporate objective for the banking industry. For years, banks the world over have sought to project images of stability, reliability, and trust. In the handling of monetary transactions and safeguarding

---

Reprinted with permission from *The Bankers Magazine*, January/February 1993, Warren Gorham Lamont.

assets, perfection has never been too high a goal for which to strive. As operators of the payment system, banks have always played a unique and mandatory role in every country and every society. Because of this role, bank standards, services, products, and prices have more often than not been dictated or at least influenced by governments that had an incentive to see only the highest levels of performance. According to the traditional meaning of quality involving accuracy, consistency, and stability, banking was probably one of the most high quality of all industries.

Today quality is taking on a new meaning. The previous measures of quality are now the minimum standards required to be competitive. The new challenge is meeting or exceeding customer expectations. The definition goes beyond accuracy, consistency, and stability. It embraces a commitment to continuous improvement and a service relationship with customers.

The growing focus on satisfying customers has led to a new view of quality related to product/service development and to the delivery process. The industry has recognized that retail banking today has to be thought of as a way to meet or exceed customer needs and wants. In other words, the business is about finding ways to satisfy customers, not ways to safeguard assets. Banks feel that a customer focus requires a process orientation to providing services and products. Functional departments can no longer operate in isolation. A cross-functional approach is required to focus on the customer. These realizations have changed the thinking about quality and its role as a competitive weapon and, indeed, a necessity.

Today quality is taking on a new meaning. The previous measures of quality are now the minimum standards required to be competitive.

Three very significant trends in banking relate to the exploitation of technology, the introduction of modern "consumer goods," marketing approaches, and empowerment of employees to improve quality. Banks are hoping to learn from other industries about product development and to take advantage of new capabilities that are possible through technology. They want to better understand what is behind customer satisfaction so that they can meet or exceed customer expectations. The expectation is that improved quality will lead to higher profitability and customer loyalty.

Quality and Technology

Technology clearly plays a major role in the worldwide banking industry. Money today is often nothing more than bits and bytes. There is no other industry in which information technology (IT) is so clearly the means of production.

IT may be critical (even essential) in other industries, but banking is somehow in a class by itself. With other businesses the customer buys a tangible product (an automobile) or some physically tangible service (electricity, a restaurant meal, a hotel room, or an airline seat). But deposits, loans, and other banking "products" are little more than debits and credits in the industry's gargantuan computer programs and databases.

Thus, there is an obvious correlation and interdependency between banking quality and banking technology. Technology improves quality by eliminating human error, but it also expands customer expectations. Thus, this connection can only strengthen in the future as IT continues to displace paper as the means for creating, storing, and effecting banking transactions.

In studying the purpose for which banks apply technology, the nature of the goals for applying technology is changing. Banks are increasingly seeing that the primary reason for deploying technology will be to meet customer expectations. Improved quality is also becoming a major reason for employing technology. These two trends are consistent in that both applications are aimed at satisfying customers.

In contrast, the two traditional objectives of the banking technology world—cost reduction and increased revenue—will be relatively less important in the future. Cost reductions do not automatically result in higher profits and neither does increased revenue. The only true security in the automated banking world of tomorrow will be a tight link with the customer.

Banks are clearly looking to technology to stir innovation. So much so that much greater competition will be created as a result. Once again technology has the capability to all at once create tremendous value for the customer while creating a competitive situation that builds profits. Banks that fail to heed the redefinition of quality in the technological world of the future may find themselves at a severe disadvantage.

> The only true security in the automated banking world of tomorrow will be a tight link with the customer.

BayBanks, a regional bank in the Northeast, has been following this strategy for its retail business for years. BayBanks has consistently been first to market with "customer valued" products and services, and more often than not technology has been the key to creating and delivering these services. They have built a reputation on meeting customer expectations through the use of advanced technology. They were the first in their market to employ a saturation strategy for deploying off-premises and advanced-function ATMs. They were also first to offer ATM access to statements of cleared checks and deposits and make available image statements.

Although much of what they have done may not seem particularly innovative, they have developed an ability to consistently be the first in their market to offer new services and delivery mechanisms. The success and value of their retail franchise can be linked to their use of technology to develop and deliver services and products.

Quality and New Product/Service Development

The product development process for banking has changed over the years. Competition from banks and nonbanks, deregulation, disintermediation, and a host of other factors have forced banks to change their approaches. Banks are now more concerned with customer wants and needs than ever before. They are using these wants and needs to become more customer-driven in developing new products and services.

The identification of new products and services has traditionally been focused on just one thing: observing the competition. Close to 80% of banks use this technique as the primary means of new product selection. However, banks are increasingly taking the customer into consideration in identifying new products and services.

The reason for this is simple. The incredible powers of information technology are making it possible to expand the features and functions of retail banking products dramatically. This proliferation of options confronts banks with a need to understand customers' needs and wants (and risks) much better than they ever did before. This is the only way they can tell which of the many product possibilities will be both appealing and provide an adequate return. Banks are aggressively expanding their use of market analysis, customer requests, and focus groups.

Banks are showing a clear desire to get customers actually involved in product development. This is perhaps more common in wholesale banking, where large customers have always gotten tailored services, whether it be in global custody, stock transfer, or zero balance disbursement accounts. In retail banking, depending as it does on serving the masses with standardized (if option-laden products, this is a revolutionary development.

In a wide variety of ways retail banks plan significantly higher levels of direct customer involvement. Involving the customer should result in products that are easier to use, instill more confidence, and add significant value for the customer.

In the past, satisfaction was often measured on the basis of complaint analysis. The fewer the complaints, the more satisfied customers were.

Quality, Empowerment, and the Customer Interface

After examining how banks are creating products and services that are of more value to the customer, it is important to consider how banks intend to deliver satisfaction to retail customers. In the past, satisfaction was often measured on the basis of complaint analysis. The fewer the complaints, the more satisfied customers were. The primary emphasis was on avoiding errors. In today's world, that is not enough, since customer expectations have grown with the industry's ability to reduce errors. Customers expect much more than error-free statements and transaction handling.

Critical to delivering customer satisfaction is the ability and desire to manage the customer relationship. The reason for interest in relationship management is clear: as competition intensifies, the customer can choose to go elsewhere quite easily. Better service to customers is one overriding theme that is emerging in the industry.

Banks are increasingly providing continuous customer relationship training to their employees. To further improve the customer interface, banks are empowering employees at the point of customer contact to make decisions (within their realm of activity). It is critical in banking that empowerment be interpreted correctly. It does not mean having tellers make credit decisions or give customers anything they want. Rather it refers to the intensely clerical nature of most retail bank customer interactions. For example, an ATM customer service telephone representative should be able to research and resolve an erroneous cash disbursement while the customer is at an ATM. Or account maintenance should be done by customer service representatives directly instead of by filling out forms that are passed along to the data entry department.

Wachovia Corporation, a Southeast superregional bank, has empowered its retail banking organization to create a personal touch. Wachovia has long been known for its use of "personal bankers" to service retail relationships. Every customer has a personal banker who is responsible for ensuring the customer's satisfaction. Each banker is highly trained, empowered, and valued. Wachovia's definition of empowerment is providing the retail bank with the skills, understanding, tools, and authority to do the "right thing at the point of contact." The bank is committed to spending a great deal of time on training and skills development relative to the way employees relate to customers.

With each banker having approximately 900 to 1,000 customers, this delivery mechanism at first would seem to be an expensive way to do business. Yet, Wachovia's culture combined with the use of "personal bankers" has consistently produced high-quality products and service in terms of meeting or exceeding customer expectations. Even more important, this combination has produced strong profits.

Typical of quality-oriented organizations, Wachovia is not comfortable standing still. The bank is continually looking for better ways to deliver and measure quality as it relates to meeting customer expectations. Performance measurement, including compensation and career development, is a key area where the importance of quality is gaining in importance. Wachovia is moving beyond the traditional measures of fee income and balance sheet growth as the primary measures of performance for their personal bankers.

The industry as a whole is also headed in the direction of identifying better quality measurements for the purpose of developing a better overall performance measurement system. The challenge is defining what needs to be measured and how to incorporate the necessary feedback to adequately measure performance and effect behavior. Those banks that are able to envision and implement the management practices that promote meeting or exceeding customer expectations will succeed in the future.

Conclusion

Ensuring quality is a difficult job because the nature of the retail banking business has changed so much. New product development, technology, and relationship management are all critical elements of the quality equation that require changed management procedures.

Until recently the customer has been the forgotten element in retail banking. A hundred years ago, banks did not lend money to individuals—period. Bank accounts were like safe deposit boxes—a safe place to leave valuables, but not a place from which to transfer value.

In the 1990s all this has changed. Today's consumers are dependent on retail banking services for travel, purchases, liquidity, asset ownership, and more. The number of retail transactions per capita continues to grow as society becomes more complex. Although the "cashless society" is not yet here, most of the important, high-value transactions are done through banking technology.

These forces are causing bank products and services to become far more customer oriented. To service customers well banks will have to develop new technologies, new relationships, new flexibility, and new levels of under-standing of their customers. Moreover, in order to adopt fee-based pricing, banks must be able to provide services that are more than mere commodities—but rather services that are valued with the customer in mind.

Banks have already begun this effort, but it will be some time before they finally achieve it. Home banking and the "smart card" containing an embedded microchip are but two examples of new technologies that, although offering great promise and while technically feasible today, will literally take decades to implement because the payment system moves so slowly.

As a final point, many banks that enjoy a high-quality reputation in the eyes of customers and industry analysts regard quality not as a single program, not as a defensive weapon, and not as just another competitive weapon, but as the only weapon. Quality is the way to give customers what they want, when and how they want it, and at a price they want. In one bank's words, "The view of quality and quality delivery is woven through everything we do."

Diogo Teixeira is a partner Joseph Ziskin is a senior manager with Ernst & Young's Center for Information Technology and Strategy in Boston.

Systems for Survival

Alex Jablonowski

Written by a managing director of Barclays Global Services, this article explains the necessity of adapting quality methods to banking in Europe, but it is equally as relevant to U.S. banking. It pays particular attention to using the concept of process reengineering to upgrade service and methods.

The key to development in British banking technology is process re-engineering—fundamentally rethinking how we do our business so that, whenever possible, data and transactions are generated automatically and pass "straight through" the system.

Increasingly, process re-engineering in a bank's operational services is becoming a necessity and not an optional extra. Banks are aiming to reduce their operating costs and provide improved service to their customers.

Where processes are complex this means combining many different functions into one workstation, thereby empowering staff to perform more functions more efficiently, faster and at lower cost.

Until this is successfully completed, banking technology will fall far short of delivering the benefits which are required of it and for which industry investment is running into many hundreds of millions of pounds.

Such developments are occurring across a wide range of operating processes, but current trends in domestic and cross-border electronic banking and payments and securities processing provide strong pointers to the way ahead.

In the US, the leading money centre and super-regional banks are familiar with process re-engineering and the way in which electronic access, cash management, payment, securities settlement, custody and trade services systems are coming together. The additional dimension and complication in Europe is that of diversity, such as the diversity of regulation and currency. The need to handle this diversity has ensured that UK banks are not merely copying what banks have been doing in the US. They are adapting the processes to pan-Europeanise them and, in order to meet the needs of their customers who operate on a global scale, to globalise them.

As the effects of deregulation spread in Europe and as the European Community coalesces, leading corporate and financial institutions are increasingly operating across borders.

In consequence, they are bringing together and centralising their cash management and investment management.

> Increasingly, process re-engineering in a bank's operational services is becoming a necessity and not an optional extra.

However, until the EC has an integrated currency, an integrated payments system and an integrated stock exchange, they will have to continue to settle in individual European countries. As corporate customers in Europe have to combine a degree of centralisation of their operations with operational decentralisation in the various European countries, they need electronic access into the various payment systems in individual European countries.

Process re-engineering enables banks to capture big transaction flows and move towards one single infrastructure which operates across borders and businesses.

So banks are now developing products which can reach across frontiers and provide cash management, trade, payment and securities settlement series not only in the UK and European arena but also on the global scale.

The more innovative and pro-active banks are forging electronic links with banks in Europe where they are employing a range of means to gain access to the various Automated Clearing Houses in the member states, exploiting the growing use of electronic data interchange (EDI) and developing new financial EDI (FEDI) systems, making the latest state-of-the-art FEDI systems available to other banks in the UK and elsewhere through third party processing on a "white label" basis.

It is now possible to collect payments by international direct debit using the global EDIFACT message standard—and the system can be used either as a stand-alone service or as an integral part of a global cash management service. Users do not even need to develop their own systems to plug into the service, as there is enabling software available which will run from any IBM-compatible PC almost anywhere.

In the field of global custody, custodian banks will be providing customers with European and global services in investment accounting, performance measurement, valuation, proxy voting, tax reclamation, stock borrowing and stock lending. They will be integrating information on cash and assets so that customers can receive information on these over a personal computer (PC) and through a single software package.

In paper-intensive processes in the banks' back-offices, image processing has reached the stage where it is now economic to use it to get rid of mountains of paperwork. Instead of documents and files being stored manually, they are increasingly being held digitally on a central database giving instant access. All the information required to deal with customer enquiries is available immediately on-screen and documents can be called up on Windows interfaces. Image-based document routing, group filing and scheduling, electronic mail and conferencing will allow PC users across a countrywide network to share and access information instantly.

Imaging becomes a particularly powerful tool when married with workflow software which can handle transaction and information processing in such a way that workstations can be set up to know where the operator wants to go and then guide them along the easiest way of getting there.

New technology, new systems, new processes, new working practices may in some cases merely supplement existing technology, existing systems, processes and working practices. In many cases they replace what existed previously. The consequences are wide-ranging.

Most of the technology is already available. The problem for banks is how to re-engineer their existing processes in order to take advantage of the technology—and how to migrate from the processes currently in use to the re-engineered. This takes time and great care, despite the urgency. A botched re-engineering can cause chaos.

Quality is a key issue. Banks must now have BS5750 accreditation if they wish to gain facilities management contracts from government departments and local authorities. While some banks see the need to satisfy the yearly and ad hoc appraisals of BS5750 as an additional overhead, it is likely that external pressures and peer pressure will lead more and more banks towards process re-engineering which gains quality recognition.

Delivering quality to the customer requires banks to change from the old culture in which they tended to tell customers what banking services were available and why customers should use them to a culture in which the customers' requirements determine the services which banks design to meet those requirements. The pace of change is often customer-led.

> *Delivering quality to the customer requires banks to change to a culture in which the customers' requirements determine the services which banks design to meet those requirements.*

Focusing on customer requirements is an important component of process re-engineering. It helps to determine the optimum way of managing the cost, budgets, timescales and resources of new developments. It is encouraging banks to see project management as a necessity which is an integral part of development from the outset of each project rather than viewing it negatively, as many have done in the past, as an optional extra adding to development costs.

What is certain is that the issues raised by the market demand for the improved quality achievable by process re-engineering cannot be dodged but have to be faced.

Banks which rise to the challenges of technological change are not merely improving their chances of staying in business. They also have the opportunity to get into new markets such as offering third-party processing. Not all banks will want or be able to justify new services coming on stream, even though they know their customers require them. The answer for these lies in obtaining the service on an agency basis from a bank which has already developed it.

The wake-up call for the banking industry now coming through from the current wave of technology is loud and clear. In the past, a bank could get away with a mediocre operations and systems capability if its customer service was excellent. Increasingly, a bank needs to be excellent both in the front and in the back office. This is not about competitive advantage. It is much more fundamental. It is about survival.

Alex Jablonowski is managing director of Barclays Global Services.

Steal This Idea

Christopher Bogan and John Robbins

One California mortgage banking company has been showcasing the quality technique of best practices of top performers as benchmarks to teach the whole company how to boost performance. This article explains how they do it.

At American Residential Mortgage Corporation, La Jolla, California, the annual occasion recognizing top performers in the company is a time of celebration. The top 20 percent of the company's loan officers named to the President's Club gather with their branch managers, operating staff and senior executives to celebrate the past year's sales achievements.

Typically, there are lots of high-spirited parties, dinners and golf mixed with business reviews and speeches exhorting this army of super salespeople to climb to even greater heights.

But this past year, the President's Club was different. It became not merely a time of celebration but a time of focused introspection on what it was that enabled these superachievers to record superior performances. And the reason for the shift in emphasis wasn't due to the fact the company was going public, or the extraordinary good spirits engendered by the company's best year on record, or the late-night karaoke party where senior management sang to American Residential employees at a local resort club. The most unusual and inspiring moments during three days of meetings were created by American Residential's best and brightest performers who had been asked to share some of the secrets of their success.

By putting the spotlight on the methods used by top achievers inside the company, American Residential was taking a critically important management step. For the first time, in a systematic way, the company began leveraging a hidden asset—the data base of "best practices" or highly effective operating techniques that enable the company's best performers to produce at far higher levels than 80 percent of their peers. During the final day of the President's Club retreat, the company focused on the best practices of its best performers—its most productive and its most innovative loan officers, closers, processors and branch managers.

What Is Benchmarking?

If we lived in a world where common sense prevailed, the tool of best-practices benchmarking would seem prosaic. It is quite simply the process of searching

Reprinted with permission from *Mortgage Banking*, December 1992, Mortgage Bankers Association of America.

for best practices that lead to superior performance. The word benchmarking has its linguistic and metaphorical roots in the surveyor's term. For surveyors, the practice of benchmarking referred to taking your bearings by sighting another geographic reference point. Building on that concept the practice of benchmarking, as it's used in modern management, leads to improved performance by comparing one's performance to that of other high performers.

Much has been written recently about using the tool of benchmarking to seek best-in-class or best-in-world performers to serve as models for upgrading corporate performance. Nevertheless, much untapped gold, in terms of superior performance technique, lies undiscovered within individual companies and within the mortgage banking industry.

> Much untapped gold, in terms of superior performance technique, lies undiscovered within individual companies.

The search for excellent operating practices to benefit your company need not be a quest for the Holy Grail, leading to such distant places as Japan, Germany or another coast. While the search for best practices often leads outside your company or industry, it also can produce significant findings and benefits by identifying highly successful operating practices within your company (see Figure 1).

Using a seven-level model to serve as a performance hierarchy against which to measure its performance, American Residential began its search for the best within its own organization (see Figure 2).

In every mortgage bank, there exists this hidden asset of best-practices experience. Frequently, it is of extraordinary breadth, depth and value. Yet,

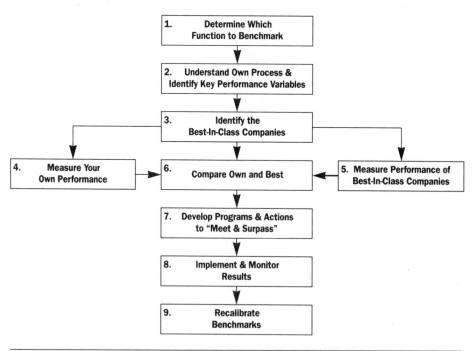

Figure 1. **The nine-step benchmarking process.**

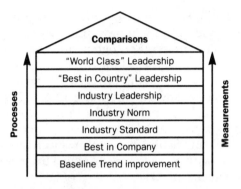

Figure 2. **Levels of performance benchmarking.**

in many mortgage banks—arguably in most American organizations—this data base of experience is often ignored, seldom understood and usually not fully valued. This experiential data base resides in the operating habits of the high performers in any corporation: those that outpace the other 80 percent in leadership, productivity, sales and quality.

The approach embraced at American Residential is not to lionize this 20 percent—but to learn from them and disseminate that knowledge to all in the company.

At American Residential, total quality management (TQM) is becoming a key part of the organization's strategy, which is based on four cornerstone concepts:

- growth through servicing and through originations;
- a balanced approach to developing different complementary businesses;
- a conservative long-term view toward organizational growth; and
- total dedication to quality.

Standard TQM concepts of customer satisfaction, continuous improvement, employee involvement and quality control are central to American Residential's approach to total quality excellence—but so is its focus on identifying, understanding, articulating and deploying the best practices of its best performers.

Why is this so important? In today's increasingly competitive and fast-moving markets, one of senior management's primary challenges is to create a fast-moving organization that can react quickly and remain agile and lean throughout sudden market swings and changing economic conditions. It's the "fast learning organization" that institutionalizes the capacity for rapid change, constant improvement and creative evolution.

In its many different guises, benchmarking or the search for best practices—both inside and outside one's own company—is a powerful tool for creating an organization in which all employees—from loan officers, underwriters and processors to senior executives, support personnel and servicing staff—accelerate the constant improvement process by borrowing or creatively swiping good ideas from other high performers.

This strategy is absolutely critical for American Residential, based in La Jolla, California, with its 49 lending offices in 17 states. The company is ranked among the top nine independent mortgage banking institutions in the country, according to rankings produced by *Inside Mortgage Finance* for all of 1991 and for the six months ending June 1992. For the twelve months ending September 1992 and September 1991, respectively, the company originated mortgage loans with an aggregate principal balance of $4.6 billion and $2.7 billion, a 70.4 percent increase.

American Residential underwent a management-led buyout in 1990 and then, during this past August, successfully completed an initial public offering of stock. With an equity infusion of $37 million and a warehouse line of $520 million from 12 major banks, the company is well positioned to take advantage of market opportunities by rapidly expanding loan production and its mortgage servicing portfolio.

TQM Dividends

Already the company's TQM initiative has started to pay dividends. It has helped American Residential effectively manage the onslaught of refinancing business without significant staff expansion. To give some idea of how staffing increases have been minimal compared with the influx in volume during the refi boom, one only need quickly review some relevant statistics. At midyear 1991 total staffing at the mortgage company was at 914, by midyear 1992 it had risen to 1,105—an increase of roughly 21 percent. But the productivity numbers dwarf the boosted staffing numbers—particularly on the production side, where the brunt of the refi boom hit hardest. As of September 30, 1991, the number of loans in the pipeline per branch staff stood at 16, but as of September 30, 1992, the number had soared by 94 percent, to 31.

Other productivity numbers that endorse the gains that the new TQM initiative has brought to the company reflect better performance per employee on the servicing side, as well. As of December 31, 1991, the number of loans serviced per servicing employee was at 618; by September 30, 1992, that had risen to 786—an increase of 27 percent. Another sign of the productivity gains posted at the company in the time since the best practices and benchmarking concepts were introduced comes from looking at the number of loans produced per origination center. That number stood at $83 million in 1991 and rose by 35 percent to an annualized figure of $112 million for 1992.

Dedication to the TQM philosophy and to leveraging the best management practices will remain a critical operating imperative if the company is to maintain its record growth and expansion without sacrificing its tradition of quality lending. In 1991, shortly after the management buyout, for instance, American Residential's 3.2 percent loan delinquency rate covering 30–90-day past-due loans was nearly 50 percent below the national delinquency rate of 6.05 percent for the industry in 1991, as shown in the National Delinquency

Survey produced by the Mortgage Bankers Association of America's economics department.

The working philosophy at American Residential is that valuable lessons are not always learned only within your own office or your own processing team. It often helps to look to others for different perspectives. That's why the search for best practices—inside and outside one's organization—is a fundamental part of the TQM process.

After internal team-based improvement efforts get under way, fast-learning individuals and teams inevitably begin to take the search outside to other branches, companies and industries, seeking the best practices in functional areas from which they might learn and accelerate their own performance improvements. The goal of all quality and benchmarking initiatives is the same: to target and achieve total performance excellence. That means to continuously improve sales, profits, cost management, customer satisfaction, employee satisfaction and all other measures of financial and nonfinancial success.

While benchmarking can involve the search for best practices outside one's own company and industry, it also relates very importantly to understanding one's own best performers.

Focusing on Top Performers

While benchmarking can involve the search for best practices outside one's own company and industry, it also relates very importantly to understanding one's own best performers. Mortgage banking institutions are excellent candidates to apply benchmarking techniques, as are many other multisite financial service companies. Variation among branches, markets, teams and individuals is a part of the common landscape. Too often, though, this variation among performers is accepted as natural and unquestioned.

In "good" organizations, those that do not summarily dismiss low performers, these modest performers are counseled and provided resources to try to help them solve their problems and meet performance expectations. But while the underachievers get this extra measure of help, too often, in many "good" and "bad" companies, the high performers are ignored. But they are the ones who always meet goals, champion new initiatives and search continuously to improve.

If your organization is typical of many American corporations, it probably applauds your best performers at an annual ceremony—and then it ignores them for the rest of the year, focusing time and attention instead on the low performers. An equally interesting—arguably far more engaging question—than "What are all our low performers doing wrong?" is the question: "What are all our best performers doing right?" After taking into account market differences, one has to wonder how can the best performers produce so much more than their peers? What highly effective approaches have they quietly developed for achieving their extraordinary levels of accomplishment?

Such people-based trade secrets can be as vital to a service organization as the closely guarded formula for concocting Coca-Cola. But the secret to the success of your own high performers can and should be freely shared and deployed within the entire organization.

This simple but powerful approach to continuous improvement and performance excellence focuses on narrowing the variation in performance levels by leveraging the learning of performers at the top. This contrasts with the typical approach of just focusing on how to improve or reform the performers at the bottom. Such an approach is well suited for marketing-driven organizations, where sales-oriented individuals are quick to pick up on good ideas that will help them improve their personal production but are sometimes slow or resistant to highly structured, variation-reducing improvement approaches, such as statistical process control, that are often associated with the quality control efforts of many fine manufacturing companies.

Since its inception, American Residential has always tried—at least informally—to recognize and celebrate its top performers. Now, to more effectively leverage its own "intellectual capital," American Residential has begun to regularly and formally focus time and attention on identifying, understanding and learning from the strategies of its own best performers. As of this writing, all branch, middle and upper management at American Residential have gone through the exercises associated with the best-practices initiative. Additionally, approximately 60 percent of the home office staff has undergone the exercises.

The Benefits of Benchmarking

The benefits of best-practices benchmarking are many. Among the many tonic effects witnessed at American Residential and in other organizations employing some version of this process, it:

- exposes people to new ideas and novel approaches;
- ensures the rigor of internal operating targets;
- helps improve quality;
- creates openness to new ideas and fosters organizational learning;
- increases the professional development of people;
- creates greater receptivity to change; and
- raises the organization's perceived level of maximum potential peak performance.

To appreciate the power that may lie untapped or poorly leveraged in your company, consider this hypothetical question: "What would be your organization's maximum potential performance if all your loan officers operated at the peak production levels of your best performing loan officers?" In American Residential's case, the company would effectively double its total production if all 230 loan officers operated at the levels of its highest performing ones— or those in the President's Club.

As dazzling as that may sound, the same theoretical potential exists for nearly every mortgage bank. Admittedly, this is something of a "blue sky" target, but what if you could achieve just half of that potential, or just 25 percent of it, by understanding and deploying the best practices of your best performers. The performance gains are still very impressive.

No one can ever corner the market on good ideas. So you should quite shamelessly borrow ideas and practices not deemed proprietary or protected by patents, copyrights, trademarks or other protections.

To begin to build a culture where creative borrowing of good ideas and practices is commonly accepted and embraced, American Residential has seeded its TQM initiative with a clear and steady focus on the many different places and forms in which highly effective operating procedures or best practices may appear. In an effort to jump start this engine of organizational creativity, the company has used a broad-reaching set of quality-improvement-related exercises—all of which are designed to plumb the deep reservoir of good ideas and operating creativity that lies within its people.

American Residential's TQM initiative is as interested in nurturing the creative swiping of good ideas that can be quickly and profitably applied in new operating areas as it is in fostering breakthrough ideas and wholly new improvements. "Keep on the lookout for novel and interesting ideas that others have used successfully," advised Thomas Edison. "Your idea has to be original only in its adaptation to the problem you're currently working on." Edison understood that the road to continuous improvement is often most quickly traveled by taking many small steps forward. So best-practices benchmarking—even of small administrative ideas—can help the organization move forward.

Consequently, American Residential's senior executive team and then later the operating units went through a series of exercises created by Best Practices Benchmarking and Consulting, Inc., called "Steal This Idea'"™ exercises, which are designed to seek embryonic best practices from within the workplace. The premise of the exercises is simple: no one individual, team, department or branch can ever corner the market on good ideas.

Developed outside the mortgage banking industry, the "Steal This Idea" exercise was initially conceived to demonstrate the power of a "borrowing shamelessly" attitude and to help foster an organizational culture that supports creativity and fast learning through benchmarking and borrowing. When applied in some organizations, it has highlighted how many traditional management systems are biased toward primarily recognizing and rewarding breakthrough ideas and inventions, while new applications of existing ideas and practices are often discouraged through the lack of recognition for such creative but nonheroic acts to improve the workplace.

This culture-setting, preliminary benchmarking exercise proved to be very powerful at American Residential, where the organization's employees used it to initially identify more than 350 improvement opportunities and good ideas. They ranged in scope and size from computer systems upgrades to customer survey development to operating procedure improvements. The exercises, which employed team-building, problem-solving and creativity themes, also proved to be cathartic in themselves, relieving some of the tension from a high-volume, fast-paced operating environment brought on by the avalanche of refinancings throughout 1992.

American Residential's TQM initiative is as interested in nurturing the creative swiping of good ideas as it is in fostering breakthrough ideas and wholly new improvements.

One senior vice president discovered the exercise and related concepts could be used deftly as a management tool. When frustrating operating issues surfaced in one of his branches, he decided to personally conduct one of the "Steal This Idea" exercises, rather than rely solely on other traditional problem-solving approaches. The exercise gave the senior manager a full opportunity to listen to branch staff. In turn, it gave them the opportunity to turn frustration into positive involvement by identifying a range of successful operating practices they had witnessed in other units and companies that could be adopted to help address many of their operating concerns.

The exercise smoothed communications between departments, and immediate implementation of some small improvements—the "low hanging fruit"—helped boost morale and performance. One example of a low-cost, morale-boosting improvement came at the suggestion of some staff attending the exercise. They expressed concern about security in the company parking lot, which was dark by the time they were getting off work as a result of working later hours to handle the refi volume. American Residential immediately put up some more lights, and the effect on morale was extraordinary as the action signaled to the employees that their personal well-being was an important concern of management. It made the staff more willing to work the longer hours and feel better about doing so; as a result the refi volume got handled in timely fashion.

Systematically Share Success Stories

Another early-stage, best-practices approach was designed to encourage people to share success stories. In every successful project, one can find the seedling of a best practice. Yet often these seedlings are planted in one part of the organization and never spread to other parts of the operation. By using an analytic tool developed for the Malcolm Baldrige National Quality Award, American Residential teams began identifying the "approach," "deployment" and "results" of their successful projects, initiatives and improvement actions. The aim was threefold: first, to encourage sharing and idea borrowing; second, to understand how even small but successful initiatives can be deployed more fully within the organization—and, therefore, be more fully leveraged; and third, to focus on what's going right—and to systematically learn from the company's successes—rather than just focus on where things are going wrong.

Here again, employees found a substantial supply of small actionable ideas scattered from the finance department to the servicing department. For instance, two branches identified successful practices in which loan officers and branch managers had developed data bases to track past borrowers and at a minimum of twice each year send out Christmas cards, birthday cards and other relationship-building communications. This particular idea, confessed one branch manager, was "borrowed shamelessly" from the life insurance industry. Another loan officer, who developed and extensively uses this type of data base, offered data demonstrating that 25 percent of the borrowers in his data base either refinance with him or actively provide him with referrals beyond the normal realtor-based referral network.

Other success stories that represented embryonic, internal best practice related to cross-training, loan processing prioritization systems, prequalification systems, effective recruitment procedures, peak-workload capacity utilization systems and cross-functional loan review teams.

The idea of borrowing good ideas may seem fairly basic when presented in an article such as this. But experience reveals that many organizations and their management systems inadvertently discourage such borrowing. Some of the most results-oriented managers have unknowingly developed operating styles that overlook the power of best practices. Many leading companies have developed operating environments where the underlying message is: "If it ain't invented here, it can't be any good."

The prejudice against borrowing starts in grammar schools, where students are encouraged to work alone—not in teams—and where sharing ideas on papers, tests and quizzes is called "cheating" and is explicitly discouraged. Fast-learning organizations, in contrast, embrace a "we can learn from anyone attitude" that encourages borrowing and creative sharing of ideas and systems that are nonproprietary.

Organizational cultures that overlook—or even discourage—creative borrowing and learning from best practices may be very deep-rooted. They are often dramatized in the way many senior executives spend a disproportionate amount of their time assisting the "problem children." This management style was dramatized during a senior executive meeting of another large financial services company.

The executive team was discussing "sales" that were closed and then fell apart. Some analysis revealed that certain units were far more subject to these problems than others. As the senior executive team was getting ready to fire a missile at the units that were the worst offenders, it was suggested that the company should examine the practices of those units and sales representatives who were high producers and seldom—if ever—had closed sales fall apart. With this suggestion, a light went on for the chief executive, who then observed: "I spend nearly all my time providing help and resources to the troubled units. The only time I ever see my best performers is at the annual awards banquet. I really don't know exactly what our best salespeople are doing to achieve such high levels of success. But it's certainly worth finding out." The incident led the company to undertake a best-practices study of their best salespeople.

Putting It into Practice

American Residential exposed its top salespeople, senior executives and managers to the concept of best practices through education and exercises presented at its President's Club retreat. Together, the top loan officers, branch managers, senior executives and operations staff gathered to work to identify the best individual sales and management practices that together constitute a "total quality sale."

Some of the most results-oriented managers have unknowingly developed operating styles that overlook the power of best practices.

What's a total quality sale? It's the ideal, customer-focused experience where all members of the mortgage bank work together as a team—not just to close the sale, but to deliver the right type of product through a fast, error-free process that extends from sale to closing to the ongoing servicing relationship. The process delights the customer and creates long-term loyalty that leads to positive "word-of-mouth advertising" and active referrals by the customer.

When viewing the sales function in this highly integrated fashion, it is easy to understand why no one person can ever monopolize an organization's or an industry's best practices. There is no one right way to market, qualify a customer, determine customer needs, gather information or establish customer trust and rapport. Rather, there is a class of highly successful and effective approaches perfected by many different top performers, most of whom excel in somewhat different ways and in different areas.

The result of the best-practices exercises and analysis undertaken by American Residential's best loan officers, branch managers and operations staff was the compilation of scores of highly successful operating practices that spanned the entire sales process. These internal best practices touched on creative marketing approaches (the company's top unit producer personally uses billboards in his home market in Utah); referral-generation systems (Massachusetts branch); ongoing product training (Utah branch); effective pre-qualification procedures (California branch); team servicing and processing practices (Washington state branch); cross-training and job sharing (Virginia branch); effective workload prioritization (California branch); as well as many other areas.

To further tap into other best practices from which the organization might learn, American Residential also implemented a survey to identify winning strategies that highly effective competitors have employed. The first-line source for such competitive intelligence is American Residential's own employees working within its network of 49 branches in 17 states. This best-practices survey identified activities where others have excelled, in areas such as training, marketing and brand development, internal communications, automation, pricing, new product development, benefits, processing and closing functions.

What's Next?

From here, American Residential will continue to scrutinize and borrow the best practices of other high performers—inside and outside the mortgage banking industry. Of course, once identified, good ideas must be implemented to have any value. For that, there is no substitute for focus and dedication by managers, loan officers, processors and staff. But if seeing is believing, then best-practices benchmarking is a valuable tool that supports successful implementation, by helping staff to recognize and support change because they are shown real evidence that other approaches may yield better results than their own. The productivity numbers cited earlier certainly offer strong evidence that this approach produces real and measurable improvement in per-formance.

There is no doubt that the quest for total performance excellence is an arduous one. But by borrowing creatively and by learning from the best, every organization can reach toward its full potential to become a higher performing company. Those that succeed at this will find they can best serve their customers by growing quickly, learning quickly and adapting quickly to change.

Christopher Bogan is president and CEO of Best Practices Benchmaking and Consulting, Inc., based in Lexington, Massachusetts, and John Robbins is president and CEO of American Residential Mortgage Corporation, based in La Jolla, California.

INSURANCE

Quest for Quality

Marian Freedman

This article on TQM in the insurance industry explains that "while the immediate goal of the quality process is to improve customer service, it ultimately is intended to provide an advantage over competitors, reduce costs, and increase productivity, boosting the insurer's bottom line."

For the field claims staff of Zurich-American Insurance Group, the time-consuming process of verifying an insured's coverage at the time of loss has always been the primary obstacle to providing good service. To tackle this problem, the insurer formed a team of representatives from the claims and commercial insurance departments, information technology services and several other divisions with a stake in claims verification. The team identified the primary stumbling block as the need to pull a policy manually from the file whenever a claim was presented. It is eliminating this bottleneck by developing a new system that provides the field claims staff with on-line information about the forms and endorsements included on specific policies.

The process Zurich-American is engaging in to develop this and other ways to improve its customer service is being repeated at insurers—and agencies—across the country. Known as "total quality management," "continuous improvement" or something similar, the process embodies concepts already firmly embraced by the manufacturing sector of the American economy and now gaining a toehold in financial services, including insurance. While the immediate goal of the quality process is to improve customer service, it ultimately is intended to provide an advantage over competitors, reduce costs and increase productivity, boosting the insurer's bottom line.

Of course, programs for improving service are not new. (Remember the quality circles and zero-defect programs popular in years past?) But what is different about TQM, its adherents say, is its comprehensiveness and the commitment it demands. In fact, a true TQM program is so demanding that few of the many insurers that have undertaken it understand what is required to make the program a success, according to some observers.

Another major problem in implementing a program, they say, is that some insurers can't decide whether their customers are their agents or their policyholders. Down the road, observers say, companies that fail to solve these problems will not be able to compete with insurers that have fully integrated TQM principles in their operations.

Under an effective quality improvement program, customer satisfaction drives all business processes. This means that divisions within a company abandon turf battles and demarcations to work together, and employees are encouraged to depart from the usual procedures when efficient service requires that they do so. Most important, all processes, from underwriting to claims handling, are examined and reorganized for greater efficiency and responsiveness to customers' needs. In the language of TQM enthusiasts, who toss about phrases like "employee empowerment," "cross-functional integration" and "horizontal management," the company undergoes a cultural transformation.

Indeed, examining the corporate culture to determine how it needed to become more adaptable and ready for change was the most important part of instituting TQM at Zurich-American in 1989, according to Robert Riker, vice president of continuous improvement. As a result of this analysis, he says, the company drew up a list of seven factors whose development it deems crucial to the success of the program. For each of the seven factors, a matrix of five steps—in order of desirability—was described. For example, for the factor "environment for change," the lowest step in the matrix is: "Change is viewed with fear. Boundaries and turf are guarded closely." The fifth step is: "Changes occur as part of normal business. Minimal fear or stress. Paradigms are challenged in order to further business goals."

After senior managers were asked to rate the insurer on where it stood with regard to each of these factors and where they would like it to be, the company began working its way up the matrix for each of the factors, while implementing a continuous improvement program by identifying and tackling specific problems. Although it takes five to 10 years to change a corporate culture in this way, Mr. Riker estimates, it is critical to the success of an improvement program. "You can't just get the process from anyone who will sell it to you," he says, referring to the courses, computer software, seminars and the like being marketed by hundreds of trainers and consultants.

Another of Zurich-American's matrix items is "management leadership and support," something observers agree is crucial to the success of a quality program. The Travelers Companies, whose program is a few years old, have achieved this support through their Quality Council, which comprises quality officers appointed by the senior vice presidents of all the major business areas.

The council, which also provides a means of crossing divisional lines, maintains the corporate quality initiative, allowing the implementation of quality principles to filter down through the organization. Each business group is encouraged to put its "own spin" on the improvement program it undertakes, says Valerie McHugh, director of the council, noting that allowing for this diversity under one corporate umbrella is particularly critical for Travelers because of the company's diverse customer base.

Sometimes, getting the commitment of top management requires a hard sell, but often a program has its genesis at the top. The best example of this, observers agree, is the service improvement program Robert F. McDermott began at the United Services Automobile Association when he became that company's chairman. This was in 1969, long before TQM, which has been popular in Japan since the 1950s, was well-known in this country. According to Gerald Gass, USAA's director of quality measurement and improvement, the chairman arrived with a vision of the paperless office and touted the importance of training and enlarging peoples' jobs. More than two decades later, USAA, a direct writer that handles approximately 90% of its business by phone, is an acknowledged leader in customer service. It stores documents on optical disks, keeping only 5% of incoming mail in its original form. This means any employee can instantly access the records of a customer who calls for help.

Making Measurements

USAA measures the success of its quality endeavors—another important facet of a quality program, experts say—by surveying its customers. It conducts an annual survey of 1% or 2% of its members and also sends questionnaires to policyholders who recently have had a transaction or claim. A monthly compilation of the information from these questionnaires is provided to senior management, and the trends it reveals help the insurer to revise its ever-higher service goals.

Mr. Gass cautions that the last thing an insurer wants is "an old, inefficient process done faster."

USAA also engages in benchmarking, another activity endorsed by TQM practitioners. It is a participant in a survey conducted by an independent firm for various industries, which allows it to compare consumers' opinions of its performance with that of other major insurers. It also benchmarks with other companies known to be doing well in certain areas, according to Mr. Gass.

While USAA obviously has used sophisticated technology to reach a high level of service, technological improvement does not necessarily equate with quality improvement, observers say. Mr. Gass notes that quality improvement should focus on "people and process and then automation" and cautions that the last thing an insurer wants is "an old, inefficient process done faster." It may be that an improvement program will result in sizable investments in technology (which should save money later), but the TQM process in and of itself requires only modest expenditures, primarily for training, observers say. And although an army of consultants pitches its wares, insurers find that they need only a limited amount of outside help. According to Ms. McHugh, many "big corporations" advised Travelers not to make the same mistake they had by spending a lot of money on consultants.

Getting Started

Nonetheless, all the insurers interviewed for this article have found the services of a good consultant invaluable, either for a particular project or to institute the whole process. According to James B. Couch, M.D., vice president, quality management at Travelers, "consultants are a necessity in the beginning to instigate the organization to change." He notes that it is difficult even for a top executive to have the credibility that is required for an organization to make a "fundamental transformation" in the way it does business. However, he says, what the company learns from the consultant should be internalized "as quickly as possible" and leaders of the organization held accountable for implementing quality.

The approach of The Institute Inc., a Houston consulting firm, is to educate senior and middle managers on the key concepts of quality improvement and to train internal consultants. After a year or so of intermittent training, an insurer can go off on its own, says Steven A. Leth, the company's president. The consultant also can "get senior management thinking," he says, by challenging sacred cows, demonstrating what other companies are doing and "bringing methods and tools to bear that have not been there before."

As part of their services, many consultants offer step-by-step programs to help insurers institute a quality program. For example, cross-functional teams in four divisions of American Family Insurance Group, which has had a quality program since 1989, follow a seven-step process typical of many that are available, according to James St. Vincent, the insurer's improvement resources director. The first step in the process, he notes, is to focus on a problem and determine a goal. Then, the team must understand precisely how the process is being managed.

> All the insurers interviewed for this article have found the services of a good consultant invaluable, either for a particular project or to institute the whole process.

Find Out the Details

To find out where things are going wrong, it is essential to "listen to people who make the process work," Mr. St. Vincent says, adding, "The supervisor usually doesn't know all the details." Consequently, the next step is to analyze all the steps in the particular process and question their variability. The final steps include proposing and testing solutions on a small scale, checking the results to make sure the new process works (if not, it is necessary to go back to the analysis phase) and, finally, to implement the best result.

Using this sequence of steps, which TQM practitioners summarize as "plan, do, check, act,"—one team sought to reduce the correspondence that flowed between the two departments. The insurer discovered that 60% of this paper was being thrown out, and by the end of the project, it had eliminated more than 5,000 pieces of mail from the weekly flow. Another project increased by $1 million the receivables deposited the day they arrive, increasing yearly interest earnings by $100,000.

Like American Family, other insurers are following one of the basic tenets of TQM when they involve employees with hands-on experience in the processes that need to be improved. At Travelers, for example, employee teams are "empowered to tear part" the processes in which they have the most expertise and, using the charts, diagrams, checklists and consensus processes that form the tools of quality management, reengineer them, says Dr. Couch. This represents a real power shift, an inversion of the power pyramid, he notes.

Welcome Challenge

It also means employees have to expend time and energy on improving processes in addition to performing their usual duties. Yet insurers insist that, in general, employees welcome this challenge. According to USAA's Mr. Gass, the improvement process enlarges jobs because in better serving customers employees gain responsibility for the end result, not just a small portion of what contributes to it. This job enlargement "definitely is motivating," and it largely accounts for the fall in USAA's annual employee turnover rate to less than 10% from 40% in the late 1960s, he says.

Nonetheless, insurers admit that generating enthusiasm can pose problems initially. Employees already are busy, notes Zurich-American's Mr. Riker, and want to know "what's in it for them." The insurer always tries to get senior managers and middle managers to buy into the quality improvement concept and "get it into the chain of command," he says. It also helps when issues are uncovered and employees can see that quality improvement will address their problems and give them the resources to meet their goals. In addition, in focusing on what customers want, the improvement initiative can result in the elimination of some routine activities, freeing up time for training in new skills.

Squeezed Out

At American Family, some team members "don't want to be there," concedes Mr. St. Vincent. But by the time the project is over, he says, they are happy to have had a role in it. Employees especially welcome the decision-making authority they are given, he says, as well as the opportunity to learn new skills, particularly the leadership training they receive through the rotation of meeting leaders.

It is middle management that "feels squeezed out," says Travelers' Ms. McHugh. Middle managers are accustomed to making decisions, and since employees are encouraged to make their own decisions under a quality program, they "don't know their role." Zurich-American made the mistake of assuming that senior management, not middle management, needed to be sold on the quality program, according to Mr. Riker. Now, like Travelers, the insurer is working on overcoming middle management's initial resistance to the quality program by educating managers on the program's advantages. At American Family and USAA, middle managers are trained as quality coaches.

Another problem, one that is unique to insurers, is to determine which customers the company is targeting in its quality improvement. Is it the policyholder or the agent or broker? Insurers are "a little schizophrenic on this," Mr. Leth says, explaining that some insurers see the producer as the customer and some the insured. The latter approach is a lot easier, he observes, and for this reason some insurers get "out of sync with their producers." However, it is necessary to accommodate both sets of customers, he notes, as well as an insurer's internal customers—its employees. If employees are not recognized as customers, it is hard for the frontline people to get their work done, he says, because they are "caught between operational processes and the consumer outside."

But the biggest problem with implementing a quality management program, observers agree, is many insurers' lack of understanding and/or commitment to its precepts. The "vast majority of insurers are playing at this," says Travelers' Dr. Couch, who is a senior examiner for the 1992 Malcolm Baldrige National Quality Award. The insurers that are just paying lip service to TQM are failing to "empower the organization by taking ownership of cross-functional processes, managing the organization horizontally or developing expertise internally to become a learning organization," he says.

Buzz and Allure

In Mr. Leth's view, TQM has so much "buzz and allure" that it has become merely a fad for some companies. At the other end of the spectrum, he notes, are insurers that see quality improvement as part of their strategic plan, a link that is crucial to a program's success. According to Mark Savory, national director of Ernst & Young's insurance industry consulting services, many insurers have not thought through what it takes to effect the cultural change a quality improvement program requires. In addition, he says, some companies have unrealistic expectations for what a quality program can accomplish and then "lose heart" when it fails to meet their goals.

Some companies have unrealistic expectations for what a quality program can accomplish and then "lose heart" when it fails to meet their goals.

Ernst & Young has seen a lot of programs "that didn't seem to be working," Mr. Savory notes, and in response developed an eight-step process to "jump start" a stalled program. The process involves hiring a quality specialist, breaking down work into distinct blocks of time to establish and conduct a quality improvement process in less than 20 weeks and focusing on problem areas. The consultant also recommends dedicating a full-time care team of 12 to 15 of the company's best people to be trained and organized into three or more quality improvement teams and equipping the team with technical and analytical training tools.

Getting Agreement

To get the support of middle management, which often "views the quality improvement process as indirect criticism of their ability to operate their department," Ernst & Young recommends "communicating and coordinating" the program with these managers and getting their agreement. The jump-start program also calls for implementing recommendations as soon as possible, using quality teams as assistants to department managers, so employees can see results, which establishes credibility, fosters change and alters people's attitudes.

However, the best way for a company new to quality improvement to see results, Mr. Savory says, is not to start by creating a full program but "to reverse the process." This involves introducing TQM principles into a new business plan or product introduction and building a quality improvement program "from the ground up." In this way, he says, when the project is completed, an employee-empowered process is left in place that will take on "a life of its own."

By incorporating TQM in a tangible change in a company's operation, Mr. Savory says, people will see a change in how the business is run and how their job is structured and react favorably. "If they try to do something outside their job description to reach a goal and are not criticized, that behavior is reinforced, " he notes. All too often, he says, insurers become discouraged when they "put their toe in the water from the top down." If a company tries to institute a TQM program and fails to see immediate results, it thinks the process is taking too long and wants to get on with its business.

But regardless of how they go about it, insurers have no choice but to focus on improving their service. After all, notes Mr. Leth, in today's competitive market, "one way to stand out is to be known for extraordinary service."

Just Won't Cut It

And Travelers' Dr. Couch points out that as suppliers of managed care services to employers, health insurers are under particular pressure to provide the superior value and service that companies in other sectors of the U.S. economy with well-established TQM programs have come to expect from suppliers of their internal customers. Traditionally, employee benefit managers, brokers and agents have created one or more layers between the insurer and the policyholder, he notes, but "with the increased hue and cry against customer-hostile practices, that will no longer cut it," particularly in the health insurance area.

Mr. Savory thinks that although the initial TQM programs in the insurance industry "have not worked very well," they will evolve into a useful management tool that will allow an insurer to compete in the marketplace. And companies with successful TQM programs can go beyond those programs' limits, as have firms in other industries, he says. This calls for taking "quantum leaps five to 10 years down the road" and determining what must be done to meet standards of competition in the future. When it is done well, TQM appears to have no limits.

Marian Freedman is senior editor of Best's Review.

HEALTH CARE

Shared Experiences

*Joint Commission on Accreditation of
Healthcare Organizations*

This article is reprinted from the book Striving Toward Improvement, *which
documents the experiences of six different hospitals in implementing
continuous improvement culture and techniques. This is a summary of what
they learned.*

The Transition and the Role of Leaders

The chief executive officer usually served as the catalyst for change within
the hospital. Leadership involvement, including senior management, board
members, and physician, nurse, and other clinical leaders, was found to be
critical for a successful transition. The first few years of the transition required considerable energy and time commitments from leaders. John
Bingham at Magic Valley estimated he spends 50% of this time on QI activities, and Philip Newbold said that in the beginning of Memorial's efforts, he
spent a minimum of two hours a day on QI. Now QI has been blended into
his daily routine. Many agreed with Newbold and felt strongly that it has
become (and should be) an integral part of daily work life that cannot be separately identified.

A steering committee or quality council, composed of senior management, provided general guidance and oversight in the transition. This group
was usually equivalent to the regular management team, although in some
cases there were variations in membership. For example, Wright-Patterson
had included their patient relations coordinator on the Quality Council, and
Bethesda's Steering Committee includes several medical staff members. The

creation of a quality council ensured leadership direction and active participation. It usually identified major areas of focus for QI efforts and guided and
approved team activities. At Parkview, for example, the Quality Council
chose five hospitalwide systems (for example, clinical results reporting) that
have become a major QI focus for the entire organization. Many teams were
created to focus on each of these five systems. The appointment of a QI
"coach" to facilitate the efforts of the quality council was felt to be useful in
the initial stages of the transition. The QI coach assists management with the
transition in areas such as education, use of QI tools, and rollout within the
organization. QI coaches frequently were members of the quality council.

Supportive board members at these hospitals were frequently involved in QI in their own organizations.

Active support from the governing body early in the process was needed
not only for approval of the new direction but also because of the magnitude
of the change involved and because resource commitments must be made
before results were realized. Supportive board members at these hospitals
were frequently involved in QI in their own organizations. For example,
Strong Memorial has a representative from Xerox, a recent Malcolm Baldrige
award winner, on its board. Board members often participated in site visits
made by leaders to other QI organizations both inside and outside health care.
The hospital leaders found such visits useful in making the initial decision
to move to QI and in determining which QI model to adopt.

Organizations adopted either an established approach to QI (for example,
Deming, Juran) or developed their own unique model, which is often a hybrid
of different approaches. For example, Parkview is devoted primarily to Deming's philosophy, while Memorial's model is based largely on Juran mixed
with Deming's and Senge's concepts. The selection of a QI model was based
on the organization's philosophical agreement with underlying concepts.
Commitment to a single approach was usually made with the expectation
that it would not be changed. The use of more than one model in an organization could lead to confusion concerning direction. The hospitals studied in
this book stressed the importance of a common language within the organization that promotes cross-functional QI efforts, enhances consistency, and
facilitates efforts to measure progress. This was felt to be best achieved by
long-term commitment to a single model.

The six hospitals reported that in a QI environment, the roles of leaders
and other managers changes from one of dictator, controller, and exhorter to
champion, mentor, and coach. These leaders exhibited behaviors consistent
with QI and demonstrated a commitment to its philosophy and methods,
commonly referred to as "walking the talk." Most senior management actively participated in QI activities by undergoing extensive education, engaging in their own process improvement efforts, personally providing training
to staff, and assigning specific senior management "sponsors" to teams. These
leaders established direction, displayed "constancy of purpose," and provided
continual guidance to encourage change in others. Sharon Fischer, QI coach
at Magic Valley, sums up the initial attitude of many middle managers and
staff at each of the six hospitals—"At first, most staff thought QI was another

fad that would pass." It took constancy of purpose demonstrated by management to change their minds.

Although QI more actively engages staff in future planning, the transition was not an egalitarian process in these hospitals; the pursuit of QI was an explicit management decision. Leaders did not delegate overall responsibility for QI implementation—they assumed it themselves. They established a structure that included a formal problem-solving process, use of statistical methods and QI tools, reliance on data, training on the appropriate use of these tools, and rewards for success. This enabled staff to address issues in a more open and, therefore, productive manner and to take ownership of the structure provided to them. There appeared to be a direct relationship between the use of this structure and staff's demonstration of a sense of inquiry, pride in work, restlessness with the status quo, and confidence that they could use their talents to make effective changes. Rather than stifling staff, the formal structure provided by management led to their "liberation"—empowerment to investigate and improve those processes that affected them.

The hospitals found that organizationwide acceptance of QI concepts was necessary before extensive change could occur. An antecedent environment that has already embraced some of the philosophical underpinnings of QI often assisted in the transition. For example, Memorial has been focusing on customer needs and staff empowerment, Bethesda has placed strong reliance on data for decision making, and Wright-Patterson and Strong have moved to matrix management at the department level, which has helped emphasize collaboration between disciplines.

Early successes were critical to maintaining enthusiasm.

Results did not appear overnight; the hospitals measure the transition time in years. Early successes were critical to maintaining enthusiasm, and leaders often ensured that such successes were achieved through the careful selection of QI projects and the provision of support and resources.

Vision

A written vision statement that broadly describes future goals of the organization was usually developed early on to focus QI efforts. The vision statement was typically developed by senior management, although in several cases the governing body actively participated. The hospitals believed that the vision must be regularly communicated to staff in order to obtain support for the transition. Different methods have been used to communicate this vision. Wright-Patterson, for example, has displayed its mission and vision on bulletin boards across the medical center and distributed a brochure outlining its QI philosophy to all staff, patients, and visitors. Several of the hospitals are also asking each department to develop a departmental vision that aligns with the hospital vision. Most organizations learned that, unless there is a shared vision and widespread acceptance of QI principles, success is more difficult to achieve.

The long-term goal for the six hospitals studied is a totally transformed organization. The leaders believe that it is not enough to be satisfied with incremental improvements in existing functions. In several hospitals, vision statements reflected this organizational transformation. Many hospitals developed measures of success to help them assess progress in reaching this desired future state. For example, senior management at Parkview developed measurements to assess key quality characteristics of the future of the hospital. In several cases, the vision was used to set boundaries for QI activities and teams engaged in projects that contributed to the achievement of the vision.

Some, such as Magic Valley, used QI as an opportunity to expand their vision beyond the walls of the hospital into the community, establishing partnerships between the hospital and those they serve.

Strategy and Rollout

While the decision to pursue QI may be due to an impending organizational crisis, it was more often the result of philosophical agreement with the concepts in the six hospitals. However, many viewed QI as providing the necessary tools to carry an organization through a crisis or to overcome negative environmental forces.

QI became an integral part of regular business strategies, and customer feedback was often an important component of strategic planning. Most, in retrospect, would have concentrated more on planning early in the process, and some had to backtrack to focus on planning. Typical to the experience of many of the hospitals, Strong formed several teams at the beginning of its QI efforts; however, because there was not a core understanding of QI goals throughout the hospital, these teams had to work in relative isolation. Now Strong is concentrating more on planning than a rapid expansion of teams. In addition, many cautioned that the QI expectations within the plan should not exceed the organization's ability to achieve them. It was suggested that planning be structured so it is consistent with the progression of staff training in such areas as quality awareness, organization vision, and process improvement.

Hospitals have found that successful implementation always takes longer than expected and a lull frequently seems to occur somewhere in the process. The lull was frequently attributed to overtraining, insufficient direction, or simply a normal waning of initial enthusiasm. Continued management commitment and, in some cases, special efforts were required to regain momentum.

QI in these hospitals was not synonymous with chartered team activities. For example, individual departments frequently were required to initiate their own QI activities, including the identification of internal customers and suppliers, development of quality plans, and intradepartmental process improvement activities. The development of an implementation or rollout plan for the hospital (including departmental priorities linked to hospital goals) usually supported the application and integration of QI principles and methods into the daily operations of the hospital. Departments typically needed management assistance early in the process with the identification of internal customers and other quality planning efforts. These department efforts involved all staff and, sometimes because of this, middle management felt threatened by a perceived loss of control or power, in important hospital processes, nurses were usually enthusiastically involved in QI efforts. The recent movement in nursing toward empowerment was seen as consistent with and useful in QI. For example, Magic Valley and Strong are adopting clinical practice nursing models that will result in greater decentralization and shared governance. At Memorial, which has been involved in empowerment and shared governance for several years, nurses have often taken the lead in department and organizationwide QI activities.

Consultants were helpful in developing rollout plans and educational materials. However, many hospitals cautioned that careful selection of the appropriate consultant and ensuring that the consultant's approach meets the unique needs of the organization is critical. Early implementation efforts can be derailed by attempting to adopt a boilerplate that is not relevant to the organization.

Quality assurance (QA) and QI were usually separate functions, particularly in the initial stages. Many hospitals felt it was important to take the time to understand how QA requirements can be met in the context of QI. The chapters on Wright-Patterson, Memorial, and Magic Valley describe approaches to this issue. Most plan to integrate these functions in the future. Several indicated that QA would become a component of QI in the future as well as a source for issues to address through the QI process.

> Early implementation efforts can be derailed by attempting to adopt a boilerplate that is not relevant to the organization.

QI Teams

Several hospitals initiated QI efforts with pilot teams to assess how well the process would work within the organizations and/or to demonstrate the effectiveness of QI methods. These pilot efforts led to improvements in team functions, such as implementing just-in-time training on tools and assigning a management sponsor to teams.

Teams tended to focus more on administrative processes than clinical issues in the initial stages of the transition because organizations felt it would be easier to achieve initial success in these areas. Several hospitals, however, have begun to explore clinical issues. Bethesda is well on its way, exploring the treatment of asthma patients, cesarean sections and hip replacements, and Wright-Patterson has a team exploring the diagnostic process for potential breast cancer, from offering mammograms to surgery. A few hospitals, including Memorial and Strong, are using critical paths to apply QI in clinical areas.

Most organizations found that initial team projects should be carefully selected by management because hospitals encountered problems when all proposed teams were allowed to form on their own initiative. Memorial refers to these as "skunk teams." In several instances, management was unable to provide the needed resources to teams (education, facilitators) or support the implementation of proposed solutions. In addition, management wanted to focus efforts on organizational priorities and wanted to ensure that teams did not conflict with macro processes. As a result, QI teams were typically chartered by the Quality Council to focus on areas identified as important to the hospital and recommendations were usually brought to the Council for approval. A structured chartering process was usually followed.

Nevertheless, unchartered teams were initiated by staff in some hospitals to explore issues within their areas of responsibility. Unchartered teams usually addressed intradepartmental issues or those that were limited in scope. Several hospitals expected that the number of such teams would increase as staff became more experienced with QI concepts and methods.

Teams needed the support of trained facilitators with QI methods and tools, particularly in the early stages of implementation. Most hospitals learned that the number of teams should be limited to the number of facilitators available because teams frequently became ineffective if they operated without facilitator guidance. Bethesda, Memorial, Parkview, and others are training additional facilitators to keep up with the demand for teams. Hospitals learned that issues addressed by teams should be narrowly focused; teams often developed charters that were too broad and as a result floundered. At Bethesda, the registration team, which was asked to investigate alternatives to or make improvements in the entire registration process, ended up focusing on outpatient registration after data showed that was where the heaviest volume occurred.

A structured process improvement method was used by each of the hospitals profiled and was applied to team efforts, in interdepartmental or intradepartmental QI efforts, and in daily activities. These methods often varied in the number of steps involved: FOCUS-PDCA has 9 steps and is used by Parkview, Magic Valley, and Wright-Patterson; Bethesda's approach has 13 steps; Strong's has 6; and Memorial's has 7. But all contained similar basic elements, such as identifying the issue, collecting data for issue clarification, identifying solutions, selecting a pilot solution, testing the solution, implementing the change, and monitoring to maintain the gain.

Internal communication was considered important for creating a common understanding and language within the organization, and for enhancing awareness of QI activities. Storyboards, storybooks, newsletters, and forums were found to be very effective in fostering such communication.

Education

All six hospitals earmarked significant financial and human resources of training all staff in QI concepts and tools. Some even identified resources for service coverage while staff were being trained.

In many cases, senior management attended external seminars for initial QI education. Most hospitals determined, however, that it would be too costly to rely on external resources for general staff education, and training materials were either developed or adapted internally to meet the unique needs of the hospital. For example, Bethesda developed an awareness course that used specific QI examples from their hospital. Many different educational vehicles were made available to staff, including courses, audio-visual materials, books and articles, journal clubs, and forums.

Training usually began at the top and was cascaded down through the organization. QI was introduced to new staff in orientation training. Typically, senior management actively participated in staff training by teaching courses.

Most organizations found it counterproductive to provide too much training at once. In the beginning, structures that allowed staff to apply new knowledge (such as functioning teams or formal departmental QI activities) were usually not in place. This is a situation Philip Newbold at Memorial referred to as "dressing everyone up for the dance with no dance to go to." In some cases, this led to frustration and a lack of future support for QI efforts. Through experience, hospitals found that the most effective approach was to provide general QI awareness training to staff followed by just-in-time training to teams and departments on QI tools as needed.

Physician Involvement

Some hospitals delayed active physician involvement in QI until the effectiveness of the methods was demonstrated and to assure that the organization could support their participation. In addition, time requirements for up front training and team participation was recognized as a barrier to physician involvement. Several hospitals identified ways to incrementally involve physicians in QI before formal introduction to the medical staff. Bethesda decided to involve physicians initially as consultants to teams addressing administrative issues rather than full members. In several cases, physicians participated on teams addressing administrative issues in areas of interest to them, such as waiting times in the operating room or emergency department; improvements in these areas demonstrated the value of QI methods to physicians. Both Magic Valley and Bethesda encouraged physicians to become involved in QI projects in their own offices.

In many cases, a physician was hired to assist with the rollout of QI within the medical staff. Initial physician involvement was also accomplished by identifying interested individuals to serve as champions for other physicians. Both approaches provided role models to encourage more widespread physician involvement. Physician interest was often enhanced when they realized QI can focus on problems relevant to them, such as variation in medical practice. They also have been intrigued by the focus on system improvement rather than individuals (bad apples), and because QI is a scientific process using sound data, QI has also helped physicians understand how they fit into the customer-supplier chain within the hospital.

QI has helped physicians understand how they fit into the customer-supplier chain within the hospital.

The language of QI may be foreign to physicians initially. Several hospitals have developed special training methods that translate these concepts into familiar terms and meet other unique needs of physicians.

QI Supports

Most hospitals identified a variety of internal and external customers that included patients, families, employers, payers, and the general community.

Regular feedback (with some variation in frequency) was gathered from identified customers, and this information was incorporated into QI efforts. Wright-Patterson, for example, identified that access to the hospital was the major concern of patients and directed QI efforts to that area. A number of techniques were used to obtain customer input, including surveys, telephone interviews, and focus groups; several hospitals combined techniques. For example, Bethesda held a focus group with physicians to gather qualitative data and subsequently conducted a telephone survey to a larger sample to gather quantitative data. Organizations used outside consultants, internal resources, or a combination of both to collect customer information. Hospitals were also making efforts to refine and increase the sophistication of data collection instruments and to reduce the possibility of biased data.

Quality relationships with suppliers were beginning to be established by hospitals. Although generally not yet widespread, these relationships involved contractual agreements, informal efforts to resolve specific issues, or supplier participation on QI teams. Memorial has an organ procurement team that involves representatives from two organ banks and Johnson & Johnson has a representative on Bethesda's wound closure team. Most expected such arrangements to increase in the future and that supplier selection would be based as much on quality as cost.

All the hospitals profiled in this book engaged in some form of benchmarking. This involved participating in comparative data bases, visiting other QI organizations and studying methods that others use for specific processes to identify opportunities for improvement. Examples of the latter included billing processes, performance feedback/reward system, and customer/guest relations. Benchmarking activities were conducted both within the health care field and with outside manufacturing and service industries.

The sophistication of information services and the ability to provide computer support for QI activities varied among the hospitals. Even in those hospitals with the most sophisticated computer systems, the data needed by teams were often not readily available in existing data bases. As a result, much information was collected manually or special programs were written to assist with data collection and analysis. Most organizations noted that there was a need for a greater integration of data systems to support QI efforts and increased staff access to data. A need for more process data was also noted. Many hospitals recognized that additional financial resources may be required to support data collection, as well as for assessing customer needs, educational efforts, and consultants.

Most organizations noted that there was a need for a greater integration of data systems to support QI efforts.

A number of these hospitals were reexamining traditional performance evaluation processes and personnel policies in the context of QI philosophy. As described in the earlier chapters, hospitals were experimenting with the elimination of traditional merit systems, introduction of "gain sharing" programs, and redesign of performance feedback mechanisms. There was some concern about striking the proper balance between recognition of group efforts and rewarding outstanding individual performance, and most agreed that the ultimate solution is yet to be found. Other forms of reward and recognition being used included individual team recognition and quality celebrations.

What Prevents TQM Implementation in Health Care Organizations?

Carol A. Reeves and David A. Bednar

This article describes a study that compares health care managers' perceived barriers to implementing TQM with those identified in the health care literature.

In spite of increasing pressure from the government and other payors to increase quality and decrease costs, the health care industry has been slow to adopt quality principles. Only a few of the more than 6,000 U.S. hospitals have started to implement quality principles and programs.[1] Interest in the management of health care quality, however, is increasing because several influential organizations are demanding action.

The Joint Commission on the Accreditation of Healthcare Organizations, for example, recently mandated that hospitals adopt and document their efforts to improve quality. The secretary of the Department of Veterans Affairs, after several critical reports on Veterans Administration (VA) medical facilities, declared that the VA system would lead government agencies in implementing total quality management (TQM) programs.

A large VA medical center located in the southwestern United States has begun a long-term effort to introduce and implement a TQM program. As part of its efforts, the center is participating in a study exploring the difficulties that top and middle managers perceive as possibly hindering successful TQM implementation in their organization. These potential obstacles can be compared to TQM implementation barriers that have been identified in literature. This comparison can increase the likelihood of a successful TQM program and help allocate resources prudently.

Relevant TQM Literature

Empirical evidence about TQM implementation processes and practices in medical facilities is limited. There exists, however, a growing body of anecdotal literature describing the factors and characteristics needed to implement TQM effectively. A summary of the factors discussed most frequently in literature is presented in Table 1.

Reprinted with permission from *Quality Progress*, April 1993, ASQC, Milwaukee, WI.

Table 1. **Key Characteristics of Successful TQM Programs Identified in Literature**

Authors	Top managers' commitment	Incentives and rewards	Long-term focus	Training	Employee commitment and participation	Middle managers' involvement	Vision	Reduce turf battles	Resources	Communication	Knowledge
Albert, Gilligan, and Deevy (1990)	X			X		X	X			X	X
Batalden, Smith, Bovender, and Hardison (1989)	X										X
Berwick (1989)	X	X	X	X					X		X
Boyd and Haraway (1991)	X	X			X			X	X	X	
Brown and Svenson (1990)	X	X		X	X		X				
Coffey, Eisenberg, Gaucher, and Kratochwill (1991)	X			X			X			X	X
Hammonds and DeGeorge (1991)	X	X	X					X			
Kazemek and Peterson (1990)	X	X					X				
McLaughlin and Kaluzny (1990)	X	X	X		X	X					X
Perlman and Zacharias (1991)	X	X	X		X			X			
Perry (1988)	X		X						X		
Sepielli and Klauser (1991)	X		X	X	X	X	X	X	X	X	
Shoop (1990, 1991)	X			X		X					
Townsend and Gebhardt (1988)	X	X	X		X	X					
Totals	14	8	7	6	6	5	5	4	4	4	5

Strong support from top management is the factor most frequently cited as necessary to implement TQM successfully. In cases where quality efforts have been effective, top management support is considered the key reason for success; in instances where quality programs have been ineffective, a lack of top management support is judged to be the primary cause of failure.[2]

Because so much energy and so many resources are needed to introduce, establish, and sustain TQM, top management support is essential. Top managers must have a vision of what quality can mean to the organization, and that vision must be incorporated into the long-term strategic plan.[3] The vision must also be communicated effectively throughout the organization. It is critical that both managers and employees understand that implementing TQM is a long-term process and will not produce easy quick fixes.

Although top managers might espouse and articulate a commitment to quality, the resources allocated to quality improvement efforts demonstrate the actual extent of management's commitment. The most important and expensive part of a quality program, especially in the early stages, is training.[4] Without appropriate and adequate training, employees will not have the knowledge and skills necessary to implement quality principles and practices. In instances where management has failed initially to devote sufficient funds to training, TQM programs have faltered and failed.[5]

The most important and expensive part of a quality program, especially in the early stages, is training.

Resources must also be used to create incentives and rewards. Monetary incentives are important, but they are not the only rewards found to be effective. Personal recognition is the primary reward used in many organizations to acknowledge employees who contribute to TQM implementation effectively.[6] Appropriate rewards provide incentives for employees to participate in quality improvement efforts and tangibly and visibly demonstrate top management's commitment.

Finally, involvement by all employees is critical to the success of TQM. Lack of participation by middle managers is a barrier that has been identified frequently. These managers are often afraid of the effect that TQM might have on their authority. By definition, TQM requires that managers let subordinates suggest changes and make decisions to improve the work environment and processes. In many successful TQM programs, middle management has been eliminated with no adverse effect on quality. Consequently, middle managers frequently and actively work to frustrate the TQM process.[7]

Extensive employee involvement encourages a multifunctional perspective to problem solving. In many organizations, one of the greatest barriers to TQM is the territorialism that has evolved over many years.[8] Turf battles frequently frustrate TQM implementation and produce other dysfunctional consequences for both individuals and organizations.

The literature just cited relies primarily on the observations of consultants and managers in hospitals that have initiated TQM programs. Only two of these studies made any attempt to gather data regarding the implementation difficulties that were encountered.[9] The study at the VA medical center, however, is gathering information on expected TQM implementation difficulties in a large health care facility. Important strategic and pragmatic insights can be gained by analyzing management's perceive barriers to TQM implementation.

The VA Study

To assess the effects of implementing a TQM program, pre- and post-intervention data have been (and continue to be) collected using a variety of methods and instruments. Data were collected from 79 top and middle managers from departments and service areas throughout the medical center.

The managers attended one of two identical two-day sessions in which TQM concepts and tools were introduced and explained. The 39 managers who attended the first session were primarily top managers (service chiefs, department heads, etc.); the 40 participants in the second session were primarily middle managers (area coordinators, assistant department heads, assistant chiefs, etc.).

On the first day of the session, participants were divided into small groups and asked to identify, using the nominal group technique, specific obstacles that could hinder effective TQM implementation at the VA medical center. To promote learning and interaction, each group had participants from many different departments and service areas. Each group produced a prioritized list of four or five anticipated barriers. A total of 11 groups (five groups in the first session and six groups in the second session) completed the exercise.

The groups from the first session produced a total of 26 barriers; the groups from the second session produced a total of 28 barriers. To identify common items and major themes, two evaluators independently grouped and classified the obstacles identified during the two sessions.[10] The two classifications were then compared.

From the 26 barriers in the first session, one evaluator identified 11 major themes while the other evaluator identified 12 major themes. Ten of those themes were identical. The evaluators classified 25 of the 26 barriers similarly.

From the 28 barriers in the second session, one evaluator identified 12 major themes, and the other evaluator identified 11 major themes. Seven of those themes were identical.[11] The evaluators classified 21 of the 28 barriers similarly. Table 2 shows the major themes identified and the number of similar items included in each theme.

The barriers presented in Table 2 are strikingly similar to those found in Table 1. Lack of top management support, the long-term nature of TQM, insufficient commitment throughout the organization, and ineffective communication were specifically identified as major barriers in the literature and by the managers. In addition, the literature and the top managers cited inadequate knowledge about and understanding of TQM and insufficient rewards as barriers to TQM implementation. Middle managers and the literature identified inadequate or insufficient training in TQM, politics and turf battles, and inadequate resources as barriers. In summary, there was agreement among the literature and both levels of management on four items, agreement be-

Table 2.   **Major Themes: Barriers to Implementing TQM in the VA Medical Center**

Major Themes	No. of similar items in the theme
Group 1	
Lack of consistent support from executive committee	5
Inadequate knowledge about and understanding of TQM	4
Lack of commitment by everyone in the medical center	4
Fear/resistance to change	3
Time required for meetings and problem solving	2
Failure to implement solutions in a timely manner	2
Unclear definitions of TQM goals, authority, and boundaries	2
Inadequate planning for TQM implementation	1
Ineffective communication of TQM mission and objectives	1
Insufficient rewards	1
Faulty group process	1
Group 2	
Apathy/lack of commitment by all employees	7
Sabotage/lack of support from top management	4
Politics/turf battles	3
Failure to implement solutions in a timely manner	2
Inadequate resources to support TQM	2
Turnover/changes in key personnel	2
Resistance to change	2
Ineffective communication about TQM	2
Inadequate/insufficient training in TQM	1
Inadequate support from executive committee	1
TQM board composition and functioning	1
Lack of confidence in program by all employees	1

tween the literature and top managers on two additional items, and agreement between the literature and middle managers on three other items (Table 3).

Two obstacles identified in the literature were not perceived by participants in this study: lack of a TQM vision and lack of involvement by middle managers. Top managers, however, did identify a similar concern when they cited unclear definition of TQM goals, authority, and boundaries as a potential barrier. Lack of involvement by middle managers might not have been perceived as an obstacle by these groups because the participants were middle and top managers. When nonmanagerial employees are questioned about barriers, lack of involvement by middle managers might be a more salient obstacle.

The differences in anticipated barriers between the two levels of management are of particular interest. The barriers identified by top managers but not middle managers were:

- Inadequate knowledge about and understanding of TQM
- Unclear definitions of TQM goals, boundaries, and authority
- Time required for meetings and problem solving
- Inadequate planning for implementation
- Insufficient rewards

Table 3.   **Barriers Identified in the Literature and by Managers**

Barrier	Literature	Top managers	Middle managers
Top managers' support	X	X	X
Incentives and rewards	X	X	
Long-term focus	X	X	X
Training	X		X
Commitment throughout the organization	X	X	X
Middle managers' involvement	X		
Vision	X		
Politics/turf battles	X		X
Inadequate resources	X		X
Ineffective communication	X	X	X
Inadequate knowledge/ understanding	X	X	

The barriers identified by middle managers but not top managers were:

- Sabotage/lack of support from top management
- Politics/turf battles
- Lack of resources
- Turnover and changes in key personnel
- Inadequate/insufficient training in TQM
- Employees' lack of confidence in program

The top managers' greatest concern was lack of support from the executive committee.

The top managers' perceptions appear to reflect a more general and organizationwide orientation toward TQM implementation. Their greatest concern was lack of support from the executive committee, consisting of the chief medical officer, director, and associate director of the medical center. Although middle managers also identified lack of executive committee support as a potential barrier, it was much less important. Top managers were also concerned about unclear directions from the executive committee regarding TQM goals, boundaries, and authority and feared that inadequate planning would result in implementation problems. They also identified time constraints and insufficient rewards as potential obstacles.

Middle managers were more concerned with the pragmatic and operational issues of implementation. Their greatest concern was apathy and lack of commitment by all employees in the medical center. They were also concerned about a possible lack of confidence in the TQM program throughout the medical center. Middle managers viewed inadequate training as a potential barrier; top managers cited the more general problem of lack of understanding and knowledge of TQM. The second greatest concern of middle managers was a lack of support (even sabotage) from top management. Thus, both levels of management identified their direct supervisors as having the potential to present significant barriers to TQM implementation.

Another difference between top and middle managers' perceptions centered on the turnover of and changes in key personnel. The medical center in this study is a teaching facility, and many of the participants in the second session had experienced problems in patient care due to the transitory nature of the medical staff and residents. The turnover of chief executive officers in the health care industry averages 25% to 30% per year.[12] Consequently, turnover is a major barrier when new programs are championed by executives who subsequently leave. The associate director of this medical center is the primary supporter of TQM, and middle managers were concerned about the long-term viability of the program, should the associate director leave.

One important obstacle identified by middle managers that was not cited by top managers was politics and turf battles. Middle managers also identified inadequate resources such as money, time, space, and equipment as a potential barrier to TQM implementation.

A Crisis

The VA study found that top and middle managers perceive somewhat different obstacles to TQM implementation. Top managers focused on organizationwide implementation obstacles, while middle managers focused on operational and process barriers to implementation. The perceived meaning of generic obstacles, such as inadequate resources and lack of management support, varied across management levels. Failure to accurately define and specifically differentiate these barriers across hierarchical levels can hinder effective TQM implementation further.

Many health care facilities—and some would argue the entire health care industry—face a crisis of survival. Decreasing reimbursement amounts from Medicare and other payors, the shortage of health care personnel, new technologies, changes in customers' expectations, and an uncertain economic environment have all contributed to the present predicament. Many health care organizations are beginning to recognize that quality is needed to survive, much less thrive, in the 1990s. The traditional style of health care organization management, however, produces many obstacles to effective TQM implementation. By understanding the perceived barriers, health care executives can more precisely define and anticipate problems impeding effective TQM implementation.

References

1. J. F. Siler and S. Garland, "Sending Health Care Into Rehab," *Business Week*, Oct. 25, 1991, pp. 111–112.

2. T. Shoop, "Uphill Climb to Quality," *Government Executive*, March 1991, pp. 17–19.

3. M. G. Brown and R. Svenson, "What 'Doing' Total Quality Management Really Means," *Journal for Quality and Participation*, September 1990, pp 32–38.

4. D. M. Berwick, "Continuous Improvement as an Ideal in Health Care," *The New England Journal of Medicine*, 320, (1), 1989, pp. 53–56; and T. Shoop, "Can Quality Be Total?", *Government Executive*, March 1990, pp. 20–25.

5. T. Shoop, "Can Quality Be Total?"

6. M. Boyd and C. Haraway, "Total Quality at Baptist Memorial Hospital," *Journal for Quality and Participation*, January/February 1991, pp. 60–66.

7. T. Shoop, "Uphill Climb to Quality."

8. S. L. Perlman and M. Zacharias, "Can the Quality Movement Succeed in Healthcare?", *Journal for Quality and Participation*, January/February 1991, pp. 36–38.

9. M. Boyd and C. Haraway. "Total Quality at Baptist Memorial Hospital"; and R. Sepielli and A. Klausner, "New Quality Challenges for Healthcare," *Journal for Quality and Participation*, January/February 1991, pp. 54–58.

10. The authors of this paper were the two evaluators who independently grouped and classified the barriers.

11. After independently grouping the barriers for both sessions, the evaluators compared, discussed, and agreed upon major themes and basic clusters. The differences in themes that occurred during the grouping and classifying of barriers from the second session were not, in the judgment of the authors, substantive in nature. Minor discrepancies resulted from different assessments of single items and subthemes; the major theme and basic clusters were identical.

12. J. F. Siler and S. Garland, "Sending Health Care Into Rehab."

Carol A. Reeves is an assistant professor in the Department of Management at the University of Arkansas in Fayetteville. She received a doctorate in strategic management from the University of Georgia in Athens. David A. Bednar is an associate professor in the Department of Management at the University of Arkansas in Fayetteville. He received a doctorate in organizational communication/behavior from Purdue University in West Lafayette, IN.

Public Sector

EDUCATION—K–12

The Educational Consequences of W. Edwards Deming

Maurice Holt

This article argues that Deming's philosophy of quality is a distinctly new way to understand the educator's mission, one that moves away from "product specifications" and toward quality in the process of educating.

If one had to name the single biggest influence on American education during this century, a strong candidate would be not John Dewey but Frederick Winslow Taylor, the father of "scientific management." Schoolboards quickly picked up ideas from Taylor's 1895 book, *Shop Management*, which recommended using product specifications to define standards of output performance. Exactly the same conceptual apparatus animates recent national documents on educational futures. The Taylor doctrine may yet dominate the next century as well.

But the management approach of another American, W. Edwards Deming, challenges this orthodoxy and has displaced it, with advantageous results, in a variety of industrial settings. Most strikingly, the Deming doctrine of generating quality by building it into the process, rather than by inspecting defects out of the end product, has been widely adopted in Japan and has contributed greatly to the Japanese economic miracle.

Reprinted with permission from Maurice Holt, professor and chair of the Division of Curriculum and Instruction, University of Colorado, Denver. First appeared in the *Phi Delta Kappan*, January 1993.

There is now growing interest in applying Deming's ideas to the educational enterprise, but efforts to establish such a relationship have tended to emphasize, under the term "total quality management" (TQM), the external aspects of Deming's approach.[1] In this article I want to go further and argue that Deming's concepts of quality and improvement cut much deeper. They embody a philosophy of action with implications that challenge current practice in both administration and curriculum.

Thirty years ago, Raymond Callahan deplored the impact of Taylor's theories on school administration, noting that educational questions were "subordinated to business considerations."[2] In curriculum planning, Taylor's influence is very evident in the "Tyler Rationale," still ubiquitous despite the powerful critique offered by Herbert Kliebard in 1970.[3] Ralph Tyler refined the notion of specifying instructional objectives in advance and then using them not only to determine the educational experience but also to evaluate it. As in an industrial process, the course of study becomes an instructional sequence, with each stage being governed by explicit objectives and judged by some assessment of performance. The overall design is determined by defined aims or standards. There is something so eminently reasonable about the model—particularly in a culture where numerical assessment has great appeal and is reinforced by educational psychologists—that its assumptions have largely passed unchallenged.

Consider, for example, the recommendations of three recent education reports. The National Council on Education Standards and Testing declares that "national standards tied to assessments are desirable" in order to "measure and hold students, schools, school districts, states, and the nation accountable for educational performance."[4] The Commission on the Skills of the American Workforce pins its hope on "a new educational performance standard" against which all 16-year-old students will be measured, using "a series of performance-based assessments."[5] And a report by the Secretary's Commission on Achieving Necessary Skills asserts that "all American high school students must develop a new set of competencies and foundation skills if they are to enjoy a productive, full, and satisfying life."[6]

Strip away the rhetorical flourishes, and the message is familiar: everything will be fine if we specify an enhanced final product and assess its formation through a series of output measures. The practical result of adopting this attitude will be the usual Tyler model of curriculum specification through goals and objectives, administered through the cognate techniques of management by objectives (MBO). In the words of Peter Drucker's standard MBO text, the whole organization "must be directed toward the performance goals of the business."[7]

Deming rejects this approach entirely: to him, MBO is "like running a business by looking in the rearview mirror."[8] The doctrine is fallacious because it focuses on outputs and assumes that the process can be corrected by deductions drawn from them. In the business world, outputs are cost and revenue figures, and most business-school graduates focus on them as the prime indicators of corporate efficiency.

> Deming rejects this approach entirely: to him, MBO is "like running a business by looking in the rearview mirror."

Beginning in the 1960s, such large organizations as the Ford Motor Company appointed these cost-oriented "bean counters" at executive level, and eventually costs came to dominate judgment. David Halberstam tells, for example, how Ford's invention of an electrolytic paint process was introduced by Ford of Europe but denied to Ford North America because, the "beanies" argued, this improvement in quality would not necessarily lead to greater profit. If the product sold readily anyway, why spend money making it better?[9] Deming's point is that Ford executives were looking at the wrong numbers: this was VNO management—looking at "Visible Numbers Only." These figures are easy to collect but fail to describe what really matters.[10] According to Deming, VNO reductionism does nothing to promote quality, which is an intrinsic good that brings its own reward. The pursuit of quality may cause profits to fall in the short term, but quality always pays off in the end.

It is not difficult to see parallels with educational management. In the belief that test scores define quality, legislators urge administrators to make the numbers look good. Teachers, in turn, are obliged to become "beanies" and count the results of tests that trivialize and distort the activities of teaching and learning. The numbers piling up in the bureaus are poor surrogates for the actual judgments of teachers, and the test results demanded by VNO management are the equivalent of short-term profit, not long-lasting quality (which would be evident in students' enhanced understanding).

Another prominent aspect of conventional management practice is the use of staff appraisal and merit systems. Deming rejects these completely: "It is necessary that people feel secure," he asserts, and trust is a much better motivator than fear.[11] If management is doing its job, workers will be doing theirs. What is the sense of generating "targets," which, like objectives, can only distort the process? In any case, cooperation is much more important to quality than competition. If some aspect of the process needs improvement, Deming's approach is not to allocate blame but to bring together all those— including senior management—who can affect the process and establish a deliberative procedure that can arrive at a credible solution. This, in essence, is what "quality circles" offer: critical reflection in a formal but unthreatening setting so as to establish what it is good to do.

It should be clear by now that Deming mounts a fundamental challenge to established management dogmas. Indeed, he has declared, "Export anything except American management. At least not to friendly nations."[12] It is evident, too, that if Deming's criticisms are valid, they have implications for education as well as for business. For not only have schools been profoundly influenced by business, but the prevailing belief is that the two should be linked even more closely. For example, America 2000 calls for "a New Generation of American Schools. . . . America's business leaders will establish and muster the private resources for the New American Schools Development Corporation."[13] Moreover, the core of America 2000 is the six national goals for education, yet the belief that specifying ambitious goals will enhance quality is part of the MBO doctrine that Deming rejects. And the goal-based strategy of America 2000 leads directly to the standards-based rhetoric of official report, familiar enough since *A Nation at Risk* appeared in 1983. But the central problem remains: talk of goals and standards is empty unless the mechanism exists to achieve them. More than that, David Seeley points out that standards either become "a crueler form of screening and pushing people out of educational opportunities, or they will be rescinded or watered down in the name of practicality."[14]

The same objectives-based thinking underpins the notion of outcome-based education (OBE), which, as its name indicates, falls into the Deming category of rearview driving. This warmed-over mishmash of the Tyler rationale, Benjamin Bloom's mastery learning, and competency-based education quite explicitly puts the natural learning process into reverse, working backward, as Jean King and Karen Evans note, "from exit outcomes to specific lesson outcomes for every student."[15] This approach may do something for crude measures of accountability, but behind the high-stepping OBE jargon of transformational outcomes, learning paradigms, and empowerment lurk behavioristic methods that are totally at odds with the Deming quest for quality.

Given this sharp disjunction between Deming's approach and traditional thinking about business and education, a number of questions come to mind. If we are to reject so much that has been taken for granted, we need assurance that Deming's approach can work here as well as in Japan, and we need more detail regarding its methods. Moreover, we must determine what these methods would imply if transferred to an educational context. On the first count, there can be no doubt of Deming's achievements in Japan. Brought to Japan by Gen. Douglas MacArthur in 1947 as a consultant, Deming advocated for nascent Japanese industries a statistical approach to quality control that had been devised by his mentor at Bell Laboratories during the war, the physicist Walter Shewhart. Given Japan's prewar reputation for shoddy goods, quality was perceived to be of primary importance, and Deming's lectures to leading engineers and managers quickly made their mark. From Shewhart's statistical foundation, Deming developed a coherent doctrine of management that many Japanese firms adopted. By 1951 the Union of Japanese Scientists and Engineers had established the Deming Prize for quality. Today, in the lobby of Toyota's Tokyo headquarters, Deming's portrait dwarfs that of the company's founder and chief executive officer.

It took much longer for Deming to find honor in his own country, but in 1981, after the broadcast of an NBC documentary examining the success of Japan's car makers, the 80-year-old Deming was invited to Detroit to meet with 30 senior Ford executives. Questioning rather than lecturing, Deming indicated that management—not technology, not worker performance—was the source of the company's problems. Despite initial resentment, Ford bought into Demingism, and by decade's end "the supremacy of the numbers men" had given way to "a new spirit of cooperation" and a much healthier balance sheet.[16]

General Motors—a citadel of orthodox rational management—succumbed to Deming only after investing heavily in expensive robots, in the mistaken belief that Japan's success stemmed from high technology and not

Talk of goals and standards is empty unless the mechanism exists to achieve them.

the attitudes of workers and managers. Various books, including Deming's own, give details of the introduction of his methods into other U.S. companies.[17] Once the shift of emphasis from product to process has been accepted, there seems to be no cultural resistance to Deming's ideas. They originated, after all, in America, and Japanese companies operating here find that Americans adapt easily to Deming-style management.

The Deming approach is not a quick fix, since it calls for a fundamental change in a company's culture. In that first meeting at Ford, the managers expected to "hear about cars, about how to transform manufacturing plants with at least 4.5 'things gone wrong' per car," but Deming focused on facilitation rather than administration and wanted to know about "processes and people and how they were managed at Ford."[18] Deming's "14 points for the transformation of management" embrace several principles that have already been mentioned. Others include:

- Quality is defined by the customer. Improvement must be aimed at anticipating customers' future needs. Quality comes from understanding and improving the process.
- Quality emanates from top management, not from workers "trying harder," or from high technology pursued for its own sake, or from arbitrary goals set without considering how they can be achieved.
- The continuing education and training of all employees is a prerequisite to adopting Deming-style management.[19]

To Deming, quality is not an entity but a way of doing things, a way in which desired states are translated into concrete processes. More generally, the concept of quality addresses the connection between theory and practice—theory being the desired state and practice being the process or device that critically influences quality.

In the industrial context, the focus on quality means controlling the variation to which processes are generally subject—hence the need for statistical techniques in analyzing this variation. Deming distinguishes between processes that are naturally stable and need no adjustment and those in which adjustment is desirable, although the cause of the problem may not be immediately obvious. All too often, Deming has found, traditional management, with its emphasis on innovation for its own sake, leads to tampering with stable processes while failing to bring adequate resources to the solution of real problems. Improvement matters more than innovation, but it is generally more difficult because its ramifications may extend beyond the worker to management, to suppliers, or even to product design. To Deming, improvement is central not merely because quality goods attract loyal customers and generate profits, but because quality is a good in itself. Quality is part of the good life for the customer, while for the worker "it is a leader's job to foster joy in work, harmony, and teamwork."[20]

We are now in a position to compare Deming's style and the traditional style of management in more analytic terms. Deming is concerned with

> To Deming, quality is not an entity but a way of doing things, a way in which desired states are translated into concrete processes.

change, not as an end in itself—stable processes should be left alone—but as a way of facilitating necessary improvement. The key element in Demingism is the way in which theory is linked with practice in order to make good decisions. Clearly, Deming sees the pursuit of quality as a moral enterprise, something good to do. His prime concern is not organizations, aims, or outcomes but the people who define the practice of an institution, for whom a structure of management is necessary—in order to provide leadership—yet subordinate to the demands of process. Deming requires that workers as well as managers be trained in statistical techniques so that they themselves can theorize about their own practice, if necessary in formal discussion with managers and other interested parties, such as suppliers and dealers.

This scheme cannot be carried out when conventional line management prevails. Decisions about the process are developed by experts (the managers) from analysis of the product and then used to determine practice. Change is the province of experts, and only rarely will workers be consulted about their practice. Far from offering workers sustained education, companies tend to provide minimal training, in keeping with the view that workers are subordinate to management, the source of the necessary theory. Linking theory and practice then requires a separate mechanism, such as a handbook or a foreman. The culture is essentially static. New ideas are equally likely to be wildly embraced or mindlessly rejected, since the concept of improvement is not implicit.

The heart of the matter is the link between thought and action, between theory and practice, and here an analysis by the philosopher Richard McKeon proves helpful.[21] To describe the possible relationships between theory and practice, McKeon identifies four modes, two of which correspond to our present concerns.[22] Orthodox rational management fits McKeon's *logistic* mode, in which theory and practice are kept separate. Theory is the province of experts and is to be joined with practice by some "science of human action." Deming, in contrast, can be associated with the *deliberative* or problematic mode, which brings theory and practice together through a process of inquiry, so that solving practical problems becomes "a task for all men, not merely for dialecticians or experts set aside by their method and knowledge from the rest of mankind."[23]

In terms of educational change, it is clear that the logistic mode dominates current practice. Documents such as *America 2000: An Education Strategy,* state mandates for curriculum and assessment, and the school districts' stipulations on scope and sequence constitute the theory. Teachers are responsible for practice, which is linked with theory by means of objectives, tests, and the other apparatus of conventional management. If radical change is needed, a "science of human action" is deployed, generally taking the form of intervention by consultants and facilitators who ease the process of implementation and achieve "mutual adaptation" between the two parties.[24]

The deliberative mode conforms to the notion of "the practical" in curriculum building, first advanced by Joseph Schwab in 1970.[25] According to this view, curriculum problems have to do, as William Reid has put it, "mainly with how to act rather than ways to know," and they are solved by practical reasoning, since they belong to Aristotle's class of practical, moral problems that cannot be solved procedurally—that is, by the techniques of "rational management."[26] I would contend that Deming's concept of process improvement is essentially Aristotelian and therefore offers particularly apt insights into education and the organization of learning. Examples from other fields can be helpful metaphors for the examination of one's own, and in this case Deming's concept brings the further advantage that it is not just another footnote to conventional management but is a quite fundamental rethinking of the activity, with an eminently respectable pedigree.

Examples of the deliberative mode applied to the school curriculum are still relatively rare, but a number of comprehensive high schools in Britain used it in the 1970s to develop integrated core curricula for students between the ages of 11 and 16.[27] In 1988 the school autonomy that had permitted such developments in Britain disappeared virtually overnight with the imposition of a national system for curriculum and assessment, along with the familiar litany of objectives, outcomes, and staff evaluations. But in the U.S. the position is more promising now than ever, since the school restructuring movement has led to site-based management and greater autonomy in a number of school districts. This so-called second wave of reform was born of the evident failure to impose the top-down prescriptions of the early 1980s—the first wave—on schools. This first wave eventually fizzled out in the conventionalities of "effective schools." Recognizing that the support of teachers is a prerequisite for reform, schools have now been accorded a bigger piece of the action, and teacher professionalism has been brought into the equation.

So far, so good. But the deliberative mode needs more than a dash of autonomy and a nod toward professionalism. It presupposes schools in which a professional culture has been established, schools in which teachers are desirous and capable of linking curriculum theory with classroom practice and so of building a more collaborative structure "that can profoundly change the way both staff and students in schools grow and learn."[28] The deliberative mode is consistent with such promising proposals as John Goodlad's for teacher preparation and professional development schools and with giving schools freedom to advance teachers' careers.[29] It is certainly furthered by the Coalition of Essential Schools and schemes like it, which build teacher professionalism as they pursue their main purposes.[30] It will need to be sustained, as Deming recognizes in the industrial case, by inservice education rather than by training directed toward particular programs. It calls for a concept of institutional practice as, in Alasdair MacIntyre's words, a "coherent and complex form of socially established cooperative human activity through which goods internal to that form of activity are realized. . . ."[31]

That vision is not easily achieved, and it must take idiosyncratic shape in each individual school, however, similar reform strategies might be within a given district. This is why Deming thinks of management not as generic but as based in a particular company, where as much staff continuity as possible is encouraged. For this reason, the current task of "systemic change"

> Deming thinks of management not as generic but as based in a particular company, where as much staff continuity as possible is encouraged.

seems particularly inept. In a Deming mode, reform is a matter of taking each individual case and developing its "internal goods." As for the rational-managerial or transmission model, its failure has been plain since the RAND Corporation research of the 1970s, and simply producing ever more grandiose goals for reform cannot conceal its defects.[32]

The difficulty of developing a vision highlights a further difficulty: the "second wave of reform" in effect concedes to schools only a degree of freedom. It allows them to determine their own methods, but the all-important *purposes* of education remain the property of legislators, who turn them into "standards" and hammer them home through assessment. In short, the capacity of schools to develop their internal values is seriously constrained when the external values are expressed as received dogma, detached from the context of the particular school and its constituency.

But what would Demingism entail in schools, and could it be transplanted into U.S. schools as readily as into U.S. business enterprises? I conclude with an attempt to answer these questions.

In schools, the equivalent of Deming's "customer" would seem to be the student and not the parent. For the customer determines the "product," which in schools is a course of study directed toward the education of the student. We improve the product by attending to the "process"—by taking account of students' responses to new programs, of society's changing demands on students, and of our deepening professional understanding of education as the development of mind and character. Parents are rather in the role of sponsors or personal agents: the school shares their concern to secure the best education for their children and sees their part of the bargain as the provision of support at home. If particular circumstances make this difficult, the task should pass by default to specialized public service agencies, which are linked to the school. The deliberative school would make special efforts to involve parents in decisions regarding curriculum and organization, seeing this as a vital aspect of improving the curriculum process.

In rejecting the "visible numbers," Deming challenges the notion that formal assessment is a good in itself.

Assessment bulks large in American schools as a measure of both teacher competence and system accountability. The evidence that grade-related tests do more harm than good continues to grow, and Deming has rejected tests for schools as firmly as he has rejected them for business. For him, trust is vital, and most forms of accountability only undermine trust. The present tendency, on the other hand, is to devise ever more elaborate and extensive forms of examination and testing. The optimism of the assessment industry is vast, but so also is its cost. Money saved by reducing assessment would allow for the continuous education and training of teachers called for under a Deming approach. In rejecting the "visible numbers," Deming challenges the notion that formal assessment is a good in itself. The educational evidence to support the benefits of formal assessment is certainly unconvincing, and the reservations of the Office of Technology Assessment regarding the recent report of the National Council on Education Standards and Testing should be taken very seriously.[33]

In a Deming-oriented school, formal assessment would be regarded as a necessary evil and only the minimum required to satisfy the school's constituency would be offered. (Informal assessment, arising from the normal processes of teaching and learning, is the "invisible" but essential element in promoting quality.) Several models of sensible assessment are available. For example, from 1965 to 1987, British schools could award Certificates of Secondary Education to 16-year-olds who took examinations in subjects of their choice. The system allowed the schools to devise their own examinations, to assess student's performance on them, and to have the results evaluated by teachers at other schools. In short, the curriculum determined the assessment, exactly as it should from Deming's standpoint and exactly as it does not with outcome-based education. The system worked remarkably well and led naturally to the decision to judge representative samples of students' work over a period of time in addition to the written responses to examination questions.[34] This is but one example of an assessment that can be associated with the individual school and its curriculum and yet provide a reliable measure of accountability to the public and the legislature.

As for the curriculum, there is no reason to doubt the capacity of American schools to link theory and practice deliberatively and thus provide outstanding learning experiences. The Foxfire project, developed at a school in the Appalachians, is a mature and distinguished example, successfully basing students' programs on their own "culture and background" despite a requirement for teachers to attend "180 state-mandated meetings over the course of the year." The project avoids the products of the "text manufacturers" and even survives "a statewide assessment program."[35] In another instance, Sara Lawrence Lightfoot studied a group of good high schools and noted the importance of "a visible and explicit ideology" (or, as Deming would put it, "constancy of purpose"), "the centrality and dominance of teachers" (the workers, as opposed to the managers), and "the easy rapport between students and teachers" (for the consumers are most important).[36] And descriptions of thoughtful, process-oriented reform in schools appear constantly in the literature.

> In short, the curriculum determined the assessment, exactly as it should from Deming's standpoint and exactly as it does not with outcome-based education.

But ability is one thing and will, another. Besides, the American school system is remarkably resistant to change—and perhaps especially to the kind of deep-structure change that must accompany Demingism. As David Tyack puts it:

> Enabling teachers to do their job better by giving them the autonomy and resources to create lively learning is quite different from traditional reform patterns of adding a new program to an existing structure. It is fundamentally an idea that needs to be developed by those who carry it out. Such reforms have historically been the most difficult to bring about.[37]

It certainly does not follow that a new philosophy of action is as readily acceptable in schools as in business, for few American businesses are embedded in social and political traditions as securely as American schools. David Labaree argues that throughout this century the schools' curriculum and organization have been subject to tension between two conflicting American ideologies; on the one hand, the "doctrine of social and vocational relevance," stemming from the pursuit of liberty and leading to a variety of courses and tracks; on the other, the "doctrine of child-centeredness," stemming from the pursuit of equality and leading to commonality and open access. The result is a "conflicted curriculum" that carries out neither prescription very well, "leaving the schools with a legacy of intellectual weakness and pedagogical ineffectiveness."[38]

The general sameness of American schools and the failure of reform programs to make much of an impact might be attributable to the stalemate Labaree describes, which in turn is attributable to the checks and balances of democracy and bureaucracy at the federal, state, district, and school levels. The situation suggests a parallel with the way in which the same people get reelected to local and national legislative offices despite the elaborate machinery that exists for displacing them. Despite the rhetoric of conflict and reform, there seems to be an inherent overstability in the system.

However, it is important to recognize that, throughout this period of school history, the rational-managerial model has animated the entire school system as pervasively as it did so many American corporations for much of that time. I have argued that this model is inherently resistant to change, and the evidence from business and industry abundantly supports this contention. Although Ford and General Motors eventually responded to the Japanese threat and switched to a quite different management style, it took them a very long time to do so.[39] The goal-oriented line-management system is characterized by great inertia, which may be even more in evidence in a statewide education system than in a single industrial company.

This tendency toward inertia may throw light on the paradox noted by Decker Walker: the distinctive American talent for invention and adaptability leads, in its school system, to a series of novelties that burn brightly but fade quickly, leaving everything much as it was before.[40] Yet, by the same token, it is not completely unreasonable to suppose that if Demingism were to spread its influence from business to schools, the gridlock might begin to break much more quickly than in the past, for it could release the innate creativity of schools as institutions. At the least, it would seem that Deming's approach has great relevance to the solution of curriculum problems. Demingism is likely, on the face of it, to effect a far more significant improvement in the quality of a school's educational program than the outmoded remedies currently being recommended at the national level.

Notes

1. See, for example, John J. Bonstingl, "The Total Quality Classroom," *Educational Leadership*, March 1992, pp. 66–70.

2. Raymond Callahan, *Education and the Cult of Efficiency* (Chicago: University of Chicago Press, 1962), p. 246.

3. Ralph Tyler, *Basic Principles of Curriculum and Instruction* (Chicago: University of Chicago Press, 1950); and Herbert Kliebard, "Reappraisal: the Tyler Rationale," *School Review*, February 1970, pp. 259–72.

4. National Council on Education Standards and Testing, *Raising Standards for American Education* (Washington, D.C.: Office of Technology Assessment, 1992), pp. 2, 6.

5. Commission on the Skills of the American Workforce, *America's Choice: High Skills or Low Wages?* (Rochester, N.Y.: National Center on Education and the Economy, 1990), p. 3.

6. Secretary's Commission on Achieving Necessary Skills, *What Work Requires of Schools: A SCANS Report for America 2000* (Washington, D.C.: U.S. Department of Labor, 1991), p. vi.

7. Peter Drucker, *Management* (New York: Harper's College Press, 1977), p. 336.

8. Rafael Aguayo, *Dr. Deming* (New York: Simon & Schuster, 1990), p. 9.

9. David Halberstam, *The Reckoning* (New York: Avon Books, 1986), p. 507.

10. Aguayo, p. 11.

11. Andrea Gabor, *The Man Who Discovered Quality* (New York: Penguin Books, 1990), p. 22.

12. Aguayo, p. 28.

13. *America 2000: An Education Strategy* (Washington, D.C.: U.S. Department of Education, 1991), pp. 19–20.

14. David S. Seeley, "Educational Partnership and the Dilemmas of School Reform," *Phi Delta Kappan*, February 1984, pp. 383–88.

15. Jean A. King and Karen M. Evans, "Can We Achieve Outcome-Based Education?," *Educational Leadership*, October 1991, pp. 73–75.

16. Gabor, p. 131.

17. See, for example, W. Edwards Deming, *Out of the Crisis* (Cambridge, Mass.: MIT Press, 1986); William Lareau, *American Samurai* (New York: Warner Books, 1992); and May Walton, *Deming Management at Work* (New York: Perigee Books, 1991).

18. Gabor, pp. 5, 127.

19. This summary is adapted from Gabor, p. 18.

20. Gabor, p. 181.

21. Richard McKeon, "Philosophy and Action," *Ethics*, vol. 62, 1952, pp. 79–100.

22. William A. Reid, "The Practical, the Theoretic, and the Conduct of Curriculum Research," paper presented at the annual meeting of the American Educational Research Association, Los Angeles, 1981.

23. McKeon, p. 94.

24. Michael Fullan and Alan Pomfret, "Research on Curriculum and Instructional Implementation," *Review of Educational Research*, Winter 1977, pp. 71–84.

25. Joseph J. Schwab, *The Practical: A Language for Curriculum* (Washington, D.C.: National Education Association, 1970).

26. William A. Reid, *Thinking About the Curriculum* (London: Routledge, 1978), p. 24.

27. Maurice Holt, *Curriculum Workshop: An Introduction to Whole Curriculum Planning* (London: Routledge, 1983).

28. Ann Lieberman, ed., *Building a Professional Culture in Schools* (New York: Teachers College Press, 1988), p. vii.

29. John Goodlad, *Teachers for Our Nation's Schools* (San Francisco: Jossey-Bass, 1991).

30. Theodore R. Sizer, *Horace's School* (Boston: Houghton Mifflin, 1992).

31. Alasdair MacIntyre, *After Virtue: A Study in Moral Theory* (London: Duckworth, 1981), p. 240.

32. Milbrey W. McLaughlin and David Marsh, "Staff Development and School Change," *Teachers College Record*, September 1978, pp. 23–45.

33. National Council on Education Standards and Testing, *Testing in American Schools* (Washington, D.C.: Office of Technology Assessment, 1992).

34. For an account of the operation of this examination in a comprehensive high school, see Maurice Holt, *The Common Curriculum* (London: Routledge, 1978).

35. Eliot Wigginton, "Culture Begins at Home," *Educational Leadership*, December 1991/January 1992, pp. 60–64.

36. Sara Lawrence Lightfoot, *The Good High School* (New York: Basic Books, 1983), pp. 320, 333, 343.

37. David Tyack, "Restructuring in Historical Perspective: Tinkering Toward Utopia," *Teachers College Record*, Winter 1990, p. 187.

38. David F. Larabee, "Politics, Markets, and the Compromised Curriculum," *Harvard Educational Review*, November 1987, p. 489.

39. Halberstam, pp. 457–510.

40. Decker F. Walker, *Fundamentals of Curriculum* (San Diego: Harcourt Brace Jovanovich, 1990), p. 336.

Transforming Schools Through Total Quality Education

Mike Schmoker and Richard B. Wilson

After visits to the Toyota plant in Lexington, Kentucky, and the Central Park East schools in East Harlem, and other schools, these educators describe how the same quality principles that work for Toyota are equally applicable for transforming the way schools operate to continuously improve the ways we educate all our children.

About a year and a half ago, we decided to visit the Toyota plant in Lexington, Kentucky. Our school district's move to site-based management was in full swing, and we went to Lexington hoping to learn more about implementing that change. Neither our experience nor the research coming out at that time indicated that site-based management, by itself, held much promise for raising levels of achievement.[1] Something was missing. We assumed that whatever accounted for the widely touted effectiveness of decentralized management at Toyota would apply to schools as well.

We got far more from our trip than we bargained for. We believe that what we learned from Toyota could transform public education and make "equal opportunity" more than an empty phrase. It would enable America finally to reach that "forgotten half" of the student population that has traditionally been deprived of a high-quality education—the group that economist Lester Thurow tells us is pivotal to a nation's ability to compete in an international marketplace.[2]

Employees at Toyota work and think together in teams. To a surprising extent, these teams are self-managing: they meet regularly to identify areas for improvement, to set many of their own goals, to gather and interpret their own data, and to check progress and adjust efforts made toward attaining their goals. In this way, they do their own quality control.

Most of Toyota's ideas for innovation and improvement—thousands of them each year—come from the employees. In any given year more than 90% of Toyota employees submit at least one suggested *kaizen*, a Japanese word for a small but significant improvement. That fact is interesting enough in

Reprinted with permission from Mike Schmoker, research analyst, and Richard B. Wilson, Superintendent, Amphitheatre Public Schools, Tucson, AZ. First appeared in the *Phi Delta Kappan*, January 1993.

itself. But what is more interesting is that more than 90% of these suggestions actually get implemented.

A surprisingly democratic atmosphere prevails at Toyota. Management allows workers a considerable degree of autonomy. The chief function of management is to encourage and support employees, or "team members" as Toyota calls them, with guidance and with continual training and retraining. It is management's responsibility to ask the right questions rather than to tell employees what to do.

On the other hand, Toyota insists on something that is seldom practiced in schools: every decision, every improvement effort must be made collectively. These decisions are made within teams and groups of teams, which, as members of the larger system, are given regular opportunities to interact. Whatever measures are taken are checked against data at every stage. Toyota believes that the key to improvement is knowing exactly how well—or how poorly—you are progressing in your efforts. A frequently heard refrain is "Give me the data." But these data are *never used to identify and blame* individual employees. They serve only to improve the overall system. No one has ever been fired from Toyota's Lexington plant.

In speaking with dozens of Toyota employees in Lexington-area bars, we learned that this approach is not only effective but appealing. It is no overstatement to say that employees seem to love their jobs. We found their enthusiasm startling. This is factory work, mind you. And yet we heard many comments like this one from an ex-jockey: "On Sunday nights, I look forward to getting with my team and hitting the ground running on Monday morning. No kidding."

> Toyota believes that the key to improvement is knowing exactly how well—or how poorly—you are progressing in your efforts.

The combination of management strategies used by Toyota, widely known as Total Quality Management (TQM), is based on the work of W. Edwards Deming, the statistician and management theorist whose success with Japanese industry has been so widely celebrated. And, as is inevitable with any large-scale movement, his theories are now being reexamined in some corners.

Deming's work emphasizes the advantages of teamwork, of investing in ongoing training for all employees to increase their value to the company, of an insistence that research and employee-gathered data guide and inform every decision and every improvement effort. As the title of a recent cover story in *Fortune* put it, these advantages account for "Why Toyota Keeps Getting Better and Better and Better."[3]

What Deming tells us is essential to the productive workplace is strikingly similar to what psychologists are learning. Professor Mihaly Csikszentmihalyi, former head of the Department of Psychology at the University of Chicago, is the author of *Flow: the Psychology of Optimal Experience.*[4] His extensive studies have recently caught the attention of educators—and with good reason. They describe those conditions that enable any of us—students or workers—to be most productive. But just as important, they point to that essential intersection between pleasure and productivity. One of Csikszentmihalyi's discoveries was that, given the right conditions, the best part of many people's lives is when they are engaged in their daily work. He cites the case of a factory employee who spends every moment of his day monitoring his own efforts and comparing them with his goals. For him, work is "better than anything else. It's a whole lot better than watching TV."

What accounts for such feelings? Studs Terkel's interviews, published in *Working*, paint a picture of work—especially routine labor—as "doing violence" to human beings.[5] What conditions ensure not only pleasure in work but productivity as well?

Deming's first and perhaps most important point is that "constancy of purpose" is critical to quality and innovation. Similarly, Csikszentmihalyi's studies reveal that people have to feel that their work is purposeful, that it has some meaning beyond collecting a paycheck. He also discovered that people work with more commitment toward collective goals than toward merely individual ones. In addition, at work as at play, we need to see that we are getting better at what we do. Because of this focus on constancy of purpose, continuous learning and a sense of improvement are essential to sustained effort. Finally, and perhaps most interesting as regards the work of Deming, this sense of improvement must be both palpable and precise. We need accurate and "constant feedback" that tells us what is working and what is not.[6]

Even a rough acquaintance with Deming makes it clear that these are the central elements of his work. The parallel between Csikszentmihalyi's work and Deming's, combined with the success of Deming's methods in industry, should counter the charge that this fascination with TQM is merely another fad. If TQM seems to be failing in some settings, the failure can be attributed to what employees in private industry not infrequently tell us: management has adopted the trappings of Deming's work without being willing to redistribute power and place unprecedented levels of trust in employees.

Anyone who knows anything about public education knows that, in general, what Deming preaches—and what Toyota does—is not happening in our schools, not by a long shot. The good news is that what happens at places like Toyota comes down to a few simple, very doable things. *Fortune* recently referred to Deming's principles as "starkly simple and effective."[7] In visiting and studying some of the most dramatically improved schools in the country, we have seen the success of these "simple and effective" methods already being demonstrated. And the schools we studied have made these changes with little or no additional infusion of funds.

A Promising Pattern

If we avoid being rigid or doctrinaire about the essence of Deming's philosophy and principles (as many who talk about them unfortunately are), an exciting and promising pattern emerges. We suggest that educators study Deming because his work codifies precisely what our schools need most. But we are further inspired by the fact that, to an impressive extent, many schools are already successfully implementing Deming's basic methods and principles, some more consciously than others. The challenge for us is to study these successes, wherever they occur, and then to replicate or adapt what we learn. The experiences of these schools give us a promising and proven pattern on which to base large-scale improvement efforts.

Central Park East

At one extreme, consider the well-known case of the Central Park East schools in East Harlem, the poorest neighborhood in New York City. Ninety-five percent of the mostly black and Hispanic students from Central Park East Secondary School go on to college. They do extremely well on standardized tests. Though Central Park East is part of a "choice" consortium in New York City's District 4, its students are in no way hand-picked: 70% of them come from the immediate attendance area.

After visiting Toyota, our visit to this school and our conversations with its director, Deborah Meier, were all the more interesting. The policies and practices she described seemed to bear an uncanny resemblance to some of Deming's teachings. But Meier had not heard of Deming when we spoke with her. If anything, the principles of Theodore Sizer's Coalition of Essential Schools more explicitly govern operations at the Central Park East schools.

Yet, in the most important respects, Meier and her teachers have created a school environment that conforms in every important way to Deming's major principles: a democratic atmosphere, supportive leadership, team and collaborative effort, a clear and unified purpose, and an insistence on regular analysis and evaluation of student performance data as a basis for continually improving on past practice to serve the school's customers.

Deming's first point of emphasis is to establish a clear and energizing sense of purpose. At Central Park East, that purpose is to help students cultivate the "habits of mind" that will enable them to succeed. Every classroom has a poster, prominently displayed, with the teacher's interpretation of those habits: variations on the ability to infer, analyze, synthesize, and extrapolate.

Like Toyota's Fujio Cho, Meier regularly meets with grade- and department-level teams. She simply asks what they are doing and calls for "evidence, evidence, evidence" that tells whether they are—or aren't—succeeding. Like Toyota's employees and managers, she and her staff focus on "data," which in their case might be how many students are succeeding on a given task or project. She examines portfolios and asks about what is coming up. She sees her role as one of "constantly articulating the school's purpose" while helping teams of teachers ensure that all effort and activity support that purpose.

Meier and her faculty do not succeed through intimidation or by assigning blame. Another of Deming's points is to "dispel fear." Neither employees nor students can work imaginatively and eagerly when they are in fear of being blamed for their shortcomings.[8] People need freedom and support in order to do work that they can take pride in. Conversations with teachers at Central Park East confirm that Meier provides that support. Ricky Harris, a humanities teacher, looks forward to Meier's classroom visits, saying, "The woman is brilliant; I always listen to a lot of what she tells me."

Meier's visits and the regular team meetings provide not just purpose, but feedback—the regular and precise evaluation that enables teachers to know

At Central Park East, that purpose is to help students cultivate the "habits of mind" that will enable them to succeed.

if they are on the right track, if the activities they are providing students are the best that they can offer. Meier and the teams examine portfolios regularly, and each spring business and community members—a school's "external customers" in the Deming lexicon—are invited to the school to evaluate the work in portfolios. The information from these public displays of students performance—"fishbowls" as they're called—then guides the following year's improvement efforts. Central Park East has conducted its own research to refine methods of reading instruction.[9] And the staff is now formalizing a study that has been going on less formally for years: tracking the areas of study that graduates, now in college, feel most and least confident in. This feedback will enable the school to continually refine and precisely adjust its efforts for its most important customers.

Central Park East doesn't waste time on feckless "mass inspection," which violates Deming's point about dispelling fear. Instead, students are trusted to do much of their own quality control. Meier says that the students must "convince us that they are ready to graduate." This is the ethos of trust and respect that prevails at Central Park East. Teamwork, collaboration, and Deborah Meier's relentless "articulation of what we're all about" ensure the "continuous improvement" that is at the heart of Deming's philosophy. The results speak for themselves.

Comer School Development Program

This program was begun in 1968 by psychiatrist James Comer as a joint effort between the Yale University Child Study Center and the New Haven Public Schools. Like Deming, Comer emphasizes the importance of recognizing that change and improvement require a "systemic" understanding of the relationships between members of the school community, including parent and social service agencies. For Comer, as for Deming, students and employees work harder, smarter, and more happily when issues of relationships are addressed, when trust and a democratic atmosphere are carefully sustained.

Comer takes a scientific approach to his work. And the resemblance to Deming's essential tenets is striking. Just as Toyota involves all employees in decisions that affect them, Comer involves all staff members and all parents "at every level of school activity." Problems and challenges are tackled through a nine-part process that resembles Deming's PDSA (Plan, Do, Study, Act) cycle. Though more elaborate, Comer's process contains the same basic elements as Deming's: systematic identification of the school's goals; planning; and then regular "assessment" of effort and progress, followed by carefully designed modification that results in improvement. Like Deming's PDSA, Comer's process is a true cycle that promotes *continuous* improvement. It takes both effort and results right back to the planning stage, where measures can be continually refined and new problems found and addressed.

There are further similarities between Comer's concepts and Deming's emphases. Comer's "staff development" echoes Deming's insistence on "training, retraining, and education."[10] Comer's "three guiding principles" include "no fault" problem solving; Deming insists that we improve processes rather than blame people and gives "accountability" a human face. Two other Comer principles, "consensus decision making" and "collaboration," are pillars of Deming's teachings that account for Toyota's success.[11]

Though Comer's initial efforts in New Haven took until 1986 to bear fruit, a recent Comer school saw remarkable improvements occur in just a six-year period. At Columbia Park Elementary, in Prince Georges County, Maryland, achievement test scores rose from the 35th percentile to the 98th percentile. This occurred between 1986 and 1991.[12]

Northview Elementary School

A more explicit example of Deming's influence is Northview Elementary School in Manhattan, Kansas. This school, which serves a lower-middle-class community, was one of the featured subjects of a public television special, "Learning in America: Schools That Work," narrated by Roger Mudd. Data provided by principal Dan Yunk show that, between 1983 and 1989, fourth-grade reading competency scores went from 59.5% to nearly 100%; sixth-grade scores rose from 41.7% to 97.1%. Fourth- and sixth-grade math scores went from 70.3% to 98.6% and from an abysmal 31.9% to 97.1% respectively.

In a telephone interview Yunk spoke of how his understanding of Deming helped him to empower his employees to bring about effective change. Not only did Yunk establish a purposeful, democratic, and collegial environment, but he also insisted on regular team analysis of achievement data to isolate problems and promote improvement. One of Deming's principles is to "break down barriers between staff areas." Only when areas and departments communicate can they solve the kinds of complex problems that require an understanding of the interdependencies that affect everyone's efforts. When statistical analysis of math scores revealed that there had been a drop in third-grade students' ability to solve certain kinds of math problems, second-, third-, and fourth-grade teams were brought together. Once assembled, they discovered year-to-year inconsistencies in emphases in the math curriculum, which the teams were then able to address. Subsequently, the scores rose significantly.

Johnson City Schools

Another case of Deming's influence can be seen in the Johnson City Schools in New York State. This enormously improved school district has become something of an educational mecca, one of the most-visited school districts in the country. Although the Johnson City Schools have only recently come under the direct influence of Deming's theories, those theories easily align with what has been going on in Johnson City for years.

In this blue-collar, lower-middle-class community, the schools were among the lowest performing in the country until the early 1970s, when a new superintendent, John Champlin, arrived. Deming believes that knowledge drives improvement, though it is human nature to resist new knowledge. John Champlin started his improvement effort by simply distributing and discussing educational research with the faculty of one school.

After some initial resistance, teachers began to see that they might be capable of helping students reach far higher levels of achievement. There was something exciting, for instance, in Benjamin Bloom's startling but well-substantiated claim that, under the right conditions more than 90% of students could achieve at levels of excellence as high as those of the highest third.[13]

During the first year, there were measurable gains in both morale and achievement at the school where Champlin focused most of his efforts. By the end of the third year, gains could be seen districtwide. After six years, 70% of Johnson City students were achieving at or above grade level—up from 45% to 50% when Champlin arrived. By 1986, 77% of Johnson City graduates were receiving New York State's prestigious Regents diplomas. (The state average for Regents diplomas awarded in a school district was 44%.)

For all its success on the state tests, the district continues to strive for improvement. The current superintendent, Al Mamary, has sought state approval to launch an initiative to suspend the district's focus on standardized test scores and move toward the development of authentic and performance-based evaluation. Mamary and his associate superintendents, Larry Rowe and Frank Alessi, have worked to create a comprehensive school improvement program they now call the Outcomes-Driven Development Model (ODDM). It includes an emphasis on noncoercive leadership and attention to both internal and external research and to data on students, schools, and the district. The statistically minded leadership routinely asks teachers and teams of teachers not "how well" something works, but how many students are meeting quality standards on units and projects. School leaders use such process data as a basis for taking corrective action.

> The statistically minded leadership routinely asks teachers and teams of teachers not "how well" something works, but how many students are meeting quality standards.

Carefully conducted pilot studies have led Johnson City to adopt such practices as diagnosing students' math skills in October and then having students attend tutoring and enrichment sessions outside of regular school hours if they need extra help. This scheme has resulted in an exceptionally high percentage of students who have truly mastered grade-level math skills before being promoted to the following grade. The district is now gathering data on a pilot project to eliminate age-grading at the primary level.

This preventive, frequent assessment of quality at every stage of the process is pure Deming. And it happens in language arts as well, where teamwork diagnosis, and careful alignment between schoolwide and grade-level goals have led to a focused and effective program. Student composition skills are regularly assessed—often by teams—and assistance is then provided for students to ensure their success on the New York competency and Regents exams.

All of these efforts are enhanced through a carefully targeted "program of training and retraining," to use Deming's language. The training equips individuals with precisely those skills that they and the district agree have the highest priority. As Champlin says, "We were doing Deming before Deming was in style."

William Glasser is well-known for wanting to show educators "how Dr. Deming's ideas can be brought undistorted into our schools."[14] He refers to the schools in Johnson City throughout his best seller, *The Quality School.* For Glasser, these are "the best quality school models around."[15]

Henry Levin and "Accelerated" Schools

An especially interesting application of the use of Deming's principles can be found in Henry Levin's "accelerated schools." Levin took classes from Deming, whose influence can be seen in Levin's six-step "inquiry process," which closely resembles Deming's four-step PDSA cycle. Levin himself calls the inquiry process "dominant accelerated practice." Like Deming's PDSA cycle, it is intended to help teams focus carefully on each essential aspect of solving—rather than merely discussing—a problem.

Levin set out not only to see what made good schools good, but also to create something that could make poor schools—indeed, the worst schools— much better. Though he carefully admonishes us not to expect quick success, Levin's program has already been immensely successful at the most difficult and failure-ridden schools, turning some of them around in as little as two to three years with little or no infusion of funds.

At schools such as Daniel Webster in urban San Francisco or Hollibrook Elementary in Houston, Texas, every effort is made to ensure both that students enjoy their studies and that they succeed at them. The object is to "accelerate" rather than to remediate students—to enable them to catch up with or get ahead of what they must learn, rather than to slow instruction down to a dull, destructive pace—a practice that has never been effective.[16] Like Deming, Levin believes that we vastly underestimate the talents and abilities of our students and teachers. He would instead have us "build on strengths" that students and teachers bring to the classroom. If artfully tapped, these strengths can result in far higher engagement and improved levels of achievement.

> Like Deming, Levin believes that we vastly underestimate the talents and abilities of our students and teachers.

Just as Toyota adheres to Deming's teachings about the importance of bringing together members from throughout the system to solve problems, Levin emphasizes group decision making that represents the "school as a whole." This is the only way to muster the consent and enthusiasm that are essential to one of his cardinal concepts: "unity of purpose." Like the "constancy of purpose" urged in the first of Deming's 14 points, unity of purpose animates all the other principles of Levin's accelerated schools.

Once purpose is established, "constant improvement" is pursued by what Levin calls "taking stock," gathering data that enable teams (or in accelerated schools, "cadres") to intelligently isolate problems of the highest priority and then to propose solutions. These solutions are in turn guided by reference to "the data."

Apparently, this approach works. Scores on standardized tests at Daniel Webster Elementary went from 69th to 23rd in the district in only three years. At Hollibrook Elementary, 85% of the students enter without being able to speak English. In 1988 fifth-graders were scoring at the 3.7 level in reading and language arts. By 1991, after Hollibrook instituted accelerated school processes, they were scoring at about the 5.3 level. In math the average fifth-grader is now a year above grade level. Staff members at Hollibrook did this with "no infusion of funding to make the difference." Even more interesting, they did it not by emphasizing dull test-preparation activities, but rather by emphasizing "hands-on programs and enrichment" that "exposed all children to the richest experiences."[17]

Mt. Edgecumbe High School

Perhaps the most explicit example of a "Deming school" is Mt. Edgecumbe High School, a public boarding school in Sitka, Alaska. The majority of its 215 students are Native American, and about 40% are at risk or have had academic problems before coming there. Though superintendent Larrae Rocheleau cautions that Mt. Edgecumbe is not a "Deming school," this is chiefly because there are still some faculty members who are not participating in the program.

Teacher David Langford, now a consultant, came back with some radical new ideas after a leave he took in Phoenix, Arizona. He saw the application of TQM less as a school-management strategy than as a classroom-level strategy. He started a business course called "Continuous Improvement." He eliminated grades but would no longer accept anything less than what he and his students regarded as quality work—a practice that William Glasser advocates. And he began to take extraordinary measures to ensure that his students participated in work they found meaningful and applicable to what they wanted from life. Langford would spend the first week of any course establishing purpose and helping students to understand the worth of what they were going to study and the contribution it would make to their personal and career goals. Many Mt. Edgecumbe teachers picked up on this idea and still make it a routine part of their curriculum. This is not unlike Glasser's remark that "we should explain much more than we do now . . . about why we teach the things we do."[18]

Just as economist Lester Thurow suggests that we tie our national curriculum to the country's need to compete in seven key industries, so Mt. Edgecumbe focuses its curriculum on the "future social and economic needs of Alaska."[19] Every effort is made to regard students as workers, as self-managers. As a result, discipline referrals have all but disappeared. Statistical analysis has also helped Mt. Edgecumbe staff members to find the root causes for tardiness, and adjustments to the system have resulted in reducing late arrivals from an average of 34 to an average of just 10 per week.

And there are other significant dividends when students assume the responsibility of managing their own learning. Teachers don't mind supervising as many as 100 students at a time, which creates more time for staff development, planning, and collaboration: an additional three hours a week so far. Their ultimate goal is to arrange things so that they can spend 50% of their time planning and collaborating in teams—without hiring any extra staff members. In keeping with Deming's belief that people desire to do quality work, grading has been eliminated and replaced in many classes with lists of "competencies," the mastery of which students negotiate with teachers.

Teacher David Langford eliminated grades but would no longer accept anything less than what he and his students regarded as quality work.

Academically, the results are not yet conclusive. Standardized test scores are up only slightly. But there are other measures of success to consider. Whereas very few Mt. Edgecumbe students used to go on to higher education, about 49% now attend some form of postsecondary school. Whereas only 2% of Native American students graduate from the University of Fairbanks, evidence indicates that a far higher percentage of Mt. Edgecumbe students are doing well in college and are expected to graduate.

Though Mt. Edgecumbe was once known for its high rate of student turnover, the percentage of eligible students returning to the school is now nearing 100%. Dropouts have been reduced from 40% to about 1% per year. And teacher turnover, once high, is now nearly nonexistent. At Mt. Edgecumbe, they must be doing something right.

Short-Term Benefits

This point has to be made carefully: Levin, Champlin, Deming, and others are quick to caution that their programs are not quick fixes and that we shouldn't expect results in less than five years. At the same time, Champlin points out that morale at the first school he worked at improved dramatically and that there were academic gains at that school by the end of the first year. There were district-wide gains at the end of only three years. Two of Levin's major efforts saw enormous gains within two to three years.

Another interesting case of positive results in the short term is that of George Westinghouse Vocational and Technical High School in downtown Brooklyn, New York. Two of the first 23 areas targeted for improvement were class cutting and course failure. By meeting in teams, identifying root causes, and then keeping statistical records, the staff was able to reduce class cutting by 39.9% in just six weeks. The school then confronted its greatest challenge: the fact that 151 students were failing every course. Staff members brought the tools and techniques of TQM to bear on the problem. Everyone, including parents, was involved in the improvement effort. Parents of failing students were asked to sign contracts saying that they would make extra efforts to ensure improvement. Data were gathered from each student, and the chief reasons for the high rate of failure were determined: lack of study and a need for tutoring. A noontime peer-tutoring program called "Lunch and Learn" was established.

Between January and June 1991, the number of students failing every course fell from 151 to 11—a 92% improvement in one semester.

The results at George Westinghouse point up what can happen when people pool their intelligence to assign priorities and then deliberately tackle problems. Between January and June 1991, the number of students failing every course fell from 151 to 11—a 92% improvement in one semester.[20]

Nearly a decade after the publication of *A Nation at Risk*, the education reform movement is still marked by rancor, ignorance, and stagnation. We have yet to begin systematically implementing the best of what we know, even though scholarship increasingly points to an emerging pattern.[21] Worse still, there doesn't even seem to be a movement afoot to help that occur. Only occasionally does the acknowledgment surface that anything like a promising pattern is emerging from beneath the rubble.

Instead, ideological battles between warring camps have reduced the "great education debate" to what George Kaplan recently called "education's thousand points of noise."[22] Education journals remind us regularly that we still manage schools as we always have and that we still rely too much on such discredited methods as drill, worksheets, and prepackaged lessons that only ensure mediocrity, boredom, and the continued and costly failure of our lowest-achieving students.[23] The waste, Deming might say, is appalling.

Deming's methods are not only effective in helping us to manage schools, districts, and classrooms; they can also help us to manage and use knowledge to our fullest advantage. We now know how to all but ensure that students enter the second grade reading on grade level; we have developed methods of teaching advanced mathematics that enable us to reach far higher percentages of students than we typically do. Deming's methods would not allow us to ignore these facts. The heart of Deming's philosophy is an insistence that management take pains to create a positive and productive climate in which employees are continually kept abreast of the most effective methods and practices—a climate in which they help one another to adapt, replicate, and refine practices.

Deming's work provides us with a proven plan that puts in place—and then continuously improves upon—what works. This is the kind of flexible and attractive program that education needs most today. Rather than divide ourselves along ideological lines, we need to promote broad, concerted participation, where the reigning controversies are not ignored but must take their proper place on our agenda of problems to be solved and practices to be improved. On a national level, Deming's work would complement that of Lauren Resnick and Marc Tucker as they seek to develop an enlightened set of national standards and assessments.[24] These standards and assessments would drive the kind of meaningful activity and help create the sense of purpose— even national purpose—that are the heart of Deming's philosophy.

> Deming's work provides us with a proven plan that puts in place—and then continuously improves upon—what works.

Amphitheater Schools

Excitement about these methods is growing here in the Amphitheater Public Schools. We firmly believe that Deming's management practices will lead not only to improved student achievement but also to increased efficiency in every department, including those nonacademic areas that truly support the instructional program.

We are convinced that the dialogue these methods engender will have profound, if indirect, benefits for us. The discussions will bring us face to face with those structural barriers that are so difficult to see but so essential for us to acknowledge if we are to change: our grading and assessment system, the practice of age-grouping, teacher evaluation policies, our assumptions about what students are capable of, employee compensation, the traditional school calendar, and the conventional certification policy. Deming's principles and practices can create a collective demand for structural change, driven by a desire for improvement on the part of those who are the real ministers of change—the employees on whose expertise we must rely.

The potential for fundamental change is both the strength and the vulnerability of Deming's principles. If the process generates fear because of the depth of the change it implies, it might be resisted. With this in mind, we are taking an evolutionary approach in our district to ensure that stakeholders understand the principle and their theoretical underpinnings. We make our case as clearly as possible at every stage of the process and constantly distinguish between a manufacturing plant and a school setting. To this end, all administrators, supervisors, and key representatives of our teacher union have attended extended training sessions.

The school board has heartily endorsed this effort, which will require a change in the role it plays. Board members have also attended workshops and formally adopted a set of basic concepts based on Deming's principles.

Several departments and some of the schools in the district have volunteered to pilot the implementation of Deming's principles immediately. Teams within each volunteering school or department have received intensive training and will now train other staff members in the unit and serve as a corps of consultants who will be available at a later date to other schools and departments. Members of these initial teams will also constitute a district-level oversight team.

Collaboration and a respect for information almost inevitably promote improvement.

For this school year, each pilot program has selected at least one goal. The teams will now gather data and then regularly analyze and make adjustments to their processes in light of the data. As we embark on this journey, we are establishing regular contact with local industries that are also making the transition to Deming's philosophy. We hope that industry and the schools can help each other avoid some pitfalls and can learn from each other's experience. We hope this will develop into a collegial relationship that will enhance everyone's efforts.

We agree with *Fortune* that Deming's methods are at bottom "starkly simple and effective" and that school improvement doesn't need to be an impenetrable mystery. Collaboration and a respect for information almost inevitably promote improvement. Much could be accomplished on the local or national level by simply asking questions such as, Are school employees working together collaboratively on the school's most pressing academic priorities? What data have been used to determine these priorities? Are we making progress toward the school's most important goals? What is working? What isn't? How can we do better?

If we ask such questions, fits and starts notwithstanding, we will be on our way toward real improvement of this country's schools and of its competitive ability. In addition, we'll be moving toward a climate in schools that is immeasurably more humane and productive. We believe that Deming's philosophy and methods best codify what the schools need most if they are to improve substantially: the ability to organize and act on the best of what we know and are continuing to learn.

Notes

1. Betty Malen, R. T. Ogawa, and Jennifer Kranz, "Site-Based Management: Unfulfilled Promises," *School Administrator*, February 1990, pp. 30–59.

2. Lester Thurow, *Head to Head: The Coming Economic Battle Among Japan, Europe, and America* (New York: William Morrow, 1992).

3. Alex Taylor, "Why Toyota Keeps Getting Better and Better and Better," *Fortune*, 19 September 1990, pp. 66–78.

4. Mihaly Csikszentmihalyi, *Flow: The Psychology of Optimal Experience* (New York: Harper & Row, 1990).

5. Studs Terkel, *Working: People Talk About What They Do All Day and How They Feel About It* (New York: Pantheon Books, 1974).

6. Csikszentmihalyi, p. 56.

7. Louis Kraar, "Twenty-Five Who Help the U.S. Win," *Fortune*, Spring-Summer 1991, p.34.

8. W. Edwards Deming, *Out of the Crisis* (Cambridge, Mass.: MIT Press, 1986), p. 62.

9. David Bensman, *Quality Education in the Inner City: The Story of the Central Park East Schools* (New York: Central Park East Schools, 1987).

10. Deming, p. 53.

11. *For Children's Sake: The Comer School Development Program*, a brochure published by the Yale Child Study Center, New Haven, Conn., 1991.

12. "District News," *School Development Program Newsline*, Fall 1991, p. 2.

13. Benjamin Bloom, "Learning from Mastery,"*Evaluation Comment*, May 1966, pp. 1–12.

14. William Glasser, M.D., *The Quality School* (New York: Harper & Row, 1990), p. 153.

15. Ibid., p. 154.

16. Martin Haberman, "The Pedagogy of Poverty Versus Good Teaching," *Phi Delta Kappan*, December 1991, pp. 290–94.

17. Ron Brandt, "On Building Learning Communities: A Conversation with Hank Levin," *Educational Leadership*, September 1992, pp. 19–23.

18. Glasser, p. 120.

19. "Reading, Writing, and Constant Improvement," *Goal/QPC's*, no. 1, 1991, p. 2.

20. Franklin P. Schargel, "School Changes Way of Doing Business," *Work America*, March 1992, pp. 2–3.

21. Carl Glickman, "Pretending Not to Know What We Know," *Educational Leadership*, May 1991, pp. 4–10; and Michael G. Fullan and Matthew B. Miles, "Getting Reform Right: What Works and What Doesn't," *Phi Delta Kappan*, June 1992, pp. 744–52.

22. George H. Kaplan, "The Great Educational Debate," *Education Week*, 8 April 1992, p. 36.

23. Haberman, op. cit.

24. John O'Neill, "National System of Standards, Exams Piloted," *ASCD Update*, October 1992, pp. 1–5.

The Total Quality Classroom

John Jay Bonstingl

Quoting Deming, this highly regarded educational consultant tells us that "the right time for attention to final outcomes in any production process — including the learning process — is at every step along the way." This article explains how and why this must happen in the classroom.

My favorite hangout is one of those rare finds in life. It's a small, family-owned neighborhood restaurant, a place where you can find just about everybody in town at one time or another. Prices are reasonable, food portions are delicious and generous, service is prompt and always given with a smile, and the table settings show a certain attention to detail.

Recently, when I went there for lunch, the place was packed. Jim, the owner, was at the door greeting incoming customers and asking those who were leaving whether they had a good time. Jim, a hands-on manager, is always at the restaurant to make sure everything is going just right. When he's not at the door, he's going from table to table, making sure his customers are satisfied. Old-fashioned quality service from a relatively young man.

He greeted me as I was shown to my table. "Jim," I commented with a smile, "I'm going to have to buy stock in this place—I've never been here when your restaurant hasn't been filled to capacity. What's your secret?"

"No secret," Jim responded, shaking his head. "We just aim to please our customers. We try to give them the best quality we can, as consistently as possible."

"Hmm," I thought aloud, "I know quite a few teachers who would love to have their students consistently producing the best quality work they're capable of doing. It seems to be getting harder and harder to motivate young people in their schoolwork."

"Sometimes it's not so easy here either," Jim replied. "Just yesterday I was training a new waiter, a college sophomore with a 3.8 average—a very bright young man. First thing, I told him, 'Here's our menu. Sit down and read it over.'

"I stressed how important it is that our waiters know absolutely everything we offer on our menu. A few minutes later, he gets up and asks, 'Okay,

Reprinted with permission from John Jay Bonstingl, educational consultant from Columbia, Maryland. The article first appeared in *Educational Leadership*, March 1992.

what do I do now?' I told him, 'Sit back down and read the menu. I want you to *know* it.' "

"And? What happened?" I asked.

Jim continued; "This bright young man tells me, 'I've read the menu. What do you want me to know about it?' It was as if he was asking me, 'What are you going to put on the exam? Tell me what you want me to know and I'll memorize it, but I won't waste my time with anything else' "

"I know what you mean, Jim," I said, thinking of the multitude of times my students have raised their hands in the middle of a lecture or experiment, cutting the process short with the bottom-line question, "Mr. B, is this going to be on the test?" The sole measure of relevance, the lone determiner or student effort wisely expended: Is it going to be on the test?

"Just yesterday," Jim continued, "a new waitress asked me how many mushrooms to put on a 12-inch pizza. Apparently, at her previous job—one of these chain restaurants—she had to follow a thick rule book, and one of the rules prescribed the exact number of mushrooms to be put onto every pizza, no more and no less.

"So I asked her: 'Do you like pizza?' and she said, 'Sure,'

" 'Okay,' I said, 'how many mushrooms do *you* like on *your* pizzas? Just do for your customers what you would like if you were in their place. You decide!'

"My toughest job," Jim concluded "is getting these kids to put themselves in the customer's shoes. I keep thinking how nice it would be if they all thought of themselves as managers. I want them to take a natural pride in their work, to make good decisions without a lot of outside advice, to act as a team, to just use their common sense. My only rule is this: Everyone who works here must always keep the customer first in mind."

I looked around at Jim's cheerful, bustling staff. "Looks like you've found the secret."

"Thanks, Jay," he responded. "But it does take a lot of hard work."

Most of the hard work Jim does with his young employees is focused on training them to take personal, thoughtful responsibility for implementing his customer-focused policy of service. "When they are first hired," Jim reflected, "many of these young people wait for me to tell them what to do, even after I put them through an intensive training program. I've got to work closely with each of them over time, to develop the characteristics I want them to exhibit—the *secret* as you put it."

Both of the employees Jim discussed with me—the college sophomore who didn't want to waste his time with the menu and the young waitress who needed instruction in mushroom placement—are actually exhibiting ideal employee behavior, according to a philosophy of work expressed early in this century by Frederick Winslow Taylor, an industrial engineer.

The Industrial Model at Work

Taylor taught American industry to view every worker as simply "a cog in the giant industrial machine, whose job could be defined and directed by

> I want them to take a natural pride in their work, to make good decisions without a lot of outside advice, to act as a team, to just use their common sense.

appropriately educated managers, administering a set of rules" (Walton 1990). Workers need not exercise any imagination or individual initiative, according to Taylor, because such action would only serve to disrupt the realization of management objectives.

Taylor's industrial model was a top-down, authoritarian structure, in which management's job was to worry about quotas and quality if necessary, while subservient workers mindlessly did management's bidding without questioning the reasons for their work or the overall plan. It was just the sort of "enlightened thinking" that Henry Ford was looking for, perfectly suited to his revolutionary new assembly-line factory. Before long, Taylor's model became the enthusiastically accepted norm among bosses throughout American industry—and quickly spread to the service and government sectors.

The Industrial Model at School

To a great extent, American education mimicked this military-industrial model of "efficient" work. Perhaps in that era such schooling was appropriate to train young people for work requiring "patience, docility, and the ability to endure boredom. Students learned to sit in orderly rows, to absorb facts by rote, and to move through the material regardless of individual differences in learning speed" (Clarke 1986).

Today's teachers and students know that system all too well. The philosophy and practice of Taylorism is still in place in many schools, industries, and government offices throughout the country. And yet, it is becoming abundantly clear that this model will not serve us well in the world of the future, where workers will need to be sharp, creative thinkers with a keen sense of intellectual curiosity and personal dedication to lifelong learning, as well as an individual commitment to the collective good.

Our entire educational system is designed to teach people to do things the one right way as defined by the authority figure.

Indeed, we are living in such a "world of the future" at this very moment. Yet our ways of responding to the challenges before us are more in tune with the perceived needs of the past than with the imperatives of our present and our future. As management consultant Robert F. Lynch tells us, "Our entire educational system is designed to teach people to do things the one right way as defined by the authority figure. We are taught to recite what we hear or read without critically interacting with the information as it moves in and out of short-term memory. In this exchange, the information leaves no tracks, and independent thinking skills are not developed" (1991).

Lynch links antiquated educational philosophies and practices with antiquated workplace philosophies and practices: "The workplace often reinforces the value of compliance. The student going into the workplace has been taught there will always be someone in charge who has the 'right' answer. Satisfying the supervisor becomes akin to getting a passing grade. Satisfying the customer is secondary or nonexistent in this system" (1991). No wonder Jim has such a difficult time training his young restaurant employees to think for themselves and to "always keep the customer first in mind."

What We Lost Along the Way

What is lost in the way we have run our schools and businesses is, of course, precious opportunities for high-quality work. We now know that, apart from the military, systems that are based on control, compliance, and command stifle creativity, loyalty, and optimal performance. In such systems, fear, cynicism, apathy, and low productivity spread like a crippling disease throughout the entire organization.

Back in the early part of the century, when literacy rates were low and common mechanical work required little or no formal schooling, Taylorism reaped abundant rewards for the industrial barons of the times. And, by the end of World War II, with foreign productive capacities decimated, American worldwide preeminence in technology, manufacturing, and trade seemed to be forever secured.

But then something happened that the leaders of American industry are just now beginning to fully understand and acknowledge. The rest of the world began to catch up with the United States. Today, competition in hundreds of highly competitive fields comes from European, Asian, and Latin American companies. Most noticeably, it comes from the Japanese, whose postwar "economic miracle" has enabled Japan, a country with virtually no indigenous natural resources, to rise Phoenix-like from the ashes to attain its current position of strength in world finance and trade.

The imperative for our nation is clear. According to a study by the National Center on Education and the Economy, America's choice amounts to this: Either we commit now to high performance in the processes and products of our schools and industries, along with the development of intrinsically motivated and highly skilled young people, or we consign more than 70 percent of our workers to increasingly lower wages and put our heritage truly at risk as the global economy washes over us.

According to this report, "What the world is prepared to pay high prices and high wages for now is quality, variety, and responsiveness to changing consumer tastes. . . . 'Tayloristic' methods are not well suited to these goals. Firms struggling to apply the traditional methods of work organization to more complex technologies, increased quality requirements, and proliferating product variety often create cumbersome and inefficient bureaucracies" (National Center on Education and the Economy 1990).

The alternative, the report says, is to reduce bureaucracy "by giving frontline workers more responsibility. Workers are asked to use judgment and make decisions." The results are enhanced productivity and improved quality, essential factors contributing to economic prosperity and greater democratic participation in the workplace and in our society at large.

> Either we commit now to high performance in the processes and products of our schools and industries, or we consign more than 70 percent of our workers to increasingly lower wages.

In the school, our students and teachers are the frontline workers. How can we rethink the schooling process so that young people have greater opportunities to develop the self-direction and creative decision-making skills so essential to success in the emerging global economy and American workplace?

Deming Enters the Picture

W. Edwards Deming has profound insights to share, as educators grapple with this challenge. Deming is the American whom Japanese industry leaders today regard as the crucial factor in their postwar "economic miracle." Hearing of his reputation as an expert in statistical quality control, the Japanese invited Deming to come to their country in 1950 to teach them how to produce consistently high-quality goods and services. Over the span of four decades, Deming taught Japanese owners, managers, and workers the principles and practices of his philosophy. Those of us who can remember when "Made in Japan" was a cause for laughter and derision are now marveling at how far Japan has come in a single generation.

Until a decade ago, Deming's teachings were largely unknown or ignored in this country. Then, on June 24, 1980, NBC broadcast "If Japan Can . . . Why Can't We?", a documentary that riveted America's attention on the "miracle" and the prophet who had helped Japan achieve it through a profound dedication of every Japanese worker and the entire Japanese society to the principles of total quality production. In October 1991, PBS aired a follow-up documentary series entitled "Quality . . . Or Else!", underscoring the urgency of our current situation.

Today, the Ford Motor Company, IBM, Xerox, Westinghouse, and a host of other companies are adopting "total quality" as their operational byword. They are redefining their reasons for existence around the requirement to service the customer first. Bureaucracies are being re-sculpted and hierarchies flattened to give more control over quality to those on the front lines.

We are beginning to realize that products of consistently high quality are the natural result of consistently high-quality processes. The most successful organizations carefully build quality of process and product into their long-term strategic planning as well as their day-to-day operations. Ford reflects this idea in company slogans: "We build quality in!" and "Quality is Job One!" When dedication to quality is adhered to at every point in the production process, quality products—those that serve the customer's needs first—are the consistent results.

American companies that have become known throughout the world for mediocre products, inefficient delivery systems, and inadequate attention to customer needs are now seeing their market share shift to foreign manufacturers whose products have established reputations for consistently high quality and consumer satisfaction.

Insights for Education

Likewise, in American education we have seen a dramatic increase in student cynicism and apathy in recent years. Media attention to low SAT and other standardized test scores, not to mention international comparisons of student achievement, have led to the current national education reform movement. Classroom teachers have very often felt the sting of public upbraiding, as blame for the inadequacies of the system have been so often focused singularly upon them.

Deming would take issue with the assertion that individual teachers are to blame for our nation's educational malaise. "Don't fix blame; fix the system," he suggests.

Our students do not come into our classrooms from a vacuum. Their families have had them in their own care for a far longer time than any one teacher will have them in a course. Families are part of the educational system, and yet this generation of young people may well be the first in our country to have grown up without learning their first lessons in responsibility, competency, cooperation, and compassion at home. The implications for education are staggering. Later lessons in these essential personal qualities will come at much greater costs, if they are ever learned at all. Consistent family support and interaction with the school is paramount for student success in education and in life.

Within the school system there must be change as well. Administrators must rethink their role, allowing greater managerial freedom to teachers in their work with students. Teachers are the administration's frontline workers. Administrators and teachers are not natural adversaries. Administrators who think of themselves as advisors and teammates with their teachers will reap great rewards in terms of teacher productivity, school morale, and community relations.

Teachers, in such a nurturing environment, will be more likely to nurture their students, to see themselves as advisors and teammates with their students, rather than power-wielders and deliverers of "the right answer." Teachers will use a wide variety of methods to help their young charges develop their ability to set goals, to apply creative ideas and consistently high-quality effort toward the achievement of those goals (alone and in cooperation with adults and fellow students), and to take pride of workmanship in their efforts.

Teachers will use tests as prescriptive and diagnostic tools, rather than as a final "inspection" of the student's learning.

Teachers will use tests as prescriptive and diagnostic tools, rather than as a final "inspection" of the student's learning. As Deming points out, the right time for attention to final outcomes in any production process—including the learning process—at every step along the way. Industry beginning to realize that quality assurance by inspection is inherently wasteful; it puts all the responsibility for the quality of the end product on the inspector at the end of the line. Total quality requires a commitment quality by everyone in the production process. In education, that commitment must be made at every level, from the superintendent, the school board, and the community, to the people who do the primary work of education: the teacher-student teams.

The whole idea of grades and student assessment must also be reexamined. Is there a place in the quality-focused school for the bell-shaped curve and other artificial determiners of success and failure? If our young people are to succeed, should a given percentage of them be made to feel inferior? What might be the results if industries in this country consciously set out to produce mediocrity or inferiority in two-thirds of *their* products?

Deming (now 93 and going strong) would suggest that undue attention to short-term benefits—whether they are monthly wages or quarterly corporate profit-loss statements or course grades—is inherently destructive of potentially positive long-term results.

Indeed, the entire issue of grades as assessment symbols will need to be rethought. If nothing succeeds like success, why do we seem to structure schooling for boredom, apathy, and marginal student involvement, rather than structuring the work that teachers and students do together for ultimate success? In what other industry do we bring people into the work environment without training them in the skills needed for success?

A Broader View of Education

Ultimately, the purpose of education must be redefined. Education, in the new paradigm, will not be a delivery system for collections of fragmented information in the guise of curriculums. Rather, education will be a process that encourages continual progress through the improvement of one's abilities, the expansion of one's interests, and the growth of one's character. Such an education would be good for the individual, good for the economy, and good for the commonweal we call society.

This vision of education will be achievable, however, only when we, individually and collectively, commit our resources to the continuous process of human improvement. Quality is our "Job One"—a commitment we must each make to ourselves, and to one another.

References

Clarke, A. C. (1986). *July 20, 2019: Life in the 21st Century.* New York: Macmillan, p. 76.

Lynch, R. F. (April 1991). "Shedding the Shackles of George Patton, Henry Ford, and First-Grade Teachers." *Quality Progress*, p. 64.

National Center on Education and the Economy. (1990). *America's Choice: High Skills or Low Wages!* Rochester, N.Y.: National Center on Education and the Economy, executive summary, p. 2.

Walton, M. (1990). *Deming Management at Work.* New York: G. P. Putnam's Sons, p. 16.

John Jay Bonstingl is an international education consultant and textbook author. Bonstingl can be contacted at P.O. Box 810. Columbia, MD 21044.

Public Sector

HIGHER EDUCATION

TQM in Higher Education

Ronald L. Heilman

This essay by consulting editor Ron Heilman, the head of the Center for Quality and Productivity at the University of Wisconsin, Milwaukee, and president of the National Educational Quality Initiative, was written especially for this book. In it, Dr. Heilman provides a succinct summary of the state of quality in higher education. For more information about Dr. Heilman and information on how you can contact him, see the Acknowledgments section in the front matter of this book.

Overview

During 1993, higher education continued to be dragged, "kicking and screaming" toward an initial awareness of TQM. Despite over 40 years of success in Japanese industry, 15 years of development in U.S. industry, and 5 years of high visibility for TQM via the Malcolm Baldrige National Quality Award, higher education remains largely in a state of denial.

The acronym TQM and the growing number of variations, such as TQA, TQI, CQI, and other such initiatives, have yet to enter the vocabulary of most disciplines. Even in the disciplines traditionally aligned with the business world such as engineering, TQM is viewed a new concept. Acceptance in business schools remains limited, but many business schools have at least introduced survey courses and integrated bits and pieces of TQM's elements into existing courses. A few business schools offer a major or a degree in Quality. A small number of universities have begun to use the TQM philosophy to restructure or reengineer administrative operations at the system, campus, and/or school or college levels. Fortunately, the stories of successes attributable to these efforts are reaching many in the academic world at a time when the public's desire for greater accountability from all public (and private) institutions is escalating rapidly. Therefore, it is a safe prediction that

TQM will be accorded for greater acceptance in higher education in the coming years than it enjoys today.

Early Starters

A very few institutions of higher education began some form of TQM effort on their own initiative in the mid-to-later eighties. Among these is Babson College where TQM was introduced by William F. Glavin upon assuming the presidency after a 34-year industry career that culminated at Xerox. Under his leadership, TQM has permeated nearly every facet of Babson's operation from administration to curriculum and research.

TQM has permeated nearly every facet of Babson's operation from administration to curriculum and research.

At Fordham University, Professor Joyce N. Orsini was instrumental in introducing the teachings of W. Edwards Deming into the MBA curriculum, which resulted in the 1992 initiation of The Deming Scholars MBA Program. The program's intellectual foundation is Deming's "System of Profound Knowledge" and features learning cycles combining classroom teaching and internships.

Quality principles were introduced at the George Washington University Medical Center (GWUMC) in 1987 at a time when it was operating in the red. Successfully implementing the principles of continuous improvement into everyday activities throughout GWUMC helped achieve turnaround—the Center is now operating profitably. The internationally renown statisticians Professors George Box and William G. Hunter at the University of Wisconsin, Madison, were early advocates of Quality. They helped create an environment at the University of Wisconsin that led to the formation of a Quality Office operating as an adjunct to the Chancellor's Office. Effective in 1992, assistance in the implementation of Quality principles in being provided throughout the University of Wisconsin System (26 campuses, 140,000+ students) through a Continuous Quality Improvement Consultant Office, which operates in a staff capacity to the UW System President.

The preceding list is far short of exhaustive. It is intended only to demonstrate that there were TQM pioneers in higher education that have had some successes.

A Wake-Up Call

In 1991, one of the higher education's many unrecognized customers issued a wake-up call. A published TQM University Challenge was issued by a consortium of leading American firms. The challenge was to develop creative and comprehensive means of introducing TQM into the curriculum of higher education, especially schools of business and engineering. Universities submitting winning proposals would have the opportunity to send 100 faculty and administrators to a week-long education symposium about TQM as practiced in the real world. Approximately 25 universities responded to the Challenge. Eight winning proposals were selected: Carnegie-Mellon, Georgia Tech, MIT, North Carolina State, Purdue, Rochester Institute of Technology, Tuskegee, and University of Wisconsin, Madison.

Later in 1991, IBM issued an additional TQM challenge to U.S. universities. It, too, was designed to encourage universities to introduce TQM into their curricula. The "carrot" was $1 million in cash or $3 million in IBM equipment or any combination thereof. Over three hundred universities responded. Again, eight winning proposals were selected: Clark Atlanta University and Southern College of Technology (joint entry); Georgia Institute of Technology; Oregon State University; Pennsylvania State University; Rochester Institute of Technology; University of Houston, Clear Lake; University of Maryland; and University of Wisconsin, Madison.

Both of these challenges received a great deal of publicity and have achieved the objective of heightening the awareness of TQM among educators in higher education. Whether heightened awareness will translate into sufficiently widespread action remains to be seen. But the initial curricular changes are being implemented in 1993 with the expectation that they will be well received thereby triggering additional integration of TQM in both curriculum and university operations.

Highlights of 1993

The year 1993 may prove to be a watershed for TQM in education. Consider the following:

- Governors continued to take a leadership role in promoting Quality in education. The success of the National Quality & Education Conference hosted by Governor Ann Richards has led to commitment for a series. The governor of Colorado hosted this in 1993, and the governor of Minnesota will do so in 1994.
- ASQC officially established an education division.
- The premier issue of the *Quality Management Journal* was published. This journal will meet a key need of faculty interested in doing research in Quality as a discipline. There had been no recognized scholarly journal dedicated to Quality, thereby denying Quality status as a discipline.
- The National Educational Quality Initiative, a nonprofit organization with nation-wide membership dedicated to introducing the Quality Sciences into all facets and levels of education, successfully completed its first full year of operation.
- The American Assembly of Collegiate Schools of Business, the national accrediting body for business schools, changed its evaluation criteria such that business schools will have to be more quality focused to pass in the future.
- The University of Wisconsin, Madison, Graduate School of Business was a finalist, not a winner, in the *USA Today*/RIT Quality Cup Award Competition.

The above milestones, together with many other achievements relating to Quality in higher education, combined to make 1993 a banner year. However, as stated earlier, many educators remain in a state of denial. In a survey sent to nearly 1,000 deans of business and engineering schools, one question was "How important is it to teach principles and methods of total quality at your school?" Of the 515 respondents, 57 percent of the deans indicated it was extremely important. However, when asked their perception of their respective facilities' views, the deans indicated that only 12 percent of the faculty would find it extremely important.

Another dampener was the experience of SRI International. In March 1993, SRI distributed a proposal throughout higher education to undertake "An Assessment and Benchmarking Survey of Total Quality Management Practices in American Colleges and Universities." SRI proposed to comprehensively assess the practices and experiences of 100 to 150 colleges and universities. Part of the output was to be a networking directory. This was structured as a subscription study. It was never started due to a lack of support.

Summary

Quality gained a significant foothold in higher education in 1993. Much resistance remains to be overcome. But the events of 1993 will launch new efforts that will help propel Quality to greater prominence in 1994 and beyond.

Total Quality & Academic Practice
The Idea We've Been Waiting for?

Peter T. Ewell

This article by a senior associate at the National Center for Higher Education Management Systems explores the potential and controversies for quality management as the proper philosphical underpinning for managing colleges and universities today and into the future.

In the academy, where doubt is a foundation of discourse, few things arouse more suspicion than the obviously fashionable. And when the fashionable is accompanied by demands to change time-honored practices, and those demands are delivered with a rhetoric of messianic conviction—as is often the case these days with Total Quality Management—instinctive distaste quickly turns to rejection.

Much of the academy's initial reaction to Total Quality (TQ) has been gut-level and negative; until this stage is passed, what good will come of TQ is hard to determine. Yet, there is undoubtedly something to the movement. Beneath the hype, TQ does seem to contain new insights about how we can and should operate in higher education. Just as importantly, these insights seem tailored to the times. Hard as they may be to digest, TQ's root concepts intrigue growing numbers of professionals in higher education, if only for their raw transformational power.

To those of us who, for the past eight years or so, have watched and pushed along the development of assessment with similar hopes of achieving real change, the dynamic is familiar. A novel set of reform-oriented concepts suddenly, against all expectations, takes off as a high visibility topic of discussion; at the same time, it engenders profound intellectual discomfort. Like assessment in its early years, many of the acrimonious debates about the merits of Total Quality occur among people who in fact know very little about it. And like assessment in its early days, the claims of both proponents and critics appear overblown.

Strikingly similar, too, are the attempts to limit domain. The commonly heard canard that Total Quality is "all right when applied to the administrative side of the house but it's inappropriate for instruction," for instance,

From *Change, The Magazine of Higher Learning*, Vol. 25, No. 3, pp. 49–55, May/June 1993. Reprinted with permission the Helen Dwight Reid Foundation. Published by Heldref Publications, 1319 18th St., N.W., Washington, D.C. 20036-1802. Copyright © 1993.

echoes earlier assertions that while assessment techniques might fruitfully be applied to basic skills or professional study, they could hardly be used to examine the ineffable outcomes of traditional academic disciplines.

Equally familiar is the mad scramble to get started. Exponential growth occurred each year in the proportion of institutions reporting assessment activities on ACE's Campus Trends survey (a proportion that topped 90 percent two years ago). The same appears to be happening now for claims of TQM efforts; a recent *Business Week* survey reported 61 percent of college presidents averring involvement in Total Quality—this compared with at best a dozen or so campus implementation efforts as recently as two years ago.

Both movements rest ultimately upon a similar image of knowledge-driven, continuous improvement. Unlike earlier management adventures such as MBO and Zero-Based Budgeting, which were *applied* to the academic enterprise, Total Quality—like assessment before it—demands fundamental change in academic *structures* and in the way the actual work is done.

But the two stories also show revealing differences. For one, the stimulus for involvement is different. Initial institutional reactions to assessment in the mid-'80s were decisively colored by the concept's early (and partly coincidental) linkage with the issue of public accountability. Assessment thus evoked the attention of institutions but, apart from a vague appreciation that something ought to be done to improve undergraduate teaching and learning, assessment *itself* did not appear to most campus parties as a needed response to a visible problem.

> Unlike earlier management adventures such as MBO and Zero-Based Budgeting, Total Quality demands fundamental change in academic *structures* and in the way the actual work is done.

The problems Total Quality presumes to address, in contrast, are palpable and urgent. The soaring attendance at "quality" conferences in higher education last year was motivated less by a general desire to improve than by institutional need to cope with an increasingly desperate set of fiscal circumstances. Partly as a result—and this is a second important difference—institutional involvement with Total Quality has often been stimulated from the top. Assessment in its early years only rarely enjoyed the active sponsorship of presidents and provosts, but those are the very people championing the TQ movement. Similarly, the institutions first identified with assessment were widely recognized as innovative but were otherwise not well known. In contrast, the Total Quality movement counts in its front ranks a large proportion of universities standing high on the reputational pecking order.

The most important difference, though is that the *reach* of TQ is from the outset more comprehensive. While only a few engaged in assessment really felt its hidden potential to radically transform teaching and learning, TQ's change agenda is up-front from the beginning. A major stumbling block to the effectiveness of assessment as actually implemented by most institutions, for instance, was the fact that the results of evidence-gathering often went nowhere because a structure of utilization was assumed, not created. But TQ claims to operate on all parts of the system simultaneously; in the compelling monosyllabic syntax of the Shewhart Cycle, "plan, do, check, act"—a scheme that not just welcomes but demands information about performance.

What should we make of these two stories? As historians habitually remind us, significant realignments require both new ideas and altered circumstances. For assessment, the ideas were surely there but too little in the structure of incentives facing institutions induced many of them to take new directions. Is the nascent "quality movement" in higher education fated to follow a similar path?

An adequate answer, I think, depends on our response to two related queries. First, are the times really different and if so, do they in fact require a new way of managing? Second, is the "it" of Total Quality really any different from the many ideas (including assessment) that have been advanced over the years to "fix" higher education—or indeed, from many of the academy's current practices, whatever they may be called? If the answer to both of these complex questions is "yes," Total Quality may indeed be the idea we've been waiting for.

Bad Times or Changing Times?

Certainly there is little disagreement that colleges and universities face difficult times, perhaps the most difficult in five decades. But though everyone will agree that things are tough, not all concur that they are *different*. A great many academics believe that higher education's current fiscal woes, however deep, are temporary, and can be managed by the usual combination of judicious belt-tightening and vigorous budgetary lobbying until the inevitable recovery occurs.

At least on the public side of higher education finance, much of the evidence now suggests otherwise. First, we appear to be up against a fundamental structural condition. In growing numbers of states, 80–85 percent of the budget is now tied up in entitlements, court-ordered spending, and restrictions of one kind or another; in this context, higher education has become the "budget balancer"—the last-in-line piece of discretionary spending remaining after mandatory expenditures are accounted for. A second element of the problem is that taxpayers simply will not support further increases, however worthy the cause—a fact demonstrated convincingly by a series of bleak state electoral results last November. These conditions, together with more general trends in the economy, suggest strongly that higher education will need to do what it does for less for the foreseeable future.

The logical cutback strategy of doing *less* by limiting access is increasingly unavailable. It rarely goes unnoticed in hard-hit states like California, for example, that attempts to reduce access in the name of financial exigency occur at precisely the time that large numbers of minorities are poised to enter higher education. Politicians have been unusually sensitive to the charge that "efficiency" or "belt-tightening" achieved this way is merely another name for discrimination.

Some people in public higher education maintain that while these fiscal conditions are real and permanent, they do not in fact require massive changes in the ways colleges and universities do business. Under their scenario, expected funding shortfalls can be made up for on the revenue side by shifting costs to students and by developing more vigorous alternative fundraising approaches. Inevitable threats to access can be addressed by funding protected classes of potential students directly—the so-called "high tuition/high aid" strategy now being visibly pursued as a policy option by many states.

But the evidence is equally unkind to this alternative, at least in the long run. The "high aid" component of this strategy is subject to the same dynamics of state budgeting noted earlier; its "high tuition" component will rapidly make public institutions aware of what the privates have known for years— that consumer choice in higher education is increasingly unpredictable but ever more demanding. Pursuing such a policy may mean accepting major changes in what public higher education offers and how it delivers it.

This combination—structurally induced fiscal stringency in the face of an increasingly demanding customer—recalls vividly, of course, the operating environment of U.S. industry over the past decade. Fundamental to this milieu is a demand for *quality service* delivered at *reduced provider cost*—a linkage that, for higher education, has been virtually unimaginable. But it was just such a linkage that spawned industry's widespread engagement with Total Quality, less out of complete conviction than through a growing awareness that traditional alternatives could forever remain inadequate. Budget shortfalls in the 15-to-20-percent magnitude were the minimum required to get industry's attention in the '80s; we have them now and they will be increasingly hard to ignore.

> Fundamental to this milieu is a demand for *quality service* delivered at *reduced provider cost*—a linkage that, for higher education, has been virtually unimaginable.

New Ideas or Just New Words?

Closely following the typical academic's initial rejection of TQ's language is a second-glance flash of recognition: when suitable translated, most of these things we appear to do already. If the first reaction moves us to righteousness, the second induces smugness; the rest of the world, after all, is only just now catching up. Smugness or no, there is more than a little truth to this contention. Many of the core ideas of Total Quality do have compelling academic counterparts. But things are also not that simple, as even a brief analysis of some of TQ's ideas will attest. Consider, for instance, how some of these ideas fare when viewed in the context of traditional academic culture.

■ *Decentralized Management and Empowerment.* Perhaps the most visible aspect of Total Quality is its call for a new kind of management. Instead of relying on traditional hierarchical structures that optimize regularity and control, TQ's philosophy emphasizes management's roles in setting broad direction and facilitating processes while decentralizing operational decisions to the level at which the work is done. Ideal managers become "coaches"—able to motivate concerted action by communicating the big picture while at the same time creating an atmosphere of openness that legitimizes new ideas and allows the creativity of all to come forward.

One of the appeals of this "new" philosophy to the academy, quite naturally, is that it appears on the surface to be quite close to what we do already.

Participatory management is obligatory in academic settings, and faculty constitute what is arguably the most "empowered" workforce on earth.

But surface parallels can be deceiving. The "empowerment of Total Quality is not about individuals but about *work teams* who for the most part are directly engaged in production—the people who cooperatively make a particular product or who own a specific process. Decentralized decision making in this context is not driven by any notions of right or entitlement but by the eminently practical insight that team members are the people who know best what's wrong and who should have the ability to fix it. With this conceptual grounding, TQ's seeming affirmation of traditional notions of individual faculty autonomy begins rapidly to fade.

How well does a focus on "teams" fit our own principal unit of academic organization, the disciplinary department? For some things, quite well. Departments do often function as work teams, and are given broad latitude to do so when it comes to such activities as the "production" of disciplinary majors or graduate degrees. With respect to research, though, despite a vague community of interest, they function more as administrative conveniences or holding companies. And with respect to such cross-cutting functions as undergraduate general education, they function politically, or not at all.

Hence the role of management. Beyond creating broad organizational vision, management explicitly comes into play in TQM organizations when an individual work team either lacks the resources to address on its own a local problem or, more significantly, when its process bumps into the interests and operations of another work team with a different agenda and mode of operation. In the latter case, a "cross-functional team" is created with authority to address the mutual problem.

At first glance again, this looks a lot like the way we handle topics like general education. But is it really? One major difference is that TQ's "cross-functional work teams" never stray far from the operational level; unlike the rotating, generalist committees that nominally preside over collegiate functions, TQ teams are built around collaborative responsibility-taking among the doers of a function.

Another difference with teams is that they typically begin with data. Rather than conceptualizing general education from first principles and negotiating its consequences, as faculty committees are likely to do, they begin with a particular *empirical* problem and trace its implications upward through the system. Such an approach to general education, again, might start deep inside the curriculum with an analysis of how specific prerequisite skills are built, and how they do or do not transfer effectively into the contexts where they are later required. And it might rest heavily on a prior look at actual course-taking behavior and student performance.

In short, for Total Quality, organization follows processes and exists to serve them. Empowerment, though a basic value, is a means, not an end.

■ *Focus on Core Processes.* As this discussion suggests, the "process" is TQ's basic unit of the analysis. And many have seen in this an apparent reversal of

> How well does a focus on "teams" fit our own principal unit of academic organization, the disciplinary department? For some things, quite well.

assessment's prior focus on outcomes—a perception reinforced by Total Quality's vocal rejection of an "inspection" route to quality assurance. Yet Total Quality depends critically upon a knowledge of outcomes, whether at the end—the resulting market reaction and customer satisfaction—or on the "shop floor," where results are continuously monitored by workers themselves at every step. Assessment occurs at all levels but is rooted in actual processes, for only there can you realize what's needed for better outcomes.

What exactly is a process? Consistent with TQ's industrial origins, its basic model is a production line consisting, in essence, of an ordered sequence of defined operations resulting in a specified product or service; critical features of a process are that it is replicable and can be documented. If it cannot be *described*, it by definition cannot be improved; hence a major preoccupation of TQ practitioners lies in identifying core processes and determining exactly how they work.

This notion of process surely fits many administrative operations in colleges and universities. The interesting question is whether the notion can help improve our central business of teaching and learning. Though loosely intended as "learning plans," most curricula are not really specified as such. Few, in fact, meet TQ's critical test of a process: the ability to flow-chart key events by noting the specific points in required course sequences at which particular skills will be acquired and reinforced. But the analogy is intriguing, and a number of campuses have found such attempts at "mapping" worth the effort—especially when they uncover places where presumed connections among courses are not happening as intended. Given typical curricular organizations in which faculty are dispersed across discrete classrooms with little incentive to cooperate, such an exercise at least provides a way to start conversations about improvement.

TQ's core philosophy, in essence, is the principles of academic inquiry applied to ourselves and what we do.

■ *Continuous Improvement.* Arguably, a belief in "continuous improvement" lies at the core of all scholarship. And indeed, organized research practice in major university settings—especially in "big science"—seems at first glance to embody fully the pattern of ongoing critique and resulting refinement that TQ proponents call for. It often proves useful as a point of departure for faculty conversation to point out explicitly that TQ's core philosophy (like assessment's), in essence, is the principles of academic inquiry applied to ourselves and what we do.

But it is hardly research that needs fixing. Our central preoccupation with quality has instead been in undergraduate education, where the established core values appear quite different. Despite the occasional ripples of the "content of the canon" debate, these values remain for most faculty essentially, and often deliberately, conservative. For better or worse, instruction at the undergraduate level is viewed by most as the transmission of a delimited domain, whether this be conceived straightforwardly as a body of knowledge, or as has become more lately fashionable, as a set of outcomes to be achieved. Ironically, in fact, assessment may have helped to reinforce this conservatism by reifying the notion that teaching and learning should be viewed from the perspective of a fixed set of instructional goals rather than, as was the movement's original intent, inducing ongoing examination of both goals and practices in the light of obtained results.

Applied to undergraduate education, therefore, TQ's notion of "continuous improvement" can help open the door not only to an investigation of potential changes in instructional technique in pursuit of fixed outcomes, but also to the question of exactly *what* those outcomes should be. But while questioning of this kind is surely healthy—and is not entirely unknown to us—TQ provides a very definite picture of what "improvement" ought to look like: "quality is conformance to requirements." In this context, "conformance" means reduction in variation, while "requirements," of course, are principally shaped by customers. Both of these concepts have interesting academic implications.

■ *Reducing Variation.* Often overshadowed by the more popular "empowerment" dimensions of Total Quality is its original grounding in the technology of statistical quality control. An important root concept here—and the principal object of this technology—is the distinction between "special" and "common" causes of variation. For proponents of Total Quality, processes are "in control" when outcome variations occur within pre-specified statistical limits, and a primary objective is to bring such systems in control through the gradual elimination of myriad "special causes" that are largely unrelated to one another. Until this occurs, improvement of the underlying process itself is impossible, because we are unable to determine systematically what is wrong.

This is a powerful insight, but in the context of improving teaching and learning, where exactly does it belong? Consider, for instance, the way we typically assign grades. Most current grading practices rest in essence upon the variation within a given non-random body of students around its own mean of performance. Instructors unconsciously reinforce the assignment of such variation to "special causes" outside the process of instruction itself. The ascribed special causes tend to be attributed to the student in the form of presumed variations in ability, motivation, and effort. Examination of the resulting grading pattern may tell us something about individual students— as indeed, it was designed to do—but it is virtually useless for informing the instructional process.

Together with a more general view of the negative consequences of evaluating individual performance, this is a reason why Deming, for one, would have us eliminate grading entirely. It is also a major reason why assessment arose initially—because current academic evaluation practices provided no good way to obtain needed data for the improvement of group performance. Criterion-based assessment schemes like those proposed by assessment are of value precisely because they *can* be used to identify and address common causes of variation.

But is reduced variation really what we want? In the development of a wide variety of basic, prerequisite, or professional skills, the answer surely is "yes": we want *all* students to learn fully what needs to be learned. But in the realm of higher-order thinking and the traditional domains of liberal education—where the development of individual voice and style becomes a paramount value—the answer is far from clear. What is important is to sort out these issues from the beginning, *before* we automatically attempt to apply TQ technology.

■ *Serving Customers.* At few points in the Total Quality conversation does discussion become so heated as around the word "customer." Partly, of course, this is because the term itself vividly signals TQ's commercial origins. More subtly, it is because knowledge "in service" to anyone—whatever their label—directly threatens the academy's core myth of independent inquiry, conducted on its own terms and for its own sake. Particularly when applied to instruction, the term also suggests a surrender of expertise and authority by those assumed to have both, to parties who by definition are unaware of what they do not know.

As the latter point suggests, it is when the term "customer" gets applied to students that things get sticky. In some cases, certainly, the label applies perfectly. Students are the direct customer of such campus services as parking, food services, registration, or the library. As consumers with particular wants and means, they (and their parents) also make the initial "purchase decision" about which college to attend or whether to attend at all, and they will continue to make such choices as long as they are enrolled. In both these areas, TQ logic seems to fit, and its admonition to know and meet customer needs is good advice. In cases where the student "customer" may be badly informed about what he or she actually needs and how best to get it, such TQ notions as "leading" or "delighting" the customer can come into play—the objective being less to react blindly to customer demands than to *shape* or *anticipate* them.

From the perspective of traditional instruction, the student becomes the "raw material" of a specified process of production.

But once inside instruction, the "customer" label no longer fits. From the perspective of traditional instruction, the student then becomes the "raw material" of a specified process of production (a point that recalls the earlier "value-added" metaphor of assessment). In cases such as basic skills instruction or technical training where the "raw material" analogy does apply, TQ practices such as mapping the process, determining its connections and how they fail, and bringing it into control make considerable sense. And because a college can apply TQ concepts in the presence of what production engineers term an "intelligent product"—one able to provide us with ongoing data about its own condition while remaining a part of the process—these techniques can in fact work even better for us than in industry. An obvious application of this logic is classroom research.

In most instructional settings, however, students are more than just raw materials. Cooperative learning settings, active learning strategies, and independent work outside the classroom render them a part of the "workforce" as well, "constructors" of their own knowledge who participate decisively in the "management" of their own learning. Though advised by college personnel, they typically make most of their own curricular choices and remain free to allocate their own time and level of engagement.

So what exactly is a student from the Total Quality perspective? On the one hand, lack of a straightforward answer suggests that TQ concepts don't fit well. More compellingly, it suggests that any "answer" depends upon the particular student role and piece of the process that we are talking about.

If students are not in all cases "customers," then who are our customers? Again the answers depend upon the level at which the question is posed. At the highest level, for public institutions especially, one viable answer is society itself. More particularly, it is the taxpayers who pay the bills and who increasingly expect a demonstrable return on their investment. Much of the escalating accountability debate in higher education can usefully be seen in this light. Arguably, our accountability agenda might be better served by a proactive perspective on our part that consciously recognizes society's rights as a customer.

Internally, at the operational level, our customers are one another—whether exchange occurs among entire institutions, as in the case of articulation and transfer, among academic units within institutions, as in the case of service course instruction and prerequisite policies, or among individual faculty as teaching colleagues. Indeed, it is often surprising when talking with faculty how quickly brick-wall resistance to the term "customer" evaporates when the term is applied not to students, to potential employers, or to society in general, but to themselves and one another in a network of customer-supplier relationships across a curriculum.

> It is often surprising when talking with faculty how quickly brick-wall resistance to the term "customer" evaporates when the term is applied to themselves and one another in a network of customer-supplier relationships across a curriculum.

As these brief musings may suggest, a number of core elements in TQ practice indeed have echoes in things we do. But by celebrating these echoes too loudly, or by picking and choosing among them, we run the risk of unknowingly making of Total Quality something that it is not. Evidence of this kind of transmutation is visible in some specific syndromes of early implementation that I've recently observed, and that can put the institutions that exhibit them badly off track.

One is a "Planning as Usual" syndrome that confuses Total Quality with old-fashioned linear goal-setting and strategic planning. Though this approach effectively picks up TQ's emphasis on strong leadership and the creation of organizational vision, it fails to appreciate TQ's essential link with operational processes and the empowerment of work teams that own them. The danger here is familiar: effective things happen in the short term through the constant intervention of committed dynamic leadership, but TQ's critical "infrastructure" of cross-functional teams never gets created at the level where the work gets done. The result is also familiar: institutional "planning" at the top never connects to the dozens of operational decisions made daily across campus.

A second trap is what might be called the "Touchy-Feely Ownership Syndrome." Here TQ's insistence upon decentralization and empowerment is confused with sixties-style participatory management—using such mechanisms as Quality Circles, T-Groups, and the like to directly foster a sense of organizational membership and empowerment. The difficulty here is a failure to recognize that TQ's notion of empowerment is intended less to serve the worker than the process—and its customers. As a result, institutions pursuing this path fail to connect these attempts to create organizational loyalty to the bottom line of actually *acting on* data or suggestions for change. We've seen this syndrome before in things such as program review: people feel good about the process for a while, but soon cease to invest their time when it fails to deliver.

A third difficulty can be labelled the "MBO Syndrome": an institution adopts Total Quality's statistical tools whole hog, but falls into the trap of using them to create fixed targets of performance. Techniques such as "benchmarking"—intended to guide continuous improvement—are instead rolled out as high-stakes, hard-point objectives against which unit and individual performance will be judged. The result is a predictable return to control-oriented management, countered by statistical gamesmanship on the part of those assigned to attain such targets. Instead, TQ proponents remind us that statistical variation is natural and that individuals cannot be held responsible and sanctioned for things over which they have no control.

A final trap is the "Pleasing the Customer Syndrome," which fabricates a strict constructionist version of TQ's core injunction about customer service and applies it directly to students. The result is a narrowly reactive approach where the recognized bottomline is immediate student satisfaction or, as one horrified faculty member recently put it, "where the inmates are running the asylum." While we surely do need improvements in service to students, this approach neglects the key TQ concept of actively shaping customer reaction by anticipating and exceeding current requirements. It also fails to recognize and develop the multiple roles of students in the learning process as a guide to improvement.

Each of these scenarios suggests the folly of direct translation and fragmentary application. The key to avoiding them, of course, is to recognize that Total Quality is *total*—its pieces must fit together. Many of the pieces *are* familiar; the "total" is what's new.

Making such varied pieces in fact fit together as part of a transformed philosophy of practice and a new organizational vision is something that will not come easily to the academy. If we are serious, we can neither adapt TQ practices piecemeal nor import them wholesale from others. As every industry has learned before us, the challenge will be to grow our own version of quality management—a task that involves a far more comprehensive process of conceptual development than has up to now marked our engagement.

But *are* we serious? Certainly the stimulus for change is present, and Total Quality ideas seem rich in potential insight. But an uncertain track record with innovation in the past makes it far too early for us to declare *this* one, at last, to be *the* one.

Peter T. Ewell is senior associate at the National Center for Higher Education Management Systems (NCHEMS) in Boulder, Colorado.

> The key to avoiding them, of course, is to recognize that Total Quality is *total*—its pieces must fit together.

Phoenix: Quantum Quality at Maricopa

Kathleen E. Assar

The author, vice president of academic and student affairs at Bunker Hill Community College in Boston, profiles the successful implementation of TQM at one of the largest community college systems in the United States. She documents the resounding success of this approach throughout the school.

Maricopa is the second largest multicollege system in the country, exceeded only by the Los Angeles system; it ranks among the nation's leading colleges in the use of computers and telecommunications. In 1992 it was selected by *U.S. News & World Report* as one of the best community college districts in the nation; Paul Elsner, its long-time chancellor, is widely regarded as one of the most effective college leaders in the nation. Given Maricopa's size, standing, and leadership, the fact of its systemwide commitment to TQM made a lot of us in higher education sit up and take notice.

This new initiative is not the result of Maricopa having surplus revenues to throw at a fancy new project. Quite the contrary, the district has had to reduce its operating budget this year, with fiscal constraints and budget-cutting expected to continue for at least two more years.

But vision is not in short supply at Maricopa. Indeed, the notion of quality improvement has been present in several enterprises of longer standing. Its Think Tank, for example, is dedicated to coalescing any and all resources to help ensure that youth remain in the education system and make the most of the educational opportunities before them. The Think Tank's new agenda is systemic change, and it knows TQM in the schools is about to become a big issue. More recently Maricopa began working with the Pew Charitable Trusts to develop an urban compact that would tie it to the schools and social-welfare agencies in ways that would make "the system" work for each child.

What, then, led Maricopa to decide that its future lies in continuous quality improvement (CQI)? How will it accomplish this goal, one of no small proportions?

From *Change, The Magazine of Higher Learning*, Vol. 25, No. 3, pp. 32–35, May/June 1993. Reprinted with permission of the Helen Reid Dwight Foundation. Published by Heldref Publications, 1319 18th St., N.W., Washington, D.C. 20036-1802. Copyright © 1993.

The Beginning

The quality initiative began, more or less, as a pilot project at one of the district's community colleges, Rio Salado. There, two years ago, president Linda Thor initiated TQM training for employees. A steering group and quality teams soon formed to employ CQI tools in several of the college's processes. Rio Salado moved along steadily with its TQM initiative. By April of this year all full-time faculty and staff and some part-time employees had gone through 40 hours of training in TQM's basic concepts and tools, and more than a dozen quality-improvement teams were at work improving various college processes. Dr. Thor reports one very telling outcome: a recent survey of Rio's full-time employees indicated that a full 94 percent say they clearly understand their roles in accomplishing the college mission.

Watching the first successes at Rio Salado, a year ago February Chancellor Elsner formed a Commission on Quantum Quality, charged both with investigating TQM programs in higher education and in government and industry, and with recommending a program for Maricopa that would focus on the central vision of the district—effective teaching and learning.

The commission's report, published last August, contains seven recommendations:

1. The Quantum Quality Initiative should begin immediately throughout the colleges and district offices that constitute the system.
2. The chancellor and a steering team should lead the initiative with actions including development of vision statements and implementation strategies with timetables.
3. Communication concerning Quantum Quality should be immediate, pervasive, and universal.
4. Quantum Quality training and education for all employees should begin.
5. Quantum Quality should be integrated into Maricopa classrooms.
6. The district should establish partnerships to ensure external support and involvement.
7. Mechanisms should be developed to monitor, analyze, and evaluate the Quantum Quality Initiative.

Quantum Quality is now fully under way at Maricopa. At the district's Support Services Center, William Waechter holds the title Vice Chancellor for Quality and Employee Development, and the Quantum Quality Executive Council, which includes the chancellor and vice chancellors, presidents, and representatives of the faculty, professional staff, and the board, has, among other things, developed a new vision statement for the Maricopa colleges. A sense of the role Maricopa is preparing itself for is captured in its opening lines: "MCCCD will be the international model for community college education and in that role will be esteemed and sustained by Arizona. This institution will focus on educational excellence for the student through a superbly prepared faculty and staff, 21st century technology, and a striking level of innovation."

Implementing Quantum Quality

Training districtwide has begun; the chancellor, vice chancellors, the college presidents, quality coordinators, and faculty leaders have all received 40 hours of training and are now certified as "coaches." All 10 colleges have selected quality coordinators—their regular jobs range from secretary to dean—and they meet regularly with Donna Schober, executive assistant to the chancellor, to plan, share, and ensure the momentum of Quantum Quality. The colleges are now forming quality coordinating teams and are well under way with training for faculty and staff.

At Rio Salado, already two years into the quality movement, the next round of training—16 hours on Employee Empowerment/Customer Satisfaction—is beginning. An exciting new development is its Quality Academy, which provides TQM training of all kinds for academic institutions, business and industry, and other organizations. Formed less than a year ago, it has already begun to "take off" with an impressive calendar of training commitments and inquiries from across the country and Canada.

Training is a key element in TQM implementation, a point readily acknowledged by Donna Schober: "Developing our training agenda has been very challenging. We are planning different types of training: basic awareness training, the 40-hour training (which is offered by Rio Salado's Quality Academy and is linked to a campus project), and enhancement or specialized training focused on an aspect of Quantum Quality like team building or driving fear from the workplace. This multidimensional training will allow us to involve everyone—on a voluntary basis—in some kind of training over a period of time."

Is Quantum Quality Important?

Predictably, faculty and staff response to Quantum Quality is not unanimous at this early stage. Not all employees yet see it as a top priority: the faculty senate at one college issued a report in response to the Quantum Quality commissions' report, raising questions about the impact of TQM on the faculty work agreement and challenging some of the basic TQM philosophy.

Dr. Paul DePippo, president of the systemwide Faculty Association, expresses reservations yet sees Quantum Quality as having genuine possibilities for the organizational aspects of a district as large as Maricopa. He is especially impressed with the potential of Quantum Quality to make committee functions more meaningful and to give faculty more say.

The weight of opinion clearly is on the positive side. Many faculty and staff are guardedly optimistic about the possibilities that Quantum Quality holds; some bubble with enthusiasm about the prospect of processes refined by quality and of campus climates strengthened by a spirit of cooperation and empowerment. Faculty member Laura Helminski sees TQM as ". . . a vehicle for student success." She describes classes in which TQM tools and

Predictably, faculty and staff response to Quantum Quality is not unanimous at this early stage.

philosophy are actively being used; students function as empowered teams, helping to set the course's goals and strategies and continuously modifying and improving them. Some faculty are experimenting with group examinations and moving toward final course evaluations based on a portfolio of educational documentation.

Students, too, seem to have caught the wind of change. At a recent meeting of the Board of Governors, several spoke powerfully and persuasively about a classroom environment where they felt part of the teaching/learning process, not mere recipients of wisdom uttered by their professors. Vice Chancellor Waechter summarizes it nicely, "Quantum Quality is really about people; it allows and encourages individuals to be at their very best. TQM is the 'people strategy' for the nineties and beyond."

The Maricopa Difference

Maricopa is not the first community college to adopt TQM; indeed, at least two—Fox Valley and Delaware County—have been at it since 1985–86. Coming a bit later to the scene, however, Maricopa does so with its own imprint; Quantum Quality is characterized by several differences from the mainstream of TQM college initiatives.

To begin with, there is the name itself. The word *Quantum* implies a special meaning at Maricopa. As Elsner describes it, "MCC would not pursue quality in the same way—sure, we are interested in continuous improvement, data analysis, empowering employees, all of which will undergird the major transformations we must face. But the *real* transformations must push the paradigms we know to the paradigms we don't yet grasp or understand. This is the Quantum aspect of TQM, the unknown, untested, the 'un-obvious' paths to change."

The "Maricopa Difference" extends beyond its name and philosophical intent. For one, its training emphasizes a "cross-functional, vertically integrated" format in which training groups include faculty and staff from different levels of responsibility and different divisions of the institutions. Most other colleges train by level and function, with faculty all in one group, administrators in another, support staff in a third.

Maricopa's efforts are directed toward effective teaching and learning and improvements in that core function.

Then there is the matter of the processes colleges choose as the focus for quality improvement. At most colleges and universities TQM's successes are reported, at least initially, in terms of turnaround-time saved in travel reimbursements or in efficiencies in the delivery of mail. In contrast, Maricopa's efforts are directed toward effective teaching and learning and improvements in that core function. According to Alfredo de los Santos, vice chancellor of academic and student affairs, districtwide groups are already conducting occupational course-by-course analyses to ensure that students are learning the competencies most required by potential employers. "The entire focus is shifting to outcomes, to institutional effectiveness," according to de los Santos; "TQM is an integral part of that."

Finally, there is the human side. Sharon Koberna, quality coordinator at Rio Salado, says the focus so far has been, "one-fourth on process improvement, three-fourths on human issues." The emphasis is on teamwork and cooperation. Vice Chancellor Ron Bleed says TQM's greatest asset is that ". . . it gets to people. It will break down bureaucracy and lead people to focus on the truly important things. Already we are seeing the benefit of working with teams; bringing cross-functional viewpoints together creates synergy."

President Thor's success with TQM at Rio Salado Community College is gaining attention coast to coast; she recently delivered a keynote address at a national conference dedicated to TQM in community colleges. Her remarks dealt with the human element of TQM. President Thor put it this way: "Some say that TQM is 90 percent culture and 10 percent tools. For me, the human aspects of TQM have been the most exciting and rewarding, namely, the fostering of empowerment and teamwork, favoring cooperation over competition, improving communications, reducing fear, increasing trust, and building pride among individual employees and the college as a whole. TQM is about the wonderfully diverse and capable people that make up our colleges."

What Will It Take for Success?

Quantum Quality is a major undertaking, especially as a districtwide initiative in a system as large and complex as Maricopa. Nothing short of total commitment is essential to its success and that commitment begins at the top. Chancellor Elsner is acutely aware of this, as is Grant Christiansen, chair of Maricopa's board. "Success will depend on the involvement of the people," Christiansen states. "To really work, that involvement must be top-to-bottom. We have the kind of personnel who can genuinely involve people. Also, we need to make sure this effort does not become a threat, rather that it becomes an opportunity."

A consensus has developed on what it will take for Quantum Quality to reach its potential:

- Training is key—as many people as possible must be trained in TQM philosophy and tools, and as fast as possible. Employees also need to be introduced to the nature and dynamics of change itself. A common ground must be reached so the vocabulary of TQM facilitates, not hinders, communication.
- Perception is often more powerful than reality. "Walking the talk" cannot be overdone. Administrators in particular must be alert to the danger of doing the same old things in the same old ways.
- Patience is critical. An institution's culture does not change overnight; a long-term commitment is basic. Maricopa looks five to ten years ahead for full institutionalization of Quantum Quality.
- Quantum Quality must become part of the everyday routine. It must be integrated into the way an institution does things, not treated as an "add on."

Chancellor Elsner describes the challenge ahead: "Quantum Quality embraces the yet-to-be-learned; the interesting risk may be the interesting

"Walking the talk" cannot be overdone. Administrators in particular must be alert to the danger of doing the same old things in the same old ways.

failures that need to be encouraged. Maricopa has gravitated to the state-of-the-art technology user, the boundary pusher—rewrites the role of community colleges as it evolves in its relationships with its partner schools, with its commitments to training a national cadre of learners, with its innovative human resources strategies—so TQM has to move Maricopa to its own quantum stage."

The Future

The teacher confers with other students about their plans and goals for the next class and discusses with them the things they think could be improved about their last class.

The year is 1999, Phoenix, Arizona; a visitor enters one of Maricopa's colleges. In a classroom, chairs and desks are scattered in groups; a list of ground rules hangs on the wall. Different things are going on all over the classroom. Energy is very high. In one area students help each other through a series of computerized multimedia lessons; in another area a team of students works on a project that will constitute a part of the final course grade; in yet another part of the room one student stands before a group, seemingly presenting a lesson in anthropology. The teacher confers with other students about their plans and goals for the next class and discusses with them the things they think could be improved about their last class. In a nearby conference room a class group meets about a major issue it has identified as an "opportunity" . . . charts and graphs line the walls . . . it is difficult to identify the chair of the group, since several individuals share facilitation of the meeting. Faculty in an office area are completing a survey asking their suggestions for improving a student-orientation process in which they took part; in the hallways, entering freshmen complete a survey soliciting their views of the same program. A member of the support staff greets a work-study student who will relieve her so she can attend a meeting of the budget team she participates in. An occupational program chair is not on campus today; she is interviewing employers for feedback about the graduates they've hired. From that information, a faculty team will make curricular revisions. . . .

Will this be the snapshot of Maricopa in the not-too-distant future? If commitment, planning, training, foresight, vision, and support are what it takes to make it a reality at Maricopa, the answer is a resounding and unequivocal "yes"! And if Maricopa leads the way with TQM, can the rest of the country's community colleges be far behind?

Kathleen E. Assar is vice president of academic and student affairs at Bunker Hill Community College in Boston.

TQM Invades
Business Schools

Paul Froiland

Quality management in the curriculum and as a way to manage is only gradually making its way into the nation's business schools. As more and more organizations demand that schools incorporate quality management principles into their courses, universities are now responding, but there is a way to go, as this article documents.

In the '80s an MBA was considered a one-way ticket up the corporate ladder. To be sure, not everyone who possessed that stamp of academic achievement was assured a corner office, but midlevel, paper-pushing obscurity was all but guaranteed without one.

Around the turn of the decade, that began to change. Both *The Wall Street Journal* and *Fortune* noted business schools' plight: declining enrollments, dissatisfied graduates and unhappy employers. Some progressive schools, such as the University of Tennessee, looked into the matter. In April 1990, Tennessee's business-school faculty invited representatives of three large firms—Xerox, Procter & Gamble and Texas Instruments—to a retreat to find out how it could improve the school. What the faculty members heard was the startling pronouncement that much of what they were teaching was simply no longer relevant.

The University of Tennessee immediately commissioned a task force to examine the problem. One of the things it discovered was a recent study by Meryl Reis Louis called "The Gap in Management Education." The study concluded that MBA students needed to be taught fewer technical and analytic skills and more people skills. They needed a clear idea of how an organization's functions are integrated and a better sense of organizational reality. Tennessee decided that the principles of total-quality management (TQM) provided the best way to redress these shortcomings.

The TQM invasion into business schools is one indicator of the paradigm shift that's been under way in industry for some time now. According to Indiana University's Robert W. Hall, the traditional, hierarchical management model dictated a business-school education that emphasized such antiquated principles as: 1) Quality is a business trade-off (i.e., the more quality, the less profit); 2) Doers are distinct from thinkers; 3) Assets are things; 4) Profit is the primary business goal; and 5) Workers ought to please the boss.

The new paradigm, says Hall, substitutes these principles, among others: 1) Quality is a "religion"—no compromise; 2) Doers must also be thinkers; 3) Assets are people; 4) Customer satisfaction is the primary business goal; and 5) Management and workers must please the (internal or external) customer.

To meet the demands of the corporate world that hires their graduates, business schools have begun to incorporate these total-quality principles into their curricula. Many have introduced courses with names such as statistical-process control, foundations of total quality, reliability development, design of experiments, strategic-quality management, principles of quality assurance, employee involvement, quality costs and quality-assurance standards, and implementing total-quality management organizationwide.

Those that dared also exchanged traditional teaching methods for student-focused methods built around TQM principles. A few radicals have gone so far as to redefine the student as the customer of the academic product (the courses being taught), and the future employer as the customer of the academic institution.

A commitment to total quality also meant redefining the instructor's role: Instead of heading the classroom hierarchy the instructor became a coach. Sometimes it meant abolishing individual grades in favor of group-project grades. And often it meant daily evaluations of instructors by their students, with instructors using the evaluations to produce continuous improvement in the delivery of their services.

This revolutionary departure from traditional classroom teaching appealed to a number of schools. Responses from 515 business and engineering schools to a 1992 survey conducted by the Total Quality Forum, an annual conference of corporations and business schools that looks at issues of curriculum, research and total quality, indicated that about 40 percent had integrated total-quality principles into as many as six to 10 courses; 45 percent had begun to practice total quality in administrative areas; and 21 percent were actually practicing total quality in the classroom and in research.

> A commitment to total quality also meant redefining the instructor's role: Instead of heading the classroom hierarchy the instructor became a coach.

The Push from Business

The initial spur to introduce the principles of total quality to academia came from business. In many cases, companies prodded schools into action with a combination of exhortations and threats. The Boeing Commercial Airplane Co. in Wichita, KS, asked area colleges and universities to develop a degree program in TQM. Wichita State rapidly developed six courses for M.S. degree candidates in business that allowed them to earn a specialization in quality. Kansas Newman College, a liberal-arts college in Wichita, did State one better by developing a TQM major in its business department and offering some of its classes at Boeing facilities.

At the same time, Procter & Gamble was making threats at various quality forums around the country that business schools had better start teaching TQM or P&G wouldn't hire their graduates. IBM offered a positive incentive by establishing nine $1 million grants in 1992 that it would give to selected schools for teaching TQM.

H. Thomas Johnson of the Portland School of Business articulated the signal business was sending to higher education in his 1992 book *Relevance Regained: From Top-Down Control to Bottom-Up Empowerment.* "The message [in the book] was that there was a lot we had to do to change the actual [course] content," he told TRAINING. "Students had to understand what it meant to be brought up to speed in a world that now had international competition. The courses taught before this were based on an old model of top-down management, not on serving the customer. The management techniques that we were teaching were just too inflexible. A lot of businesses were starting to find that out, but the universities were falling behind."

Certain business schools, mostly smaller ones outside of major urban centers, moved swiftly to establish total-quality courses at their schools. Some of them modified classroom procedures to follow total-quality principles. In some cases, entire universities began quality initiatives in the administrative management of the school (see accompanying story). And many universities developed partnerships with local businesses that were already implementing TQM principles.

"If I were suggesting strategies for growth to a college," says Anna McLeod, the TQM-program director at Kansas Newman College, "I would say partnering with business is the name of the game. If you don't have partnering, you will remain stagnant. When our students graduate they go to companies for jobs, and their training is in line with what the companies want."

In Kansas Newman's case, partnering was accomplished through several willing businesses. Besides Boeing, there was Cessna, two large area hospitals, a bank, a group of cardiovascular physicians, and even a community college, which was actually a competitor for KN's Associate of Science degree program.

George Heinrich, who teaches at Wichita State, agrees with Kansas Newman's partnering philosophy. "I think that there has to be a partnership between business and the university," he says. "The businesses feel that they have to implement TQM to be competitive internationally, and that the universities need to prepare students for this world. We also have to plant seeds and talk about things that companies are not implementing now that may need to be implemented three or four years down the pike."

At the University of Wyoming, all business-administration majors soon will be required to take a previously elective TQM course. In this course they will be participant observers in an existing quality team on the university's administrative side or at a local hospital. The course requires students to give regular reports to the class on the status of the group they're working with.

"Some of these student teams are working with teams that are just getting started, so they see how the teams get formed and figure out what they are and what they are supposed to do," says assistant professor David Snook-Luther, one of the teachers of the course. "Some of the older teams have been quite effective, but they've had turnover in leadership and are losing some of their fire, so the students see how that happens, too. By sharing these reports with each other, they are getting a cross-sectional perspective on TQM implementation. Basically, we show them how to become good anthropologists."

The University of Wisconsin offers a variation of Wyoming's plan. Not only do the students go out and join teams in existing organizations, but the school requires these organizations' teams to come in and take the course along with the students. "So we actually have the managers come in and take the course," says Mark Finster, a Wisconsin School of Business professor. "We team grad students up with them, and then they learn the theory here and [practice the] methods there." The system seems to be a success, at least judging from enrollments: Wisconsin currently has four times more student demand for TQM courses than it has faculty to supply them.

TQM as Curriculum

Even as there is some variation in how different businesses define and practice TQM, there is variation in how universities address it in their curricula. Kansas Newman offers eight required courses in TQM in its B.S. program. Another undergraduate school, Marian College, in Fond du Lac, WI, offers 14 courses in what it calls its quality and productivity-management program.

Wisconsin currently has four times more student demand for TQM courses than it has faculty to supply them.

The University of Tennessee, which instituted its first quality-oriented course in 1981, began to transform its MBA program as a result of the challenge from Xerox, P&G and Texas Instruments in 1990. Today it offers 11 TQM courses.

On the other hand, Oregon State has only one course, but it received one of IBM's $1 million grants to design another that will be offered jointly through the business and engineering schools—a rare interdepartmental phenomenon at any university. Dave Gobli, an OSU professor and a "chief initiator" of the TQM thrust there, believes that "there will come a time when it just becomes part of the curriculum everywhere."

Another school that offers just one course in quality is The Simon Graduate School of Business Administration at the University of Rochester in Rochester, NY. The course is now an elective, but it will likely become an MBA requirement. Phil Lederer, an instructor at the school, believes that only one TQM course is necessary. "Is a statistics course in which you teach about control charts a quality-management course or just a statistics course?" he asks. "I don't really think it's a quality course. [In our one course] students learn many of the tools of quality management, and they can then use them in many of the [other] courses."

The school that can perhaps boast loudest about its TQM curriculum is the Columbia Business School in New York City, which features quality legend W. Edwards Deming as a faculty member. "About seven years ago I convinced Ed Deming that he could do something for us," says Martin K. Star, a faculty member at Columbia and a TQM advocate. "We had him come in to talk to our faculty and administration about the applications of quality. We went on a week-by-week basis, and he was a great convincer. He got a lot of

A QUALITY ADMINISTRATION

Some colleges and universities do more than include total-quality management in their curricula. Some are also putting quality-improvement practices to work in the administrative side of their operations. These schools have developed work teams, streamlined student registration, and given students a voice in matters such as campus housing and food service.

At the University of Wyoming, for example, work teams have come up with some money-saving ideas, says faculty member David Snook-Luther. "One team in the physical plant replaces the filters in the heating systems. It had been spending something like $100 per filter, counting the time it takes to buy, clean, wash and so on. The team figured out a way to do the whole thing for about $25 by using materials that were just as effective. We've had a number of things like that going on."

Often, one of the first steps universities take is easing the bureaucracy students must battle. At the University of Tennessee, for example, the length of the registration process was cut from two weeks to a half-hour. Students register over the telephone and are faxed verification of their class schedules. Wyoming also began telephone registration this year.

Schools also have taken steps to improve the quality of life for students, although, as Columbia business professor Martin Star wryly notes, "No one has yet gotten around to the quality of the faculty life." At Wyoming, students are involved in planning menus for the food service, and they have changed both the selection of food and the hours of the campus snack bars, as well as the hours and offerings of several other student services.

Wisconsin, Columbia, Tennessee and the Portland School of Business are implementing TQM throughout the administration. Wyoming began the process five years ago. And Oregon State, which began three years ago, already has 80 teams in place.

On the other hand, Wichita State and Rochester's Simon School have not taken a total-quality approach to administration, although Wichita State had hoped to use grant money to implement TQM at the administrative level in its unsuccessful bid for one of the nine 1992 IBM Total Quality grants.

people to start what I call 'the process' in short order. Deming is still with us [as] a faculty member. Some of the largest classes in our school are his classes."

TQM in the Classroom

When schools actually begin to align classroom operating procedure with the TQM principles they are teaching, they are likely to draw fire from faculty.

Students, on the other hand, generally enjoy being treated like customers instead of like barely worthy underlings sitting at the feet of the great teacher. Most of the college faculty and administrators interviewed for this article report enthusiastic responses from students.

TQM in the classroom often means that students work on team projects. Many schools grade students as a team as well. Columbia is a notable exception. "We still use traditional teaching methods," says Star. "We grade on a curve, and students want that. Deming says that everyone gets an A in his class. But when you tell students that, they say, 'I want to stand out so I can get hired by the best company.' [So] we try to do the A-B-C curve, [but] it's a very slight distinction [from A to C]. Everyone passes in that system. We don't have students who are getting D's. The admissions process is so severe that we are talking about students of obvious capabilities. I'm always amazed at how good the students are who are not at the top."

> TQM in the classroom often means that students work on team projects. Many schools grade students as a team as well.

In Star's classes, students form groups of their own choosing having between three and five members. They are graded mostly as a group, although they do receive grades on individual projects as well. "If they see their group slipping," says Star, "they come to me and I tell *them* to do something about it. That's the real world, I say. Each group is graded on a curve. They have a vested interest in having their group be as good as it can be. In the last course, 12 percent had A's and 10 percent had C's. The rest had B's."

A true commitment to TQM would mean giving no grades at all, Star acknowledges. "Grading is a very time-consuming process that is not informative in the real sense. It makes people who get a C feel that they are 'C persons.' That's Martin Star talking with Ed Deming's approval."

Kansas Newman gives group grades, but in the face of opposition from some students who want to use a high grade-point average to get into graduate school. At the same time, says KN's McLeod, other students endorse the position of Deming, wanting to eliminate grades altogether. " 'You are setting [up] a philosophy of teamwork,' the students say, 'but you are giving us a grade.' "

Other schools take a variety of approaches. University of Tennessee students are in the same team for the first year and earn team grades. The Simon School assigns students to teams, but gives the individual grades. Wyoming's single TQM course gives team grades on team assignments and individual grades on individual assignments.

Faculty: The Reluctant Buyers

Clearly, the toughest sell of TQM in academia is the faculty, which cherishes its autonomy and tends to prize the thinking of individuals over the thinking of groups. Part of the problem is that quality zealots in business schools often insist that the entire university would benefit from turning classes into hotbeds of quality processes and procedures. Yet even business-school professors aren't universally convinced; many still consider the movement an infringement on their academic freedom.

They are joined by a chorus of liberal-arts faculty, who generally oppose notions such as having students learn in groups; being evaluated daily by their students; and putting the whole context of education into terms like *product, service* and *customer.* Some professors also have difficulty swallowing the idea that grades—which Deming considers a scourge—are an impediment to learning and should be done away with.

Lowry Burgess, an art professor at Columbia, finds the whole idea of the student as customer and the teacher as vendor to be anathema. "The function of a university is entirely different than that of a business," he says. "Our time frames are entirely different in terms of what we are aiming for and where we are coming from. We [in the university] are both reaching out into the future to ascertain what is not known, and we are also trying to reach back to that which is beyond memory. In a hyperbolic sense, I have said that our customer is the truth. Our customers tend to be the very abstract principles. We are responsible to those customers rather than to the momentary student customer."

On the whole, business-school faculties put total-quality principles into practice with the same level of enthusiasm found among most veteran first-line supervisors in the corporate world. In other words, they are reluctant to embrace the changes required. Professors and administrators offer delicately phrased descriptions of faculty receptiveness to TQM. At Tennessee the adjustment by faculty to such practices as using teams in the classroom and abandoning the approaches of traditional textbooks was "very difficult," says Ann Mayeux, associate director of the university's Management Development Center. "When someone has created a course and has taught it for years, they get very proprietary. It takes awhile to convince them that there is a new and better way to do things. And we are not all the way there; there are still faculty that think this approach doesn't have value."

> On the whole, business-school faculties put total-quality principles into practice with the same level of enthusiasm found among most veteran first-line supervisors in the corporate world.

At Columbia, says Star, "We have a core of faculty—about 25 percent—who are very gung ho, including me. And we have some who are not." At Wichita State, there is "a lot of skepticism"; at the Simon School there is "resistance to change"; at the Portland School it "[causes] some wrenching change for the faculty"; at Oregon State "There's enormous variance in response: Some think it's a joke or fad, others have totally bought into it." OSU's Gobli notes that Deming would consider this variance "a system out of control."

At Wisconsin, long known for its liberal tradition, there is no attempt to sell TQM to faculty, even though the graduate school offers courses that emphasize quality-training procedures and techniques. "Being in an academic environment we don't try to sell things to people," says Finster. "As people learn about it, they either buy into it or not. I'm glad that there are people challenging it at every turn. If you start making something into a religion and everyone has to believe it, I don't think that's healthy. A country that only recently ceased to exist spent several decades proving that that doesn't work. If it isn't presented in such a way that people choose it, it won't work."

In fact, some of the basic tenets of quality-improvement efforts generate considerable controversy among faculty members. Take a relatively straight-forward exercise: defining your customer. "Traditionally in academia we didn't even clearly define the customer," says Kansas Newman's McLeod. "Is it the student, the parent, the community, the future employer? I recall one faculty meeting in which we used the word *customer* instead of *student*. Some people became unglued. We said we were selling a product. They said we are not selling a product; we are educating. That was two years ago. Now we call them student/customers, and it seems to be no problem."

The competition in the education market is such that academics have in the past perceived the customer as the research community.

The Simon School has also wrestled with this issue, according to Lederer. "Who the customer is is a very important issue," he says. "This is the problem as I see it: The competition in the education market is such that academics have in the past perceived the customer as the research community. Now there is a greater focus on teaching, and there is a resistance to putting more of a focus on [the student] community.

"Of course, we have to think of both the students and employers as our customers. It's my view that business school's primary responsibility is to produce 'products' that people want to hire, and I think ultimately students will be best served if we focus on what they will need to be employed and have good careers."

Paul Froiland is associate editor of Training *Magazine.*

GOVERNMENT

Total Quality Management in the Public Sector

A. Keith Smith

Part 1

This article, documenting the systematic adoption of quality management techniques in government, appeared in two parts in successive issues of Quality Progress. *In part one, the author discusses the importance of customer service as a guiding principle, and in part two, he discusses the nuts and bolts of the TQM effort in government.*

During the past two years, there has been an explosion of interest in the application of total quality management (TQM) in the public sector. Many government processes are, by nature, repetitive, standardized, error-prone, and customer-hostile. These processes are ripe for TQM philosophy and methodology.

Rising Public Expectations

There is increasing demand for the public sector to improve service even as budgets shrink. Private companies are competing with the public sector on the basis of the quality and cost of their services. Companies such as Federal Express (a winner of the Malcolm Baldrige National Quality Award) are competing in areas that were once the exclusive domain of government and are providing service that is recognized as exemplary. Private enterprise has entered areas heretofore the sole concern of government, further expanding the

---

Reprinted with permission from *Quality Progress*, June and July 1993, ASCQ, Milwaukee, WI.

competitive arena. Meanwhile, as federal, state, county, and city budgets tighten, competition among public agencies for limited dollars increases. Government agencies must meet the cost and quality standards set by the private sector because these are the standards by which all organizations are judged. The survival of some government agencies is at stake.

The continued health of an agency directly depends on its credibility. That credibility depends on the taxpayer's perception of the importance of the agency's mission and the quality of services provided. Thus, it is self-evident that public agency management must describe the agency mission clearly to the ultimate customer—the taxpayer—and must ensure congruence between the mission and a clearly perceived public need. Outstanding customer service must also be a key organizational objective. This is equally true whether the customer is internal or external to the government.

The perceived value of the services provided by an agency relates directly to cost and benefit. A tenet of the quality movement is that the higher the quality of the product or service, the lower the cost. Thus, the service quality improvements and cost savings that TQM can provide make it an effective strategy for continued organizational health in a time of limited resources.

Many public sector TQM efforts founder because agencies adopt canned improvement models that stress the use of teams and tools but do not incorporate the planning necessary to manage the implementation effort at every level of the organization. Without an understanding of both the transformational nature of TQM on the management of the organization and of the unique factors faced by managers in the public sector, any TQM effort in government is likely to be only marginally effective.

Balancing Conflicting Constituencies

Politics is the balancing of conflicting priorities. Different customers for a government service might have conflicting views about the appropriate missions for a department. For example, restrictions on the release of public information such as drivers' addresses might be supported by drivers but opposed by commercial users of this information. Government must often decide between such mutually conflicting constituencies, guaranteeing that one group inevitably will be dissatisfied. Executive leaders must clarify the predominant public needs in the mission of the agency so managers can make informed operational decisions. For example, traffic safety is a predominant need; therefore, releasing addresses is justifiable in the case of a vehicle recall, but not for a direct marketing effort.

Government is often required to include the needs of other agencies in both decision-making and service processes. For example, both sales tax collection and vehicle emission control compliance are a part of the California vehicle registration process. Multiple and sometimes conflicting needs might be imposed on a process, making streamlining difficult. Requirements of one agency can affect the ability of another to improve the efficiency of work systems.

The inevitable changes in political balance can cause an agency's mission to reflect such changes. Change in mission inevitably leads to lack of a consistent vision for the future, which in turn can derail long-term planning. This conflict can have a profound effect on the design of service processes. Should we make the qualifications for entitlements difficult, or should we ensure that the broadest range of applicants qualify with minimum difficulty? Do we provide quick driver licensing service and run the risk of licensing drivers who are minimally qualified? If we focus on highway safety and make drivers' tests more complex, we ensure greater disruption for the customer. Customers can hold both goals valid, so customer satisfaction depends on how the process affects the individual and the people around him or her.

Elective politics and government is the system we have adopted to resolve issues that divide us. Government is, therefore, often in the business of defining societal missions and resolving problems. Continuous improvement of this system is one of the highest priorities and greatest challenges in the quality movement.

Balancing Customer Expectations

Government is expected to treat and serve its customers equally. The tendency is to design a service to fit everyone. Customers, however, expect personalized service, especially when problems arise. Deciding when personalized service is appropriate and balancing this with government's need for equity and minimal cost adds complexity to service delivery planning.

The tendency to design one service to fit all makes it difficult to respond to the variety of customer service need. Is it equitable to provide faster processing if the customer is willing to pay a premium to fund any added service costs? Should weekend service be instituted at added cost to the taxpayer to accommodate those who are unwilling or unable to do business during normal business hours? These dilemmas are faced by those who manage within a political system. Decision criteria, such as profit and loss or market share, are clean and simple by comparison.

> Deciding when personalized service is appropriate and balancing this with government's need for equity and minimal cost adds complexity to service delivery planning.

Balancing Service and Compliance

Managing an improvement effort in the service arena is inherently more difficult than in manufacturing. Both service delivery and the customers' perceptions of quality depend heavily on person-to-person interactions. As noted by Karl Albrecht and Ron Zemke, service is produced at the moment of delivery by people beyond the immediate influence of management.[1] The service, once provided, cannot be inspected or recalled. The customer's perception of quality is as much influenced by the behavior of the service provider as it is by the results of the service process. Thus, both aspects of service must be the focus of any improvement effort.

A second complicating factor is that most government agencies have a responsibility to ensure compliance with laws and regulations. Compliance might involve such issues as entitlements (welfare), capability (driver's license), equity (affirmative action), revenue (taxes and fees), or societal goals (vehicle emission control inspections). These compliance requirements can negatively affect the customer's overall perception of the service. It is management's responsibility to make compliance a service by communicating to the customer why compliance is necessary and by making the compliance process easily understandable. While enforcing compliance issues is important, government must be sensitive to the special circumstances that will inevitably occur. The ability of the service process (designed by management) and of the frontline people to balance the customer's expectations of service and government's need to ensure compliance is an essential part of service management in the public sector.

These compliance requirements can negatively affect the customer's overall perception of the service.

Creating a Service Strategy

In *Service America,* Albrecht and Zemke describe managing the service triangle as the key to service quality.[2] Figure 1 describes the elements that must be managed simultaneously in an effective TQM effort. The first element is a service strategy.

An effective service strategy requires a comprehensive understanding of the environment in which the organization functions and a knowledge of customers' requirements and expectations. The service strategy provides a clear and simple vision of the desired future state from both the customers' and the organization's perspective. It identifies the balance between conflicting constituencies by clarifying a primary mission. A values statement establishes the organization's internal and external behaviors and helps define the balance between service and compliance. Finally, the service strategy identifies key issues (processes that must be transformed) and describes goals that must be achieved to accomplish the vision (see Figure 2).

Environmental Scanning

Before embarking on a planning process, it is essential to understand both the organization's external environmental and its current status. In the public sector, external issues include:

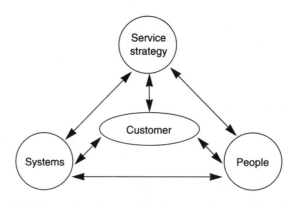

Figure 1. **Elements that must be managed simultaneously in an effective TQM effort.**

Figure 2. **Elements of a service strategy.**

- Customer requirements (type of service)
- Customer expectations (quality of service)
- Customer complaints and praise
- Current and proposed legislation
- Political and social factors
- Technological futures
- Customer and employee demographics
- Economic factors
- Supplier performance

A review of internal organizational issues should include:

- Service quality as perceived by the customer
- Effectiveness of service delivery systems
- Costs
- Customer and employee safety
- Employee satisfaction and commitment
- Adaptability of service delivery infrastructure (people, automation, facility, procedures, etc.)
- Management processes
- Prior years' objectives

The most critical element in environmental scanning is the organization's knowledge of its internal and external customers. It is important to identify and prioritize the most valuable constituencies or customer groups in each major service area. Their current and future requirements and expectations must be determined through surveys, focus groups, frontline contact, or other means. Where requirements conflict, determine the primary requirement(s) and measure how the service delivery system is meeting them.

Customer expectations reinfluenced by the performance of other government and private organizations performing similar functions. Federal Express overnight delivery has set a standard for a public agency: the post office.

One excellent way to heighten awareness of the external environment is to undertake benchmarking studies. Internal benchmarking compares one operating unit against another performing a similar job. More powerful, though, is benchmarking against world-class external providers of each major function, no matter what the exemplar's agency or industry.

Identifying the gap between current performance and world-class performance and understanding what new or improved service is possible can mobilize management's commitment to change.

Creating a Shared Service Vision—Customer Service

Once management understands future customer requirements and expectations and has evaluated current performance, it must create a vision of the future service. The vision should be such that it meets the customers' requirements and seeks to exceed the customers' expectations. New and enhanced service delivery systems (e.g., weekend service, extended hours, telephone service, and automated teller machines) and new or redefined services (e.g., drivers' licenses not only as proof of ability to drive but also as a secure form of identification can be conceptualized. New standards for customer service performance can be envisaged. Clear vision of the organization's future customer services facilitates decisions on needed transformational changes and identifies improvement opportunities.

Organizational Behavior

New support systems, organizational behaviors, and employee and management skills must be developed to achieve the needed changes.

New information systems will be needed to evaluate customer needs, current service quality, and comparative benchmarks and to identify improvement opportunities. New planning processes to bring the voice of the customer into design and delivery of service will be necessary. A quality improvement process must be developed to manage the improvement of today's delivery systems.

Developing skills such as effective customer service behaviors, team leadership and participation, quality improvement, and supervisory coaching will be required. Aligning the hiring, evaluation and feedback, and reward and recognition systems with quality service values will be necessary.

Finally, a strategy to communicate the vision throughout the organization must be developed. Management must communicate the key issues and goals and, most important, affirm its personal commitment to the goals through its behaviors and decisions. Management must provide leadership, support, training, and resources.

Mission and Values

A comprehensive and coherent mission statement is an important force for change; it brings members of an organization together to work toward a collective purpose. The mission statement should reflect the core purposes of the organization and should describe the products and services that are to be delivered to the customers.

In the public sector, the primary mission generally involves service and/or compliance and is usually defined by legislative language. Reducing conflict between constituencies and creating balance between service and compliance depend on leadership and negotiation. The mission statement should provide enough clarity about the primary purpose of the organization and the requirements of the major customers to allow informed management decision making in areas of conflict or unclear direction.

How the organization plans to carry out its business can be incorporated into the mission statement or be separated into a statement of organizational values. The value statement should reflect the beliefs and operational philosophy of the organization and support the desired organizational culture. It often reflects the desired relationship between the organization and its customers and between management and employees or describes desired behavioral norms. This value statement should answer the question of whether the current values of the organization support the vision and how much behavioral change is necessary.

Both mission and value statements focus all employees on the core purpose of the organization. Properly used, these statements can be important motivational tools, energizing and challenging all employees to achieve attainable goals.

> In the public sector, the primary mission generally involves service and/or compliance and is usually defined by legislative language.

Key Issues

The next step is to identify key issues, processes that must be transformed to successfully accomplish the vision. For service delivery processes, it is important to work on issues that have some or all of the following characteristics:

- Are important to the customer
- Create substantial cost of poor quality
- Happen frequently
- Have substantial impact
- Create substantial delay

A number of such key issues are common to many service organizations:

- **Quality.** Provide a continuously improving level of accurate, courteous, and timely service.
- **Delivery.** Provide convenient and dependable access to services for all customers.
- **Safety.** Operate in a manner that ensures the safety of both customers and employees.
- **Cost.** Ensure that operations run at minimum cost to the taxpayer while improving service to customers.

- **Organizational responsibility.** Demonstrate concern for the communities served and for employees.
- **Infrastructure.** Ensure that service delivery systems are adaptable to new and changing requirements.
- **External relationships.** Establish and improve communication with customers, suppliers, legislative bodies, other government agencies, and taxpayers.
- **Customer protection.** Ensure that customers' property and financial interests are protected.
- **Compliance.** Ensure clear explanation and fair and equitable application of laws and regulations.

For organizational processes, it is important to work on issues that:

- Affect the beliefs and behaviors of those in the organization
- Affect the organization's ability to deliver world-class service
- Enable the organization to identify and capitalize on opportunities for improvement

Examples are:

- Executive leadership
- Planning processes
- A focus on the customer
- Use of data, management by fact
- Training and recognition
- Empowerment and teamwork

Selecting three to five key issues focuses the attention of the organization on those areas in need of improvement and change. These are the areas in which innovation and continuous improvement activities are concentrated.

Goals

Identifying key issues leads to the development of specific goals related to the changes needed to accomplish the vision. For example, in the area of service delivery, customer contact might have shown that a substantial number of customers would prefer to do business over the phone or outside of government hours. The ability to spread large payments over time might be important to some customers. An increasing population of non-English speaking customers might be increasing talk time, rework, and repeat office visits.

Goals to improve delivery systems might include:

- Evening and weekend service hours
- Alternative delivery systems such as telephone service centers or automated kiosks
- A variety of payment options (credit cards, etc.)
- Clearer forms and instructions and simplified procedures
- Forms and instructions in multiple languages and access for those who are hearing or visually impaired

Customer contact might have shown that a substantial number of customers would prefer to do business over the phone or outside of government hours.

The organization might be under increasing demand to provide services in new areas. Goals to improve the adaptability of the infrastructure might include:

- Automated supply systems
- Improved employee training programs
- Integration with supplier and customer data bases
- Improved intra-organizational communication
- Attractive and adequate facilities
- Fast, flexible automation

Defining the service strategy for an organization helps employees understand changes in systems and behaviors that are necessary to achieve the vision. Defining specific goals and behavioral changes will start to change the responsibilities of every employee in the organization and is the first step toward legendary customer service.

References
1. Karl Albrecht and Ron Zemke, *Service America* (Homewood, IL: Dow Jones Irwin, 1985).
2. Ibid.

Part 2

Effective TQM implementation leads to improvement in all of an organization's processes. Every member of the organization should have an opportunity to participate in improvement activities. Many improvement efforts have failed because many middle managers have been excluded from meaningful roles in the process. Decisions to form workplace improvement teams are often made without involving middle management in either the targeting of significant issues or in team participation and leadership. A parallel quality improvement organizational structure, including new reporting relationships, is often formed. This almost guarantees the active resistance of middle managers. Until new organizational structures develop as a result of the TQM process, it is advisable to manage the improvement process within the existing organizational framework. Described is a model for organization-wide involvement in improving work processes. The behavioral skills and the statistical, problem-solving, and analytical tools needed to accomplish the changes have been clearly described by others.[1,2]

TQM is a managed process that seeks organizationwide improvement through:

- Planning for new products and services
- Innovation in existing services
- Continuous improvement in all existing service processes

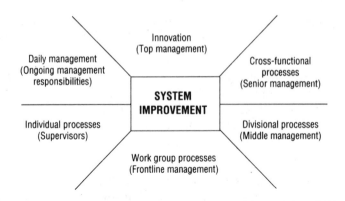

Figure 1.   **System improvement model.**

■   Daily control of service processes

Goals generated from the key issues must be incorporated into action plans and integrated throughout the organization. Managers at every level of the organization must include those goals in their planning. Coordinating these plans between units is essential if the improvement efforts are to work for the organization overall. Techniques such as policy deployment can integrate these plans and document the required links.

The use of technology to dramatically improve productivity and customer service is an essential and increasingly cost-effective strategy.

Figure 1 shows how all management levels can lead and participate in improvement efforts in their areas of responsibility.

Innovation—A Top-Management Responsibility

Science and technology are rapidly changing the face of business and government. In the 1950s, hiring employees was inexpensive and technology was expensive. Today, a powerful desktop computer can be bought for the price of one month's salary and benefits. The use of technology to dramatically improve productivity and customer service is an essential and increasingly cost-effective strategy.

Products and services that exist today were science fiction 10 years ago. A computerized search of crime-scene fingerprints against a data base of digitized criminal prints can identify suspects. This same technology can use a driver's thumbprint to ensure that only one driver's license is ever issued to each individual. Driver license data can be carried on a magnetic strip and can be used by law enforcement to electronically create a traffic ticket, considerably improving the speed and accuracy of that process.

Innovative change is often technology based. Such changes require long-term planning, are high in cost, and are frequently performed in conjunction with outside experts and suppliers. Top management generally conceptualizes new products and innovative ways to deliver existing services. Areas include:

■   Automation and technology
■   Alternative service delivery systems

- Equipment planning
- Service site selection

The key issues identified by the service strategy point to how innovation can create new or improved processes to serve internal and external customers. Quality function deployment can help bring the voice of the customer into the planning.

Cross-Functional Processes—Senior Management

The key issues might not indicate the need to create innovative services or technologies, but rather point out the need to dramatically improve existing service processes. Typically, these are cross-functional processes—significant processes that involve the coordinated efforts of several work units. For example:

- External customer relations
- Customer education
- Management information systems
- Employee safety
- Internal communication
- Policy making and procedure writing
- Cash handling
- Internal and external mail systems
- Telephone services
- Management development
- Reward and recognition systems
- Hiring
- Discipline

Customer feedback and performance measures help management determine which processes have a major effect on the customers' perception of service quality and where the greatest potential for improvement lies. These processes are selected for study and improvement using cross-functional teams.

Often, individual unit managers in a cross-functional process manage only the functions performed by those units. Most process problems, however, occur in the white space between units, the supplier unit, and unit-customer interfaces.[3] Creating a cross-functional team of the major players (including external customers and suppliers if appropriate), ensures that the whole process is studied, including all unit interfaces. Teams are led by senior managers, who are designated as system owners. Placing overall responsibility for improving major service processes on a senior manager ensures the participation of this management level in the improvement effort. The teams are charged with conducting a comprehensive review of the current process; analyzing the redundancies, delays, rework, errors, and so on; and designing a new service delivery system.

Coordinating plans and improvements between the units is essential to the success of these improvement projects. Improvements often require only moderate expenditures of time and money and might require the approval of top management to implement.

Divisional Processes—Middle Managers

Middle managers might be members of teams responsible for the design of new delivery systems or of cross-functional improvement teams. Often, however, managers at this level have no defined role in the improvement effort.

Each division owns processes that might not be a part of these efforts. While these processes might depend on outside suppliers and require, for example, data processing support, they are acknowledged as the province of one division. Changes in these processes will not substantially affect others. Often, identifying the need for improvement in these processes results from analyzing delays, errors, or rework within the division. Improving these processes is the province of teams led by divisional middle managers. These processes include:

- Customer information
- Customer complaint resolution
- Error reduction
- Form simplification
- Personnel and budget allocation
- Supply systems
- Technical training
- Workload balancing

Improving the internal customer-supplier relationships between units and reducing processing errors are often good projects for teams led by middle managers and can often have a significant effect on the efficiency of the service process.

Work Group Processes—Frontline Managers

Work unit teams are the staple of many quality improvement efforts. They can address opportunities for improving processes in their own work groups, such as personnel scheduling, work flow, equipment usage, equipment maintenance, workload balancing, response time improvement, and on-the-job training.

Unit managers and supervisors should lead these teams because they are responsible for the issues their personnel address. Unit processes in need of improvement should be selected using data analysis, not by vote or by opinion. Selecting a systematic approach to quality improvement should ensure that this requirement is met.

The Improvement Process

Many of these improvement efforts can benefit from a flexible analytical process. It is essential to train team participants in process analysis, data collection

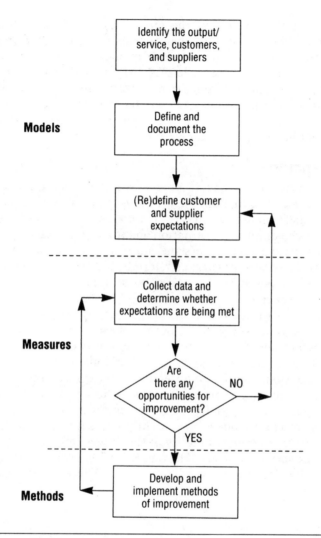

Figure 2.   **A six-step improvement process.**

and analysis, and service process solution options.[4] As the complexity of the process under study increases, more tools can be introduced through just-in-time training. The six-step process described by Randolph I. James is a useful and generally applicable introductory model (see Figure 2).[5]

Individual Processes—Supervisors

Most suggestion systems recognize only the ideas that successfully navigate a cumbersome review process bent on finding ways to say "no." Often, the process of analysis is more costly than the savings realized. What is needed is a process that recognizes participation as well as suggestion acceptance; the more suggestions that are made, the more they will be of value. The first evaluation should be placed in the hands of those with responsibility for the process, often the frontline supervisor or manager. Initial responses to suggestions should be quick. The gainsharing that is part of many current systems should be retained, and recognition for the number of suggestions made should be added. Frontline employees should be encouraged to suggest ways to make the job simpler. Planned experiments to test new ideas should be a fact of life at all levels of the organization.

Daily Management

Maintaining control of daily work processes is an ongoing management responsibility. Key factors that are important to the customer should be part of daily work measurement systems. Four hierarchical levels of measures are needed to provide complete information about a process: customer behavior, customer satisfaction, end-process measures, and in-process measures (see Figure 3). Customer behavior tracks referrals and retention, with particular emphasis on why customers give or receive service referrals or go elsewhere for service. Customer satisfaction measures overall impressions of service quality and value. Particular attention is paid to critical incidents of service failure and to customer suggestions. Both of these measures are learned from customer contacts, surveys, and interviews. End-process measures are factors such as timeliness, rate, volume, accuracy, and class that directly relate to customer satisfaction. Significant differences between customer expectations in these areas and actual performance are identified as problem areas. In-process measures focus on the quality of the process that delivers the service or product. These might include error rates or process times for each step of the process. Understanding the variability of the process and identifying statistically significant variations lead to the identification of special causes of problems and to the design of control measures. These same measures can

> Key factors that are important to the customer should be part of daily work measurement systems.

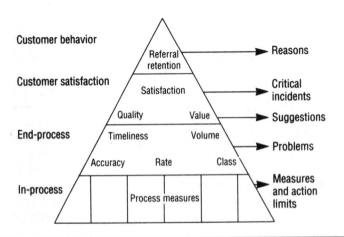

Figure 3. **Daily managment.**

demonstrate the results of efforts to reduce process variability and the common causes that impede peak process performance and degrade customer service.

Customer-Friendly Employees

What customers require of any service organization, including government, is courteous and customer-friendly employees who provide the products and services promised. Many complaints about poor government service involve employee behavior. Customers expect:

- Care and concern on the part of public contact employees
- Problem-solving capability in frontline personnel
- Flexibility in the application of policies and procedures
- Recovery, or the ability of frontline employees to make things right when errors are made.

In the service arena, the interaction between server and customer is an integral part of the product. It is equally important that the process works and that service representatives are customer-friendly.

Customers judge the performance of an organization through moment-of-truth episodes in which they come into contact with any aspect of an organization and get an impression of the service quality.[6] To manage these episodes, managers must identify the moments of truth and learn how the customers define success. They must:

- Create a service behavior model for employees
- Hire, inspire, train, and develop customer-oriented frontline employees
- Measure behavior
- Give feedback and take action on the results
- Empower employees to solve problems for customers
- Recognize employees (see Figure 4).

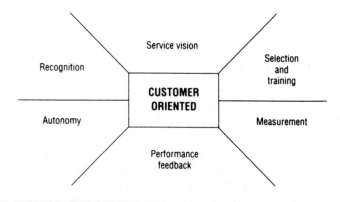

Figure 4. **Service orientation model.**

Service Vision

Management's first responsibility is to establish a clear vision of superior service. This should be done by questioning customers, studying customer feedback and complaint data, identifying behaviors that are important, and creating definitions for those behaviors. One model created in a large public contact government agency is the seven C's of customer service: courteous, clear, concise, correct, complete, concerned, and clean. Each of these C's is further defined in Figure 5. These customer service behaviors are taught as part of all introductory training.

The seven C's of customer service: courteous, clear, concise, correct, complete, concerned, and clean.

Courteous
- Welcome customer
- Acknowledge customer's presence
- Make eye contact and smile
- Use a pleasant tone of voice
- Be polite and helpful
- End on a friendly note

Concise
- Respond quickly
- Explain delays
- Give concise explanations and instructions
- Verify customer's understanding
- Focus on the business issues

Complete
- Provide complete service
- Ensure complete documentation
- Give complete instructions and answers
- Understand policies and procedures
- Do it all the first time

Clean
- Look appropriately well-groomed
- Maintain a neat, safe, and pleasant work area
- Take responsibility to keep all areas clean and uncluttered

Clear
- Clarify using questions
- Give clear instructions
- Use understandable explanations
- Speak clearly
- Do not use jargon
- Use the customer's language if possible

Correct
- Ensure correct documents
- Correctly enter data
- Correctly answer questions
- Learn from inevitable mistakes
- Do it right the first time

Concerned
- Take time to listen
- Give the customer your full attention
- If you are unsure whether someone needs help, ask
- If you can't help, find someone who can
- Be willing to explain
- Know where to direct customer for service

Figure 5.   **The Seven C's.**

Selection and Training

Good interpersonal skills along with the ability to learn the technical aspects of the job, are essential for any customer-contact employee. Interviewing and job testing is, at best, an inexact science. At a minimum, written tests and interviews should probe as many of the necessary behavioral skills as possible. A better but more time-consuming approach is to expose potential employees to simulated real-world situations through, for example, video modeling and to have them choose one of several alternative responses to the situations depicted. Careful design of such testing can help identify those who are not customer-friendly

Training is consistently neglected in government. It is often the first area to undergo budget cuts and is often underfunded. At least four areas of training are essential for every customer-contact employee in an organization dedicated to continuous improvement:

- Job-specific technical training
- Customer relations behaviors
- Quality improvement and problem solving
- Team participation

New supervisory skills, such as team leadership, measurement and data analysis, feedback, and coaching, will also be needed.

In the future, frontline employees must develop multiple job skills, add data collection duties, and develop diagnostic and problem-solving talents.

Measurement

The advent of automation in the public sector has brought with it a tidal wave of data but very little information. Organizations need to separate performance data that are essential for the budgeting and planning process from the data that reflect service quality. While volume, rate, and cost data are essential for budget planning, they are of little or no value in assessing whether the organization is meeting the customers' requirements. Measures such as timeliness, service availability, courtesy, and responsiveness to problems are the measures that are important to the customer. These measures are best collected from customers, processes, frontline workers, and supervisors' observations. These measures are the driving force of quality improvement. An example of a survey that relates to the seven C's of customer service is shown in Figure 6.

Performance Feedback

James describes a performance feedback model that involves the management of six elements:[7]

1. **Expectations.** Clearly defined expectations enable employees and work groups to assess performance.
2. **Data relevance.** Data should show how customer requirements and expectations were or were not met.
3. **Data clarity.** Data should be easily understandable.
4. **Source credibility.** The closer the data source to the customer, worker, or job, the better.
5. **Delivery schedule.** Delivery should be frequent and timely (while there is still time to act on the data).
6. **Power.** Management should be willing and able to act on the data.

Each of these elements is part of a well-designed performance feedback system.

Measures such as timeliness, service availability, courtesy, and responsiveness to problems are the measures that are important to the customer.

Your comments are important to us.

Dear customer,

Our goal is to provide you with the best possible service. Recognizing that sometimes we succeed and other times we fail, we would like to know how well we are doing. Your comments will help us serve you better.

	No opinion	Strongly agree	Agree	Disagree	Strongly disagree
Technicians were courteous					
Explanations and instructions were clear					
Technicians were quick and efficient					
The work was completed accurately					
Complete information was provided					
Technicians were helpful					
The office was clean and the employees had a businesslike appearance					

Is there a technician you would like
to commend?   Name:_____

If you disagree or strongly disagree _____
with any of the above statements,   _____
please share your viewpoints.   _____

_____

Date of visit: _____ Time of visit: _____
Name: _____ Tel. number: _____
Address: _____

Figure 6. **Customer service questionnaire.**

Empowerment

Ensuring compliance with laws and regulations will always be one of the government's main responsibilities. Many government agencies tend to demand compliance on most issues. This limits the ability of frontline managers, supervisors, and staff to act on behalf of the customer by making reasonable exceptions to policy. The result is often the creation of several hundred-page manuals that attempt to define rules for every circumstance. Locating relevant policy is frequently difficult because most manuals are neither current nor clearly indexed.

The goal of public sector management should be to identify as compliance issues only those that are essential to maintaining the integrity of the system. For example, personal identification is at the core of the driver licensing and driver record systems. Processes to ensure unique identification for each driver must, of necessity, be compliance-driven with only limited room for exceptions.

An example from the vehicle registration process shows where an exception to established rules was appropriate. Many returning Desert Storm veterans found, on their return, that their vehicle registration had expired and that they were subject to a 40% late penalty. The rules had no exceptions for such circumstances, but management quickly set up a procedure to waive the late charges. This ensured customer satisfaction and prevented numerous legitimate complaints.

Current compliance issues should be reviewed by management. First, decide whether the issue is central to the integrity of the process. If it is, then clearly define it as a compliance issue to all employees. If any exceptions are possible, identify who has the authority to decide.

Critical review should identify many issues where the flexibility to act with common sense and discretion on behalf of the customer would enhance service and not jeopardize system or fiscal integrity. Establish reasonable boundaries for decision making (dollars, time, missing items, etc.). Start a managed process to gradually empower frontline managers, supervisors, and employees to make decisions.

Customer problems provide the opportunity for decision making. A good general rule in disputed situations is to accommodate, compromise, or add value for the customer if the value of goodwill exceeds the need for compliance. Rather than create yet another manual for decision making, educate employees by recognizing good decisions and by sharing examples and the decisions made throughout the organization.

> The goal of management should be to strike the appropriate balance between compliance and flexibility.

The one issue that must be handled with care is the incorrect decision. When an incorrect decision is made in a compliance area, corrective action might well be appropriate. An incorrect decision in an area of flexibility should be treated as an opportunity for counsel and guidance, not as a disciplinary issue. Repeated poor decision making by an individual in an area of flexibility should lead to removal of the authority to make decisions, not to a new rule for everyone. The goal of management should be to strike the appropriate balance between compliance and flexibility.

Recovery

Mistakes are inevitable. Employees should strive to prevent problems, but when they do occur, employees can effectively recover. The ability of frontline employees to make things right for the customer is a vital service element. Much has been written about recovery.[8,9] Up to five actions are appropriate when errors have been made:

1. **Apology.** Employees should apologize for the inconvenience the customer has been through.
2. **Action.** Employees should offer to fairly and quickly fix the problem.

3. **Empathy.** Employees should treat customers in a way that shows concern about fixing the problem.
4. **Atonement.** Employees should add value to compensate for the inconvenience.
5. **Follow-up.** Employees should follow up with the customer to ensure he or she got what was promised.

Autonomy to act on behalf of the customer is a principal customer expectation. This aspect of frontline behavior must be managed like any other.

Recognition

Recognition should be timely, frequent, and related to specific performance that the organization wishes to encourage.

Positive recognition is a powerful motivator. Feedback is the constant flow of information that people and teams need to do a better job. Recognition highlights specific positive results and demonstrates the appreciation of the organization. It also shows to others the kind of behaviors and results the organization values. Recognition should be timely, frequent, and related to specific performance that the organization wishes to encourage. What is considered recognition is unique to every team or individual. Be creative and varied in the range of available rewards.

Fully implemented, TQM is a transformational process. It will have significant effects not only on the service delivery process, but also on the entire structure and behavior of the organization. It will focus the entire organization on its true purpose: service to the citizens, to whom the government belongs.

References

1. Randolph I. James, *The No Nonsense Guide to Common Sense Management* (Orangevale, CA: James and Associates, 1990).
2. Peter R. Scholtes, *The Team Handbook* (Madison, WI: Joiner Associates, Inc., 1988).
3. Geary A. Rummler and Alan P. Brache, "Managing the White Space," *Training*, January 1991, pp. 55–70.
4. T. F. Gilbert, *Human Competence: Engineering Worthy Performance* (New York, NY: McGraw-Hill Book Co., 1978).
5. Randolph I. James, *The No Nonsense Guide to Common Sense Management*.
6. Karl Albrecht. *The Only Thing That Matters: Bringing the Power of the Customer Into the Center of Your Business* (New York, NY: HarperCollins Publishers Inc., 1992).
7. Randolph I. James, "Building an Effective Performance Feedback System," *Journal of Performance & Instruction*, October 1983, pp. 20–21.
8. R. Zemke and C. Bell, "Service Recovery: Doing It Right the Second Time," *Training*, June 1990, pp. 42–48.
9. C. W. L. Hart, J. L. Heskett, and W. E. Sasser Jr., "The Profitable Art of Time," *Harvard Business Review*, July–August 1990, pp. 148–156.

A. Keith Smith is the chief of field operations at the California Bureau of Automotive Repair in Sacramento, CA. He has a bachelor's degree from the University of Bristol in England.

State Governments' Growing Gains from TQM

James J. Kline

Starting with a quote from then Governor Bill Clinton, this article documents what state governments are doing to implement quality management, including a variety of specific examples from states such as Arkansas, Colorado, Florida, Minnesota, Missouri, South Carolina, and Wisconsin.

Change is never easy and undertaking a new management philosophy is hard work. But I have seen the difference quality management can make, I encourage every company in Arkansas to become involved—immediately—to ensure a bright future for our state.

—Governor Bill Clinton (May 1991)

Total quality management (TQM) is an organizational philosophy and management approach that is rapidly being adopted in both the public and private sectors. The intensity of the private sector's involvement in TQM is mirrored in the interest in Malcolm Baldrige National Quality Award applications. In 1987, the first year of the award, 12,000 applications were requested. In 1989, the number increased 542 percent to 65,000. Approximately 230,000 applications were requested in 1991, a 354-percent increase.

On the government side, both the U.S. and Canadian federal governments have adopted TQM. The provinces of British Columbia and Ontario and over one hundred North American city and county governments have instituted TQM programs. In addition, Arizona, Arkansas, Colorado, Connecticut, Massachusetts, Minnesota, Missouri, North Dakota, Ohio, South Carolina, Vermont, and Wisconsin have implemented TQM statewide. It is reported that Kansas, Pennsylvania, Tennessee, and Texas also have set up TQM programs and that a number of states—among them California, Hawaii, North Carolina, Oklahoma, and Oregon—have individual agencies using TQM.

Although the rapid adoption of TQM seems almost faddish, it is, in fact, a practical response to a number of forces that are pushing the public and private sectors to change their management philosophy and approach. And the economic and efficiency gains that result from TQM programs further spur their adoption. In addition, the recent presidential election has made TQM a politically correct philosophy. President Clinton is the first U.S. President to have been a quality-improvement team leader. He has also been active in promoting the adoption of TQM.

Faced with the need to ensure that U.S. businesses are competitive internationally, and to fulfill a promise he laid out with Al Gore in their book, *Putting People First—How We Can All Change America*, to encourage greater labor-management cooperation by setting an example in the "federal government by eliminating unnecessary layers of bureaucracy and putting more decision-making authority in the hands of front-line workers," President Clinton can be expected to continue his promotion of TQM. In promoting quality, President Clinton will be building on a solid foundation that he, as governor of Arkansas, and other governors, state and local officials, and concerned business leaders have laid. This article provides an overview of this foundation.

The Forces Pushing for Change

Two factors are driving the private sector's adoption of TQM: profit and fear. According to the CEOs of American Express, IBM, Procter & Gamble, Ford Motor Company, Motorola, and Xerox, TQM results in higher-quality and lower-cost products and services, quicker response to customer needs, closer contact with supplier and customers, and an increase in the ability of employees to contribute to customer satisfaction and business health. Specifically, they note that their companies have been able to cut product development time in half, decrease "things gone wrong" in products shipped by 75 percent, and save $1.5 billion in scrap and rework costs over five years.

A General Accounting Office study of twenty-two finalists for the Malcolm Baldrige Award in 1988 and 1989 noted a number of other benefits. The report found that the use of TQM resulted in better employee relations, higher productivity, greater customer satisfaction, increased market share, and improved profitability. Marlow Industries, a Texas company that was a 1991 Baldrige Award winner in the small business category, found that adoption of TQM helped improve its competitive position worldwide. Since 1987, when TQM was implemented, Marlow Industries has been able to increase its share of the world market by 50 percent. In addition, employee productivity increased an average of 10 percent per year, and scrap costs, rework, and other nonconformance errors were cut in half.

Just as TQM's benefits are becoming clear, a consensus is developing on the consequences of *not* being quality-competitive. Robert Benson, the president of Viccorp Restaurants, Inc., of Denver, Colorado, stated the issue clearly in *Colorado Business Magazine*: "The winners and losers of the 1990s are going to be separated by who can deliver on quality." In an article in *Nation's Business*, Michael Barrier echoed this sentiment when he noted that TQM is not only "a way for small business to improve the quality of its products and services," but "may very well be the key to survival." In his book *America and the New Economy*, Anthony Carnevale was equally blunt:

Two factors are driving the private sector's adoption of TQM: profit and fear.

"Today's consumers can afford something better than they used to. They demand, and new technologies allow, quality, variety, customization, convenience, timeliness, and mass-production prices. And in the global economy, if American industry does not meet these standards, somebody else will."

A Massachusetts Institute of Technology (MIT) study on U.S. manufacturing productivity and competitiveness, entitled *Made In America*, found that Japanese companies were consistently better than U.S. companies in product optimization, design for manufacturability, fabrication methods, and quality. The comments on the loss of the U.S. position in the semiconductor market are important for what they say about the speed with which market share can be lost and the potential impact of not being competitive: "The loss of U.S. leadership across a wide range of semiconductor technologies in the short span of about a decade has enormous implications. Semiconductors are the basic building blocks for a rapidly expanding spectrum of high-growth, high-technology industries that touch every market sector: business, industry, consumer products, and defense. They are the most critical components for computers, telecommunications, factory automation and robotics, aerospace, radar, and many consumer products. They provide controls for still more products, including automobiles, appliances, machine tools, and military equipment."

The MIT study also noted six actions—most of which are related to TQM—that the best U.S. manufacturers were taking to make themselves competitive and regain market share: (1) focus on simultaneous improvement in cost, quality, and delivery; (2) establish closer links with customers; (3) establish closer relationships with suppliers; (4) make effective use of technology for strategic advantage; (5) establish a less hierarchical and less compartmentalized organization that allows greater flexibility; and (6) institute human-resources policies that promote continuous learning, teamwork, participation, and flexibility.

It is important to note, however, that it takes time to train managers and employees to understand the importance of and implement these six actions. In addition, training is costly. For small businesses in particular, this cost may be prohibitive. A further complicating factor for the suppliers of intermediate goods and services, most of whom are small businesses, is that there is a limited time frame in which to become quality-competitive. This is because a basic precept of TQM is the use of a few quality-oriented suppliers. The fourth of Deming's fourteen points says: "End the practice of awarding business on the price tag alone. Purchasing departments customarily operate on orders to seek the lowest-price vendors. Frequently, this leads to suppliers of low quality. Instead, buyers should seek the best quality in a long-term relationship with a single supplier of any one item."

Despite these obstacles, surveys of major manufacturing companies conducted in 1990 and 1991 by *Purchasing* show that companies are becoming more quality-conscious. From 1990 to 1991, the timing of supplier quality reviews changed appreciably. In 1990, 42 percent were conducted annually, 26 percent quarterly, and 32 percent monthly. In 1991, 26 percent were conducted annually, 5 percent semiannually, 46 percent quarterly, and 23 percent monthly. Manufacturers are monitoring the quality of the products they purchase more frequently. When quality does not measure up, the 1991 survey found, 54 percent assist in correction for a specific period of time, 26 percent drop the supplier right then, and 20 percent demand self correction within a specified period of time. As competition increases, the number of suppliers a company uses will be reduced. In its comeback drive, Harley-Davidson cut the number of its suppliers from 320 to 120. Xerox reduced its suppliers from 5,000 to 300 and Harris' Electronics Systems Sector cut theirs from 2,500 to 270.

As in the private sector, a number of forces in the public sector are causing state governments to reevaluate the way they do business. Fiscal stress and voter resistance to taxes are well documented. In addition, as the private sector's level of service and product quality improves, pressure will mount on all levels of government to do likewise. The International City Managers' Association clearly noted this pressure: "Citizens have become accustomed to good service and quick responses from private-sector business, and they are coming to expect the same from local government." The association's recommended solution is to "develop a customer orientation that is based on market research and emphasizes high-quality service and responsiveness to customer demands."

"Citizens have become accustomed to good service and quick responses from private-sector business, and they are coming to expect the same from local government."

Also sparking the movement toward TQM is the persistent belief that government is inefficient and provides poor-quality products and services. A 1987 Gallup Organization survey for the U.S. Advisory Commission on Intergovernmental Relations found that most respondents felt that all levels of government only "sometimes" or "hardly ever" performed their duties efficiently and at the best possible cost (federal 71 percent, state 60 percent, and local 50 percent).

When government is rated for the quality of its products and services against the private sector, it does not fare well. Gallup surveys conducted in 1985 and 1988 for the American Society for Quality Control (ASQC) found that local government, which is always rated as the most efficient level of government, was consistently rated last when compared with private-sector organizations. Banks topped the list, followed by airlines, hospitals, hotels, insurance companies, and auto repair shops.

The 1985 ASQC survey asked respondents the causes of their complaints about quality. For all services, the major complaints were poor performance or failure to get the work done properly, slow service, cost of the service, and indifference of service personnel. For local government alone, the most frequent complaint was slowness of service (40 percent). Thus, reductions that further slow service reinforce the negative opinion about government and continues a negative cycle.

TQM on the State Level

An increasing number of state officials are recognizing that to deal with fiscal stress and the perception of inefficiency and poor quality, a new approach must be taken. For them, the new approach is TQM.

State quality efforts are called by different names. Minnesota calls its effort Strive Toward Excellence in Performance (STEP); Florida has Total Quality Leadership; and Wisconsin has set up Quality Improvement. However, the most common designation, in both the public and private sector, is total quality management.

TQM can be defined as a process-oriented, results-driven organizational philosophy and management approach, which seeks to bring about congruence between the quality of the services and products provided by the organization and the quality expectations and desires held by customers and stakeholders. As an organizational philosophy, TQM stresses meeting customer quality requirements and expectations the first time and every time. This philosophy is implemented through the use of a management approach that (1) identifies and corrects problems by means of data, not opinions or emotions; (2) empowers employees and uses teams to identify and solve problems; and (3) seeks to continuously improve the entire organization's ability to meet the demands of customers and stakeholders.

Structurally, the TQM effort is overseen by a quality council. Membership in such councils varies. For example, the Massachusetts council consists of one member of the House of Representatives, one member of the Senate, five members from executive branch agencies, three individuals from the private sector who have TQM experience, two individuals from public-sector labor unions, and two members representing the judicial branch. In Florida, the council, called the Florida Quality Management Committee, is composed of executives from leading Florida corporations. In Minnesota, a Quality Steering Committee, composed of executive department managers, oversees the state's STEP effort. However, private-sector partners are sought for specific quality-improvement team projects. They provide technical advice, access to networks and information, and help in designing surveys, products, and services.

The quality council is generally staffed by a quality-improvement coordinator. Colorado's central quality management staff consists of 1.5 full-time employees. Staffing of Minnesota's Quality Steering Committee comes from staff in the Department of Administration. Staff provide quality training and technical assistance to departmental quality coordinators and help review and authorize team projects. Minnesota's Quality Steering Committee uses these four criteria to select team projects:

- Provide front-line service delivery improvement.
- Demonstrate a high degree of employee participation.
- Create a quantifiable product.
- Show evidence of the agency's commitment to provide time, personnel, and out-of-pocket costs.

Both state government and the business community benefit from each other's involvement with total quality management. For state government there are three key benefits: the ability to tap into TQM's positive image; in-kind contributions, which lead to reductions in the learning curve and implementation costs; and increased productivity and effectiveness. For private

> Both state government and the business community benefit from each other's involvement with total quality management.

businesses, the most important benefits result from efforts that facilitate adoption of TQM, reduce training costs, and shorten the learning curve.

In states that have implemented TQM, the private sector has responded with substantial assistance. An analysis of the fifty-nine Minnesota STEP projects completed between 1985 and 1990 found that 75 percent actively involved private-sector partners. Fifty-one percent of the partners came from the business community. Team partners contributed $225,000 annually in free labor. In Florida, the business community has provided $160,000 of in-kind services to get the state's quality effort started. In Connecticut the following companies have agreed to adopt a state agency and assist with TQM implementation: GET, Olin, Pitney Bowes, Perkin-Elmer, Champion, General Electric Capital, and Xerox. In Arkansas, Arkansas Eastman loaned the state its quality management coordinator for one year to help set up and run the state's TQM effort.

For the private sector the biggest benefit of the state's involvement with TQM is the creation of an atmosphere that facilitates the adoption of TQM. Such an atmosphere reduces resistance to change and heightens the concern for quality. When combined with efforts to reduce training costs and shorten the learning curve, businesses are able to stay quality-competitive and, in some cases, gain a comparative advantage. There are two ways states are accomplishing this. The first is by creating or supporting community-based quality councils; the second is by sponsoring a state quality award.

There are over seventy-five community quality councils in the United States. The largest concentrations are in states that actively support TQM. For instance, Arkansas has eleven, Minnesota seven, and Wisconsin two regional councils and a number of local councils. Consortiums of local businesses, labor, educational institutions, and government, community quality councils have five major objectives.

1. Increase the competitiveness of local industries by teaching management and labor how to compete in the quality-competitive world economy.
2. Support local economic development by providing better quality and more efficient local governments and schools.
3. Organize sessions that highlight the experience of local companies or consultants with special expertise.
4. Conduct training classes for team members.
5. Hold celebrations in which teams present the results of their projects and are recognized for their accomplishments.

Arkansas, Minnesota, and Wisconsin represent three approaches that have been taken in nurturing community quality councils. In Arkansas, the council is the responsibility of the State Industrial Development Commission. Minnesota funded the Minnesota Council for Quality to make the phrase "Produced in Minnesota" mean quality second to none. In 1989, the council became a not-for-profit, self-sustaining organization. Wisconsin has two large regional quality networks, Madison Area Quality Improvement Network (MAQIN) and Northeast Wisconsin Quality Improvement Network (NEQIN), which developed without direct state assistance. Even so, public officials were heavily involved in MAQIN, which was cofounded in 1985 by the mayor of Madison. In addition, a large number of state agencies managers are members of MAQIN.

Experience indicates that community quality councils reduce training costs and enhance productivity. The city of Searcy, Arkansas's Quality Council attributes over $11 million worth of savings to the work of project teams in banks, steel tubing manufacturing facilities, industrial laundries, ice cream plants, and other companies.

The Erie County, Pennsylvania, Council of Excellence cites the following benefits reaped from its TQM training program.

Experience indicates that community quality councils reduce training costs and enhance productivity.

- County government is saving $50,000 a year using intensive probation as an alternative to housing inmates at prisons outside the county.
- An industrial hardware distributor decreased computer errors 750 percent.
- A manufacturer improved several processes and reduced the completion time from thirty to three days.
- A department store doubled the single-visit spending of its buying customers.

To further facilitate the spread of TQM, the states of Connecticut, Florida, Minnesota, New York, North Carolina, and Wyoming; Erie County, Pennsylvania; and the cities of Phoenix, Arizona, and Austin, Texas, have established quality awards. These awards generally are modeled after the Malcolm Baldrige National Quality Award and their purpose is clearly noted. For example, North Carolina expects its Quality Leadership Award to stimulate:

- Education and training of the management work force, both current and future, in technical and behavioral areas.
- Improvement in performance and resource management to achieve excellence of products, service, business processes, and supplier relationships for greater successes in a competitive environment.
- Exchanges of experience in implementing successful efforts toward self-assessment and continuous improvement, including regional councils and industry associations.

A 1991 study for Forward Wisconsin, that state's public-private economic development corporation, indicates the impact that a private sector-public sector relationship can have on quality awareness. The study found that 80 percent of Wisconsin manufacturers think quality control programs reduce cost, compared with 68 percent nationally. Forty-four percent of the companies with Wisconsin operations have measured the cost of quality, whereas only 31 percent of the national sample had. It was also noted that Wisconsin companies increased exports to quality-conscious Japan by 22 percent between 1989 and 1990.

The Impact of TQM on State Agencies

The types of TQM productivity improvements and cost savings commonly seen in the private sector also can be found among state agencies.

Arkansas—Arkansas adopted TQM statewide in 1989. The enacting legislation contains two elements that distinguish its program from those of other states. It ensures that no employee will lose his or her job because of the TQM effort. It also allows the Quality Management Board, after legislative review, to reallocate resources within any agency of the executive branch. As of July 1, 1990, sixty-eight project teams had started analyzing problems. For example:

Arkansas ensures that no employee will lose his or her job because of the TQM effort.

- Brainstorming was used to identify and rank problems with the publication of Arkansas's Fiscal Notes. Once identified, solutions to problems were sought. The objective was to eliminate rework errors from the publication process. A second objective was to determine what information should be included and who was interested in the publication and who wasn't.
  Solution: Set up a three-person editorial team to review the publication before printing. Survey readers on interest and desired content.
  Results: Zero errors in the first issue reviewed by the editorial team and a reduction of printing costs. The projected annual savings is $2,100.

- A team in the state's Revenue Tax Administration identified four specific problems that inhibit speedy individual income tax form return processing:
  1. Poor identification of forms.
  2. Poor form design.
  3. Massive amounts of rework.
  4. Significant work hours in processing.

  Solution: New forms were designed and processing procedures changed.
  Results: These included:

  1. Time to process refunds was reduced by four weeks.
  2. Time to process a rejection letter was reduced by two to six weeks.
  3. Ease of starting returns allows sorters to process fourteen to twenty forms per employee per day, up from twelve to sixteen per day.

4. The new form design allowed the section to eliminate the "Early Recognition System" (ERS), which will eliminate $5,388.80 in salaries.
5. The eight seasonal workers eliminated in ERS will be used in other areas.

Colorado—In January 1989, the Governor's Commission on Productivity Organization Management Systems recommended that the state begin a quality management effort. In March, the Office of State Planning and budgeting presented the governor with a draft program plan. On September 13, 1989, the first team-building retreat was held. One year later, Governor Roy Romer issued an executive order implementing TQM statewide. Colorado's TQM effort has four guiding principles:

1. Participation should be voluntary.
2. Emphasize development of interpersonal skills and team building more than the analytical skills and tools.
3. Go slow, experiment, and be flexible.
4. There should be central guidance, but not central control.

Ten state agencies have active quality-improvement teams. For example, the Social Services Child Support Enforcement Team developed a work-flow diagram to see if any of the steps in collecting delinquent child-support payments were unnecessary. Questionnaires were developed to identify the need for the steps and paperwork requirements. The responses indicated that the delinquency notices were needed less than 1 percent of the time. A check with the attorney general's office indicated that there was no legal requirement to send the notices.

Results: The routine mailing of more than 13,000 notices was stopped. The estimated annual savings are $60,000 in staff time, computer use, mailing cost, and records storage.

Florida—In August 1991, Governor Childs implemented TQM statewide. Ten agencies are currently implementing Total Quality Leadership. The Department of Transportation began its quality-improvement effort in 1985. In July 1991, the various quality activities were consolidated into the Quality Management Office. Over 150 quality-improvement team projects have been implemented. Thirty-seven of these have been costed out, with a net dollar savings of approximately $750,000. In addition, there have been an equal number of spin-offs—that is, beneficial results or solutions directly attributed to the quality-improvement teams. These addressed minor problems, and not the major problem on which the team was working. One example of each follows.

- Personnel Paperwork Errors Team
  Problem: Fifty-nine percent of the paperwork submitted to the personnel office is incorrect.

Solution: Update the personnel manual and detail how to fill out each personnel action form.

Results: Reduced paperwork errors by 50 percent. The updated annual cost $586 to produce. The savings in personnel cost due to the reduced errors is estimated to be $11,954. The net productivity increase is thus $11,368.

■ Trash Removal (spin-off) Team

Problem: The high cost of trash removal at the Panama City Maintenance Yard—approximately $4,697 annually.

Solution: The trash removal cost at Panama City Maintenance can be reduced from $4,697 to $848 annually. At present, the state's Department of Transportation personnel and equipment are removing the trash, which is reflected in the cost. It is proposed to (1) have the Panama City Sanitation Department pick up the trash using a dumpster, (2) train supervisors to ensure their crew members off-load trash daily into the dumpster, and (3) prepare a site including access for the dumpster.

Current Annual Cost	$4,697
Cost To Implement Program	1,372
First-Year Savings	3,325
Annual Cost To Remove Trash	848
Continuous Annual Savings	$3,849

Minnesota—Minnesota implemented STEP in 1985. Between 1985 and 1990, sixty STEP projects were initiated to address such problems as marketing and customer service, human-resources management, communications and information management, and financial management. The Public Safety's Drive and Vehicle Service Division provides an example of the combined effects teams can have. Teams reduced error rates, improved the computer system, and reorganized the work process in a way that reduced the need for thirty people, without sacrificing service.

Missouri—The state began its TQM effort in the summer of 1989 with the creation of an Advisory Council on Quality and Productivity that oversees the state's TQM effort. The first step was to provide TQM awareness training to agency heads and conduct an employee survey. The survey was used to identify and evaluate critical organizational issues. In 1991, seven agencies began pilot projects to deal with such issues as administration of training classes, telephone call response time, expediting bridge inspection, and improving printing services.

A team in the Highway and Transportation Department looked at the development of microcomputer applications, training, and procedures. The new system that was developed was clearer and more consistent, and enabled easier access to data, decreased the number of errors caused by redundant data entry, and reduced the volume of paper filed. It is estimated that the new

Teams reorganized the work process in a way that reduced the need for thirty people, without sacrificing service.

system saved the department $100,000 in the first years. Future savings should increase as the system becomes more complete and customers become familiar with its capabilities.

South Carolina—Prompted by the success of two Malcolm Baldrige National Quality Award-winning companies, Westinghouse Commercial Nuclear Fuels Division in Columbia (1988) and Milliken and Company of Spartanburg (1989), several agencies began examining TQM. The first were the Tax Commission, the Department of Archives and History and the Department of Probation, Parole, and Pardon Services. In 1990 the agencies using TQM formed the South Carolina State Government Quality Network. "The network," says Nathan Strong, manager of product and quality services in the Division of Human Resources Management, "is a voluntary association of individuals representing state agencies who meet to share information resources, and educational materials on quality principles." The Division of Human Resources Management provides staff support and facilitates the network and its executive committee. The five members of the executive committee, four of whom are agency heads, provide direction for network activities.

The network has just drafted a strategic plan. In March 1992, the Budget and Control Board passed a resolution endorsing the network's activities and authorizing it to act on the state's behalf in furthering the adoption of TQM. It was emphasized, however, that agencies will not be required to adopt TQM. Currently, 35 of the 110 state agencies are implementing TQM. Among the efficiency gains made in South Carolina are:

- The Tax Commission reduced the staff time spent processing tax returns and speeded up identification of fraudulent claims.
- After reviewing its mailing system, the Department of Social Services identified areas in which several changes could be made. These changes included hiring outside contractors to presort mail and changing the size of some computer-generated mailers. It is estimated that the changes will save the agency $220,000 annually. It is also estimated that team efforts to reduce rework on the production and distribution of agency manuals will save $163,000 annually in staff time.
- The Quality Steering Committee of the Department of Archives and History has overseen the implementation of 358 quality-improvement forms. The forms, combined with a new zip code recognition process, resulted in savings of $43,000. In addition, numerous work processes have been simplified and customer satisfaction has increased.

Wisconsin—Governor Tommy G. Thompson adopted TQM statewide in 1989. A five-year plan has been developed that includes a quarterly review requirement, development of joint training programs between the central council and departments by 1992–93, and development of criteria for assessing the organizational culture by 1992–93. In addition, every supervisor must complete a series of supervisory classes that include quality improvement through participatory management.

The Wisconsin Department of Revenue began TQM training in 1985 and was the first agency to implement it. Currently, 90 percent to 95 percent of the 1,200 agency personnel have been provided with Quality Improvement (QI) training. There are forty trained facilitators and more than fifty QI teams in operation. The department's TQM team studied the steps a tax return goes through when it arrives. It found that many returns claiming refunds could be diverted from the normal tax processing system.

Results: The department reduced the average turnaround time from six to eight weeks to an average of two weeks. It is estimated that this change affects 1.2 million of the 1.7 million tax filers.

A Win-Win Situation

There is a growing consensus on the benefits—increased profits, improved efficiency, improved morale, and fewer grievances—that occur when businesses implement TQM. Equally clear is the fact that not being quality-competitive could mean loss of market share and even closure. Recent experience shows that states that create an atmosphere conducive to the adoption of TQM protect their economic base. Further, by reducing training costs and shortening the learning curve, they also strengthen the relative quality-competitive position of their businesses.

Support for community quality councils and quality awards are increasingly seen as ways states can create the atmosphere needed to implement TQM. Community quality councils are particularly useful because they help facilitate and reinforce adoption of TQM by making it a community-wide effort. They also reduce training costs by spreading them among more companies and provide a forum for sharing TQM project successes and failures, thereby reducing the learning curve.

Implementation of TQM creates a strong relationship with the business community.

State officials are finding that adoption of TQM provides a number of other noneconomic benefits. First, they are able to tap into the positive attitude associated with quality-improvement efforts. Second, implementation of TQM creates a strong relationship with the business community. Major corporations have shown a willingness to provide substantial in-kind support for TQM efforts to help shorten the learning curve and reduce the cost of implementation. Finally, by focusing on quality improvement, states are able to improve their own productivity, reduce red tape, and lower costs.

James J. Kline is a consultant in Portland, Oregon. He has over eight year's experience in state and local government and has managerial experience in both the public and private sectors.

Implementing Quality

Part Three presents a collection of articles, almost all published in 1993, that deal with the strategic and tactical issues surrounding the implementation of total quality management. Reflecting what organizations have learned over the past several years, we have organized the material in this part into four logical groupings: *Quality Transformation, Quality Tools and Techniques, Functional Processes*, and *Standards and Assessments*. Within each of these groups, you will find practical advice and techniques relevant to all types of organizations.

Quality Transformation

Quality management is **not** just a set of techniques to add to your management repertoire (as we discussed in the article that opens this book). It requires a long-term commitment at the top and a disciplined, informed transformation of company culture. Managers **must** focus on supporting and developing the people who carry out the interrelated processes that characterize organizational work. This section includes an array of articles on *leadership, cultural change, customer focus, communication*, and *training*. Our selection is designed to give you a clear sense of the attitudes and approaches necessary to successfully make quality work and *how to make it happen*.

Quality Tools and Techniques

In 1993, the two techniques that most caught people's attention were *reengineering* and *benchmarking*. Some of the best publications to appear in recent years on these subjects came out in 1993. We have included an assortment of those articles to help you think about these techniques and how to implement them. Included among these is a chapter from Hammer and Champy's *Reengineering the Corporation*.

How and what to *measure* is often a mystery to managers, yet absolutely vital to implementing quality management. To shed light on this topic, you'll also find a section from

Eugene Melan's recent book on process management that lays out the principles and how to's of measuring performance.

Functional Processes

Important work is underway in many industries at the functional level (e.g., accounting, sales, and human resources), making it possible to begin documenting their successes and procedures. We have noted this and chosen to highlight six areas: *sales and marketing, suppliers* and *purchasing, product development, information technology, accounting and finance,* and *human resource practices.* Our guideline here was thoughtful practicality, and these articles describe how quality principles can help shape and improve practices in all these areas. Our most extensive section is on human resources, working with and through people to make quality happen. Featured pieces include Peter Scholtes' article on what's wrong with performance appraisal, as well as a piece on employee recognition.

Standards and Assessments

The final trend that continued and accelerated in 1993 is the expanded interest in ISO 9000 certification. Throughout the industrialized world, ISO 9000 continued to gain momentum as the de facto quality standard to achieve. This is an often-confusing area, and we have selected an article designed to clearly explain this subject for nontechnicians. Finally, we look at the Baldrige criteria as a way to audit and implement quality throughout an organization. In a fine article from the *California Management Review*, George Easton, a Baldrige examiner, assesses the state of quality management in the United States from a Baldrige perspective. You'll also find an article by Curt Reimann and Harry Hertz on the Baldrige award that compares this award with ISO 9000 registration.

* * *

We again want to refer you to the detailed bibliography in Part Four. Some of the fastest growth areas, in terms of documented case studies of successes with quality practices, are in benchmarking, reengineering, sales, supplier relations, and ISO 9000. You'll find an extensive listing of current articles and books covering all these topics plus many more.

LEADERSHIP

Quality: If at First You Don't Succeed . . .

Tracy E. Benson

This article comes from a special report in Industry Week *and presents a primer to help managers sort through the confusing maze of quality approaches and a shopper's guide to help in selecting the right consultant. It also documents "The Anatomy of One Initiative," at Kieffer Paper Mills of Brownstown, Indiana.*

In ten short years, total quality management (TQM) has become as pervasive a part of business thinking as quarterly financial results. And while it would be difficult to find anyone to disagree with the need to boost the quality of U.S. goods and services, the consensus ends there. In fact, business leaders are as widely divided about how to approach quality as the Democrats and Republicans are about how to reduce the federal deficit. Those on the far left preach the gospel of "Quality as a Philosophy." Focusing on culture as a means to improvement, they advocate spending most, if not all, of a company's budgeted time, energy, and money on vigorous campaigns to end employee apathy. The premise seems to be that real operational improvement can be pursued only once the workforce has been collectively convinced of its virtue.

The rightwingers, on the other hand, put their money exclusively on tools and training. Shunning T-shirts, banners, and logos as wasteful corporate jargon, their modus operandi is rooted in two uniquely American tendencies—

one toward action and one away from long-term planning. The polarity that prevails between the two camps and its subsequent clamor often serve to undermine the need to get something done. During the last five years, a growing group of moderates has begun to press for the need to integrate the best of both extremes. Delivering tools and training without aligning them with strategic goals is like giving someone "2,317 parts that go into an automobile and then saying 'drive it,' " notes Chuck Holland, president of Knoxville-based QualPro.

Bill Ginnodo, executive director of the Quality & Productivity Management Assn. (QPMA), Schaumburg, Ill., agrees. If you're focusing on activities like problem-solving teams, training, and process improvement without putting them into the context of improving customer satisfaction, improving the quality of the product, and improving market share, "You're missing the point," he says.

Simply adopting quality as a philosophy without the regular use of tools and methods, on the other hand, is equally dangerous. Without a way to apply it practically, the concept remains abstract, and the message on the front lines is that "they don't really mean it."

The key to choosing a path, says Paul T. Hertz, president of the Paul Hertz-Group, Miami, is to know where you want to go. Most companies "make the false assumption that total quality is a generic concept, like everyone's going to Quality World," he says. "There are a lot of levels of quality, and there are a couple of things that will automatically dictate where you wind up. One is the approach that you're going to take, another is the method you're going to use, and another is the implementation that you're going to be using." The critical question that most companies forget to ask is, "Is this going to get us where we want to go?"

Simply adopting quality as a philosophy without the regular use of tools and methods is dangerous.

Lessons Learned

It's no secret that the path to quality is bumpy. Recent headlines about "failed" programs sent shock waves through organizations and frustrated consultants who declare their efforts have been misunderstood.

Whether quality initiatives have indeed derailed or simply hit a minor speed bump, organizations that are considering how to implement quality and companies that are retooling their existing efforts can learn valuable lessons from those who went before. Following is a list of some of the most common reasons some quality initiatives hit the wall and effective methods for salvaging what may seem like a "failed" attempt.

Inappropriate motivation: When the impetus to adopt a quality initiative comes from setting a goal to win an award (such as the Malcolm Baldrige National Quality Award) or pressure from a customer to become a certified vendor, companies are most likely to take a "fix-it" approach, says Michael Taggart, executive director of the Unified Technologies Center (UTC), the business-and-industry arm of Cuyahoga Community College, Cleveland. "The biggest challenge is that companies don't want to take the time to really

THE ANATOMY OF ONE INITIATIVE

One of the most frustrating aspects of a quality manager's job is the management of expectations within the organization. That's because most people have read enough about TQM to know that significant and dramatic changes can take place that will allow the organization to compete more effectively. What interests people most is where we are now (how bad it is) and where we are headed (how good it can get). Very little time is spent considering what has to be done to get there. That attitude can often undermine the highly disciplined methodology that must be applied in order to get results. Once people know what they're getting into, though, they may be far more helpful and supportive of the entire initiative. Following is a condensed historical snapshot in journal form of two years of a quality-improvement initiative at Kieffer Paper Mills Inc., Brownstown, Ind., taken from the files of QualPro, a Knoxville-based quality-improvement consulting firm.

- **Absentee owner** and Chairman Thomas Phelps attends a conference for top executives, hears a speech on quality, and decides to install a program at the paper mill.
- **Large banners** proclaiming "We will be a quality producer" are hung around the plant, and notices are distributed encouraging employees to do only quality work. There is no perceptible improvement.
- **Mr. Phelps decides** he needs outside help and begins interviewing consultants. After checking references, he chooses QualPro. Basic training in quality principles is delivered by QualPro to managers and union leaders.
- **Mr. Phelps meets** with union leaders and learns that plant workers are aware of quality problems, but have resorted to filing grievances to get management's attention. Union leaders recognize the need for improvement, but voice concerns over management commitment and the ability of workers to handle basic math.
- **Kieffer announces** a $25 million expansion project to produce "engineered" pulp from recycled paper waste. A new 21st-century pulp mill with 40 employees will adjoin a 19th-century Kieffer paper mill that employs 100. QualPro's quality-improvement methods will be used for the first time in a new start-up.
- **To establish** the need for change, QualPro consultant David Pruett and newly trained project teams begin to document and analyze problems. They find Kieffer is steadily losing old customers and has survived only by developing new niche products and then finding customers to use them. They also learn lost customers are not being tracked.
- **One team discovers** problems such as the lack of a good basis-weight scale, which prompts the shop to "guess" at the weight per square

Continued—

The Anatomy of One Initiative (continued)

foot of paper they are about to ship. "Guessed" weight results in paper that is 9% more costly to the customer than was ordered. This irritates customers, causing them to take their business elsewhere. There is no indication of how long the company has been working with faulty data.

- **The need for basic education** is becoming obvious. Managers learn that two workers who are illiterate are worried. The plant engages a high-school instructor to teach reading to anyone who is interested. Six employees sign up.

- **These and other findings** gradually convince managers of the need for change. More project teams are formed and assigned specific tasks. Teams use methods learned in training and work with the coordinating consultant until their skills are fully developed.

- **The need for a measurement system** becomes obvious and critical. A major customer returns a shipment complaining the paper is "not stiff enough." Employees develop a unique "stiffness test" The homemade "droop-test" method works, and later a commercial instrument is installed.

- **A crisis develops** at the pulp mill when the dewatering press leaves "crush marks," which cause the sheets to tear, prompting the manager to shut it down. The plant is at a standstill while many solutions are attempted, all unsuccessfully. The pulp mill manager, newly trained in quality-improvement methods, pinpoints the major cause in one hour using a five-factor eight-run DOE (design of experiments—see note). The procedure shows a warped belt on the press is responsible and that higher tension will help. No marks are found after adjustment is made.

- **The concept** of customer satisfaction is gaining ground in the paper mill. A procedure is refined to track rejected shipments by customer, by weight, and by total number of units shipped instead of by total weight alone. Results are closely analyzed and charted, leading to new refinements. Also, a customer profile listing the most important characteristics for each customer is given to the production force.

- **The consultant notes** that operators have become accustomed to control charts and are able to spot trouble sooner. Self-directed, unsupervised six-person work teams in the pulp mill are gaining confidence in their ability to run the process. They learn all jobs in their operation, and test data are made available to all on a computer network.

- **A major customer** of the paper mill is ready to discontinue buying because of paper dirt spots. A work team examines the problem and initiates process changes and improvements. The result: Kieffer is able to guarantee that 98% of shipped product will meet or exceed

Continued—

The Anatomy of One Initiative (continued)

specifications. The customer stays and subsequently increases its or-ders.

- **One quality team finds** a way to reuse a $50,000 screen with only $200 in modifications.
- **The paper mill wins** a major order for a national magazine insert re-quiring stiff and bright heavyweight paper. The plant manager says the plant could not have handled this before DOE demonstrated the need for improved sizing.
- **Chairman Phelps says** the quality-improvement program, which saved more than $1 million, is responsible for the survival of the com-pany during severe price wars during the previous year. Though some problems persist, Mr. Phelps says that overall quality from the pulp mill is so good that customers are finding new products in which to use recycled pulp.
- **Mr. Phelps announces** a 30% expansion of the pulp mill, which is running over designed capacity. The mill is running seven days per week because of the elimination of variation in process as well as in product.

Note: Design of Experiments (DOE) is a sophisticated quality-improvement tool that meas-ures the relative impact of several factors in a given process area. The impact of all factors in question is measured simultaneously, eliminating the need to conduct independent and extensive testing on each variable. DOE is generally used to isolate opportunities to refine a process or for process redesign once a set of problems within the process has been stabilized.

get off to a good start because they're under pressure to get so many people trained or get something launched."

No upfront assessment: Because so many companies perceive the quality quest as generic, they often fail to take a studied look at where they are now and compare it with where they want to go. "When that is done," says QPMA's Mr. Ginnodo, "the facts are laid out: 'Our customers think our serv-ice stinks,' or 'Look at our unit's production costs compared with our com-petitors' costs.'" That sort of "gap analysis" not only serves to orient the whole initiative, but also demonstrates the need for change to those who will be responsible for carrying it out.

Training as a miracle cure: Although it is a critical component of the overall quality picture, training in and of itself will not produce results. "When the trainer walks away and there's no infrastructure [in the] organi-zation to make quality happen, no plan, no gap analysis, no follow-up, no management support, it's just going to die," says Mr. Ginnodo.

Lack of role definition: It's easy to talk about quality—by now everybody knows the language. But to transform rhetoric into reality, every person within the organization needs to understand specifically what quality means

To transform rhetoric into reality, every per-son within the orga-nization needs to un-derstand specifically what quality means to him or her.

to him or her. "What does the president do differently once total quality is implemented, for example?" asks Dr. Hertz. "Does he or she know that? Do they know how they are going to be acting or thinking differently?" Getting away from abstract conceptual statements, he says, is the only way companies can achieve a permanent transformation of culture.

Failure to address individual management style: Companies often set about improving their working environment by teaching people how to work together on teams. What they usually forget, though, is that the dictatorial management style that exists even in pockets of the organization will obstruct these efforts. "Somebody can be on three teams and have a supervisor who's autocratic, and they're miserable," says Dr. Hertz. "They have to live with that supervisor 90% of the time."

Bumping heads with the company's infrastructure: In most cases, companies appoint an individual or department whose sole mission is to coordinate the company's quality-related activities. Unless these individuals work hard to tie elements of the quality initiative directly into things like reward and appraisal systems and career development, "ownership" of the initiative will continue to reside outside of the various operational areas of the company. Bypassing the organizational structure—not making quality values a part of everyone's job—means that quality will never become integrated into the way people work.

Disconnect between strategic objectives and quality improvement: Quality-improvement projects that are not tied directly into key business needs are apt to send the signal to employees that the whole effort is aimless and ill-conceived. Companies need to identify four to six key quality success measures "that can be understood and addressed by everybody," notes QPMA's Mr. Ginnodo. Without these key measures, such as market share, customer satisfaction and employee perception of quality, "you really don't have any way of keeping people apprised of your progress and orienting them correctly."

Mismanaging the transition: Organizations often underestimate the pressure of keeping the old system running until the new system is completely installed. "They'll have a batch of bad product, and they know the new system says you really shouldn't send that out," says Dr. Hertz. "But the old system says we have a commitment to the customer—maybe we'll try to slip it by." The result is that managers will "let it slide," but often out of their own frustration will fail to explain the decision to their employees. "For people who go to a training seminar, get turned on by the philosophy, and then come back and see business as usual, they say, 'Quality's dead.' They look at it as a very negative signal."

Giving it up too soon: Because the dramatic improvements tend to come early on, companies whose initiatives seem to slow in the second or third year often make the mistake of seeing their effort as stalled. This is particularly dangerous if there is a perceived setback with a major project or team. Some managers, driven by a self-fulfilling prophecy, will take this opportunity to proclaim, "I didn't think it was going to work in the first place." That can be tragic, notes UTC's Mr. Taggart, "because if they just tough it out over that one little hump, they may find the breakthrough they need to propel the effort forward."

How to Salvage a 'Failed' Attempt

Whether or not a stalled quality-improvement initiative can be salvaged depends to a large degree on how the managers involved perceive the problem. If the prevailing tendency among management is to say, "I told you so," there's not a lot of leverage to move the effort past the plateau. If, on the other hand, there is a sufficient number of executives (or even one very strong one) who support quality management as a means to increase competitiveness, they can exert enough influence to get the effort back in gear. Either way, there is nothing more dangerous than to allow a quality-improvement initiative to languish in apathy.

Face facts: In the end, it takes unwavering and genuine support from senior managers for a quality-improvement effort to thrive. And even though most executives openly declare their support, many don't take it seriously enough to change the way they behave. When that happens, the power of a quality coordinator to influence change becomes dramatically limited, and his or her ideas will become increasingly ineffective.

> There is nothing more dangerous than to allow a quality-improvement initiative to languish in apathy.

To get the effort back on-line, says QPMA's Mr. Ginnodo, the quality manager needs to orchestrate a "sit-down, drag-out conversation" amid a cross-functional gap representing both management and employees. The idea is to address on a fundamental level everything from progress the company has made to areas of disappointment. Often this sort of open disclosure between people whose expectations have been raised and then dashed will result in a renewed trust and commitment to make it work.

One way to facilitate this dialogue is to conduct an internal survey. By sharing the results with senior managers, says QualPro's Mr. Holland, "we can see if they understand the necessity for having dramatic improvements, if they understand that that's the missing piece of the puzzle they've been working with." When top managers officially sign on, they're ready for action.

Do something!: By this time in a typically stalled effort, the company has digested enough rhetoric to sustain another five management fads and has undergone enough training to receive college accreditation. What the company needs now is results. Mr. Holland suggests selecting a few (no more) processes that are key to the customer and working toward improving these dramatically within six months. "In that kind of situation you can be sure they haven't focused on dramatically improving what's important to the customer. We've got to show them that this stuff works here. We'll be putting the car together for them."

Don't try to move mountains: By and large, quality managers know that to effect lasting change they must tie quality improvement into the company's infrastructure. That can be daunting, though, if what that really means is that systems such as reward and recognition, appraisal, and promotion need to be completely overhauled. Dee Gaeddert, co-author of *Quality on Trial*

(West Publishing Co., 1992), suggests that the *existing* systems can, in fact, be used to drive quality improvement into every level of the company.

"You probably have a performance-appraisal system in place, and within that system you may have 15 factors on which you evaluate any given individual. One of these factors should have to do with how you manage your customer relationships." Avoid using global language like, "Manage your customer relationships more effectively," she asserts, and use this opportunity to get specific. "When you describe what you expect, say, 'I expect you to conduct 10 interviews with your customer this year.' Now there's no doubt in my mind what you expect from me. I know how to accomplish that."

Be honest: Nothing engenders trust, loyalty, and commitment among employees more strongly than integrity. Nobody expects the changes that companies and individuals are undergoing to take place overnight. Moreover, employees know that if the transformation is real—that is, if it's more than grist for the corporate public-relations mill—managers and processes will occasionally stumble. The key is to be open. When a manager faces a situation that demands "business as usual," explains Dr. Hertz, "tell your people and your customers why. Tell them, 'We know this isn't the right way, we know it's not the way we're going to be doing it, but based on these conditions, we have to do it this way.'" It boils down to "knowing where you want to go," he says, "knowing that you can't get there overnight, and being open."

Employees know that if the transformation is real managers and processes will occasionally stumble.

Picking a Consultant

Choosing a consultant to guide your company's quality-improvement initiative is like moving to a new town and selecting a primary-care physician. You want someone who comes highly recommended by those whose opinions you trust, has a depth of background, is up on the latest developments in the field, is an excellent diagnostician, and is either directly affiliated with or in a position to arrange necessary care from the best specialists in the field. Beyond these basic considerations, more subtle issues are likely to affect your search for the right consultant.

For one thing, you need to establish your expectations of the client-consultant relationship from the start. If you want to drive the entire effort yourself—from design to training and through implementation—you'll want to amass a number of firms that specialize in the various components of TQM. If you'd rather rely wholesale on the expertise of one consultant, you'll play a more traditional customer role.

Another alternative is to approach the relationship as a strategic partnership, much the way manufacturing companies are beginning to relate to their suppliers. The Unified Technology Center's (UTC) Michael Taggart says that a situation in which "both parties come to the table with the knowledge of their issues, concerns, and what they want out of it" offers the highest leverage for transformational change.

Beyond offering the best opportunity to lend skills, partnering allows both the client and the consultant to remain true to the objectives. Because of internal pressures to show results, for example, there will undoubtedly come

BEWARE THE QUALITY QUACKS

As an operating concept, quality is certainly not new to American business—the ASQC recently celebrated its 47th Annual Quality Congress. As a management philosophy, however, TQM has begun to pick up serious steam during the last five years. And just as in the case of "green" or environmentally friendly marketing a few years ago, dedicated practitioners of quality management have had to run hard to fend off advances by those just out to make a buck. These days, it seems, almost anyone can hang a shingle and declare himself to be a quality expert.

- **A consulting company** developed a quality-improvement "technology" designed to boost productivity. Called "The Least Valuable Employee," the tool was promoted for use on work teams, where "no one would want to be singled out as the least-productive member."
- **A fired vice president** of a Southeastern manufacturing company was hired by a quality-improvement consulting company even though he had no background in quality improvement. On his first day, he was sent by himself to do quality-improvement consulting with the top-management team of a large manufacturing company.
- **An organizational psychologist** who had no background in quality improvement bought a book on simple statistical tools and read it over one weekend. The following Monday, she had her business cards changed to read "Quality Improvement Consultant."
- **Three men** had worked for a company that won a Malcolm Baldrige National Quality Award. However, all had left the company at least three years before the company won the award. Yet together they started a quality-improvement consulting company and advertised that they had helped their old employer win the Baldrige.
- **A minister** with no background in quality improvement attended a five-day quality-improvement seminar. Two months later, he mailed out brochures indicating he was an expert in all aspects of quality improvement.
- **A textile company** took an ex-manager who had been a repeated failure in several positions and named him its corporate quality manager.
- **A large accounting firm** wanting to get into quality-improvement consulting took one of its existing partners, who knew nothing about the field, and named him "Manager of Quality Improvement Consulting."
- When the quality education and consulting business got "hot" in the early 1980s, **a firm specializing in human-resources consulting** switched its so-called specialty to quality-improvement consulting. Yet it continued to use the same staff and do the same things.

Lesson to be gleaned? When shopping for quality counsel, be vigilant about researching a candidate's credentials to avoid becoming a lab experiment by quacks like these.

a time when the client company's quality manager will press the consultant to deliver more and deliver it faster.

"Anyone who really has your best interests in mind will be strong enough to look you in the eye and say, 'I know you're anxious to get off the ground, but I strongly encourage that you take the time to do these things.' That's a good test," Mr. Taggart observes, "because later on down the road, you may need to be challenged about what you think you should be doing, and you need to know that you've got a consultant who's willing to be straightforward."

Without establishing a win-win agreement up front, both parties stand to get hurt if the effort fails down the road.

If the client company insists on calling the shots, for example, it may not distinguish that fact later on. "When it doesn't go right," says Mr. Taggart, "they're going to say to the consultant, 'You're the one who did this for us.' "

Successful outcomes are as important to the consultant as they are to the client, says QualPro's Mr. Holland, because "in this business, 'it is by their fruits that you shall know them.' "

Companies often make the mistake of overlooking valuable resources other than traditional consulting companies. Educational institutions, particularly community colleges, offer a wide variety of services to today's industrial companies. "There are over 1,100 community colleges throughout the country," says Mr. Taggart, "most of which have a business-and-industry training component of some sort." Their common mission, he says, is to help companies get competitive advantage through education and training.

The UTC offers northeast Ohio businesses everything from executive-level conferences to training-needs assessment to the development and maintenance of on-site learning centers. And the center partners with the industry arms of other leading community colleges to coordinate and deliver training for clients who operate plants in more than one city.

Whether you select a one-man shop or a larger, more established firm, or choose to tailor a program with your community college, you'll want to be sure the following issues are addressed.

Avoid generic one-size-fits-all treatment: Consulting firms often seek to bolster the credibility of their services by lavishly promoting successes reaped by their secret "formula." Although there is merit in many of these working models (how would TQM have spread without them?), consultants should be open to customizing around a client company's particular business concerns. "All companies do not suffer from the same ills," says QualPro's Mr. Holland. "It's kind of like saying we've got a hospital, and everybody who comes in is going to get penicillin. They've got different ills—you have to provide different treatment."

Upfront assessment: Regardless of the approach, every consulting engagement should begin with some sort of assessment. Like a complete physical exam, it allows the consultant to correctly diagnose the "ills" and then tailor the appropriate treatment. Moreover, it represents an opportunity for the consultant to "get to know the organization," says the UTC's Mr. Taggart, before he or she begins recommending changes.

Look to build internal capability: A good consultant often acts like a therapist. He helps the client get to the root of the problem, guides him toward a long-term practical solution, and then steps out of the way so that the client can solve it. In order to sustain the early improvements that lead to competitive breakthroughs, a company must learn to stand on its own feet, because "at some point, the consultant is going to leave," Mr. Taggart notes.

To avoid falling into the dependency trap, the company should designate a group of people who will ultimately take responsibility of quality improvement throughout the organization. This cross-functional team should be supported through ongoing training and should be fully in place by the time the consultant is ready to cut the company loose. Ideally, these folks should represent most, if not all, of the key operational areas of the company so that their expertise is evenly distributed throughout the company's key processes.

> To avoid falling into the dependency trap, the company should designate a group of people who will take responsibility of quality improvement throughout the organization.

Ensure availability for follow-up: Some consultants are so heavily booked the client companies may find it difficult to get them to move as quickly as they'd like, notes Mr. Taggart. Effective and timely follow-up, though, can often determine whether a project flies or falls. Ask candidates whether they can provide just-in-time training and informal telephone consultations when teams or projects get stuck, he suggests. And find out ahead of time how to make arrangements for these and other types of visits.

Willingness to adjust the plan: Although it is important to trust the consultant's judgment when it comes to things such as assessment and training needs, operational recommendations, and overall timing, flexibility is a must. "You don't want to have someone who feels locked into the direction and may not be as comfortable about changing schedules or priorities," Mr. Taggert says. In the end, you need to know that the sometimes-changing needs of your company drive the plan—as opposed to the plan driving the plan.

Walking the Talk at GE

Noel M. Tichy and Stratford Sherman

Jack Welch wanted to make changes at GE, but somehow things weren't working, and at first he couldn't figure out why. Then he understood that management must demonstrate at every level of the organization through its leadership that empowerment, productivity, and commitment to customer satisfaction were real at GE. Thus began what one GE consultant called "one of the biggest planned efforts to alter people's behavior since Mao's Cultural Revolution."

General Electric CEO Jack Welch was frustrated. It was a warm September afternoon in 1988, and Welch was leaving GE's Crotonville management-training center, accompanied by Jim Baughman, GE's manager of corporate management development.

For the zillionth time, a bunch of middle managers had bombarded Welch with complaints about the way things worked at their local GE outposts. Stripped of particulars, the grievance was always the same: The speaker believed in GE's shared values, but his or her boss didn't.

The CEO kept hearing such comments as these:

- "The goal of downsizing and delayering is correct. The execution stinks. The concept is to drop a lot of less-important work. But it just hasn't happened. We still have to know all the details and follow all the old policies and systems. We have no time and more demands than ever."
- "If this is the best business in the world, then why do I go home feeling so miserable?"

Welch had been CEO for almost eight years, and he knew that far too many GE managers still weren't "walking the talk."

By almost any other measure the GE revolution had made enormous progress: The corporate productivity rate, for instance, finally had broken into the 4 percent to 5 percent range, roughly twice its previous level. Welch was basically satisfied with GE's portfolio of businesses, and the worst of the layoffs had ended long ago. Progress was visible almost anywhere you looked. Resistance had become rare.

Yet, they lingered—these unimaginative, frightened, bureaucratic bosses from hell, the ones who demanded that fewer people do everything that once had been done by many more. These were the managers or supervisors who snored through the videos of Welch's speeches and then pushed their subordinates to work weekends and nights under intolerable pressure, with no end in sight, often to accomplish tasks that seemed irrelevant, senseless, or worse. When anyone complained, they blamed corporate headquarters.

Welch had to find a way to get past those people, to directly touch the great mass of GE employees. The boundaryless organization he envisioned couldn't work without the active participation of the whole workforce—but he couldn't expect people to participate in something they didn't understand.

How could he reach them?

On that particular day in 1988, the GE revolution reached its turning point. Jack Welch experienced an epiphany that enabled him to embody his whole understanding of business in a single, very practical idea. It was a big idea, the sort of transforming thought that comes along only once or twice in a lifetime.

Walking with Baughman to the helicopter that would fly them from Crotonville (in Croton-on-Hudson, New York) back to GE headquarters in Fairfield, Connecticut, the CEO was angry enough to pound nails with his fist. He'd been hearing the same complains from "GEers" for years. Unless something changed, Welch feared, he'd still be listening to the same broken record when he reached retirement age.

Welch remembers speaking with Baughman as they boarded the helicopter: "I must have had to say, 'I don't know' about 20 times today," he said to Baughman, "or 'That's not my job; that's your job,' or 'I'm sorry, I don't know why you do that stupid thing, and why you don't fix this.'

"It wasn't much of a learning experience," Welch says. On the helicopter that day, he told Baughman, "Jim, we've got to change this. We've got to get these issues dealt with. We've got to put the person who knows the answer to these frustrations in the front of the room. We've got to force leaders who aren't walking the talk to face up to their people."

Says Welch: "That was the start of Work-Out."

Baughman designed Work-Out to Welch's specifications: an ambitious, 10-year program that Harvard Business School professor and GE consultant Len Schlesinger has called "one of the biggest planned efforts to alter people's behavior since Mao's Cultural Revolution."

"Productivity Growth Is Essential to Survival"

Welch's desire to make believers of GE's middle managers was based on pragmatism as well as passion. By 1988, as he has often said, GE had done about all the "slashing and burning" it could do. In certain areas GE still lagged behind such productivity champions as Toyota, Honda, and Canon, but it had largely matched or exceeded the achievements of its direct competitors. At that level of accomplishment, just maintaining GE's productivity rate required enormous effort.

And Welch still believed GE had to improve. As he later wrote, "Without productivity growth, it is possible to lose in 24 months businesses that took

Unless something changed, Welch feared, he'd still be listening to the same broken record when he reached retirement age.

a half-century or a century to build. Productivity growth is essential to industrial survival."

By 1988, GE's top-level executives understood Welch's ideas and embraced them. The Corporate Executive Council—a group of GE's 30 top executives, who meet with him for two days each quarter to discuss business issues—had become an effective mechanism for pushing shared values. CEC members were accustomed to mining good ideas in one part of GE and moving them quickly to the rest of the company. In fact, the CEC had spawned similar councils at all of GE's 13 major businesses, engaging another layer of GE executives in the new style of management.

But as the complaints voiced at Crotonville indicated, managers further down in the organization were far less likely to share the new GE values. Middle- and lower-level managers still did not see any urgent need to change. Despite delayering, GE still had a substantial hierarchy; a few levels down in most GE businesses, junior managers were still filling out unneeded reports, taking superfluous measurements, and coping with Draconian goals.

As Welch will cheerfully concede, the intellectual underpinnings of Work-Out, from worker involvement to continuous improvement, are familiar to the point of being shopworn. The uniqueness of the program is its vast scale, which is evidence of GE's commitment.

By mid-1992, more than 200,000 GEers—well over two-thirds of the workforce—had experienced Work-Out. On any given day, perhaps 20,000 are participating in a related program. Within another few years Work-Out will have touched every single person at GE. By contrast, Crotonville programs annually can reach just 10,000 people, an elite 4 percent of the corporate population.

A mechanism to change minds, Work-Out is designed to deliver the Crotonville experience to the great mass of GE employees. Crotonville can powerfully affect those who go there, but it can't touch those who hear about it second, third, or fourth hand, because the experience depends on personal participation. You've got to be there.

Trying to replicate that rich experience for 300,000 people was like trying to design a mass-market Rolls Royce, but GE found a way. Work-Out began with four major goals:

- **Building trust.** GEers at all levels had to discover that they could speak out as candidly as members of the executive council do, without jeopardizing their careers. Only then would GE get the benefit of its employees' best ideas. Welch regarded this goal as so important that he allowed the program to proceed for years without proof that it was working.
- **Empowering employees.** The people closest to any given task usually know more about it than their so-called superiors. To tap workers' knowledge and emotional energy, the CEO wanted to grant them much more power. In return, he expected them to take on more responsibility. "There's both permission and obligation," he says.

- **Eliminating unnecessary work.** The quest for higher productivity was only one reason for pushing this goal. Another was the need to provide some relief for GE's stressed-out workers. And Welch hoped to generate enthusiasm for the program by showing employees some direct, tangible benefits of Work-Out.
- **Creating a new paradigm.** Ultimately, the CEO wanted Work-Out to define and nurture a new, boundaryless organization.

"Unnatural Acts in Unnatural Places"

Once Baughman designed Work-Out, he formed a small GE team at Crotonville to implement it. He retained two dozen outside consultants, all world-class experts on organizational change. Each was assigned to work with the top management team of a GE business to implement the generic design and tailor it to specific needs.

Baughman and his Crotonville team, responsible to Welch, led the companywide effort. Their role was to integrate the Work-Out activities of the GE units and their consultants, and to facilitate the sharing of best practices throughout GE.

Work-Out began in October 1988. The first stage was a series of local gatherings patterned after New England town meetings. In groups of 30 to 100, the hourly and salaried employees of a particular business would spend three days at an off-site conference center discussing their common problems. Dress was causal. The setting and behavior was so different from business as usual that Work-Out consultant Steve Kerr called these meetings "unnatural acts in unnatural places."

To ensure that people could speak candidly without fearing retribution, bosses were locked out during discussion times. And Welch made it clear to managers that he would treat any obstruction of Work-Out as "a career-limiting move." Facilitators, all outside consultants at first, ran the workshops.

Meeting in small groups, the employees would define problems and develop concrete proposals. On the final day, the bosses would return. According to Work-Out's rules, they had to make instant, on-the-spot decisions about each proposal, right in front of everyone. Some 80 percent of proposals got immediate yes-or-no decisions; those that needed study had to get decisions within a month. As Welch had hoped, the process quickly exposed GE managers who didn't "walk the talk."

At first, people spent much of their time griping. In a 1991 story on Work-Out, *Fortune's* Thomas A. Stewart quoted an electrician from GE's Aircraft Engines plant in Lynn, Massachusetts, who explained, "When you've been told to shut up for 20 years, and someone tells you to speak up—you're going to let them have it."

But in the course of complaining, GEers also would identify a lot of problems that could be fixed without too much effort. Picking such "low-hanging fruit," as GEers called it, was a way to build momentum and trust in a hurry.

A middle manager tells how the Work-Out process worked at one plant:

According to Work-Out's rules, they had to make instant, on-the-spot decisions about each proposal, right in front of everyone.

"We were getting screws from one supplier that were not so good. The bits would break off the screw heads, and scratch the product, and cut people's hands—we had one guy get eighteen stitches. Tempers flared, but management never fixed [the problem]. They said, 'OK, we'll get you some screws from the good supplier.' But the bad screws would always reappear.

"So a shop steward named Jimmy stood up at Work-Out and told the story. This guy was a maverick, a rock thrower, a nay-sayer. He wanted to test us, to see whether we really wanted to change.

"He knew what he was talking about. And he explained the solution, which had to do with how deep the bit could be inserted into the screw head. . . .

"We listened, and then said, 'OK, what do you suggest?'

"And he replied, 'We need to go tell the supplier what the problems are.'

"Well, I was nervous about it, but I decided to charter a plane to fly Jimmy and a couple other guys to the plant in Virginia where they made the bad screws. They left that very night.

"Jimmy got the problem fixed, and it sent a powerful signal to everyone here. He became a leader instead of a maverick, simply because we gave him the forum and allowed him to have some ownership. Now we don't even have supervision in his part of the plant. He carries a two-way radio, and if he needs help he asks for it."

> He became a leader instead of a maverick, simply because we gave him the forum and allowed him to have some ownership.

"We Knock Down the Walls"

As the GE revolution progressed, the pace of change continued to accelerate. By 1988, Welch had clearly defined his vision. Through trial and error, he had reduced it to a few simple ideas: integrated diversity, boundarylessness, global leadership, and the "business engine," which is Welch's way of explaining how each of GE's businesses fits into the corporate whole.

In technical and political terms, GE already was largely transformed; the time had come to change its corporate culture.

Preeminent among Welch's ideas is boundarylessness. In a GE annual report, Welch described the boundaryless company as one in which "we knock down the walls that separate us from each other on the inside, and from our key constituencies on the outside."

The boundaryless company, he said, will remove barriers between functions, levels, and locations. It will reach out to key suppliers to make them part of a single process, in which, "they and we join hands and intellects in a common purpose—satisfying customers."

Only through boundarylessness, Welch argued, could the corporation reach its productivity goals.

"This is an admittedly grand vision, requiring unprecedented cultural change," Welch said. "And we are nowhere near achieving it. But we have an idea of how to get there—an idea that is rapidly becoming reality. . . . It's called Work-Out."

Boundarylessness was a challenging proposition. It implied much more than just eliminating bureaucracy. "Ultimately," Welch said, "we're talking about redefining the relationship between boss and subordinate." He envisioned the replacement of hierarchy with cross-functional teams, the transformation of managers into leaders, and a radical empowerment of all the workers who were still getting bossed around.

"My view of the 1990s is based on the liberation of the workplace," he said. "If you want to get the benefit of everything employees have, you've got to free them—make everybody a participant. Everybody has to know everything, so they can make the right decisions by themselves.

"In the old culture, managers got their power from secret knowledge: profit margins, market share, [and] all that. But once you share that information with everyone, it often turns out that the emperor has no clothes.

"In the new culture, the role of the leader is to express a vision, get buy-in, and implement it. That calls for open, caring relations with every employee, and face-to-face communication. People who can't convincingly articulate a vision won't be successful. But those who can will become even more open—because success breeds self-confidence."

> The key was an insistence on emerging from every session with a list of "actionable items."

Work-Outs took place all over GE, hundreds of them. As Stewart wrote in his 1991 *Fortune* article: "Like kernels of corn in a hot pan, they began popping one at a time—in GE Plastics' silicones unit in Waterford, New York; at NBC; in the lighting business—[and] then in a great, noisy rush."

By 1989, the pent-up demand for change was enormous. Work-Out's carefully designed stagecraft made employees feel safe, freeing them to voice their complaints. Managers added to the momentum by sharing once-secret data. In those early Work-Out sessions, GE picked a lot of low-hanging fruit.

The key was an insistence on emerging from every session with a list of "actionable items"—things people were committed to start working on right away. At the Schenectady turbine plant, for instance, hourly employees complained about the milling machines they used. They won authorization to write the specifications for $20 million worth of replacement machines, which they tested and approved themselves.

The result: Cycle time—the time needed to mill steel—dropped 80 percent, lowering inventory costs while increasing responsiveness to customers.

"Legitimate Plagiarism"

While Work-Out was getting started, a related movement called Best Practices got underway. One of GE's great weaknesses always was its susceptibility to the "not invented here" syndrome. The corporation had been so accustomed to producing good ideas for so long—ever since company founder Thomas Edison, really—that GEers rarely bothered to find out what other folks were thinking. Figuring that no company could corner the market for good ideas, Welch forced the organization to look outside.

During the summer of 1988, Welch assigned Michael Frazier of GE's business-development staff to develop a list of companies worth emulating and then to study their achievements. Frazier and his team selected nine companies to study, worldwide, including Ford, Hewlett-Packard, and Chapperell Steel.

THE RENAISSANCE OF JACK WELCH: "THE NICE THING ABOUT JACK IS THAT HE KEEPS GROWING"

The epiphany that GE CEO Jack Welch experienced in the helicopter with Baughman—when the Work-Out idea was born—was emblematic of his transformation as a leader.

The CEO's earlier interactions with subordinates had been characterized by a cranked-up ferocity. By 1988, that approach was giving way to a more wholesome attitude—an urge to respect and empower people—which seemed genuine. Having started out as the man with the bullhorn, in effect yelling at subordinates who couldn't keep pace, Welch evolved into a coach, willing to pause (for a nanosecond or two) to help others along.

To some observers, the change was astonishing.

"I've watched the rebirth of Welch, or the renaissance of Welch, or whatever has happened to him," says one GE manager. "I don't know all the elements that went into his being born again, and I don't even care what they are. But I'm sure glad it's happened. He's a different man than he was in 1981."

Welch disagrees. "I haven't changed a thing!" he insists. "I try to adapt to the environment I'm in. In the seventies, when I was helping grow new businesses . . . I was a wild-eyed growth guy. And then I got into the bureaucracy and I had to clean it out, so I was different in 1981. And now I'm in another environment. But that's not being 'born again.'

"The ideas were always the same. We've been talking about reality, agility, ownership, and candor since the beginning. We just got it simpler and more carefully articulated over time. Work-Out, eight years later, is a more meaningful way of communicating the idea of ownership—but it's the same idea.

"You don't get anywhere if you keep changing your ideas. The only way to change people's minds is with consistency. Once you get the ideas, you keep refining and improving them the more simply your idea is defined, the better it is. You communicate, you communicate, and then you communicate some more. Consistency, simplicity, and repetition [are] what it's all about. . . . We never changed; we just got better at it. And after a while it started to snowball."

It seems to be true that Welch's thinking has remained consistent from the first. But many people still think the man himself has changed. Says Gertrude G. Michelson, a senior vice-president of R. H. Macy & Company, and a GE director since 1976, "He's changed from competitive to cooperative, in the broadest sense—he understands that's the real top-leadership role."

"I do think there was a change, vividly," says Larry Bossidy, CEO of Allied Signal and former GE officer, "from yelling and screaming for

Continued—

The Renaissance of Jack Welch (continued)

performance, to a much more motivational kind of approach. He became a lot more understanding, much more tolerant—'Hey, if you get the job done even though your style is different from mine, that's fine.' He wasn't that way in the beginning.

"The nice thing about Jack is that he keeps growing. The Jack Welch who took over GE is not the Jack Welch you see today."

Work-Out is evidence of a major change in Welch's thinking. He used to argue against incremental change, on the theory that only quantum leaps made enough of a difference.

Work-Out represents Welch's personal commitment to the Japanese idea of *kaizen*, or continuous improvement. This is really a cultural attitude that guides people to seek constantly for ways to get better; small improvements are as important to the process as big ones. By 1988, *Kaizen*-style methods had produced impressive results at some GE businesses, and Welch had become a convert.

Another major shift was "from hardware to software," in Welch's words. Once the organization's survival was no longer at risk, Welch had the luxury of working on the "soft" issues of corporate culture and employee behavior, requiring different behavior from the CEO. You can't boost people's self-confidence by yelling at them.

Welch has always been interested in the soft side of management. Now he is beginning to appreciate its power.

The Best Practices team's 10 members fanned out around the world and spent a full year collecting on-site data at the nine companies. Although they absorbed a lot of minutia, they retained an Olympian perspective. They were seeking answers to the question, "What is the secret of your success?"

Their report argued that the accomplishments of the world's productivity champs depended on common traits:

- They managed processes rather than people. Instead of tracking *how much* they produced, they focused on *how* they produced.
- They used process mapping and benchmarking to spot opportunities for improvement. (Process mapping involves writing down every single step, no matter how tiny, in a particular task. Benchmarking means comparing oneself to an objective standard, such as a competitor's performance.)
- They emphasized continuous improvement and lauded incremental gains.
- They relied on customer satisfaction as the main gauge of performance. That overcame the tendency to focus on internal goals at customers' expense.

JACK WELCH'S SIX RULES FOR SUCCESS

- Control your destiny, or someone else will.
- Face reality as it is, not as it was or as you wish it were.
- Be candid with everyone.
- Don't manage; lead.
- Change before you have to.
- If you don't have a competitive advantage, don't compete.

- They stimulated productivity by introducing a constant stream of high-quality new products designed for efficient manufacturing.
- They treated their suppliers as partners.

No less valuable to GE than these overarching ideas were the mind-blowing stories of the nine companies' achievements.

A typical one came from a leading producer of washing machines in Japan. According to GE's case study, this company had realized by 1984 that demographic changes would soon fragment its market into niches. That implied a need to switch from producing a few washing-machine models in high volumes to producing a broad selection of models, which would sell at lower volumes. The challenge was to accomplish that without creating profit-threatening assembly-line snafus.

The company crated a flexible production system designed to respond directly to the ebb and flow of sales. In five years the company tripled the number of new washer models it introduced. The washer factory became accustomed to 11 model changes per day, versus two-and-a-half per day in 1985.

Spending only $2 million to $3 million each year to make all the changes, the business doubled both its manufacturing capacity and the dollar amount of sales per employee. At the same time, quality dramatically improved.

After hearing the Frazier team's presentation, Welch became an instant convert. He ordered up a major new Crotonville course on Best Practices, and assigned to Work-Out teams the task of spreading Best Practices throughout GE.

He frequently quoted a favorite Baughman line: "Best Practices has legitimized plagiarism."

"Is the CEO Crazy to Set Goals So High?"

In the second phase of Work-Out, which gathered steam through 1990, GE shifted to unnatural acts in natural settings. Now the sessions began to involve groups of people who would ordinarily work together, such as the cross-functional teams of finance, manufacturing, purchasing, and marketing experts responsible for particular products. A session would begin with a clearly defined problem and a mandate to solve it.

With that shift, Work-Out began to become a regular part of the GE way of life. And self-sufficiency became a key goal: GE trained its own people as facilitators to replace the outsiders.

Work-Out now depended heavily on tools acquired from the Best Practices study, process mapping in particular.

In business after business, GEers would gain control over processes by identifying every step in them. Some process maps were so complex that they covered whole walls and resembled diagrams of the wiring in computer chips. The maps noted even such seemingly minor matters as the signatures required to approve purchases or shipments. Since a document tends to sit on a desk for a day before it's signed, cutting out a few unnecessary approvals can significantly speed up a process. (When process mapping failed to help, it usually was because the attention to detail got out of hand.)

Self-sufficiency became a key goal: GE trained its own people as facilitators to replace the outsiders.

To forge a shared commitment to speed and customer satisfaction, GE invited customers and suppliers such as 3M and Sears to join in these sessions. The gatherings were effective at building trust, but they weren't always pleasant.

At one session, complaints were registered by three companies that worked with GE Aerospace—a Union Carbide division, a major ship-builder, and a large construction consulting firm. Point by point, executives from those companies demonstrated how arrogant behavior by GEers was costing them business. Obviously, this part of GE still had its "backside to the customer and its face to the CEO."

An early example of GEers vaulting over the high bar was the Quick Response program at GE's Louisville-based appliance business. Process-mapping there showed that while a fifth of the parts in any given appliance model were unique, only 5 percent were expensive enough to substantially affect inventory costs. GE found that it could speed manufacturing and cut costs by keeping ample stocks of the cheap components, while working out just-in-time programs with suppliers to deliver the others quickly, as needed.

The biggest gains of all came from controlling the sequence in which parts were delivered from a plant's loading dock to its assembly line.

Measures such as these enabled the appliances group to reduce its inventory by $200 million—and to increase return on investment by 8.5 percentage points. It cut by more than 75 percent its 80-day cycle time from receipt of an order to delivery of a finished product.

Then, Welch put the appliances group on a pedestal, touting it as an in-house example of best practices. Louisville became a regular stop for executives from all over the company. But this was more than a corporate tourist attraction: To create a corps of Quick Response experts, each GE business sent a few managers to take a full year of "action learning" in Louisville. By the time these people returned to their own units, they had mastered the intricacies of Quick Response and could serve as effective advocates.

More recently, GE's Aircraft Engines group used Work-Out to help it figure out how to meet an ambitious 1992 income target. A big winner during the defense-spending spree of the Reagan years, the unit had produced stellar results through the 1980s, avoiding the need to do much hard thinking about productivity. But demand for military engines is slowing down. "Where's the enemy?" Welch asks with a shrug.

In 1992, Aircraft Engines' sales were declining slightly from 1991 levels of about $7.9 billion. Yet the CEO challenged the business to reduce its inventories by $1 billion to help reach a net income goal of $750 million—as much as it had made in its very best year.

To achieve that, it seemed logical that the group had to match its revenue cuts with cost cuts. For months, Aircraft Engines' managers searched for ways to achieve the massive productivity gains they needed to meet their earnings target. During Work-Out, they decided that the business could increase its efficiency enough to halve the time between customers' orders and the delivery of finished engines. That would boost cash flow and enable Aircraft Engines to cut its inventories by up to 40 percent, reaching Welch's goal.

Is the CEO crazy to set goals so high? He doesn't think so:

"What right do I have to do that?" Welch asks. "It always works. And it's rational. This is not a business that's going to recover any time soon, so it's reasonable to squeeze. And there were lots of inefficiencies built in during the boom times.

There were lots of in-efficiencies built in during the boom times.

"In a growing business, it's hard to know whether you've picked the right goal. You pick one based on the peak returns of other global businesses—but maybe that's too low.

"During a slump you have to find out what you can do. Our Aircraft Engines business is going to get to four inventory turns a year—then five, seven who knows? We've been trying to get them there for three years. . . . Now they're going to do it, because it will reduce the number of employees they would otherwise have to let go."

GE spent nearly a decade getting in shape; then, in just a couple of years, Work-Out enabled it to bust through the wall. The same phenomenon has been happening all over the company during the past couple of years: GEers aren't resisting much any more. They understand the imperatives of global competition, and they're determined to win. So instead of complaining when the bar is raised, they focus on how to surmount it.

"I Held 21 Meetings, So Now It's Over"

The third phase of Work-Out began in 1992. Called the Change Acceleration Program, or CAP, it is a systematic attempt to use Work-Out to breed a new type of GE manager. Welch wants all of GE's leaders to be professional change agents rather than mere managers. The idea behind CAP is to disseminate to top managers all of GE's accumulated knowledge and wisdom about the change process itself: how to initiate change, how to accelerate it, and how to make it stick.

Work-Out is a forum for teaching the skills that Welch expects to be the most valuable in the years ahead. It is where GEers explore the implications of boundarylessness. It is where competence becomes more important than position, and where nobody can hide behind a title or a desk.

If the CAP training works, outside facilitators won't be needed. Program graduates will fan out throughout GE to spread the revolutionary message.

"In seven years," says Welch, "people who are comfortable as coaches and facilitators will be the norm at GE. And the other people won't get promoted. We can't afford to promote people who don't have the right values."

Work-Out has not been perfectly successful. Cynical GEers have described it as "Work-In." Many stressed-out GEers still regard liberation as little more than a distant dream.

And there remain some fascinating issues that Work-Out has yet to address. An important one is compensation. Work-Out parcels out authority, but not money, according to individual merit. Eventually, GE probably will have to devise more equitable gain-sharing systems, to share the rewards of improved productivity with those who are most responsible for it—regardless of rank.

By now, so much low-hanging fruit has already been picked that it may be reasonable to wonder how much longer GE can sustain the momentum of the last few years. But as the Work-Out process becomes more powerful and people grow to trust it, more opportunities for improvement come into view. The supply of low-hanging fruit may be inexhaustible.

A Work-Out session led GE Medical Systems, for instance, to patch a major supplier into its internal electronic-mail network. The two companies also decided to build new-product prototypes jointly. As they work more closely together, they keep stumbling over additional opportunities to improve designs, lower costs, and speed processes. As in human relationships, intimacy can become its own reward.

The supply of low-hanging fruit may be inexhaustible.

Work-Out's success is hard to measure. As Welch explains, that's intentional.

"It's best to present big ideas without time frames or rigidly defined goals," he says, "because there is resistance to every idea that's different from the current norm. If you allow the nay-sayers to measure and quantify your idea, they can come back and blow it away before it has a chance to work.

"For the first year of Work-Out, some people would have loved to measure it. Then they'd have been able to say, 'I held 21 meetings and 591 people attended, so now it's over.'

"How will we know if Work-Out is successful? We'll know because over time we'll become more productive. Our attitudes will be better, people will be happier, [and] better ideas will flow."

As a formal mechanism for sustaining a revolutionary process—and for transferring real power to employees—Work-Out is unsurpassed. But those who are tempted to try the program themselves should beware: GE's already successful transformation is what enabled Work-Out to succeed. Without that foundation—without all the pain and difficulty of Welch's early years—Work-Out's techniques would not have had much effect.

As Welch says, "You better be lean before you play these games."

Noel Tichy, a professor at the University of Michigan School of Business, is a longtime consultant to General Electric. Stratford Sherman is a senior writer for Fortune.

CULTURAL TRANSFORMATION

Ten Reasons Why TQM Doesn't Work

Oren Harari

This intriguing article documents the kind of goals that can displace what is really at the heart of TQM: continuous improvement at satisfying customers. The author argues that companies often get so hung up on the mechanics of TQM that they forget why they began its implementation in the first place. As the article at the beginning of this book reminds us, TQM is not a particular set of procedures or roles; it is a more realistic way to make sense of what organizations do. This article shows what happens when managers forget this.

Many managers are beginning to rethink their love affair with TQM. By TQM I mean all those programs promising big boosts in quality, and yes, I know the title of this article could get me into trouble. Somebody's bound to trot out a TQM program that has achieved incredible results. No doubt successful programs exist. But for every success story, I'll show you two disappointments, or more. Put together all the independent research conducted by consulting firms Arthur D. Little, Ernst & Young, Rath & Strong, McKinsey & Co., and A. T. Kearney, and you come up with the conclusion that only about one-fifth—at best one-third—of TQM programs in the United States and Europe have achieved "significant" or even "tangible" improve-

Reprinted with permission of the author. This first appeared in *Management Review*, January 1993, published by the American Management Association, New York, NY.

ments in quality, productivity, competitiveness or financial returns. This is a frightening conclusion given the hype that has accompanied TQM for years. It's even more serious given the fact that three-quarters of reasonably sized American firms claim to have invested in some form of TQM.

The findings themselves no longer surprise me, and that doesn't make me special. Managers are beginning to realize TQM is not synonymous with quality. Quality is essential for organizational success and competitive advantage. TQM is only one of many possible means to attain quality. In other words, quality is sacred; TQM is not. There's another difference: As we shall see, quality is about unbending focus, passion, iron discipline and a way of life for all hands. TQM is about statistics, jargon, committees and quality departments.

Yes, of course, the two concepts sometimes converge, but there are at least 10 reasons why they are likely not to. The remainder of this article is a frank attempt to explain the disquieting research findings cited above. In that spirit, let me propose 10 reasons why TQM programs often don't work even in organizational environments that desperately cry out for quality improvements.

> Quality is about unbending focus, passion, iron discipline and a way of life for all hands.

1. TQM Focuses People's Attention on Internal Processes Rather than on External Results

Despite all the lip service to the contrary, the actual day-to-day mechanics of most TQM programs hypnotize—if not require—managers and nonmanagers to become internally focused, even as all the action is happening externally. Consider the preoccupation with internal performance measurements, conformance indices and technical specifications. That preoccupation inevitably diminishes managers' attention to external factors like constantly shifting perceptions and preferences of customers, as well as all the marketplace choices available to them, all the technological advances occurring that might positively impact them, and all the potential product and service enhancements they might respond to. Thus, what an internally focused company actually does may result in a product or service that in the eyes of the customer is outdated, blandly conventional, insufficient or just plain irrelevant. As one manager told a colleague of mine: "Before we invested in TQM, the rap on our company was that we churn out poorly made products that customers don't want. Now, after TQM, things have changed. We now churn out well-made products that customers don't want."

I've noticed another insidious consequence of this internal focus. It is difficult to sell TQM to nonmanufacturing, nonoperations groups like sales, marketing, design, engineering and, for that matter, anyone in any organization who is providing intangible services. These are people who could and should be influenced by strategies to add value to end-users, which is the ultimate goal of real quality anyway. Since TQM activities don't explicitly address this issue, they often are perceived by these in-house professionals as only marginally relevant to their concerns, and rightfully so. Hence, many of them wind up attending the classes and plotting the innumerable charts, only under duress.

The Baldrige Award is actually counterproductive when it reinforces this internal preoccupation. It does so by allotting only 250 or so possible points out of 1,000 to the actual results of a firm's quality efforts; the remaining are allotted to internal process improvement. Internal process improvement is a good thing, but if that's where managers focus their primary attention, the firm becomes more "efficient," but less responsive, flexible and interesting, hence less "effective."

2. TQM Focuses on Minimum Standards

Zero defects products and no rework efficiency are laudable goals, and they must be pursued. If TQM can help, well and good. But those are minimal standards these days. Attaining them means you get to play in the arena; they're the price of entry, not guarantees of success. Unfortunately, TQM seduces many people into believing that minimum standards define quality. They do not. In today's frenzied global economy, quality also includes the capacity to offer customers things that add excitement, ease and value to their lives. Quality means offering your customer products and services and personal experiences with your company that they will find easy, useful, intriguing and even fun. In customers' definitions of quality, zero-defects is merely one small part of that package, and it's a given.

> Quality means offering your customer products and services and personal experiences with your company that they will find easy, useful, intriguing and even fun.

Tom Peters has a wonderful analogy on this point. Remember the scene in the film *Amadeus* where young Mozart plays before Emperor Joseph II? First he plays a mechanically perfect and uninspiring Salieri score, then he begins to improvise, and suddenly the music soars and the listener is immediately stirred. Salieri's music was zero-defects TQM music. Sure, Mozart could play TQM music; without the technical proficiency to do so, he wouldn't have been allowed to sit at the piano in the first place. But if that's all he could do—if he couldn't add value to the notes with creativity, flair and beauty—Mozart's name and music wouldn't be what they are hundreds of years after his death.

This point has global implications. One survey found that most U.S. companies project significant improvement in their quality practices three years from now, but concede that by then they will reach levels that many companies in Japan, Germany and Canada have already attained. Notes Joshua Hammond, president of the American Quality Foundation: "They're so far ahead of us that quality is no longer a competitive issue. Now we've got to get into it to survive."

And where we need to go is beyond minimal standards. A *Consumer Reports* article notes that "Americans are building nice average cars but few 'gee-whiz-look-at-this' cars." TQM programs do not deal with "gee-whiz" or "wow!" factors—or what Paul Sherlock of Raychem labeled the "bewitch" and "bedazzle" effects—that are so essential to how customers view quality nowadays.

3. TQM Develops Its Own Cumbersome Bureaucracy

Many TQM programs implicitly assume (in fact, consultants market it as such) that quality is an orderly, sequential, linear and predictable process. To a rather small extent it is. But ask any executive who's been successful in engineering a quality turn-around, and he or she will tell you that real total quality emerges from a chaotic, disruptive emotional process that rips open the guts of any organization and rebuilds it from the bottom up.

If one accepts the myth of order and predictability, however, as most TQM programs do, it is natural to build an orderly, predictable bureaucracy around it. Of course, we don't call it a bureaucracy; we merely create reams of paper and sign-offs, a formal hierarchy of councils and committees, a plethora of meetings and techniques that must be adhered to, and a steadily growing staff that does little but monitor—some would say "police"—it all.

This has little to do with energetic, lithe market-driven quality. Quite the opposite. Moreover, many people start viewing the whole concept of quality as a number-crunching paper-chase or as a "whip." In one company, an hourly worker told me he was so fed up with the paperwork that "I've signed off on the crap because I don't want to hassle with it any more." In another company, a line manager of a successful operation practically begged me to tell corporate to "stop force-feeding their formula on us; they don't work here and they don't listen!"

The Florida Power & Light company is a case that TQM adherents once loved to cite. True, it won the 1989 Baldrige, but despite a quality department of 85 full-time individuals monitoring 1,900 quality teams immersed in a highly statistical "quality review" system, the gains in quality were actually pretty modest. The gains in employee depression and stress were much more impressive. And as one outsider remarked, people seemed more interested in the appearance of quality and jumping through the internal TQM hoops than on quality itself. Recently, Florida Power & Light has shrunk its bureaucracy dramatically; the quality department is down to six, for starters. And I recently read that British Telecom has dismantled its quality bureaucracy and "focused on the customer instead." What a novel idea.

> Quality can't be delegated. It must be assumed and lived by everyone on the payroll.

4. TQM Delegates Quality to Quality Czars and "Experts" Rather than to "Real" People

This is a big one. Quality can't be delegated. It must be assumed and lived by everyone on the payroll. It must be central to company strategy, operations and individuals' job roles. I remember sitting at a dinner a year ago with a senior manager of Milliken, the South Carolina-based textile manufacturer. Milliken is a Baldrige winner that has been appropriately cited for a true customer-obsessed, companywide quality process. We both had presented speeches to an audience of pharmaceutical manufacturers earlier that day, and during our dinner we were approached by a participant who told us that her company had recently created a quality improvement department and she had just been appointed (or should I say anointed) director. She asked us if we had any sage advice.

The Milliken fellow and I immediately looked at each other, eyebrows raised. "Uh-oh," I said. He nodded, querying, "I wonder who's going to be responsible for quality?" We took turns explaining to the participant that it sounded like she was being set up to be a staff department charged with making quality "happen" while others—senior line managers, middle managers and nonmanagers—could go about their business absolved from authentic and complete accountability for "total quality management."

And it's true that the first thing many TQM programs do is anoint somebody or some group within the company as the grand poo-bah of quality. This is a problem. Xerox and Honda define quality as "the way to do business." They're right, but does one then need a director or department in charge of the way to do business? If quality truly is the centerpiece of doing business, it becomes everyone's responsibility and the cornerstone of strategy and operations, including budgeting. The problem with quality departments, quality directors, quality councils and the like is that they slowly become isolated from the realities of strategy and day-to-day operations while simultaneously taking on the brunt of responsibility for the destiny of quality. Steve Young, one of the A. T. Kearney study authors, is blunt: "You don't need a director of quality."

Another issue: The poo-bahs spend a lot of time conferring with "experts" like consultants, and according to Joshua Hammond, the "proliferation of consultants" aggravates the problems rather than solves them. That is because each consultant and consulting company preaches its own pet strategies and techniques and insists that the company adhere to them. The Ernst & Young study found 945 different quality-management tactics being peddled in the TQM market. Sounds like a pretty confusing market to me, but obviously it's a lucrative one for the vendors.

If we're talking about real people, let's not forget that empowered employees and informed, involved customers are crucial for shaping quality interventions. But consider these statistics: American computer and auto companies involve only 12 percent and 28 percent of their employees respectively in idea suggestion. Customer complaints are considered of "major or primary importance" in only 19 percent of banks, 26 percent of hospitals and 26 percent of computer makers.

Meanwhile, 60 percent and 73 percent of computer makers in Germany and Japan respectively use customer complaints. Employee suggestions are crucial to 34 percent of Canadian banks and 78 percent of Japanese car makers.

Suggestions are really only a small part of the picture. The key to quality is threefold. One, that front-line people "own" the process. It's their show and, within broadly defined parameters, they've got access to whatever information (including financials), budget and decision-making authority they need to implement ideas. Two, customers are actively involved in the process, providing continual feedback and literally working on quality-related teams with in-house personnel. Third, management is truly committed to the process. I use the word "commitment" very carefully. Here's why:

Consider a continuum of management reaction to quality effort. The continuum ranges from "resistance" to "fence-straddling" to "support" to "commitment." I've seen too many senior and middle managers who at best "support" quality. A manager who "supports" quality allows the dollar investment in TQM efforts, makes a periodic attendance to a quality team meeting, and encourages the TQM consultants who are on-site. That's no longer enough. Commitment is what's enough, and commitment involves a sense of urgency, passion, time allocation and heaps of personal attention. Commitment means that customer-driven quality permeates meeting agendas, budgeting and personnel decisions, e-mail, memos, personal reports and daily calendar appointments. (More on this next month).

Quality can't be delegated.

People at all levels are "boss-watchers," and they pay attention to what the boss pays attention to. If the boss is personally preoccupied with quality, they will be too. All too often TQM allows management to get off the hook simply by "supporting" a discrete program divorced from any requirement of substantive change in management's personal habits.

Quality can't be delegated. Commitment, ownership and involvement by real people at all levels is what characterized success stories like Motorola, Milliken, Federal Express and Harley Davidson. Don't let anyone fool you that it was TQM alone.

5. TQM Does Not Demand Radical Organizational Reform

You've heard this one before: If your organization is weighted down with excess management layers, bloat in corporate staff and a proliferation of functional feifdoms, all the TQM training in the world won't jack up your quality. The plain fact of life is that authentic quality improvements demand the flattening of structures, the liberation of line management from corporate control, the liberation of front-line people from line management, and the breakdown of functional foxholes. The last point is crucial: Cross-disciplinary cross-departmental efforts, which include "outsiders" like customers and suppliers, must become the institutionalized norm as "the way we do things around here." Interdisciplinary collaboration must replace a system in which one department does its thing and then throws it over the wall. Studies reveal that quality improvements using fully empowered, self-contained cross-functional teams show 200 percent to 600 percent improvement over their traditional functional pass-off counterparts.

Authentic quality improvements demand the flattening of structures.

The problem is that while TQM gives these issues lip service, it rarely confronts them head on. Too often in TQM, tough, painful, structural changes play second fiddle to the more visible carnival of motivational balloons and wall posters, innumerable classes with big binders and slick presentations with fancy graphics.

6. TQM Does Not Demand Changes in Management Compensation

How much more straightforward can I be? When quality indices become important determinants of management compensation, as they have been at Motorola, Ford and Federal Express, then people really start taking quality seriously. Usually, since TQM genially divorces itself from compensation issues, the audio of TQM and the video of pay don't match up, and the integrity of the quality process suffers, which means, of course, that ultimately the company's financials suffer. The Ernst & Young study found that in the auto, computer, banking and healthcare industries, for example, quality performance measures, like defect rates and customer satisfaction measures, play a key role in determining senior management pay in fewer than 20 percent of organizations. Profitability still matters the most in all four industries. Maybe that's why we have so many troubled companies in those industries.

7. TQM Does Not Demand Entirely New Relationships with Outside Partners

Profitability still matters the most in all four industries. Maybe that's why we have so many troubled companies in those industries.

Since TQM is inner-directed and since it needs to avoid confronting the issue of radical structural change, it's not surprising that the organization's "intangible" relationships with suppliers, joint venture partners and other company business units are not highlighted. Nowadays, with so much work being subcontracted and outsourced, often globally, and with the need for lightning-fast top-quality turnaround work, new nonadversarial, nonlegalistic relationships among partners become crucial for total quality. These new relationships are based on soft, squishy concepts like trust, honesty, inclusion, mutual support and candid, nonlegalistic expectations of both parties' responsibilities. These intangible relationships are absolutely essential to quality. This is why companies as diverse as GTE, Milliken, Xerox, Baxter and Ford are no longer willing to jerk around suppliers in order to save a couple of dimes. Instead, they are pruning down their supplier lists dramatically. They are bringing in the survivors as long-term partners, giving them training, sharing data and cost savings, allowing them to access central databases via electronic data interchanges, and working collaboratively with them on common problems, new ideas and potential opportunities.

The same applies to sister facilities (plants, labs, offices, etc.) within firms, and to joint venture partners. All too often, the bloody turf warfare among these siblings and "partners" would be amusing if it weren't so tragic. One can't simply declare "partnership" or "synergy" and then have it magically appear. Like any relationship, it has to be worked on with trust and caring. If a real relationship doesn't exist, neither will quality.

General Motors is always good for a lesson in what not to do. How does the "new" GM deal with its suppliers? Under recently appointed global purchasing executive J. Ignacio Lopez de Arriortua, the company has arbitrarily ripped up established contracts, shared confidential suppliers' blueprints and bids with others to see if they can get lower prices, and has demanded unilateral price cuts of more than 20 percent with no guarantees of future work. If I was a betting man, I'd give you good odds that the fear, distrust and loathing experienced by suppliers towards the "new" GM does not bode well for GM quality. What does traditional TQM have to say about such goings-on? Not much.

8. TQM Appeals to Faddism, Egotism and Quick-Fixism

On the surface I'm being too harsh on TQM on this point. After all, is TQM responsible for American managers' preoccupation with quick, painless, no-harm to the P & L results? Is TQM responsible for many managers' inability to deal with a process that by definition is never-ending? Is TQM responsible for many executives' obsession with winning the Baldrige for reasons of personal aggrandizement and corporate public relations rather than as a reward for real quality improvements?

No, of course not. But let me go out on a limb and suggest that in their efforts to sell TQM seminars and programs, too many vendors have subtly pandered, perhaps inadvertently, to these weak traits among managers. I've seen representatives of some well-known consulting and seminar outfits promote their own companies and wares by presenting a fantasy picture of a lean, orderly, straightforward, eminently logical user-easy path to success, with some ego-gratifying quickie results promised for good measure. Good marketing it may be, but good quality it ain't.

9. TQM Drains Entrepreneurship and Innovation from Corporate Culture

Bluntly speaking, TQM programs attempt to standardize and routinize internal processes with a carefully developed set of measurements and methodology. This is fine if the world outside is routine and standard. But it is not. As we discussed earlier, customer preferences and choices are constantly evolving and changing and, therefore, product and service offerings must be constantly evolving and changing too.

Now let me raise the bar. Continuous improvements on current operations and products are necessary, to be sure. But obsessing internally until one achieves a zero-defects "do-it-right-the-first time" routine is a dangerous luxury that often slows down new breakthrough developments in products and services. It is the latter that is the cornerstone of business success.

We appear to be faced with a paradox. On one hand, a company must pursue constant improvement toward perfection in what it is doing now. On the other hand, a company must encourage risk and tolerate errors in pursuit of the destruction of the status quo and the creation of the new. Typical TQM, at best, only addresses the first part of the equation, and then often myopically, as noted in points #1 and #2. It does not address the second part of the equation at all, which means that the organization's entrepreneurship and innovation become seriously impaired.

I can't emphasize this point enough. For a company that wants to survive against the onslaught of myriad global competitors, many of whom rely on economies of scale, routine is death. Distinguished Japanese scholar Ikujiro Nonaka proposes that business success in the 1990s and beyond will be dependent on management's ability to "induce and amplify organizational chaos." Peter Drucker argues that successful organizations will be "destabilizers. ... organized for innovation." Like economist Joseph Schumpeter, Drucker defines innovation as "creative destruction."

The reason that Microsoft has a higher stock market value than either Boeing or General Motors, even though Microsoft's sales and physical assets are a fraction of Boeing's and GM's, is because investors anticipate that Microsoft's earnings will be higher. And the reason they anticipate higher earnings is because they know that Microsoft consistently and creatively destroys its current offerings and replaces them with new products and features that customers will gobble up. Apropos of "zero defects," Microsoft's newly released products usually have a few bugs in them. Naturally, the company zealously pursues constant improvement toward the elimination of those bugs, but its top priority is to accelerate the development cycle for new userfriendly products. It is that market-driven entrepreneurship and innovation that drives up market value, not an obsession with doing it right the first time.

10. TQM Has No Place for Love

We are all learning that quality is more than correct processes.

By this outrageous statement, I mean that when all is said and done, TQM attempts to make quality happen via an analytically detached, sterile mechanical path. What's often missing, frankly, is emotion and soul. Go out and look at all the sincere individuals diligently following the step-by-step processes they've learned in the TQM (and, for that matter, customer-service) training classes, and ask yourself: "Where's the *love* of our product and our customer? Where's the *joy* of the pursuit of excellence? Where's the *passion* in the doing and creating? Where's the *fun* in being here? Where's the *rage* and *agony* in the slightest snag in product or service quality? Where's the *thrill* in accomplishment?" If you can't find evidence of these, you probably won't find real quality either. Dr. Frankenstein learned that humans are more than anatomically correct bodies; Mr. Salieri learned that music is more than correct notes. Similarly, we are all learning that quality is more than correct processes.

Business writer Paul Cohen has written extensively about Maine-based Thos. Moser cabinetmakers. With an array of exceptional products and service, this 90-person company is winning the loyalty of a growing army of highly demanding consumers around the country. Moser quality, of course, is superb, even though statistical process control charts and quality committees are conspicuously absent. Thomas Moser explains his company's approach to quality by noting that, first, most products today "lack soul," and, second, "There's a set of values resident in our furniture that attracts customers. They're not just buying something to sit in, something well made and well designed, or something the neighbors will envy. Those are all motivations, but there is a strong emotional component to the objects themselves that motivates people to buy." Moser goes on to say that what his company brings to the picture is "soul," including craftsmanship of "absolute integrity," and an in-house delivery service (itself a profit center) that guarantees gentle, caring, precise, on-time delivery across the country. Small wonder that Moser can say with all sincerity, "We don't sell furniture."

Not your usual TQM lingo. I believe that Debbie Coleman, ex-CEO of Apple computer, was right on target when she said, "You have no right to manage unless you care passionately about what you are doing."

And while the words may be a bit hyperbolic, even I—an ex-professor of statistics and psychometrics—can buy the spirit behind the highly respected Herman Miller Chairman Max DePree, who said, "Managers who only understand methodologies and quantification are modern-day eunuchs."

Dear reader, with these 10 points, I hope I have not placed myself on your hate-mail list. Keep in mind that I didn't create the findings unearthed by Arthur D. Little, McKinsey, et al. I am merely trying to explain those findings and why TQM programs you are personally familiar with might still be stuck in first gear.

To be sure, even traditional TQM can provide a genuine service when it gets people sensitized to the concept of quality, when it helps people get disciplined in their efforts to attain higher quality, when it offers people some pragmatic tools to help them in that process, and when it injects some commonality in language and goals into the company culture. But as I've argued, when one strips away the hype, what TQM really does is at best a small part of quality, at worst a distraction from the real thing.

And what is that real thing? As customers, we know. We know when we experience real quality; we know which vendor provides the real thing and which one doesn't.

Oren Harari is a professor at the University of San Francisco and a consultant with The Tom Peters Group in Palo Alto.

The Learning Trip
Enhancing an Organization's Ability to Learn

James W. Lawton and Matthew D. Williams

Using a division of Hewlett Packard as an example, these authors offer a novel and practical suggestion for organizations seeking to enhance their capacities for deep learning. And they point out that it is only through such learning that an organzation can sustain any competitive advantage. We can see from this article the central place of learning in a culture of quality.

"The rate at which organizations learn may become the only sustainable source of competitive advantage."

Ray Stata, CEO at Analog Devices

Mr. Stata is not alone in his assertion. How organizations address the issue of learning will be critical to competition well into the next century. However, while the learning organization is easy to agree with in principle, describing one is difficult, and creating one is uncharted territory. Most agree, however, that critical to enhancing organizational learning is fostering an environment that promotes challenging the mental constructs through which one views the world. One way of addressing this issue is the concept of the learning trip, a trip to environments very different from one's own for the purposes of stimulating non-normal ways of thinking and fostering lateral problem solving. In experimenting with this concept at Hewlett-Packard's (HP) Analytical Products Group, the learning trip proved useful. This paper describes learning trips, the experiment conducted at HP, the findings from this experiment, and factors for guaranteeing the success of such trips.

Why Learning Is Important

A recent study at Royal Dutch/Shell documented that one-third of the industrial companies on the 1970 list of Fortune 500 had gone out of business by 1983. The average life expectancy of an industrial company is less than half that of a human being. According to Arie deGeus, former planning director at Shell, the organizations that survived did so because they mastered the ability

---

Reprinted with permission from *Target*, July/August 1992, published by the Association for Manufacturing Excellence, 380 W. Palatine Road, Wheeling, IL 60090.

to conduct "experiment in the margin," that is, to continually explore new business and organizational opportunities. He notes that the world is rapidly changing, and concludes that organizations that know how to learn will be most likely to survive.

Lester Thurow, an economist and Dean of MIT's Sloan School of Management, addresses the issue from the standpoint of competition. He describes how the historical bases of a nation's wealth have been resources, capital, technology, and human resources. For example, the economic development of Great Britain can be tied to an abundance of coal ore and the development of various technologies such as the Spinning Jenny. However, with the advent of the green revolution, a global capital market, and a high level of technological sophistication, Thurow contends that the only means of competition left will be human assets.

The average life expectancy of an industrial company is less than half that of a human being.

Thurow goes on to say that traditionally it has been easy for a rich country to remain rich, noting that over the past 130 years, only one country (Argentina) has fallen from the list of the ten richest countries in the world. However, with this shift in a nation's source of wealth toward human resources, remaining a rich country will become more difficult and the list of the ten wealthiest nations will become increasingly more volatile.

> "Leave my factories but take away my people and soon grass will grow on my factory floors. Take my factories, but leave my people, and soon we will have new and better plants."
>
> Andrew Carnegie

Why Creating a Learning Organization Is Difficult

Ironically, the ability to learn is something that scientists consider to be inherent in all of us. Humans are born with an innate desire to learn, and given a cultivating environment, will do so until inhibited. Consider the questioning spirit and thirst for knowledge that young children display. They ask dumb questions, make strange combinations, and think in a way unrestricted by custom, tradition, or societal norms. As children we are at the creative and imaginative zenith of our lives. Children learn tasks and skills, and digest information at a pace that will steadily diminish throughout their lives.

Society gradually erodes this inborn trait. Where failure was once considered an acceptable part of the learning process, a premium is now placed on success. One rejoices when an infant takes a first step and falls, even congratulating the baby for trying and failing. But in school systems, a student makes a mistake and receives a low grade instead of an "A." Children learn that nothing succeeds like success, and nothing fails like failure. In short, the U.S. educational system does not promote learning, rather it promotes performing according to another person's standards.

The U.S. educational system promotes performing according to another person's standards.

Educator John Arnold writes, "We put our children in classrooms and expect them to guess what the teacher is thinking." And in doing so, it teaches our children something else, namely that someone always has the answer.

ABOUT HEWLETT-PACKARD COMPANY AND THE AVONDALE SITE

Hewlett-Packard Company (HP) was founded in 1939 in California by two Stanford University engineering graduates, Bill Hewlett and Dave Packard. Today Hewlett-Packard is a major international designer and manufacturer of computers and precision electronic equipment for analysis, measurement, and computation.

The Avondale site, formed when HP purchased F&M Scientific in 1965, is one of three sites that make up HP's Analytical Products Group. The Avondale site encompasses 230,000 sq. ft. of building space on 55 acres of land. Approximately 800 employees work here.

HP-Avondale is a leading manufacturer of gas and liquid chromatographs, data handling systems, and automated chemical systems. It is also the site of HP's Analytical Direct operation.

Avondale's product lines and related consumables are used in education, government, and the petroleum, environmental, pharmaceutical, and chemical industries.

Some applications for HP-Avondale products include: detection of drugs in blood and urine, organic analyses for the environmental monitoring of water pollution, consumer protection studies, petrochemical refinery process monitoring, and law enforcement.

The teacher. The consultant. The winner of the Malcolm Baldridge Award. But some other person always has the answers.

The downward spiral continues into the working world. As W. Edwards Deming puts it, "Our prevailing system of management has destroyed our people." Managers tend to seek conformity and try to find new ways to "improve the numbers" How frequently does one observe managers attempting to invent a new numbering scheme? While this type of thinking can produce results, is there not another mode of operation that can do so as well?

Clearly, fostering learning is not as easy as it may appear. From an early age, one comes to realize that performance, and not learning, is what is valued. Changing a person's thought patterns is a challenging task; creating a learning organization is extraordinarily difficult.

The learning organization will always be somewhat loosely defined. Specific prescriptions are probably not possible. The extent to which guidelines, suggestions and leads can be developed is frequently debated. Most agree, however, that critical to enhancing an organization's ability to learn is fostering an environment that continuously challenges the mental constructs through which one views the world. While mental constructs permit the abstraction of vast amounts of information, they can also limit one's thinking.

Challenging Mental Constructs Critical to Learning

Each individual views the world through a lens or construct. Peter Senge, Director of MIT's Organizational Learning Center, refers to these lenses as mental models. They are the embodiment of stereotypes, assumptions, preconceived notions, and beliefs. These lenses strongly influence not only how people think, but also what they see. Two people with different mental models can observe the same event and describe it very differently, because their lenses filtered out different details. When two people walk into a crowded party, they both take in the same basic sensory data, but each picks out different faces. The important point is that no one can truly view the world objectively. Regardless of how scientific a person's approach, that person is being subjective. Psychologists say that humans observe selectively.

The important point is that no one can truly view the world objectively.

To help illustrate the power that mental constructs have on one's thinking, Mr. Senge tells a story.

A tribe of Bornean natives was discovered on an island a few years ago. The tribe, untouched by any aspect of modern civilization, provided a rare, unspoiled opportunity to witness the past. Two researchers went to the island and studied the Borneans extensively. Near the end of their research, they took one member of the tribe to Singapore for a few days to observe his reactions to civilized society. They were startled to find that upon returning to the island, the Bornean rarely spoke of his visit to his fellow tribesmen. Later, when asked of his experience, his only comment was: "I saw a man carrying more bananas than any man I had ever seen before."

During his visit to Singapore, this Bornean native was presented with literally thousands of potential ways to make his life better, but all he "saw" was a man carrying more bananas? Unfortunately, he did not have constructs for interpreting most of this information. Why? Because the Bornean had never seen a bicycle, much less a car. What he saw in Singapore was so different than anything back in Borneo, he could not make a comparison. His constructs and mental models of how the world works kept him from seeing the opportunities right before his eyes.

The issue with mental models lies not in whether they are right or wrong; all models are, by definition, simplifications. In fact, they are necessary. The issue is that mental models are tacit; they exist below the level of awareness. How might the Bornean's observations have differed if he were exposed to some fundamental concepts about modern society before his trip to Singapore?

Mr. Senge addressed this issue nicely in his recent book, *The Fifth Discipline*:

> New insights fail to get put into practice because they conflict with deeply held internal images of how the world works, images that limit us to familiar ways of thinking and acting. That is why the discipline of managing mental models—surfacing, testing and improving our

Traditional Trips		Learning Trips
Specific topics	*Topic Selection*	Understand environment
Limited	*Level of sharing*	Broad
Low	*Risk level*	High
Easy	*Ease of preparation*	Hard
Straightforward	*Choice of companies*	Abstract
Focused thinking	*Participants*	Open-minded
Similar	*Similarity of environments*	Very different
Linear/Vertical	*Problem-solving approach*	Lateral
Easy	*Translating solutions*	Difficult

Figure 1. **Differences between traditional trips and learning trips.**

internal pictures of how the world works—promises to be a major breakthrough for building learning organizations.

Learning trips are designed to address this aspect of learning.

The Learning Trip Concept

A learning trip is a trip to environments very different from one's own for the purposes of stimulating non-normal ways of thinking and fostering lateral problem-solving. Doing so challenges deeply-held assumptions and beliefs about how the world works and adds to the experience base from which to solve problems. In many traditional environments, first-line supervisors and individual contributors participate in very specific, narrowly-defined fact-finding trips. Likewise upper management tends to pursue more broadly-scoped topics, but frequently limits their investigations to other sites within the same company. On a learning trip, a small group embarks on a broadly-defined, but very focused, set of visits to environments external to their company as an experiment in challenging mental constructs and promoting new ways of thinking.

Figure 1 outlines the major distinctions between traditional trips and learning trips. The more important ones are described below.

By far the most significant difference between traditional and learning trips is its choice of places to visit. On traditional trips, the locations visited are based on the topic of the trip. Selecting the locales is usually fairly straightforward. On a learning trip, choosing places to visit is much more abstract. The intent is to find environments to visit that are very different than one's own. If you visualize all of the possible places to visit in n-dimensional space, where n is the number of different ways of describing a location, the intent of a learning trip is to explore many different portions of the n-dimensional space. The key to choosing sites to visit is contrast, so make the portfolio of locations is as diverse as possible.

For example, typical trips at Hewlett-Packard are usually to other sites within HP. In the event that a trip does venture outside the company, the visiting team might go to Motorola, Digital Equipment, or IBM. On a learning trip, a group would go to a small-volume candy manufacturer, Federal Express, or NASA.

Another critical success factor lies in the ability of the visiting team to engage their hosts in true dialogue and to deeply penetrate the organization in a way unlike superficial, tour-like presentations. The very nature of many of the discussion topics make it important that the team be able to quickly establish a relationship to guarantee the interaction that is deemed essential. Considering this, the level of preparation for a learning trip is significant. Each company's products and operations must be researched. Detailed topics of interest need to be developed. A proposed agenda must be prepared. Comprehensive phone conversations are necessary to build rapport with the hosts. The level of preparation is more extensive than most traditional trips.

On traditional trips the topic of discussion is usually the focus of the trip. For example, a group of people may be visiting another company's facility to learn more about how they manage their surface mount process. On a learning trip, the topic of conversation is used as a vehicle for understanding the environment. A group may focus on a company's surface mount technology, but only as a means of understanding the operation of the environment. In this case, the topic of discussion is not necessarily significant.

When a group returns from a traditional trip, they will most likely attempt to implement what they learned. The level of similarity of product and process is high, which makes this translation straightforward. On learning trips, translating a solution to the home environment is more difficult. For example, in the case of the group visiting various surface mount facilities, they may be able to return and implement a new method for guaranteeing consistent solder bumps. On a learning trip, the visiting team must be able to translate what they witnessed at the small-volume candy manufacturer into a solution suitable for a surface mount process. Further, traditional trips usually result in specific, technical learnings, whereas learning trips encompass a much broader spectrum of learnings. Many learnings border on the philosophical. While these translations are more difficult, the rewards can be extensive.

On a learning trip, the visiting team must be able to translate what they witnessed at the small-volume candy manufacturer into a solution suitable for a surface mount process.

The Intent Is Not to Benchmark

It is important to note one final distinction. Learning trips should not be confused with benchmarking visits, which are focused much differently. In the case of benchmarking, the objective is to seek out excellence in a particular area. On a learning trip, the objective is to seek out non-normal ways of thinking—thinking that is different, and not necessarily best-in-class.

For example, the Analytical Products Group is currently benchmarking its supplier selection process. In this project, we will do a detailed investigation to determine which companies in the world are considered exceptional at selecting suppliers. In the case of a learning trip, one might choose to visit a small-volume candy manufacturer, not because they are necessarily good at making candy, but because making candy is different than assembling gas chromatographs. The intent in choosing sites for a learning trip is to seek out environments that will challenge the way your environment functions. Excellence is simply not implied in the selection process.

Likewise in the case of a benchmarking trip, comparisons are being made of a product or process. Thus a company will visit environments where solutions can be translated for that particular product or process. As an analogy, assume the objective is to discover a good dessert. Liking apples, the benchmarking team might sample five different apples and pick the best one. The result is that the benchmarking team ends up with a really good apple. On a learning trip, the team tastes an apple, a biscuit, brown sugar, and vanilla ice cream. And if the team is open-minded, they end up with apple cobbler.

> Innovation is usually the result of connections of past experiences,
> But if you have the same experiences as everybody else, you're unlikely to look in a different location.
>
> Steve Jobs, CEO at NeXT Computer

On a learning trip, the team tastes an apple, a biscuit, brown sugar, and vanilla ice cream. And if the team is open-minded, they end up with apple cobbler.

The Experiment

The first experiment of the learning trip concept was conducted last fall at HP's Avondale Site, the largest site in the Analytical Products Group. A small team was assembled to visit five different environments during a five-day period. Considerable emphasis was placed on exposing the participants to environments that would significantly challenge their thinking, where the hosts were open and willing to share information and stories.

The team spent time up-front characterizing the environment at HP's Avondale site so as to establish a baseline for comparing the various companies under consideration. The search then began for companies that operate under dramatically different assumptions and models than those at Avondale.

Several alternatives were considered, such as working in a fast-food restaurant for a day, helping a stage company set up for a rock concert, and visiting a ship-building yard. The first site chosen was A. David Moore, a six-person craftsman operation located in the hills of Vermont that builds large, mechanical pipe organs for churches. Working out of a barn in Mr. Moore's backyard, the team works on all aspects of the organ's construction, from wood carving the fascia to rolling tin for the metal pipes. The operation is extremely vertically-integrated; the major incoming materials are trees, cut on the same property, and lead billets. Every step of the process including the design, construction, testing, tuning, and installation at the customer is done by Mr. Moore and his staff. Mr. Moore even does all of the photography and layout for his advertising.

A typical organ takes nine months to construct and costs approximately $200,000. The company has an impressive reputation among music circles for its ability to produce extremely high quality and beautifully ornate organs in the traditional style. Their organs adorn such well-known chapels as the

Old North Church in Boston, MA and Grace Episcopal Church in Washington, D.C.

At the other end of the spectrum, and chosen for that very reason, the second company selected was Boeing Commercial Aircraft in Seattle, WA market leader in commercial passenger jet aircraft with over 60 percent market share. One of the largest manufacturing facilities in the world occupying over 100 acres, the Everett plant contains an operation that rolls out a 747 every four days. A typical plane sells for $150,000,000 and contains over four million parts.

The Boeing Company and A. David Moore are known for their expertise. Both companies are very successful and very different. The contrast between these two facilities is phenomenal. Boeing is highly-structured, complex, very hierarchically organized. A. David Moore is very informal, unstructured, and has a simple managerial style. In both cases, the environments are very different than HP's Avondale site.

The third and fourth companies selected were MIPS Computer Systems, located in Santa Clara, CA, and NeXT Computer, located in Fremont, CA. Both companies make computer workstations. The two companies are competitors. Yet both companies are taking a much different approach to selling computers.

MIPS chose to develop its own RISC-based microprocessor architecture for use in its workstations. The designs are given to a large, semiconductor house, which manufactures the chips. Most of the components are off-the-shelf. NeXT, on the other hand, chose Intel's microprocessor architecture. Where NeXT invested significantly in its manufacturing capability, creating a truly world-class facility, MIPS chose to take a more incremental approach, investing in manufacturing as the need arises. The differences between these two companies provide an excellent opportunity for the learning trip participants to see both ends of the spectrum, and more importantly, learn from the contrast.

The last location selected was the Massachusetts Institute of Technology (MIT). The team reasoned that opportunities for learning need not be confined to the business community. After all, history has shown that many revolutionary business concepts were initiated in academia. The time at MIT was structured around tours of several laboratories and meetings with various faculty for the purpose of exposing the visiting team to the leading-edge research.

Learnings

Each environment on the trip provided a rich opportunity for learning. The two that stimulated the most thinking are discussed below. In both cases, the learnings are not things that were explicitly stated by the hosts, nor are they the immediate observations made by the visiting team at that time. Rather, in both cases, the learnings existed just below the surface of the organization, and only became apparent as the team reflected on their visits later.

One of the learnings was discovered by contrasting A. David Moore with Boeing; the second stemmed from observations made at A. David Moore. For each, the learning is discussed and related to the environment at HP-Avondale. It is important to note that there are no prescriptions or specific to-do lists in the following examples. However, to the extent that these learnings can be applied to an environment, they may provide any organization with many returns.

Contribution to Society

At A. David Moore and Boeing, the team observed that employees seem to have a very clear understanding of how their particular product, whether it be a 747 or a pipe organ, contributes to society. Not that they simply understand what the product is and how it functions, but these people comprehend how what they were working on contributes to the betterment of the world community. The people at Boeing understand how airplanes that they are personally involved in creating transport people and cargo to the farthest corners of the earth. They understand that without planes, the world would be a much different place. The people at Boeing are not building nameless widgets, they are building a critical piece in world operations.

The people at Boeing are not building nameless widgets, they are building a critical piece in world operations.

At A. David Moore, workers take similar pride in their work. They know that for more than 100 years after they complete their work, church congregations, music teachers, and composers will listen to their handiwork and marvel at the beautiful sound. People will admire the intricate decoration and the handsome sturdiness of the organ.

What the team discovered at Boeing and A. David Moore was more than just product knowledge, it is product-impact knowledge. By identifying with the product's purpose, the people at these two companies develop a strong bond with the product and assume a stake in its success. One wonders if this is not one of the keys that allows Boeing to "make four million parts fly in close formation", and enable A. David Moore to create some of the best-sounding and most beautiful organs in the country using trees cut from the hillside behind Mr. Moore's house and talent from the local high school.

What the team discovered at Boeing and A. David Moore was more than just product knowledge, it is product-impact knowledge.

Relating the concept of understanding a product's "contribution to society" back to HP's Avondale site, the team concluded that the linkage is not as strong as it is at A. David Moore or Boeing. There appear to be two major reasons for this. First, HP-Avondale's products (instrumentation for chemical analysis) are highly specialized and are rarely used in settings visible to the non-using public. Most people, including Avondale employees, will never see one of the products in a practical setting, such as a chemist's laboratory or research center.

Second, the product does not use common technology or fill a generally recognized need. For example, at Boeing, employees are reminded of their products' importance every time they glance up in the sky and see one fly overhead. A. David Moore employees are reminded of their contribution every time they see an organ or hear organ music. Unfortunately, one rarely sees a gas chromatograph in operation.

The team did reason, however, that while the linkage is not as clear at HP, it can be. HP analytical products are making significant contributions to society, of which most people are simply not aware; one area is in environmental testing. Samples are examined in search of contaminants that could be harmful to humans or the environment. HP instruments were used in the clean-up of the Exxon Valdez disaster. During the 1988 summer Olympics, an HP mass spectrometer uncovered Ben Johnson's use of steroids.

The next step for HP-Avondale is to show how the site's products contribute to society. Efforts are already underway to develop people's product-impact knowledge.

Intrinsic Motivation

Most people have said at some time or another that there are more important things in life than work, such as family, church, and friends. One goes to work to make money. Indeed, there are many important aspects of life, but this message has a twist to it. By saying that other things are more important, work becomes a necessary, but less-than-ideal, part of life—a seemingly disappointing way of spending one third of a lifetime.

At A. David Moore, the Vermont organ craftsman, the team came to realize that this is a faulted perception. What the visiting team observed was a small group of people committed to making beautiful instruments. These people are doing what they truly desire to do, making a product and working in an organization that really makes a difference to them. These are self-actualization issues, such as doing what one wants to do as opposed to what one has to do. Someone once wrote that organizations fail at fulfilling a person's higher order needs like self-esteem and self-worth. After visiting A. David Moore, the team cannot help but believe this is true. This is intrinsic motivation.

> These people are doing what they truly desire to do, making a product and working in an organization that really makes a difference to them.

Relating intrinsic motivation back to HP-Avondale is difficult. At A. David Moore, David hires people who really want to learn, teaches them the entire process, gives them a major hand in the organ's creation, and lets them go. The organizational context at HP makes a seemingly simple concept distressingly complex. After all, HP-Avondale is not an organization of six people; it is an organization of more than 600.

Discussion

In thinking about learning trips, it is important to note that the learnings, or benefits, can take one of two forms. At one end of the spectrum, a learning may be immediately and directly applied to ones own environment. When the learning trip team uncovered contributions to society, it became apparent to them that they could increase the product-impact knowledge of the workforce at HP-Avondale, and potentially have an immediate positive impact. And as mentioned, efforts are already underway to develop people's product-impact knowledge.

At the other end of the spectrum, a learning may be more far-reaching in nature, more philosophical, and thus more speculative. Intrinsic motivation is an example. Even in an environment as people-oriented and open as HP, the concept of intrinsic motivation provided the learning trip team with a

AT THE HEART OF A. DAVID MOORE

On a snowy Friday morning in November, we visited A. David Moore in Pomfret, VT. Located a couple of hours outside of Boston, it sits placidly off one of Vermont's many unlabelled rural routes in the conifer-covered hills of the Lesser White Mountain range. Nestled in the woods, where he still cuts most of the lumber that goes into his organs, and the sloped pasture, where the family's cows graze contentedly, sits the barn, the tractor-powered sawmill, and the wood drying house that make up this operation. They make pipe organs here, some of the best in the world.

As we parked our car, we were greeted by Mr. Moore—bearded, wearing worn chinos and an untucked flannel shirt. He shows us his business: how they cut the wood, stack it to dry, select particular pieces, and eventually craft it into an organ. He shows us how they melt tin and lead into sheets that are rolled into the pipes that make up the vocal chords of the instrument. David fashions a pipe while we watch. He tunes it; the skilled master at work.

David shows us his current project, a 12 foot-wide creation stretching some 15 feet up toward the ceiling in his workshop. It is beautiful. All polished wood and stark metal. He describes the various characteristics of the organ. David Moore makes organs in the traditional way—all mechanical operation, bellows, and hand carved air channels as opposed to electronic solenoids and digital controls. He does this not for the sake of tradition, but because traditional mechanical organs provide more lasting value to the customer. Electronic controls may last ten years, David's last a hundred.

He digresses, telling us about how he began making organs as an apprentice in another shop down in Massachusetts. He left to start his own operation many years later. Since starting his own business, he's crafted organs for churches, schools, and conservatories from Florida to Maine. He designs and makes organs from the ground up, taking them apart, delivering and setting them up himself.

When he seems finished describing his passion, we ask him a few questions. Why do you do it? "I enjoy building and playing organs," he replies, "I like the way they sound." Everyone working with David agrees.

Speaking of those who work for him, who are they? They're not the grizzled, spectacled veterans you might expect. They're all young, some barely out of high school. As a matter of fact he hires them because he says he knows how hard it is for young people to find jobs these days. Dave trains them all personally. He pays based on knowledge. "You start over here. You learn how to do this, you get an extra buck; learn that and you get another. It works great." We say, "Organizations struggle for years trying to do this." He laughs; we sense he thinks we're idiots.

We ask him about quality, what does he do to ensure it, how does he measures it? He seems taken back, looking at us strangely "What do you
Continued—

At the Heart of A. David Moore (continued)

mean, 'defect?' We don't have any. Why would we? We do it right!" We come to understand later that, in this organization, the idea of not doing a job right just doesn't exist.

We ask him about his competition. David knows all 14 of his competitors. He knows who is good, who's bad. They communicate frequently, share trade secrets, exchange ideas, visit each other, and critique each others' work. They don't think of themselves as competitors. They don't make organs to compete or make a buck. They're in this because this is what they want to do. Consider that last statement again. These people take pride in designing and crafting something of tremendous value with their hands. To them, an organ is not a product. It is art, the ultimate hobby, a lifetime dedication, worthy of their absolute highest attention. They go to work to self-actualize, not to bring home a paycheck.

Although we had difficulty understanding him at first, we came to envy this man. We came to wish we could live as he does. This was not work to David Moore. This was the love affair of a man with a true purpose in life.

David Moore made us challenge many of our beliefs about business. instead of making our organization into whatever form it takes to maximize profit, what if we made an organization what we really wanted it to be? Scary thought, isn't it? It runs contrary to much of what we've learned about business. Business is business and play is play. Right? The main reason we're here is to make money. Right? Maybe not.

"shock to the system." But the nature of the learning prevents one from immediately implementing it. Rather, intrinsic motivation provided the team with a foundation upon which they may build a stronger understanding of the nature of work.

Undoubtedly, coming to understand intrinsic motivation and the idea of designing an organization around what people want to do, as opposed to what they have to do has had a profound impact on the learning trip team. But large-scale cultural and philosophical issues are not ones to be hastily implemented across large sections of an organization. For now, the learning trip team sees their role as a promoter, attempting to share the concept of intrinsic motivation understanding, plant seeds, and develop pockets of success.

Full-scale organizational changes may not take place for years. This is not necessarily bad, however. An area of discussion and contemplation has been formed. Future learning trips may help the concept grow, deepen its understanding, and then possibly result in a revolutionary shift in HP-Avondale's manners of business.

Both immediate and longer-term learnings grew out of the learning trip experiment at HP. The team has implemented some immediately. On others, the team is still thinking, but thinking differently. Both types are valuable. Contribution to society and intrinsic motivation have impacted the learning trip team's thinking; neither will soon be forgotten.

A Unique Plan for Sharing

One characteristic of a learning organization is the ability to synthesize diverse information, and share it quickly and broadly across an organization. A format must be developed for disseminating this information in a way that is conducive to learning. Traditional trip reports and bullet-point presentations are usually not the most effective vehicles. They are frequently impersonal and do not engage the audience.

> Rather than write a trip report, a series of informal, highly-interactive, story-telling type presentations were developed and presented as brown-bag lunches.

In the experiment conducted at HP-Avondale, significant effort was invested in an attempt to improve information sharing. During post-trip discussions, the visiting team contrasted the different environment visited with each other and to HP-Avondale. Based on these discussions, the team assimilated meaningful learnings. Rather than write a trip report, a series of informal, highly-interactive, story-telling type presentations were developed and presented as brown-bag lunches. Each session focused on specific learnings. For example, one centered around the two learnings described in this paper, contribution to society and intrinsic motivation.

The brown-bag lunches were well-received. Aggressively publicized, each session filled HP-Avondale's largest conference area, leaving standing room only. Attendees included everyone from upper-level managers to design engineers to production operators. The format proved so successful that many managers asked the learning trip team to repeat the presentations for those who couldn't fit into the conference area.

For most trips, the primary beneficiaries are the participants. Learning trips are no different; they are a very personal and emotional experience. But a thoughtful sharing plan can leverage the learning trip experience throughout the organization.

Learning Trip Is a Useful Tool

Creating a learning organization requires change. Instigating change in an organization, as all of the change literature demonstrates, is difficult to achieve. As a research topic, this territory is still largely unexplored. A few frameworks have been proposed; some models of learning have been developed. However, it will be many years before a sophisticated understanding is developed.

The learning trip addresses one piece of the learning organization, namely that of challenging the beliefs, assumptions, and constructs that affect what we see, and ultimately, what we learn. In the learning trip experiment at HP's Avondale site, the visiting team accumulated a wealth of understanding. The learnings were diverse and more broadly-scoped than expected, encompassing new manufacturing techniques to novel reward systems to new philosophies about the nature of people's work.

- Emphasize up-front preparation
- Keep team small
- Encourage dialogue
- Work on relationship building
- Look for contrasts in company selection

- Record observations and thoughts real-time
  Consider media devices (VCR, dictaphone, camera)
- Schedule time for participants to reflect
- De-emphasize plant tours and prepared presentations

Figure 2. **Tips for making a learning trip a success.**

Concentrating on visiting contrasting environments was very beneficial. The sheer immensity of the 747 assembly operation, the keen sense of customer awareness displayed at MIPS, the pride with which NeXT spoke of using manufacturing as a competitive weapon, and the simplicity of David Moore's approach to business are examples of the enriching experience. For those organizations considering taking a learning trip, Figure 2 lists some tips for guaranteeing success.

When embarking on a learning trip, prospective practitioners and supporters need to be open to new ideas and are advised to understand that returns are frequently speculative, and many times, not immediately apparent. While a carefully-developed sharing plan will help disseminate learnings, it is important to remember the primary beneficiaries of a learning trip are the participants as the trip is a personal and emotional experience. While conducting all trips according to the leaning trip concept is extreme, increasing the percentage of trips carried out in this way seems justified.

At HP, the experimental learning trip increased the understanding of learning concepts throughout the organization. "Can you recommend any articles or books on the topic of learning?" "What's next?" "How can I help?" "Are we perhaps viewing this problem too narrowly?" The results are encouraging. In addition to planning future learning trips, the authors are developing other tools and mechanisms for promoting the development of a learning organization.

Enhancing the ability of an organization to learn is not an easy task. Many organizational barriers need to be overcome. To the extent that learning trips contribute to this objective, the concept serves as a useful tool.

Leadership and learning are indispensable to each other.

John F. Kennedy

References

deBono, Edward, *Lateral Thinking*. New York: Harper & Row, 1970.
deGeus, Arie P., Planning as Learning *Harvard Business Review*, March–April, 1988, pp. 70–74.
dePree, Max, *Leadership Is an Art*. New York: Doubleday, 1989.
Gluck, Frederick, "The Unbuttoned Organization." Keynote address given to the Fourth Annual Strategic Management Conference, Philadelphia, PA, October 10, 1984.

Langer, Ellen, *Mindfulness*. New York: Addison-Wesley, 1989.

Nonaka, Ikujiro, "The Knowledge Creating Company." *Harvard Business Review*, November—December, 1991, pp. 96–104.

Senge, Peter M., *The Fifth Discipline: The Art and Practice of the Learning Organization*. New York: Doubleday, 1990.

Shaw, Robert B., and Dennis N. T. Perkins. "Teaching Organizations to Learn." Unpublished, 1990.

Williams, Matthew D., "The TBC Creativity and Thinking Course: A Course In Discovery." Unpublished, 1992.

James W. Lawton is Strategic Operations Planner at Hewlett-Packard's Avondale Site in Pennsylvania. Matthew D. Williams is Distribution Manager at Hewlett-Packard's Avondale Site in Pennsylvania.

Where "Quality" Is a Language

Michael Barrier

We all know that language and culture are closely related. Spurred by the local chamber of commerce, quality as a way of doing business is endemic in Spartanburg, South Carolina. Indeed, this aspect of the local way of doing business is one reason BMW decided to locate its U.S. plant there. This article explains how this all came about.

In 1983, the manager of a Monsanto Corp. plant in Spartanburg, S.C., came to the local chamber of commerce for help. The plant had made textiles until 1980, when it began manufacturing silicon wafers, from which computer microchips were made. Monsanto's silicon wafers were sold in a global marketplace that was ever more competitive, and the plant's manager was seeking ways to improve quality and productivity.

A decade later, the ripples from that meeting are still spreading—and they are starting to touch and benefit small firms.

The Spartanburg Area Chamber of Commerce learned that other businesses in Spartanburg County shared the Monsanto managers's concerns, and it set up a committee to explore ways to address them. The committee decided that a far-reaching quality program, based on the ideas of W. Edwards Deming, would best meet the needs of Spartanburg businesses.

Deming has probably given the tenets of the quality movement their purest and most rigorous expression. Those tenets include the use of customer satisfaction as the ultimate criterion of quality; worker empowerment; reliance on statistical process control rather than final inspection; and continuous improvement of production processes.

Deming demands that managers adopt not just new techniques but a new philosophy—in particular, that they rethink their roles and become leaders and mentors rather than bosses.

The chamber worked with QualPro, a then-new quality-management consulting firm based in Knoxville, Tenn., to develop what it called its Quality in the Workplace program. At the heart of the program were four-day seminars laying out the basics of quality management in terms generally consistent with Deming's views.

Conceived as a short-term effort, Quality in the Workplace has instead picked up steam over the years. The chamber says that 3,000 people have attended QualPros's Spartanburg seminars—there are 10 to 14 a year—and that around 40 of the county's 50 largest companies have been represented.

Participants have spread the quality gospel to their own companies, and those companies have influenced their suppliers by making new demands on them based on quality-management concepts.

QualPro's presence in the community has given shape and coherence to quality efforts that might otherwise have foundered. For example, Frederick B. "Rick" Dent, president of Mayfair Mills, a large textile manufacturer in Arcadia, S.C., just outside Spartanburg, recalls that he attended a week-long Deming seminar in Detroit about 10 years ago. In that seminar, Deming emphasized the importance of statistics. "When I came back," Dent says, "all of a sudden we had charts everywhere; but we didn't know how they interrelated."

Then, he continues, "we stepped back, with the assistance of QualPro, and realized that statistics are a tool for implementing an overall change in philosophy. With that in mind, we made big headway." Even now, a QualPro instructor visits Mayfair once a month to observe what the company is doing and to offer comments.

The seminars have facilitated quality efforts in subtler ways. "The QualPro courses provide a common language, to some degree," says Dan J. Hargett, the current manager of what used to be the Monsanto plant (it was sold in 1989 to a German chemical company and is now known as MEMC Electronic Materials). "After a while, you tend to put things in quality language."

But as important as the seminars have been, it is in their other dimensions that the chamber's efforts may have had their greatest impact. "A lot of the chamber's activities are built around networking," says Wayne I. Steinberg, the chamber's vice president for quality programs. "Any company can go find training somewhere; they don't need the chamber for that. But networking is a real value that we can provide that they can't get on their own."

The chamber encourages networking through bimonthly "quality dinners" for 100 to 150 participants, and through monthly, and much smaller, "networking round tables."

By networking with other companies, you hear the wrong way to do it.

Training, as in the QualPro seminars, can educate companies in the right way to do things, Steinberg notes, "but by networking with other companies, you hear the wrong way to do it." There's a very strong correlation between success and being open about mistakes, he says: "the ones that are all positive about their quality programs probably don't have that great a program."

Says MEMC's Hargett: "We feed off each other. It gives us a commonality. 'What are you guys doing?' is almost the first question that you ask" when business people in the area get together.

There is no way to measure precisely how much the Spartanburg chamber's quality programs have contributed to the area's prosperity, but the figures are striking nevertheless. From a high of 13 percent during the recession of the early '80s, the county unemployment rate shrank to below 4 percent in the late '80s, rising to only a little above 5 percent even during the recent economic doldrums.

The Spartanburg area's quality consciousness has undoubtedly made it more attractive to foreign manufacturers. The Spartanburg chamber puts total foreign investment in the county (which has a population of around 230,000) at $1.5 billion, which the chamber says is the highest per-capita foreign investment for any county in the U.S.

"It keeps building on itself," Steinberg says. "Back in Europe, the word gets around that Spartanburg is a good place." In the most recent piece of good news, the German auto manufacturer BMW announced that it would build a $1 billion plant near the airport that serves Spartanburg and neighboring Greenville.

The quality movement has spread beyond for-profit companies into the non-profit arena; the United Way of the Piedmont, for example, adopted a quality program in 1990, with "mentoring" from the Chamber's Wayne Steinberg. "I don't think that the not-for-profit sector is really different from the for-profit," says Vincent M. Pulskamp, United Way's president. "We ought to produce a return on investment to [the members of] the community, who are our stockholders."

Small companies have not yet been major beneficiaries of the chamber's quality efforts. "We've been so consumed with just meeting the needs of the larger companies that we have not had the time or the resources to have a major focus on small business," Steinberg says.

Larger companies "were the ones to embrace it and ask for it," he says of the Quality in the Workplace program. "They were getting a lot of pressure from their customers to improve, and they were the ones typically facing international competition."

There is, however, evidence that interest in quality management is quickening among small firms in the Spartanburg area. "We've had 50 or 60 benchmarking visits the last 12 to 18 months," says H. L. "Dunk" Hale, MEMC's quality-improvement manager, referring to the technique by which companies measure themselves against outstanding firms as a way of determining where they most need to improve. "Probably 90 percent of those are small businesses."

In general, though Steinberg says, smaller companies don't want to invest the money and time that a serious quality effort requires. The chamber is now trying to come up with a seminar aimed at small businesses, to be offered for a few hours in the evening each week.

What really holds small companies back, says Jerome V. Bennett, the dean of the business school at the University of South Carolina at Spartanburg, is "the perception by the chief executives that they just don't have time to devote to the training effort. They're too busy running the shop. The fact that ABCO has come around to doing it makes it an awfully good role model."

The ABCO to which Bennett refers is a Roebuck, S.C., company that makes chemical products for the textile industry—products that the average consumer would never be aware of but that are critical to the look and texture of many fabrics. One such product ABCO makes is sizing, which is, in effect, a temporary plastic coating that is applied to fiber so it can be woven.

ABCO, now a 125-employee firm, started as a family firm, although a few key nonfamily employees now own a large part of it. A. B. "Al" Bullington Jr.'s father started ABCO in 1961. Al joined the firm, as he says, "on Day One" and has been president since his father retired in 1973.

In the late '80s, Bullington recalls, ABCO executives surveyed the textile industry and decided that the best opportunities for growth lay outside the U.S. "That probably had some influence on our decision to change our management style," he says.

In addition, says Vice President Edward E. "Ned" Page, "our customers were pressuring us." That pressure came not in the form of direct demands that ABCO adopt a quality program. Instead, Page says, he was dealing with people—"people I eat lunch with a lot"—who were talking about their own quality effort in a way that made him "feel somewhat envious."

ABCO executives called Steinberg and met with him, and they followed his counsel to put top executives through a QualPro seminar. When they started the seminar, they had no idea how much change awaited them, Page says. "We were incredibly naive about the whole thing."

Bullington had thought he had so many problems on his desk that he wouldn't have time to get involved in quality management. "But after going through some of this training," he says, "I realized that I didn't have to handle all of these problems. I had people who could handle them for me. I had to learn to sit back and let them do it."

In the spring of 1990, with the first round of training behind them, ABCO's top executives began trying to figure out how a quality program might work at their firm, Page says, "without damaging the company, or taking up too much time."

In forming employee teams, ABCO started first, in May 1990, with a team to deal with, as Page says, "something easy to measure, something tangible, something that we knew could be a success story." That so-called "steam team" studied the energy that ABCO consumed in the form of steam. The team, which included some employees who knew nothing about steam before working on the team, produced savings of more than $60,000, mainly by renegotiating ABCO's contract with its steam supplier. As Page says, "It was unheard of for someone outside of management to do that."

ABCO's executives went one step further: They tried to give their employees an *emotional* understanding of what the company wanted to achieve. In 1991, they did that through training that encouraged employees to examine their own lives, in the same way that the company was examining itself. Individual employees wrote their own "mission statements" for their private lives, and "all kinds of wonderful things happened," Page says. "We had people who were sending flowers to their wives, and people going back to church who hadn't been to church in a long time. It was so easy to tie that into quality management, and what our company was going to be faced with."

Thanks to that emotional comprehension of quality management, ABCO has been able to move much more rapidly than most experts would say is possible. For example, at MEMC—in many ways, a model quality-management facility—the formation of "high-performance teams" began in 1989 and won't spread throughout the plant until late in 1993. At ABCO, where quality efforts didn't get well under way until early 1991, about 80 percent of the employees already belong to teams.

The introduction of teams didn't go altogether smoothly—"we fell into the pit," Bullington says, because the teams didn't get enough guidance from management at first—but the initial confusion has long since cleared up. "Today," Page says, "people knock each other down getting into a meeting, because they see it as a way to get rid of their problems. Before, you couldn't drag them into a meeting."

What happened at ABCO is thus an excellent example of one of the paradoxes of quality management: Small firms are often slow to move into it, but once they do, they usually find that it meets their needs even better than it meets the needs of large companies. The cultural changes that may take years in a big company can come much faster in a small firm where people know each other, and their customers, very well.

If there's a downside to quality management, Page says, it is that teams' good ideas can create demands on a company's resources. "Using these resources widely is what ramps us at a greater rate than our competition," he says, "and we're trying to do a better job of that."

ABCO has already met what Wayne Steinberg calls "the biggest challenge: to get top management not only to accept that they need to change but actually to do it."

Al Bullington suggests that all it really takes is for top managers to taste the sweet rewards that quality management can bring. "We all of a sudden find that we've got some free time," he says. "I have time to study and focus on where the company is going."

Early in the quality effort, Bullington admits, "I struggled hard; I floundered." But today, he says, the demands of his job "are less than half what they used to be." He meets now with close to 80 percent of ABCO's employees every month, he says, by sitting in on team meetings: "All of a sudden, I know what's going on again." And in what has to be the strongest possible endorsement of quality management, he says, "I've even got where I enjoy coming to work." Probably a lot of other people in the Spartanburg area could say the same thing.

Michael Barrier is a writer and editor for Nation's Business.

> At ABCO, where quality efforts didn't get well under way until early 1991, about 80 percent of the employees already belong to teams.

The Nature of Customer Satisfaction

Charles R. O'Neal
Part One

Good Enough Is No Longer Good Enough

This is a three-part review of just what is involved in understanding and implementing a customer-focused organization. In part one, "Good Enough Is No Longer Good Enough," the author documents the relation between customer satisfaction and the bottom line. Part two, "Identifying Your Customer: The First Step to Customer Delight," talks about the importance of developing a mission statement identifying who you are in business to serve and a strategy that allows you to do that. Part three, "Understanding Your Customer: The Most Critical Step to Customer Delight," explains how to go beyond satisfying customers to truly delighting them, time over time, and the necessity of doing this to sustain competitive advantage.

Four decades ago, Peter Drucker cut to the bottom line with his statement, "There is only one definition of business purpose: to create a satisfied customer."[1] He went on to say that because of this purpose, any business

Reprinted with permission from *Target*, May/June, July/August, and September/October 1992, published by the Association for Manufacturing Excellence, 380 W. Palatine Road, Wheeling, IL 60090.

enterprise has only two basic functions: marketing and innovation. Interestingly, he described marketing not as a specialized activity, but as the whole business as seen from the point of view of its final customer.

Unfortunately, during the decade of the 1980s, American consumers were not very well satisfied with the product offerings provided by domestic producers. The devastating impact of global competitors providing customer satisfaction—and more—cut across broad sectors of U.S. industry. Consumer electronics was virtually abandoned by U.S. companies. During the 1980s, U.S. automakers watched their share of the domestic market erode from 71 percent to 62 percent. The domestic share of the U.S. computer industry plunged from 94 percent to 66 percent. Few U.S. industries and companies remain immune.[2]

What's the Problem?

MIT addressed this question in the late 1980s with its massive research study summarized in *Made in America: Regaining the Productive Edge.*[3] The study team discovered major weaknesses: outdated strategies, short-time horizons, technological weaknesses in development and production, neglect of human resources, failure of cooperation, and a government at cross purposes with industry. Robert Kaplan and Thomas Johnson added to this list of weaknesses the lack of relevance of management accounting systems used for internal decision making, citing their failure to track and measure the true drivers of process costs.[4]

These factors are indeed weaknesses of the U.S. development—production—delivery system, but an even more significant shortcoming has transcended the whole set—the lack of market orientation by many, perhaps most, U.S. companies.

Market-Orientation: A Missing Link

Much empirical evidence shows that American companies have been much more product or technology-driven than market-driven despite the feeling by many manufacturing people that sales and marketing "run the show."

Robert Cooper, after 10 years researching new product failures and successes, found in a study of 114 industrial product firms that marketing research was either poorly done or omitted altogether.[5] He found that market research is the most serious deficiency in the entire new product development process, and that product successes are significantly influenced by an understanding of market needs. His findings are supported by studies of hundreds of other innovations. The high failure rate of new products and loss of market position by many American companies, and entire industries, confirm that this has not been well communicated, or accepted.

Cooper emphasizes that before moving into product development it is critical to carefully define the "target" by answering four questions:

1. Who is the customer?
   Construction fleet owners for whom downtime is a critical and costly problem.

> Much empirical evidence shows that American companies have been much more product or technology-driven than market-driven.

2. How will the product be positioned or perceived by the customer and differentiated from competitive offerings?
   A truck that can be repaired overnight and back on the road in twelve hours no matter how serious the breakdown.

3. What benefits will the product deliver to the customer?
   Higher profitability resulting from full utilization of the entire fleet on a daily basis with increased revenues, lower capital investment, and reduced repair and maintenance costs.

4. What are the product requirements? What does the customer need/want/prefer in terms of features, attributes, and specifications?
   A modular, minimum downtime truck with every major "trouble component" engineered to be removed and replaced quickly and easily—engine, transmission, rear axle, front axle, electrical systems, radiator—with parts available from a variety of local sources.

> A superior protocol activity defines a product that is unique and superior in the eyes of the customer.

Agreement on these questions by all the people and departments involved in project separates the winners from the losers. Cooper refers to this as the "protocol activity." A superior protocol activity defines a product that is unique and superior in the eyes of the customer.

The Transformation Begins

In the late 1980s the importance of customer satisfaction was beginning to be driven home. On a macro-level there were signs of stability, in some instances, of recovery by U.S. firms as demonstrated by the edging up of the share of GNP represented by manufacturing, and the share of world manufacturing held by U.S. firms.

The term "quality" took on special significance during the late 1980s as the many definitions began to converge—with the customer as a common focal point, not just customer satisfaction, but a total experience of fulfillment with incidents of delight.

Baldrige Criteria Right on Track

The establishment of the Malcolm Baldrige National Quality Award—the most significant nationwide quality event of the '80s—served as a catalyst for developing a market orientation among U.S. companies. Its customer focus is evident from the heavy emphasis placed on customer satisfaction in the evaluative criteria—300 of the 1000 points available. It also emphasizes competitive analysis and comparisons with competitors throughout the relevant criteria. Finally, cross-functional coordination is stressed, especially section 4.0 relating to human resource development and management, and 5.0 covering the management of process quality.

The Baldrige Award's emphasis on the customer is one of the factors that has caused organizations which understand the meaning of market orientation and are deeply committed to it, to become the first recipients of the award.

- Xerox uses a myriad of marketing research techniques to find out what customers want and need, and once this is determined, it continues to involve the customer in every step of the process to assure the delivery of 100 percent total satisfaction.
- IBM-Rochester transformed its quality culture from reliance on technology-driven processes to market-driven processes directly involving suppliers, business partners, and customers.
- Cadillac's simultaneous engineering teams, responsible for defining, engineering, and continuously improving all products, fully integrate suppliers and dealers alongside employees and customers in the process.
- Motorola marries its technology development with a deep understanding of customers' needs, and not just their communications needs, but their business needs. As a result Motorola can design products its customers can't even imagine. Motorola's process serves the customer across the functional units within the company, using an integrated team approach, starting with the supplier and moving across—not up and down—the organization. Each functional unit understands how it can contribute value to the customer. The objective is total customer satisfaction with a six-sigma level of customer-focused quality.

A growing number of companies use the Baldrige criteria as a blueprint for making the transition from product-driven to market-oriented organizations.

Customer Satisfaction Goes to the Bottom Line

Recent research relating customer satisfaction and bottom line financial performance has dramatically demonstrate that customers whose expectations have been met or exceeded become loyal customers and significantly impact the bottom line of the organization. Three major research streams confirm the relationship between market orientation and profitability.

The Quality-Profitability Connection

The massive database of the Strategic Planning Institute's PIMS (profit impact of marketing strategy) has provided valuable insights into market-oriented quality and profitability.[6] In the study of the relationship between "relative quality," as perceived by the customer, and return on investment, the results (See Figure 1) show repeatedly that organizations with higher relative quality are able to differentiate their products, and either charge a premium price for the higher relative value, thus increasing their margins, or maintain a competitive price and increase market share, lowering costs through scale economies. The result is higher profits (B). They also show that higher quality

Three major research streams confirm the relationship between market orientation and profitability.

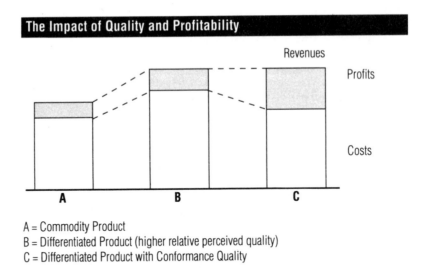

The Impact of Quality and Profitability

A = Commodity Product
B = Differentiated Product (higher relative perceived quality)
C = Differentiated Product with Conformance Quality

Figure 1.

processes result in improved conformance quality which lowers the overall cost of quality—leading to a further increase in profits (C).

The Value of Customer Retention

Bain and Company's research on customer retention has certainly caught the attention of management. Its careful examination of over 100 companies from more than two dozen industries uncovered a performance measure it believes to be the best—and probably the simplest—measure of the ability of a company's products and services to provide customer satisfaction. It is the rate at which the company retains its customers.

While common logic would suggest a quality-customer retention connection, less obvious is the powerful impact on profits of even small shifts in a company's retention rate. For example, the study found that a five percentage-point improvement in the customer retention rate drives profits up by 25–85 percent for a wide range of industries. It has concluded that customer retention is a direct result of customer satisfaction, with customers reporting higher satisfaction levels demonstrating significantly greater loyalty.[7]

Figure 2 illustrates the profit contribution profile of individual customers as they are retained over a longer-term period. Research by Bain and Company has shown that a company actively managing its retention rate is helped by a solid base of repeat sales, by referrals from satisfied customers, and by a trend, that has been confirmed, for net sales per account to rise almost steadily as the age of the customer account increases.

On the cost side of the equation, experienced customers are generally less expensive to serve. New customer acquisition costs benefit from lower turnover. In addition, some companies find that consistent, good service to long-established accounts provides the opportunity for charging a premium.

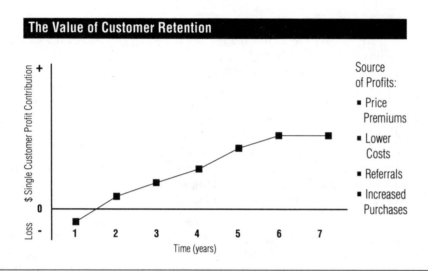

Figure 2.

Taken from "Zero Defections: Quality Comes to Services," by Frederick Reichheld and W. Earl Sasser, Jr., *Harvard Business Review,* September–October, 1990, p. 108.

The Market Orientation Impact

A recent research stream initiated by John Narvin and Stanley Slater examines the relationship between market orientation and profitability. They tested the concept of "market orientation" in an industrial product setting.[8] Market orientation, according to their empirically-developed description, has three basic elements.

1. *Customer orientation*—the sufficient understanding of target customers to be able to create superior value for them continuously. This requires that the seller understand the customer's entire value chain—product/process design, development, materials management, production, delivery, and service support—not only as it is today, but also as it will evolve over time.

   The seller creates value to the customer by either:
   a. *Increasing benefits* to the customer in relation to costs—designing the part for automatic centering in assembly (error-proofing) at an additional cost to the customer of two cents per unit, but a savings in assembly of five cents per unit, or
   b. *Decreasing the customer's costs* in relation to customer benefits—reducing the order cycle from eight days to two days with an equivalent reduction in the customer's raw material inventory cost.

   The seller must understand not only the cost/revenue relationships of its target customers, but also of its customer's customer, if they do not represent the final buyer in the industry value chain.

2. *Competitive orientation*—understanding the short-term strengths and weaknesses, and long-term capabilities and strategies of key competitors, including potential competitors. This analysis must include the entire set of technologies capable of satisfying the current and expected needs of the seller's target customers. This requires analysis well beyond the industry in which present competitors are operating since competitive/technological threats frequently come from outside the industry. For example, the leading electronic tube producers of the 1950s were not the leading discrete semi-conductor producers of the 1970s, and the latter are not the leading microprocessor chip producers of today. This presents a major challenge of identifying and analyzing the industries/technologies representing the chief competitors of the future.

3. *Cross-functional coordination*—creating superior value for target customers does not rest on the shoulders of a single department. It is achieved by the carefully-planned integration of each of the value-adding units through cross-functional teams with target customers as the primary focus. This is a very tough assignment since it requires that the traditional vertical management orientation be transformed into a horizontal management process to match the natural flow of customer-oriented development, production, and fulfillment processes. It is best illustrated by the concurrent engineering (CE) team which forms as market need and technology capability are matched by the organization. The CE team translates these needs into appropriate internal technical requirements, and ensures the communication of these requirements to all individuals in the organization that contribute, in any way, to delivering them.

Creating superior value is achieved by the carefully-planned integration of each of the value-adding units.

The test of the relationship between market orientation and profitability were significantly positive when applied to 140 business units of a major forest products company. The results were consistent for small, medium, and large business units producing commodity products (logs, wood chips, dimension lumber, plywood); specialty products (laminated doors, hardwood cabinets, particle board, roof truss systems); and for distribution businesses serving building-supply retailers, contractors, and exporters.

These recent research streams are consistent. Their basic theme is customer satisfaction. Quality, as perceived by the customer, is how well the product/service meets the needs/expectations of the customer. Customer retention is a direct result of customer satisfaction. Customers reporting higher satisfaction levels demonstrate greater loyalty. Finally, a key element of market orientation is customer orientation—the providing of customer satisfaction. The other two elements—competitive orientation and cross-functional coordination—serve as facilitators.

Customer Satisfaction Does Not Ensure Loyalty

While customer satisfaction is generally accepted as a measure of market success, it has limitations, especially for the organization striving for world-class status. One of the shortcomings is the failure of customer satisfaction scores to measure performance relative to competitors. How would your scores compare with ratings provided by your competitors' customers? Bradley Gale of Market Perceived Quality Systems makes the important point, "Your customers may give you higher customer satisfaction scores while you lose position versus your competitors."[9]

Another very relevant consideration is the "degree of customer satisfaction" with a supplier's quality compared with retention/loyalty of the customers. The Customer Satisfaction Research Institute has found that customers responding as "satisfied" with respect to level of satisfaction, and "good" and "same" as measures of quality levels/competitive comparisons, do not necessarily become brand loyal.

In a British Airways study, customers compared it with competitors. The results: 20 percent rated it "better," 65 percent "the same," and 15 percent "worse." What are implications for customer loyalty? While 85 percent were "satisfied"—the 20 percent plus the 65 percent; 80 percent would switch—65 percent plus the 15 percent. Only 20 percent were brand loyal—those who rated British Airways as better than competition.

Extensive research by Ray Kordupleski of AT&T supports the above results. One of his findings, shown in Figure 3, was the dramatic impact of customer rating on customer loyalty (retention). A four-times greater customer defection rate was likely among those customers rating AT&T as "good" (40 percent defections), compared to those giving a rating of "excellent" (10 percent defections), Kordupleski concluded "good is not good enough." While a rating of good may be equated with customer satisfaction, an excellent rating has an element of customer delight.

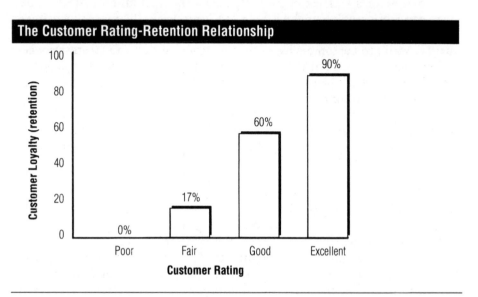

Figure 3.

Wayland Hicks of Xerox Corporation, which recently introduced a 100 percent customer satisfaction guarantee, emphasizes that "very satisfied" customers are six times more loyal than "satisfied" customers. He also points out that as quality rises, customers' expectations rise. Exceeding expectations becomes essential. He emphasizes the importance of enhancing the customer relationship by anticipating customer needs. This provides customers with exciting quality as they receive important, but unexpected, value enhancements.

Customer Loyalty Requires a Total Quality Offering

The product- or technology-driven organization focuses on the quality level of the physical product—attributes such as performance, durability, and reliability. These are certainly important to the customer. But some of the softer quality characteristics may be of equal, or even greater, importance—intangibles, such as availability, order cycle time, on-time delivery, service response time, call backs, accessibility of contact personnel, general attitude, openness, cooperation, and empathy.

These attributes and many other softer quality characteristics make up the total product offering. It consists of the total set of "marketing exchange" attributes that are perceived by the customer as providing value. In the case of organizations marketing a service—airlines, hospitals, banks—most of the product offering is a set of intangibles.

A total quality offering meets or exceeds customer expectations across all product offering attributes which the customer perceives to be important. A few illustrations will help clarify this point.

In each of these instances, the development of a robust product offering—a total quality offering—required process changes beyond the physical product.

When Alcoa's Warrick operations, producers of aluminum sheet for beverage can fabricators, launched their TQC initiative, they were focusing on critical width, thickness, and surface dimensions in providing excellence in quality. Visits to customers by TQ teams revealed that the greatest concern of their customer was not the basic product dimensions, but what to do with the very large pallets, plastic wrap, and strapping material accompanying each giant coil of aluminum.

Nike, in equipping its sales force with customized Compaq laptop computers, found them to be extremely valuable in increasing the productivity of its sales teams. However, the attribute that differentiated Compaq from competition was not the basic product so much as the outstanding product service provided by Compaq's authorized dealer network—a much softer quality attribute.

Motorola, in talking to its prospective pager customers, learned that what bothered them most was not so much the product quality, but its delivery and billing mistakes, the softer product offering attributes.

Procter and Gamble, in developing its "Excellence in Customer Service" program with major customer-partners, learned that the single most significant customer problem was not the basic product or transaction, but excessive damage in transit. A QFD analysis discovered the source of the problem—a one-half inch overhang of the carton when loaded on the shipping pallet. Extremely difficult to discover, extremely simple to correct.

In each of these instances, the development of a robust product offering—a total quality offering—required process changes beyond the physical product.

Scandinavian Airlines, benchmarked by many U.S. companies, is an excellent example of a company with robust-designed customer service. The familiar story, recounted by Jan Carlzon, president of SAS, provides an outstanding illustration.[10]

Rudy Peterson, an American businessman was planning to fly SAS from Arlanda (north of Stockholm) to Copenhagen. He arrived at the airport realizing he had left his ticket in his hotel room in Stockholm. He resigned himself to missing the flight and his business meeting since everybody knows you can't board an airplane without a ticket. But wait; when he explained his dilemma to the SAS ticket agent, an unusual thing happened. Rather than saying "sorry," she smiled and said "don't worry, Mr. Peterson, here's your boarding card, and a temporary ticket. Tell me your hotel room number and your destination in Copenhagen, and "I will take care of the rest." And she did! Why? Because SAS is a market-oriented airline that has empowered front-line employees not just to satisfy their customers, but to delight them. Their empowerment is a key element in the robust service they provide.

References

1. Drucker, Peter F., *The Practice of Management*, New York, Harper and Row, 1954.

2. Stewart, Thomas A., "The New American Century: Where We Stand," *Fortune*, Special Issue, 1991, pp. 12–23.

3. Dertouzos, Michael, Richard K. Lester and Robert M. Solow, *Made in America: Regaining the Productive Edge*, Cambridge, MA, The MIT Press, 1989.

4. Johnson, H. Thomas, Robert Kaplan, *Relevance Lost: The Rise and Fall of Management Accounting*, Boston, Harvard Business School Press, 1987.

5. Cooper, Robert G., *Winning at New Products*, Reading, MA, Addison-Wesley, 1986.

6. Buzzell, Robert D. and Bradley T. Gale, *The PIMS Principles*, New York, The Free Press, 1987.

7. From "The Power of Consumer Retention," A presentation by Frederick Reichhold, at the Third Annual Consumer Satisfaction and Quality Measurement Conference, Co-sponsored by ASQC and AMA, Washington, D.C., April, 1991.

8. Narver, John C., and Stanley F. Slater, "The Effect of Market Orientation on Business Profitability," *The Journal of Marketing*, October, 1990, pp. 20–35.

9. Gale, Bradley T., "Bringing Customer Satisfaction and Market Perceived Quality to Life," a presentation at the Third Annual Customer Satisfaction and Quality Measurement Conference—ASQC & AMA, Washington, D.C., April, 1991.

10. Carlzon, Jan, *Moments of Truth*, Cambridge, MA, Ballinger Books, 1987.

Part Two

Identifying Your Customer:
The First Step to Customer Delight

"**W**ho's the customer?" is a deceptively simple question frequently addressed very superficially. Identifying the "wrong customer" has big pitfalls:

- selection of inappropriate product-market growth strategies
- failure to adequately segment the market
- not focusing on the vital few customers within an appropriate
  segment
- missing important indirect (intermediary) customer organizations, and
- overlooking critical decision influences within key target organizations.

Delighting the customer begins with identifying the "right customers"—
those customer organizations with the potential for the greatest long-term
payoff for both organizations. It continues with the identification of the key
decision influences—the primary value-adding units—within each selected
customer organization. (Once identified, every value-adding unit within the
seller organization needs clear understanding of precisely who these "customers" are so they may focus all of their efforts and resources on delighting
them.)

We can visualize this process as one of focusing on the customer through
a series of lenses, each of which provides a sharper definition of the customer
to be served (see Figure 1).

The Mission Statement—The Customer from 30,000 Feet

The parameters for customer identification are set by a series of prior organizational decisions beginning with the mission statement which flows from
the vision of the organization. The mission statement must address four vital
questions:

- Who are we?
- What do we do?
- Whom do we do it for?
- Why do we do it?

The truly successful organization answers these questions by looking at
its business from the outside—from the customers' point of view.

Steelcase, Inc. has taken this approach in developing and applying its customer-focused mission statement—"Our mission is to provide the world's

Figure 1.   **Focusing on the Customer—a multi-stage process.**

best office environment products, services, systems, and intelligence designed to help people in offices work more effectively."[1]

This carefully developed statement guides Steelcase in all its activities. It defines who it is—"the world's best." This also prescribes the culture of the organization—the attitude and commitment of each employee. Every employee carries a card with the mission statement inscribed on it, a step in the internalization of this goal. It specifies what it does—"provides office environment products, services, systems, and intelligence." It also establishes, very broadly (at 30,000 feet), the market being targeted by Steelcase—"people in offices." Finally, Steelcase specifies why it does this—"to help (people in offices) work more effectively." Notice the customer focus used by Steelcase in response to the final question.

The mission statement provides the general ballpark it will use to satisfy these needs, and the technology, or approach, it will use in satisfying these

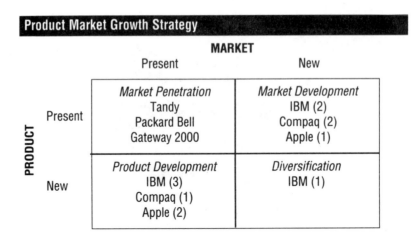

Figure 2. **Alternate strategies for profitable growth. (1) = primary; (2) secondary; (3) tertiary.**

needs. In larger, multi-division organizations, the individual units must identify a "piece of the ballpark" in which it will complete.

Directions of Growth

The first lens defines the general ballpark, the second focuses on the direction of growth, giving further definition to the question "who is the customer?"—moving to 3000 feet. The four options appear in Figure 2. They are not mutually exclusive, but the organization with limited resources is wise to select a single primary product-market growth strategy. The theme woven throughout the customer identification analysis is one of focus—"doing what you do best for those customers who are best served by it."

Market Penetration

The organization selecting this option as its primary growth strategy will center on developing a better understanding of the needs of target groups already served. It will strive for growth through more aggressive marketing of current products by centering on pricing, marketing communications, product accessibility, and value-added services. Several PC producers illustrate successful market penetration strategies:

- **Gateway 2000,** a recent market entry, with the lowest prices for what's perceived in the market as a viable product, and enjoying early market success. Its strength lies in its low-cost operation. It serves as a product assembler outsourcing all components, sells only through phone orders in response to media advertising, and has assembly worker labor rates starting at $6.00/hour in its South Dakota plant.

- **Packard Bell** is becoming the king of the mass market with its low prices and broad distribution network through consumer electronics retailers.
- **Tandy** (Radio Shack), a PC pioneer, draws strength from its vertical integration—from components manufacture to captive retailing. It offers very broad distribution, substantial and accessible service support, and very competitive prices.

Market Development

This strategy centers on finding new applications for present products, or marketing them beyond the geographical region currently served.

- **IBM** has followed a market development strategy by considering the world its market, and by marketing its basic products into most of the major market sectors—business, education, home, and government.
- **Apple** placed its initial emphasis on the educational market to help it gain access, through student experiences, to the home, and later, the business markets.
- **Compaq**, whose initial focus was the U.S. domestic market, has more recently made a major move into the international market, especially Western Europe. Compaq's international sales now comprise well over half its total revenues.

Product Development

This strategy places the greatest emphasis on moving beyond present technology to serving customer needs. While the market penetration strategy may examine enhancements to the basic PC, such as capacity, speed, monitor clarity, the product development strategy searches for new solutions as represented by portable, laptop, and notebook designs. This presents a much greater challenge to the marketing-design team in market needs assessment and in product definition.

- Compaq has followed product development as its primary strategy since its inception, with the introduction of the first PC portable. Its stated objective is to build computers recognized by customers as the "best in the world." It challenges IBM on performance and features, but not on price.
- IBM, a late entry in the PC market, set the standard with its original PC in 1981. Its dominant position in mainframe technology and excellent service reputation catapulted IBM into the lead position with a 25 percent share of the PC market by 1985.
- Apple provides an alternative, excellent product to PC users. Its strength is drawn from the ease of use and superior graphics capabilities of its products.

Diversification

This strategy often places the organization in a new ballpark, and may require a modification to the basic mission statement. It has not played a dominant role in the business plans of most major PC producers. IBM has used a concentric diversification strategy as it has moved out from its original mainframe business into minicomputers and PCs and related communications products. This strategy is higher risk and requires a very substantial resource base.

The product-market strategy decision sets the direction of growth and eliminates large sectors of prospective markets by default. The focal lens strategically located within the product-market quadrant selected to be served provides the focus for the descent from 3000 feet to ground zero in three stages: selecting target segments within the served quadrant; identifying target organizations; and focusing on key decision influences within chosen customer organizations—the true customers.

Segmenting the Market

Every large heterogeneous market includes numerous, relatively homogeneous submarkets or segments, each with a rather unique set of needs and buying behavior. Attempting to cut across these segments with a single product means a set of design compromises that satisfies none of them. The objective is to carefully select one or more segments that provide the best match between the seller organizations' capabilities and resources, and the customers' needs. This is most effectively done in two stages—macrosegmentation and microsegmentation.

Attempting to cut across these segments with a single product means a set of design compromises that satisfies none of them.

Macrosegmentation carves up the market based on organizational demographics using information available from external sources—government census data, trade publications and associations, research organization reports, etc. A first cut at the microcomputer served market, based on end-user as the macrosegmentation variable and using the PC firms discussed earlier, would look something like Figure 3.

Microcomputer Market Segmentation				
	Business	*Education*	*Consumer*	*Government*
Apple	x	x[1]	x	x
Compaq	x			x
Gateway 2000			x	
IBM	x[1]	x	x	x
Packard Bell			x	
Tandy	x	x	x[1]	

Figure 3.

Those firms serving multiple segments began by focusing on a single segment (designated by [1]), and later chose product market strategies that moved them into additional segments. Macrosegmentation based on a single variable as in Figure 3 is too broad to provide meaningful customer data to the seller organizations. Additional cuts are required with relevant variables such as types of business end users (service organizations, manufacturers, retailers), organizational characteristics (size, location), and product application. For example, Compaq may focus on large financial service organizations with extensive networking requirements, while Apple may select medium-size advertising agencies with significant desktop publishing needs.

Macrosegmentation is very helpful, but it is not sufficient for establishing useful market segments. Additional cuts using microsegmentation variables focusing on specific response behavior—benefits sought, sensitivity to price, importance of the product, brand loyalty, etc.—are often required. Information on these variables must come from a look inside the organizations; and while it is more difficult and costly to obtain, it is much more useful for establishing specific target segments.

Identifying the Customer Organization

This process begins as microsegments are developed. Specific markets are defined, and sets of customers with common needs are identified. Specific organizations to be targeted include those for which the product offering has the potential to provide the most positive impact. This is consistent with J. M. Juran's definition of the customer as "anyone impacted by the product."[2]

These organizations are highlighted as we analyze the industry channel, or value chain, for the product offering. Figure 4 illustrates a typical channel

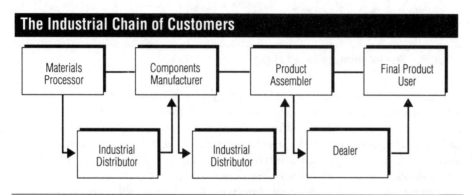

Figure 4. **Direct customers and intermediaries (indirect customers).**

configuration of the PC industry as we include upstream supplier organizations. It flows from the materials processor (substrates) to components manufacturer (chips) to product assembler (completed PC) to the end user.

In the case of the materials processor there can be as many as six downstream customer organizations whose needs must be assessed and met—two producers, three intermediaries (indirect customers), and the final user. The final product assembler will have a single customer set if using direct marketing (Gateway 2000, two customer sets if marketing through a dealer network (Compaq), and a combination of these if using both channel alternatives (IBM). The more direct the path the simpler the needs assessment and need satisfaction tasks.

The importance of each downstream customer cannot be overstated. For example, the PC producer using an independent dealer network to serve the final users, such as Packard Bell and Compaq, must consider the needs/requirements of these indirect customers as fully as those of the final users. Both are equally important "customers." In fact the dealer organizations may provide them with their unique competitive advantage. Similarly, moving upstream, the component manufacturer (Intel) must consider the requirements of its industrial distributors, its PC producer customers, and the final product users of PCs with Intel components.

> The importance of each downstream customer cannot be overstated.

Looking Inside the Organization

The "customers" just described are organizations, and organizations do not buy products and services. We must look inside each of these to identify organizational units—value-adding activities that will be significantly impacted by the product offering. These will become the specifiers or decision influences as the product offering is being developed, produced, delivered, used, and maintained over its lifetime. Figure 5 includes the primary value-adding units.

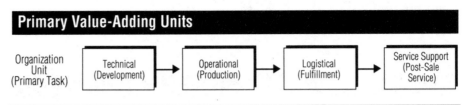

Primary Value-Adding Units

Organization Unit (Primary Task) → Technical (Development) → Operational (Production) → Logistical (Fulfillment) → Service Support (Post-Sale Service)

Figure 5. **The internal customer chain.**

Each customer organization, including intermediaries, has this common set of internal units which generate value for the organization. The importance of each unit within a single organization is determined by the organization's basic objective, and the primary strategy it uses to differentiate itself in the marketplace. These establish its critical needs, and must be thoroughly understood by the seller organization choosing to serve it.

For example, the PC manufacturer with the objective of maintaining technological leadership will emphasize up front R&D (technical) activity centering on innovative designs and will need suppliers with leading edge capabilities to work closely with it in produce development. The technical unit becomes a key internal customer to the supplier.

On the other hand, the PC assembler emphasizing superior value through quick response with established, proven designs will emphasize operational and logistical activities, needing JIT suppliers that can match its operational (inbound logistic, and manufacturing) requirements. The operational units become the key internal customers of supplier organizations.

The PC producer must use the same approach to identify the key internal customers of its downstream customer organizations.

Illustrating the Process

Compaq has an amazing record as a marketer of personal—desktop, portable, laptop, and notebook—computers. By 1990, only eight years after its inception, Compaq's sales reached $3.6 billion with earnings of $455 million, an achievement resulting from Compaq's mission to provide "phenomenal customer experiences." Compaq selected product development as its basic growth strategy with emphasis on being the "best in the world."

Compaq uses a multi-product, multi-segment approach to serving its markets, cutting across many market segments. It has learned that the traditional approach to customer identification and needs evaluation is inadequate to allow it to go beyond customer satisfaction to delighting its customers.

In developing meaningful segments Compaq analyzes its markets by type and size of organization, type of application, and brand/type of products owned. It has discovered that "range of technical sophistication" of customers is an extremely meaningful microsegmentation variable. It tends to be related to company size as well as to brand and type of product used (Apple versus IBM). Customer sophistication ranges widely across products, and rather widely within products. This influences the types of questions Compaq can ask prospective customers. For example, a person deeply involved in networking applications can answer different questions than the user who knows very little about the machine's capabilities.

Compaq has identified four rather distinctive constituencies—internal customers within target customer organizations and indirect customers—that significantly influence the purchase decision process:

1. Influential users (operational) who have opinions about the products and advise others formally, and/or informally.
2. MIS directors (technical) that have formal authority to recommend/specify product offering characteristics.
3. Executive managers (economic influencers)—that have formal authority to make the final product decision. This group may have very different interests from the MIS managers.
4. Authorized dealers with a major concern about how well Compaq supports them. These play a key role in Compaq's success by providing outstanding logistical performance and service support.

Critical internal customers within these organizations are units directly involved in inbound logistics, and in customer service support.[3]

Determining Segment and Customer Attractiveness

The multi-stage segmentation process provides information for assessing the attractiveness of individual customer segments. The key measure will normally be anticipated profit over some acceptable time horizon. This will be the result of the revenues generated from offering superior value, less the costs of providing that value. Three very important factors in this determination include:

- Individual customer potential,
- Match of the selling organizations competencies with customer needs, and
- Vulnerability to competitors.

This information will be readily available from segments in which the seller organization has substantial experience. It will be much more difficult to obtain in new segments.

Selecting the Vital Few

The woods are full of "customers." The trick is to sort out the vital few that will result in the most mutually satisfying/delighting and profitable relationships over the long haul.

This requires a product-market growth strategy that is most consistent with the organization's mission and resource base. It also demands a segmentation strategy that draws out those organizations whose needs most closely match the capabilities and resources of the seller organizations. This provides the customer pool.

Use the Pareto principle to provide the definitive response to "who is the customer?" First apply it to the customer pool to isolate the "winners"—those organizations destined to be successful in the global marketplace. These are excellent candidates for long-term partnerships. Once these potential partners are identified, the Pareto principle is applied to the decision influences/value-adding units within each of these organizations. It serves as the lens in focusing on the vital few units that will be significantly impacted by the product offering.

We've now covered the full distance form 30,000 feet to ground zero—into the office of the "true customers." Once inside their offices, the organization must focus on delighting these customers.

References

1. Dutkiewicz, Ken, "Competing through Excellence in Product Delivery," presented at the Index Alliance Working Session, Chicago, IL, August, 1990.

2. Juran, J. M., Juran on *Planning for Quality*, New York: The Free Press, 1988.

3. Sources include: a presentation by Andrea Morgan, market research manager, Compaq Corporation and Douglas Haley, senior vice-president, Yankelovich, Clancy,

Shulman at the third annual ASQC/AMA Customer Satisfaction and Quality Measurement Conference, Washington D.C., April 1991; conversations with, and material provided by Jeff Kibodeaux, corporate quality specialist, Compaq Corporation, and the Compaq Corporation 1990 Annual Report.

Part Three

Understanding Your Customer: The Most Critical Step to Customer Delight

We have demonstrated that a market orientation, with its three key components—a customer focus, a competitive orientation and cross-functional coordination—directly influences business performance. The common element in this linkage is the degree of customer fulfillment delivered. Just satisfying the customer is no longer good enough. Customer loyalty calls for an exciting quality offering that goes beyond satisfaction to delight the customer.

The process of delighting the customer begins "at 30,000 feet" with the mission statement broadly defining the customer set. It proceeds through a series of stages, each providing a sharper definition of the customers to be served, until it reaches ground zero—the identification of the true customers. It then continues by focusing on understanding the needs of this vital set of target customers.

A Critical Process

Most of you will agree that understanding your customers' needs is important—perhaps the most important step to achieving customer satisfaction/delight.

Robert Cooper, with his extensive research in the new product development process, confirms this statement by concluding "more than any other single element of the success formula, the ability to identify and understand customer needs, wants, preferences, and benefits, is the critical deciding variable."[1]

Also a Neglected Process

Then what's the problem? Why do such a high percentage of new products fail? Cooper goes on to report that market activity, in contrast to technical and production activities, is the most serious deficiency of the entire process. Understanding customer needs, while vitally important, is undoubtedly the most neglected step in the total quality process.

Why the Neglect?

Most mission statements today emphasize that the organization must be market-driven. However, market-driven is more of a buzzword than a philosophy for many organizations. Let's examine two prevalent misconceptions that go a long way toward explaining this paradox.

1. Organizations assume they already understand their customers' needs. Why shouldn't they? They have been serving many of these customers for years and should have a solid understanding of their needs. Right? Not according to Peter Drucker. He maintains, "What the people in the business think they know about the customer and market is more likely to be wrong than right."[2] He goes on to explain that only one person really knows: the customer; and only by asking the customer, and by carefully examining the customer's behavior can you learn about customer values, preferences and expectations.

    DuPont has confirmed Drucker's contention in dozens of recent studies of customer needs. It has invariably found that managers of most of their businesses feel they have a good understanding of the needs (values) of their customers. But they have consistently failed the tests that match managers' perceptions with customer responses on important quality attributes. They also experience significant variation within teams of business managers—sales, marketing, manufacturing, and R&D—when they attempt to identify and rank these important attributes.[3] (You may want to test this in your own organization.)

2. Organizations believe they can fill the information gap by asking the customer. This is the most common method of getting needs information. While it is a vital information source, it misses two very important sets of information. The first is unspoken needs, which may include important attributes that the customer assumes will be provided, such as ease of operating comfort, and safety, but are not expressed by the customer. The second includes those quality attributes that are important to the customer but are not expected. They may even be unknown by the customer, such as the Ford Taurus design team including a netting in the trunk—to prevent grocery bags from turning over.

Requirements for Satisfaction/Delight

Figure 1 shows these three levels of needs and their potential impact on customer satisfaction/delight.

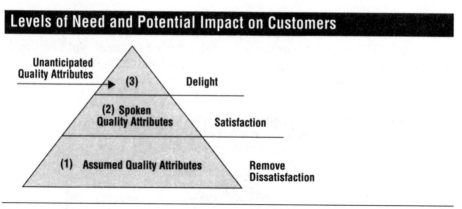

Figure 1.

Providing assumed (unexpressed) quality attributes is essential. This removes potential dissatisfaction and establishes the foundation for customer satisfaction. The second level of quality attributes are those that are expressed by the customer as desired, often considered the "specification." When these are provided at the expected level, and the assumed set is also delivered, the customer is satisfied. When important, but unanticipated, quality attributes are delivered, along with the assumed and expressed attributes, the customer is delighted.

Transforming Potential Delight into Dissatisfaction

Now for a recent personal illustration. My automobile was ready for its routine 5000 mile maintenance service—a simple lube, and oil and filter change. I also had been experiencing a couple of minor problems (starter and brake). I called for an appointment and explained to the service manager that my car needed the 5000-mile maintenance. I also explained the two sets of symptoms. When I delivered the car, the service manager carefully documented the symptoms. Later in the morning I received two calls from him, explaining the two problems and assuring their solution.

When I went to pick up the car:

- The service manager confirmed that both the starter and brake problems had been solved—this fulfilled my set of important, expressed quality attributes (second level needs).
- The cashier said she would have the car brought to the door for me. This was a new unexpected service, and provided an important unanticipated quality attribute (third level needs).
- The bill for the repair service was lower than I had expected—another unanticipated value attribute (third level).

This service encounter had almost all the ingredients for a "delightful" experience. There was only one missing element. My audit of the repair bill on my forty-mile drive home revealed that the routine maintenance, which I had not explicitly enumerated, but had assumed would be completed, had not been done. This accounted for the lower bill. Was I delighted? No! Was I even satisfied? No! The first level needs which established the foundation for satisfaction/delight had been overlooked, requiring a return visit.

Alternative Expectation-Fulfillment Outcome

Quality Attribute Perceived as Fulfilled?

		No	Yes	
Quality Attributes Expected?	Yes	(2) Dissatisfied	Expectations Met	Expectations Exceeded
			(3) Satisfied	(4) Delighted
	No	(1) No Effect	(5) Delighted	

Figure 2.

The Two Paths to Customer Delight

Figure 2 provides another view of this process. It considers each of the quality attributes (needs) perceived by the customer as important, and expresses the impact in terms of customer expectations and perceived fulfillment.

Figure 2 demonstrates two paths to customer delight. One is the result of an experience in which fulfillment exceeds expectations on important quality attributes (4). The other is the result of the fulfillment of a quality attribute that is important, but not expected to be fulfilled (5). In the previous illustration, if the routine maintenance had been completed, I would have been delighted with the cost as billed (exceeding expectations on a value attribute) or with the delivery to the door (an unanticipated quality attribute). Both of these paths are available to product/service organizations, and pay off handsomely when provided.

The Important Quality Attributes

The quality attributes needed/expected by customers are very situation specific. The total list would be unending. However, two excellent streams of research have developed two rather complete systems of important quality attributes that are applicable to product quality[4] and to service quality.[5] Since few products are delivered without elements of service, and many services have tangible characteristics, the following list is applicable to most products, and many services that are marketed. The first set focuses on the core product/service, the second on the softer provider attributes.

A. Core Product/Service Attributes
  1. Aesthetics/tangibles—How does it look/feel?
  2. Conformance—Does it meet the specification?
  3. Features—What will it do?
  4. Performance—How well will it do it?
  5. Reliability—Will it do it every time?
  6. Durability—How long will it continue doing it?
  7. Serviceability—How easy is it to service?

B. Product/Service Provider Attributes
  8. Responsiveness—How willing are you to provide helpful, prompt service?
  9. Assurance—How knowledgeable and courteous are employees, and do they convey trust and confidence?
  10. Empathy—How understanding, caring, and attentive is your organization?

A thorough understanding of the customer begins at the bottom of the list, with empathy. Take the perspective of the customer and ask each of the preceding questions about your product/service—the acid test of customer focus.

But where do the answers come from? They come from your targeted "true customers"—from the customers you presently serve, have formerly served (lost customers), have never served (competitor's customers), and would like to serve (potential customers using alternative technologies).

> A thorough understanding of the customer begins at the bottom of the list, with empathy.

Building the Framework for Understanding

An excellent way to begin developing an understanding of customer needs is to ask the target customers. If there are several, or a large number of organizations in the target segment, focus groups of a cross-section of representative organizations are a rich source of qualitative information. Mike Oilar, vice president of Market Decisions Corporation, explains its extensive use of focus groups drawn from present/prospective product specifiers and users of its clients products and services.[6] They provide useful information on present needs. They also generate customer wish lists and dreams. The results can provide a very valuable, and very sensitive, idea pool that can be sorted into:

- things you (the potential supplier) already do
- things you can do better
- things you might be able to do, and
- things you will probably never be able to do.

While focus groups lay the groundwork for understanding customer needs, they generally require a more formal quantitative research study to validate the results and to provide precise measures of company performance, importance ratings, and competitive evaluations on key quality attributes.

Compaq Computer makes creative use of formal survey research by developing what they call a "strategic cube" that graphically displays findings on the three dimensions of attribute importance (motivating power), its own performance, and key competitors' performance, on each of 34 quality attributes, as perceived by the respondent.[7] While there are many possible outcomes of this evaluation process, three key outcomes are shown in Figure 3.

Alternative Importance-Ratings Responses			
Quality Attribute	Attribute Importance	Company Rating	Key Competitors Rating
1	High	High	Low
2	High	Low	High
3	High	Low	Low

Figure 3.

Each of the three quality attributes in Figure 3 is judged by respondents as important (highly motivating). The company has a perceived advantage on the first attribute. This is a strength it will want to maintain. On the other hand, it falls short of competition on the second attribute. This must be quickly overcome for it to be successful with these customers. The third outcome is unique in presenting what may be a break-through opportunity that could delight the customer. It is an important attribute that is presently unfulfilled.

This approach to analysis allows the company to focus on the vital few quality attributes which customers/prospects consider to be important in their purchase decision. It can establish priorities based on the performance gap analysis.

Fleshing It Out

We have established one important set of quality attributes—the second level. We are missing the first level (assumed) and third level (unexpected). The latter may also provide break-through opportunities.

How are they determined? By getting closer to the customer. By understanding its business, and often its customers' business, including the processes, the people, the operating environment, the mission/objectives, and the total culture. Only with this level of understanding can the full extent of problems encountered and opportunities presented by the customer be fully understood, and creative solutions be integrated into the total product offering. Companies are beginning to develop innovative approaches to getting closer to their customer.

In 1990 Hewlett-Packard (HP) implemented a new selling process that allows it to identify factors that are critical to its customers' success. The company uses this information to diagram the information flow and to determine the solution set for solving specific business problems of its customers. The process has led HP to build a high level of industry-specific expertise for target industries.

Blount, Inc. develops detailed studies of the entire business process used by its customers, including users, OEMS, dealers, and distributors, as part of the customer set. This provides a much fuller understanding of customers' existing and potential problems/needs.

AT&T, rather than taking the traditional view of customers, looks at the customer as an operational system with certain performance objectives. As a supplier, AT&T becomes a component of this larger system. To enhance its customer's performance, every member of AT&T's product delivery team must have a complete and precise understanding of the quality attributes vital to this enhancement.

One of the secrets of IBM's success with the AS/400 was its involvement of representatives of all types of customers—business partners, end users, operators—from the beginning of the development process. It listened to these customers and developed a product that was not only easy to use, but easy to install and maintain, with an electronic customer support system offering constant remote testing and on-line hardware and software assistance.

Intel made a major shift from a product-driven chipmaker to a customer-focused supplier as it developed the 586 chip. The 586 required engineers to envision how it would fit into large computers as well as into PCs. Designers visited every major customer and important software houses to determine customer needs. The result was a list of 147 specific features—many ranked differently from what Intel expected, with the elimination of many changes in later stages of development. The process also caused engineers to begin thinking like customers.

Everybody Needs to Become Involved

Meeting and exceeding customer expectation requires an understanding of customer needs by individuals at all levels of the organization, and a responsiveness based on that understanding.

Senior executives need to get closer to their customers. Bob Galvin was well aware of this need and became an excellent role model for Motorola's non-sales executives by making customer visits. Not visits to their counterparts in customer organizations, but to the *users* of their products and services. The visit may begin at the customer's receiving dock and follow the path of the delivered product as it moves through successive processing operations, an excellent source of first-hand, immediate customer feedback.

AMP has an adopt-a-customer program for managers who do not normally make customer contacts. They are assigned customers to whom they make personal visits to plant sites, take plant tours, and serve as ombudsman for these customers.

Xerox has executives spend one day a month handling customer complaints in their "Care" program. They are charged with "making the complaint go away" within a two-day period.

The practice of direct customer contact by executives and managers outside the marketing area removes the "insulation" and gives them a customer focus from their own unique perspective.

What about the individuals at the lower end of the organizational hierarchy? In the first place, many organizations are beginning to turn their organizations upside down, placing front-line employees at the top, with management service as the support staff. Opportunities are provided for these employees to have important direct customer interaction. For example, Dupont technicians spend time in customers' plants to figure out new applications for their products and to get researchers and manufacturing employees to think more about the customer.

> Many organizations are beginning to turn their organizations upside down, placing front-line employees at the top, with management service as the support staff.

Nissan employees outside the marketing unit call each new customer to ask how they like their new car. In a visit to Consolidated Diesel Corporations's (CDC) North Carolina plant, we observed a three-person team from a Japanese fuel line supplier assisting in the redesign of the assembly process, essentially eliminating the in-process inventory, no doubt delighting CDC. By the same token, CDC, with an outstanding record of customer satisfaction, sends an engineer along with each of its new products to act as a liaison/consultant in the early stages of customer application.

An increasing number of organizations are building into their work schedules a time in which line operators can visit customer plants. It provides opportunities for them to observe how their product and services are used, and how they interact with their customers' products and operating systems. These first-hand customer encounters capture many of the soft issues that can only be understood by careful observation, with trained eyes, product-process interaction, and face-to-face dialogue with users along the product's path. Direct contact brings a new dimension of understanding to those who serve the customer—identifying those quality attributes that the customer assumes will be included in the product/service, and discovering opportunities to provide important unanticipated quality attributes.

Living Together Enhances Understanding

A growing number of organizations are finding that living together significantly enhances mutual understanding of total needs. This can be achieved by arranging to live in with your key customers, an idea generally referred to as early supplier involvement (ESI). Inviting key customers to live in with your organization, early customer involvement (ECI) or both. In each case "continuous" would probably be more descriptive than "early," since the intensive relationship continues throughout the product definition, development, production, and delivery process. In its purest form it means physical co-location.

The Bose Corporation presents a classic example of ESI. As part of its JIT II® process referred to as "the ultimate in partnering and concurrent engineering," Bose has key supplier representatives located in its purchasing organization, replacing both its buyer and its suppliers' sales representative.

With seven years' experience, Bose considers the process extremely successful for both sets of organizations.

On the flipside we have ECI, the in-house co-location of lead customers. Boeing is an excellent example of a company that is using both ESI and ECI in the development of its B777, scheduled for release in 1995. United, a lead customer and member of the design team, has co-located a number of engineers at the Boeing facility. Honeywell, a key electronics supplier, has also joined the design team and is co-located on site.

The practices of ESI and ECI—two sides of the same coin from a different perspective—are growing as organizations recognize their value in enhancing total understanding of their partners' needs and capabilities. The degree of "living-in" ranges from short visits to permanent residence.

Understanding customer needs is a complex, never-ending, process. It requires formal market research as well a mosaic of informal customer interaction by all value-adding units, at all levels of the organization. There is a payoff, as George Fisher, CEO of Motorola, explains, "When we marry our technology development with a deep understanding of our customers' business needs, and their communications needs, we can develop products/systems they can't even imagine—but that are immensely valuable to them." The result: delighted customers!

References

1. Cooper, Robert G., *Winning at New Products*, Reading, MA, Addison-Wesley, 1986.

2. Drucker, Peter, *Managing For Results*, New York, Harper and Row, 1964.

3. Day, George S., *Market-Driven Strategy: Processes for Creating Value*, New York, The Free Press, 1990.

4. Garvin, David A., *Managing Quality: The Strategic and Competitive Edge*, New York, The Free Press, 1988.

5. Zeithaml, Valarie A., A. Parasuraman, and Leonard L. Berry, *Delivering Quality Service: Balancing Customer Perceptions and Expectations*, New York, The Free Press, 1990.

6. Oilar, Mike, "Market Segmentation," a presentation at the Association for Manufacturing Excellence Time-to-Market Seminar, Seattle, WA, April 1991.

7. Morgan, Andrea Z., and Douglas F. Haley, "From Bean Counting to Marketing Intelligence," a presentation at the Third Annual ASQC/AMA Customer Satisfaction and Quality Measurement Conference, Washington, D.C., April 1991.

Charles R. O'Neal is a professor of marketing at the University of Evansville, IN with teaching and research involvement in strategic industrial marketing.

Beyond the Smile
Improving Service Quality at the Grass Roots

Ken Myers and Jim Buckman

Using what they call "breakthrough action teams," the authors demonstrate how to help make the voice of the customer predominant in any organization. The article provides practical tactics for breaking through quality service barriers, one quantifiable step at a time.

For years, improving service quality at the grass roots meant more smile training. Employees, particularly those on the customer frontline, were given intensive bursts of human interaction skills laced with the latest organizational slogans. This approach has changed markedly as improvement processes such as total quality management (TQM) have taken hold in service organizations. Obviously, interaction skills, coupled with job knowledge, are important. But TQM has added a dimension. Where the suggestion box once served, now legions of service employees offer their experience in unit-level quality teams. With their managers and peers, they seek continuous improvement of service processes. They are sanctioned to analyze and often take action on opportunities backstage and front. These empowered employees add value to the organization as never before imagined.

TQM literature and training provide first-rate analytic tools that have been successful at the grass roots (e.g., statistical process control). Recent experience with unit-level teams, however, indicates a need to add to the tool box. In particular, team members need to know *where* to look, not just *how* to look, which is the main focus of existing tools. Several field-tested tools point out where to look to improve service quality for internal and external customers.

BAT: The Basic Unit of Analysis

People become involved with quality improvement in many ways; however, TQM has demonstrated the wisdom of a planned process, whose implementation cascades from the top. With TQM, the rubber really meets the road through the involvement of significant numbers of service employees in unit-level improvement teams. Such teams have been given many labels. Since the teams' primary purpose is to help the organization break through to new

Reprinted with permission from *Quality Progress*, December 1992, ASQC, Milwaukee, WI.

levels of performance, an appropriate name is breakthrough action teams (BATs).

BATs are knowledgeable, motivated, and trained groups of five to eight employees, supervisors, and managers. Sometimes the members are volunteers, but as a TQM process unfolds, such assignments are typically part of normal duties. More often than not, BAT membership crosses functional lines in the same way many system problems or improvement opportunities do. BATs are frequently guided by a trained facilitator and use relatively simple but powerful tools to identify the critical few improvement opportunities. These opportunities are researched through intensive problem-solving and cost-benefit analyses. Finally, the convincing analyses and likely solutions are presented for appropriate management sponsorship. BATs are often empowered to implement the solutions and track progress until the project is complete.

Experience suggests that empowered BATs generate incredible energy and remarkable solutions.

Perhaps the real key to BATs is the teams' selection of bite-size improvement opportunities, called breakthrough projects, which are pursued to measurable outcomes. BATs break through quality service barriers one quantifiable step at a time, helping the organization consistently set new standards of excellence. Experience suggests that empowered BATs generate incredible energy and remarkable solutions. They also nurture a great deal of grass-roots ownership in the never-ending process of improving quality and customer service. Thus, BATs are an organization's basic and most important unit of analysis—real windows to a quality future. But BATs must know where to look as well as how to look.

Where to Look

There are several building blocks basic to any organization's ability to provide quality services to its customers. Many are obvious; others are often overlooked or taken for granted. Here are six foundation blocks upon which to base measurable improvement.

1. *Knowing your customer.* If you are not on the front line serving the organization's external customers, you should be serving someone who is. It is important to understand that almost everyone in an organization has customers (internal or external), and these customers must be identified.

    This process is not as simplistic as it sounds. Both individuals and units must actively identify their customers and suppliers and then energetically clarify and negotiate their roles and relationships with them. This process re-establishes communication, clarifies expectations and territory boundaries, and often leads to the discovery of obvious opportunities of improvement. An added benefit is that the process makes others explicitly aware of what you do for them. Explicit awareness helps both internal and external customers sense the individual's, unit's, or organization's concern for them.

2. *A seamless experience.* What does high-quality service really mean? Most internal and external customers seek a seamless experience. They don't

want anything to fall through the cracks. They want what was expected, when and where they were led to expect it. Customer satisfaction (or delight) increases the closer you come to this mark. If you want to leverage the perception of high-quality service, go a step further and push the seamless experience beyond the customer's expectation. Obviously, meeting or exceeding customer expectations requires a good deal of customer knowledge and ongoing information.

If you want to leverage the perception of high-quality service, go a step further and push the seamless experience beyond the customer's expectation.

3. *Information and communication.* You must get and give a great deal of information when pursuing service quality breakthroughs. The rule is communicate, communicate, communicate. Employees, managers, customers, and suppliers must be in the communication loop. Information on the organization's vision, management's expectations, and organizational and employee performance must be communicated to employees if they are to feel motivated, be committed, and clearly understand their tasks. Communication helps managers lower employees' resistance to change and gain their continued support. Communication also helps the organization obtain an ongoing stream of performance information from customer and suppliers and develop benchmarks.

4. *Organizational environment.* The organizational environment can help or hinder performance improvement. For example, it is hard to make unwilling or unable employees do much beyond the minimum work requirements. Thus, managers should foster a positive work culture and provide adequate training, time, and physical resources. In particular, managers must remove problems from the work environment. For example, if you tip the balance of fairness by restricting when some (but not all) employees can take their vacations, you'll find it difficult to get anyone interested in grass-roots improvement.

5. *Continuous improvement.* Continuous improvement is vital to building high-quality customer service in any unit or organization. Technology, processes, and customer expectations change over time, and competitors keep raising the bar in the quality high jump. Thus, continuous improvement is necessary just to keep up, let alone to build, a competitive edge. BATs are highly effective at grass-roots continuous improvements. They analyze a situation, create a plan, obtain needed assistance, and then pitch in to eat the elephant one bit at a time.

6. *Celebration and reward.* People take jobs, assume tasks, and are paid to get work done. Often they hear managers lament: "You get a paycheck, you really oughta wanta. . . ." Beside a paycheck, however, people like to receive a little recognition. Who doesn't like to hear praise, get a pat on the back, or receive some other token of appreciation for a job well done?

If you want to improve quality, acknowledge progress early and often. When you notice people making improvements, praise them. You might also try using small unpredictable rewards (token rewards such as taking an individual or group out for pizza) to recognize incremental improvements. Make sure that your formal reward system is tuned to the improvement process.

The Service Setting

Did you ever get lost or feel out of place in new surroundings? Did you ever grow tired of waiting in line or trying to find a person to help you? When these things happen in a service setting, not enough attention has been paid to the setting's utility value or user-friendliness. Internal customers are routinely left to simply accept whatever happens. Many times, they respond to this situation by treating external customers similarly. Thus, attention must be paid to the following six service setting dimensions for both internal and external customers:

1. *Orientation.* A service setting needs to be user-friendly, providing relevant, well-located information to keep customers from getting disoriented. Check facilities and service cycles (multiple streams of service activities) for proper clarity and continuity from the user's perspective. Make sure both the system and process steps are legible (i.e., have nonverbal or other signals) at and between points of contact. Make sure that informed employees are available and authorized to help solve problems and expedite matters.
2. *Waiting.* Waiting can frustrate and even provoke anger in customers. A negative waiting experience can deaden an otherwise superior performance. Often waiting is effectively managed by a queue. For example, customers might be guided by chrome posts and velvet ropes into forming a line where a "first come, first served" or other fair rule is invoked. Information, distractions, and other tools can be used to build a neutral, even positive, queue experience.
3. *Physical environment.* The physical environment goes a step beyond orientation and waiting. The physical environment must match the image you want to project. Is it safe and warm or harsh and noisy? Does the decor convey the desired message? Is the room layout adequate for the service context? (For example, open bull pens are hardly adequate for confidential information exchanges.) Is the environment functional? Does it make the customer feel and respond appropriately?
4. *Social environment.* The service provider's appearance, demeanor, knowledge, enthusiasm, and approach must be appropriate. Empathetically review how customers are controlled and moved. Examine employees' routine tasks to ensure they facilitate service delivery. Make sure the service providers meet or exceed standards at the moments of truth (points of contact with the customer) and reward exemplary performance. Finally, observe the service providers to see whether they seem to care about the customer and determine whether they add value to the service they are providing.
5. *Tangible service.* The more tangible the service, the better customers become at appreciating high-quality service. Without being obtrusive, make the service more visible by increasing the number of "felt contacts" (mini encounters). While seamless service is the goal, customers should be given enough signs and verbal messages that they pause and take notice of the

service process. This awareness is a basis for internalizing and reporting a high-quality experience.

6. *The rules.* Purposeful organizational activity could hardly exist without rules. Yet nothing galls customers more than rules they perceive as unclear, inappropriate, or obtrusive. Thus, rules should be reviewed to see whether they can be simplified, limited, or made more user-friendly. Employees on the front line should be empowered to make appropriate adjustments to the rules if needed. If you like living by the rules, others might perceive your service as dying by them.

Action Levers

One of the most important aspects of quality service is properly managing moments of truth with customers. Research and common sense indicate that at least six factors positively influence customers' perception of service quality:

1. *Being on target.* Set and meet the customer's expectations. Do what was promised, when and where it was promised. Heighten the customer's awareness of the service provider's actions.
2. *Care and concern.* Be empathetic. Tune in to the customer's situation, frame of mind, and needs. Be attentive and willing to help.
3. *Spontaneity.* Empower service providers to think and respond quickly. Allow them to use their discretion and bend, rather than quote, procedures.
4. *Problem solving.* Train and encourage service providers to be problem solvers. Service providers have the customer's undivided attention when that person is experiencing a problem. A positive response to a problem will stick in the customer's mind. Capitalize on this opportunity to show the organizations capabilities.
5. *Follow-up.* Follow-up captures customers' attention and is often sincerely appreciated. It is associated with caring and professionalism, so follow up with flair and create a reputation for legendary service quality.
6. *Recovery.* Customers experiencing problems often have low expectations for their resolution; thus, they are exceedingly mindful and appreciative of speedy solutions. Making things right quickly is a powerful factor in creating an enduring image of high-quality service.

Service Analysis

The checklists just presented outline many of the essential elements in providing high-quality service to internal and external customers. Ultimately, you want to provide customers with a high degree of satisfaction by meeting or exceeding their expectations, but first you must continually communicate with customers to find what those expectations are. Nine service analysis tools foster communication:

1. *Service inquiry.* Formal or informal service inquiries can prevent an organization from flying blind or substituting assumptions for knowledge.

In inquiries, data on customers are gathered and analyzed. Inquiries often begin by simply walking around, observing the environment and interactions, asking questions, noting answers, and analyzing comments and trends.

Questionnaires are another way to gain information. They can be very effective, but the conditions under which surveys are administered greatly affect whether and how they are filled out. Surveys also tend to set expectations about follow-up communication and action. (Crushed expectations are the bane of any improvement effort.) Thus, someone knowledgeable about surveys should help you design and administer the questionnaire.

Focus groups are another rich source of information. Marketing, human resources, and communication department colleagues should be able to help you form focus groups. An informal method is to gather a few customers or suppliers in the same room and ask them about their experiences with your organization. The discussion usually builds and feeds on itself. Remember, it is important to listen, not explain.

2. *Customer or supplier mirror.* The mirror can be insightful and interesting each time you use it. First, you must identify your primary customers or suppliers. (This activity is useful in itself.) Next, for each customer or supplier, write down your answers to three questions:

- What specific services are provided?
- What services are being performed well?
- What are the opportunities for improvement?

Then ask each customer or supplier to write down his or her candid answers to the same questions. With both lists in hand, you can confirm who your customers and suppliers actually are, understand any important differences between your view and their views, and gain specific improvement ideas. Depending on the circumstances, you might choose to openly discuss (rather than write) the answers or exchange lists with the customer or supplier. Again, listen to and understand the information you are receiving; don't explain why your organization does what it does.

3. *Moments-of-truth critique.* To begin, list all the routine points of contact between members of your unit and your customers (even suppliers). Next, observe the actual moment of interaction and take note of the elements previously discussed in the service setting and action levers sections. You are mainly trying to determine the quality of the process. Other information you gather (such as how long customers have to wait and the rules they must follow) will further influence your observations. Finally, ask customers what the experience was like for them and how they felt about it. If they tell you that your service is a grinding experience, keep looking for why it is a grind.

4. *Fairness analysis.* People judge whether they are treated fairly in their personal and business lives. People who feel unfairly treated might react out of frustration and try to get even in some way. For example, internal

customers might act in political spite and refuse to help with future projects; external customers can turn to a competitor's service and even spread malicious information about your organization's service.

In sharp contrast, those who are treated fairly or even pampered often respond with positive actions. For example, if you immediately solve an external customer's problem and go a bit further by giving them a discount coupon, the customer might spread the word about how well he or she was treated. Your action helps re-establish basic fairness, leaving the customer with a high regard for the organization.

Fairness analyses are usually conducted in tandem with other analyses. When using other tools, listen for comments about fairness. You can also ask questions, such as "All things considered, are we treating you fairly?" If there is any hint of unfairness, keep on talking with that individual until you find out how and why he or she was unfairly treated. Then fix the injustice and let others know it is fixed.

5. *Service cycle blueprint.* Diagramming the service cycle is an important part of any analysis. A "cycle" is one complete sequence of service from beginning to end. A single retail sales cycle runs from the moment the customer steps into the store to the moment the transaction is completed. The cycle can also be extended to include preparation activities for the customer's arrival and post-transaction activities. Complex operations have many individual service cycles.

   Even a simple blueprint adds graphic clarity to a service analysis. One easy method is to draw a circle and, moving clockwise, indicate with tick marks the cycle's key moments of truth in chronological order. Annotate each moment of truth to show precisely what happens at that point (behavior, quality factors, technology involved, materials, complexity, staffing, timing, etc.) You can separate front-stage moments (those seen by the customer) and backstage moments and note any customer participation in the process.

   Beyond documentation, drawing a blueprint helps isolate problems and increase efficiency. Appropriate auditing, cost analyses, and what-if analyses can be coupled with blue-prints.

6. *Service audit.* Performing a service audit involves following the internal customer service trail and asking key questions. Suppliers can also be asked the same questions. The audit questions include:

   - Who is your customer?
   - What service do you provide to your customer? (Answer in detail.)
   - What value do you add to the process and outcomes?
   - How did the customer critique the service? How did the customer critique the relationship? Is the customer's view different from yours? How and why?
   - What can be improved? Is more or less required or desired?
   - What standard procedures exist to get ongoing feedback or foster continuing dialogue?

7. *Problem audit.* Many people won't tell a person when he or she has bad breath. Similarly, customers are usually reluctant to indicate when a unit

or organization unknowingly is providing low-quality service. One way to determine whether your unit or organization is providing substandard service is to simply ask your customers whether they are experiencing any problems. To make this process easier for everyone, ask the customer to describe the problem using concrete examples. Be prepared to listen nondefensively and try not to explain why things are done the way they are. Pay close attention to any point the customer emphasizes or says with hesitancy—this might indicate a priority problem.

Customers are usually reluctant to indicate when a unit or organization unknowingly is providing low-quality service.

8. *Empathy walk.* To truly understand the caliber of your organization's service, you must experience the service cycle from beginning to end in your customer's footsteps. During the walk, note the following:

- Is there a logical, coherent system?
- Is needed information available?
- Is there appropriate assistance?
- Are the processes and procedures smooth and user-friendly?
- Is there a positive feel to the process?
- Is each contact of high quality?
- Is the service environment suitable?
- What roles do the various manager and supervisors play? Are they supportive and do they offer assistance?
- What are customers currently in the cycle saying about their experiences?

9. *Seam negotiations.* You can't simply say, "The customer is always right." Reality and resources suggest that a middle ground on which there is a high standard of service is needed. Seam negotiations can be used with internal and external customers and suppliers when the parties are feeling a problem (i.e., when a seam in the service cycle is ripped open).

These negotiations, which are particularly effective for internal customers, can also be used to clarify employees' or units' roles, responsibilities, and territories. Although you could go to your boss for a decision when there's a problem, seam negotiations usually provide lasting solutions that everyone involved owns.

To negotiate, each person (or party) separately details his or her view of the issue and notes explicit factors he or she believes might be the basis for resolution. Then the people involved meet and trade lists to compare positions. Together they equitably negotiate what the problem is and its solution. Finally, they negotiate clear future roles, procedures, or other issues to provide continuity. Remember, it is important to use concrete examples when working with problems. In addition, the examples and their effect on quality should be presented in an informational, not "gotcha," manner.

Quality Service Lives Beyond the Smile

By coupling the use of traditional quality analysis tools with these additional techniques, you can leverage TQM at the grass roots of your organization.

The marriage will help unit-level improvement teams know where to look for improvements as they continue their quest to achieve service quality breakthroughs.

Ken Myers is the principal of The Breakthru Group in Minneapolis, MN. Jim Buckman is the president of the Minnesota Council for Quality in Bloomington.

COMMUNICATION

A Failure to Communicate

Roger J. Howe, Dee Gaeddert, and Maynard A. Howe

In this chapter from the book Quality on Trial, *the authors argue convincingly that communicating quality initiatives must involve more than rhetoric by organization leaders and managers. Without clear actions, without practicing what they preach, all such rhetoric just reinforces employee and market cynicism and, ultimately, mediocrity.*

Shimmering heat waves radiate off the pavement of the south Georgia highway. The hot, humid air hangs heavy, like a wet wool shirt. It's too hot for birds. The only sound is the mesmerizing clip clip . . . clip clip of thrashing hoes swung in metronome motion by the shirtless chain gang chopping roadside weeds. In the distance, skimming the water-like mirages glistening on the blacktop, a long, black car approaches. It brakes to a stop, showering the prisoners in a flurry of chaff.

Looking every bit the role of the petty tyrant prison warden, an exasperated Strother Martin emerges from the front seat of the car. Two burly guards drag a man from the back seat. Martin scowls at a bloodied but unbowed Paul Newman lying on the ground where the guards disposed of him. Speaking in a slow southern drawl, he delivers the signature line of the movie "Cool Hand Luke": "What we have here," he says, "is a failure to communicate."

Communication, or rather the failure to communicate, is the scapegoat for a growing number of the world's ills, from the failure of personal relationships, to business failures, to disasters like the ill-fated cold-weather launching of the space shuttle Challenger (the result of a failure of communication

---

Reprinted with permission of the authors, Chapter 3, from *Quality on Trial*, St. Paul: West Publishing Company, 1992.

between project engineers and senior management in charge of the project). Lack of communication is also frequently cited as the reason for failing quality initiatives. Most frequently the blame falls on the company CEO. "He didn't give the program any visible support" or "She just isn't a charismatic leader" are typical of the arrows fired at management when a quality initiative fails.

We believe that such criticism is not justified as frequently as it is used. Charisma creates its own problems, and what is seen as lack of visible management support is really the lack of a comprehensive strategy for moving from quality objectives to the integration of those objectives in the ongoing activities of individual employees.

It is during the Rhetorical Component of a quality movement—before the Activist Component—that quality initiatives tend to bog down. The need to communicate quality objectives is a given. Communication is the right "what to do;" the "how to do it" is where companies are failing.

Some companies take a Strother Martin "the flogging will continue until morale improves" approach to communication in support of their quality objectives. They turn up the heat and flog away at employees, shotgunning a variety of communications approaches and methods, hoping employees will finally "get the message." Communication is one-way—management talks and employees listen and obey. As one corporate citizen lamented, "Ours is not to think or ask, ours is but to type and fax."

Other companies take a "whips and whistles" approach to quality communication, promoting slogans over substance. They are typified by a *Wall Street Journal* profile of Fidelity Investments, which in 1988 joined the ranks of leading American organizations creating executive-level quality positions. Company executives tapped a marketing manager as their quality guru. Immediately she struggled to avoid having her mandate trivialized. The first suggestion from top officials—which she rejected—was "logos, buttons, and mugs." "They wanted to turn it [the quality initiative] into a marketing campaign," she is quoted as saying.[1]

> Quality awareness is not *sufficient* in and of itself to ensure the successful integration of quality into ongoing business practices.

Having recognized the need to improve quality, companies like the investment firm immediately shift the corporate communications department into high gear, pumping out slogans, designing logos and ordering buttons and mugs printed with the quality message for every employee. When challenged, management at these companies responds that these methods "build quality awareness." Although quality awareness is certainly a *necessary* element of success, equally certain is that quality awareness is not *sufficient* in and of itself to ensure the successful integration of quality into ongoing business practices.

A communication strategy that focuses exclusively on creating awareness creates a state not unlike narcotic addiction. A quality awareness campaign provides an immediate rush and a lot of frenzied activity. To keep the momentum requires another enthusiasm fix—another "Quality Day," another button, a catchier slogan. And like progressive addiction, each successive awareness event must be bigger, better, and more stimulating than the one before just to achieve the same high. An awareness focus for quality communication spawns an endless cycle of activities, each lacking the power to sustain the quality initiative. The quality initiative will stall in the Rhetorical Component of the movement, and quality will never become integrated with the ongoing normal operations of the business unless there is a specific call to action.

Issue a Call to Action

A critical success factor for a quality initiative is a call to action that links quality objectives with new behavior and the new behavior with improved business results. The leader of the quality initiative must not only define the organization's quality objectives (the stuff of awareness), but he or she must also communicate the process—the specific behavior changes that employees must make—that will move the organization from objectives to measurable results.

Contrast that approach with the more typical quality kick-off approach of launching a quality initiative with a four-star quality spectacular exclusively focused on quality awareness. "Change people's attitudes," the communication people tell the CEO, "and behavior changes will naturally follow." However, psychological research and practical experience dispute that advice.

Although it is true that people can be motivated to change their attitudes, a change of attitude in and of itself cannot ensure *behavior* change—and behavior change is the ultimate objective. As a would-be leader of your company's quality initiative, it is important to your communication effort to recognize that, in general, attitudes are not always the best predictors of behavior. However, some attitudes are better predictors than others, and it is clear that attitudes predict behavior much better when they are linked to action, not just awareness.

For example, when an attitude is formed by direct experience, it usually leads to a change in behavior. Employees may be exhorted to "focus on the customer," but until they have actual, direct experience with customers, the words of the customer focus message are just that—words. It is the attitudes that employees develop while working directly with customers that will ultimately determine their behavior.

Another case where attitude predicts behavior is when expression of the attitude is narrowly focused and associated with a specific behavior. A general attitude expression like "I'm committed to quality" says little about what a person might do if the "quality" at issue would cost his or her organization to slip a development schedule by several months. However, "When quality and schedule collide, we will do what's right by the customer" is a more specific expression. It is not predictive in the sense that it will tell you what action a person will take, but it does indicate the basis or the rationalization the person will use for the course of action ultimately chosen.

At the far end of the spectrum, attitudes are poor predictors when behaviors are codified as habits. A person may express the attitude "Smoking is bad for you," but if that person has a three-pack-a-day habit, his or her attitude

It is the attitudes that employees develop while working directly with customers that will ultimately determine their behavior.

does little to predict behavior. If a company habitually makes decisions based on cost and schedule rather than the impact on the customer, a "customer focus" campaign will accomplish little in terms of actual behavior changes.

The point is that all too often, quality initiatives stop short of taking that final step linking quality attitudes to quality behaviors. Trying to demonstrate a "visible commitment to quality," business leaders paint elegant visions of the grand scheme, but they do not tell employees what their *specific* roles are or what actions they should take. Employees are left with a mandate as vague and informative as "do good and avoid evil."

It is reasonable to assume that without a specific call to action, employee attitudes toward quality and the customer are *not* formed from direct experience, not specific to targeted behaviors, and in many cases the politically correct quality platitudes portend attitudes that are contradictory to prevailing habitual behaviors. The CEO's inspiring speech catapults the quality movement into the Rhetorical Component; however, employees leave the quality kick-off meeting charged and ready to go, but with no idea what *specific actions* they should take to participate in the CEO's brave new agenda.

The "Be a Tiger" Syndrome

There are a lot of Dinsdales in the business world. Dinsdale is a character in a Jerry Van Amerongen *The Neighborhood* cartoon. One of Van Amerongen's single-panel cartoons illustrates Vice President of Sales Dinsdale at the rostrum wearing a tiger hand puppet. Clutched in the cat's mouth is a sign reading "Be a tiger." A shoe clangs off Dinsdale's head and the caption in Van Amerongen's trademark understatement reads, "Dinsdale underestimates the sophistication of his sales force."

When it comes to quality, one of the biggest mistakes business leaders make is underestimating their audience. Contrary to what many business leaders believe, the employee population today is not poised and pulsating for another burst of executive quality enlightenment. They may not heckle or launch their footwear, but make no mistake about it—when the executive preaches quality, he or she is facing one tough crowd.

In research for their book *The Cynical Americans*, Kanter and Mirvis found that 43 percent of the American working population fit the profile of a cynic—an individual who believes "lying, putting on a false face and doing whatever it takes to make a buck are all part of our basic human nature." Although some of these cynics describe themselves as realists, most are unvarnished cynics, who see selfishness as fundamental to people's character and believe that people inwardly dislike putting themselves out for others. They also believe that the unselfish are taken advantage of and think that people are simply dishonest by nature.

Without an action plan associated with the rhetoric, those expectations can't possibly be met.

Kanter and Mirvis classified 16 percent of the remaining 57 percent of the work force as wary—those who believe that people are motivated primarily, but not solely, by self-interest. Only 41 percent of the work force in the Kanter/Mirvis study could be described as having an upbeat view of the world.[2]

What is the underlying cause of this cynicism? Kanter and Mirvis explain it as the failure of society to meet the expectations it set in the minds of the people. The cynical cycle is set up because of unreal expectations reinforced by politicians, the media, schoolteachers, success-oriented lecturers and clergy. One is expected to be happy and win. When the inevitable happens and many people do not win, cynics have their built-in explanations, which seldom take into account their own excessive expectations, personal short-comings, or even rotten luck.[3]

To state Kanter and Mirvis's theory in terms of your quality initiative, a communication strategy that focuses on changing attitudes sets up the expectation that things will change for the better. Without an action plan associated with that rhetoric, those expectations can't possibly be met. The result is not just no gain—the result is more scar tissue on the basic cynical attitude prevalent in today's work force. If employees don't see things change, they become even more skeptical.

Communicating a Strategy for Change

So here you are. As a company leader, it is not enough to use your corporate pulpit to preach quality. And every time you do take to the stump for the big "Q" more than half your employee audience is sitting silently cynical of everything you say. And yet, everywhere you turn today, there is a quality "true believer" preaching that the success of a quality initiative depends on the "commitment of the leader" and the leader's "visible support" of the quality initiative. There are more than enough quality terrorists lurking in the corporate woodwork ready and willing to beat management upside the head for a lack of dedication to quality. Can leaders only conclude if they aren't a combination of Knute Rockne, John Kennedy, and Martin Luther King, Jr., then they haven't a prayer of leading their companies to the economic milk and honey of Qualityland?

Many would have you think that is the case. We do not. Inspirational communication is a plus, but it is only a part of the communication equation. It is the balance of the equation—communicating the call to action and the *plan* for achieving quality objectives—that makes or breaks a quality initiative. Providing feedback on performance closes the loop.

True, great leaders are associated with grand visions and great rhetorical skills. "Ask not what your country can do for you, ask what you can do for your country," is how we remember John Kennedy, not by the arcane details of his tax reform act. Few know the economic theory of Franklin Roosevelt's depression-era recovery programs, yet most people associate FDR with "Fireside Chats" and know that he told Americans that they "have nothing to fear but fear itself." If you need a single example of the power of the Rhetorical Phase of a social movement, imagine how America might be different today if Martin Luther King, Jr., had traded in his "dream" and addressed the masses with the stirring refrain—"I have a strategic plan."[4]

All great leaders have the ability to inspire. But the converse—that the ability to inspire does not in and of itself make a great leader in the world of

> It is the balance of the equation—communicating the call to action and the *plan* for achieving quality objectives—that makes or breaks a quality initiative.

social or quality reform—is often overlooked. Nor is lack of a charismatic communication style an unconquerable curse. Here we might draw an analogy from the world of sports.

At every level of athletic competition, from amateur leagues to the pros, are coaches who envision themselves as reincarnations of Knute Rockne. Every game is preceded by a "win one for the Gipper" speech that sends the team onto the field on a wave of enthusiasm. However, without a game plan that the team believes in, without each player knowing what he or she must do to contribute to that plan, wins are few and far between. And with each successive failure, the pre-game speech loses a little more credibility.

Successful business leaders, like successful coaches, understand that inspiration can take you only so far. In the case of a quality movement, "awareness" can move a quality initiative to the Rhetorical Component, but not beyond. It can influence what people think about and talk about, but inspiration alone does not provide an outlet for people to actually do something that yields *results.*

Whether you look at business or sports, the business leaders and coaches who consistently come out on top are those who blend inspiration and perspiration and communicate a winning strategy for change. That strategy is two-fold: First, it provides a definitive set of objectives to the organization; second, it communicates concise, easy-to-understand actions that individual members of the organization can take in order to do their part in achieving those objectives. In organizations where a culture change is required, it is the definition of expected behavior changes, not a statement of objectives, that indicates to the organization that the current practices are no longer acceptable and that there will, indeed, be change.

John Kennedy didn't leave people asking what they could do for their country—he created programs like the Peace Corps that provided the opportunities. Franklin Roosevelt didn't leave people to ponder the question of fear—he changed the role of the federal government and created thousands of jobs to involve the people in economic recovery. And when Martin Luther King, Jr., revealed his dream, he and his people took to the streets in a nonviolent, but rebellious, statement that the status quo had changed.

A One-Two Punch

Communicating the quality strategy is a two-fold process: First, the leader must provide a clear sense of direction to the organization that focuses the organization externally on the customer. Second, he or she must communicate concise, easily understood actions that employees can immediately take to do their part in moving the organization in the desired direction. The latter requires that you build three key points into your quality message.

First, your message must contain a specific call to action. Second, clearly defined behaviors must be in place that provide an outlet for people to heed the call to action. Third, the action must be directed at specific results so people have a means of measuring their progress.

The best means of realizing the power of the one-two punch of objectives *and* action plan is looking at a case study—a manufacturing company of approximately 2,000 people.

For many years, the company in question enjoyed a market share for its product of approximately 85 percent. However, in a relatively short period of time, two Japanese companies and a second American company aggressively went after its customers. In just two and half years, the company's market share declined to 47 percent. During this dramatic decline, the company remained internally focused, concentrating on reducing internal costs rather than focusing on the marketplace. Instead of looking for ways to grow, it began the process of reducing costs and headcount. Employee morale was low and was having a negative impact on productivity. Business results did not improve, and ultimately the CEO left the company "to pursue other interests."

One of the new CEO's first actions was to rent a very large auditorium and gather all company employees together. He provided employees with a realistic picture of the decline in market share the company had suffered, and further explained that the company was on the verge of losing business with other major customers. The quality of both the company's products and service had been exceeded by the competition.

At this point, however, he departed from what might be the normal course of action. He did not exhort employees to "try harder and do better." He did not lay out a strategic plan that told employees how the company was going to make a comeback. Instead, he showed a single slide with the names of the company's three major competitors.

"What I need you to do," he told employees, "is help me understand how we're going to beat these guys." He asked that each employee sign up for a competitor team. He asked each employee to learn everything they could about the competition. In addition, he asked each employee to interview customers, both existing customers and those lost to the competition. Finally, he asked that in eight weeks each team make a presentation on their findings. Keep in mind that the majority of the employees in this company were hourly, line manufacturing employees.

By this effort, the CEO identified behaviors that would turn the perspective of the organization outward. He did not ask them to identify what was wrong inside the company. He asked them to find out what it took to serve their customers. He empowered employees to understand who their customers were, and what their customer's requirements and expectations were.

During the first week following the presentation, 25 percent of all employees had signed up for a team. By the second week, 60 percent were on board, and by the third week, 85 percent of line employees were out talking to customers and researching the competition.

After eight weeks, the CEO reconvened all employees. On stage were representatives from the three competitor teams. Each team made a presentation on what they had found out—and they found out plenty. From privately held companies they found out gross sales, cost of production and inventory levels. They dissected the competition's product. They presented lists of customer requirements and expectations garnered directly from talking with customers—both current customers and customers who had defected to the competition. Finally, they presented recommendations based on the findings. Following through on his commitment to the process, the CEO empowered employees to carry out those action plans.

In two years, the company's share of the market rose from 47 percent to 77 percent. Although they never reached the 85 percent level again, today their market share has stabilized at 80 percent.

The CEO provided a call to action and defined behaviors that motivated employees to get involved and have an impact on their own futures and the future of the company.

The key to this company's success was that the CEO did not just state the need for change. Instead, he provided a call to action and defined behaviors that motivated employees to get involved and have an impact on their own futures and the future of the company. He committed to an action that visibly showed employees that current business practices were no longer acceptable. Essentially, he took a depressed organization and provided them a clear objective—meeting customer needs and exceeding customer expectations—that got them externally focused and actively working for a cause greater than themselves. He gave employees a simple process that provided identity, purpose and hope.

Communicating a Mechanism for Change

The leader who can provide a message of hope, a message that focuses the individual on something larger than self, will find a receptive audience, despite any underlying cynicism. "The life committed to nothing larger than itself is a meager life indeed," writes Martin Seligman in his book *Learned Optimism*. "Human beings require a context of meaning and hope." Traditionally, that context was found in a belief in the nation, in God, in one's family or in a purpose that transcended an individual's life. However, as Seligman points out, events during the past 25 years have "so weakened our commitment to larger entities as to leave us almost naked before the ordinary assaults of life."

Notes Seligman, an individual "stripped of the buffering of any commitment to what is larger in life, is a set-up for depression." When individuals face failures they cannot control, they become helpless. Helplessness becomes hopelessness, and may escalate into full-blown depression.[6]

Often, when individuals are depressed, they turn inward. Their thoughts and conversations are self-centered. They feel powerless to change their situation. Without a larger context in which to find meaning, they attribute commonplace failures or disappointments to permanent, pervasive and personal causes. At the extreme, individuals become immobile, both emotionally and physically.

The same sense of depression can overcome an organization when it becomes internally focused. The more a company focuses on internal processes and activities, the more it tends to view commonplace business problems as signs of permanent, pervasive and personal failure. The result of this kind of rumination essentially immobilizes the organization, making it incapable of adapting to changes in the external environment. This state, in which employees feel powerless to influence the company's (and hence their own) future, is already occurring in organizations today. Fewer than half of the employees we surveyed feel they have the freedom to do what it takes to get their jobs done, a paltry 11 percent feels management is responsive to employees, fewer than one-third feel free to make constructive suggestions, and only 37 percent feel their jobs contribute to the success of the business.

One method of treating depressed individuals is to change the individual's cognition from an internal to an external perspective. The person's thinking must be reversed. As part of the treatment plan, the therapist may even give the individual a set of structured activities that focuses the individual outside of themselves, often on the needs of others. Serving others provides a purpose that cannot be fulfilled by a preoccupation with self.

Organizations that are depressed require the same treatment—transferring the organization from an internal to an external focus. The focus must be shifted from internal processes to the external needs of customers. That message is know who your customers are, what requirements they have, what expectations they hold and what you must do to meet those requirements and exceed those expectations. Meaning for the organization comes from the value it creates by serving its customers. Because of the social movement nature of quality, how a leader communicates the quality message—as mere rhetoric or as a clear call to action—can be either the right therapy for a company or the final push into spiraling decline. However, and this is the point of the above discussion, that message alone is not enough. As in the treatment of individual depression, organizational depression must be treated with a structured set of behavior changes that will focus the organization externally.

Defining and communicating the mechanism for change (not just a set of objectives) is the quality leader's primary task during the Rhetorical Component of a quality movement.

In summary, how do you avoid "the failure to communicate"? Your task—communicating the quality message—is clearly not an easy one. Your audience is tough—at best predominantly cynical, at worst depressed and hopeless, most likely resistant to any implication in your message that they haven't been trying to do quality work all along. Your environment is probably one of constant change. Buttons, mugs, and quality slogans simply won't cut it. Flogging away until quality improves isn't the answer. Pulpit-pounding inspiration ("Be a quality tiger") is likely to get the speaker whacked by a wing tip à la Dinsdale. Is the environment difficult? Yes. Is the task impossible? No.

The CEO in our example faced all of these issues at once, and yet he succeeded in pulling his organization back from the brink. He did it by using communication to integrate quality into the real-time concerns of his employees and into their on-the-job behavior. He succeeded by following a few key precepts. *You can too.*

Your "quality objectives" must focus your organization on knowing your customers and their requirements and expectations. Those objectives must

> Meaning for the organization comes from the value it creates by serving its customers.

be linked to a call to action—employees must be charged to do something different. That call must be accompanied by defined behaviors that when implemented provide employees with direct experience with customers that converts attitude into actions.

All quality communication should support that progression. Recognition for those who respond to customer requirements and expectations should be integrated into normal, ongoing business practices. Every channel of communication should be used to focus employees on their customers. The message should always focus on creating committed customers, not merely satisfied customers.

Communicating the quality message is not so much a communication project as it is what marketers Reis and Trout call a "selection process."[7] If you want to achieve customer-focused, sustained behavior from your organization, you have to set the stage in a manner that is likely to break through the sheer volume of information transmitted in today's corporate world where a person must check an electronic mailbox, listen to recorded phone messages and check the fax file before finally tackling the in-basket. Where do you think that management memo exhorting employees to "do quality" fits in the employee's hierarchy of things to do?

By providing a method for behavior change, the CEO in the example broke through the everyday clutter that was keeping his employees from talking with their customers. The key was not so much what he said, nor how he said it. The key was empowering employees by providing them with the opportunity to act—to change their behavior in a way that would have an impact on the organization.

Notes

1. "Gurus of Quality Are Gaining Clout," *The Wall Street Journal,* November 27, 1990.
2. Donald L. Kanter and Philip H. Mirvis, *The Cynical Americans.* Copyright 1989 Jossey-Bass Inc., San Francisco, CA.
3. Kanter and Mirvis. *Ibid.*
4. Reference to Martin Luther King Jr.'s "strategic plan" used by Sheila Sheinberg in a presentation to the International Association of Business Communicators.
5. Martin Seligman, Ph.D. *Learned Optimism.* Copyright 1990 Martin E.P. Seligman. Alfred A. Knopf, Inc.
6. Seligman. *Ibid.*
7. Al Ries and Jack Trout. *Positioning: The Battle for Your Mind.* Copyright 1981, 1986 McGraw-Hill, Inc., New York, NY.

Eight Communication Channels for Fast Tracking TQM

Roger Tunks

Just as its title suggests, this chapter from Roger Tunks' book provides a review of eight practical ways to communicate the company's commitment to quality, customers, and helping employees succeed.

Once, while talking about the value of keeping employees informed about Quality processes in the organization, a company president said, "You can't communicate with your customers if you can't communicate with your employees." This manager is certainly an insightful leader. He recognizes the importance of keeping staff well-informed, so as to enable them to serve and communicate with their customers, particularly external customers.

Clear, consistent communication with employees builds and strengthens employee understanding about the Quality processes in the organization. It helps them see where they can actively participate in the Quality advancement process. Keeping employees informed also fosters personal commitment to TQM and to the company. It helps them catch the full vision of TQM and what it can do for the organization, for their department or work group, and for themselves.

FAST-TRACK TIP

If you can't communicate with your employees, you won't be able to communicate with your customers. Clear, consistent communication is a key to developing employees who are able to meet or exceed their customer's expectations.

Keeping lines of communication open with employees isn't a short-term process. It is something that must become ingrained into the very fabric of the organization as a way of doing business. Organizations committed to advancing Quality must be willing to devote the time and resources needed for

Reprinted with permission from *Fast Track to Quality: A 12-Month Program for Small to Mid-Sized Businesses*, New York: McGraw-Hill, Inc., 1992.

clear, consistent employee communication if they are to succeed with TQM. Mid-sized to large companies often assign a full-time staff member or even a small department to the sole duty of employee communications. Some companies, particularly smaller ones, opt to hire independent communication consultants to handle employee communications rather than pay for full-time communication staff. Regardless of whether you use internal or external staff to get the job done, the extent and frequency of the employee communication program and its emphasis on keeping staff informed about Quality advancement will reflect the commitment of the organization's senior management—particularly the president or CEO—to TQM.

As with any effective communication process, no one vehicle or approach can ensure that the right messages are getting across consistently to every employee. Just as educators and psychologists have identified different types of learners, people receive messages in different ways. Some may respond to a general company communique like a newsletter, while others need a personal letter or a seminar. To ensure reaching everyone, you have to be willing to use a variety of communication channels. Some of the most effective communication channels for keeping employees informed and involved with the TQM process are discussed in the following sections.

FAST-TRACK TIP

Different employees respond to different messages. Use a variety of communication vehicles to reach everyone with the quality message.

Channel 1: Fax and Photocopiers

A group of senior managers were discussing their lack of effectiveness in communicating with employees. The problem was compounded by the fact that they have field offices in three states. Their concern was for more than being able to keep employees informed, but being able to provide immediate recognition to employees for special achievements. The solution was at their fingertips, yet overlooked. The solution was a special use of the fax machines located in each office. Together we designed a form with the heading in large, bold print, "News Flash." A border was included with adequate space to type or write in the hot news item. This made it easy for managers throughout the organization to fill in the news item and to quickly disseminate it throughout the organization.

> By having a prepared form, each office became a distribution center to convey hot items describing employee accomplishment in advancing Quality.

By having a prepared form, each office became a distribution center to convey hot items describing employee accomplishment in advancing Quality. Photocopies of the fax received at each location were made to distribute the news item. To retain the identity of the "News Flash" to Quality advancement and employee recognition, senior managers agreed to limit its use to Fast-Track TQM.

FAST-TRACK TIP

Develop and use a "news flash" form to disseminate hot news items about employee achievements. Use a fax or photocopy machine to broadcast the news items throughout your organization.

Channel 2: Newsletters for Quality

Newsletters are certainly not the easiest channel of communication, but they are one of the most cost effective. Even small companies with 100 or so employees typically have some kind of in-house newsletter to keep employees informed about the activities of the organization. It's here that you can begin your Quality communication emphasis.

FAST-TRACK TIP

Newsletters can be one of the most cost-effective methods of consistently communicating the Quality message to your employees.

When Quality advancement is just beginning in an organization, it's common to add a special column or page devoted to advancing product or service Quality in the current in-house newsletter. Eventually, it will be important to have a separate publication for advancing Quality, whether it is an extension of an existing newsletter or an additional publication.

By giving Quality advancement its own communication vehicle, you send a strong message about its importance in the organization.

Too often, organizational newsletters are boring and seldom read by employees. You can avoid this if you follow two important rules:

1. Maximize the number of employee names listed in the newsletter.
2. Maximize the number of employee photographs.

Everyone likes to see his or her name and picture. Employees do too. Seeing their names and photographs in the Quality newsletter creates pride in employees, who come to identify with the company and with the TQM processes. Typically, employees featured in the organization's Quality newsletter share the newsletter with family and friends. They may save the issue in a scrapbook or post it on their office wall. While it may seem a small thing, being recognized in the organization's Quality newsletter builds and reinforces the value and importance of the employee to the organization and increases employee self-esteem.

Controversial topics can also add spice to the newsletter. You can have both sides express their opposing views on a chosen topic, and let employees reach their own conclusions. Not only does it build understanding of sometimes complex issues, it also fosters tolerance for differing opinions and sends the message that people don't necessarily have to agree to work cooperatively together.

Size, Frequency, and Format

The biggest mistake companies make with their Quality newsletter is that they become too ambitious. They start off with a publication that is too large and too frequent to sustain over the long run. Often, companies will produce a large, multipage newsletter and announce it will be published on a monthly or semimonthly basis. The first issue of a Quality newsletter is always easy to prepare. At this point, there is a lot of excitement and enthusiasm about the Quality process. New and unusual events have taken place, and it's easy to include articles about them in the first issue.

The next issues become more problematic. How do you keep the newsletter newsy and interesting for employees? If you talk to any staff member who has had to consistently produce a Quality newsletter, they'll tell you that the fun and excitement diminishes very quickly and that the publication can become a real burden.

A more realistic approach is to publish the newsletter on a quarterly basis and limit its size to a single 11 × 17-in. sheet, folded in half. This yields four pages and, in some cases, even this size can be very ambitious for a continued publication. Using plenty of high-quality photographs will make the publication graphically interesting, keep employee interest high, and use up space when news items are limited. The format should be two or three columns, with a balance of text and photographs. Give byline credit to employees who write special articles.

Keep in mind the publication of a Quality newsletter is a management performance agreement. Management has stated that they will publish this document on a consistent schedule. They've said that this vehicle is an important part of communicating with employees about the Quality process. If management doesn't follow through consistently on the publication, employees will question management's commitment to Quality, and the all-important trust and credibility between employees and management will suffer.

Keep in mind the publication of a Quality newsletter is a management performance agreement.

FAST-TRACK TIP

Don't be overly ambitious with your Quality newsletter. In the beginning, publish no more frequently than quarterly and keep the size down to four pages or less.

Newsletter Content

An established newsletter format makes subsequent issues easier to prepare. Often a template can be created on a computer that speeds up the placement of regular columns and features faster, and gives the newsletter a consistent look. Here are some of the topical areas that should be addressed regularly in each publication:

1. *Employee recognition:* A minimum of 50 percent of the publication should be devoted to names and photographs of employees in articles that describe their action and involvement in the Quality process. Whenever special events to improve Quality take place and employees are involved, their names should be included in the descriptive articles.

   A word of caution: Often, organizations expect their managers and supervisors to be so excited about the Quality process that they will write and submit newsletter articles. It won't happen. While managers, supervisors, and employees are enthusiastic and want to see their department or work group featured, most have neither the time nor the skills to write newsletter articles. If you don't have someone with the necessary writing and editing skills on staff, you may have to hire an independent communications consultant to write and edit your publication. Whoever is responsible for publishing the newsletter must interview the managers, supervisors, and employees—and write the articles. The newsletter editor should ensure that not only are the articles professionally written, but also that the names of everyone mentioned in the newsletter are spelled correctly. While this may sound like a minor point, it's vitally important. A name is an important part of a person's identity and value. It's imperative that the publication—particularly a publication on Quality advancement—be free of spelling or other defects.

   As mentioned, photographs play an important part in both employee recognition and in the professional look of the publication. It is important to have a camera available to ensure that photographs are taken of employees actually participating in Quality events. Nothing is more boring than having a series of "mug shots" of people not doing anything but smiling into the camera.

2. *Celebrations:* Include articles about celebrations both large and small that take place around significant accomplishments.

3. *Employee suggestions:* The newsletter can be the vehicle for a running dialogue between employees and management. Employees can make suggestions about advancing Quality, and management can respond with comments on how the suggestions were implemented or with explanations for not implementing them. Employees, seeing their ideas in print, are encouraged to make more suggestions. Publishing employee ideas also encourages "hitchhiking"—that is, tagging onto other ideas—thereby expanding and improving on others' suggestions.

4. *President's message:* Every issue of the newsletter should have space devoted to a message from the company president. While some senior officers may see this as a burden, it is an important part of their commitment to advancing Quality in the organization. It isn't necessary for the president to actually write the message him- or herself. The staff member or consultant producing the newsletter can interview the president or CEO,

write the piece, and then have the senior officer fine-tune the article. Occasionally it's a good idea to use an interview question-and-answer format in the president's column. It provides a quick and easy read, and can make for an interesting article because it is in the president's actual words.

5. *Schedule of events:* It's important to keep employees informed about activities going on in the organization that support and advance the Quality process. The schedule of events may include special classes, speakers, or seminars. The lack of a consistent flow of upcoming activities on a quarterly basis is a good indication that the organization isn't doing enough to advance Quality. It underscores that the time has come to reevaluate the organization's commitment to TQM. Keeping a consistent flow of Quality-oriented activities going takes special effort, but it's an important part of keeping the excitement and enthusiasm alive in the Quality-advancement process.

6. *Customer interviews:* A portion of each publication should be devoted to one or more interviews with external customers. This reminds employees that Quality advancement is really all about meeting or exceeding customer expectations. Seeing photographs of customers and hearing stories about the products and/or services they receive creates a real picture of customer service for employees. Customer interviews can help employees answer the question, "How well are we serving our customers?" Over time, customer interviews can help employees see the changes and improvements they're making in the company's products and services. They also give employees another form of recognition for a job well done.

7. *Employee interviews:* These features reinforce employee commitment and help employees get to know one another better. An easy format to duplicate is the one used by the *USA Today* newspaper that has a photograph of the person, a single question, and a brief paragraph of response.

> The lack of a consistent flow of upcoming activities on a quarterly basis is a good indication that the organization isn't doing enough to advance Quality.

FAST-TRACK TIP

If you don't have communications/public relations professionals on staff, consider hiring a professional writer/editor to produce your newsletter.

Channel 3: Letters from the President

In addition to supporting management forums, letters from the president can also be used at any time to provide the special recognition from the senior officer that is so important for TQM success. Word processing has made it very easy for presidents and CEOs to send a special letter in a mass mailing to all managers and employees, or to a select group of managers and employees. You can personalize the letter even further by having it addressed to the individual's home address.

Letters become a special form of recognition. They can announce an upcoming event or provide instruction and guidance about an activity taking place in the organization. While it may be a form letter, using the individual's name and having the president sign it makes it personalized. It's a good idea to have the president's signature in a different color to make it easy for the recipient to recognize that the president, in fact, took the time to sign their letter.

Channel 4: Computer Screen Messages

In organizations in which employees log onto a mainframe computer, it's easy to insert messages that appear on the screen as employees enter the system. This channel of communication must not be used in such a way as to suggest that "Big Brother" is keeping an eye on people. When used to communicate special announcements or upcoming events, or to recognize the particular achievements of an employee, it can be very effective. Cute or humorous sayings become tiring, and after a while become a form of derisive humor, particularly toward management. The computer screen is a channel for Quality information that may even replace employee bulletin boards in importance.

FAST-TRACK TIP

Computer screen messages can be effective at communicating with employees. But they must not be viewed as a "Big Brother" tactic. Limit the messages only to special announcements or recognitions.

Channel 5: Brown Bag Lunches

Several years ago, when I was the director of organizational development for a large corporation, a new president came on board who was anxious to get to know the employees and understand more about the organization. I arranged for him to meet informally with employees and managers in a series of brown bag lunches, each lasting about 45 minutes. The company supplied the lunches, as twice a week the president met with groups of employees and managers to share lunch. The informal lunches enabled the president to share his ideas and views and to answer questions. Even more importantly, they allowed employees to express their ideas and suggestions.

While having lunch with the boss may not seem particularly significant, the employees were amazed that the president would actually take the time to eat and talk with them. The informal setting encouraged candor and openness in both the employees' questions and the president's responses. It not only created a new level of understanding among employees, it gave the president real insight into the concerns of the employees and ways the company could be more effective in creating a satisfied workforce. The president's brown bag lunches were so popular that they evolved into an ongoing affair regularly scheduled throughout the year. It became a valuable forum for open dialogue between the president and employees.

You can easily adapt the brown bag lunch idea to your own organization to advance Quality and ensure open communication. Not only can the president establish brown bag meetings, divisional or department managers or work group supervisors can use this informal format on a regular basis. You'll find it's an effective way not only to stop unfounded rumors and gossip, but also to keep employees informed about the Quality process.

FAST-TRACK TIP

The informality of brown bag lunches with management and employees can foster the open and honest exchange of concerns and ideas.

Channel 6: Payroll Stuffers

Announcements in payroll envelopes are effective ways to communicate with every employee in the company. But beware. Overusing this communication channel can quickly render it ineffective. Payroll stuffers should be limited only to special announcements or special recognition for employees who have made significant accomplishments.

Channel 7: Visual Identification of Quality Processes

Banners, posters, special mottos are all ways of making quality processes visible. But it's a communication channel that's frequently abused. Many managers become so excited about the Quality advancement process that they want to decorate the entire company with special banners and slogans. The danger is that Quality advancement will be seen as a special program, not as a way of doing business on an ongoing basis. If you choose to use visual identification of Quality processes in your company, keep it simple and don't overdo it. The message should be short, identifiable, and meaningful. The Ford Company's "Quality is Job One" is a good example. All employees, regardless of their positions in the company, can relate to it.

FAST-TRACK TIP

Be careful not to overuse banners, slogans, and mottos that can give the impression that Quality advancement is a program that will end.

Channel 8: Employee Bulletin Boards

Some organizations devote a special bulletin board or portion of one for announcements and information regarding Quality in the organization. The board can become an important communication channel for posting special announcements and scheduled events and for recognizing extraordinary employee efforts. But be aware that this is another one of those performance agreements—if you're going to start it, be prepared to sustain it. Lack of continued effort in employee bulletin boards will be seen as a decrease in the importance of Quality in the company. Keep the bulletin board new, fresh, and filled with ideas and information, and employees will see it as another message that Quality is important to you and to the organization.

Roger Tunks is president of the Richard-Rogers Group, a management consulting firm specializing in total quality management training.

Training for Quality

H. G. Menon

This article, taken from a chapter in Menon's book on the people side of TQM, explains in concise terms why and how to train people so they can continuously improve their abilities to contribute to the company's purpose of profitably satisfying customer needs.

One of the most important facets of the TQM system is the participation of every level of personnel within the company to the quality process and getting appropriate inputs from them. This process can be accelerated and improved by providing appropriate tools to all levels of personnel. While the rest of this discussion ponders the importance of direct quality training, there are other aspects of training, such as cross training in other functional departments to ensure a better understanding of other related functions.

Why Train Your People?

Before beginning your training programs, it is necessary to ask the question, what is the purpose of training? The answer could be one or several of the following:

- Foster an attitude of change.
- Make all employees view the business from the customer's point of view.
- Demonstrate management commitment to continuous improvement.
- Develop skills in workers, leading to solutions to problems.

Reprinted with permission from H. G. Menon, *TQM in New Product Manufacturing*, New York: McGraw-Hill, Inc., 1992.

- Encourage employee decision making.
- Encourage group problem-solving skills.
- Provide the tools necessary to provide quality service to customers.
- Build a team spirit among the workers.

Who Should Be Trained?

This one factor will be the critical variable in determining how successful the TQM system will be. Training should not be short-term, but should be a continuous reinforcement of the learning process. Depending on the level of the personnel in the organization, different levels of quality education and training are required. Basically, organizations can be divided into four levels:

1. Top management, including owners, presidents, and vice presidents.
2. Middle managers, including department chiefs and plant managers
3. Engineering, design, and R&D personnel
4. Supervisory personnel and operators

Some of the training offered will overlap or be omitted, depending on the defined organizational responsibility. For example, some of the training offered to the engineering personnel may be offered to the SPC facilitator and the supervisors, but not to the operators. Offering a common course which introduces the concept of quality control, including aspects such as zero defects, continuous improvement, and other general concepts of quality such as nonconformance is critical to creating a uniform mindset throughout the organization. The training offered has to be put to use within the organization for running a successful quality management system. The teachings of one of the TQM gurus such as Deming or Juran can be used as the basis for introducing the TQM system and this is dealt with later in this chapter. The level of training and other training-related issues can be decided using a systems approach, as shown in Fig. 1.

Four important considerations in determining a training program are

1. Clearly define the objectives of the training program.
2. Develop a training program to match the objectives of the training program.
3. Training programs should not be exclusive of either technical or behavioral content.
4. Get the input of the participants, in a formal or informal manner, to improve the quality of the training program.

The various types of training programs that should be considered essential to the successful implementation of the total quality management program are as follows.

1. *Leadership.* This training has to be different from conventional training, since management has to be trained to share decision making

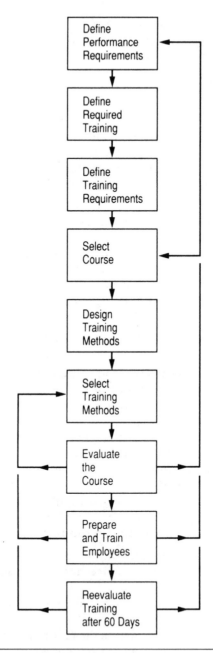

Figure 1. **A systems approach to TQM training.**

responsibilities. They have to forget the conventional route of managing employees through discipline. This also means that the top management has to go out and emphasize the importance of the contributions of the employees and show their appreciation for them. Many members of top management teams have an inherent reluctance to share power by delegating decision-making authority lower down the organization ladder. Without a top management vision, there can be no total quality management. The leadership training programs should attempt to teach the leaders of the organization these skills, the most important being the vision of seeing quality as an issue of conforming to requirements, and seeing what a TQM strategy can do.

Another problem leadership faces is the resistance to change. Leadership must instill the understanding that business cannot continue as it always has. Nurturing change is another important task for top management. Change has to come about as a result of understanding the importance of the use of statistical methods for managing quality. Top management has to have a strong conviction in the effectiveness of using statistical methods as the basis for improving efficiency and reducing waste.

2. *Strategic planning.* This is an important skill top and middle managers have to learn. The strategy of the company should revolve around the quality management systems, and planning should be such that a quality product results. Conventional strategic plans have revolved around the methods to increase market share, increasing sales, increasing profitability, and such. These goals are automatically attained by using TQM strategies in your planning process. TQM strategies improve your competitive position and, in turn, result in a cost-effective, quality product and a resulting increase in market share. The strategic planners should see that an overall quality management strategy automatically leads to improved profitability, increase in sales, and market share.

3. *Supplier involvement.* The first step in involving suppliers is training your own buyer to demand and expect only quality product from your suppliers. The next step in the process is to train the supplier in the TQM philosophy adopted by your company and what is expected of them. Many of the larger companies do offer such training to their suppliers.

4. *Internal and external customer satisfaction.* Normally, the manufacture of a product requires the use of numerous steps. At each point the person getting the input is the customer and should be treated as any external customer to the organization would be treated. Most external customers will not accept anything less than zero defects, and all personnel should be trained in the concept of internal and external customer.

5. *Statistical analysis.* This may consist of numerous aspects, from simple graphing, histograms, Pareto analysis, and X-bar and R charts to complex statistical methods such as design of experiments, training in these methods has to be offered to all levels of employees. Depending on the level of the personnel, suitable levels of training may be offered to them. Many

larger organizations do offer training to the employees of their suppliers as a part of getting the supplier to meet the quality requirements.

6. *Cost of quality.* The concept of cost of quality has been dealt with earlier, and by the most commonly accepted definition is the cost associated with producing a nonconforming part. Usually the information is documented by someone in the accounting or quality control department. All levels of personnel should be trained in interpreting the charts depicting costs of quality so that they can understand how much it costs to produce a nonconforming part. The understanding of cost of quality charts often leads to operator endeavors to correct numerous problems either by bringing them to engineering's attention, or, if possible, fixing them themselves.

7. *Continuous improvement.* For remaining competitive, it is necessary to improve the processes continuously. Training for continuous improvement is an important part of the TQM strategy. Many of the statistical tools offer operators important skills in identifying problems with the process and offering suggestions to improve the process. A very important part of the continuous improvement process is training the machine operators to correctly identify problems and suggest possible solutions.

8. *Employee involvement in a team environment.* While employee involvement in the decision-making process is not a new concept, employees working as teams is new in most American work environments. To avoid bitterness among the team participants, each member must be trained in team dynamics and how to work effectively with team members.

To avoid bitterness among the team participants, each member must be trained in team dynamics.

The first step in the process of implementing a TQM training program is to determine which of the areas described above require maximum attention. This can be attained by interviewing the employees at all levels.

Top Management Training

The first step in the process of implementing a TQM system is the orientation of the top management in the dynamics of TQM with an in-depth analysis of reasons for failure of such systems:

- Failure to bridge the gap between training and implementation.
- Partial training, where only some of the members of the organizations are trained in the use of statistical process control.

Top management must also be trained in the executive management's roles and responsibilities, required long-term investment and strategic and operation planning, and the difference between management commitment and endorsement of TQM. The leadership or the top management is critical to the success of the TQM process for the following critical reasons:

1. They are required to provide the vision to unify all the quality improvement projects.
2. They are the chief motivators during the massive changes in philosophy as a result of applying TQM.

3. They have the power to change manufacturing systems and parameters before a crisis stage is reached.
4. They have the ability to allocate resources necessary for solving the problems and effecting continuous improvement.
5. Priority for continuous quality improvement at the levels offered to manufacturing, R&D, and marketing can be attained only if the top management wishes for it.
6. Only the leadership can allocate adequate training time for every level of the organization.

Middle Management Training

The next level in the organization that must be trained is the middle management. Middle management should be trained similarly to top management, with less emphasis on strategy and more on the overall management of quality. Considerably more emphasis is placed on tools and techniques of TQM and SPC. The actual implementation of the methods is dependent on this level of management having a clear understanding of the techniques available for use.

Training Technical Personnel

Once middle managers are trained in the tools of TQM, the next step in the process is training the technical personnel, who, depending on the organizational responsibility, should be trained in every aspect of TQM. The various courses in training will depend on the responsibilities. Design and verification personnel would have to be trained in CAD simulation, prototype building, design, and development tests. Manufacturing engineering and process verification would have to be trained in various aspects of SPC, reliability tests, problem-solving techniques, and so on. Technical quality assurance personnel would have to be trained in coming quality assurance methods, including SPC, product process control, and supplier process monitoring. Depending on the manufacturing process and the product, it may be necessary to offer certain specialized training to the personnel. For example, in case of electronic components, it is necessary to statistically analyze the results of burn-in tests; this is not applicable to other products.

Middle management should be trained similarly to top management, with less emphasis on strategy and more on the overall management of quality.

Operator Training

Finally, training the operators is a critical aspect of the successful implementation of the TQM system. Operators should be trained in SPC and actual operation of the machinery and the gaging systems used. The SPC training must essentially be in the form of programmed learning where the operators are taken through SPC in simple incremental steps. Depending on the size of the organization, an SPC facilitator or trainer may be used. Using a separate SPC facilitator offers considerable advantages over letting one of the technical personnel or supervisors train the operators, since for any training to be effective it is necessary for it to be a continuous process. The classroom training should be repeated at regular intervals for all levels in the organization so that the initial enthusiasm for using the SPC methods is not lost. The operators should also be trained in basic problem-solving skills, where they learn to define the problem, identify the root causes, and take action if necessary to rectify the problem in systematic, scientific fashion as far as possible. This problem-solving course can be used to help operators highlight any problems that arise to the technical personnel who may be adequately equipped to solve them.

At each level of the organization, appropriate problem solving should be practiced so that the training sessions do not remain in the classroom. It may be necessary to form teams of a company steering committee consisting of a cross section of employees that gathers information from various work areas, provides recommendations to the committee, and is empowered to implement the recommendations.

How to Implement Training Programs

There are numerous aspects to training that must be determined by top management, including where the training should be held, how much information should be imparted at various levels, and how fast information should be given. The material and content of each of the courses offered at various levels should be determined, and this is a part of the strategic planning for quality. The steps needed for quality training are defining the requirements; identifying the training requirements based on which course content is selected; designing instruction; and selecting methods and training aids such as notes, video displays, tape recording, and so on. Care should be taken to reinforce the training through repetition.

Customizing Training Programs

The best method for training operators is programmed learning.

Many canned training programs are readily available, but more often than not the examples used are not related to the actual manufacturing process. Most of these canned programs use combinations of slides, video tapes, and workbooks, but are often not relatable to your own manufacturing environment. This is particularly true for operator-level training for SPC. When the operator is not able to relate to the training program, then getting him or her to use the methods will be extremely difficult. From our own experience, the best method for training operators is programmed learning, where the operators are answering simple multiple-choice questions or fill-in-the-blanks to enhance the learning process. I used a sample dimension from our shop floor as an example for creating an easier understanding of the SPC mechanism.

One more direction to look into is the possibility of using an outside consultant to implement the SPC programs. This is advantageous when the conventional wisdom of quality management has to be changed to a TQM philosophy. But this may not work as well as expected because the outside consultant may not have a good evaluation of the system existing within the company. However, if a decision is taken to hire an outside consultant, then it is usually a good idea to check if his or her views of TQM match yours, what he or she expects to change as a result of TQM systems being adopted by the company, and how these systems should be implemented. Besides this, it is also useful to check the consultant's reputation and performance with other clients. Using a consultant on a continual basis may not prove cost-effective, so more often than not the sensible course to take is to start off with an external training program followed by internally developed training programs. The importance of reinforcing the learning process by repeated training cannot be overemphasized. Besides reinforcing learning, the use of repeated training tells employees that they are important for the organization.

Where to Train

This is an important question, usually decided by the level of the person in the organization and the resources of the company to develop and implement training programs. These are important considerations, but the attempt here will be to answer the question of whether the quality management program should be conducted in-house or outside the company. The key benefits of using in-house training, whether conducted by an internal or an external trainer, are

1. Reduced training costs.
2. Reduction in time taken for travel.
3. Flexible training schedules with the trainees being able to change the times depending on the tasks being performed on the shop floor.
4. Trainees can continue performing most of the day-to-day tasks.
5. Workers learn more about the quality orientation of the company and relate information learned to the actual working environment.
6. The distractions are fewer. This may not be true if the trainees are asked to attend to shop-floor problems right in the middle of the training sessions.
7. Training can be matched to class size and composition. Training outside the company may require sending people at different levels to different training programs.

H. G. Menon is a manufacturing engineer for Jernberg Industries in Chicago, Illinois, where he is responsible for their total quality management system.

How To Get Your TQM Training On Track

Patricia A. Galagan

TQM training must be on-going and continuous. The author points out that "a common belief among companies just starting to pursue quality is that it can be learned quickly." She then demonstrates the fallacy of this belief and how to implement TQM training successfully, with a special emphasis on small and medium businesses.

Of the 20 million small businesses in the U.S., only a handful are practicing true Total Quality Management. A few more are somewhere on the steep learning curve that gets companies to the point that they're ready for TQM.

For the rest, it's business as usual.

The pioneers have discovered that it takes training, training, and more training to be a quality company. Not just formal training in a classroom, but a whole range of learning experiences, from reading books to inventing new work processes as a team.

A common belief among companies just starting to pursue quality is that it can be learned quickly. The basic principles—focus on the customer, and continuously improve your product or service—seem simple enough. Until, that is, you start trying to apply them.

"You read about the need to be patient, and after a year of trying, I can say it's true," acknowledges Charles Jett Jr., of Premix Industries, a maker of just-add-water bagged concrete. The company, based in Chesapeake, Va., has 165 employees.

"Quality takes a long time to learn, and I wish we had accepted that earlier," Jett says. "It would have saved us a lot of anxiety and frustration. TQM turned out to be a much more encompassing philosophy than we thought. We thought we'd read a Deming book [management consultant W. Edwards Deming is a TQM pioneer] and maybe a book on teamwork and be done."

Lengthy preparation for the real action is common in small and midsize companies. People spend what seem like huge amounts of time reading about quality or going to training courses, only to realize they don't know much and their company hasn't really started quality management.

"The TQM journey has a lot of surprises in it," says Pat Lancaster, president of Lantech, a manufacturing company of 330 employees in Louisville, Ky. Lantech makes machines that wrap large items in plastic.

"One of the surprises is the length of time it takes to actually begin," he says. "In our case it took two years."

Elaine Biech, a partner in "ebb associates" of Portage, Wis., has been a TQM consultant and trainer for several years. "The biggest problem we have is to put reins on people," she says. "They want to train everybody at once because training has been touted as the answer to all their quality problems." But the critical first step, she says, is to train the managers and supervisors thoroughly, "so that when the rest of the staff comes out of training they won't get shut down for practicing their new skills."

Building a friendly environment for TQM—what quality consultants call a culture—is some of the hardest work they've ever done, say people who've been through it.

"I was surprised at the degree of organizational shock we had to go through," Pat Lancaster recalls. The top managers in his family-owned business had to make a commitment to change some of their deeply held views about how to run things. Wrenching as that was, it was only the first step.

"An organization that has a belief in TQM and a commitment to it is only about 10 percent of the way there," Lancaster warns. "The key is to change behaviors and overcome resistance to those changes."

But what kind of training is most likely to bring about such change? You can choose among hundreds of versions of TQM. Whether sold by a single consultant or by a large training organization, each program reflects the values and beliefs of its inventor.

> Whether sold by a single consultant or by a large training organization, each program reflects the values and beliefs of its inventor.

Most TQM training should cover some or all of a basic set of skills, says Richard Wellins, senior vice president of Design Dimensions International, of Pittsburgh. DDI is one of the biggest TQM vendors, with annual sales of $60 million. Those skills, he says, fall into three areas:

Leadership skills. These skills must be acquired by managers and supervisors. They must change their leadership behavior to become more receptive to ideas from others, to be coaches rather than controllers of people, and to facilitate things rather than mandate them.

Teamwork skills. TQM often involves working in teams. "Most people won't necessarily have the skills to work in teams as leaders or participants," Wellins says.

Technical skills. Sometimes called quality tools, these include dozens of methods for studying a problem and displaying the results of analysis.

"A big mistake that companies can make about TQM training is to put people into classes without first figuring out what skills they need," warns Richard Chang, of Richard Chang and Associates, Inc., a consulting firm in

Irvine, Calif. "Not everyone will need the same skills. It will depend on what business processes they work on, and who their customers are."

Many people in search of a TQM consultant or training program feel that they are about to swim in shark-infested waters. After several years of seeking help, Pat Lancaster warns: "There is bad information out there and a fair number of consultants who don't have the backbone to belly up to the client's table and get straight."

Premix Industries' Charlie Jett started by looking in the Yellow Pages under "Consultants." He says, "We interviewed them all and didn't like any of them." The local chamber of commerce directed him to the Total Quality Institute in Portsmouth, Va. It provided the course in group facilitation that Jett wanted.

Jim Zawacki, owner and president of Grand Rapids Spring & Wire Products, in Grand Rapids, Mich., with 160 employees, put his early money and training effort into "getting people to understand why we're in business" and into building "trust, relationships, integrity, and communications." He had no formal guide or mentor for this, only his own beliefs about quality management.

"I really believe that TQM starts with culture," he says, "and culture is the responsibility of management. It's taken years, but today we share financial statements with our people. They know that when we talk about improving an operation from a quality standpoint, we're not trying to eliminate jobs."

Zawacki says he also spent "a lot of money" on formal technical training, starting with statistical process control (SPC). Before these courses could begin, some employees needed to learn basic math skills. Zawacki taught those skills himself. For the SPC courses, he hired community college teachers.

A high level of care for employees and a big investment in training paid off for Grand Rapids Spring & Wire, Zawacki believes. In the past five years, on-time delivery has gone from 60 percent to over 95 percent. Inventory has gone down 30 percent, and sales have doubled.

Lantech, the stretch-wrap machine manufacturer, bought mainly big-brand-name consulting and training for its TQM effort. Like Zawacki, Lantech's president, Pat Lancaster, spent a lot of time—a year, in his case—building commitment to the idea of TQM before buying training. To do this, teams of employees, including Lancaster, held many discussions about the human values in the company's vision and strategy.

Lancaster says he got his ideas about how to proceed "from the TQM salad bar" of books and theories. Then he hired a business consulting firm to assess the levels of quality awareness of Lantech's top managers, middle managers, and people on the shop floor.

"They gave us a rather grim report," he recalls. "We hired them to help us along, and we started some projects that were probably too large and grandiose."

A year later, Lantech hired a second consulting firm to assess its position again. "They reported we were pretty close to where we were the first time,"

Lancaster admits. At that point, Lantech decided to do some in-house training because, he says, "we couldn't find training about quality that was consistent with our values."

From the president of another company Lancaster learned about the training firm Design Dimensions International. "We had a value alignment with DDI," he says. "They believed, as we did, that self-esteem boosts productivity, and that it's leadership's job to enhance self-esteem. We made an enormous investment in training, thousands of hours of training for over 300 employees."

Lantech now works with another large consulting company, Time-Based Management. Lancaster describes it as "a sort of graduate school for us." Time-Based Management provides technical training and has helped Lantech's engineering and manufacturing operations pick up their pace by encouraging employee teams to focus less on how they made decisions and more on how they carried them out.

After five years of effort and a major investment in training, TQM seems to be working at Lantech. In a typical change, a process-improvement team, made up of floor workers, managers, and engineers, redesigned the process for building semi-automatic stretch-wrapping machines. Instead of building 10 machines at a time, as before, they now produce machines as customers order them.

Very few small companies can afford to buy TQM training directly from big-name vendors, as Lantech did; they must be more inventive in seeking help with TQM. But the motivation behind their search should be the same as the motivation behind Pat Lancaster's: to seek out the avenue to TQM that best fits their companies' values and circumstances.

The small company that approaches TQM in that spirit will find that it has plenty of options, even when its training budget is lean. Among them:

Hire small or midsize consulting firms. With lower overhead than the giants, they often can offer more-attractive deals.

Buy off-the-shelf training programs. Such training programs cost less than programs designed for specific customers. A middle-range option is to buy a packaged program from a supplier who can adapt it for your company, for a fee.

Form partnerships with local educational institutions. One way to enjoy the expertise of big-company consultants at small-company prices is to search out community colleges and vocational schools that will form training partnerships with small businesses. The schools license training from major training suppliers to avoid the costly and time-consuming task of developing training programs themselves. Zenger-Miller, an international training and consulting firm based in San Jose, Calif., has been taking part in such partnerships since 1983 and now serves schools in 23 states.

In any case, what is absolutely critical is not choosing a particular path to TQM, but making the unqualified commitment to find the path that is right for you. Lantech, for example, was able to keep pressing toward TQM, despite all its false starts and disappointments, because its owners and managers knew what they wanted to achieve.

"We didn't have the Japanese coming over the ocean and cleaning our clock," Pat Lancaster says. "No customer or competitor was pushing us. But there was something out of sync about our internal focus. The big cultural shift for us was to recognize that we are really here only to satisfy the customer."

Patricia A. Galagan is editor of Training & Development magazine, published by the American Society for Training and Development, in Alexandria, Va.

Cascading Quality Through the Training Process

Gerard R. Tuttle

Not only is regular training vital to a company's ability to improve continuously its processes and the quality of its offerings, it must also seek to do exactly the same thing with its training—learn from experience and continuously improve it. This article explains this insight and how to make it actionable.

When Xerox Corporation received a Malcolm Baldrige National Quality Award in 1989, the companywide, total quality management (TQM) training program mandated by David Kearns, its chief executive officer, was identified as one to be emulated as a benchmark and was considered world class. The Xerox training system, known as "cascading," required supervisors, including senior leaders, to participate in the training of those they supervised. This process created a cascade of information through the work force. While Xerox became the industry benchmark for TQM training, Kearns thinks the toughest problem training professionals have is intercepting and integrating new ideas into training.[1]

In attempting to emulate Xerox's training program, organizations might have selected TQM instructors who were neophytes in TQM implementation and who had not learned to apply the concepts of TQM to their own instruction processes. This is likely to produce instructors who can state what the training manual dictates but who are unable to integrate the concepts themselves or explain to their students how to apply the concepts of TQM as they apply to various jobs and professions.

What key concepts must be integrated into any training process to ensure TQM is taught at an understanding level rather than simply a knowledge level? And how do we teach instructors to integrate TQM concepts into their instruction? These questions must be answered by the training manager in the organization that wants to successfully initiate or revive its TQM training program.

Reprinted with permission from *Quality Progress*, April 1993, ASQC, Milwaukee, WI.

Context for Change

According to Masaaki Imai, an internationally known expert on quality management implementation, TQM training flourishes in certain cultures. He thinks the concepts of TQM are readily adaptable in Japan because of kaizen, a traditional Japanese philosophy that identifies the goal of work as an "ongoing improvement involving everyone."[2] It is a process-focused, rather than problem-focused, concept of thinking. Kaizen requires workplace strategies that support continuous improvement and is dependent on the interaction of employees and management.

Kaizen requires workplace strategies that support continuous improvement and is dependent on the interaction of employees and management.

TQM tools fit naturally into the concept and strategies of kaizen, but for TQM to be commonly accepted throughout the United States, the American workplace culture will require adjustments. In this regard, the TQM literature is replete with statements that identify the necessity for cultural change. Yet W. Edwards Deming thinks it can take decades to change a corporation's culture.[3]

From a narrow-based beginning, TQM has spread throughout the United States. Ford Corporation, which has followed the path of continuous improvement since 1975, has incorporated these concepts and tools into the development of the Taurus model line. As a result, the Taurus was the second-best-selling car in the United States from 1985 to 1990.[4] Florida Power and Light won the Deming Prize in 1989, becoming the first international winner of Japan's prestigious quality improvement award.[5] In 1990, the U.S. Air Force Logistics Command (AFLC) was recognized with the Presidential Award for Quality and Productivity Improvement as the leader in the federal government.[6]

The service sector has shown an increasing interest in quality improvement. A 1991 study of TQM in higher education showed that 103 of the 160 universities that responded both teach TQM and implement its principles in their administrations.[7] In health care, the Joint Commission for Accreditation of Healthcare Organizations requires evidence of continuous improvement initiatives prior to re-accreditation.[8] The U.S. Navy Bureau of Medicine has adopted total quality leadership training requirements for all its medical department heads.[9]

Combining Concepts

The philosophy and concepts of kaizen were merged with the techniques and tools of TQM by the staff of the Center for Quality Education at the Wright-Patterson Air Force Base in Ohio to improve the quality of its training and service.

The center was established in January 1990 to provide required core TQM course training to the approximately 13,000 employees of AFLC and the Defense Electronic Supply Center located in Dayton, OH. The staff of 20 instructors had little or no experience in education and training. Because TQM was relatively new to the Air Force, few instructors had experience implementing the concepts of TQM.

Chosen for their interest and willingness to work as instructors on self-managed teams, the instructors not only had to be trained as trainers but had to learn to "walk the talk." Center management determined that the best way for the new instructors to truly understand what they were teaching would be through applying TQM to their training processes. By wrapping the philosophy of kaizen around the tools of TQM and using the structure provided by benchmarking, departmental task analysis, and quality function deployment (QFD), the instructors would experience what their students would experience. Understanding would occur through planned, structured implementation within their organization. The center staff would serve as trainer and model for the rest of the organization in TQM implementation.

The traditional problem-solving model used by U.S. manufacturing and service industries requires pushing responsibility and authority to increasingly higher organizational levels. That is where the funding, but not necessarily the expertise, exists for problem solution. With constrained resources, this is becoming a less valued option. Alternately, part of the TQM foundation is work force empowerment. Empowerment is an act of building, developing, and increasing power through cooperation, sharing, and teamwork. It is more than problem solving at the appropriate level of intervention; it is an interactive process.

The management plan was to empower employees through self-managed work teams. Given the authority to manage courses, the instructors helped develop management's plan for continuous improvement. They were held responsible for managing teaching schedules, maintaining their instruction quality, and revising their processes (with a strong recommendation to ensure customer input). They were granted ownership.

The empowered instructors were expected to continuously improve their training processes based on defining and meeting or exceeding their customers' requirements.

The goal of TQM as defined by AFLC was to provide products or services that met or exceeded the customers' expectations. The customer was to be the ultimate judge of the quality of the goods produced or the services provided. Tying this goal to kaizen, the empowered instructors were expected to continuously improve their training processes based on defining and meeting or exceeding their customers' requirements. Using materials that had been developed to serve as training courses for all 90,000 AFLC employees, the instructors decided to use student critiques to define their priority areas for improvement. Instructors, however, were generally dissatisfied with the existing command-approved critique. It essentially measured form, not substance. The consensus was to obtain or develop a more effective, more useful instrument.

Benchmarking

The instructors reviewed student critique forms from educational institutions in the Dayton area to obtain useful data. This process, known as benchmarking, helps organizations identify and emulate the best in their class. Instruments from a local community college, a university, and the Air Force Institute of Technology were reviewed. A consensus instrument, which increased the number of substantive areas requiring student evaluation, was developed and tested. Using a Likert-type scale ranging from poor to excellent, the critique responses became readily quantifiable, producing numerical values that, among other things, identified an overall customer satisfaction rating.

Thus, quantifiable data were available to begin measuring processes. Statistical process control (SPC), which is a collection of statistical and analytical tools used for continuous improvement of critical process characteristics, was available to the teams, but its specific applicability was not necessarily understood by individual members. Initially, the teams hand calculated and charted one statistic: overall customer satisfaction. But this was tedious, considered additional work, and resented. In an effort to make their lives more pleasant, one instructor introduced the staff to spreadsheet software as a labor-saving device. Another applied the data to a graphics software package, developing run charts that could be used to monitor any of the 21 individual items from the critiques.

Figure 1. **Managers' course.**

It was serendipity at its best when the first run chart printed by the computer showed variation in customer satisfaction when new instructors were introduced, and a continued downward trend for the five classes (see Figure 1). Through analysis, the instructors identified a change they had introduced into their training process at the start of the downward trend as the potential cause of the decreasing level of customer satisfaction. They reviewed the comments sections of the applicable student critiques and confirmed their hypothesis. The area of dissatisfaction was related to their newly implemented change. They adjusted their activity, monitored it over the next seven classes, and discovered a corresponding improvement in student satisfaction. Thus they learned that SPC can be used to improve customer satisfaction.

Departmental Task Analysis

One of the primary responsibilities for a team using TQM is identifying its customers' requirements. But in the training environment, who are the customers? The initial assumption was that the student was the primary customer, with feedback required from the organization to determine if what was taught was being applied in the office.

In addition to the critiques previously discussed, surveys were sent to both managers and graduates asking whether the students had been able to effectively implement the training provided. The assumption was that these surveys would help the instructors better understand the effectiveness of the training and would indicate the level of customer satisfaction. In reality, the responses were not helpful in defining customer needs.

To counter this deficiency, the center staff (including the administrative support team) was led through an exercise developed by Boeing Aerospace Company, known as departmental task analysis (DTA).[10] DTA is a systematic organizational review that focuses the staff on answering the following questions:

- Who are we?
- Whom do we serve?
- Who supplies us?

As a result, the center staff rewrote the mission statement, redetermined the organizational responsibilities, redefined the primary customers as the organizations of AFLC and the secondary customers as the students and employees of AFLC, and proposed a feedback process to ensure that continued improvement took place.

Quality Function Deployment

Identifying the organization as the primary customer and the trained student as a value-added TQM resource led the instructors to review the question "Are the customers' needs being met?" Traditional surveys ask the customer "Are you satisfied?" The alternative is incorporating QFD into DTA, which asks "What do you need?"[11,12] QFD is a planning tool with a primary goal of overcoming a disregard for customer requirements. In QFD, cross-functional teams are used to facilitate communication between customer wishes and functional responsibilities. It is essentially a series of matrixes that translate customers' needs into behaviors, behaviors into objectives, and objectives into course content.

To accomplish this, nine managers from several customer organizations were asked to assist the center staff by defining what they thought they needed in relation to TQM from a student who completed center training. They translated these needs into behaviors and objectives, and the team members compared them with those being taught. They found an approximate 20% mismatch, which required readjustment in the course objectives to meet the stated customer needs. The instructors then adjusted the content to meet customer needs.

Process Evaluation

The feedback process chosen to ensure continuous improvement was developed by the AFLC inspection team. The command leadership was refocusing its mission to embrace TQM and recognized that quality cannot be inspected into a product or service. This led to a change in the inspection philosophy, transferring the responsibility for quality assurance from the inspectors to the process owners. Empowered employees must ensure the ongoing quality of their processes.

The command leadership was refocusing its mission to embrace TQM and recognized that quality cannot be inspected into a product or service.

The process evaluation checklist is a set of questions for any process owner wanting to establish continuous improvement methods. It focuses on identifying the requirements of all internal and external customers, methods of measurement to ensure continuous improvement, benchmarking, and flowcharting. Applied as a test in one of the center courses, it provided a road map of steps to ensure continuous improvement.

The teams used flowcharting, an integral part of process evaluation, to identify the flow, or order, of operations through each process. Process flowcharts identify which operations depend on the successful completion of earlier operations. Problems found in the end product can be traced back, through data collection and statistical analysis, to identify those operations in the flow where unacceptable levels of variation were introduced. Additionally, non-value-added steps can then be identified and removed. Thus, classroom setup time was identified as being haphazard, without standardized processes and requirements, and varied significantly within courses. This caused problems with the availability of student materials, teaching aids, and instructors. In addition, the instructors saw themselves as internal customers whose needs were not being met. As a result, they redefined their requirements, redesigned the processes, and set up measures to ensure the reworked processes would be monitored for continuous improvement.

When processes that required improvement were identified, it became necessary to prioritize them. Initially, the instructors tended to respond by paying attention to the process they felt was more important or more easily accomplished or fixed. In TQM, however, the customer's identification of concerns should determine the priority of efforts. After collecting six months' worth of customer comments from the student critiques, the instructors developed Pareto charts, an SPC tool that helps establish which subprocesses offer the greatest potential for return on investment (see Figure 2). This allowed them to display, in the order of importance, the sources their students identified as contributors to process problems. The instructors defined actions that would improve these processes, formulating the basis of the team's management plan. Successful improvement in the top three areas of customer

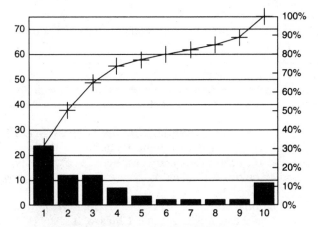

1. Provide more role playing, practice, and definition
2. Improve organization of materials, directions, and objectives
3. Improve quality of handouts, overheads, and student guides
4. Place less emphasis on how-tos of presentations
5. Use more films
6. Do not use Massey videotape (a film containing offensive language)
7. Offer class for company leaders
8. Do not repeat material from previous classes
9. Increase length of course
10. All other responses

Figure 2. **Facilitator Pareto chart.**

concern during the next year will directly affect 66% of their students' identified concerns.

Continuous Improving

Institutionalizing continuous improvement is the main objective of process evaluation. As trainers, the instructors learned to walk the talk. As team members, they accepted the responsibility as well as the authority to manage their processes. They return continually to the question "What are the customers' requirements?" They constantly measure their processes and learn new ways to apply TQM concepts and tools. Now they are being benchmarked by their students, other managers, and newer "quality training schools" in the federal government. They have participated in a changing culture in the military bureaucracy, and they recognize that they have only scratched the surface.

Cascading in the training process is possible. Emulating the training program developed by Xerox Corporation requires educators and trainers to define customer requirements. Continuous improvement principles can be institutionalized in all types of organizational training. It requires training professionals at all levels to intercept and integrate changing ideas, not training processes. The development of quality training processes is reiterative. To paraphrase Ishikawa: Quality begins and ends with training.[13]

References

1. Patricia A. Galagan, "David T. Kearns: A CEO's View of Training," *Training and Development Journal,* May 1990, p. 42.
2. Masaaki Imai, *Kaizen* (New York, NY: Random House, 1986).
3. W. Edwards Deming, *Out of the Crisis* (Cambridge, MA: Massachusetts Institute of Technology Center for Advanced Engineering Study, 1986), pp. 149–155.
4. James B. Treece, "New Taurus, New Sable, Old Blueprint," *Business Week,* September 1991, p. 43.
5. Brad Stratton, "A Beacon for the World," *Quality Progress,* May 1990, pp. 60–65.
6. "1991 Presidential Award for Quality and Productivity Improvement," a letter from President George Bush to Secretary of Defense Dick Cheney, May 31, 1991.
7. Suzanne Axland, "Looking for a Quality Education?" *Quality Progress,* October 1991, p. 61.
8. "Third Annual National Forum on Health Care Quality," Joint Commission on Accreditation of Healthcare Organizations, Chicago, IL, Nov. 1–2, 1990.
9. Robert K. Zentmyer and James A. Zimble, "The Journey From Bureaucracy to TQM," *Quality Progress,* September 1991, pp. 61–66.
10. "Total Quality Improvement: A Resource Guide to Management Involvement," Boeing Aerospace Company, 1987.
11. Lawrence P. Sullivan, "Policy Management Through QFD," *Quality Progress,* June 1988, p. 18.
12. Andrew A. Kenney, "A New Paradigm for QA," *Quality Progress,* June 1988, p. 30.
13. Kaoru Ishikawa, *What is Quality Control? The Japanese Way* (Clifton, NJ: Prentice-Hall Publishing Co., 1985).

Gerard R. Tuttle is a colonel in the United States Air Force and director of academic plans and policy at the National Defense University in Ft. McNair, Washington, DC.

BENCHMARKING

Benchmarking: An Overview

Calhoun W. Wick and Lu Stanton León

This excerpt from a chapter in Wick and León's new book, The Learning Edge, *provides a practical review of what benchmarking is and how companies may effectively use it to gain competitive advantage.*

Benchmarking is an eye-opener. Goodloe Suttler, a general manager at Analog Devices, was one of 25 senior managers from five companies who were assigned to create a Center for Quality Management in Boston. Suttler says that during that 5-week assignment, the time he spent observing outstanding companies lit a fire under his learning.

"I learned more in that 5-week period than I had learned in the previous several years, at least with respect to some of the quality management issues. It was an intense learning experience that has helped me formulate an agenda not only for how this division should run but how the corporation should run, too," Suttler said.

"We thought we had done pretty good," he continued, and then we went out and saw some of these Deming and Baldrige prize winners and we were just blown away by what they had done. The practices that we observed both in Japan and the United States were incredibly motivating and moving. After I came back, I had enough to propel myself for several years."

Reprinted with permission from Calhoun W. Wick and Lu Stanton León, *The Learning Edge: How Smart Managers and Smart Companies Stay Ahead*, New York: McGraw-Hill, Inc., 1993.

Benchmarking Defined

Robert C. Camp, a leading advocate of benchmarking, defines it as "the search for industry best practices that lead to superior performance."[19] The idea is to use the best to become the best.

As it applies to your learning plan, we define benchmarking as seeking out people or organizations who are the best in their field and putting their knowledge to work for you. Again, using the best to become the best.

Benchmarking's popularity is due, in part, to the Malcolm Baldrige National Quality Award, which requires that all entries benchmark. But its growth is more directly due to fierce global competition that forces companies and individuals to seek out the best, wherever it may be, and, when possible, adapt it to their situation.

The word benchmarking originally was used as a surveyor's term, referring to a point of reference. Xerox Corporation is credited with popularizing the term in the business world in 1980 when it was used to describe a quality program at the company.

Then in 1982, Xerox's match up with L. L. Bean, a Maine-based retailer, became the first benchmarking case to gain national attention. Xerox was searching for ways to boost productivity in its logistics and distribution unit and looked to L. L. Bean as a model of excellence. The result was a 10 percent gain in warehouse productivity, 3 to 5 percent of which Xerox attributes directly to studying Bean.

"What is fundamental is recognizing that benchmarking involves uncovering best practices wherever they exist," Camp says.s1 Wherever includes one's own organization, competitors, and organizations in totally different fields.

That kind of cross-pollination makes for odd couples. Who would have foreseen Xerox pairing up with a sporting goods retailer? Or Motorola benchmarking with Domino's Pizza in its effort to reduce cycle time between order receipt and delivery of its cellular telephones?

Many of the largest companies in America have some kind of benchmarking program in place. Books have been written on it, magazine and newspaper articles debate its virtues. Consultants scramble to help with its implementation.

> We define benchmarking as seeking out people or organizations who are the best in their field and putting their knowledge to work for you.

Benchmarking for Individuals

While benchmarking most often is used to identify best-in-class organizational practices, we have found that it can easily be adapted to provide a powerful tool in helping individual managers choose and achieve learning goals. You can use it to promote your own learning or, as a senior manager, to accelerate the learning of your organization.

Managers and organizations need to benchmark how much their counterparts know and the rate at which they are learning. If they discover someone else is outlearning them, they need to find ways to increase the rate of their own learning.

By benchmarking the abilities of counterparts at major competitors, you'll gain insight into what you should be learning and where you stand in relationship to others in your field. By benchmarking best practices in your own company, you take advantage of information that's easily available. By looking across entirely different fields, you get a more complete picture of what is currently the best and what tomorrow's best will be. Problems and insights know no occupational boundaries.

Opening Your Eyes to New Ideas

Theresa Eyre, education manager at Hewlett-Packard, said benchmarking has given her company "a different sense of what is possible as an organization."

"We were interested in understanding more about how the roles of managers, particularly middle managers, were changing in complex organizations," Eyre said. "We had read a lot about the new management roles, but we hadn't seen a lot of change in what our managers actually did at work. So we sent teams of middle managers to talk with their peers in other companies about how their jobs were changing."

Benchmarking helped Hewlett-Packard's middle managers in Cupertino, California, see other management models. "Because Hewlett-Packard is recognized for its successful management practices, it is tempting to believe that our way of doing things is the right way," Eyre said, "yet our success depends on our ability to continue to improve."

At Hewlett-Packard, benchmarking and learning go hand-in-hand. "Benchmarking management practices is an important component of our overall management-executive development process," Eyre said.

Typically, the company sends teams of two to four managers to meet with peers in other companies to exchange ideas about leadership and organizational practices. After the visits, the benchmarking teams exchange observations.

"We encourage the managers to look for ways to generalize beyond their specific observations, such as what conclusions can they draw about leadership in general? Then we encourage them to examine their own practices relative to these conclusions," Eyre said. "Benchmarking can help managers develop concrete mental pictures of people doing things that may be different from how we do things here."

Admitting You Don't Know It All

The most difficult part of benchmarking is recognizing that you don't know it all. American companies, particularly those seen as industry leaders, have difficulty entertaining the possibility that they can learn something from a competitor or another organization.

"The idea that somebody out there might be better is a tough thing to come to grips with. Overcoming that myopia is very, very important," Camp says.

If you want to become the best, or stay the best, you have to know not only what your competitors are up to, but where to find the best business practices, wherever they exist.

Benchmarking can be awe-inspiring. "I think that at some level, when you are there on the benchmarking trip, it can be overwhelming," Eyre said. "You feel like 'Oh my gosh. There is all this out there that I never knew about or that I never gave credibility to before.' "

Kay Whitmore, chief executive officer of Eastman Kodak, says that being a globally successful company can make benchmarking more difficult. But being aware of external best practices is a must if a company wants to remain on top. He explained:

"One of our burdens at Eastman Kodak is that we have been very successful for a very long time. That has given us some habits and cultural entities that were an advantage at one time but, as the world changed, became disadvantages.

"In my mind, some of the more successful companies are those who walked right up to the edge of disaster and said there are two choices: over the edge or change. And they changed. Companies that have not been forced right to that edge are slower to change.

"Right now, in certain businesses, we have been pressed to the edge. Getting us to change was a problem, so we said 'benchmark.' "

Getting started wasn't easy because the company had such a high opinion of itself. Whitmore gave this example:

"I asked the managers, 'How good are you?'

"They answered, 'Well, we're really great.'

"So I said, 'How do you know?'

"And they said, 'Well, we've always been great so we'll always be great and we just know that.'

"Then I said, 'Let's benchmark.'

"They replied, 'Yes, we'll go call somebody and check.'

"Then they go through the motions of looking like they are benchmarking when in fact they are not."

Instead, explained Whitmore, they just seek to reaffirm their own superiority. He speculates that the problem stems from a desire to create rather than adopt. "As a company, we have taken the 'not invented here' syndrome to a rather high art," he said, meaning that if it's not invented at Kodak, they don't think it worthwhile. "And I don't think we're distinctive in that."

When a company is very good at what it does, the problem often is how to make managers recognize that another company may do it better, and then learn from them. Because managers at Kodak weren't ready to take that leap, the company decided to benchmark internally first. (See Exhibit 1.)

Other companies have a completely different mentality. Compare the mindset at Kodak to that of Corning, where a vice president of quality said, "We will 'steal' any idea we can," meaning they are willing to adopt best practices from any source. Then he used the example of needing to improve Corning's process quality. They found that Westinghouse already had done a significant amount of work in that area and had a great program to do it.

"We just went out and bought it from them, which probably saved us 24 months of trying to invent our own, plus people's time. So it's better than we could have produced, and we're getting it 18 months to 2 years before we could have produced it ourselves."

Apple Found the Truth Hard to Swallow

In 1990 Apple Computer Inc. found out the hard way that they had been surpassed by a competitor. After the company introduced its first portable computer, weighing in at a hefty 18 pounds, Compaq Computer Corporation came out with a 6-pound notebook machine.

"We took it apart and we were stunned because we realized that Apple couldn't make anything similar," one Apple Executive told *The New York Times*.[23]

Although belatedly, they learned. In late 1991 Apple introduced its notebook computer, priced beginning at $2,295 and weighing from 5.1 to 6.8 pounds.

KODAK CLASS: INTERNAL BENCHMARKING

Being a very large company with many divisions and sections, Kodak believed that they did most things quite well somewhere in the company, but quality wasn't uniform. Whitmore tells what happened:

"Take an example out of manufacturing. We spool Kodacolor film in lots of different places. Some places we do that at higher quality and lower cost than we do at other places.

"So we can do some internal benchmarking. We have a thing called Kodak Class in which we go around and look at the Kodak world. We get some very tight parameters on how to measure quality and cost effectiveness. Then we provide that data for all locations. It shows where somebody does it better than somebody else.

"Benchmarking internally has gotten people started. It's been a methodology of first, 'How do I learn from locations inside the company?' and then, 'How do I learn from an organization external to the company?'

"It's the way you become world-class. If you are to be competitive long-term, you've got to do most things as well as anybody in the world, and you've got to do a few things better.

"We still assume we know everything there is to know about photography. If it is important to think about, we would have thought about it. So if somebody else thought about it, it must not be very important because we didn't think about it first.

"There is an arrogance in the learning sense of a successful organization that is really difficult to get past."

Exhibit 1. **Eastman Kodak uses internal benchmarking to speed organizational learning.**

And Compaq Almost Choked on It

At the same time, Compaq was facing its own problems. Success had made the company smug. Additionally, Compaq was focusing on the wrong competitor as 'best in class.'

In 1991, Compaq saw its shares drop from nearly $75 to about $26 as its market share fell and domestic sales stalled. Late in the year Eckhard Pfeiffer, who was named chief executive after a management upheaval, told *The New York Times* that Compaq had been blinded by past success.

> "The company had been so successful over the past nine years that there hadn't been any doubt that the success formula was working, but it masked, in a way, the changes that were happening. The company failed to recognize the changes necessary to cope with the environment of the 1990's. . . .
>
> "One other major flaw . . . was our almost exclusive focus on I.B.M. You know, 'I.B.M. did this and how can we outdo them, how do we make it better, faster?' It was our total focus. The addition of second-tier pricing wasn't welcome because it deviated from that focus. We didn't recognize who the new competition would be."
>
> That competition came from the upstarts like Dell, CompuAdd, and AST Research, and companies that didn't even register on Compaq's radar screens, like Northgate and Gateway 2000. A telling example was in the nearly simultaneous product announcements from Dell, AST, and Compaq the week before Compaq's upheaval.
>
> Compaq introduced an 18-pound color portable that needs to be plugged into an outlet and costs $10,000. Dell and AST introduced 7-pound color portables that run on batteries and cost $5,000.

Compaq had been exclusively benchmarking with the wrong competitor. By contrast, when Ted Hutton took over as president and CEO of Baltimore-based Waverly, Inc., a publishing and printing firm, he assumed he had a lot to learn. He made it a point to benchmark against as many competitors as possible and cull whatever knowledge he could.

"I found it very valuable to interview competitors," Hutton said. "Most of the time your competitors will be reasonably honest. In some businesses that's not possible because there is cutthroat competition."

The Benchmarking Process

We use a modified version of the benchmarking process described in Camp's *Benchmarking*.

1. *Brainstorm what you need to learn.* You need to identify: what is important to your company's success in the next 2 to 3 years; what proficiencies you will need for success in the company as it will become.

2. *Identify the best.* Studying a mediocre company or individual wastes time and results in lowering your expectations rather than lifting them. Equally

disastrous is concentrating on the wrong company. The Compaq Computer Corporation example described earlier in this chapter offers a case in point.

Be creative in searching for best practices and who the best really is. It isn't necessary to go to large companies. Thom Harvey, CEO of Harvey & Harvey, Inc., the waste management company, benchmarked with George Clement, CEO of Clement Communications, to learn the best way to build a senior management team. In return, Clement benchmarked with Harvey to learn better ways to handle the disposal of chemicals used at his manufacturing plant.

Be creative in searching for best practices and who the best really is.

3. *Discover everything you can about the company or individual you are studying. Never try to wing it. Keep your specific goal in mind.* You can choose one of many processes for benchmarking investigations. The object is to gather as much information as possible, remembering to keep it goal-specific. Eyre, at Hewlett-Packard, said that keeping a focus is crucial.

    "It's almost too challenging of an experience to go into a company for a couple of hours or a day and expect to learn everything about the way they do business," she said. "So I think putting some structure on it and being clear on what you want to learn is important.

    "Our managers return from benchmarking trips with a wealth of new ideas and are excited about sharing them. Yet, without clear focus, the benefits may be limited to hearing some interesting stories about how things are different in another company."

    The key for encouraging organizational learning, Eyre said, is to work with the managers to establish goals and a method of reporting their findings back to their peers. That way, their benchmarking visits are more focused and key learnings are better defined.

    If you are benchmarking with an individual, you should read everything you can about the person and the job he or she holds. Then arrange for an interview. Make it clear that the other person also will benefit from the exchange. Think through what you have to offer the other person, not only not only as a way to convince them to participate but to make the person feel they've gained something of value.

    Camp writes that "It has been found from experience that the basic willingness to share—provided the information is not proprietary or confidential—is based on a mutual desire to uncover and understand industry best practices." You have your professional experience and judgment to offer.

    If your benchmarking culminates with an interview or an on-site visit, do as much homework as possible. Sources of information include magazine and newspaper articles, professional publications, annual reports, and internal publications such as newsletters. You also may want to talk to analysts who keep track of particular companies.

    Also prepare a package of materials about yourself or your company, depending on whether you are benchmarking as an individual or an organization. Provide this package to your benchmarking counterpart ahead of time so that they, too, can expect to learn something about you and from you.

4. *Calculate the performance gap and how you can benefit from what you have discovered.* At this point in the process, you have gathered all of your information, made an on-site visit, if applicable, and are ready to analyze what you discovered.

   There are times when you will realize that you outperform the person or organization being benchmarked. But because your purpose was to learn from someone else, usually you will find a negative performance gap. To close that gap, you must study what you have observed. What procedures or ideas can you adapt to your own work?

   At Hewlett-Packard, benchmarking benefits to managers have been obvious. Eyre said:

   "The individual managers who participate in the benchmarking trips find the experience highly developmental. It gives the managers new ideas about what is possible.

   "Part of what I believe, and what studies have shown in the past, is that expertise is really just a collection of experiences. It's just building for yourself a very rich repertoire of experience from which you can draw.

   "I think that benchmarking can accelerate the development of this repertoire and you can build it faster by building it deliberately."

5. *Have a clear idea of how you'll use your findings. Develop and implement action steps to close the gap and put your new knowledge to use.* You should give this step some thought before you begin benchmarking. Discovering best practices may be exhilarating, but unless you have a plan to put your new knowledge to use, it remains a mental exercise. Write out your action steps, being as specific as possible. When listing each step, identify what consequences you anticipate. Be clear about what you want to get out of it. Erye, of Hewlett-Packard, said this is a step that often is shortchanged: "When you are benchmarking, you need to think through what you want to do with the information when you get back."

6. *Actually use the information you have gained.* Goodloe Suttler offers a good example from Analog Devices. When he went to benchmark with Florida Power & Light, Suttler was impressed with how they presented their quality improvement stories on 3 × 5 boards that were like displays at a state fair. In a step-by-step process, you could see the entire story, from the problem to the analysis to the solution. He said:

   "We came up with a format that is on a metallic magnetic board so that we can add these nice story boards for the teams that go out and pick off a problem and solve that problem.

   "We're trying to get out the idea that here is the process by which you solve classic cross-functional departmental problems. Here is the way by which you institute process control, and here is an example less than 3 days old as to how to do that, who did it, and who team members were.

"So it provides recognition. It provides a kind of closure on the process. And it spruces up the factory because it's a nice board. Quality story boards were a very specific thing I got out of Florida Power & Light that we are instituting here."

Calhoun W. Wick is president and founder of Wick & Co., a Wilmington, Delaware-based research and consulting firm specializing in executive and leadership development. Lu Stanton León is a writer, editor, and journalist.

Linking Strategic Thinking with Benchmarking

Gregory H. Watson

Not only can firms use benchmarking as a tool to enhance business processes, it is also a useful concept for improving business strategy. This excerpt from the new book by Gregory H. Watson explains benchmarking and its value in strategic planning.

Benchmarking involves the application of process benchmarking techniques and methods to the development of an increased understanding of strategic business issues, with the cooperation of companies that participate in long-term business alliances. Bill Lehman, managing partner of the Price Waterhouse Manufacturing Management Consulting Practice, has observed that strategic benchmarking is similar, in application, to benchmarking of operational processes, but it is different in scope. "Armed with this [strategic benchmarking] information, the process of developing a vision of the changed organization can be very rich indeed."

What issues are addressed by strategic benchmarking as opposed to "operational" benchmarking? Among the issues are: building core competencies that will help to sustain competitive advantage; targeting a specific shift in strategy, such as entering new markets or developing new products; developing a new line of business or making an acquisition; and creating an organization that is more capable of learning how to respond in an uncertain future because it has increased its acceptance of change.

In the mid-1980s, when Jack Welch, a forward-thinking CEO of General Electric, wanted to position his company for the coming decade, he asked his strategic planning group to study how successful companies positioned themselves for continuous improvement. The General Electric benchmarking team conducted internal interviews of leading GE divisions and visited nine companies in the United States and Japan. They found that the companies that had set aggressive goals (such as halving the product development cycle time, or tripling the level of productivity) had high levels of sustained improvement. These leading companies viewed productivity as a combined issue of customer satisfaction and competitiveness. The benchmarking team also observed a common approach to change: driven by top-down changes in the

> These leading companies viewed productivity as a combined issue of customer satisfaction and competitiveness.

management system, the emphasis was on process rather than on programs (or, in their words, input over output). The conclusion of the study provided an operating definition of a company that is a world-class competitor:

- Knows its processes better than its competitors know their processes;
- Knows the industry competitors better than its competitors know them;
- Knows its customers better than its competitors know their customers;
- Responds more rapidly to customer behavior than do competitors;
- Uses employees more effectively than do competitors;
- Competes for market share on a customer-by-customer basis.

Aside from its interesting observations, why is this particular GE study significant? Note its parallels to the earlier discussion of core competence and process capability. GE applied benchmarking in the area of strategy to address the same basic issues, and the GE results reinforce the need for an integrated approach to understanding competition, in order to satisfy customers in the long run. In its approach to benchmarking, GE observed the change in strategic direction and company culture (values and vision) over a three-year period. Each of its benchmarking partners joined the study for the long haul. They participated by allowing the GE interviewers to visit multiple facilities over the duration of the study. The study was, in effect, an extension of GE's approach to forming strategic alliances with technological partners by seeking strategic partners who could help GE learn the lessons of adaptation for the future. A final interesting observation is that the GE study was directed out of the strategic planning function, which clearly illustrates the contribution of benchmarking for developing long-range plans.

Strategic Benchmarking as an Element of Planning

The job of planning is to take into account the uncertainties of the future and make preparations that will carry the organization through that time, especially by setting achievable goals that will bridge to the future. How can challenging, yet achievable goals be set to direct an organization's vision of the future? One lesson that needs to be learned is that the different stakeholders in the organization—customers, stock analysts, employees, and management—have different perspectives and values for making their judgments about its goodness. All share a common perspective in wanting the organization to continue to improve and create value for them. This requires the organization to learn how to adapt to a changing environment faster and more effectively than its competitors will. In an article on performance measures, Robert S. Kaplan and David P. Norton observe that benchmarking is a technique that companies use to set goals based on external standards: "[T]he company looks to one industry to find, say the best distribution system, to another industry for the lowest cost payroll process, and then forms a composite of those best practices to set objectives for its own performance." This is the essence of strategic benchmarking and the link to a company's planning process. Companies selected for benchmarking because of their key business process knowledge and performance indexes can serve as a basis for establishing challenging, yet realistic and achievable goals. When John Young was driving Hewlett-Packard toward tenfold improvement of its hardware reliability during the 1980s, he encouraged management not to think "the same old way." He deliberately chose goals to stretch the organization—to challenge it to do things differently. The goals were out of the reach of its current process capability so that it could not finesse a goal by doing things the "same old way." Change was necessary or it wouldn't be able to meet the goal. Roger Milliken has observed: "Insanity is doing the same thing the same way and expecting a different result."

What is the process for applying strategic benchmarking to a company's planning process? This activity tends to be a staff function, as the GE example indicated; it supports the development of objectives by the senior staff, and guides the selection of appropriate goals during the catchball with middle management. A process flow of planning considerations illustrates how strategic benchmarking fits into the development of the strategic plan (see Figure 1) and then flows into annual or functional plans. Note that head-to-head comparisons are made between the company's own strategy and that of

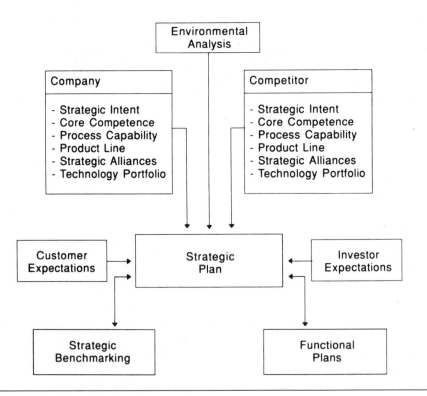

Figure 1. **The application of strategic benchmarking.**

the major competitor. In addition, customer expectations and investor expectations must be factored into the strategic plan along with an environmental analysis (considerations from government regulations, technology developments, economic conditions, and similar factors). Strategic benchmarking studies address particular issues in the strategic plan: development of organizational infrastructure, establishment of goals and objectives, selection of key business processes for improvement, identification of technology areas targeted for development, and so on. The scope of the strategic benchmarking study is established by the senior management team, but the method for conducting the study is the same as for all process benchmarking studies.

Influencing a Plan for the Future

A company that is developing its strategic approach to benchmarking should consider establishing long-standing relationships with a limited number of companies that will serve as a network for sharing strategic direction and methodology. A company should consider its natural alliances as a starting point for developing a small number of strategic partners. (GE used nine companies and planned to increase it to no more than 16.) The natural alliances include those with customers (major accounts and product distribution channels, in particular), suppliers (preferred suppliers, in particular), stockholders (major institutional stockholders or companies with large interests), strategic alliances (companies in which the benchmarking company holds a significant interest, or with which it has technology, patent-sharing, manufacturing, or OEM agreements). These companies may be supplemented by others that have earned management admiration for their business performance. No matter how the initial list of companies is formed, it is important to establish a set of objective selection criteria, in order to identify the companies that have the best possible long-term contribution toward understanding of strategic alternatives. This use of networks, alliances, or even "good friends" permits the influence of a consistent external perspective in the process of developing strategic direction.

External perspective is a value normally described for external members of a company's board of directors. Strategic benchmarking studies are based on facts culled from direct observation within the context of the organization's own problem; the members of the board of directors must rely on recollections of personal experiences, and these, most probably, are restricted to conditions that are different from those facing the current management team. The external board of directors can apply seasoned judgment to a particular situation, but the strategic benchmarking study can complement this judgment with a solid factual basis, providing "fodder" for the debate on which directions to set.

The stakeholders in a company have a right to understand and influence the direction of that company. Stakeholders are stockholders, industry analysts, customers, employees, managers, and, like it or not, the government—local, state, and federal. The most active participants in the stakeholder role of advisers to management tend to be the community of investors, customers, and employees. These groups share a common trait: "Everyone is a volunteer." None of these groups has to invest its energy or resources into the organization; each has a choice of where it will invest, purchase, or work. The volunteers must be convinced that they should "re-enlist" as participants in the company's future. The bridge to the future is in the lessons that an organization learns today and in its ability to apply the lessons rapidly for growth in the future. Core competencies and process capabilities may be invisible to the external stakeholders, but their importance is fundamental to their best interests. Communicating the lessons learned from a company's overall learning strategy is essential; all stakeholders will then understand the strategic direction, and the organization can align its goals in a congruent manner. However, the ability to satisfy the various stakeholders of the company is only as great as the company's ability to internalize the lessons of benchmarking.

Gregory H. Watson is the Vice President, Quality, Office Document Products Division of the Xerox Corporation. He is the author of three other books on benchmarking.

How to Build a Benchmarking Team

Michael J. Spendolini

How do you select a team to undertake benchmarking in your organization and make sure the information they find results in improvement of your processes? This article, written by the author of The Benchmarking Book *(AMACOM, 1992), addresses this question with specific, practical, how-to advice.*

There is nothing that can wreck a well-intentioned benchmarking plan faster than selecting the wrong people for the team. Take the company that chose staff members who didn't have enough credibility within the organization to sell their benchmarking team's recommendations to senior management. The team did an excellent job, but without the clout to get their recommendations approved, their efforts failed.

One of the primary factors that has contributed to the success of the benchmarking efforts in such organizations as Xerox Corp., AT&T Co., Motorola Inc., and Milliken & Co., Inc. is the careful selection, training, and help given to employees who perform benchmarking activities. As a recent study we conducted of 23 U.S. best-practice benchmarking companies demonstrated, these firms know that the long-term value of benchmarking as a useful and practical tool depends on attracting effective benchmarkers and making sure that they are successful with this process so that they will repeat it themselves and attract other effective benchmarkers through positive word-of-mouth.

What Type of Team?

Although individuals can benchmark effectively, most benchmarking is done by teams to take advantage of the diversity of knowledge, skills, and perspectives that groups offer, as well as to balance workload and time requirements. Various types of teams have produced valuable benchmarking results.

The most typical is the *intact work group*, composed of a manager and a number of direct reports. These teams usually benchmark topics that are directly under their control and reflect their primary area of responsibility. The main advantage of this type of team is the close linkage of benchmarking activities to their normal work environment and job responsibilities.

Reprinted with permission from Journal of Business Strategy, March/April 1993, Faulkner & Gray, Inc., New York, NY.

Cross-functional teams usually include representatives from such functions as manufacturing, engineering, and finance that have a stake in the product or process being benchmarked. A team that benchmarked methods to reduce overall cycle time for new product development, for example, was made up of representatives from strategic planning, engineering, manufacturing, finance, and marketing.

Functional teams usually include individuals from a single function such as finance or human resources, but representing, perhaps, different locations or divisions. For example, a Xerox engineering benchmarking team included engineering representatives from two domestic divisions as well as representatives from the Fuji Xerox affiliate in Japan. These types of teams can benchmark activities that are common across their own internal business segments while taking advantage of internal diversity and geographical proximity to their benchmark partners.

Most benchmarking teams employ simple divisions of labor that allow some individuals to focus on data collection and analysis and others on such specific tasks as team leader, process mentor, and data analyst or compiler. In many benchmarking teams, the team's senior manager takes on the leader's responsibilities. On teams composed of peers (with respect to grade level), leadership responsibilities are often assigned either by a senior manager outside of the team or by team members themselves. Other teams rely on volunteers to fill key roles, or they may rotate assignments based on some agreed-upon schedule.

Most benchmarking teams employ simple divisions of labor.

How Many Players?

The size of benchmarking teams varies. However, for many experienced benchmarking organizations, the average size seems to be about six, with the range generally between three (more common in smaller organizations) and ten. Six is the average because it ensures a good cross section of skills and abilities while balancing the overall workload. Also, if one member of the team should be absent, there are still enough team members remaining to keep the process going.

This number is also desirable when the results of benchmarking interviews are being reviewed. With a manageable number of team members, each person has enough time to discuss in detail what he or she has learned from each benchmark partner. When teams get too large, the level of qualitative review and analysis by individual team members decreases proportionately, often rendering the analysis too superficial. Finally, the logistics and the expense of managing large teams of benchmarkers often makes the process difficult to manage and prohibitively expensive.

What Types of Players?

What are the most desirable traits team members should have? Our respondents' answers varied, but five characteristics were almost always identified. Obviously, not every team member will have a high level of each of these

STRIKING A DEAL

In the past, many companies agreed to be benchmarked out of professional courtesy. But as more and more companies turn to benchmarking, they are beginning to see the value in providing access as a *quid pro quo*. Negotiations and counter-proposals are getting much more common, and savvy benchmarking candidates are beginning to say, "What's in it for me?" Conversely, experienced benchmarkers with something to offer are aggressively marketing themselves to prospects. Negotiating for fees, which runs counter to the spirit of benchmarking, is frowned upon. But chances are you'll have to offer a benchmarking candidate something in return for opening up his business to you. Here's a range of options:

Show and tell. At the very least, be willing to share your reasons for choosing a prospect. Review your strategy and explain your shortcomings and goals in the area you're benchmarking. It won't end up costing you much and will give the other company a context for its expertise.

Value added. Offer to prepare a report of your investigation, including what you learned from any of the other companies you benchmarked. You don't necessarily have to name names, but you should identify the larger trends in the area of study. This will give benchmarkers something tangible in return for their input.

You've got a friend. Offer reciprocal access to an area of your company related to the one you're benchmarking. If you delve into one firm's bonus plans, open the doors to your salary structure.

Carte blanche. This is the most liberal option—offering reciprocal access to any area of your company. But match strength for strength. For example, if you're known for robotics, but desperately want to study another firm's marketing strategies, offer access to your state-of-the-art factories.

Whichever option you choose, know what you're willing to give up before approaching anyone. And don't look at this only from one side of the table. If a company approaches you for permission to benchmark, see what you can get in return. Maybe you'll learn something.

---

characteristics. However, the key for a successful team is to achieve a balance among team members.

Functional Expertise Effective benchmarkers represent the best and the brightest from your organization in terms of the process being benchmarked. Not only do these individuals know the right questions, they can also interpret responses from benchmark partners. Highly skilled benchmarkers can make distinctions between information that is simply "different," information that may represent an improvement opportunity for your organization, and information that may represent valid best-practices insight.

In addition, companies often ask to discuss benchmarking subjects with the best representatives they can find in other organizations. It is, therefore, important that you match experience and expertise with your benchmark partners, especially if they are interested in information about your organization. New or inexperienced individuals generally won't ask the best follow-up questions, nor will they be able to control the pace and focus of interviews with more experienced individuals. As one benchmarker from AT&T remarked, "Benchmarking is not a process to give new people a learning experience; it is an opportunity to have your best employees talk to their most able counterparts in an effort to transfer knowledge from one organizational environment to another."

Internal Credibility: Because many of the recommendations produced from a benchmarking investigation represent significant changes and departures from the status quo, the individuals presenting this information and proposing change should be well respected *within* the organization. Although benchmarking findings and recommendations should be judged on their own merits, not on the merits of those delivering the message, successful benchmarkers are often internal opinion leaders, which means a benchmarking recommendation from them is likely to be taken seriously.

Communications Skills: Effective speaking skills ensure that questions are presented clearly and succinctly to the benchmark partner. In many cases, complex subjects have to be discussed with relative strangers over the telephone. Only a skilled interviewer can ask questions clearly and answer questions thoroughly and accurately.

The effective benchmarker must also be a good listener. A benchmarker from Boeing estimated that the typical benchmarking interview was about 25% speaking and 75% listening. Unfortunately, many effective speakers are not effective listeners. Given that, and the fact that tape recorders may not be permitted in certain situations, it's useful if the benchmarker is an effective note-taker during both telephone and live interviews.

Effective Group Interaction Skills: The effective benchmarker needs to interact as a team member, often with other individuals who are not members of his or her natural work team. Often, this relationship goes on for months at a time in locations removed from the normal work environment. Benchmarkers need to be able to work as a team under these types of circumstances and demonstrate high levels of group interaction skills—effective listening and providing feedback and support to team members.

Motivation: Benchmarking with a team of motivated individuals is stimulating and challenging. Benchmarking with people who would rather be somewhere else or who have been forced to participate can be frustrating and negative.

Developing an Effective Network

How can a novice benchmarking organization develop a highly qualified, highly motivated core of benchmarkers? What strategic issues should be considered by those responsible for launching and sustaining a formal bench-

Successful benchmarkers are often internal opinion leaders.

marking effort? To nurture a long-term benchmarking process that will produce high-level results and be stimulating and rewarding to those who
participate in the process, consider the following recommendations of the
excellent benchmarking companies surveyed. All have sustained the process
for at least five years; a few have kept it going for more than ten.

Think Strategically: Rather than using benchmarking to fight fires or
solve short-term problems, begin with a consideration of the company's long-
term business strategy and business objectives. Benchmarkers at the best-
practice firms consider how each benchmarking initiative links to the bottom-line business objectives of their corporation, their business unit, their
functional group, and their immediate work group. Unfortunately, many
firms start backwards—developing a benchmarking initiative quickly and
rushing out to collect information. Then they review the mass of data that
they have produced and try to link it to the business in some meaningful way.
Considering, too, that the benchmarking process often takes six to eight
months—with the average benchmarker dedicating 10–15% of his or her time
to the process—benchmarking only makes sense in terms of a long-term or
strategic context.

> Begin with a consideration of the company's long-term business strategy and business objectives.

Create Internal Process Champions: Implementing a benchmarking process means that management must rely on the expertise of those who can
effectively communicate about the process, guide others in the use of process
tools, evaluate progress and offer constructive feedback to novices, and work
to improve its application in specific organizational settings. Internal process
champions develop a level of expertise that allows them to perform these
functions. However, they may have to dedicate a significant portion of their
time to developing this level of expertise; in some cases, this responsibility
may even evolve into a part- or full-time job.

During the first critical years of any new process, it is often desirable to
appoint an individual who is identified as a process expert. This person will
serve as a resource to new and experienced benchmarkers and be a "keeper of
the process." Make sure multiple process champions in your organization are
aware of each others' presence and that they have the opportunity to network
with each other to share what they have learned.

Create a High Level of Awareness Among Employees: Link benchmarking
with other quality processes and tools, such as formal problem solving and
statistical process control (SPC), that already exist in the organization to avoid
the perception that processes like benchmarking are somehow competing
with other processes or tools that already exist.

Rely on Volunteers During Early Stages of Process Implementation: Begin
applying the benchmarking process with those who actually understand the
implications of using the process and who want to participate. Many organizations appoint benchmarkers based on their position or expertise. While this
may seem practical, it often produces teams that have the requisite skills, but
not the necessary level of motivation. The result is often a team that needs
continuous reassurance and prodding, and one that is often resentful (particularly when their non-benchmarking workload hasn't been reduced). One

SUPPLY-SIDE AGGRAVATION:
A BENCHMARKING CASE STUDY

The problem: A major computer hardware manufacturer had become disenchanted with several of its suppliers, reaching its breaking point in 1991. The suppliers were not meeting delivery deadlines and were throwing the company's production schedules off track. When supplies arrived on time, they were often in the wrong quantities, and the rate of defective parts was unusually high. Feedback from customers and outside advisors convinced management they stood to lose business if they didn't improve supplier quality.

The plan: At a meeting on supplier quality, the company's vice president of manufacturing announced he was putting together a benchmarking team. He assigned a manager with overall responsibility for supplier quality to be team leader. Rounding out the team were two QA (quality assurance) managers, four people from manufacturing, one from engineering, and the company's TQM (total quality management) manager.

The company dispatched the team of nine to several corporations with superb supplier networks, including Ford, Xerox and Motorola. After six months of study, the company established two goals: cut the number of suppliers by 70% in three years and establish a program to improve the quality of their supplied parts. From Ford, the company learned how to clarify quality guidelines. At Motorola, they saw the importance of regular visits to suppliers' facilities. Xerox taught the company that nothing would improve without good communication with suppliers.

The first step of implementation was getting proactive. The company established standard quality guidelines, and cut suppliers that didn't use SPC (statistical process control) measurements to track production errors. Quality control teams began making regular visits to supplier facilities. The next step was opening up communication. The company began holding monthly supplier briefings and kept suppliers in the loop during production forecasts so they would know when to expect a surge in orders.

The results: After a year and a half, the company has cut its suppliers by 50% and is on line to cut another 20% by the end of 1994. In addition, the performance of the company's suppliers has improved significantly. Shipment errors and defective parts are down about 25%, and the on-time delivery rate is approaching 95%.

benchmarking manager at IBM stated that her personal choice was to "preselect potential benchmarkers based on skills and let them self-select based on motivation."

The Role of Mentors

Mentors have usually participated in at least one successful benchmarking effort and have volunteered to help others in their functional or geographical area implement the process. They assist benchmarking team leaders in planning the benchmarking calendar and in preparing for team meetings and activities. Having lived through the start-up phase themselves, mentors usually have a more realistic perception about scheduling, planning, and budgeting than do novices. Unrealistic time expectations are usually due to underestimating how long it takes to contact knowledgeable individuals in the partner's organizations, as well as the amount of time that those people will need to adequately prepare for benchmarking interviews.

Mentors also serve as "process coaches"—helping new benchmarkers adhere to established benchmarking practices and maintain an acceptable level of process discipline. Shortcuts new benchmarkers may take without a mentor along might include a lack of adequate internal process analysis prior to examining the work processes of other organizations, brainstorming a list of potential benchmarking partners instead of dedicating adequate time to investigating valid best-practice information sources, and rushing to implement ideas that seem to represent opportunities for improvement without considering all the information that might be available.

In many of the excellent benchmarking organizations, process mentors occupy formal positions and dedicate more than half their time to training and mentoring benchmarking teams and individuals.

A network of benchmarkers can serve as a reliable pool of potential mentors to those who are just beginning to use the process. New benchmarkers can often receive valuable information and support by contacting local members of the benchmarking network.

New benchmarkers might also consider forming and supporting informal networks. These need not be elaborate and may consist of simple systems linkages by means of such internal communications channels as computer "notes," bulletin boards, and electronically distributed memos.

The development, implementation, and maintenance of an effective benchmarking process depends, in large part, on an organization's ability to motivate the right types of individuals to participate in the process. Attracting the right kind of individuals, organizing them into effective teams, and mentoring them though their start-up phases are all critical for effective benchmarking.

While virtually any organization can get any group of employees to do something once they're under the guidance of a process expert, the true test of benchmarking success is the realization on the part of employees that the search for best practices is an ongoing part of the job and must be repeated as part of the unending quest for continuous improvement.

> Mentors usually have a more realistic perception about scheduling, planning, and budgeting than do novices.

Michael J. Spendolini is principal of MJS Associates, Laguna Beach, CA. He is the author of The Benchmarking Book (AMACOM, 1992) and a managing partner of The Benchmark Partners, Oakbrook, IL.

PROCESS REENGINEERING

The Hunt for Reengineering Opportunities

Michael Hammer and James Champy

In this chapter from Hammer and Champy's best-selling book, the authors point out that what organizations do is reengineer processes not departments or divisions. *This excerpt explains how companies identify their business processes and suggests techniques for selecting the processes that should be reengineered.*

Processes, not organizations, are the object of reengineering. Companies don't reengineer their sales or manufacturing departments; they reengineer the work that the people in those departments do.

The confusion between organizational units and processes as objects of reengineering arises because departments, divisions, and groups are familiar to people in business, while processes are not; organizational lines are visible, plainly drawn on organization charts, and processes are not; organizational units have names, and processes most often do not.

This chapter illustrates how companies identify their business processes, suggests techniques for selecting the processes that should be reengineered

---

and the order of their reengineering, and stresses the importance of under-standing specific processes before attempting to redesign them.

Processes are not something that we invented in order to write about them. Every company on earth consists of processes. Processes are what companies do.

Processes in a company correspond to natural business activities, but they are often fragmented and obscured by the organizational structures. Processes are invisible and unnamed because people think about the individual depart-ments, not about the process with which all of them are involved. Processes also tend to be unmanaged that people are put in charge of the departments or work units, but no one is given the responsibility for getting the whole job—the process—done.

One way to get a better handle on the processes that make up a business is to give them names that express their beginning and end states. These names should imply all the work that gets done between their start and finish. Manufacturing, which sounds like a department name, is better called the procurement-to-shipment process. Some other recurring processes and their state-change names:

> *One way to get a better handle on the processes that make up a business is to give them names that express their beginning and end states.*

Product development: concept to prototype
Sales: prospect to order
Order fulfillment: order to payment
Service: inquiry to resolution

Just as companies have organization charts, they can have process maps that give a picture of how work flows through the company. A process map also creates a vocabulary to help people discuss reengineering.

Figure 1 is a high-level process map (slightly simplified) of Texas Instru-ments' semiconductor business. Four especially interesting characteristics of TI's process map stand out. The first is its simplicity as compared to an or-ganization chart of the same company.

The process map shows only six processes for a $4 billion business. "You know," commented a TI executive about this map, "until we drew this picture we thought we were a lot more complicated than we really are." TI is not unusual in this respect; hardly any company contains more than ten or so principal processes.

At TI's semiconductor division, the main business processes are strategy development, product development, customer design and support, manufac-turing capability development, customer communications, and order fulfill-ment. Each of these processes converts inputs into outputs.

The *strategy development* process converts market requirements into a business strategy, which identifies markets to be served and products and services to be offered. The *product development* process uses this output as input in order to produce new product designs. In some of TI's business lines, general product designs have to be customized for particular customers. The *customer design and support* process creates these so-called "qualified"

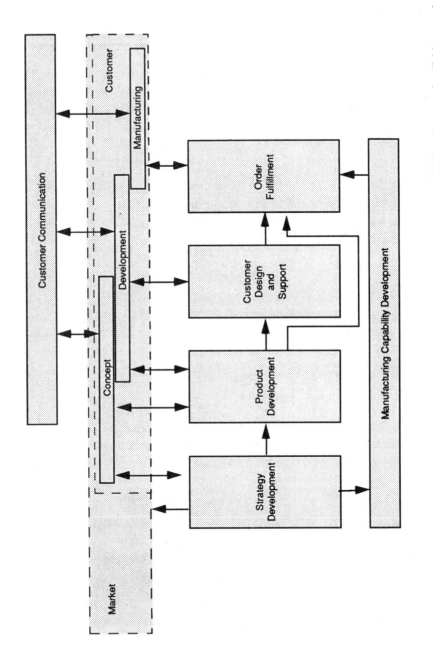

Figure 1. **TI Semiconductor Business Process Map**

Source: Texas Instruments (Reprinted with permission)

designs as its outputs, using standard product designs and customer requirements as inputs.

The TI process map shows three other high-level processes. Two of them
have names that are probably unfamiliar: *manufacturing capability development* and *customer communications.* The manufacturing capability development process takes a strategy as its input and produces a factory as its
output. Customer communications inputs are customer questions and inquiries; its outputs are heightened interest in TI products and consolidated
responses to customers.

Order fulfillment is the company's payoff. Order fulfillment converts an
order request, a product design, and a factory into a product that is delivered
into a customer's hands.

The process map displays a clear and comprehensive picture of the work
at Texas Instruments' semiconductor division: Strategy development creates
a strategy; product development generates an overall product design; customer design and support produces a custom design; manufacturing capability
produces a plant; customer communications answers customer questions and
inquiries; order fulfillment delivers what the customer wants.

The second important point to be made about TI's process map is that it
includes something that is almost never displayed on a company's organization chart: the customer. On the process map, TI's customer is right in the
center.

> The second important
> point to be made
> about TI's process
> map is that it includes
> something that is al-
> most never displayed
> on a company's or-
> ganization chart: the
> customer.

Point number three is that the TI process map also includes non-customers in its view of processes. These non-customers, who are all potential customers, are included within the "market" label on the map. These non-customers provide important input to the strategy development process.

Fourth, the process map reflects TI's recognition that its customers are
companies with processes, too. The customer is not seen as a monolith, but
in terms of three key processes with which TI interacts: concept formulation,
product development, and manufacturing. This perspective indicates that TI
appreciates how its customers' business works and how it can contribute to
that work and the customers' processes.

A few processes one might expect to find are not on the map. Manufacturing, for instance. Texas Instruments is a chip maker, but the process portrait does not depict manufacturing as one of its main processes. Instead, manufacturing is a subprocess of order fulfillment—just one of the subprocesses
that must get done to deliver a chip to the customer. "Sales" doesn't show up
in the picture, either. Sales is not a process, but a department—a collection
of people. Salespeople, however, are involved in many of the processes.
They're involved in order fulfillment because another subprocess of order fulfillment is order acquisition, which is primarily performed by salespeople.
Salespeople will also be involved in the customer communication and in product development processes.

Clearly, then, this map does not represent everything that happens at TI.
It shows only the high-level processes. But each of these can explode into
various subprocesses—usually numbering no more than half a dozen or so—

on separate subprocess maps. Together, the process and subprocess maps give a simple but effective picture of what TI—or any company—does.

Process maps don't require months of work to construct; several weeks is the norm. But this task does induce headaches, because it requires people to think across the organizational grain. It's not a picture of the organization, which is what people are used to seeing and drawing, but a depiction of the work that is being done. When it's finished, the process map should not surprise anyone. In fact, people may wonder why drawing it took as long as it did, since the finished map will be so easy to understand, even obvious. "Of course," people should say, "that's just a model of what we do around here."

Choosing the Processes to Reengineer

Once processes are identified and mapped, deciding which ones require reengineering and the order in which they should be tackled is not a trivial part of the reengineering effort. No company can reengineer all its high-level processes simultaneously. Typically, organizations use three criteria to help them make their choices. The first is dysfunction: Which processes are in the deepest trouble? The second is importance: Which processes have the greatest impact on the company's customers? The third is feasibility: Which of the company's processes are at the moment most susceptible to successful redesign?

Broken Processes

Typically, organizations use three criteria to help them make their choices: The first is dysfunction. The second is importance. The third is feasibility.

In looking for dysfunction, the most obvious processes to consider are those that a company's executives already know are in trouble. As a rule, people are clear about which processes in their companies need reengineering. The evidence is everywhere and generally hard to miss.

A product development process that hasn't hatched a new product in five years can safely be said to be broken. If employees spend time typing data from a computer printout into a computer terminal or from one terminal into another, whatever process they're working on is probably broken. If people's work cubicle walls and their computer screens are papered with Post-it notes reminding them to fix this or look into that, the processes in which they're involved are probably broken too.

Let's look behind some of these symptoms of process distress or dysfunction to the diseases that usually cause them.

> *Symptom:* Extensive information exchange, data redundancy, and rekeying
> *Disease:* Arbitrary fragmentation of a natural process

When employees are keying data taken from one computer into another, it is a symptom of what we call "terminal disease." The efficiency minded manager's typical response to a case of terminal disease is to look for a way to rekey the material more quickly or, if the manager is more technologically oriented, to find a way to link the terminals, so the material can travel electronically from one system to another. Both solutions treat the symptom, not the disease.

When the same information travels back and forth among different organizational groups—whether it's rekeyed each time or transmitted electronically—it suggests that a natural activity has been fragmented. Well-designed natural organizational units should send finished products to one another. Extensive communications is a way of coping with unnatural boundaries. The way to fix the problem is to put the pieces of that activity or process back together. Another name for doing that is cross-functional integration, which allows organizations to capture data just one time and then share it, instead of finding faster ways to ship it back and forth.

Cross-functional integration allows organizations to capture data just one time and then share it.

Terminal disease doesn't involve only computerized data. If people in different parts of the organization have to telephone one another frequently or send a lot of memos or E-mail messages, that probably means a natural process has been inappropriately broken apart. The typical response to this form of terminal disease is to give the people affected by it more communications links—another phone line, a fancier fax, and so forth. But that treats the symptom not the disease. Indeed, the new devices often fail to treat even the symptom. Our version of Parkinson's Law says that "work expands to fill the amount of *equipment* available for its completion." Give people more communications capacity and they will communicate more and still feel it's not enough.

The fact is—although collaboration may be necessary for some processes—people should not be calling one another *more;* they should be calling one another *less.* To treat the disease, we have to find out why two people need to call one another so often. If what they do is so closely linked, maybe it should be done by one person, a case worker, or by a case team.

Good organizational boundaries should be relatively opaque. In other words, what goes on inside one organizational unit should not be seen or matter very much to people outside it. Organizations should have a thin pipeline connecting them to the rest of the world. If the boundaries of two or more organizations have to be transparent to one another, they probably ought not to be different organizations in the first place.

Symptom: Inventory, buffers, and other assets
Disease: System slack to cope with uncertainty

Many companies are moving to JIT—just-in-time inventory; their current reality in most cases is JIC—just-in-case inventory. Companies, and organizations within companies, know that they will have to supply their output to customers, internal or external. Usually, they're just not certain when the demand will come or how much the customer will need. So they always squirrel just a little extra away somewhere (and sometimes they squirrel away a lot). We are not just referring to just physical assets, either. People create little buffer caches of work, information, cash, and even extra workers against unexpected demand.

The conventional reaction to JIC inventory is to create better inventory management tools. What a company really should work on is getting rid of the inventory. It is there only to take up the slack introduced into the system by uncertainty. Remove the uncertainty, and we have no slack to worry about, so we won't need the inventory.

One way to rid an organization of uncertainty is by structuring processes so that suppliers and customers plan and schedule their respective work together.

Symptom: High ratio of checking and control to value-adding
Disease: Fragmentation

A lot of work goes on in organizations that does not add value to the company's product or service. We have a simple test for distinguishing work that adds value from work that does not. Take the customer's perspective and ask, "Do I care?" If the answer is no, the work adds no value. Does the customer care about a company's internal controls, audits, management, and reporting? Absolutely not. That sort of checking and control work doesn't benefit the customer, only the company. It does not contribute to the value of the product or the service.

As long as companies consist of people, some amount of checking and control will be unavoidable. The issue is not whether non-value-adding work exists in an organization, but whether it forms too great a portion of all the work the organization performs.

Checking and control work is, of course, a symptom, not the disease. The root cause—the reason executives and managers think they must perform checking and control work—is the incompetence and mistrust that can come from fragmentation. The objective in reengineering is not to make checking and control more efficient, but to eliminate its root causes.

Symptom: Rework and iteration
Disease: Inadequate feedback along chains

Most often rework and iteration are the consequence of inadequate feedback in a long work process.

Rework and iteration both involve doing work again that has been done once—repainting a part that was painted the wrong color or writing a document several times over. Most often rework and iteration are the consequence of inadequate feedback in a long work process. Problems are not caught when they happen but only much later in the process, requiring more than one step to be redone.

The objective in reengineering is not to get the rework done more efficiently, but to eliminate it entirely by doing away with the mistakes and confusion that necessitate it.

Symptom: Complexity, exceptions, and special cases
Disease: Accretion onto a simple base

When most processes begin life, they are usually quite simple. But they grow complex over time, since every time a new wrinkle or contingency develops, someone modifies the process by adding a special case or a rule to deal with exceptions. Soon the simple process is buried under exceptions and special cases. We may then struggle to simplify what has become unbelievably complicated, but we will fail.

In reengineering we uncover and restore the original, clean process, then create other processes for the other situations. That means we end up with two or more processes instead of just one.

Organizations have become accustomed to standardizing, which means trying to satisfy every contingency with a single process. They create one standard—and complicated—process that has decision points along its entire length. We now know that in process design it is better to install a decision point up front that can send work along one of several simple processes.

The examples listed identify a set of common symptoms or dysfunctions that we often encounter in companies and the diseases, or process problems, to which they are usually connected. But, as we continue to stress, reengineering is as much an art as it is a science, and symptoms don't always point organizational physicians to the correct diagnosis. Sometimes the symptoms can be seriously misleading. In one organization with which we've worked, the order fulfillment processes were badly flawed, but the company's customers didn't think that was the case; they thought the order fulfillment process was superb. They received exactly what they ordered when they wanted it. Superficially, the process appeared healthy. Where did the problem lie? It turned out that the company's sales were limping badly. Was the sales process broken? No. Rather, the order fulfillment process was in such bad condition that customers received their products on time only because salespeople went to the warehouse, picked up the orders, and delivered them themselves. That pleased the customers, but salespeople were making deliveries instead of selling.

In such a situation, we call the slipping sales a secondary sign of dysfunction; a process is broken over here, but the symptoms show up over there. Many times the evidence that a process isn't working exists but it appears somewhere other than in the obvious places. So, while data may indicate that *something* is broken, it may not indicate accurately *which* process isn't working well.

Important Processes

Importance, or impact on outside customers, is the second criterion to consider when deciding which of the company's processes to reengineer and in what order. Even processes that deliver their outputs to customers inside the company may be of major importance and value to outside customers. However, companies can't simply ask their customers directly which processes are most important to them, because customers, even if they are familiar with the process terminology, have no reason to know in much detail the processes their suppliers use.

Customers are a good source of information in comparing the relative importance of various processes, however. Companies can determine what

Customers are a good source of information in comparing the relative importance of various processes.

issues their customers care strongly about—issues such as product cost, on-time delivery, product features, and so on. These issues then can be correlated with the processes that most influence them as an aid to creating a priority list of those processes that need reconstruction.

Feasible Processes

The third criterion, feasibility, entails considering a set of factors that determine the likelihood that a particular reengineering effort will succeed. One of these factors is scope. Generally, the larger a process—the more organizational units it involves—the broader its scope. A greater payoff is possible when a process larger in scope is reengineered, but the likelihood of its success will be lower. Broad scope means orchestrating more constituencies, affecting more organizations, and involving more managers who have their own agendas.

Similarly, high cost reduces feasibility. A reengineering effort that requires major investment in an information processing system, for example, will encounter more hurdles than one that does not.

The strength of the reengineering team and the commitment of the process owner are also factors to be considered in assessing the feasibility of reengineering a particular process.

We must emphasize that the method used to decide among reengineering opportunities is not a formal one. The three criteria we have outlined—dysfunction, impact, and feasibility—must be used with wisdom to help make choices.

Management might also ask whether a particular business process has a significant effect on the company's strategic direction. Does it have a high impact on customer satisfaction? Is the company's performance in this process far below the best-in-class standard? Is it unable to gain more from this process without reengineering? Is this process antiquated? The more yeses to questions such as these, the stronger the argument for reengineering that process. No two organizations will weigh all of those questions equally. They are, however, the kinds of questions that managers should raise in their search for reengineering opportunities.

Understanding Processes

Before a reengineering team can proceed to redesign, it needs to know some things about the existing process.

Once a process has been selected for reengineering, a process owner designated, and a team convened, the next step is not redesign—not yet; the reengineering team's next step is to "understand" the current process.

Before a reengineering team can proceed to redesign, it needs to know some things about the existing process: what it does, how well (or poorly) it performs, and the critical issues that govern its performance. Since the team's goal is not to improve the existing process, it does not need to analyze and document the process to expose all of its details. Rather, the team members require a high-level view, just enough so that they have the intuition and insight necessary to create a totally new and superior design.

Nonetheless, one of the most frequently committed errors in reengineering is that at this stage reengineering teams try to analyze a process in agonizing detail rather than attempt to understand it. People are prone to analyze because it is a familiar activity. We know how to do it. It also feels good, because analysis gives us an illusion of progress. We come to the office every morning, and we have calls to make, interviews to perform, data to graph. We produce lots of paper, and it all feels comfortable and satisfying. But analysis doesn't necessarily move us any closer to real understanding.

Detailed process analysis of a conventional sort may be useful to help persuade others in the organization that reengineering is necessary or desirable, but that task is part of change management. What the team is now looking for is knowledge and insight. So, in that the team doesn't have to collect and analyze volumes of quantitative data, understanding a process is less complex and time consuming than analyzing it. However, it is no less difficult. In some ways, understanding is harder than analysis.

Traditional process analysis takes the process inputs and outputs as given and looks purely *inside* the process to measure and examine what goes on. Process understanding, in contrast, takes nothing for granted. A reengineering team attempting to *understand* a process does not accept the existing output as a given. Part of understanding a process is comprehending what the process's customer does with that output.

The best place for the reengineering team to begin to understand a process is on the customer end. What are the customers' real requirements? What do they say they want and what do they really need, if the two are different? What problems do they have? What processes do they perform with the output? Since the eventual goal of redesigning a process is to create one that better meets customer needs, it is critical that the team truly understands these needs. Understanding customer needs doesn't mean asking customers what those needs are. They'll say only what they *think* they want.

For example, in the case we discussed earlier involving Wal-Mart and Procter & Gamble, P&G might simply have asked Wal-Mart, "What would you like our invoices to look like?" Or, "Do you want the goods delivered faster?" But that is not what happened.

Instead, P&G and Wal-Mart together stepped back and asked, "What is Wal-Mart's real challenge?" The answer in this case was maximizing its profits from selling diapers. Then P&G could ask, "How can we help you sell diapers more profitably? What problems do you have? What do you need?" This is very different from, "How can we help you improve the quality of the existing interaction between us?" Understanding means considering the customer's underlying goals and problems, not just the mechanics of the process that links the two organizations together.

This understanding cannot be obtained merely by asking customers what they want, since they will tend to answer from their own unexpanded mind-

> The best place for the reengineering team to begin to understand a process is on the customer end.

set. They'll say they want it—whatever "it" they already get—a little faster, a little better, a little less expensively. Customers, when asked, will respond with not very surprising ideas for making incremental improvements to the existing process. That is not what a reengineering team is after.

Rather, a reengineering team has to understand the customers better than they understand themselves. Toward that end, the team, or some of its members, might move in and observe and/or actually work with customers in their own environments. Doing this is another way in which gaining understanding differs from analysis. In traditional analysis, people collect information through interviews that take place in offices or conference rooms. They don't interview at real work sites, because it is considered much too noisy and distracting there. So, analysts take people out of their work environment, sit them down, and ask them to explain what they do. What people tell analysts, however, is what they *think* they should be doing, what they happen to remember, or what they've been told to say; they do *not* tell what they actually do. What people do and what they say they do are almost never the same.

A better way to acquire information about what customers do is to *watch* them do it. A still better way is for team members to do it themselves. Neither observation nor participation will make experts out of team members after a few days or weeks, but they will come away from the experience with a better idea of what is important and what is not than they would from any interview.

Being there, not just hearing about being there, can help team members see beyond the customers' blinders as well as their own biases. The point is not to learn how to do the customers' work but to understand their business—and to gather ideas.

Ideas will spring from team members seeing and comprehending how the customer uses the output of the process. If, for example, the customer has to partially disassemble the output before using it, maybe the output should be shipped in a partially assembled state. The team is looking for ideas about ways the process can better serve the customer.

Once the team understands what the process customer might need, the next step is to figure out what the process currently provides—to understand the current process itself.

Observing and performing the process is the best way to develop insight into it.

The goal is to understand the what and the why, not the how, of the process, because in redesign the team is less concerned with how the process works today than in what the new process will have to do. Knowing what and why, the team can begin its redesign with a blank sheet of paper. To learn the what and why, the reengineering team can take almost all of what we have just said about observing, and participating in, customers' work and apply those same remarks to the process itself. Observing and performing the process is the best way to develop insight into it. However, the team must be vigilant about avoiding the temptation to over-study. The goal must be to move quickly to redesign.

Before concluding we should comment on another tool that is available to reengineering teams, namely benchmarking. Essentially, benchmarking means looking for the companies that are doing something best and learning how they do it in order to emulate them.

The problem with benchmarking is it can restrict the reengineering team's thinking to the framework of what is already being done in its company's own industry. By aspiring only to be as good as the best in its industry, the team sets a cap on its own ambitions. Used this way, benchmarking is just a tool for catching up, not for jumping way ahead.

Benchmarking can, however, spark ideas in the team—especially if teams use as their benchmarks companies from outside their own industries. For example, the idea around which Hewlett-Packard reengineered its materials purchasing process came from a senior manager who joined the company from the automotive industry. He brought with him a completely different mind-set—and a new purchasing model.

If a team is going to benchmark, it should benchmark from the best in the world, not the best in its industry. If a team's company is in the consumer packaged goods business, the question is not who is the product developer in packaged goods, but who is the best product developer—period. That's the company from which the team might get great ideas.

There's an old story that when Xerox decided to improve its order fulfillment process, it didn't compare itself to other copier companies, but to the mail-order clothing retailer, L.L. Bean.

There's still a danger, however, even in using benchmarking to generate new ideas. What if it doesn't turn up a new idea? It is possible that no one in another company has had a great idea yet that is applicable to the process that the team is seeking to reengineer. Just because that's the case, however, doesn't give the reengineering team an excuse to be complacent. Rather, team members might consider it a challenge: *They* can create the new, world-class benchmark.

Keep in mind that by diagnosing the company's current processes, the reengineering team is learning a great deal about them, but not so that it can fix them. Old processes can take only so much fixing before the marginal benefits aren't worth the bother. Besides, reengineering teams don't look for marginal benefits, but order-of-magnitude improvements. Just fixing the old processes is not enough.

Instead, the team is trying to study the existing processes so it can learn and understand what is critical in their performance. The more team members know about the real objectives of a process, the better they will be at its redesign.

Dr. Michael Hammer is the originator and leading exponent of reengineering and the founder of the reengineering movement. He was formerly a professor at MIT. James Champy is chairman of CSC Index, Inc. and the leading authority on the implementation of business reengineering initiatives.

The Basis of Successful Re-engineering

Daniel Morris and Joel Brandon

In this excerpt from a new book on reengineering, the authors review the seven organizational capabilities necessary to undertake reengineering successfully. Without these capabilities, the authors tell us, "re-engineering becomes difficult to manage, unpredictable, as well as being restricted to delivering only a small fraction of its potential benefits."

We have found that seven capabilities must be part of re-engineering to make it succeed:

1. The ability to conduct re-engineering in accordance with a comprehensive, systematic methodology.
2. Coordinated management of change for all of the affected business functions.
3. The ability to assess, plan, and implement change on a continuing basis.
4. The ability to analyze the full impact of proposed changes.
5. The ability to model and simulate the proposed changes.
6. The ability to use these models on continuing basis.
7. The ability to associate all of the management parameters of the company with each other.

Without all seven of these capabilities, re-engineering becomes difficult to manage and unpredictable, as well as being restricted to delivering only a small fraction of its potential benefits.

The significance of each of these seven success factors is explained in the following paragraphs.

Reprinted with permission from Daniel Morris and Joel Brandon, *Re-engineering Your Business*, 1993, New York: McGraw-Hill, Inc.

Note: Some authors use a hyphen in the word "reengineering" and some do not. Hammer and Champy do not; Morris and Brandon do. We have honored these authors' spelling preferences in reproducing their articles.

1. *Systematic Methodology for Re-engineering.* Re-engineering is too important and complex to be done on the back of an envelope. A fully systematic approach to re-designing the business processes should always be used. Furthermore, this methodology should always begin with a detailed mapping of the current business process.

2. *Coordinated Management of Change.* Business operations must respond to changes initiated by four forces: competition, regulation, technology, and internal improvement. To best react to change, an operation must be flexible and it must be designed for ongoing modification. Re-engineering represents a systematic response to change. If properly used, it becomes a change methodology, a standard approach for modifying operations. As such, it will encompass many components of the business, such as marketing, corporate planning, quality initiatives, human resources, finance, accounting, information technology, and even physical plant. Because of the high degree of interdependence among these activities, a re-engineering project that ignores these areas will probably fail during implementation. For this same reason, the reverse is also possible: an action external to the re-engineering effort can reduce its effectiveness.

    The need to coordinate all the factors involved in corporate change is paramount. The most effective approach is to place re-engineering and all other change activities in an overall framework of change management.

3. *Continuing Change.* Business process re-engineering almost always encounters two very difficult problems. The first results from the sheer size of the projects; they tend to be very large. Management is justifiably intimidated by re-engineering projects that seem to put the whole fate of the company at risk. Also, some projects require so much elapsed time that their effect will not be realized in time to solve the problems at hand. The second difficulty that seems inherent in re-engineering is that the improvements will give competitive advantage for only a short time.

    There is a solution to both of these problems. Re-engineering can be done on a continuing basis. Instead of trying to implement a major project that will restructure the entire corporation, a series of smaller projects can alter the business a little at a time. This approach not only reduces the risk and shortens the delay in getting benefits, it enables the company to keep up continually with its competition, government regulation, and the changing business environment.

    Another advantage of continual re-engineering is that this approach allows the company's quality program and re-engineering to be completely and effectively integrated. This continuing approach to quality improvement is, in effect, the implementation of W. Edwards Deming's quality concepts. If properly implemented, a re-engineering methodology can greatly improve the effectiveness of quality efforts by helping them look at whole work processes and also to plan and evaluate the impact of improvements.

4. *Impact Analysis.* Since processes typically cross organizational lines, a re-engineering approach should provide the ability to analyze the impact

> Instead of trying to implement a major project that will restructure the entire corporation, a series of smaller projects can alter the business a little at a time.

that changes in any process will have on all organizational units. Also, because processes normally interact with one another, the ability to anticipate the impact of any change on all the associated processes throughout the business is critical. To do this, it is necessary to understand all the relationships among organization, operation, business function, planning, policies, human resources, and information services support. Based on these relationships, any change can be followed through its associations, to determine the full potential impact of a proposed action.

5. *Modeling and Simulation.* Fundamental to the re-engineering effort is the ability to simulate the changes that are being proposed. This allows the testing and comparison of any number of alternative designs. This ability is based on the use of business process models and some method by which the costs and benefits of each suggested design can be assessed. A computerized modeling system, of course, provides the easiest way to simulate these alternatives.

   It would seem rather risky to do re-engineering of processes without any attempt to simulate the results, but it has been tried. In these cases, the business itself becomes the test-bed for the new process, with only limited opportunity to rectify any part of the design that was found to be unsatisfactory.

6. *Continuing Use of Designs.* The designs drawn for the new business processes should not be used only in the implementation of the new processes and then discarded. Nor should they be stored on a shelf to gather dust and become obsolete. The re-engineering process costs too much; the designs are too valuable.

   The obvious use for the re-engineering designs and models is supporting future re-engineering efforts. If a total quality initiative is implemented, the company will need to change its processes on a frequent basis as improvements are implemented. For control, these activities should be performed following re-engineering methods and all documentation should be updated.

   A second and less obvious use of the designs is to support daily business operations. The designs contain information that can be useful in making daily operational decisions, in training and in controlling work performance.

7. *Association of Corporate Management Parameters.* To begin re-engineering, the project team will require rapid access to all of the information related to the business processes being re-engineered, the company's plans, the current information systems, organization charts, mission statements, and job descriptions, as well as many other details of business administration and work organization. As important as all this data is to the project, the relationships among the data items are equally so. The re-engineering approach, therefore, must have the ability to gather and combine this management information.

A Methodology that Works

Early attempts at re-engineering, both successful and unsuccessful, lacked systematic methodologies. More recently, several methodologies have been suggested for re-engineering phases; some examples are described in the following chapters. The primary purpose of this book is to present systematic methods for the entire spectrum of business change management, from the beginnings of repositioning to post-re-engineering change control. These methods have been developed by the authors to support their consulting practice; they are proven to work effectively.

The overall method is shown in Fig. 1, and briefly introduced in the following paragraphs. It begins with the determination of changes that will help gain competitive advantage, and continues through the various activities that lead to real changes in the business. However, the approach presented is not the plan of a single project. It is best itself employed as a standing business process, used as often as is needed, with each major change proposed becoming a project in itself.

Determine Goals and New Market Position

The first step in moving the company to a new market position is determining what that position should be. Factoring marketing into corporate business plans has always been difficult, but starting with marketing solves many old problems. An analysis of the marketplace comes first. A realistic assessment is made of the company's current position. What will it take to move upward? What about five and ten years in the future? Once an educated business judgment has been made, the corporate goals can be set (perhaps optimistically at this time). These goals should be very ambitious; in today's business world it is usually much better to fall just short of very lofty goals than to meet easy ones and be soundly beaten by the competition.

In today's business world it is usually much better to fall just short of very lofty goals than to meet easy ones.

Establish a New Business Environment

The marketing, expense, quality, pricing, product differentiation, market share, and other business goals that are developed in the positioning process are followed by the establishment of a new business environment. This is formed by examining the conscious and unconscious assumptions that form the paradigms of the company and questioning the ones that are no longer valid. The most important of these is the current attitude toward change and the company's willingness to change when there is a business reason to do so. The new paradigm is one in which change is used to win competitive advantage. As such it must not only be enabled, it must be made entirely acceptable to every member of the corporate staff. The objective of this action is to put the company in a position where change will be implemented without resistance.

Map the Current Business

Once the company has determined its target position and the staff is set for change, the next tasks are to gather information about the company's current business operations and create a model of the business processes being studied. The authors call the basic model a Business Activities Map (BAM). The careful mapping of *current* processes is often given token attention in re-engineering efforts, but, where used, it has been found to be effective and is highly recommended as a starting point for any analysis of business processes.

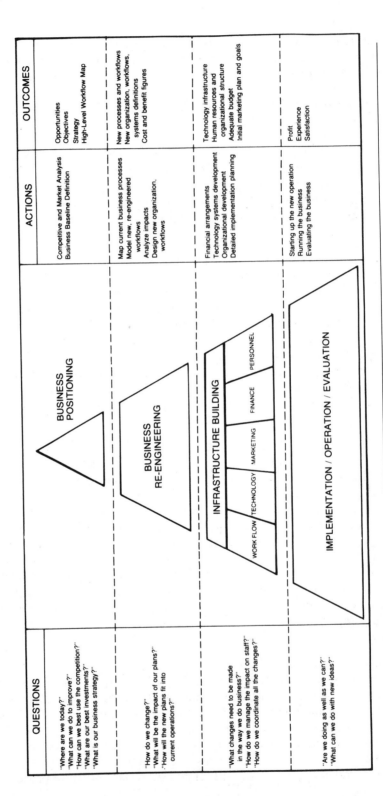

Figure 1. **Dynamic business re-engineering model.**

Business Activity Maps describe the flow of work in each business process. They are first drawn as very general pictures, showing the main business processes, with no detail and only a few notes related to quantitative information. For example, the average length of time that a process requires may be included. The general, high-level maps are then broken down into more detailed ones, until a very fine level of detail is obtained for all tasks in the process. At detailed levels, more numerical data is obtained and included. The process of adding levels of detail, called "leveling" or "factoring," is not difficult, but it does require the involvement of the staff who actually perform the work. Additional tables, or matrices, are used to capture supporting information for the processes, such as the answers to the basic questions who, what, why, when, how, and where? Facts concerning the use of information in each business process are also sought, as is the usual organization chart data and any existing business plans.

Redesign: Using the Map as a Model

The reward for gathering the details of the current system comes in the next activity: creating a new business process design. The redesign effort uses the BAMs to model the new business operation work flow. The redesign process becomes a modeling activity, with guesswork reduced to a minimum. The first model can be a real attempt at designing the final process, or a "straw man" can be used, in which all similar work activities are combined. This can be called a least-cost design, in which all duplication of effort and redundancy is removed. The least-cost scenario is seldom feasible, however, because other desirable characteristics are sacrificed. In most cases, the managers reviewing the design will create some duplication in successive new versions of the design.

The least-cost scenario is seldom feasible, however, because other desirable characteristics are sacrificed.

Each version of the model is reviewed by managers and staff to ensure that the work functions are adequately facilitated. The versions are also subjected to cost and timing analysis, so that the attainment of quantified goals can be tested. Using paper or, better still, computerized models to simulate a new operation serves business far better than using trial and error on the organization itself. Usually, the actual implementation is required to be nearly perfect, as most companies will tolerate only a minor fine tuning after a reorganization. However, without modeling, the probability of any reorganization being fully successful is small. This is borne out by industrial experience with reorganizations motivated by cost cutting in recent years.

When the modeling process has produced a satisfactory design, the result will be a map of the new business operation in the same format as the map of the current business. It will be understandable, because it is written in terms of the way things are done. The project will have produced business process designs that are likely to work very well, that have been reviewed by the managers who will work within them, and that can be easily implemented.

Build the Foundation

The new processes will need more than a new organization chart and work flow diagram. The design of the new business is examined by experts in training, staffing, information technology, marketing, accounting, and finance to determine the needs for new support from those areas. These support elements are usually put into service long after the business process has been operational, and they are seldom coordinated. The processes of repositioning and re-engineering provide an opportunity to do better. At this time the impact of support can be assessed, often quantitatively, planned and fully coordinated. Equally important, the support elements can be helpful in smoothly implementing the newly designed processes.

The third level of the Change Model pyramid in Fig. 1 represents a level of planning in which the support infrastructure and the architecture of the business are designed. The support infrastructure is composed of the activities that support a business process without being a direct part of it: for example, human resources, travel, and procurement are all support activities. The business architecture is the overall design of the processes and support activities that work together to form the entire enterprise or a large part of it, such as a division. Like an architectural design, the structure of the business is the basis of the architecture, and the support elements are each deigned to have a specific role.

The design of the infrastructure includes consideration for information use, whether or not any technology is required. Information systems and technology are given a high priority in this phase of re-engineering, due to the long lead times and possibly high costs involved. In most medium-sized and large businesses, information technology is a basic requirement in many work processes, and it will grow in importance as competitive advantage is increasingly based on the creative use of information. As new systems will require fairly long lead times for implementation, and new equipment will require some time to obtain and set up, this support element may determine the overall implementation schedule for the re-engineering project.

The next support issue to be addressed is the human capital required for the new business processes. The infrastructure related to human capital may be built by specialists in organization development, staffing, training, and other human resources topics. It consists of position descriptions, training, and staffing requirements, and various methods to achieve teamwork, quality, and focus. One very important human capital consideration is the method by which the new business processes will be staffed from the old ones. The objective is to avoid the usual personnel problems that seem to be an unavoidable feature of reorganizations. Business re-engineering can help achieve this objective.

Marketing, which contributed heavily at the beginning of the re-engineering project, may re-enter it at this point. Marketing may be linked to a business process to provide support to both the operating and marketing efforts. For example, if order processing is being re-engineered, Marketing may be able to help define address requirements and may want to know as soon as possible when standing orders are canceled. These relationships may or may not be important enough to be noted explicitly in the Business Activity Map models. When such marketing linkages are important to the business, their presence in the Business Activity Maps will assure that they will be given consideration when the new infrastructure is being designed.

Obviously, infrastructure includes such common support as facilities, power, heating, ventilating, air conditioning, telephones, lighting, and office equipment. Given a fully detailed map of the new business processes, these elements can be installed, renovated, converted, or just reassigned with great accuracy. In some cases, however, specialized equipment or facilities will be required and special considerations must be made for putting them into production and for phaseover from the existing equipment.

Finance and Accounting should not be forgotten when building infrastructure. Accounting, in particular, can provide much more direct support to the business operations than is customary in most companies. This phase of re-engineering presents an opportunity to establish meaningful cost accounting for the new processes and to build a management budget structure that directly helps managers.

Implement and Operate

Implementation planning, implementation, and the operation of the new business processes comprise the last level of the Change Model in Fig. 1. This last step is where the payoff occurs.

Generally, implementation of a reorganized or restructured business operation is difficult. If there is the slightest hint that management and staff workforce reductions will be a part of the effort, it can be a nightmare—undoubtedly the greatest challenge that a manager can face. The methods that we suggest can help considerably, however. First, management will have comprehensive before and after pictures of the business to work with: the maps of the current and the new, re-engineered business operations, plus the organization charts and other supporting documents developed in earlier phases. Having these tools will place management in much greater control than when organization charts, and perhaps mission statements, were relied on.

Another important aid to phaseover is the prearrangement of infrastructure. Having support already determined avoids scrambling under the pressure of production requirements at the time of phaseover, or even after the fact during operations, in full view of customers. Prearrangement essentially places all of the company's capabilities in support of the implementation, instead of their seeming to be opposed to it.

Operations after the phaseover is completed will continue to be affected by the re-engineering effort. The measurements shown in the Business Activity Map for the new process become the production goals for the new process. The efficiency and performance of the process and its staff can be measured using these numbers and the framework of the Business Activity Map, which clearly shows what is supposed to happen. The re-engineering documentation is also used to support ongoing improvement by assisting all managers and the production workforce in the continual redefinition and attainment of quality in every detail of the work being done.

Daniel Morris and Joel Brandon are principals of Morris, Tokarski, Brandon, & Co., a Chicago-based management consulting firm specializing in business positioning and re-engineering.

A Methodology for Reengineering Businesses

D. Brian Harrison and Maurice D. Pratt

"Business process redesign across a wide range of industries is uncovering new ways to organize work, that, in turn, is creating breakthrough improvements." With that as its premise, this article provides yet another perspective on what is involved in undertaking reengineering.

Here's the radical manifesto of business process reengineering:

- All activity that matters to customers can be described as a set of interrelated business processes. (A business process is a sequence of activities that fulfils the needs of an internal or external customer.)
- Excellence in business processes and their continuous improvement is the secret formula for meeting the customer requirements in the Nineties.
- Business process teams will displace functional disciplines as the critical organizational unit of world-class companies.

Business process redesign across a wide range of industries is uncovering new ways to organize work that, in turn, is creating breakthrough improvements. A process approach to organizational performance has produced a number of innovations: Quick response logistics systems; invoiceless accounts payable systems; "six sigma" quality achievements; accelerated new product development cycles; and the one-day accounting close.

The New Analytic Framework

New team concepts, tools, and methodologies are emerging to support process analysis, improvement, and management:

- Cross-functional teams, organized around processes, are rethinking traditional, functional perspectives of the business; eliminating departmental red tape; and taking charge of overall process performance.
- Rapidly improving computer economics and more flexible data communications are changing ideas of what is possible. Electronic

This article is reprinted from *Planning Review*, March/April 1993, with permission from The Planning Forum, The International Society for Strategic Management and Planning.

models are replacing new product mock-ups and pilot projects and creating innovative ways of streamlining new product development. Dispersed processing is enabling team collaboration by making information and expertise available anywhere, anytime. Data-base technology is eradicating traditional territorial attitudes toward data, broadening access, reducing waiting times, and lowering costs.

- For the past decade, process analysis methodologies have been helping us satisfy customers more effectively. Quality function deployment helps embed the "voice of the customer" into products and services. Process design of experiments helps isolate defects or variations that have the most impact on quality and customer satisfaction. Design for manufacturing helps reduce manufacturing costs and cycle times by standardizing parts and tools, simplifying designs, and selecting product features to facilitate factory operations.

New Ways to Organize Work

The new analytic framework is helping to challenge traditional thinking on how businesses operate and inspiring management teams to find new ways to organize work:

- **Extended Enterprise Concepts.** World-class companies are managing business processes beyond conventional organizational boundaries. Car makers are improving product design by including suppliers' experts on product development teams. Retailers are sharing demand information among channel partners to improve forecasting accuracy and to accelerate replenishment. Manufacturers are forming supplier alliances to shorten manufacturing cycle times.

- **Concurrency.** Process steps that have traditionally been sequential are being performed concurrently. The best new product design organizations are multidisciplinary teams working concurrently. World-class order entry processes permit order specification, inventory commitment, production scheduling, packaging, labeling, documentation and routing to be resolved in a single telephone call from a customer. Production process flows are being rationalized by integrating equipment, tools, materials handling, and maintenance into multifunction manufacturing cells.

- **Displacement.** Information technologies and software, coupled with process reengineering, can displace specialized functions, reducing costs and improving cycle time. For example, quality inspection is being replaced by quality validation during product development; receiving inspection is being displaced by supplier quality certification; and traditional order-entry functions are being displaced by direct customer order placement through electronic data interchange.

■ **Simplification.** Creative business process redesign teams are challenging the need for traditional activities and functions and eliminating those that are no longer necessary. By linking vendors into production-scheduling systems, Ford has eliminated parts ordering. Another innovative firm has eliminated invoice processing for minor purchases by mailing the payment with the order.

Breakthrough Performance Improvement

In the new vision of enterprise performance, companies are redesigning underlying business processes to create simultaneous improvement in quality, cycle times, service and productivity—often by orders of magnitude. From another viewpoint, if our aim is to shorten cycle times, we invariably have to start with quality improvement by "doing it right the first time."

Companies are redesigning underlying business processes to create simultaneous improvement in quality, cycle times, service and productivity.

Motorola was among the earliest North American companies to demonstrate the power of process reengineering. Between 1984 and 1987 a process-improvement program aimed at greatly reducing defects also cut cycle times in half and reduced costs by almost $1 billion.

Transforming the Organization

While functional organizations and accountabilities will be with us for some time, cross-functional organizations and teams are becoming a common organizational characteristic. The best organizations are assigning clear accountability for process performance and realigning functional objectives and performance measures to support process performance goals.

New, more malleable information technologies are being built into process designs. Information systems used to be considered an adjunct to the business process, but now they're being embedded in process designs. Old, rigid, centralized architectures are being replaced by flexible, dispersed networks that enable process improvements that enhance performance.

Organizing for Change

A successful transformation program needs a clearly defined organizational structure, roles, and accountabilities. Our experience suggests that four groups play a key role in successful change (see Exhibit 1):

■ **Executive Steering Committee.** The CEO and the senior management team champion the change process, set the goals, assign the resources, expedite progress, support change and remove barriers.

■ **Process Evaluation Teams (PETs).** Cross-functional teams provide the baseline, benchmark the existing process, construct the vision of the future process, design the improvements, and oversee implementation. Subteams—created by the PETs when needed—resolve complex problems or capitalize on high-potential opportunities.

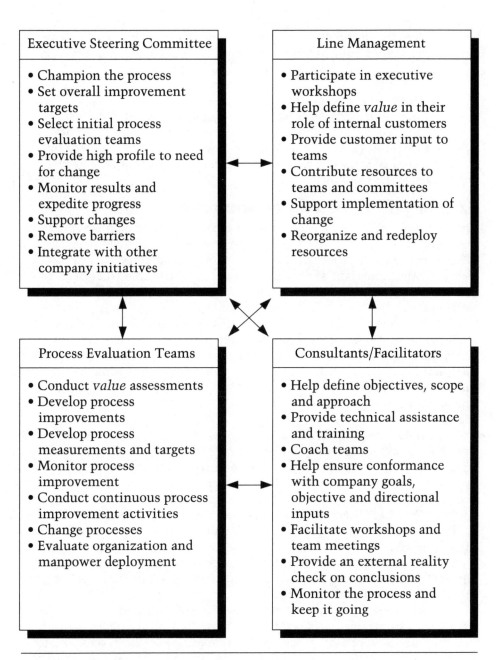

Executive Steering Committee

- Champion the process
- Set overall improvement targets
- Select initial process evaluation teams
- Provide high profile to need for change
- Monitor results and expedite progress
- Support changes
- Remove barriers
- Integrate with other company initiatives

Line Management

- Participate in executive workshops
- Help define *value* in their role of internal customers
- Provide customer input to teams
- Contribute resources to teams and committees
- Support implementation of change
- Reorganize and redeploy resources

Process Evaluation Teams

- Conduct *value* assessments
- Develop process improvements
- Develop process measurements and targets
- Monitor process improvement
- Conduct continuous process improvement activities
- Change processes
- Evaluate organization and manpower deployment

Consultants/Facilitators

- Help define objectives, scope and approach
- Provide technical assistance and training
- Coach teams
- Help ensure conformance with company goals, objective and directional inputs
- Facilitate workshops and team meetings
- Provide an external reality check on conclusions
- Monitor the process and keep it going

Exhibit 1:   **Organizing for change.**

- **Line Management.** The line organization provides resources to the change effort, then implements the agreed changes. Because implementation is the most difficult hurdle in any change program, line management involvement and buy-in is a critical ingredient for success.
- **Consultants/Facilitators.** External consultants help deliver results. They assist in the design of the programs, train and facilitate the teams, provide tools and methodologies, import industry and technical knowledge, provide an external reality check, and challenge the thinking.

Executing a Methodology for Structured Change

Our approach strikes a balance between changing existing processes and redesigning them. Sometimes business processes can't be redesigned with a clean sheet of paper; the methods already in place may be tied to physical assets or other constraints that can't practically be overlooked. In such cases, process reengineering starts with the existing framework and focuses on improving it.

On the other hand, some business processes are so bound up in antiquated thinking or outmoded technology that they defy repair. The only solution is to completely replace them. In these cases, process reengineering emphasizes analysis of the existing process and focuses on creating the vision of the future process. But whether we are improving an existing process or designing a replacement, our goal is always for breakthrough, not incremental improvement.

Typically, the point of departure for the change initiative occurs when the chief executive officer articulates the strategic context and mandate for change. The CEO typically chooses an internal forum, such as the executive committee, as an arena for debating and agreeing upon the business imperative. Our methodology for supporting this change is:

Step One: Set Direction. During an initial two-to-four-week planning period, the steering committee decides which business processes will be redesigned, in what sequence, and by what teams. The members of the steering committee set macrotargets for overall performance improvement. They identify the processes most critical to competitiveness and those offering the greatest opportunity for improvement.

Because thinking in terms of processes may encounter powerful resistance in many organizations, the steering committee may need to spend some time defining the scope of each process and articulating specific process-improvement goals. This sets the stage for deciding which functions need to be represented on each cross-functional PET. Next comes the selection of the leader and members of each team, while also taking steps to ensure that the organization continues to function in the absence of several key people.

The steering committee then designs and launches a communications program to announce the change initiative and to disseminate ongoing information on the process. By the end of the planning period an action plan is in place, processes have been designated, PET members have been appointed and briefed, and the organization understands that a major change is underway.

Step Two: Baseline and Benchmark. Next, the process-evaluation teams may spend up to six weeks learning all the ins and outs of the existing process. The PETs articulate the business process mission and objectives. They identify the customers for the process outputs. And then they conduct surveys of customers to understand their requirements, the current levels of customer satisfaction and value criteria.

The PETs then map the "as is" process flows, activities, and technologies. They establish a baseline for transaction volumes, cycle times, defect rates, and costs. They benchmark the practices and performance of comparable organizations in order to set their own aggressive but achievable goals. They identify or reevaluate performance metrics and begin to shape the steering committee's macrotargets into process-specific objectives.

"Early wins" invariably surface from the baseline analysis. These are opportunities to make immediate improvements, and line management is responsible for implementing them. Early wins are critical because they increase cash flow and demonstrate the value of the methodology. They also provide a shakedown cruise for the various teams—they discover firsthand the difficulties of implementing real-world change.

Step Three: Create the Vision. While they scrutinize the existing process, the PETs also begin to visualize the future process. This requires PET members to break out of the conventional thinking about how their organization works and launches them into the broader world of possibilities.

Because breakthrough thinking can only originate outside the organization, the PETs need to spend time interpreting benchmarking results, understanding marketplace and industry trends, and familiarizing themselves with emerging information technologies. Consultants can contribute significantly to broadening the PETs perspective, and so can suppliers and customers invited into key team meetings.

The result of the visioning process is not just an idea. To be truly successful it requires total organizational buy-in.

PET members also need to spend time off-site in visioning workshops to help them shift mindset. These workshops can be exciting events filled with truly creative thinking. They often result in new ways of organizing processes for breakthrough results. Once the vision has been created, the PETs document their new ideas, then communicate and explain the future process to the steering committee and line management. The result of the visioning process is not just an idea. To be truly successful it requires total organizational buy-in.

Step Four: Launch Problem-solving Projects. At the same time that the baseline and visioning steps are proceeding, the PETs initiate projects to investigate detailed problems or capitalize on high-potential opportunities. Such projects typically deal with a wide range of issues—for example, changing product identification codes, changing account-management practices, or implementing a measurement system.

The detailed problem-solving projects are assigned to temporary subteams or sub-PETs under the leadership of a PET member. This approach enables people close to the problem, or to the opportunity, to be included on the team. This, in turn, expands the resources available to the PETs, involves a broader cross-section of the organization in the change process, and allows the PETs to stay focused on overall process issues.

The result of each problem-solving project is typically a recommendation for change or improvement that is handed over to line management for implementation. This means that the projects build on and continue the implementation activity that began with the early wins.

Step Five: Design Improvements. The baseline and vision steps generally draw to a close 12 to 14 weeks into the change initiative. At this stage each PET has both assessed the priority opportunities for improving the existing process and established a vision for what the future process should look like. The PETs have probably set a number of early-win opportunities in motion, and are also managing four to six sub-PETs undertaking detailed improvement projects. By continually measuring performance improvement on a regular basis, the PETs have a clear grasp of their impact on business results so far.

At this point the PETs begin to consolidate their analyses and develop a comprehensive plan for process improvement. They prepare a blueprint that outlines the future process and a supporting technology architecture that describes the supporting information systems at the design criteria level. Taken together, the process blueprint and technology architecture form a road map that integrates major process and supporting systems changes. This road map then becomes the primary vehicle for communicating the intended changes across the organization.

In addition, the PETs prepare an integrated action plan showing how the blueprint and architecture will be implemented. The action plan describes future changes to the organization structure and staffing levels in support of, or resulting from, process redesign. The PETs establish process performance measures and targets; set the implementation agenda for line management; and scope out the necessary information technology projects. Included in the action plan documentation is the business justification for any capital investments or significant operating expenditures needed to change the business process.

Step Six: Implement Change. Implementation begins up front in our methodology with the early wins and continues as the PETs spin off problem-solving projects. The full-scale improvement program builds on these initiatives and elevates the activity level to a point where virtually the entire organization is involved in the change process.

Full-scale implementation involves assigning change accountabilities to line managers and setting targets and timetables for actions and improvements. A. T. Kearney research shows that a significant percentage of change programs fail because line management drops the ball. To avoid this pitfall, the PETs become heavily involved in communicating recommendations and building support and buy-in from line managers. Pilot or demonstration processes are established to demonstrate and validate the process changes and new technologies before the full-scale rollout. Training programs are initiated to teach employees needed skills. PETs also track and report achievements against targets, and communicate and celebrate performance-improvement successes.

Step Seven: Embed Continuous Improvement. The ultimate step is to embed teamwork behavior throughout the organization in place of traditional management methods. Teamwork is a well-defined and observable set of behaviors in the day-to-day management of the business. These behaviors include upward, downward, and lateral communication; ongoing measurement and team review of performance against clearly defined targets; feedback from and reinforcement of team members; and continuous improvement of performance through performance-tracking systems and problem-solving skills.

Instituting teamwork throughout a traditionally managed organization is a major undertaking. An organization of 3,000 employees, for example, contains about 250 executives, middle managers, and supervisors, each in turn responsible for managing a team. All 250, from the CEO down, need to be trained and coached in a new set of teamwork skills and behaviors, which typically takes about a year.

At the end of this step, participative management and continuous improvement have become a reality in the workplace. Not only is the line organization better equipped to implement PET recommendations, it is actively building on the PET changes on an ongoing basis. The teamwork behaviors established in the workplace have set the stage for the introduction of self-managed work teams—if the organization chooses to go in that direction. The groundwork has also been laid for advanced, team-based, pay-for-performance compensation systems.

This methodology does not have an end point—the change process is ongoing. The PETs become permanent organizational groups, the custodians of their respective processes. Once the process blueprint and information architecture are in place, the PETs regularly monitor process performance, benchmark emerging best practices, and make continuing recommendations for process improvement. After the line organization has been trained and coached in teamwork behaviors, continuous improvement becomes an ongoing feature of the day-to-day management of the company.

D. Brian Harrison is a vice president of the Chicago-based consulting firm of A. T. Kearney, and president of its Canadian unit, headquartered in Toronto. Maurice D. Pratt is a principal of the firm's information technology practice.

> The ultimate step is to embed teamwork behavior throughout the organization in place of traditional management methods.

MEASUREMENT

Measurements: The Heart of Managing a Process

Eugene H. Melan

This excerpt from Eugene H. Melan's book on process management provides an overview of the basics of measurement of any business process. Knowing how and what to measure is among the most misunderstood areas of management. This piece provides a start for clearing up this misunderstanding.

After establishing control points, determining the parameters to be measured is the next logical step in process management. Measurements are the heart of managing a process. They are needed not only to determine defect or error rates but to assess whether the output is conforming to requirements. Measurement may encompass simple sampling or auditing to complete inspection of every item. In business processes, the kinds of measurements that are performed fall into five categories:

Measures of conformance
Measures of response time
Measures of service levels
Measures of repetition
Measures of cost

Measures of Conformance

Conformance measures involve an inspection or verification as to whether the work product or service meets either a specification of some other re-

---

quirement. Implicit in these measures is that they reflect customer requirements directly or indirectly. Clerical and source translation type errors such as miscodes are conformance errors that are measurable. The acceptable error rate may range from zero to some low percentage value, depending on the business or economic impact of these errors. An example of conformance measurements performed in a staff department is the following:

> The Technical Writing Services department reduced the defect rate in its technical publications by 97.3 percent in 16 months, beginning with a critical analysis of the entire writing and production process. The program called total defects per unit (TDPU) measures the ratio of defects detected in a 13-week period to the pages of technical literature completed. An average page of copy contains about 5,200 opportunities for defects. But, by using an elaborate quality screening process that makes the writer the monitor of defects, the average number of defects per page went down to about 2.00 per page within five weeks. At the end of 16 months, the defects per page had dropped to 0.54 or 14 defects per million.

This example resulted from work performed at Motorola, a 1989 Baldrige Award winner, as part of its Six Sigma Program.

When output is in a state of nonconformance, one of three situations can occur:

- Work is accepted as is.
- Work is rejected and returned to the producer.
- Work is accepted by the customer and modified to conform to some desired state or condition.

These three conditions imply either that an ineffective inspection has been done on the work product or that no inspection is performed and nonconformity is detected solely through discovery in subsequent operations. Because of the consequences of nonconformance, verification controls are built into many processes.

Measures of Response Time

Response is measured from the arrival of the request until the completion of service or from the start of the actual performance of service until completion. For service facilities such as fast foods, package delivery, or the ten-minute oil change business, response time is crucial. It provides a competitive edge and serves to differentiate a firm from its competitors. Federal Express, for example, has emphasized nationwide overnight delivery service from its beginning in its attempt to differentiate itself from similar delivery services. Response or cycle time is generally an important measure for most service and support type operations.

In the case of product development, the cycle time in developing a product is critical to the competitive posture and market share of a firm. Cycle time

Response or cycle time is generally an important measure for most service and support type operations.

measures are also used in various staff and administrative functions. An example of this is the following:

> One comprehensive process being used at Motorola is cycle time management. While primarily a manufacturing term, cycle time can be applied to service tasks. . . . All administrative and staff functions at Motorola are working on cycle time reduction with success.
>
> The patent department, for example, has reduced the time it takes to file a patent from as much as two years to fewer than 90 days by getting patent attorneys involved with engineering, business and marketing people early in the process.

General Electric has used cycle time measures to improve the delivery time of an order and reduce inventory costs. In GE's appliance group, the average production cycle for its consumer appliances was reduced 70 percent and the time between receiving an order and delivery for electric ranges and refrigerators was brought down to six days from sixteen weeks. These improvements have reduced inventories by greater than 50 percent and translate to annual savings of over $300 million by 1993.

Measures of Service Level

The term "service level" means the degree to which a service or a facility is available to a user.* For example, an information system facility or data center might commit to provide on-line terminal availability to users 99 percent of the time during a month. This is known as a service-level agreement and is often embodied in a document. To determine that the service level agreement has been met, management would measure the percentage of time that the system is, in fact, available to the user during the month. In this case, the target value is 99 percent.

Measures of Repetition

Repetitive events are generally a reflection of wasted and unproductive work.

Measures of repetition involve measures of recurring events or the frequency of occurrence of an activity. Measuring the number of times a typed document is redone or the number of design iterations before the final design is reached are typical examples of a repetitive measure. Repetitive events are generally a reflection of wasted and unproductive work. Repeated rejection of a document that has not been typed properly adds significant cost to clerical activity.

Measures of Cost

Cost has always been a primary measure of business performance. However, the cost of product and service waste did not receive widespread attention by

---

*The service level concept appears to have originated in inventory management where, for a particular inventory item, a stock-out risk is assigned. Service level is 1—Stockout Risk. Thus, for a stockout risk of 5 percent, a service level of 0.95 exists. Depending on the type of inventory system and model used, an inventory reorder level is established for this item consistent with a service level of 95 percent.

management until the advent of quality improvement in the United States. This cost concept known as "cost of quality" was promulgated in the 1950s by J. M. Juran and A. V. Feigenbaum and further publicized by P. Crosby. Cost of quality has provided a powerful business approach for assessing the economic impact of waste in product manufacturing and service. For example, costs associated with scrap and rework of material, documentation errors, service and administrative errors of various kinds, as well as measures of loss such as stock-out and lost sales have been estimated to be in excess of 20 percent of sales for many companies. In large firms, quality costs can run in the tens of millions of dollars and even higher in some instances.

Quality costs are traditionally divided into three major elements:

1. *Failure or nonconformance costs.* Failure costs are those directly related to not meeting requirements. A nonconformance may be an incorrect insurance policy or a product not meeting specifications. Costs of product and material scrap and fixing defects or errors of various kinds are also failure costs. For an insurance policy, the cost of correcting a document having a wrongly calculated premium or an error in coverage would be considered a failure cost.

   Failure costs are often divided into costs of internal and external failure to enable management to focus on the appropriate areas of the business. An external failure cost would be that resulting from a warranty claim. An internal failure cost would be the scrap costs incurred because of faulty material used or generated in a production process.

2. *Appraisal costs.* Appraisal costs are those costs attributable to human and machine activity required to detect nonconformity in work. The cost of inspecting or auditing work as it proceeds from one operation to another is an appraisal cost. The labor cost of checking an insurance policy for accuracy would be considered an appraisal cost.

3. *Prevention costs.* Costs associated with preventing future occurrences of nonconformance are deemed prevention costs. The cost of developing a process improvement such as an automatic checking scheme for assessing the accuracy of a policy would be an example of prevention cost. Typical cost-of-quality assessments show that investments in prevention are small compared with appraisal and failure costs—a reflection of the short-term focus of business.

> Typical cost-of-quality assessments show that investments in prevention are small compared with appraisal and failure costs—a reflection of the short-term focus of business.

The quality cost approach, though by no means a standard, provides a comprehensive way to determine areas of an operation that are incurring waste and, therefore, require improvement. It can also show the savings in the failure and appraisal cost components when a preventive investment is made.

The more frequently used method in many business applications employs a straightforward computation of direct and indirect labor and equipment involved in an operation. Costs are based on the estimated cost of a nonconformance and any associated costs for repairing the error. In the case of response time, cost is based on labor time saved in producing a product or service.* Where time computations involve bringing a product to market earlier, estimates of the increase in sales are required in order to compute profits. For service-level agreement measures, the cost of lost sales (opportunity costs) or the cost of idle labor when a set of terminals is inoperative can be calculated.

Examples of various measures used in service and administrative operations are given in Table 1. These are not all-inclusive but are intended to provide the reader with an idea of the various types of measures that can be implemented.

Considerations in Selection and Implementation

Measurements must be meaningful, timely, accurate, and useful. Clearly, measures that are lacking in any one or more of these attributes will prevent proper control of an operation. In the selection and implementation of measurements, the following steps may be found helpful to the reader:

- First, determine what is to be controlled. It is useful at this point to determine (or review) the critical success factors of the process** and customer requirements. In many instances, response time is of primary importance. This makes a timing parameter such as cycle time or the elapsed time between the time an input is received until the output is transmitted an appropriate measure. In other cases, defect-free output is a critical requirement so a defect attribute such as errors becomes the right measure.
- Second, examine existing data bases for measures that are currently in use (if any). The question to be asked is: can what is available be used or can it be modified to extract the needed measures? This often occurs in the case of financial measures such as costs.
- If nothing is available, the question to be answered is: can a business case be made for new measurement tools, or should measurements be performed on a manual basis?
- Finally, given the type of measurements to be made, an appropriate sampling method, sample size, and measurement frequency must be determined. Here, the possibilities range from sample measurements of every item to sophisticated sampling techniques, depending on the application, intellectual understanding, skill, and statistical tools available.

---

*Westinghouse, for example, uses a cost-time management concept for measuring process improvements. A cost-time profile is used in measuring an existing process; costs of materials, services, and equipment are depicted as vertical lines on a chart. Diagonal lines represent labor costs as a function of time spent on the process. Process improvements manifest themselves in reduced cost-time profiles and graphically show the reduction in both cost and time that results.

**The critical success factor concept was developed by N. Rockhart in connection with the application of information systems. The concept is useful in examining any business process in terms of its critical success factors—business parameters that are crucial for the success and survival of an operation. For a firm, a critical success factor may be market share. For the marketing process, however, a critical success factor may be accurate assessment of the market for a product.

Table 1.   **Examples of Service/Administrative Measurements**

1. Accounting and finance
   - Accounting report errors (by type and quantity)
   - Number of reports issued after due date (% per month)
   - Number of account reconciliations per month
   - Number of lost discounts per month
   - Payment error rate
   - Billing errors per month by error category
   - Number of defective vouchers per reporting period
   - Clock card or payroll transcription errors
   - Ledger reruns (time and frequency)
   - Deviation of predicted budgets from actual
   - Payroll errors (number per month by type)

2. Administrative
   - Employee turnover and transfer rates
   - Number of safety violations (per month by type)
   - Response time to inquiries
   - Typing errors (per month by type)
   - Keypunch or data entry errors (per month by type)
   - Time spend in locating filed material
   - Filing errors (per month or quarter)
   - Internal mail delivery time (average turnaround time by month)

3. Computer center services and programming
   - Computer outages (time and frequency)
   - Job turn around time
   - Number of program runs to a successful compile/test
   - Number of coding errors in inspection and test
   - Program error resolution time
   - Number of documentation errors

4. Engineering
   - Number of engineering change releases (per month by type)
   - Success rate in meeting product schedules
   - Response time to bid requests
   - Adherence to contract budget
   - Number of change requests due to design errors discovered in manufacturing and field
   - Design errors found in release packages

5. Field service
   - Number of repair callbacks (per month, by type)
   - Response time to service requests
   - Response time to spare parts demand
   - Time to repair (by type of repair)

6. Marketing
   - Customer inquiry response time
   - Order errors
   - Billing errors
   - Response time to special bids
   - Accuracy of market forecasts (predicted vs. actual)
   - Contract errors
   - Number of customers gained or lost per month
   - Number of late deliveries per week or month

A useful technique for detailing and summarizing the type and frequency of inspection is shown in Table 2. Here, the measurement parameter, its unit of measure, and frequency of measurement are listed for each activity. This listing serves as an accompaniment to the flow chart and becomes a central source of measurement information for the process.

Table 2. **Process Measurement**

Process step (activity name)	Control parameter(s)	Unit of measure	Frequency	Remarks
A_1 Document inspection	Document defects – Missing – Illegible – Out of sequence	Percent of total errors by category	Every job	100% inspection
A_2				
A_3				
$\vdots$				
A_N				

Graphical Methods

Measurements of many business processes can be summarized by simple statistical charts such as trend charts and bar graphs (shown in Figure 1), pie charts and histograms, and even more complex charts such as box plots. Some business processes are amenable to control chart techniques as Dmytrow and McCabe have shown. McCabe has also given several examples of administrative types of control charts for mail delivery and purchase order errors. These examples are shown in Figures 2 and 3.

Target Ratcheting and Improvement

In the case of trend charts, one may consider establishing sliding targets to reflect a continuous drive to improve the process as shown in Figure 1. The technique of "ratcheting" targets has been found to be an effective management technique to facilitate improvements. Target ratcheting involves the periodic reassessment of actual defect data in comparison with its target or objective value. When the actuals are consistently below target for a period of time, the target is adjusted to the actuals or below. In this manner, new goals are set periodically that support a philosophy of continual improvement. Targets may be derived from process capability studies, benchmarking, or traditional competitive comparisons.

An example of target ratcheting is IBM. In the 1980s, management of the IBM Poughkeepsie plant (which produces computer mainframes) began to hold manufacturing meetings with its counterparts in Montpelier, France and Yasu, Japan. These locations were considered "sister" plants in that the same type of product was being made at the same time by similar manufacturing processes. At these meetings, which were held quarterly, various topics such

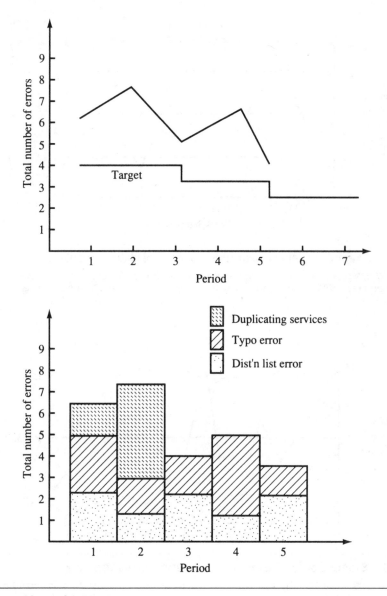

Figure 1. **Measuring the process.**

as process yields, product and process quality, process improvements, and costs were reviewed and information exchanged. During the quality reviews, each location would present its in-line performance data describing defects being encountered in its manufacturing process, its root cause analysis of the defects, and actions taken to prevent their recurrence.

The performance of each process sector would be presented in graphic form by a trend chart showing defects versus time. Each sector would have

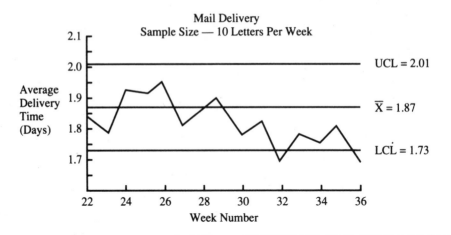

Figure 2.   **Example of service measurement control chart (variables).**

(Source: W. J. McCabe, "Quality Methods Applied to the Business Process," Transactions 40th Annual Quality Congress, 1986; © American Society for Quality Control, 1986; Reprinted by permission.)

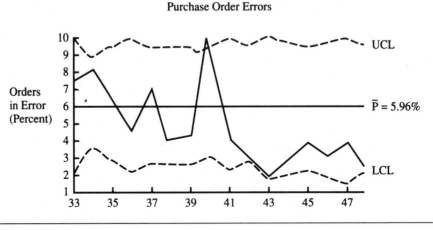

Figure 3.   **Example of service measurement attribute control chart.**

(Source: W. J. McCabe, "Quality Methods Applied to the Business Process," Transactions 40th Annual Quality Congress, 1986; © American Society for Quality Control, 1986; Reprinted by permission.)

an established target, which was set both by past history and by judgement as to what the process is capable of giving. As the quarterly reviews progressed, it became clear to the Poughkeepsie plant manager who attended each review that each manufacturing location had its own quality target. Moreover, for essentially the same process, each sector was achieving a different level of quality performance. In addition, it became obvious that no one plant was consistently superior to the other two for any period of time so that a detailed root cause analysis could be made. It was also apparent that any learning curve differences could not explain these marked contrasts in quality.

The Poughkeepsie plant manager then proposed that a uniform target for each process sector be established and that the lowest (in terms of defect levels) one of the three be chosen. The Yasu and Montpelier plant managers readily agreed to the proposal and a target standard went into effect immediately. For some sectors, the targets were set by Poughkeepsie; for others, the Japanese and French plant management set the target.

As the quarterly reviews progressed, it became evident that the sectors were beginning to reach the new targets as the plan-do-check-act methodology of measurement, root cause analysis, and defect elimination became an integral part of the manufacturing process.* The rates of quality improvement differed by sector, by plant location and, to compound matters, differed in time. During the course of a year, the plant having the highest overall quality level shifted in what appeared to be a random fashion among Montpelier, Poughkeepsie, and Yasu. In fact, what was occurring was an interplant quality competition. As Poughkeepsie personnel saw that its defect levels (measured in parts per million) were somewhat greater than either or both of the other two plants, increased motivation to improve quality occurred. This, in turn, unleashed additional improvement efforts which resulted in further defect elimination and increased quality levels surpassing that of the sister plants. When this occurred, employees of the sister plants were goaded into further action to reduce defects and the cycle repeated itself.

At a point in time, all three plant locations were approaching targets. Each plant manager was faced with a dilemma: maintain the targets and be satisfied with their achievement, or change them. Each of the three knew about, and subscribed to, the concept of continuous improvement, hence, change was the only alternative. The question became how to do it? At the next quarterly review meeting, the Poughkeepsie plant manager proposed that, as each target was reached, a new target be automatically set to the actuals being achieved by the first location to break the target value. No location would be permitted to reset to a higher defect level. The Yasu and Montpelier plant managers readily agreed to the proposal and the concept of the ratcheting target was born. Since then, this concept was adopted at other locations and for other products within the company with excellent results.

Measurements, if performed correctly, provide a factual and quantitative basis for improvement. Referring back to Figure 1, the trend chart or line graph shown leads us to conclude that the documentation process is improving over time because there is a general decline in total errors. However, because errors can originate at several different steps in the process, control and improvement can only result from analyzing the process and examining the individual, or piece-part, contributions to the errors in the output.

Measurements, if performed correctly, provide a factual and quantitative basis for improvement.

---

*Interestingly, this problem-solving approach was used without knowledge of the Shewhart plan-do-check-act cycle or training in the Deming method. For the Poughkeepsie manufacturing personnel involved, it was simply a natural and logical way to isolate causes of defects and prevent their recurrence.

Functional Processes

SALES AND MARKETING

A Sales Force Strategy for Quality

James W. Cortada

This chapter from a new book by co-editor James Cortada describes specific strategies for implementing quality programs in sales organizations. It examines key elements of these strategies including measurements, organization, compensation, and education. *This material provides a clear statement of the quality paradigm and its practical application in managing a sales force.*

> We realize that we are in a race without a finish line. As we improve, so does our competition. Five years ago we would have found that disheartening. Today we find it invigorating.
>
> David Kearns, Xerox

The challenges facing sales management are to define how customer-contact employees should behave, what services customers should be provided besides simply a product, and to what extent offerings are "pushed" on customers as opposed to executing a "pull" strategy. Many factors influence choices: competition, the nature of goods and services, industry practices, economic realities, quality of the sales force, and so forth. Yet even at the

---

sales force level, the basic elements of TQM can and are being applied to implement marketing strategies.

The Theory of Quality in Sales

However you choose to implement quality principles, the elements are the same, regardless of whether they are imposed on manufacturing or any other part of the business. All good quality plans should have the following elements:

1. customer delight (customer satisfaction and feedback)
2. leadership involvement (directs and inspects)
3. continuous improvement (process focus)
4. employee involvement (commitments and empowerment)
5. quality assurance (assessment and process)
6. measurements (including self-assessments)
7. supplier partnership (sharing same disciplines of management)
8. strategic quality planning (by all involved)

> However you choose to implement quality principles, the elements are the same, regardless of whether they are imposed on manufacturing or any other part of the business.

At all levels of a sales organization, activities are looked at as collections of processes. All should contain each of the eight elements of TQM assembled into a cohesive plan that is implemented. Managing the effectiveness of these elements within processes is an important way to improve sales. Increasingly, leading with quality, rather than with price, is proving to be the more effective strategy.

Three Effective Attitudes Toward Quality in Sales

Three perspectives apply at the sales level when implementing quality. First, activities performed always should be looked at as part of a collection of processes. Processes are the heart of any quality movement. Thus you can look at the order entry process, commission and compensation process, customer feedback process, and so forth. Customer-contact personnel can improve their efficiency by looking at their activities as a series of processes and, as they are asked to study these (because they are closest to the issues), they in fact can improve effectiveness with little or no management involvement.

Second, all processes, tasks, and measurements of effectiveness have an outward, or customer focus. Measuring how fast an activity is performed is of little significance if the customer does not care. For example, of what importance is it to a customer how fast your organization collects outstanding accounts receivables? It is very important to you, but if they are collected too effectively you might lose a customer. Much too frequently the tendency is to measure with inwardly focused indicators. The evolution of measurements should be to more outward, customer-focused indicators.

The third perspective calls for reductions in the time in which a cycle of events takes place. Cycle time reduction is of particular value in customer-contact situations for a number of reasons. For one thing, when you reduce the amount of time it takes to provide a service, customers like that and come back for more. That is why banks and fast food restaurants constantly worry about customer lines at counters and continuously try to figure out how to shorten them. For another, cycle time reduction means customer-contact personnel can service more customers, hence increasing both's productivity.

Reducing the amount of time it takes to execute a process often leads to reduced numbers of errors because, in many instances, cycle time reduction can only be achieved by simplifying the process you have today. That requires taking out more steps. Each time a step in a process is eliminated, you reduce the risk of an error. That is theory and often reality. However, since you can also create unanticipated new problems, it becomes critical to document the changes (so you can go back and see what is different). It also becomes crucial to measure the consequences of as many steps as possible, in order to learn how you are improving, what causes fewer or more errors, and to suggest possible opportunities for continued improvement. The errors will still occur, the changes will not always please you, but in aggregate, the process improves.

Common examples of simplification include reducing the number of approvals and "signoffs" required, the number of forms to be filled out (thereby eliminating redundant data that might be entered incorrectly anyway), and the number of people who have to touch a process. That is why more authority and responsibility is increasingly being placed in the hands of those actually performing tasks. Another approach is to delegate responsibility for an entire process to a small team (typically fewer than 10 individuals), who can decide at a tactical level how best to perform tasks. Both approaches decompartmentalize activities, *integrating* them more closely. The result is that they get done faster and more accurately.

Why You Should Focus on Customer Satisfaction and Cycle Time Reduction

Customer satisfaction and cycle time reduction represent the two most useful points of attack when searching for better ways to run a business. By asking how we might increase customer satisfaction, we immediately place ourselves in the position of our customers. We become more inclined to find out what they want next, crafting new offerings as a result. All the literature on quality and marketing harps on being fanatical about customer satisfaction; experience indicates that this is a good perspective. However, too often, even in well-run organizations, internal views are too dominant. Thus the culture constantly must be redirected outward toward customer satisfaction. This can be done by implementing measurements of customer satisfaction as opposed to tracking internal productivity achievements and by building processes that address customer needs before those of the firm.

Cycle time reduction can be used to lead employees to new ways of thinking about process reengineering. This is a technique well-understood in manufacturing. Ford executives like to cite the example of accounts payable, where they went from having hundreds of employees in each plant to fewer than a handful. They asked the question, How can we do accounts payable more quickly with fewer employees? By setting expectations on what "more quickly" meant, they forced thinking away from incremental improvements

Customer satisfaction and cycle time reduction represent the two most useful points of attack when searching for better ways to run a business.

in their accounts payable process to fundamentally new approaches. Now suppliers get paid as soon as parts are shipped, not 30 days or more later.

Using the Eight Elements of Quality

The same can be done in sales. By setting a dramatically high level of expectations for a particular process, by default you force the process owners to develop bold new approaches. Along the way they can add customer satisfaction indicators, make more decisions based on fact that can be trapped more effectively than before, and give both customers and employees confidence about the possibility of even better service.

Process owners play a special role. They "own" responsibility for improving a process and should enjoy the fruits of their success. Since "their" process usually crosses conventional organization lines, they must be given responsibility to act and recruit cross-functional teams (people from various departments), as well as to be held accountable for results. These responsibilities often mean, in practical terms, that the process owner has to be high enough in the organization to understand how the process will be affected by the reduction of corporate coordination of activities across various departments and divisions. In other words, process owners must understand the context in which their responsibilities lie. My notion of ownership is crucial to the successful implementation of a process because it is best handled in the same way as, for instance, the delegation of responsibility for generating sales, using all the same motivational tools such as compensation, rewards, and accountability.

Figure 1 summarizes on the right the kind of behavior wanted in a quality-driven organization and on the left the kind of behavior that generally exists today. To move from left to right, you use the eight key elements of TQM and rely on customer satisfaction and cycle time reductions as compasses to guide you. The necessary task improvements can be done using the process management reengineering techniques we are increasingly studying and applying today.

CULTURE CHANGES IN SALES ORGANIZATIONS

Transactions ▶	Relationships
Product ▶	Service
Centralized Management ▶	Decentralized Management
Individual Performance ▶	Team Performance
Bureaucratic ▶	Entrepreneurial
Inward (Upward) Focused ▶	Outward (Customer) Focused
Slow to Change ▶	Quick to Change
Measures Efficiency ▶	Measures Effectiveness

Figure 1. **The transformation of a sales organization.**

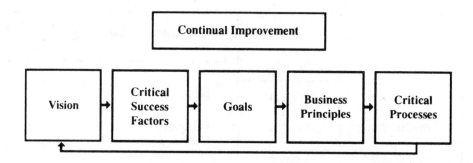

Vision:

A view of our environment that will enable our tremendous future success.

Critical Success Factors:

Areas requiring continual improvement through quality to successfully implement our vision.

Goals:

Measurable targets that support our vision and ensure focus on the critical success factors.

Business Principles:

The manner in which employees approach their responsibilities to achieve our goals.

Critical Processes:

The most important processes requiring a discipline to support the actualization of our vision.

Figure 2.   **A simplified blueprint for excellence.**

Figure 2 illustrates conceptually how all of these elements work. As you develop a plan for quality improvements, it is helpful to document these actions in a visual manner so that everyone understands how specific activities fit into the big picture. Figure 2 is a simplified form of an actual blueprint for excellence employed by a sales organization.

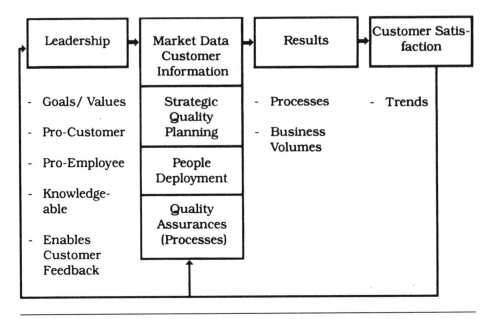

Figure 3. **Process view of a market-driven sales organization.**

Existing models of how quality-driven organizations view themselves apply in a sales enterprise. For example, Figure 3 looks at sales as one large process and uses the Baldrige framework to express its various components. As with the pieces depicted in Figure 2, we see common elements:

- the leader driving a vision that is heavily value-based (e.g., market-driven, customer-focused, quality-dependent)
- the collection of information used in fact-based decision making, planning and deployment, and improving the processes of the enterprise
- the measurement of both results and customer satisfaction

Results then influence the leader's vision and the process starts all over again.

The Role of Processes

The core of a quality-driven sales organization's activities is its collection of processes with which the business is run. In addition to providing leadership and measuring results, the lion's share of the work in transforming an organization rests on the collection of tasks performed on a daily basis. The sooner you can identify these, measure their current effectiveness, assign process owners, and begin improving critical processes, the faster you get going on the quality journey.

How to Apply Planning Elements

The beginning is the creation of a vision of where the organization is going. Visioning as a process is more appropriately discussed by experts on leadership and need not detain us here. However, having a leadership vision, as well as a mission statement about what the role of the sales organization should be, are preliminary steps to working with processes.

The mission statement should be profoundly customer-driven. For example, "thriving by helping our customers gain competitive advantage in their markets through the use of our services," suggests a focus. Some organizations also add a statement concerning their employees for example, "We are also committed to continually improving the skills, performance, and job satisfaction of all employees." Most will also make a statement of success: "A key measurement of our success will be our growth in revenue," or "in customer satisfaction."

Traditional critical success factor analysis typically leads a quality driven organization to the conclusion that improving customer satisfaction is the most important issue to focus on, followed very closely by employee success (morale, skills, and so forth). Other critical success factors involve an organized approach to identification of sales opportunities, application of teamwork, use of process reengineering, and so forth. Results usually are measured in one of three ways:

- customer success or satisfaction
- employee success or morale
- company revenue or profit success

Typically, indicators of success and continuous improvement are developed for all three categories, as it is impossible to do well without performing effectively in all arenas. Examples of quality indicators are percentages of telephone calls answered, measures of how fast proposals are answered over time, or surveys of how customers feel about particular service or offering.

Goals help point to the specific processes that must improve and become more effective. Goals also serve as a good link back to vision and categories of successes. In sales organizations effective common goals are statements of values and expectations. Examples include:

- delighting customers
- improving employee skills
- implementing "world class" quality
- enjoying market share growth
- experiencing increased profitability

Setting Priorities for What Gets Done

Firms that have experienced successes in the implementation of quality in sales organizations, such as IBM, Motorola, and Xerox, will argue that (1) you cannot fix all processes at the same time because boiling the ocean will take too much focus off day-to-day business and (2) thus you must set priorities on processes targeted for improvement. Experience shows that working on a few at a time (say a half dozen or fewer) in a disciplined manner is extremely effective. Once a set of processes is improved, stabilized, and put on a course

---

IMPORTANT SALES PROCESS

Opportunity Identification	Competitive Analysis
Customer Feedback	Compensation
Communication	Employee Feedback
Skills Development	Order Processing
Accounts Receivable	Distribution/Delivery
Service and Repair	Recognition
Revenue and Profit Accounting	Pricing
Telephones	Business Partners
Supplier Relations	Facilities Management
Advertising	Sales Planning
Quotas and Measurements	Suggestions
Resource Deployment	Inventory Management
Organization	Strategic Planning
Quality Assessments	Personnel Practices
Complaints	Market Segmentation
Product Liability	Brand Management

Figure 4.   **Important processes in a sales organization.**

of continuous improvement (and with some early results achieved to encourage others), then the next tier of processes can be addressed.

It is not uncommon to catalog a list of 15 to 20 critical processes that need improvement.

It is not uncommon to catalog a list of 15 to 20 critical processes that need improvement. Figure 4 lists some of the more obvious ones evident in all sales organizations. Yours probably has some additional ones. No list is absolute except the one your organization creates. But any list is very long.

Depending on which planning methodology is used, it is best to lump all obvious processes into groups based on importance to the organization and to its customers. Linkage analysis methods, for example, point out dependencies among processes, which leads to one list of what gets worked on first, then second, and so forth. Self-interest and management philosophies about how things get done will lead to another. Sporadic or even thorough surveying of customers generates a third. Any of the major planning methodologies in use today will generate useful lists. In the final analysis, your list will be a blend of what is important to customers, your employees, and the firm as a whole.

However, experience shows that there are several very obvious processes and issues to begin with, regardless of what list is used. They are (1) measurements, (2) organization, (3) compensation, and (4) education on quality. All four are admittedly inward-focused, pay too little attention to customers, and allow maximum politicking in the existing culture. However, they are the crucial early processes to work on because they represent the bedrock of incentives that historically have encouraged employees to perform the way you want. By the same logic these tools, when managed as processes, can be applied to improve all other processes, to learn about quality improvement techniques, and ultimately to change behavior to conform to the vision. Organizations that have transformed their sales organizations understand the logic of why these four are first and in the order listed; the literature on quality is only just beginning to catch up with this reality.

Measurements

People work on those tasks for which they are being measured. That is one reason Deming, Juran, and all the other quality gurus spend time on the pros and cons of various types of measurement systems. In order to improve continuously, processes have to be measured statistically; yet even before going to work on a process, individuals must have incentives to perform well. Part of how that is done is through measurements. Nowhere is this more so than in a sales organization, where we have developed a type of worker whose performance is rewarded according to measurable results, usually sales volumes or profitable sales volumes. Their managers are also products of a system that rewards them with money and promotions based on their performance against a measurement system. Often this measurement system created incentives for individual results, not for team results. The incentives also encouraged many sales regardless of what the market (customer) wanted—the "push" approach.

People work on those tasks for which they are being measured.

Sales personnel traditionally compete against each other, as well as against other competitors outside of their firm. By not cooperating across a larger base of customers, they suboptimize the capabilities of the entire enterprise to get many sales in order for the individual to gain a few orders in a particular sales territory.

In a shared circumstance, someone with deep skills in a particular aspect of your services or product line could focus just on that, bringing in more sales because of his or her continually improving skills. But when more skill is focused on a narrower area, a larger territory or customer set is required. This is the reason for finding ways to share resources across a broader customer set.

The theory behind traditional measurement systems is that sales personnel work best when rewarded for individual achievements (sales) and that they will not attempt high performance if not measured and rewarded on a transaction-by-transaction basis, in other words, by commissions and quotas. A backward look in time indicates the wisdom of this approach, as most successful sales organizations have compensated and rewarded their staffs that way.

How Measurements Influence Your Sales Team

However, it is becoming increasingly evident that the nature of measurements profoundly supports or inhibits the cultural transformation of an organization, particularly manufacturing sales teams that need to become more service-oriented. It is difficult to get the attention of a salesperson to improve a customer-related process if he or she is only being measured on sales achieved this month. In other words, the measurement system in an enterprise must support the vision, goals, and objectives in terms that are quality-driven.

The measurement system in an enterprise must support the vision, goals, and objectives in terms that are quality-driven.

Jump-Starting Transformation with Shared Measurements

Several very simple methods are frequently used to jump-start the transformation. First, in order to get disparate sales offices or sales units working together to optimize the use of resources, have them share a common quota. If an individual's reward/compensation/career is dependent on the success of specific others, he or she will quickly want to learn to function in a team environment. The process is most successful if managers of a sales office within a district are first put on the district manager's quota, because then they have an incentive to alter their own and employee's behavior.

This shared measurement approach should not be limited just to quotas but should include expenses, resource allocation, market share, and over all customer satisfaction. By being forced to help others be successful in order to succeed individually, executive management can then turn to this team to determine better how to allocate resources across various sales offices, share resources, or combine processes to improve overall effectiveness. In time, the sales organization can also improve the measurement and reward processes of the firm to reflect the new realities values.

How far down the organization should shared measurements go? The cautious approach is to begin with just sales management at the district and sales office levels sharing common measurements. However, it quickly becomes evident that unless a common measurement system exists up and down the line from sales representative up to sales executive, contention and conflict occur. Therefore, common measurements have to be pushed as rapidly as possible down the organization. Team successes then become more valued.

Initial reaction to such an approach is anything but wildly enthusiastic, particularly among outstanding sales personnel who fear commissions being "socialized" as they "carry" weaker performers. They also experience difficulty relating to successes that are much larger than they are accustomed to tracking. For example, if salespeople used to chasing $100,000 worth of revenue annually and are now being asked to contribute to the success of an organization selling $5 million in goods and services, they may not relate their contribution to the $5 million as easily as to the lower number.

However, if expectations of how much individuals should generate for the common good are defined and the results of those salespeople and the enterprise are communicated constantly, they soon come to relate to the welfare of the whole. For example, asking salespeople to grow their sales volumes by what is anticipated across their industry, knowing that expectations may rise or fall during the course of the year depending on how the whole team does, helps move the process along. Then broadcasting how the entire enterprise is doing monthly, quarterly, and annually lets management communicate whether as a team everyone is on track to success or if additional efforts are required.

Thus measurements in a quality-driven organization tend to be broader in scope than in traditional sales structures. Instead of just measuring an individual's sales revenues or number of products sold, other measurements, such as customer satisfaction indices (for which you need a customer feedback process), skill levels, profitability, and team participation, are added. This requires reward and recognition systems to change so that a salesperson can actually thrive because of outstanding contributions in areas other than just revenue volumes. For many, that notion is radical, a profound departure from how we have measured sales personnel in the past.

> Other measurements, such as customer satisfaction indices, skill levels, profitability, and team participation, are added.

A Case of the New Measurements

Perhaps no greater stereotype of the traditional commission-hungry predatory salesperson exists than that of a car salesperson. Yet it is this community that provides a dramatic example of what happens when measurement systems are changed. Carl Sewell's Cadillac dealership—the most successful luxury-car business in the United States—illustrates the lesson. Sewell begins with the concept that if something is important then it should be measured so you know how you are doing. Second, he believes in setting measurable targets for performance, e.g., number of cars sold, bills collected, customers satisfied, and so forth. He argues that "the secret is to set goals that are in the best interest of the business," which ties back to the vision of what the business should be all about. Sewell believes in competition and thus makes available to all employees results of individuals. But he also expects the team as a whole to be successful.

Sewell argues that measurements can be compared to baseball performance. You want measurements that indicate whether or not the baseball team won and individual statistics on the performance of each player. Using the same analogy, individual performance indicators can be accumulated for the team while the team has a common goal: to win today's game, to get to the World Series, to be world champions. As individuals—and thus the team as a whole—perform better, expectations can be raised and measurements can document results. Thus a combination of what the individual and the enterprise do together provides the design point for measurement systems that encourage continuous improvement.

Sewell preaches the gospel of measurements. Simply put, his experience shows that you should measure things that employees can relate to, affect, track easily, and understand. One added-value tip from Sewell is to state your measurements in positive terms, not as targets missed but as progress toward a goal. His success is built on the vision of customer satisfaction; no measurement is implemented that does not support that notion. The result: his is one of the most successful automobile businesses in America as measured by repeat business, growth in sales, and earnings of sales personnel.

Focus on Measurements

Lesson Number One. Focus early in your transformation on what gets measured; later we will look at what gets rewarded as linked to performance against measurements. Changing measurements may in fact be the easiest element of a transformation process because the senior manager of an organization can almost single-handedly implement these. He or she would then require the help of staff to trap data on these measurements and ideally would engage employees in designing measurements in the first place to gain buy-in and understanding.

Organization

Chances are your organization is a marvelous example of what your firm needed to perform well in the past. It probably is not well structured for today's market realities because it is very difficult to change structures. Changes are attacks on little kingdoms, sanctuaries of inefficiency, and comfortable zones of operation. Most companies reflect a time when efficient organizational structure involved a command-and-control approach to business. That required many layers of management and staff, often leading to ratios of staff to customer-contact employees of 5 to 1 up to 8 to 1. Changes to policies, practices, and offerings had to work their way through a hierarchy to ensure that coordination occurred across the empire and that innovations were the "right" ones.

Times have changed. Symptoms are everywhere. Product introductions need to come every year or two, not every three to seven years. New competitors appear from out of left field, especially from overseas. Market opportunities are identified more quickly, and you have less time to take advantage of them before they change, disappear, or are occupied by a rival. Microcomputers and telecommunications have democratized access to information in all organizations, allowing a decision maker to act faster. This access reduces or bypasses traditional staff functions. Costs are too high, given what goods and services have to be sold for, so overhead must be slashed, and quickly.

Then, of course, change is not what it used to be. In a marvelous book, *The Age of Unreason*, Charles Handy shows that change is not part of a pattern but appears more "discontinuous" than ever before; thus it's disturbing to decision-makers. He argues that "it is the little changes which can in fact make the biggest differences to our lives" and that "changes in the way our work is organized . . . will make the biggest differences to the way we all will live." We do not need to go through his defense of these ideas because we all are already noticing the effects on our businesses.

What Today's Organizations Must Look Like

Let's get to the heart of the matter. We need to structure organizations that satisfy several basic requirements reflecting current realities:

- the majority of workers placed in direct customer-support functions; fewer in staff positions
- fewer levels of management, driving down overhead costs while shortening the decision-making process
- flexibility to change quickly to support new sales opportunities
- continuous improvements in the effectiveness of the enterprise

As sales increasingly move toward a market reality that involves adding services to products, deliverables become more of what an individual does in front of the customer. Instead of just delivering a product, you frequently have to perform a service associated with that product. That circumstance can call for more labor-intensive tasks and, at a minimum, requires people in front of customers. In a market-driven organization, backroom personnel are of less value to customers. So, from a design point of view, we need more sales and service personnel and less staff. It is no accident that major corporations throughout the world are slashing staff functions in order to supply sales offices with people.

As market conditions change, the ability to make decisions more quickly and to deploy resources equally as fast requires us to reduce decision-making cycle time. The only way to do that is first, by reducing the number and levels of decision makers, and second, by giving greater authority to make decisions to lower levels of an organization. The ideal situation is a customer with a salesperson who has been properly trained, who can negotiate a profitable deal on the spot, and who can close some business without having to run to a manager for permission. That is cycle time reduction at work!

It is no accident that major corporations throughout the world are slashing staff functions in order to supply sales offices with people.

The smaller the transaction value, the easier it is to empower employees to make quick decisions:

- the waiter who rips up a dinner bill because the meal was poorly prepared
- the automobile salesperson who adds a half dozen oil changes to clinch a deal or to thank a repeat customer
- the clerk who takes back a piece of merchandise with no questions asked because customer satisfaction is paramount

We have all heard about the extreme cases of people renting helicopters or jumping out of airplanes to deliver goods, and Japanese store clerks delivering flowers and products to people who bought faulty electronics. But realistically, the required decision making is more than just having customer-contact employees enjoy greater leeway in making decisions. It also involves giving managers greater responsibility and authority to decide what products to sell, what services to offer, and how best to organize without having to seek permission. That is the goal you should strive for in restructuring organizations.

Why We Need to Change Organizations

The logic for changing organizations to meet new market conditions is fairly straightforward. Organizations function best when they support groups of work activity and if these groups of work activity respond in time to existing marketing opportunities. So the ability to change an organization's structure quickly is very important. It's also significant to have measurements that encourage an organization to change in a timely fashion in response to market conditions.

An example illustrates the case. IBM in the 1980s did a fine job in selling computer hardware. It became very obvious as the 1980s passed, however, that the slowest growing portion of the market was hardware and that the two fastest expanding segments were software sales and services (e.g., programming, project management, and consulting). Being outstanding in the fastest shrinking segment of the market was not going to be a long-term winning strategy. IBM therefore poured dollars and people into software and services. That led to major reorganizations as resources shifted to these growing market segments. As a result, contract services business grew at double-digit rates in the late 1980s and early 1990s, rapidly contributing larger portions of the overall revenue of the corporation. A whole new consulting business emerged that, by mid-1993, had become a very large enterprise in itself, generating hundreds of millions of dollars in revenue around the world. Meanwhile hardware revenues, still enormous, remained relatively flat as product costs declined and expenditures by customers shifted to software and services.

Hardware firms that did not make the shift quickly enough either suffered terribly or went out of business. IBM, although it was not entirely immune to the negative effects of the transition, nonetheless moved rapidly from being just a vendor of machines to being a service company with positive results. Internally, the same kind of impatience exhibited in process reengineering and cultural change appeared with the movement to new markets. Executives wanted the process of migration to software and consulting to go faster than it did; but change came and at about the same speed as in other firms that transformed their businesses.

Other examples abound. Airline companies now think of themselves as service companies, with their "moments of truth" coming when customers deal with employees. Sewell uses the notion of service more frequently than the concept of sales to attract business. Today all the literature on marketing and manufacturing identifies with the concept of service.

How to Change an Organization

Alteration of spans of control in turn forces managers to become facilitators of change, cheerleaders, and visionaries.

The fastest, easiest way for organizations to change is to reduce their size. That means taking out layers of management, changing spans of managerial control from 5 or 6 employees to 10 or 30 employees. Alteration of spans of control in turn forces managers to become facilitators of change, cheerleaders, and visionaries, because otherwise they become huge bottlenecks for employees. Changing spans of control also forces organizations to delegate more responsibility and authority to the lowest levels. If you have intelligent, positively motivated employees who are well trained to make decisions and support and understand the vision, the process works. Those closest to a situation or a problem often are the best individuals to find a solution. Organizations, therefore, become smaller, hence easier to change, and migrate to structures that support the work that has to be done.

There is no ideal organization. At one enterprise sales and administration may form a team to concentrate on a specific set of clients while at another, a group of product experts may band together to increase market share in a specific geographic area. In the consulting world, teams of experts from all over the nation come together for a specific engagement and then disband at the end of that effort. Often they operate with little management interference because all are being measured by a common system focused on making the engagement successful.

Increasingly evident is the rapidity of "unofficial" changes in organizations. Traditionally, management announces a restructuring and produces an organization chart with people's names in boxes. We have all seen examples of how in practice people cluster together differently than on the "org chart" to get tasks done. What is happening more today is that the informal organizational structure is the norm, and that it changes much faster. Access to telecommunications, data bases, micro-computers, fax machines, and air travel has democratized business structures, taking away from senior management the authority to design the organization. The challenge for management is to make those changes public to improve their efficiency and effectiveness.

Individuals increasingly are working out of their homes and cars, may or may not be card-carrying members of your firm, and already are specializing with deeper skills in narrower functions. Charles Handy has statistics that bear out this reality; the point is you have to make organizations work in this new world.

Focus on Organizational Change Early

Lesson Number Two.   Make organizational change as early as possible in the transformation of a sales enterprise to a quality, market-driven one. Encourage change organizationally and use measurements, flatten enterprises, share resources across traditional departments (e.g., sales office to sales office, store to store, district to district), delegate more responsibility (empower) to employees. To make that happen, all have to be accountable for common results, share a universal set of measurements applicable to various types of organizations (e.g., customer satisfaction indices, profit targets, etc.), and be knowledgeable about a common business plan.

Compensation

No issue creates more controversy faster in a quality-driven organization than how sales personnel are paid. The debate is an unresolved one and yet it strikes at the core of what an organization values. In the eyes of sales personnel "walking the talk" is most reflected in their compensation plan. The jury is still out on what constitutes the best strategy for balancing revenue generation with continuous improvements within a customer-focused enterprise. However, the battle lines are drawn and you have to choose which side to fight on.

The traditional school of thought holds that salespeople perform best when they are paid for transactions (things sold, billable services performed) in the belief that only in this way will their productivity be maximized. In this paradigm sales representatives are usually paid some salary (or none) and then commissions for either goods and services sold or how they do against preassigned quotas. There may or may not be any limits to their earnings, and all are encouraged to make more money by selling more products. For over a century this approach has characterized the sales compensation plans for most manufacturing companies with direct sales forces and for retail sales operations.

The benefit of such an approach is that sales personnel have to hustle to get paid and also fear being fired for not making objectives. It fosters self-initiative and independent action, and it keeps sales personnel focused on results, usually in individual territories.

The downside of this approach is that salespeople do not have incentives to develop relationships with clients that go beyond the sale of specific types of products. Concern, for example, for the overall welfare of a customer has to take a back seat. Resources are collected by sales people into concentrated masses focused only on their territory with little or no regard for the welfare of the enterprise at large. In their world it is more important that *they* make quota than the corporation. Sharing of resources and help is less evident in this kind of environment. Development of additional skills also is minimized since it takes away from selling time. Frequently products that get sold most are those on which there is a bonus.

Problems with Traditional Compensation Methods

Besides these drawbacks, given what has been occurring in the world economy, the debate on how to compensate sales personnel has once again surfaced. For one thing, in a quota-driven environment, it becomes difficult for an organization to gain the full cooperation of sales personnel in identifying sales opportunities. Sales personnel fear that once additional leads are identified, their quotas will go up and hence put their earnings at risk if performance is measured against percent of quota attained. Yet sales personnel frequently have the most detailed view of opportunities, even if theirs is a constrained view (based only on what they see on the horizon in specific accounts). Not to use salespeople as full players in opportunity identification makes it difficult for a firm to respond quickly to changing market conditions.

A second problem is that a transaction-based compensation plan does not sufficiently encourage relationship-building as the organization becomes more service-based in performance of its marketing and sales functions. As it becomes increasingly important to employ teams working continuously or in narrow engagements with customers, the old compensation system is perceived simply as not motivating cooperation. Sales personnel tend, therefore, to "work the sales plan" to their advantage, which would be fine if corporations developed sales plans that elicited the exact kind of behavior wanted from the sales force. Few ever do, however; they always seem not quite perfect.

> Not to use salespeople as full players in opportunity identification makes it difficult for a firm to respond quickly to changing market conditions.

New Ways to Compensate

Against this background is another school of thought very different from what sales management has ever known. Deming, for instance, attacks quotas since they do not account for either quality or methods. He argues that to make quota, a salesperson will burn up as much of the company's resources as he or she has to.

Put in a more positive way, there is a school of thought that says, pay your salespeople a good salary and then allow them the opportunity to earn bonuses based on their performance in a number of areas, of which revenue generation is only one. This approach says that you pay less attention to "pushing" specific products on customers and more on encouraging (pulling) customers toward you, by emphasizing relationship-building instead of just transactions performed.

In order to alter behavior to mimic service-sector performance more closely, bonuses are paid based on management's assessment of performance in specific categories that are often defined in some detail in performance plans developed jointly with employees. These might include bonuses for achievements in the following categories:

- revenue generation
- team participation
- quality process improvements
- suggestions implemented
- skills developed
- customer satisfaction improvements
- sales opportunities and leads identified

Various models of bonus structures exist to implement these. Most are consistent from salesclerk and representative up through ranks of sales management.

Approaches vary. One way would be to assign point values for each category and then allocate available bonus money divided by the number of points, then multiply the number of points earned by an individual during a specific appraisal period by the bonus amount per point. Another would place an employee in one of four levels from high to low and assign bonuses as a percent of assigned salary with the people in the highest level earning the greatest percentage of salary (e.g., 40 to 90 percent) and those in the lowest level receiving nothing. This approach protects the ideal of attempting to feed the eagles and starve the turkeys. It has the added advantage in that the bonus pot is never overspent, as happens frequently in traditional percent-of-quota-attainment-based systems.

What Customers and Employees Want You to Do

Compensation systems are viewed very differently depending on where you perch in the customer-sales personnel chain. So far we have talked about a sales perspective. What about customers and the firm? Customers generally want sales personnel to treat them fairly and honestly keeping their short-

and long-term interests at heart. At the other extreme is the firm which desires to influence the activity and results of both sales personnel and customers.

Salespersons in the middle want a link to the firm that pays their salary and compensation at least commensurate with the results they achieved, and ideally with the efforts they expended. Studies on motivation notwithstanding, there is a higher percentage of individuals working in sales who are motivated by money than in most other professions, and salespeople have less regard for job security than many other professionals. Those are the realities facing sales and marketing managers designing compensation plans.

The Conference Board, in a 1979 study about sales force motivation, learned that the top five motivators for sales personnel, ranked in descending order, were:

1. Recognition for outstanding performance
2. Promotional advancement opportunity
3. Management encouragement
4. Personal bonus incentives
5. Incentives in the form of commissions

Overall compensation was sixth, skills development seventh, and prizes eleventh. As an incentive, quotas were twelfth!

So should you assign quotas or not? In either extreme you can or cannot; what you do is a function of what your culture can tolerate. More important, which approach alters behavior to achieve what you want the entire organization to display?

A third variant, usually applied in addition to a base compensation and bonus plan, is some form of profit sharing. This approach is becoming increasingly popular in organizations that want (1) employees to work as teams, (2) employees to watch bottom-line expenses, and (3) to reward the effectiveness of the organization as a whole. The corporation assigns a percent of its profits to a bonus shared by all employees. The bonus is either a flat amount paid equally to each employee or a percentage of an individual's salary. Thus a salesperson who made more money this year than another would receive a larger profit-sharing bonus in recognition of his or her greater overall contribution to the corporation's profitability.

A middle ground between the old commission structure and the "let's get rid of all quota" approaches has been employed successfully by Sewell in his Cadillac business. Individual targets are set, results publicly posted, and payments made against revenue and other targets achieved. The business as a whole has targets that are communicated continuously to employees. At IBM, a combination of salary, product sales and/or behavior (e.g., acquisition of skills, implementation of process improvements, etc.) is generally in use, and in 1992, a profit-sharing bonus was implemented.

Develop a Compensation Plan that Supports Your Vision

Lesson Number Three. Getting to the right compensation method crucial for an organization. Two suggestions work well.

First, form a team of sales personnel and sales management to develop a compensation methodology consistent with what the enterprise expects in the form of rewardable behavior, namely an overwhelmingly procustomer emphasis with an eye cast on the bottom line, too. The will do the job better than any personnel or compensation consultant because they are closest to the situation.

Second, treat compensation as a process that needs to be studied and continuously modified as circumstances warrant. If employees come to see that it is *their* process, they can be expected to take ownership of tying its rewards to their business objectives.

Now let me complicate the process further by reminding you that as sales personnel get older, their interests change. Between roughly ages 20 and 30, people are developing, learning, and exploring possibilities, and therefore they are very interested in things such as improving selling skills, job satisfaction, and positive feedback. In the next period—roughly from about age 30 to 45—research shows that career enhancement is of utmost importance while their managers are viewed less as guides and more as role models. Rewards have to be more than money; promotions are crucial. In the period from the late thirties to early fifties, competition for success and promotion generally declines, employees see themselves as guides, and immediate rewards have to be monetary. They worry about making money, relationships with coworkers, and how their job identifies with specific organizations. As they approach retirement, sales personnel begin to change their images, identifying with other interests outside of their traditional career. They are more interested in what psychologists and sociologists would call "lower-order rewards," like money.

So why go through all of this? As you change your organization into one valuing continuous improvement and renewed customer focus in a service-based world, each age group has to be treated differently. This is particularly difficult with older employees, a problem since 22-year-old salespeople are becoming as rare as hen's teeth thanks to demographics throughout North America and Western Europe.

> As you change your organization into one valuing continuous improvement and renewed customer focus, each age group has to be treated differently.

The problem is fixed the same way smart sales managers have always properly fixed sales contests. Involve the right age mix of sales personnel to design your reward and compensation system to conform to your requirements and values and to their needs and desires. Treat it as a process and the incentives to motivate correctly will emerge.

Quality-focused firms find that compensation strategies can be developed that support business objectives. Hewlett-Packard pays better than the average company and for merit—with bonuses, commissions, and base salary an outgrowth of sustained performance. Many of its competitors follow a similar approach. Honeywell pays competitively by business type, fairly in comparison to other employees in equal positions; the process is communicated and each business division is responsible for establishing and administering its plans.

Quality Education

The fourth process that must be attacked early and with enthusiasm and care is education to make employees aware of the principles of process reengineering, the realities of changing markets, and the definition of their role. Some skills transfer can also occur in this early stage of movement to a more quality-driven company culture.

Just as measurements, organizational changes, and compensation systems remain forever with the enterprise, so too does education on quality. Each of the Baldrige winners in the United States and Deming Prize winners in Japan will tell you that it is not uncommon to spend up to 4 percent of their budgets educating people on quality continuously for a number of years. Why? Because the results can lead to a 10 to 40 percent reduction in waste and associated costs while gaining several points of market share within three to four years of initial investment in quality education. Money in the bank or invested in stocks hardly matches those yield rates.

Every case of quality transformation I have studied has placed education at the forefront of implementation. Larry McMahan, vice president of human resources at Baldrige-winning Federal Express, stated what the first task has to be: "All managers must be required to take company unifying courses in teamwork, customer/supplier alignment and systematic quality." Brenda Sumberg, director of quality at Motorola University (Motorola was also a Baldrige winner) argues that "initially, training's role is to change the attitude of the people, then skill-based training encompasses quality tools, related to their jobs." I could fill pages with such quotations, but the message is obvious enough.

It is important to note that just as the first three most crucial processes should be attacked in the first six months of a move to quality-based management, so too should quality education.

Two Strategies for Quality Education

There are two typical approaches to quality education. The first approach, and the one most appreciated by sales personnel, involves a one- to two-day awareness class on why the enterprise needs to apply quality techniques, identification of TQM's basic elements, and some exposure to statistical methods of measuring activities. This is then usually followed up later with seminars on process reengineering (usually one or two to five) in which specific problems are worked on. At this point employees are exposed to statistical process control (SPC) tools such as Pareto charts, fishbone diagrams, and so forth.

A second path, the fire-hose approach, sends everyone off to five to fifteen days of education on the above topics and then drops them back into their work environment. If the measurement system has been altered to give incentives for process reengineering, then results can reasonably be expected; if not, then you can count on having wasted their time while frustrating employees now hopeful that things will change.

I personally have found incremental education programs substantially more effective. Providing adults with training when needed with a "just-in-time" approach works better and creates expense only when needed, when it makes sense. Each successful education program recognizes that employees need hard skills to transform their business and that those skills involve process reengineering, problem identification, analysis, and resolution. Education must allow employees to link their quality activities back to their real jobs. Finally, good education programs must by necessity evolve over time as the skills and needs of employees, individual by individual, change.

The better programs, like those at IBM, Xerox, Milliken, Federal Express, and Florida Power & Light, are also aimed at altering cultural values. For example, at IBM, a two-day class, known as "The Journey Continues," is given a year after initial TQM exposure to show employees the power of vision, the benefits of working more closely in a team environment, and how to encourage and support each other in quality improvements. It is based on the work of James M. Kouzes and Barry Z. Posner. Theirs is a simple message: to get extraordinary things done in an organization, five practices must be alive and well:

Education must allow employees to link their quality activities back to their real jobs.

- challenging the process
- inspiring a shared vision
- enabling others to act
- modeling the way
- encouraging the heart

The job of leaders is to make these five practices come alive. By challenging the process, you search for opportunities to change the status quo, with risk-taking allowed and encouraged. Inspiring a shared vision calls for envisioning a better, specific future and attracting others to the common purpose of implementing the vision. Enabling others to act is simply fostering collaboration and teamwork and sharing power and information. Modeling the way is setting the example, leading by doing. Encouraging the heart is recognizing contributions, linking rewards to performance, and "valuing the victories."

The class is unique in that it works on the values of an employee as applied to quality and not on the mechanics of applying process reengineering. Many of the same sentiments are reflected in Stephen R. Covey's *The 7 Habits of Highly Effective People.* Approximately 25 percent of the course content is directed to altering attitudes, another 25 percent to teaching skills, and the remainder to transmitting knowledge about transformation, vision, and so forth.

Nobody is exempt from quality education. In many firms the standard approach is for the initial awareness education to be taught by the highest ranking official of the firm to his or her direct reports; they in turn teach their direct reports, and so on down to the lowest level. This process ingrains in management the principles and values involved and is proof of commitment to employees up and down the line. Later, when skills, such as statistical analysis and problem solving, are of greater importance, instructors on staff (full- or part-time) usually do a better job in providing the training.

Increasingly, particularly with industrial products, customers are asking for proof of a vendor's commitment to quality. This is done not just to ensure quality goods and services but also because manufacturers are finding it more cost effective to have fewer suppliers, upon which they become more dependent. To have a supplier that is not dedicated to providing high quality goods can be disastrous. Thus just to be competitive, many suppliers have to prove what they are doing to implement TQM. For instance, at one point Motorola insisted that its suppliers compete for the Baldrige Award!

We already saw that customers at the retail level are increasingly relying on quality of products to make buying decisions rather than just on price.

Invest in Employee Education

Lesson Number Four. Educating employees about quality is thus a crucial and early requirement.

Tips on Knowing If It All Is Working

A large number of processes has to be improved to make an organization more effective. The real test of whether or not the initial attack on quality, with its attendant recharging of the customer-contact community to place customer satisfaction at the top of its priorities, begins by assuming nothing. A number of tests to gauge progress should be performed, starting at about the six-month point and continuing periodically afterward.

To begin with, the first four processes targeted—measurements, organization, compensation, and education—are inward-looking and do not involve customers or take into account where your competition is on quality. However, nobody goes to market without first doing some preparation internally, e.g., building a product or service to offer. So it is with transformation to a quality-driven organization. The initial measurements are simply a step to alter behavior and will be replaced with others more specifically tied to tactical processes of concern to customers. Organizational and compensation actions are taken to align resources with the vision of your firm's future. Education simply greases the wheels of progress.

The skeptics are the best allies because once converted they can be the nucleus of a new way of doing business.

However, while a new vision and focus may look good on paper, in reality they will be resisted. First, there are those who feel that the way things are today is just fine, so why change? A second group will conclude that the kinds of changes being asked for are different from what made them successful so far. A third perspective will be that these changes just will not work. This group—usually cynics—will argue that they have seen this all before: quality circles in the early 1980s, excellence as the program *du jour*, and so forth. The skeptics are the best allies because once converted they can be the nucleus of a new way of doing business and they ensure that reality does not give way to euphoria and wild abandon to TQM.

But because change is difficult for many people, the nature of the difficulty must be understood. That is why formal assessments are very helpful. Several techniques work well in taking the pulse of the transformation.

How to Assess the Status of Quality Among Employees

Employee opinion surveys are very useful tools; many companies apply them effectively. If you do not have such a tool, get to work on one right away and make sure its anonymity is preserved no matter what the cost, because the knowledge gained can set the quality agenda for years. As you begin to preach the gospel of quality and customer focus, two or three questions in employee opinion surveys allow you to determine progress or at least buy-in. If the questions are asked exactly the same way over the next several years, the first round serves as a base line against which to measure progress over time. The kinds of questions to ask include:

- To what extent do you believe senior management is committed to quality improvement at XYZ Company?
- To what extent are you personally willing to apply principles of quality improvement to your job?
- To what extent is your manager (or department) committed to quality improvement?

You also want to know how your managers feel about these issues both as employees and as leaders of the firm because in the final analysis, if management is not on board with quality, it will not come on its own. Senior management needs to monitor commitment on the part of those individuals who ultimately have the authority and capability of energizing the entire enterprise toward quality.

Statistically measure responses to the questions on the roles of management, department, and individual. Then also measure answers to the following:

- To what extent do you understand the company's quality improvement strategy?
- Which of the following best expresses your views on being customer-driven? (Pick 3 to 5 variables relevant to your industry and business.)

Incremental improvements in buy-in of 5 to 10 points per year would not be uncommon.

Initial responses will probably range from a low of 20 percent positive to perhaps a high of 50 percent. Incremental improvements in buy-in of 5 to 10 points per year would not be uncommon, meaning that the *total* transformation of the culture will require up to nearly ten years, although three to five years is more normal. As successes mount along with peer pressure (due to growing buy-in), some will leave your firm, others will be eliminated for taking too long to convert, and the rest will embrace the new approach at their own pace. The point is that it takes time to gain buy-in and to effect a real service-oriented transformation. But it then sticks as a permanent part of the corporate culture. Figure 5 illustrates the quality transformation.

Using Quality Indicators

To use measurements as a tool to influence activities as early as possible, begin by developing a short list of quality indicators that measure progress against goals and add to it as necessary. Practical criteria for these should include:

- one page of measurements only
- quarterly publication

Business Response Changed

◆   **Cycle Time Reduction**   ➡   **Competitive Advantage**

◆   **Added Services to Products** ➡   **Differentiation**

◆   **People Make a Difference**   ➡   **Services Focus**

Profound Culture Change

◆   **New Values**

◆   **Process View**

◆   **Rise of the Customer**

Figure 5.   **The quality transformation.**

- numeric (percent, index, ratio, etc.)
- easy-to-understand trend indicator
- this year's achievement goal (a number)
- measurable from salesperson to sales executive

There is no black magic involved. For example, I worked in one sales organization that set five goals involving customer satisfaction, employee morale, quality, financial contribution, and community involvement. Ultimately we had 2 to 5 measurements for each category, and all of them fit on one piece of paper, serving as a barometer of the health of the business.

For customer satisfaction we began with what was available: a national blind survey that generated a satisfaction index. We then added local surveys, a complaint process measurement, and so forth. For employee morale, we began by using results of a national survey, added a local one to generate data on our issues and then a skills index (which measured the percent of skills we had to go after quantifiable opportunities). Then we added percent of employees submitting suggestions (as an indicator of ownership for change) and other measurements as new processes came on-line.

For quality we did a Baldrige assessment, graded ourselves terribly with an awfully low score, and then built upon that platform.

Financial contribution was obvious: customers voted with their money, which we could measure with existing data: percent of revenue growth, index of market share, and profitability.

Community involvement was measured by the number of employees active in community affairs (e.g., political office, charities, United Way, and so forth).

Another tactic is to put together a team representing various segments of the organization to advise, preach, and report on progress. Respected floor leaders can craft a program for quality while preaching, explaining, and defending its purpose.

One final recommendation: ask peers in other firms about how much progress they made and over what period of time. Their advice is priceless; they too want to ask you the same questions. Many firms find it expedient to form councils made up of customers or peers to trade war stories and get advice. Suffice it to say that asking others about their initial processes and programs is just good benchmarking and common sense. The support they give is vital in this early stage when most employees have doubts and are insecure about the outcome of what obviously does not appear on the surface to be good old-fashioned tactical selling activities!

Conclusions

Earl C. Conway, director of corporate quality improvement at Procter & Gamble, stated the message clearly: "Quality is the unyielding and continuing effort by everyone in an organization to understand, meet, and exceed the needs of its customers." Others have lined up behind this same message to all managers. An editor-in-chief of the *Harvard Business Review*, Rosabeth Moss Kanter, spoke for many executives when she warned that "cowboy management is a disaster for the company that seeks quality." If you have any doubts about the need for quality, remind your employees that customer focus in a global economy is the central issue. "The Japanese are consistently disciplined. They seem to have the ability to stick with a task until they reach a goal. And that's not true for Americans," says Marilyn Zuckerman, quality manager at AT&T. I could fill many pages with similar statements, but they would all simply reinforce the same message and provide sales management with a wonderful reaffirmation of what we have always known: that the customer is king and the king wants quality. And isn't the customer always right?

References

Bowles, Jerry, and Hammong, Joshua. *Beyond Quality: How 50 Winning Companies Use Continuous Improvement.* New York: Putnam, 1991.

Covey, Stephen R. *The 7 Habits of Highly Effective People.* New York: Simon & Schuster, 1989.

Handy, Charles. *The Age of Unreason.* Boston: Harvard Business School Press, 1989.

Kouzes, James M., and Posner, Barry Z. *The Leadership Challenge: How to Get Extraordinary Things Done in Organizations.* San Francisco: Jossey-Bass, 1990.

Rackham, Neil. *SPIN Selling.* New York: McGraw-Hill, 1988.

Ries, Al, and Trout, Jack. *Bottom-Up Marketing.* New York: McGraw-Hill, 1989.

Ries, Al, and Trout, Jack. *Marketing Warfare.* New York: McGraw Hill, 1986.

Sewell, Carl, and Brown, Paul B. *Customers for Life: How to Turn That One-Time Buyer into a Lifetime Customer.* New York: Doubleday, 1990.

Where Will You Get Your Next Sale?

Barry I. Ptashkin

This article describes a tactical approach based on quality principles to maintain and build business among current customers as a way to increase business during a slow economy. It focuses on improving a company's understanding of customer needs and developing formal customer service plans to better meet those needs.

During previous economic downturns, many commercial and professional service businesses relied on simple, sometimes drastic cost reductions as their strategy for survival. Today, however, these same businesses have gone far beyond cost reductions to focus on ways to generate revenue and sufficient cash flow to keep their enterprises going.

Traditional, well-planned marketing and sales programs for industrial markets (as opposed to consumer markets) might not produce results for six to nine months. Developing new customers can be a lengthy process involving research, targeting, advertising, promotion, networking, and coordinating sales with market communication. On the other hand, current customers provide companies with established business relationships, some level of knowledge and predictability in buying behaviors, and short-term opportunities for expanded sales.

Most businesses do not have formal plans and actions for current customer service and sales. Customers are often taken for granted or neglected. Excessive time is spent with troublesome customers instead of those with whom the money is and can be made. The sales emphasis becomes maintaining the current activity volume, not expanding it.

Given the limited resources you have available, where would you focus your employees and their time to get sales from your current customers? If you knew where to focus your resources, what would your objective be?

The objective in customer service planning is to expand sales and increase profits—not merely to increase volume and perpetuate business problems. Several questions need to be answered:

- What opportunities will most likely provide more sales and more profits?

Reprinted with permission from *Quality Progress*, May 1993, ASQC, Milwaukee, WI.

- How should these opportunities be approached?
- Which troubled customer relationships can be upgraded or turned around? Which cannot?

Figures 1 and 2 will help you classify and analyze your customers and, in turn, help you allocate your resources. The customer service model will enable you to classify your customers in terms of how profitable and successful they are in their own businesses and how much potential they have to increase your business' sales and profits.

To use the customer service model, you can classify your customers based on objective financial, credit, and/or performance reports or on your subjective

Characteristics	General needs
1. Best accounts	
Your most profitable customer relationships	
Highly visible	Frequent contact
Highly profitable	
10%+ growth during each of the last three years	Proactive advice; problem solving
Aggressive, competent management	Fast response
Above-average growth potential	Timely delivery
Uses outside professionals wisely and frequently	Immediate or one-hour access to owner, partner, assigned troubleshooter, salesperson, or manager
Has outstanding supplier relations	
Good debt-to-equity ratio (bankable)	
Expansion oriented	
Edge of technology in industry	
2. Underserved	
Your high-profit-potential customers providing you with less sales volume	Same as best accounts, but some reluctance to use you or to pay fair prices or fees. Or, unaware of your complete product and service menu
Characteristics same as best accounts	
3. Core accounts	
The majority of your customers providing you with medium to low profits in your business	Timely service with known assigned customer responsibility
Profitable	
Stable to moderate growth in last three years	
Competent management for size of company	Competent service
Stable future	
Low to moderate interest/need for nontraditional/professional services	Relatively quick or one-day access to owner, partner, assigned troubleshooter, salesperson, or manager
Average debt-to-equity ratio	
Lack of internal sophistication	Knows your key employees and is generally aware of your product and service menu
Longevity in the market	

Figure 1. **Customer classifications for the customer service planning model in Figure 2.**

Characteristics	General needs
4. Marginal	
Inconsistent profitability levels	Reasonable access to your key employees
Inconsistent growth	
Lack of management depth or competence	Problem solving
Short-term-oriented high flyers	
Seems to want superior products and services, but is unwilling to pay fair market prices or professional fees	Access to your full array of products and services
Thinly capitalized—does not retain earnings	
Demands unrealistic product or service delivery—either results or time lines	
5. Problem	
Has attributes of marginal to best in terms of profit or potential, but . . .	Same as marginal with a lower likelihood of achieving your desired profitable sales
Difficult to deal with	
Unrealistic expectations	Reasonable access to your key employees
Unwilling to pay fair prices and fees	
Autocratic management style	Problem solving
Constantly complains about everything	Access to your full array of products and services
Blames personal/company failures on everyone but top management	
Does not accept responsibility for own errors or lack of performance	
Promises leads and referrals but never or rarely delivers	
6. New customers	
Within your target market(s)	Same as marginal
Apparent/uncertain profitability	
Unknown management skills and style	
Unknown commitment to volume or full array of your products and services	
Obtained by discounting prices	
7. Submarginal	
No growth potential	Service on as-available basis only
Marginal profitability	
Incompetent management	Set timetable to upgrade, outplace to another supplier, or terminate business relationship
Cannot pay fair prices or fees even for modest products and services	
Below-average performance in industry	
Poor long-term prospects	
Failing industry or niche	

Figure 1. **Customer classifications for the customer service planning model in figure 2, *continued.***

perception of profitability and potential. As you proceed, keep in mind that the classifications are not static; you can upgrade customer classifications based on economic improvements or mutually improved behaviors. You should revise the classifications periodically.

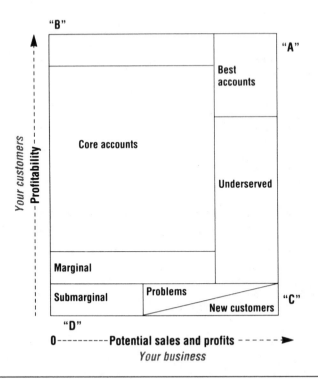

Figure 2. **Customer service planning model.**

Starting Your Program

There are four steps you should follow when starting your customer service planning program:

1. Classify your customers by their profitability and by the sales and profit potential for your company.
2. Prioritize these classifications as follows to determine how and where to assign and focus your employees first:
    - ■ A—Move quickly to strengthen and preserve relations with your current high-profit-potential customers.
    - ■ B—Bolster relations and improve profit margins with customers that have successful businesses but have restricted your profitability (i.e., low margins are a function of the commodity nature of the product). Set prices to retain your sales base and expand volume and concentrate on new product and new business development.
    - ■ C—Build or improve relationships and, in turn, intensify sales efforts with customers that have high potential to you, but questionable viability in their businesses.

- ■ D—Be fair but firm in your conviction not to sell to those customers that have not and will not benefit your business; while there might be an emotional reluctance to terminate a customer relationship, the decision and action should not be delayed. The timetable for upgrading the customer relationship should be set at the same time that "A" priority action plans are developed.

3. Perform a situational analysis for each customer, starting with your "A" priority group; document what is important to your customers; and determine how to help or, more important, how to add value to your customers.
4. Plan and execute calls and meetings to follow up with your customers.

Case in Point

Recently, a manufacturer of industrial metals that had been in business for 100 years was struggling through the recession. The president of the company became painfully aware of how vulnerable the business was to reduced and lost sales. Certain base metal products continued to be sold with little or no added value processing. Pricing of these metals was contrived, difficult to understand, and competitively high due to the company's historical quality reputation. The sales force was small. The sales approach was not targeted and was conducted in a superficial good-old-boy style. All sales personnel operated in an order-taking, rather than order-motivating, mode. Customer relations were a function of orders received. The company had a few highly talented research and development (R&D) employees who operated in an unfocused crisis mode and often missed deadlines and commitments. This staff was capable of producing unique and leading-edge products, but the existing product menu had not been assessed for ongoing viability and expanded value-added applications. There were no marketing or sales plans.

To get an immediate resurgence in profitable sales, the pricing structure on base metal products was simplified, and prices were reduced to below the premium level, but with sufficient margin built in. Within two weeks, the number and size of base metal sales increased.

To provide an orderly structure for market and product planning, the existing product and service menu was analyzed to determine needs for upgrading, repacking, or purging current products as well as identifying new product opportunities. This effort produced prioritized projects for product improvements and new product development. The participative efforts of sales, operating, and R&D personnel led to improved efficiency and effectiveness in their respective functions. The R&D staff became more focused, completed assignments, and became more credible to the sales force. With more current technical product information, the sales force was able to focus more on problem solving.

To focus the small sales force on getting near-term profitable sales, the current customer base was classified and prioritized using the profitability matrix. Lacking adequate customer performance data, the president called a team meeting of the sales force, the R&D staff, and the manufacturing managers. He insisted on straightforward classifications regardless of the size or duration of the customer relationship. Following classification and prioritization, the customers that fell into the "A" and "D" priorities were assigned to smaller work groups for needs assessments and solution planning. Each customer plan became a project and culminated in a meeting and a follow-up program with the respective customer.

The early results of this effort have shown add-on sales of different products to old customers and the preservation of relationships that were vulnerable to competitors. Relationships with several troublesome customers have improved, and a few have become current in their payments and are increasing their number of orders. The president's instincts were sound.

Continuing Customer Service

The process of assessing and resolving customers' needs is continuous:

- Don't put off getting started. Your current customer base is critical for both survival and growth; customer service planning is an integral part of the total quality management program.
- Your best source for intelligence about your customers' behaviors and needs is your own employees.
- Customer service planning should be a team effort; participation from sales, R&D, administrative, and operations personnel will yield greater understanding of customer needs and, in turn, will help you respond with more specific and meaningful product and service solutions.
- As the needs assessments continue, establish more formal means for obtaining input from your customers to determine their needs.
- As you agree on approaches to meet your customers' needs, each prioritized customer situation should be transformed into a project with budgets, personnel responsible for tasks, and scheduled start and end dates.

The emphasis is on developing a rationale for focusing resources on your customers, responding to your customers' needs, delivering results, and building credibility.

Barry I. Ptashkin is the managing associate of performance improvement at Coopers & Lybrand in Chicago, IL.

Functional Processes

SUPPLIERS AND PURCHASING

What Does TQM Mean to Purchasing?

James F. Cali

This excerpt from a new book, TQM for Purchasing Management, *discusses the value of the insights of TQM for better managing purchasing decisions and dealing with suppliers in general. There are also brief synopses of how several prominent firms are applying these ideas to the purchasing process.*

Introduction

Purchasing is a key ingredient in the implementation of TQM for a very simple reason. To see why, take a look at Figure 1. This study by General Electric shows that the cost associated with finding a problem during inspection of a product at delivery is just 3 cents, while the cost of finding the same problem after the product has been installed is $300.

In the 1970s it was considered good business to sell a product requiring recurring service. (Remember the term *planned obsolescence?*) In today's climate, however, such a product will not sell—or will not sell more than once.

Senior executives consider the role of purchasing critical to improving quality. In a survey conducted in 1989 by the American Society for Quality Control, 601 senior executives indicated that more control over suppliers was one of the top ten areas in which quality could be improved throughout

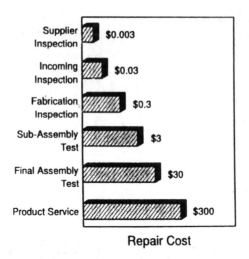

Repair Cost

Figure 1. **Fault-repair costs.** *(General Electric)*

American business. (Other target areas were employee motivation, employee education, process control, and quality improvement teams.)

While most companies understand that 60 to 70 percent of the cost of most manufactured products is materials, we have only recently realized that the cost of buying materials and services is more than just the unit price. Figure 2 illustrates the many components of the total cost. The other components can amount to as much as, if not more than, the unit price. Moreover, the concept that the market dictates the price and the buyer has little influence may be appropriate for the unit price, but buyers *can* influence the other

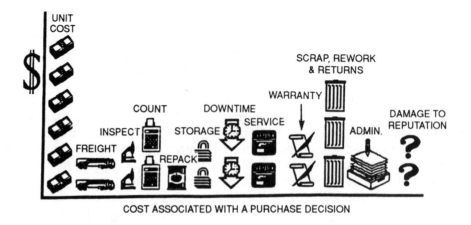

COST ASSOCIATED WITH A PURCHASE DECISION

Figure 2. **The "color of money"—costs associated with a purchasing decision.** *(Coopers & Lybrand)*

parts of the total cost. This is another reason why there is a new focus on purchasing in TQM.

Suppliers and customers alike have never been as motivated as they are today to improve the quality of products and services to a level previously believed impossible. In many companies the burden of achieving this new level of supplier quality has been placed directly on the shoulders of the purchasing department.

The experts tell us that the solution is for purchasing to become more efficient and to have greater supplier involvement. This kind of general guidance is great, but how should it be applied. To understand this, it is appropriate to look at how purchasing is changing under TQM.

Several traditional elements of purchasing are changing:

- The role of purchasing
- Acquisition strategies
- Buyer/supplier relationships
- Purchasing performance measurements

The Role of Purchasing

TQM is changing purchasing's traditional role. Before TQM, the supplier viewed the buyer as the customer. In this approach there existed a balance of power. The supplier usually knew more about the product it sold, while the buyer made the decision in selecting the supplier. Under TQM, the buyer views the supplier as the customer. The buyer is required to provide the supplier information, such as drawings, specifications, and required dates, that will allow the supplier to provide products or services as needed. This new role gives the supplier an unfair advantage, but the risk to the buyer is offset if the supplier and the buyer share mutual goals and benefits.

Under TQM, the buyer views the supplier as the customer.

Before the advent of TQM, the buyer's role was to select suppliers and place orders. Under a TQM system, the buyer's role is to serve as the team leader of multiple functions within his company (engineering, quality, and manufacturing). The team is charged with supplier selection as well as with providing the supplier with appropriate training. Training will help ensure that the goods and services provided meet the needs of the buyer.

Acquisition Strategies

Acquisition strategies have also changed:

Traditional Acquisition Strategies	TQM Acquisition Strategies
Use multiple sources	Qualify supplier base (reduce/expand)
Market dictates price; buyer has little influence	Buyer looks at total cost, not just at price
All technologies developed in-house	Buyer uses suppliers' technology
Suppliers get drawings and determine whether they can supply the parts or services as specified or must request changes in specifications	Suppliers are involved in design

The illusion of multiple sources leading to assurance of supply has been replaced by reduced-source or single-source strategies. The trend today is to reduce the supplier base and to use multiple sources only when a unique technology is required or when one source cannot provide all the parts. The strategy of Ford Motor Company, for example, is to rely on a single source for parts wherever possible. A notable exception in Ford's case is tires, since one tire company cannot supply all Ford's needs.

The buyer's influence on unit price is limited. The market tends to determine price levels, so that transaction is little affected by the buyer-supplier relationship. However, other elements—total cost, freight, downtime, and so forth—can be heavily influenced by the buyer's relationship with the supplier.

The concept of vertical integration (developing all technologies in-house) is no longer economical for most companies. The complexity of many of our products today requires more use of our supplier's technology.

The use of suppliers in the design stages of a product not only takes advantage of the suppliers' technology but also provides an opportunity for supplier input. This input allows a supplier to effectively utilize the supplier's manufacturing processes in the final design of the product.

Supplier Relationships

TQM's greatest impact on purchasing has been in the area of supplier relationships.

Traditional Buyer/Supplier Relationships	Buyer/Supplier Relationships in a TQM Environment
Buyers and suppliers work in constant conflict (a win-lose situation)	Buyers and suppliers work in partnership (a win-win situation)
Buyers are always considered right (implying that suppliers are always wrong)	Suppliers are considered experts in the commodity they supply
Buyer-oriented supplier asks: "What can I do to get the business?"	Supplier-oriented buyer asks: "What can I do to help you become a better supplier?"

Developing partnerships does not eliminate the need for good negotiations. However, the objective of negotiations is for both parties to benefit. The old tendency, when problems with supplier's products arose, was to blame the supplier. Today, the approach is to find out how each party can help the other to improve performance. The buyer's ongoing role is to help ensure that the supplier has the right tools to provide good services and products.

Today, the approach is to find out how each party can help the other to improve performance.

Purchasing Performance Measurements

Purchasing has a second customer, the requisitioner. Purchasing has always been considered an internal service organization, but within a TQM environment the emphasis on meeting all the customer's needs is more pronounced.

Under the TQM umbrella, assessing purchasing's performance includes not only measuring the efficiency of the individual buyer and of the purchasing department (and determining the cost of issuing a purchase order), but also measuring how well the needs of both the internal customer (the requisitioner) and the external customer (the supplier) are being met. The latter assessment involves measuring the control of the supplier base, a process that develops supplier's resources to achieve a competitive advantage in the seller's marketplace. The resources include the supplier's technology, processes, quality, and cost. The following table compares purchasing performance measurements within a traditional environment and within a TQM environment.

Traditional Measurements of Purchasing's Performance in Meeting the Needs of the Requisitioner (the Internal Customer)	TQM Measurements of Purchasing's Performance in Meeting the Needs of the Requisitioner (the Internal Customer)
Requisition cycle time	Requisition cycle time
Meeting required dates	Meeting required dates
Quality of product/service	Quality of product/service
	Responsiveness to requisitioner

The priorities of the requisitioner under TQM include not only receiving products and services of sufficient quality on time, but also being able to count on purchasing for a response to specific needs. For purchasing, this means being available to answer questions in a timely manner and giving the requisitioner access to such supplier resources as technology and product/service capabilities.

Measuring the control of the supplier base includes meeting the needs of the supplier in addition to measuring the supplier's performance regarding quality and delivery.

Traditional Measurements of Purchasing's Performance in Meeting the Needs of the Supplier (the External Customer)	TQM Measurements of Purchasing's Performance in Meeting the Needs of the Supplier (the External Customer)
Sufficient data	Sufficient data
	Training of supplier

In addition to providing information to enable the supplier to provide the product/services needed, purchasing must also give the supplier training in process improvement and continuous quality improvement.

In a TQM environment, measurement of the supplier's performance covers additional areas.

Traditional Measurements of a Supplier's Performance	TQM Measurements of a Supplier's Performance
On-time deliveries	On-time deliveries
Quality of product/service	Quality of product/service
	Number of problems solved
	Responsiveness to inquiries
	Control of processes

In a TQM environment, the assessment of a supplier's ability to provide quality products in a timely manner is supplemented with an assessment of the supplier's performance in solving customer problems (such as technology needs). Also measured is the ability of the supplier's manufacturing processes to provide products with reduced variation in specification limits—i.e., products that are consistently made to conform to a specific target, such as .5 mil., etc.

The best supplier I ever had was one that not only delivered quality products on time but also tried to keep me out of trouble. He advised me in advance when he thought I should reorder, based on his records and on changes in technology that he thought might have an impact on the products he provided my company.

> The best supplier I ever had was one that not only delivered quality products on time but also tried to keep me out of trouble.

What Are the Leaders Doing?

Introduction

Purchasing professionals nationwide are aggressively pursuing programs to improve supplier relationships. However, some of them suggest that the whole idea of building such networks is in danger of becoming a meaningless slogan. Nevertheless, new ideas can be generated and lessons learned by reviewing the approach taken by several companies. These companies have had success with various actions resulting from the changing roles of purchasing.

Although each company's approach to TQM and suppliers is different, there are common themes that all seem to adhere to:

- Benchmarking provides the goals to strive for.
- Reducing the supplier base and heading toward single sources of supply provides a better vehicle for improved quality.
- Trust is the one element that will cement the relationships established.

- Investment in the training and technical support of suppliers is key to success.
- Focus on continuous improvement must become a way of life.
- Involving suppliers in the product design process yields the greatest benefits.
- Using metrics to measure performance is necessary to determine whether improvement is occurring.
- The sharing of information, risks, and rewards with suppliers is the only way to establish long-term mutually beneficial partnerships.
- Multidiscipline involvement in supplier selection and relationships strengthens the relationship.

The following companies will be discussed below in alphabetical order:

Apple Computer	ITT Defense
Bell & Howell	Kurt Manufacturing
Black & Decker	McDonnell Aircraft
Briggs & Stratton	Morton & Co.
Caterpillar	Motorola
Chrysler	Navistar International
Corning	NCR
Cummins Engine	Outboard Marine
Delta Faucet	Raytheon Small Missile Division
Ford	Thiokol
Harley-Davidson	Toyota
Haworth	Westinghouse
Honda	Xerox
IBM-Rochester	Yale Materials Handling

Apple Computer

Apple Computer's purchasing people firmly believe their success can be traced to their relationship with their suppliers. This claim is supported by contributors to the *Harvard Business Review*. Apple focuses on purchasing's involvement in the design cycle. This ensures that the best possible integrated circuit can be devised to provide leading-edge technology for high-quality product with short life cycles.

The tightness of Apple's supplier relationships can sometimes be measured in hours. Its purchasing staff claim their suppliers receive hourly updates on Apple's needs to facilitate delivery. Apple has five objectives for purchasing:

Apple's purchasing staff claim their suppliers receive hourly updates on Apple's needs to facilitate delivery.

1. *Quality.* With emphasis on design, supplier, and buyer's process.
2. *Velocity.* Defined as the competitive use of time and rate of change.
3. *Cost improvement.* Total life-cycle cost throughout design, development, test, and manufacturing process.

4. *Technology.* Purchasing has a lot of input into design.
5. *Risk management.* People are taught to calculate risk.

Bell & Howell

Bell & Howell focuses on certification to reduce its supplier base. Suppliers rated well in a preliminary assessment are invited to submit a detailed, written quality plan. These plans are analyzed to determine if they complement Bell & Howell's own business plans. An on-site audit is then conducted.

Certification means a multiyear partnership of up to five years, and in some cases certified suppliers will handle 100 percent of the business in certain commodities.

Black & Decker

Black & Decker has a rating system that is the primary basis for supplier selection. The system features quantitative ratings in four primary areas: quality, technology, delivery, and commercial. The program includes supplier on-site evaluations by Black & Decker in-house experts in the four areas.

Briggs & Stratton

A supplier quality engineer is assigned, sometimes full-time, to a supplier that does not conform to Briggs & Stratton's *Supplier Quality Manual* and whose manufacturing systems are not capable of producing the caliber of product required. With ten to twelve suppliers participating, the results have been the resolution of problems in one-quarter to one-half the normal time.

Briggs & Stratton has also created a new position, manager of supplier development, and launched a Certified Supplier Award based on quality performance, pricing, and technical capability.

Caterpillar

Caterpillar has a Quality Institute that has educated one thousand individuals representing four hundred suppliers.

Chrysler

The objective of Chrysler's program is to achieve an overall performance level of zero defects. Included in its program are the following elements:

1. All buyers attend in-house training four hours a day for three months.
2. Purchasing achievement teams nominate individuals who have excelled at their jobs and have contributed to Chrysler's goals.
3. Awards, ranging from plaques of recognition to month-long assignments of executive parking spaces, are given to reward performance.
4. Long-term contracts are established with suppliers. Twenty-seven suppliers are asked to quote on two-to-four-year requirements.

5. The supplier base has been reduced by 20 percent.
6. Key suppliers are informed of short- and long-term plans and strategies.
7. All suppliers are advised that their prices may not increase.
8. Suppliers are asked to indicate how Chrysler requirements have cost them money and to suggest ways to reduce costs. Many suggestions have been the same as those coming from internal engineers.

Corning

Corning relies heavily on the Malcolm Baldrige criteria for their purchase program. The Baldrige Award establishes benchmarks and provides guidelines for companies attempting to develop their own internal programs and supplier rating systems.

Cummins Engine

Cummins sets targets for suppliers to shoot for and then helps suppliers reach these goals. The targets are established in four key areas: quality, technology, piece price cost, and administration.

The administration category includes the supplier's account services, frequency of visits to customer plants, and electronic communications capabilities that allow the supplier total access to Cummins' computerized scheduling bulletins.

Once a year each supplier makes a formal presentation to Cummins, assessing its progress toward the specific objectives set for that company.

Delta Faucet

In its first year, Delta Faucet's supplier performance program has developed partnerships with 80 percent of their suppliers that do at least a $40,000-a-year business with Delta. The program assesses quality, acceptance, delivery, and price. Under the partnership approach Delta forecasts up to a year's orders with some suppliers, with the first two months firm.

Ford

Ford spends $50 billion worldwide per year and has an impressive performance record. Thus far, Ford has

1. Globalized its supply base by establishing worldwide centers of excellence in design, engineering, and purchasing. To respond to global requirements, some suppliers are forming joint ventures or business associations with former competitors
2. Optimized its supplier base by trimming the base by 40 percent
3. Placed 70 percent of its North American suppliers under long-term contracts
4. Placed practically every production part for a given model single-sourced under a long-term contract

5. Focused on early supplier involvement and awarded 70 percent of its purchases to suppliers that assume concurrent engineering responsibilities for components
6. Taken a highly centralized purchasing approach, with the body and assembly plants doing very little of their own purchases except for some blanket orders and maintenance
7. Established the American Supplier Institute to bring suppliers up to date on new quality techniques, notably those based on the ideas of Japanese quality guru Genechi Taguchi

Since 1980 Ford's quality has increased by nearly 70 percent and reportedly leads the Big Three with the fewest defects per car. Ford was awarded the 1990 Medal of Professional Excellence by *Purchasing* magazine.

Harley-Davidson

Harley-Davidson's program focuses on generating savings. It has

1. Developed and conducted seminars for suppliers
2. Decentralized its purchasing department and located buyers in the shop areas close to the product and the people
3. Increased the number of buyers from five to nine
4. Requested from suppliers a 2-percent price reduction and an extension of terms to 60 days
5. Trimmed its supplier list in half—from 820 to 415
6. Arrived at single-sourcing for each part
7. Involved suppliers in product engineering
8. Allowed suppliers a 16-week window to the production schedule

The results have been an increase in inventory turns from $4\frac{1}{2}$ to 23 and an increase in market share from 23 percent to 40 percent.

Haworth

Haworth has developed unique relationships with its suppliers. The supplier designs and manufactures a product and Haworth markets it. This relationship is cost-effective for Haworth, which can develop more products with fewer Haworth people. The relationship is a source of more business for the supplier and allows the supplier to concentrate on manufacturing.

Haworth uses capability ratios and statistical formulas (Cpk) that hone in on the first piece and the capability of the supplier's tooling.

Honda

Honda has a top-selling car in the U.S., the Honda Accord. Honda's program:

1. Requires purchases to be 30 to 100 percent of suppliers' volume
2. Dedicates 120 engineers to deal with incoming parts and supplier-quality issues
3. Dedicates 40 engineers to work with suppliers to improve productivity

4. Helps suppliers develop employee involvement programs
5. Dedicates technical support to suppliers
6. Assists suppliers with business problems (i.e., rapid growth)
7. Conducts a loaned executive and a guest engineer program
8. Conducts frequent supplier visits

As a result, 40 current suppliers ship 100 percent defect-free, 100 percent of the time, and virtually all parts go directly to the assembly line. There is no inspection of the product when it is received at the buyer's dock or receiving department.

IBM Rochester

IBM replaced competitive bidding with competitive supplier evaluation. Suppliers are evaluated on:

- *Quality posture.* An evaluation of the supplier's quality system and SPC capability
- *Technical expertise.* A match of technical expertise with IBM's needs
- *Delivery.* A capacity for continuous flow basis and a willingness to reduce inventory and minimize product lead time

IBM insists that its suppliers use SPC and look for suppliers that have adopted Malcolm Baldrige principles. Although IBM doesn't require its suppliers to apply for the award as Motorola does, IBM has asked its suppliers to work with IBM in doing self-assessments.

IBM has already cut its supplier base by 35 percent in the last five years and plans to continue to reduce the base. IBM has moved toward suppliers delivering parts directly to the line and has tried to reduce lead times by having suppliers close to home.

In 1990 buyers received 40 hours of training. It is expected that in 1991 each buyer will receive 80 hours of training. IBM has developed a Certified Purchasing Manager (CPM) training program to help buyers get CPM-certified.

The new purchasing approach is credited with helping IBM win the 1990 Malcolm Baldrige Award.

ITT Defense

ITT utilized Quality Functional Development (QFD) to determine its customers' needs and select appropriate purchasing strategies (see Chapter 7). In addition, ITT developed a process to assure that suppliers were ready to meet its needs. The process is known as Supplier Readiness Assessment and is described in Appendix F.

Kurt Manufacturing

Kurt, a precision machine parts manufacturer in Minneapolis Minnesota, focuses on getting information into the hands of suppliers as a key element in establishing good partnerships. The most important information falls into three categories: realistic quantities, accurate production start and stop dates, and correct market information.

McDonnell Aircraft

McDonnell Aircraft has a plan to reduce its supplier base from 2875 to 1000 with 500 suppliers designated as part of its Certification of Preferred Suppliers.
Certification consists of three distinct parts:

1. *Assessment of business processes.* The elements assessed include management, quality, delivery, cost, technology, and customer support.
2. *Application of process control/SPC*
3. *Product performance.* Supplier Performance Evaluation and Rating System (SPEARS) measures quality (the percentage free of quality defects), delivery (performance to purchase order schedule), responsiveness (multidiscipline assessment), and price trends (at a part-number level).

A performance progress report is issued quarterly to suppliers. The report reviews the past 12 months' performance in terms of delivery and quality (including attention paid, during the final quarter, to fixing quality problems). The report also identifies items needing improvement.

Morton & Co.

Morton & Co., based in Wilmington, Mass., is a small company that manufactures precision parts. Its program has several key characteristics:

1. Open and consistent communications with suppliers
2. A comprehensive qualification program for evaluating and selecting suppliers
3. Long-term commitment to suppliers
4. An understanding of the total-cost concept
5. A can-do attitude

Motorola

Motorola is also a winner of the Malcolm Baldrige Award. Its purchasing program:

1. Benchmarks the Japanese
2. Has established a tenfold improvement in ten years
3. Has established a target of 6 sigma = 3.4 PPM defect rate
4. Requires all suppliers to develop plans for the Baldrige Award

Navistar International

Navistar has component management teams that employ a decision-analysis system to rate potential suppliers for many components of its trucks and diesel engines. The team consists of specialists from engineering, manufacturing, quality, transportation, marketing, and materials management (purchasing). The team completes mandatory training in a problem-solving and decision-analysis approach developed by Kepner-Tregoe Inc. of Princeton, New Jersey.

NCR

NCR's purchasing job is supply-line management. Purchasing is a key element of NCR's corporate overhaul, holding the reins on overall material expense rather than just on price, keeping the company technologically competitive, and also building relationships with suppliers of key technologies. The key qualifiers for NCR suppliers are quality and leading-edge technology. The following table illustrates NCR purchasing policies before and after the overhaul.

NCR Purchasing Policies Then	NCR Purchasing Policies Now
Contracts renegotiated yearly	Evergreen contracts
Incoming inspection	Benchmarking
Purchasing components	Securing technology
Over 2000 suppliers	150 suppliers
Spotty parts quality	50 to 100 ppm rates on incoming parts

Source: *Electronics Purchasing.*

Outboard Marine

Outboard Marine's director of corporate purchasing, C. W. Cross oversees buying for 11 domestic and four overseas plants and does central buying from 500 active suppliers. Outboard Marine's focus is on the development of an objective, quantifiable rating system that lets suppliers know where they stand.

Raytheon Small Missile Division

The manufacturer of the Patriot missile focuses on redoing its supplier base and training supervisors in techniques like statistical process control.

The 200-person purchasing department spends $300 million annually for 200,000 different production parts from 7000 suppliers. Its goal is to cut the supplier base by up to 40 percent by 1993.

Buyers measure the performance of suppliers and look for an acceptable parts-per-million defect rate, high performance in meeting delivery commitments, and quick response to problems.

The corporate group, headed by Marty Kane, director of corporate purchasing, evaluates the purchasing departments annually on the quality of incoming parts, delivery, the overall performance of suppliers, ethics, and the management of subcontractors.

Thiokol

Thiokol's supplier-partnership approach is a three-phased program:

1. *Long-term supplier relationships.* Thiokol applied this phase to Maintenance Repair Orders (MRO). The objective was to eliminate or reduce the cost of inventory, minimize the labor required to handle MRO suppliers, simplify invoicing, and improve customer service. The approach included getting Thiokol's internal users involved in the development of the program, briefing the suppliers on the program expectations, and issuing contracts for three to five years to successful bidders. The contracts are a three-year stockless supply contract with stationary suppliers, with items stocked at the suppliers. Suppliers deliver directly to each user within 24 hours. The user releases all shipments with no formal purchase order issued. Each user reconciles monthly deliveries and authorizes payment.
2. *New program partnerships using concurrent engineering to focus on manufacturability.* Competition is utilized on the front end to satisfy government contracting regulations. The best overall supplier is then selected to participate on a long-term basis. Usually only one source is used, with both parties sharing cost information in order to focus on cost-reduction opportunities. Cost savings are shared by Thiokol and the supplier.
3. *Supplier certification.* A supplier model was developed after visits to companies demonstrating leadership in supplier base management. The model has five major elements: leadership quality, delivery, cost, and technology. A supplier assessment program selected the candidate suppliers who would participate in certification. The assessment process is not a pass-or-fail system and evaluates suppliers on the five elements from the model. The questions are generic in nature to make the program universal and flexible. Open-ended questions are designed to encourage supplier input and participation.

Toyota

All suppliers must have a TQM program and be certified. Toyota gets involved in the suppliers' business right down to the manufacturing process. Toyota uses a system called *keirestu* that involves a network of suppliers with which Toyota has deep ties—and often financial links. These suppliers are privy to Toyota's secrets and are often willing to sacrifice some profits for the parent's sake. Toyota has been accused of trying to create a keirestu in the United States.

Westinghouse

Westinghouse's small central corporate purchasing group is headed by Thomas V. Doyle, director of purchases. Doyle's group serves as a catalyst for the purchasing groups in the 15 self-sufficient business units. The mission of the group is to "provide leadership through projects aimed at improving the total quality and cost effectiveness of the sourcing process throughout the corporation." The ten people at corporate headquarters serve 880 management and professional purchasing people in 70 different locations. Westinghouse relies heavily on special-interest councils, such as the small disadvantaged business steering council, in this decentralized environment.

One key role the corporate group serves is to help individual units take advantage of the buying clout that Westinghouse has as a $5.2-billion purchaser of goods and services. Corporate purchasing uses commodity surveys to identify candidate products and services for national contracts. Then commodity teams and Technical Advisory Committees (TACs) plan and execute contracts. Divisional representatives spend a day or two putting the strategy together, defining the requirements and specifications and identifying the potential bidders. Then engineering and manufacturing representatives are called in to form the TAC.

The corporate group issues a material price forecast quarterly to all the purchasing managers and controllers in the corporation. The forecast provides price projections on 47 commodities used at Westinghouse and an assessment of various commodities' vulnerability to supply interruptions from economic or political disruptions around the world.

Westinghouse's recipe for finding talent includes recruiting on college campuses for direct, entry-level purchasing positions in the field or for positions in their Purchasing Development Program (PDP), a six-month training program. At promotion time, the corporate group is used as a resource to identify people to fill openings.

Alan J. Meilinger, vice president for corporate services at the company, believes that purchasing will be a critical element in building the new Westinghouse as a result of 40 percent of the sales dollar being spent outside the company.

Xerox

Xerox, winner of the Malcolm Baldrige Award in 1989, achieved the following goals in dealing with its suppliers:

1. Reduction of its supplier base from 5000 to 350 worldwide, making for a concentration of economic leverage, more stable demands on suppliers, an ability to focus on a few high potential suppliers, and an ability to develop "model suppliers"
2. Use of a sole-source policy worldwide
3. Minimization of reliance on competitive bidding through the use of a target-cost method, while encouraging participation in design
4. Provision of extensive quality training for suppliers in Statistical Process Control (SPC), just-in-time purchasing, cooperative costing, set-up reductions, and Total Quality Management
5. Establishment of long-term (three-to-five-year) contracts
6. Adoption of a continuous supplier-improvement program that includes product design participation with open sharing of business and technical information
7. Formation of central commodity management teams

8. Use of competitive benchmarking for continuous measuring of processes, services, and practices against the toughest and best competition and functional leaders in the world
9. Establishment of multilevel communications with suppliers

As a result of these techniques, Xerox has realized an overall reduction in material costs of 50 percent. With improved designs, concentrated purchases, new technology, and internal efficiencies, Xerox has reduced defects from 10,000 parts per million (PPM) to 300 PPM.

Xerox representatives discuss "model suppliers" as they travel the country talking about how they won the Malcolm Baldrige Award. Model suppliers expect Xerox to be a model customer. The characteristics of a Xerox "Model Supplier" (MS) and "Model Customer" (MC) are as follows:

MS Company History: Shows organizational stability and demonstrated expertise

MS Financial Status: Has a stable position with growth potential

MS Management Attitude: Has customer satisfaction as a driving force; possesses a vision of the future; shows a willingness to change and progress

MC Management Attitude: Demonstrates honesty and avoids false promises; communicates openly about strategies and business constraints and expectations; provides a single-point business interface; is a significant customer; rewards performance with business growth

MS Quality: Products have defect levels in parts per million below the best in the industry. Embraces Total Quality Management concepts; practices statistical process control; is certified by Xerox and has its own certification program for its suppliers

MC Quality: Shares quality responsibility with suppliers; provides test specifications; develops universal quality metrics; provides competent subtier suppliers when required; communicates problems; fosters closed-loop corrective-action systems

MS Costs: Knows and controls cost elements and prices on cost, not market

MC Costs: Establishes realistic cost targets; provides benchmarking assistance; shares costs of change; provides prompt payment

MS Delivery: Demonstrates flexibility; delivers just-in-time, not just-too-late

MS Delivery: Strives for minimal schedule changes; develops realistic schedules and priorities

MS Service: Provides spares support and problem follow-up

MC Service: Provides training; shares design, commodity, and technical knowledge; provides simple and common communication systems

MS Technical Capabilities: Utilizes state-of-the-art production technologies; can process technical changes efficiently; has process, tool engineering, and prototype capabilities

Yale Materials Handling
Yale hosts and invites suppliers to participate in full-day seminars. One seminar is for executives, sales and manufacturing senior management, and quality supervisors. Another seminar is for the everyday doers, the frontline people. Yale has cut its supplier base from 1100 to 800 and is headed toward 300. Ideally, it wants two partner suppliers for each of the 91 separate commodities purchased.

James F. Cali is Director of Materials at Harvard Industries/Elastic Stop Nut Division. He has more than 20 years hands-on purchasing experience in both the commercial and defense sectors.

Functional Processes

INFORMATION TECHNOLOGY

Empowerment: Key to IS World-Class Quality

Harvey R. Shrednick, Richard J. Shutt, and Madeline Weiss

Using Corning Incorporated's Information Services Division as an example, this article explains in practical, down-to-earth language how empowered self-managed teams are the key to effective employment of information resources to deliver total customer satisfaction.

Introduction

Companies today face fierce competition from successful global competitors, most of whom have made continuous improvement and rapid response to market needs a way of life. Adopting total quality management has become imperative.

Although each company's approach to establishing a total quality environment varies, certain common elements underlie the variations: leadership, information and analysis, planning, human resource utilization, quality assurance of products and services, quality results, and customer satisfaction. These elements are the seven basic criteria for the prestigious Malcolm Baldrige National Quality Award, given since 1987 to firms that have made

Reprinted by special permission from the *MIS Quarterly*, Vol. 16, No. 4, December 1992. Copyright © 1992 by the Society for Information Management and the Management Information Systems Research Center at the University of Minnesota.

outstanding contributions to the pursuit of quality. The National Institute of Standards and Technology sets the criteria and selects the winners of the award. According to Curt Reimann, associate director of NIST's Quality Programs, quality absolutely depends on information. Information services (IS) organizations play an important role in meeting each of the seven criteria. In order to deliver services that support the organization's use of information technology, IS must create quality processes and systems within its own function.

Corning Incorporated has been instituting a company-wide quality program since 1983. The Information Services Division (ISD) has been an active proponent of the program, as have its business partners throughout the corporation. While ISD has incorporated all the key elements of total quality into its approach to conducting business, we believe the innovative high-performance work system embodying significant employee empowerment is noteworthy. The work system is characterized by self-managing teams—groups of interdependent people with responsibility, authority, and accountability for accomplishing a common mission with little or no supervision.[1]

For years, Corning employees have participated in cross-functional quality improvement teams (QIT) and corrective action teams, in addition to regular work assignments. These teams are accountable for improving the quality of services and products as well as processes. Participation on such teams in ISD now exceeds 90 percent. This culture of involvement and commitment laid the groundwork for the self-managing teams now springing up across ISD. Teams weave empowerment into the very fabric of how business is conducted in ISD, fundamentally and profoundly changing the way work is organized and how service to internal customers throughout Corning is delivered. Through Corning's experience, we are discovering that empowerment underlies all Baldrige elements of quality in the following ways:

> To deliver services that support the organization's use of information technology, IS must create quality processes and systems within its own function.

- **Leadership.** Corning's senior ISD management team evolved through a vision of empowerment and tries to manage through that vision in day-to-day decisions and actions. The leadership structure is being transformed into a "flatter" organization where everyone accepts ownership for delivering quality products and services.
- **Information and analysis.** Teams seek information on customer satisfaction through surveys, interviews, and informal exchanges analyzing feedback to determine how to serve their customers better.
- **Planning.** ISD members take responsibility for understanding customer requirements for information technology and for developing plans to meet and even anticipate those requirements.

---

1. Unlike self-managing teams proliferating in plants and some service areas, our teams do not necessarily consist of individuals with the same skill sets performing similar activities.

- **Human resource utilization.** Self-managing teams of IS professionals operate in several departments across ISD. Team members—those closest to customers, products, and end results—have the power, authority, and responsibility to satisfy their customers. They are also encouraged to grow by learning and using new skills and knowledge.
- **Quality assurance of products and services.** Team members have accountability and skills for continuously improving their delivery of quality products and services.
- **Quality results.** Teams develop their own quantitative and qualitative measures of quality based on overall ISD quality goals, and they take actions based on results of the measurements.
- **Customer satisfaction.** Teams are encouraged to develop a close relationship with their customers in order to understand changing requirements and ensure they are met, if not exceeded. They are also empowered to resolve customer problems quickly and efficiently, with minimal bureaucratic encumbrance.

Impact of the New High-Performance Work System

While self-managing teams are relatively new—the oldest, Operations Services, recently celebrated its third anniversary—their impact on both ISD and its service to customers throughout Corning has been substantial. Teams have significantly improved customer satisfaction because team members are better positioned to understand customer requirements and move quickly to meet them. Service and productivity have increased partly because team members can feel free to approach anyone in the organization to solve problems and to provide excellent customer service. Time is not wasted working through supervisors or managers. Team members answer directly to customers. According to one Operations Services team member, "We no longer have supervisors between us and customers." Moreover, newly acquired financial knowledge, coupled with a broader business perspective, help all team members feel a strong sense of ownership for the ISD business.

A prevalent myth says that increased customer service must carry a higher price tag. In Corning's case, costs have been reduced, principally by eliminating management layers and positions, then relocating the displaced people to other needed positions within ISD and Corning. The advantage to the employee is a greater opportunity to learn and use new skills and knowledge, and the savings to the company are already over $500,000 annually.

Team members who previously kept to themselves now believe they can make a difference beyond their own individual jobs.

Team members who previously kept to themselves now believe they can make a difference beyond their own individual jobs. In addition to contributing substantially to their own teams, they have become influential participants in the overall management of ISD. For example, some of the biggest contributors of time, creativity, and energy to ISD-wide quality improvement teams are self-managing team members. According to one team member, "Even those who didn't want to build leadership skills and make decisions are finding they're liking it." In many ways the most important result is that people are growing, learning, and developing at remarkable rates. IS professionals who are committed, energetic, skillful, and highly knowledgeable hold the key to ISD's (and Corning's) success.[2]

Examples of the New High-Performance Work System

This section describes some specific cases of team successes in various areas of the ISD.

Computer Utility

The Computer Utility (CU), comprised of Operations, IBM and VAX Technical Services, Help Line Services, and Process Support, operates entirely as an empowered organization of self-managing teams (Figure 1). There is only one level of management between teams and the senior vice president of information services. In a benchmark study conducted by an outside firm,[3] the CU was cited as among the best in its class. According to the study, Corning runs its data center "with an impressive 29 percent fewer persons than the average for the MIPS [millions of instructions per second] group. The Operations staff has the greatest difference with 48 percent fewer persons." In

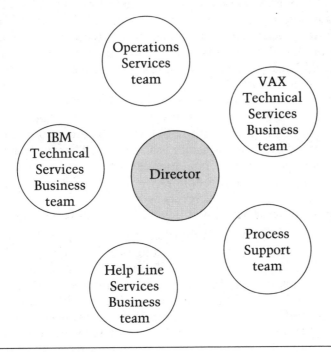

Figure 1.   **Computer Utility.**

2. Additional information on the impact of teamwork can be found in *Business Week* (1989).

3. The study was conducted by Real Decisions, a company that provides information to organizations on how they compare with others in their category using similar measures.

addition, the study noted that the cost per person is 11 percent lower in Operations and 4 percent lower in Technical Services than the MIPS and industry groups.

In 1992, ISD changed its business relationship with its internal customers from a chargeback to a services-for-sale arrangement. In effect, the businesses outsource to ISD, which must compete with outside IS service providers. CU members are convinced this conversion would have been much more difficult had they not been cognizant of budgets and financial management.

Accepting the challenge of surviving and thriving in this new environment, they continually look for both cost reduction and new revenue opportunities. Teams actually created the CU business plan for 1993. Representatives from each team studied the business planning process and then conducted a series of interviews to identify customer needs. They then divided up the tasks and created a business plan grounded in customer input and their own creativity and newly developed business savvy. The result was a visionary , creative, and controversial department plan.

Teams actually created the CU business plan for 1993.

Functions that received inadequate attention in the past can now be performed well and with fewer people. Two former managers now serve as advisors to CU teams. As teams require less help from advisors on day-to-day activities, advisors are able to focus more on strategic issues and coaching, as well as ISD-wide activities such as facilitating redesign and re-engineering efforts in other ISD departments. Another former manager serves as financial guru for the CU, using the same business perspective so needed in the services-for-sale environment.

Over 60 ISD members in leadership positions recently rated each ISD unit on the effectiveness of its relationships with other units. The CU's ratings far surpassed those of any group within ISD, with 80 percent of the respondents indicating *very effective* relationships with the CU. There were seven positive ratings for every negative one. No other department even came close. While there are no comparable past measures, we feel confident that these ratings reflect a major turnaround from several years ago.

The following descriptions highlight some Computer Utility team results.

Help Line Services Team   This division, which handles almost 3,000 calls per month from internal customers throughout Corning, upgraded the help line from its previous mediocre level. Team members sought additional education so they could expand services from mainframe to mid-range and personal computers. The percentage of calls resolved on the spot is now over 90 percent, compared to 75 percent when the help line started in July 1988; and customer satisfaction has jumped from 78 to 100 percent. To assure it has the data for continuous improvement, the team has started a raft of initiatives to measure quality, including monthly surveys of selected customers, tracking of call handling and abandonment, follow-up calls the day after customers are helped, and informal lunch-hour focus groups. Noticing a trend toward increased call volumes and abandonment rates, the team proposed converting another budgeted (exempt) position in the CU into an additional help line (non-exempt) position. Management readily agreed, applauding the team's initiative.

Not content to limit improvement to their own boundaries, the team has initiated regular sessions between themselves and communications teams in the Lynx Communications Services (LCS) Department to resolve long-standing coordination problems. Now, team members across departments actually help each other. After major network changes or outages, LCS team members provide information and answer questions alongside Help Line Services team members on the Corning help line.

The team continues to find new ways to delight ISD's customers. Recognizing that they collect valuable information about ISD's customers that would benefit other ISD units, they asked for the opportunity to share those insights at an ISD quarterly all-managers' meeting. Their presentation met with such approval that they will probably become a regular feature at quarterly meetings.

The team continues to find new ways to delight ISD's customers.

Viewing themselves as business managers as well as service providers, they think strategically about their "business." Unlike other parts of ISD, they are still funded through corporate overhead. But they have begun searching for ways to actually measure their value in order to justify their service as a corporate overhead expense in the future.[4]

Operations Services Team   This team consists of all operators of corporate mainframe and mid-range computers. Improved teamwork within and across the three shifts has led to dramatic reductions in operator errors. In 1990, 70 percent fewer errors were made than the year before—even though there were 20 percent fewer operators. The team treats the computer room as its own shop, taking great pride in preventing problems, improving operations, and saving money. When Operations acquired new tape cartridge technology, a vendor submitted a proposal to create internal and external labels on the cartridges for $45,000. Team members decided to do the job themselves—and did so at a cost of only $500 in overtime and temporary help.

Operations Services team members have gradually increased their skills at giving each other open, honest performance feedback during evaluation sessions they conduct themselves. And they actually recommend final performance ratings for each other. They recently decided that team members could evaluate each other's performance more effectively if they better understood the work done on each shift. So, despite personal inconvenience, members agreed to work for two weeks on each unfamiliar shift.

IBM Technical Services Team   Traditionally known as the back office folks, these people previously interacted with their customers only when requested to do so. In contrast, they now work as active partners with customers to identify and solve problems. It began with the Control function at Corning, which asked the IBM Technical Services team to help solve performance prob-

---

4. The Help Line Services team is featured in an article on total quality management. See Digital Equipment Corporation (1991).

lems during critical period closings. The solutions implemented significantly improved the process. Buoyed by their success, team members proactively approached other customers they serve and suggested resolving longstanding problems. Their success rate to date is impressive. Not only do they meet with customers to fix problems, but they attend periodic customer reviews, using these opportunities to discover innovative ways of contributing to plans.

Buoyed by their success, team members proactively approached other customers they serve and suggested resolving longstanding problems.

VAX Technical Services Team   This team is the first to acknowledge its shift in focus from technology to the customer. Customers no longer need to withstand delays as technical services employees wait for their supervisor to make decisions. Instead, they make decisions on the spot. A customer recently asked a team member to purchase more disks for a VAX machine. With both his knowledge of the budget and the authority entrusted to him, the team member was able to agree at once. Team members feel responsible for "delighting their customers"—for proactively finding ways of improving their service. During a recent major change in the electronic mail facility, the team worked all weekend, displaying a remarkable level of camaraderie despite daunting vendor-related problems, to ensure that its customers' electronic mail capability would be available first thing Monday morning.

Previously, team members scheduled systems outages without much regard for customer needs. Today, they coordinate down times with IBM Technical Services and network specialists so that customers are minimally inconvenienced.

Several months ago, team members explored inefficiencies in carrying out team functions. After careful analysis, they redesigned their work process using Corning's IMPACT (Improved Method for Process Analysis of Cost-Time) methodology. Instead of generalists who perform all functions on their own VAX systems, they became experts on particular aspects of all systems. Duplication of effort has been drastically reduced and the team has been able to support an expanding portfolio of VAX systems without a commensurate increase in its own membership.

Corporate Staff Services

For the past year, a Corporate Staff Services (CSS) team has been redesigning the department, which consists of applications development groups, to create an empowered organization with self-managing teams focused on providing excellent customer service. After conducting a survey of the department's customers to determine which areas were doing well and which needed improvement, the team mapped and then redesigned selected core processes. Significant improvements are already evident. Weekly departmental meetings are now held to share project information and discuss common issues. As a result of the design team work and these meetings, CSS staff have greater appreciation of each other and understand issues beyond their own groups. They also attend customer meetings to enhance their business knowledge and improve communication.

Administrative Center IS Team   One self-managing team was formed two years ago as part of a consolidation of corporate administrative services ranging from accounts receivable and payable to payroll and insurance. This team develops and supports the Center's information technology applications. Working closely with its Administrative Center customers, the team evaluates requests and sets priorities across the Center. Previously, priorities were set individually with each administrative group, resulting in suboptimization of priority decisions and IS resources. Team members are developing expertise on all administrative information systems, thereby increasing overall flexibility and eliminating the previous "key person" syndrome. They play an active role in planning the team budget and take responsibility for hiring and firing team members. When their former advisor was promoted to a new position within ISD, they selected a replacement, breaking new ground in team empowerment. They also share programming practices and solutions and have developed formal standards and procedures. Not long ago, they set very high standards for themselves in customer service categories and created their own version of the Domino's guarantee. They call it their "pizza" measure. If a customer is dissatisfied with the IS team's responsiveness, the team delivers a free pizza to that customer.

When their former advisor was promoted to a new position within ISD, they selected a replacement.

Support for their customers exceeds traditional expectations. For example, IS team members now replace insurance claims employees at the telephones so the claims employees can attend training sessions. This also benefits IS team members, whose deeper understanding of the insurance claims function suggests new ways to support it.

Lynx Communications Services

Lynx Communications Services (LCS), which consists of the Integrated Network Services, Consulting, Customer Service, and Product Strategy teams (see Figure 2), has re-engineered its functions, simplifying work flows, reducing cycle time, and establishing self-managing teams. LCS added a customer service function for network services and helped design a new front-end to a billing system to support Customer Service team members, eliminating one position in the process. Employees who were locked in the same job for over 20 years were able to move into new areas and learn new skills.

Teams in LCS have improved cross-department communication and coordination by establishing a series of coordination meetings. Department-wide daily production meetings are attended by LCS team members, while weekly meetings are attended by both LCS and CU team members. In addition, an inter-team council meets monthly to discuss cross-department plans and issues. Improved cooperation is evident when new systems, changes, or problems occur, and when teams need back-up assistance.

Organizations sometimes suffer a downturn in customer service during the early months of transition to teams. However, service form the LCS improved during these first months despite the extra time required to establish teams. Although there are no comparable metrics for before and after, we know that a customer survey conducted before teams were established

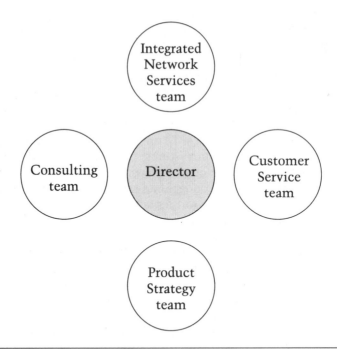

Figure 2. **Lynx Communications Services.**

recorded myriad complaints about responsiveness and work quality. Current ongoing surveys initiated by teams indicate significantly more positive responses in these categories.

The following descriptions highlight some Lynx Communications Services team results.

Customer Service Team After designing processes for their newly formed team, members developed and implemented a plan to train and cross-train each other on new responsibilities. At first team members (mostly telephone operators) were skeptical of their ability to take on self-management or customer service responsibilities. Yet within months, they began performing many management functions such as scheduling work, arranging for temporary help, and searching for ways to improve operations. Former telephone operators now perform a wide range of customer service functions, and the former receptionist has taken on system administration responsibilities.

By answering customer calls related to all network services, the team provides one-stop shopping, affording customers of network services a simpler, more direct route to LCS. In addition, Integrated Network Services team members can not focus on establishing new services and correcting problems because the Customer Service team now handles many requests previously handled by the Integrated Network Services team. Team members have grown as they have sought additional responsibilities and have searched for improved ways of serving customers.

Integrated Network Services Team   This team has developed a sense of ownership and commitment not previously experienced. By setting their own objectives, team members feel greater commitment to achieving them. By participating actively in developing their budget and tracking revenues by product, team members understand their business and make fund allocation decisions that best meet LCS needs. Before team formation; individuals would grumble when requests for training were turned down by their manager. Today, the team as a whole determines who needs training and allocates the budget accordingly.

The team also developed a postcard that requests feedback on service (quality of work done, timeliness of work, level of satisfaction, and comments). The card, which contains the technician's name, is given to every customer upon completion of work.

Consulting Team   Team members have taken on responsibilities previously reserved for managers. For example, LCS recently changed its primary telecommunications services vendor—a change that should result in a savings of millions of dollars. An analyst on this team played a major role in negotiating the contract.

Team members also collaborate with customers in solving joint problems and developing better processes. They recently held a series of working sessions with representatives of Corporate Staff Services to improve corporation between the groups. After surveying members of both organizations to uncover all problems, they thoroughly analyzed and solved the issues. Next, they initiated meetings with other groups within ISD that support local area networks to clarify roles and set such common practices as naming conventions.

> Team members have taken on responsibilities previously reserved for managers.

ISD-Wide Quality Improvement Teams

As mentioned earlier, the number of quality improvement teams (QITs) has been steadily growing at Corning. While there are a half-dozen now operating across ISD, the Empowerment QIT is particularly noteworthy. Instead of assigning the responsibility for leading the empowerment effort throughout ISD to the IS management team (the traditional leadership group), an Empowerment QIT was established and is comprised of volunteers who represent a diagonal slice of the organization. The team's first project was to conduct a survey of ISD staff to assess feelings about their level of empowerment. Based on the results, the team decided to conduct working sessions to convey business needs for transforming the organization's culture to one of empowerment, to present a vision and principles for empowerment (Table 1), and to take some first steps toward creating the new culture. Recognizing that current managers needed to make the biggest adjustments to the new environment where power is shared, they chose to hold a four-day working session in January 1992 for current managers, supervisors, and advisors. In addition to heightened awareness about empowerment, all left the session with individual action plans and commitment to create department-wide plans for enhancing empowerment. Those plans have since been published and distributed. Actions taken to date include liberalizing approval levels and

Table 1.   **Empowerment Vision and Principles**

Vision

Information Services will be an organization in which employees are vested with both the
responsibility and authority to deliver total customer service.

Principles

In order to achieve empowerment vision, Information Services subscribes to the following operating principles:

■ An integrated, well-communicated division direction guides each individual's actions such that a
  sense of commitment, dedication, and power exists within each employee.

■ An openness exists throughout the organization that facilitates communication, minimizes bureaucracy, and speeds decision making.

■ Responsibility for the success of the empowerment effort rests with all IS employees. Responsibility for creating an empowered environment rests with the IS management team.

■ Increased responsibility, authority, and accountability reside at the action initiation or customer
  interface points within the organization.

■ Coaching, mentoring, and collaboration skills are emphasized and are the dominant organization style.

■ Processes are simplified to allow broader involvement in direction- and priority-setting.

■ Continuous improvement is expected and is measured by a periodic empowerment survey

establishing principles—rather than rules, regulations, and policies—to conduct various aspects of Corning's business. These principles provide guidance
and boundaries for everyone while empowering individuals and teams to use
the principles in making decisions best suited to their needs. A follow-up
working session for all 270 ISD members was held in July 1992.

Benchmark for Other Organizations

Benchmarking, industrial research or intelligence gathering that allows companies to compare their functions to those in other companies, has become
an integral part of the quality process. Increasingly, IS organizations are identifying, then visiting, other organizations that represent best practices in particular areas.[5] ISD receives calls and visits from information services organizations throughout North America interested in learning from Corning's
experiences with empowerment. In fact, the CU hosts quarterly education
sessions for interested organizations.[6] Several have since embarked upon the
journey to empowerment with self-managing teams.

---

5. For more information see Freedman (1992).
6. Companies that have attended education sessions include General Electric Corporation, LTV
Steel, Eastman Tennessee Chemical Company, Hills Pat Foods, and Schreiber Foods.

ISD's quality manager participates in interorganizational working groups to learn more about what others are doing to improve quality in information services. In February 1992, he made a presentation to members of Ernst & Young's Total Quality Management for Information Services Leadership Program. Participants included representatives from Ameritech Services, Inc., Apple Computer, Inc., AT&T, Carolina Power & Light, Eli Lilly and Company, First Chicago Corporation, IBM Corporation, Milliken, Coca-Cola Company, Eastman Kodak, Texas Instruments, and Xerox Corporation—many of whom are acknowledged leaders in organizational empowerment. The many follow-up calls requesting further information is another indication that Corning is perceived as a leading practitioner in deploying empowerment in information services. In addition, ISD has been an active participant in the Society for Information Management's working groups on quality.

Key Success Factors

By now it should be evident that we are describing a profound cultural change rather than merely a tinkering with boxes on an organizational chart. This change requires a shift in paradigms from control to commitment and coaching (Table 2). Our experience so far confirms several key success factors for implementing empowerment strategies in information services organizations:

> We are describing a profound cultural change rather than merely a tinkering with boxes on an organizational chart.

Table 2. **Required Paradigm Shifts**

From:	To:
Control—Supervisor or manager	Commitment and coaching
Many levels	Flat organization
Directive decision making	Consensus decision making
Competitive	Cooperative
"Tell me what to do"	"How can we work smarter?"
Low risk-taking	Innovation
Reacting to change	Seizing opportunities
"We'll think about it and set up a committee to study it"	Do it faster than the competition
Internal organization driven	Customer driven
Rules-bound and slow	Flexible and fast
Doing things right	Doing the right things
"I only work here"	"I am the organization"
Power over staff	Empowered staff
If it's not broke, don't fix it	Continuous improvement
Acceptable quality and service	World-class quality and service
Status counts	Ability and contribution count more than status
Rewards reflect time in job and who you know	Rewards reflect real contributions

1. Start with a vision and clear goals.

Key members of the ISD senior management team must demonstrate leadership in stating and promoting ISD's vision of empowerment as the primary enabler in meeting ISD's "vital one" goal of total customer satisfaction. That vision has helped the senior management team communicate its desired future work system and continues to serve as a "lighthouse" as teams navigate through inevitable conflicts.

2. Ensure management commitment, visible support, and willingness to take risks.

This new work system leads to change—in roles, relationships, management styles, and work flows. The senior management team must continually demonstrate their commitment and willingness to take the risks inherent in such dramatic changes, such as truly sharing power and information. The team now acknowledges early misgivings about whether managers would give up power and teams would act responsibly, possibly causing "organizational upheaval." Yet despite doubts, support must be active because when managers pay lip service to empowerment but fail to nurture an environment that supports empowered behavior, others in the organization quickly become cynical.

One written comment after the empowerment event illustrates the importance of visible support: "I was impressed with Harvey's [Shrednick, ISD director] expressed commitment to empowerment. Now we will all be watching his feet." Since this event, people have quickly flagged management actions not consistent with the vision of empowerment. For instance, Harvey was recently admonished in public for not accepting the recommendations of a QIT empowered to identify applications development methodologies for ISD.

3. Pay particular attention to middle managers and supervisors.

It is not uncommon for middle managers and supervisors to view announcements of impending empowered work systems with suspicion, uncertainty, and resistance. Some view the change as a threat of loss of power, influence, and importance over which they have minimal control. When they come to understand that their repertoire of management skills, often developed from years of experience and struggle, will become at least in part obsolete, they worry that they won't successfully master new coaching and facilitating skills.

A former manager who now serves as advisor to two teams expressed this concern most poignantly: "At first it was a big shock. All of a sudden, everything changes—your benchmarks and reference points of what's expected of you. You have to totally change your style. It's difficult not to make decisions when you're used to doing so and the answers are so obvious to you. And any slip-up is viewed negatively by the team." This manager has risen to the challenge with great success, but some others are struggling to make the transformation. These advisors need support from their managers and peers (especially those who are further along in their transitions).

ISD's January empowerment event was one commitment designed to help middle managers and supervisors succeed. Other commitments involve training in new skills, which should include setting boundaries and communicating them to teams. Coaches, like parents, need to set limits and then back off as good judgment in decision making is demonstrated.

4.   Involve staff in all phases of the project.

In addition to building commitment and ownership, involvement ensures that plans incorporate the valuable insights and experience of those who do the work. Based on experiences with their associates, the CU design team expressed concern that some teams would be more willing than others to take on full self-management within a short period of time. Consequently, a scheme was developed for different starting levels of self-management. This scheme has proven successful in giving team members a greater sense of choice and control. Moreover, active involvement helps team members internalize new team concepts. During one meeting before Operations became a self-managing team, the Operations supervisor asked, "Will the team take over the responsibility for being on call on weekends?" At the time, this responsibility was rotated among various ISD managers. One computer operator provided the traditional response: "Of course not! That's a supervisor's job." However, another operator countered with: "Wait a minute. We're taking on the supervisor's role. What kind of credibility will we have if we don't take on this responsibility?" The others agreed. At that point a key aspect of the new self-managing team was internalized by all.

5.   Communicate, communicate, and communicate some more.

Inevitable uncertainty accompanies significant work system changes. Communication is a strong antidote. Uncertainty was addressed at the onset by communicating our commitment not to terminate people as a result of the new work system. In addition, those involved with the design of the new work system must keep communication flowing to all stakeholders. Communication involves distribution of minutes, regular briefings, and "rollout" meetings. The CU team that designed the new work system ran into an interesting challenge when it was ready to conduct its final "rollout" to other members of the utility: they had been so thorough in communicating that there was nothing new to say.

> Uncertainty was addressed at the onset by communicating our commitment not to terminate people as a result of the new work system.

Timely communication of relevant information within teams and across ISD, as well as with senior IS managers and customers, continues to be crucial. Teams need to receive information on many more aspects of the business in an environment where they are expected to make business decisions. At the same time, teams need to keep more people informed of their actions and decisions. Basking in their newly acquired empowerment, teams can easily neglect to keep IS management team members in the communication loop.

6.   Keep your eye on the ball.

The ball in ISD's case is the business it must run. There is a natural tendency for teams to focus inwardly, especially during the early stages of development. Managers and advisors must play a crucial role in helping to focus teams outwardly on their customers and other teams with whom they must coordinate to satisfy customer expectations. On the other hand, teams must be wary of getting so focused on the business that they lose sight of their empowerment objectives that ultimately will help them achieve business objectives.

7. Educate all those involved.

Education and training continue to be high priorities. Educating managers on how to assure a leadership role in an empowered organization is critical to success. Managers must learn how to coach and facilitate rather than direct. They must understand how teams develop over time and how they can facilitate that growth. Team members must also understand how teams develop over time and how to work effectively in a team environment. Education in team skills, as well as technical and business skills, must be an ongoing activity among team members, not simply a one-time activity when teams are first established. Formal seminars continue to be held on relevant subjects. More important, team members learn by experience—with guidance from their managers and advisors.

Managers must learn how to coach and facilitate rather than direct.

8. Develop a reward system that promotes success.

Corning has an extensive system of rewards for recognizing individual accomplishments in improving quality. We saw the need to augment the reward to recognize team accomplishments. Teams are now rewarded for meeting both individual and team objectives. Teams evaluate themselves as a whole on how well team objectives were met at the end of the yearly performance cycle. In more mature teams, members conduct performance evaluations on individuals as well. Additional ways of formally and informally rewarding team performance are being explored including goal-sharing programs. The Administrative Services team is currently part of a pilot goal-sharing plan that covers all Administrative Center employees. The plan includes incentives for spending within budget, customer satisfaction, process improvement, and cost reduction.

Approach for Developing and Sustaining the New Work System

Until recently, assistance in designing and implementing new work systems came from outside consultants. Now this assistance increasingly comes from internal ISD people who have gained experience and skills through participation in redesigns and implementations in their own areas. For instance, CU and LCS advisors serve on an advisory council to the CSS design team. A CU advisor actually facilitates design team meetings.

Structured approaches are used to design and establish teams in ISD; and in retrospect, using these approaches has probably been a major factor in our success to date. A steering committee and design team work closely throughout the process. Senior managers on the steering committee create or validate the vision, and then sponsor, guide, and support the change process. Those who will need to use the new work system play an active part in creating it through participation on design teams. As part of the design process these teams perform many duties.[7] They

- Conduct benchmarking;
- Survey customer and staff members to determine what is going well and what needs improvement;
- Explore anticipated changes in the organization's external and internal environment that might impact this project;
- Review current work practices, systems, tools, and results;
- Recommend redesigned work practices, structures, systems, and tools to achieve the vision created by the steering team;
- Develop implementation plans, including training and measures for monitoring project success; and
- Serve as change advocates and communicators.

The design teams themselves are comprised of individuals who are part of the work system under study in this paper. This make-up was chosen for many reasons: (a) active involvement builds ownership and commitment; (b) involvement ensures that recommendations incorporate the valuable insights and experience of those who do the work; (c) involvement teaches work team members how to collect data, analyze their work system, and find ways to improve it—skills all work team members need in order to facilitate continuous improvement beyond this project; and (d) active involvement helps team members internalize new team concepts. This collaborative approach is clearly more time-consuming up front than more traditional methods, where consultants or managers identify needed changes and then mandate them. However, we found that the collaborative approach not only leads to more effective implementation by committed individuals who own their solutions, but to better long-term results.

> We found that the collaborative approach not only leads to more effective implementation by committed individuals who own their solutions, but to better long-term results.

Redesign and implementation are just the beginning. Existing teams require sustenance if continuous improvement is to become a way of life. Managers must meet regularly with teams to address issues and concerns. And teams should evaluate their own performance frequently, making improvements as required to enhance customer service, quality, productivity, and work life. One method is to include reviews as regular agenda items at team meetings that address such questions as (a) What have we done well as a team? (b) What are some problems or potential areas for improvement for our team? (c) How can we address these problems or areas for improvement? In addition, formal assessments offer a more objective "airplane view" of how the teams

---

7. For further reading about organizational design process, see Hanna (1988).

are doing. They help put successes in perspective and highlight areas for improvement and suggestions for moving to the next steps.

Continual Learning

In order to sustain the major cultural change taking place at Corning, the management teams must learn to adjust their thinking and behavior. The IS management team must be transformed from the command and control managers they were taught to be into true leaders who give self-managing teams responsibility, accountability, and authority to deliver first-class customer service. While the IS management team appreciates having more time to develop overall strategy and marketing, they admit that letting go is difficult. Making decisions in light of business impacts comes naturally to them. But patiently explaining the external environment and boundaries for a decision, and utilizing less-than-ideal team decisions as springboards for coaching do not come as naturally. There are many examples of the subtle ways teams can fall into old patterns. One senior manager highlighted some of these pitfalls: "Unless I carefully state that I am giving my opinion, team members hear it as a decision. And those leery of taking on responsibility look to me for approval. I have to be wary of falling into the trap of approving or disapproving too much. I recently expressed some reservations about a candidate being interviewed by one team. The team heard the reservations as disapproval of the person even though that was not my intention." To counteract these tendencies, the teams discuss what each has done recently to foster empowerment and IS management team meetings.

There are many examples of the subtle ways teams can fall into old patterns.

While managing by the numbers is an integral part of total quality management at Corning, the IS management team must now be even more vigorous in its measurements (because they are less involved in day-to-day decisions in many cases) and in sharing results of all measurements with the self-managing teams. And they continue to search for the most effective ways of rewarding individuals and teams based on results.

The IS management team must also learn to play the key role of "barrier buster." During this time of transition, many practices and systems throughout Corning are not yet geared to the empowerment level of the teams. Supervisory signatures are still expected for job descriptions, expense reports, and other administrative actions. Many senior managers in Corning's divisions are not yet comfortable receiving phone calls directly from team members. Management team members must reduce the many subtle and unwitting barriers to empowerment. Adding to the challenge is the reporting structure—Corning is a traditional hierarchical organization.

Despite all the learning, the IS management team occasionally falls into old ways of doing business. When a new director for the CU was hired, none of the IS team members thought to involve CU team members in the hiring process. They were thoroughly embarrassed when team members pointed out the transgression.

Augmenting ISD's Portfolio of Capabilities

Work system innovation in ISD has taught the team how to help ISD's customers reap similar benefits. As business process re-engineering is incorporated into the IS team's work with internal customers, the team's expertise in work system innovation becomes extremely valuable.[8] The following example illustrates this point.

A member of Applications Development Services is consulting with Corning's Science Products Division in its redesign of the customer contact function to create empowered teams that will better serve Science Products' customers. Building an ISD expertise in process mapping and redesign as well as creating empowered work teams, the Science Products design team reviewed its work and information flows and identified processes performed by each of the six separate customer contact units within the division. The resulting matrix of key processes and units helped the design team recognize the benefits of combining all customer contact functions in to one organization of empowered teams. Requirements for an information system to support these teams have been identified.

There has already been significant benefit from the improved communication and understanding of information flows. Team members have realized substantial time savings (over 65 hours per week or the equivalent of one and a half staff members) as well as enhanced customer service. For example, time previously spent in processing rebates has been reduced by 90 percent by issuing monthly rebates to each distributor instead of issuing a rebate for each invoice. Savings of $54,000 annually in overhead costs are anticipated.

For years, customer contact staff complained about pricing practices that had detrimental effects on customer service, but assumed they had no power to change these practices because "they have always done pricing this way." Emboldened by their new skills and successes, the design team initiated meetings with key stake-holders in Marketing to convince them to change from current pricing practices (which require frequent calls to Marketing and resultant delays) to computer-generated pricing tables based on marketing-supplied information (which are projected to enhance accuracy and consistency while greatly shortening response times).

Assisting our customers in implementing innovative high-performance work systems is one more meaningful way of delivering world-class service.

Competing to Serve Our Customers

ISD's new services-for-sale arrangement means that IS must be run as a business and must compete with outside IS service providers. ISD accepted this challenge in order to expand its services without the limitations of corporate spending constraints. Because of its strong foundation of quality, their chance of success was high.

---

8. For further reading, see Davenport and Short (1990).

During this first difficult transition year, the revenue generated by the CU and LCS (two departments operating with self-managing teams) is exceeding projections. Overall, energy, creativity, commitment, and ownership in ISD have been unleashed. The sense of pride in satisfying—even delighting—the customer is evident throughout the teams. The director of Corning's Administrative Center, a long-time ISD customer, describes the difference as night and day. "We experience a different kind of energy and enthusiasm. The teams want to do things right the first time. They are truly customer-focused and really care. That was not true two years ago."

Total customer satisfaction has become ISD's "vital one" objective. Total quality management is not only a key element of its approach to providing Corning with the information technology support it needs to compete globally, but it is ISD's most powerful weapon in the competition to serve Corning customers. We are convinced that empowerment through work systems such as self-managing teams is the means for enlisting the minds, hearts, and spirits of ISD members toward delivering world-class service that its customers value.

The sense of pride in satisfying—even delighting—the customer is evident throughout the teams.

References

Business Week, "The Payoff from Teamwork," July 10, 1989, pp. 56–62.

Davenport, T.H. and Short, J.E. "The New Industrial Engineering: Information Technology and Business Process Redesign," *Sloan Management Review*, Summer 1990, pp. 11–27.

Digital Equipment Corporation. "Quality Through Time," Special Report of *Enterprise* (15:1), Spring 1991.

Freedman, D. "Those Who Can, Teach," *CIO*, September 1, 1992, pp. 46–51.

Hanna, D.P. *Designing Organizations for High Performance*, Addison-Wesley Publishing Company, Reading, MA, 1988.

Harvey R. Shrednick is senior vice president of Information Services and a corporate officer of Corning Incorporated. Richard J. Shutt is director of Applications Development Services at Corning incorporated. Madeline Weiss is president of Weiss Associates, Inc., a consulting firm specializing in management and organizational issues related to information services and technology.

ACCOUNTING

The ABC Innovations

Peter B.B. Turney

This excerpt from Turney's book on activity-based costing *explains this approach to accounting for costs, not based on products produced but on activities involved in the creation of the products. It lays out a more realistic way for an organization to accurately measure costs in terms of value-added and non-value-added activities.*

Cost information should reveal problems to tackle and opportunities to exploit. But, as previous chapters show, that's not always the case. Conventional cost systems *actually* hide problems and fail to identify opportunities.

Conventional cost information is like the sea that hides dangerous rocks. On the surface, all appears calm and smooth; there's no inkling of unprofitable products and customers, and there's no hint of waste in the operations. And, like the unwary mariner, the good ship *World Class* sails on, oblivious to the dangers lurking below.

What the ship's officers need is a look below the surface of misinformation. This would reveal the rocks and shoals of poor quality, high cost, lack of responsiveness, improperly designed products, overpriced products, and neglected customers. These are the very things that sink the ships of enterprise in today's competitive world.

And nearby, lurk sharks of all kinds. Some may be hungry competitors looking for the opportunity to bite off parts of your business. Others may be hostile asset-strippers or hungry conglomerates. Trouble is the smell of blood

Adapted, with permission, from Peter B. B. Turney, *Common Cents: The ABC Performance Breakthrough*, Beaverton, OR: Cost Technology, 1991 and 1992.

to these sharks. Overpriced products, neglected markets, and underperforming assets are their feeding grounds.

Can the aspiring world-class company be saved from these perils?

Yes. It can.

Part of the solution is to lower the sea of inventory to reveal the rocks. This involves eliminating inventory buffers and long lead times that mask problems. As those problems become visible, they can be tackled. Set up times can be reduced, sources of poor quality can be eliminated, people can be trained and empowered and machines can be properly maintained so they don't break down.

A second part of the solution is to provide activity-based information about the rocks lurking below the surface. This information complements visual inspection of the rocks. It identifies what each one is, describes its importance (some rocks are more costly than others), and shows how successful you are in eliminating its threat.

Activity-based information also reveals those tasty morsels so prized by the sharks of competition. Which products and customers are unprofitable? Which products are improperly priced? Which profitable products and customers are being neglected? What opportunities are there for reducing the cost of products?

Activity-based costing allows you to identify problems and plot safe courses to solutions and opportunities.

To answer such questions—to avoid the rocks and sharks—today's corporate ship needs a world-class navigation system. Activity-based costing (ABC) is just such an information system. ABC allows you to identify problems and plot safe courses to solutions and opportunities. It does this by providing cost and nonfinancial information about activities and cost objects.

Activities are descriptions of work that goes on in a company. Entering the details of a customer order at a computer terminal, setting up a machine, inspecting a part, and shipping a product are examples of activities.

Cost objects are the reasons for performing activities. They include products, services, and customers. Entering the details of a customer order at a computer terminal (*the activity*), for example, is performed because a customer (*the cost object*) wishes to place an order.

Activities and cost objects are basic to the ABC concept. This chapter shows you how ABC uses them to:

- Report more accurate cost information, and
- Provide useful information about activities.

You'll also find out:

- What ABC reveals about the rocks and sharks that lie in wait for the unwary, and
- How well ABC fits the information needs of aspiring world-class companies.

It's also important to realize that navigation by ABC information is imperative whether times are good or bad. The tide is in during boom times, covering up the rocks and sharks. Don't wait until the recession hits and the tide is out. You may already be on the rocks, with the sharks tearing you to pieces.

How ABC Gives You Accurate Cost Information

The underlying assumption of ABC is quite different from that of conventional costing. Conventional costing assumes that products cause cost. ABC is more realistic. ABC assumes that activities cause cost and that cost objects create the demand for activities.

ABC is more realistic. ABC assumes that activities cause cost and that cost objects create the demand for activities.

As an example of how activities and cost objects work, let's say you're involved in auditing the quality of printed circuit boards. Auditing is an activity. It involves checking the thickness of the circuits, the placement and sizes of holes and pads, and the flatness of the board.

Performing the audit activity requires various resources. These include the salaries of individuals doing the work, equipment and software to measure and record the checks made on the boards, and floorspace for the work.

The auditing activity is performed on boards received from the finishing department. Receiving a batch of boards from finishing is the trigger that initiates the work associated with the activity. The boards themselves are the cost objects that demand activity (more boards means that the auditing activity must be performed more frequently).

ABC's underlying assumption makes intuitive sense when applied to an activity such as quality auditing. But why does it make a difference to the accuracy of reported cost information? To understand this, let's take a closer look at how ABC helps in costing the quality auditing activity.

The 1st Innovation—Assigning Costs to Activities

The first innovation of ABC is assignment of costs to the auditing activity. This assignment is based on measurements of resources used.

Salary costs, for example, are assigned based on determinations of who is doing the work and how much of their time is spent on auditing boards. *Figure 1* shows the costs assigned to the auditing activity.

Knowing what activities cost helps in identifying important activities— those with the greatest potential for cost reduction. Knowledge of activity

Test equipment depreciation	$58,000
Salaries and benefits	88,000
Space	61,000
Supplies	6,5000
Fixtures	120,000
Total activity cost	$333,500
Number of boards tested	667,000
Cost per board	$0.50

Figure 1. *__The cost of a quality auditing activity.__* **Cost information directs attention to high cost activities and confirms that savings have been achieved subsequent to improvement.**

cost also allows you to model the impact of cost reduction actions and to subsequently confirm that savings were achieved.

By and large, however, activities *are not defined* in conventional cost systems. You can learn about the cost of the quality control department, but you'll rarely find any information about the cost of the auditing activity within the departmental accounts.[1] This is unfortunate because activity cost knowledge is important.

In contrast, cost assignment in a conventional cost system is to departments or cost centers. The auditing activity, for example, could be a cost center in a conventional cost system. In some cases, cost centers are defined so narrowly that they are equivalent to activities.

The 2nd Innovation—Cost Assignment to Cost Objects

ABC's second innovation is the way in which costs are assigned to cost objects. *ABC assigns activity costs to cost objects based on activity drivers that accurately measure consumption of the activity.*

An activity driver is a measure of the consumption of an activity by a cost object (such as a product). The number of hours devoted by engineers to each product, for example, measures each product's consumption of engineering activity.

In the case of the auditing activity, for example, *number of batches* best measures the consumption of the activity by each type of board. This is because the quality audit is only performed on one board in each batch received.

Figure 2 shows how this works for two different types of printed circuit boards. The activity driver *number of batches* assigns two times more ABC cost to Board B than it assigns to A. This is correct, because Board B is audited twice, whereas Board A is audited only once.

Quality Auditing Activity

Cost per batch	$50
Cost per direct labor hour	$25

	Product A	Product B
Number of direct labor hours	4	2
Number of batches produced	1	2
Conventional cost (DLH)	$100	$ 50
ABC cost (batches)	$ 50 ✓	$100 ✓

✓ Accurate product cost

Figure 2. *Accurate product costs.* ABC assigns cost to products based on their use of activities, which is cost per batch in this example. The result is accurate product costs.

The audit cost per batch in *Figure 2* is the same for both products ($50). This assumption is correct if the quality audit of each board takes roughly the same length of time and uses the same resources regardless of the product checked.

If this were not true (if, for example, Board A requires significantly more checking time because it has more holes), then a different activity driver would be used. *Number of holes checked,* for example, might then be a better activity driver, because it would capture variations in effort from one board type to another.

Now, let's take a moment to look at how conventional costing treats the same auditing example.

Conventional costing uses direct labor hours as the activity driver. Direct labor hours is a measurement of the "touch labor" needed to produce a unit of the product.

In *Figure 2,* the cost assigned to B by direct labor hours is half that assigned to A. This is because B uses half the labor hours of A.

This would only be correct, however, if the amount of direct labor cor-related well with the number of batches. In this case, it doesn't, so the two products are miscosted by substantial margins. Product A is overcosted by 100%, and Product B is undercosted by 50%.

The inaccuracy in conventional costing for this example is no accident. It results from limitations in the activity driver used to assign cost; direct labor hours *does not* accurately measure the use of the auditing activity by the products.

> Direct labor hours *does not* accurately measure the use of the auditing activity by the products.

ABC corrects for this inaccuracy by choosing an activity driver that does accurately measure cost consumption by each product. In this case, the driver is the number of batches. However, it could have been the number of holes checked, the number of checking hours, or the number of direct labor hours if the facts had been different.

In short, ABC is generally superior to conventional costing because it reports more accurate product costs. This occurs because ABC uses *more* activity drivers and more *types* of activity drivers than conventional costing. Like a toolkit that contains a wide range of tools, ABC uses different activity drivers to fit different circumstances.

The Number of Activity Drivers. It's common to find ten to thirty activity drivers in the typical ABC system. However, some ABC systems have as few as two activity drivers and some have as many as a hundred. Conventional systems, on the other hand, usually have one activity driver; occasionally they have as many as three.

More activity drivers allow ABC to "do it more ways" than conventional cost systems. Most companies have many activities that are consumed in different ways. It's unlikely that one activity driver (such as direct labor hours) can capture this diversity even in a small company.

Types of Activity Drivers. Another fundamental innovation of ABC is the recognition that there are different levels of activity in most organizations. Different activity levels require different types of activity drivers *(Figure 3).*

Activity	Activity driver
Unit	
Assembly	Direct labor hours
Stamping	Machine hours
Batch	
Moving material	Number of movements
Inspecting first piece	Number of runs
Product	
Modifying product design	Engineering change notices
Maintaining routing	Number of part numbers
Customer	
Processing customers orders	Number of customer orders
Sustaining	
Managing the plant	(No good activity driver available)

Figure 3. *Activity and driver levels.* **ABC recognizes that activities relate to cost objects at different levels and different levels require different activity drivers. In the case of sustaining activities, it is not possible to meaningfully assign the cost to products or customers.**

Let's start by looking at three levels of activities that exist in many manufacturing companies:

- *Unit* activities are performed on units of the product. Tapping threads in a metal elbow is an example of a unit activity.
- *Batch* activities are performed on batches of products rather than individual product units. Setting up a machine to produce a batch of products or inspecting the first piece of the batch are examples of batch activities.
- *Product* activities benefit all units of a particular product. An example is preparing a numerical control (NC) program for a product.

Accurate assignment of the cost of unit activities is accomplished by using measures of the product unit. The number of direct labor hours needed to tap threads in a metal elbow, for example, accurately measures operator effort.

Unit activity drivers are the *only* activity drivers found in conventional cost systems. Direct labor hours, machine hours, material cost, and product units are all used as unit activity drivers.

The problem is that unit activity drivers do not accurately cost non-unit activities. You need batch activity drivers for batch activities, and product activity drivers for product activities.

Let's see why this is the case.

In *Figure 4*, making tools and dies is a product activity; it benefits all the units produced of each product type. The cost of this activity ($1,000) is assigned to the two products using a *unit activity driver* (the number of units) and a *product activity driver* (the number of products).

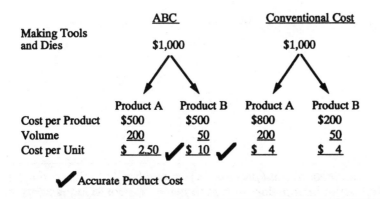

Figure 4. ***Accurate cost assignment.*** **ABC traces the cost of sustaining products to each product type. As a result, high-volume products correctly receive less cost per unit than low-volume products.**

Under ABC in *Figure 4*, the product activity driver assigns an equal amount of cost ($500) to each product. This assumes that each product requires the same amount of effort to manufacture tools and dies.

Product B, however, is a low-volume product, so its cost per unit ($10) is much higher than that of Product A ($2.50). This makes sense, because Product A is able to share its activity cost over a larger number of units ($500/200).

Under conventional cost in *Figure 4*, the unit activity driver assigns cost directly to the product units. This has two results. First, each unit receives an identical amount of cost ($4). Second, Product A has more product units than B, so in total, A receives the lion's share of the cost ($4 × 200).

Both of these conventional costing results are wrong. *It's the products that benefit equally, not the units.* The high-volume product shouldn't pick up more cost simply because it's successful.

ABC avoids these conventional costing errors by picking activity drivers that match the type of activity. Setting up a machine to produce a batch of parts is costed using the number of set up hours or the number of production runs. Changing the engineering specifications of a product is costed using the number of engineering change notices or the number of engineering change hours.

Assignment to Customers. ABC's activity cost assignment innovation works just as well for customers as it does for products. The difference is that the cost of customer activities is assigned to customers rather than products.

Examples of customer activities are processing customer orders and providing engineering and logistics support. Activity costs are assigned to customers using activity drivers such as the number of customer orders and the number of customers.

ABC provides new perspectives about service to customers and opens up opportunities that don't exist in conventional cost systems.

Quality Auditing Activity

Type of activity:
  ■ Non-value-added

Cost drivers:
  ■ Number of holes
  ■ Density of circuitry

Performance measures:
  ■ % of boards returned
  ■ % of boards not marked

Figure 5. *Information about performance.* **In addition to to the costing benefits of ABC, nonfinancial information, such as shown here, permits judgements about performance.**

ABC also makes customer profitability analysis possible. It provides new perspectives about service to customers and opens up opportunities that don't exist in conventional cost systems.

The Reporting Limitations of ABC.   There are limits to ABC's ability to report accurate product costs. This is because there are always some activities not directly associated with products or customers. Activities that sustain a plant, for example, are very difficult to assign to products. Such activities include cleaning, securing, and landscaping the plant.

It's fairly easy, however, to assign cost to these sustaining activities. The cost of an alarm monitoring service, for example, can be assigned directly to the plant security activity. The cost of a landscaping service can be assigned to the landscaping activity.

But you can't assign the cost of these activities to products directly. You don't landscape products (or customers), and it's not possible to obtain information about the landscaping cost of each product.

There *are* two possible solutions. The first is *not to assign* the cost of sustaining activities to products. This recognizes the difficulty of assigning these costs to products in any meaningful way.

The second solution is to assign the cost of sustaining activities using nonmatching activity drivers. For example, the cost of landscaping can be assigned to products based on direct labor hours (a unit activity driver). Alternatively, the cost can be distributed evenly to each product. This ensures that the cost reaches the products, but it's not clear that the result has any economic meaning.

The lesson is this: ABC reports more accurate costs than conventional costing, but it isn't perfect. Use ABC information with confidence *and* with care.

The 3rd Innovation—Information About Activities
The third innovation of ABC is the improved quality of information about activities. In addition to cost information, you find nonfinancial information about the work that is done.

For example, there's a lot of useful nonfinancial information you should know about the quality auditing activity *(Figure 5)*. The number of holes in the circuit boards and the density of the circuitry determine how much effort is required to perform the activity. (More holes and greater density require more work). These determining factors are called *cost drivers*.

It's also important to know how well the activity is carried out. Indicators of the results achieved in an activity are called *performance measures*.

The primary performance measure for quality auditing is the frequency of warranty returns. This measure should be zero if the audit is done right every time. A second measure is how often the checker's inspection mark is missing from a board. A batch that isn't stamped as checked will be returned by the customer.

The ABC analysis in *Figure 5* shows that the auditing activity is a *non-value-added* activity. A non-value-added activity is one that *does not* contribute to the value received by the customer.

The purpose of the auditing activity is to catch defects in the printed circuit boards. The defects can then be corrected prior to shipment to the customer.

This is a valuable contribution as long as the quality of prior processes is suspect. But the customer does not value the auditing per se. Instead, the customer values the quality of the boards.

A better cost solution is to improve the quality of prior processes so much that the auditing activity is no longer necessary to ensure that the customer receives a quality product. At that point, the auditing activity can be discontinued without any negative impact, and cost is reduced.

> A better cost solution is to improve the quality of prior processes so much that the auditing activity is no longer necessary.

Providing nonfinancial information such as this may be the most important contribution of ABC. Its purpose is to help improve the activity. It is, after all, better to improve or eliminate work than to more accurately assign the cost of unnecessary work to products or customers.

ABC supplies a powerful combination of nonfinancial and cost information. These two types of information work together to help manage and improve the performance of the company.

Peter B. B. Turney is the President and CEO of Cost Technology, Inc., the activity-based training and consulting firm. Formerly the Tektronix Professor of Cost Management at Portland State University, Dr. Turney is an internationally known author, trainer, and consultant. He can be reached at (503) 645-2434.

Valuing TQM Through Rigorous Financial Analysis

Richard D. Spitzer

This article documents a procedure for determining the future value of investing in TQM today. This is an insightful approach that shows how to use net present value *calculations to demonstrate the financial benefits of TQM.*

Undeniably, quality is now the buzz-word for most participants in today's globally competitive industries. Advertisements continuously boast of Company A's commitment to quality, regardless of Company A's actual system of operation. Admittedly, many U.S. companies are making significant strides in implementing total quality management (TQM) systems, regardless of whether the impetus is competitive necessity or is a preemptive move against the competition.

The majority of U.S. companies, however, are still struggling through the early stages of maturity in their progress toward a totally integrated quality system.[1] Several factors—such as cultural impediments, industry protection, or resource limitations—might explain this seemingly sluggish rate of progress. Evidence suggests, however, that many senior managers still perceive quality as an amorphous concept bearing mostly soft benefits with no obvious, significant cash flow implications.[2]

Many senior managers still perceive quality as an amorphous concept bearing mostly soft benefits with no obvious, significant cash flow implications.

Most analyses attempting to quantify the benefits of a TQM system consider only the cost reduction implications of such a system. Frequently, these analyses poorly address quantifying such improvements by applying invalid methods of financial analysis, i.e., return on investment (ROI), internal rate of return (IRR), and payback period. Managers need a more rigorous method of financial analysis that not only values the cash flow implications of cost improvements properly, but also values increased customer satisfaction and the option to invest in future projects that provide further operational benefits.

TQM and Its Roots

Armand V. Feigenbaum described total quality control as "an effective system for integrating the quality-development, quality-maintenance, and quality-

---

Reprinted with permission from *Quality Progress*, July 1993, ASQC, Milwaukee, WI.

improvement efforts of the various groups in an organization so as to enable production and service at the most economical levels which allow for full customer satisfaction."[3] This definition still rings true today, although most managers tend to redefine TQM using their companies' terminologies.

While the techniques of quality improvement might seem difficult to some (given the sometimes heavy use of statistical methods), the idea is quite simple. Quality is determined by the internal customer (next operation) or external customer (end-item user). Therefore, products and processes should be designed and controlled so as to maximize customer satisfaction at the least possible cost.

The mechanics of achieving maximum customer satisfaction at the least cost is quite involved and necessarily requires corporate commitment (both philosophically and financially) to be successful. Financial commitment primarily involves capital investment for employee education and training, as well as expenditures for process improvements. TQM requires employees to be empowered to make decisions regarding process and product troubleshooting. To ensure that rational decisions are made, however, employees must first be properly educated and trained in the process analysis techniques necessary to correct any out-of-control processes or unsatisfactory products.

Note that the terms "process" and "product" are not confined to the factory floor, but relate to any process performed for, or product delivered to, any internal or external customer. Depending on the specific educational needs of the work force, employees typically need to be educated and trained in elementary statistics, statistical process control (SPC), design of experiments (DOE), quality function deployment (QFD), problem-solving tools (Pareto analysis, cause-and-effect diagrams, and process flow analysis), and other areas.

Benefits of TQM

Although some argue that a properly implemented TQM system yields a plethora of benefits—such as improved process yields, motivated employees, and satisfied customers—the benefits can be placed into two basic categories: revenue enhancers and cost reducers.

Significantly improved product performance, features, reliability, conformance, durability, serviceability, aesthetics, or perceived quality relative to that which the competition is supplying, should increase demand for Company X's product or service, assuming that these dimensions of quality are still significant to the customer.[4] This increased demand translates into increased market share and (usually) increased revenues for Company X. These improvements are revenue enhancers.

Another source of revenue enhancement provided by a TQM system relates to the time-to-market or total product cycle time for a product cycle time for a product or service. The timeliness of a new product introduction, product changes, or the simple delivery of existing products are all dependent on a company's cycle times. Cycle time is defined as the length of time it takes for a product to travel from point A to point B. Total product cycle time would then represent the time it takes for Company X to translate the consumers' needs into a finished product that is delivered to the consumers. Obviously, several interim steps determine this time interval, some of which add value to the product, and others which do not. TQM, which seeks continuous improvement of processes and products, would press the organization to eliminate or reduce all unnecessary or nonvalue-added activities involved in the production cycle. The benefit or revenue enhancer arises from improved ability to deliver the product or service in less time. For most producers, late deliveries lead to customer defections that lead to lost sales and income.[5] Thus, revenues are enhanced or prevented from declining by increasing the time-related efficiency of operations.

Cost reducers represent the most obvious benefit of a TQM system. TQM tools and methods (such as cause-and-effect diagrams, SPC, DOE, or supplier-customer partnerships) systematically reduce the cost of materials, direct labor, overhead, working capital, and expenses; each has cash flow implications.

For example, consider the concept of supplier partnerships, a business practice intended to minimize the cost of purchased materials or services (which can represent up to 60% of sales for many manufacturers). The partnering process promotes win-win relationships between customers and suppliers. Each helps the other in such areas as training, design consultation, or resource sharing. The benefits of this sharing process are distributed equitably between the partners. Several U.S. manufacturers and retailers, including Motorola, Ford, Hewlett-Packard, and Xerox, have instituted such a program, and the results have been significant (see the sidebar "Partnership Success Stories—Xerox Inc.").

Potential economic benefits to be derived from TQM implementations pertain to quantifiable improvements in:

- Purchased materials cost
- Direct and indirect labor costs
- Accounts receivable financing costs
- Space requirements
- Inventory levels
- Total product cycle time
- Costs of quality

While actual benefits of a TQM system will vary, case studies suggest that the cash-related benefits typically experienced for companies adopting such a system are:

- A 10% to 20% reduction in purchased materials cost
- A 10% to 20% reduction in direct and indirect labor costs
- A 10% to 20% reduction in accounts receivable costs
- A 30% to 50% reduction in space requirements
- A 30% to 90% reduction in average inventory levels
- A 40% to 60% reduction in total product cycle time
- A 30% to 50% reduction in the cost of quality (COQ)

PARTNERSHIP SUCCESS STORIES—XEROX INC.

In 1982, Xerox's share of worldwide copier revenue had fallen to 41%, a 50% drop from its share of the market in 1976. Xerox responded by creating a supply management function that practiced the concept of supplier partnerships. By systematically reducing its suppliers (from 5,000 to 400) and teaming with the suppliers in both training and design efforts, Xerox was able to achieve the following improvements (from 1981–1986):

- Product cost reduced by 10% per year
- Design cost reduced by 33%
- Materials cost reduced by 12% per year
- Prototype cost reduced by 50%
- Inbound logistics reduced by 13% per year
- Production lead time reduced by 65%
- New product development reduced by 50%
- Market share increased by 20%

Xerox was one of the 1989 Malcolm Baldrige National Quality Award winners.

Sources: Keki R. Bhote. *Strategic Supply Management* (New York, NY: Amacom, 1989), and David N. Burt: "Managing Suppliers Up To Speed." *Harvard Business Review* July–August 1989.

COQ addresses a catch-all category for cost improvements. It includes the costs associated with achieving or not achieving product or service quality. More specifically, quality costs represent the total costs associated with investing in the prevention of nonconformances to requirements, appraising a product or service for conformance to requirements, and failing to meet requirements. COQ can be defined in layman's terms as the cost of ensuring that things are done right, plus the cost of correcting them when they are not done right.

Some people propose that companies just beginning to implement a TQM system are experiencing costs of quality that approximate 25% to 40% of sales.[6] COQ categories include prevention, appraisal, internal failure, and external failure. As the company progresses or matures with the system, these costs fall dramatically, nearing 2% to 4% of sales in some cases. These reductions are reflected in reduced cost of failure and appraisal, such as warranties, field service, rework, scrap, inspections, and management oversight. In theory, the sum of all these benefits is reflected in a reduced COQ relative to sales.

Investment Analysis—Finance Theory vs. Traditional Approaches

A TQM system necessarily cuts across all business lines. The decision to adopt such a system must be addressed during the company's strategic planning process. During this process, the economics of TQM are analyzed; financial analysts drive for numbers, and strategic analysts search for conditions of market imbalance and competitive advantage.

TQM proponents frequently argue that monetary value cannot be assigned to many of the resulting benefits, such as satisfied customers and motivated employees. Many TQM proponents, however, are not trained in the principles of modern corporate finance and tend to enter this process with less than adequate financial analysis tools. TQM proponents often base most of their investment justification on the intangible benefits of such a system or point to success stories in related industries.

Financial analysts, however, also tend to underperform in this valuation process by relying on either irrelevant or incomplete measures of investment performance. A number of financial analysts continue to evaluate capital investments using traditional methods of financial analysis, such as payback period, ROI, or IRR.

The payback period method quantifies the period of time it takes before cumulative forecasted cash flows equal the investment. Projects are accepted or rejected based on a cutoff period. Projects that have a payback period less than this cutoff period are accepted; otherwise, the project is rejected.

The ROI method determines the rate at which accounting profits are returned to an average annual investment. Again, a cutoff value is used to determine project worthiness, where accepted projects are those with a predicted ROI greater than the cutoff ROI.

The IRR method calculates the discounted cash flow rate of return for a given project. Similar to the other methods presented, projects are evaluated based on a cutoff IRR, usually defined by the company for various types of projects representing different levels of risk.

Financial economists have frequently disproved the validity of these common methods of analysis, and their proofs are well documented.[7] Briefly, ROI fails due to its dependence on a non-cash item, accounting profits, and its inability to discount the cash flows at the opportunity cost of capital for the project at hand. Meanwhile, payback period ignores both the time value of money and cash flows generated beyond the cutoff period. IRR provides a rate-of-return number, but is irrelevant in that this number has nothing to do with the opportunity cost of capital for the project of interest. The relevant measure of investment performance agreed on by most financial economists for determining the acceptability of a project with certain expected cash flows and opportunity cost is net present value (NPV).

NPV is simply the difference between the present value of cash inflows and the present value of cash outflows expected to be generated during the project's life. All projects producing a positive NPV should be accepted. Advocates of IRR note that this measure is acceptable assuming the company has unlimited access to capital; but if capital constraints exist, then the company should seek to get the most bang for the buck. Capital constraints most often are self-imposed, however, and are not the reality of the capital markets. If constraints do exist, then the proper measure for determining the most bang for the buck is NPV per dollar invested (also known as profitability index), not IRR. In either situation, NPV still prevails.

Practical use of NPV does become problematic.[8] Difficulties—such as estimating the opportunity cost of capital, forecasting cash flows, and estimating cash-flow dependencies across investments—must be addressed. But even if financial analysts can overcome these issues, there still remains one problem that limits the use of NPV in valuing strategic approaches such as a TQM system: the link between today's investments and tomorrow's opportunities for additional investment.

Valuing Real Options

Many investors are at least familiar with options created for financial assets, and some effectively use the option pricing model developed by Fischer Black and Myron Scholes.[9] Less well-known, however, is the use of this model in pricing options on real assets. Two important options found in capital investment projects are to wait and learn before investing and to make follow-on investments if the initial investments still look attractive. The second option refers to the scenario presented earlier in which NPV cannot be applied. Here, the focus is on valuing this form of a real option because it represents the only means for valuing many of the benefits arising from a TQM system.

The conventional discounted cash flow method does not properly value follow-on investments that are dependent on today's decisions because the follow-on investment is an option and the company is not committed to take it. The option to invest in follow-on projects represents a call option. For financial assets, the value of a call option is dependent on the price of the stock, the exercise price, the risk-free rate of interest, the time-to-exercise date, and the stock price volatility or variance. The same is true for real assets, where stock price is now represented by the present value of cash flows projected for the follow-on investment(s). The exercise price is the amount of investment necessary for the follow-on project. Stock price variance is the variance of the estimated present value of future cash flows for follow-on investments. The time-to-exercise date is measured from the present to the date when follow-on investment should occur. The risk-free rate of interest is the same for both real and financial options. Figure 1 provides an example using the Black-Scholes option pricing model to value a call option on a share of common stock. The following discussion applies the same option valuation technique in valuing real options provided by a TQM system.

The Mowzer Company manufactures golf equipment (clubs and balls) with annual sales of $40 million and a net income of $5 million. Mowzer's senior managers recently committed to implementing a TQM system, but are now reconsidering this commitment due to the magnitude of capital investment needed to initiate the program. A consulting group of quality specialists had surveyed Mowzer, seeking to identify the quality maturity of the company. Based on their findings, the consultants recommended initial employee education and training in basic skills development, such as team building, group problem solving and elementary statistics, supplemented with pilot

VALUING A CALL OPTION ON A FINANCIAL ASSET

The Black-Scholes formula for valuing a simple call option is:[1]

$$\text{Call option value} = PN(d_1) - EXe^{-r_f t} N(d_2)$$

where: $d_1 = (\log(P/EX) + r_f t + \sigma^2 t/2)/\sigma\sqrt{t}$

$d_2 = (\log(P/EX) + r_f t - \sigma^2 t/2)/\sigma\sqrt{t}$

$N(d)$ = cumulative normal probability density function

EX = exercise price of option

t = time-to-exercise date, years

P = current stock price

σ^2 = variance per period (year) of (continuously compounded) rate of return on the stock

r_f = annual (continuously compounded) risk-free rate of interest

Example: IMB common stock sells today for $140 per share. Value a call option on this share of stock if the exercise price is $145, the time-to-exercise is six months, the risk-free rate of interest is 8%, and the variance of stock returns is 16%.

Richard A. Brealey and Stewart Myers simplify this solution by providing tables that allow this problem to be solved with the following two calculations:[2]

1. $\sigma\sqrt{t} = (0.4)\sqrt{0.5} = 0.28$
2. Asset value/PV (exercise price) $= 140(145/(1 + 0.08)^{0.5}) = 1$

With these two values, one can refer to the tables provided by Brealey and Myers and find that the simple call option is worth about 11% of the current share price, calculated to be $15.40.

References

1. Simple or European call options cannot be exercised until the exercise date. American call options can be exercised at any time prior to the exercise date.

2. Richard A. Brealey and Stewart Myers, *Principles of Corporate Finance*, third edition (New York, NY: McGraw-Hill, 1988), Appendix Table 6.

Figure 1.

projects that provided hands-on experience with these skills. Education training, and pilot projects thereafter would involve more sophisticated techniques such as statistical quality control, SPC, QFD, DOE, customer quality assurance, and value engineering. Estimated investment required for the initial phase of education and training totaled $1 million, while follow-on education and training required an additional $3 million. The education, training, and pilot programs were expected to occur over two years. Given the magnitude of the investment, and the less-than-obvious cash flow benefits, the executives decided more research would be necessary and postponed the program.

The executives' skepticism is commonplace among executives in both the manufacturing and service industries. Yet as noted earlier, several cash-flow-related items can be positively affected by a TQM system. Two categories of cash flow will improve cash flow from operations (CFFO) and incremental working capital investment CFFO (calculated as net income plus depreciation) will increase with improvements in the cost of goods sold and customer defection rates. Cost of goods sold (as a percentage of sales) is reduced through improvements in purchased materials cost (through supplier partnerships), overhead (through elimination of inspection and other non-value-added activities), and direct labor (through process simplification). Customer defections represent those customers who stop buying Company X's product and/or service due to their dissatisfaction with the product and/or service quality. As Frederick F. Reichheld and W. Earl Sasser Jr. note, these defections likely produce a significant value loss to the supplier.[10] Customer quality assurance programs (a part of TQM) systematically reduce this defection rate, providing additional income to the company. The second category of cash inflow, incremental working capital investment (where working capital is defined as current assets minus current liabilities), will also decline given the improvements in inventory and accounts receivable turnover.

Estimating these cash flow improvements can be accomplished by a benchmarking process. Benchmarking involves measuring the performance of best-in-class companies (which are not necessarily industry competitors) with respect to these improvement areas. Using best-in-class benchmarks, the company can estimate the cash flow effects of improvements that are included in the option pricing model.

Recall that the option being valued is the option to make follow-on investments. In the Mowzer example, the follow-on investment is for additional, more sophisticated training. This follow-on investment provides cash inflows, the future value of which is highly uncertain. To value the option, one must determine the present value of expected cash inflows, the variability of these cash inflows (annualized), the elapsed time from the present until the second investment becomes necessary, the amount of the second investment, and the risk-free rate of interest. Once these parameters are estimated, valuing the call option becomes a simple process using the Black-Scholes model. Figure 2 presents the cash flows expected for Mowzer based on benchmark findings.

A benchmarking process identifies improvement opportunities, and the cash inflows affected by these improvements will be seen sporadically over time. In Mowzer's case, a small portion of each category's cash inflow will be affected in the initial investment, while the remaining larger portion will result from the follow-on training investment. For instance, the initial training should produce a 10% reduction in working capital investment and a 5% after-tax CFFO increase. For simplicity, these inflows are shown occurring as one inflow at the end of the first year (realistically, these flows would occur continuously throughout the year). Therefore, a portion of the total investment value of this product is represented by the net present value of the initial

VALUING TQM AT MOWZER COMPANY

Cash Outflow:

Initial Investment	$1,000,000
Follow-On Investment	$3,000,000

Cash Inflow:

Decreased Working Capital $1,000,000
   (achieved by reducing inventories and accounts receivable)
Increased After-Tax Cash Flow From Operations (CFFO)
   (achieved through lowered cost of goods sold
   and customer defections) $1,000,000

Net Present Value (NPV) of Initial Investment:

$$NPV_1 = -\$1,000,000 + (0.05)(\$1,000,000)/(0.15) +$$
$$(0.1)(\$1,000,000)/(1.15) = \qquad\qquad -\$579,710$$

where weighted average cost of capital = 15%, and increased after-tax CFFO is valued as a perpetuity.

Option Value of Follow-On Investment Using the Richard A. Brealey and Stewart Myers Tables in *Principles of Corporate Finance*, third edition (New York, NY: McGraw-Hill, 1988):

Time t	= 2 years
Variance of present value of follow-on cash flows, σ^2	= 35% per year
Present value of follow-on cash inflows (asset value)	= $((0.95)(\$1,000,000)/(0.15)/1.15^2 +$
	$(0.9)(\$1,000,000)/1.15^2$
	= $\$4,788,910 + \$680,530$
	= $\$5,469,440$
Follow-on investment (exercise price)	= $\$3,000,000$

Step 1. $\sigma\sqrt{t} = (0.60)(1.41) = 0.84$

Step 2. Asset value/PV (exercise price) =
     $\$5,469,440/(3,000,000/1.15^2) = 2.41$

Table value (using 2.5 instead of 2.41) indicates that option value is 63.6% of the asset value ($5,469,440) or $3,480,000.

Total Investment Value:

The value of the investment is equal to $2,900,290, which represents the sum of NPV_1 and the option value of the follow-on investment.

The timing and magnitude of these cash-related benefits will differ across the industry types, and efforts should be made to approximate the pattern of cash flows, such as the use of mathematical modeling techniques (exponential growth, linear growth, etc). The magnitude and pattern of cash inflows given here are based on simplifying assumptions made in an effort to avoid confusion.

Figure 2.

investment. Here, NPV is determined by discounting the cash inflows at Mowzer's opportunity cost of capital—assumed as Mowzer's weighted average cost of capital—and then subtracting from this value the initial investment. Figure 2 indicates this value to be—$579,710.

The remaining portion of the investment's value is represented by the value of the call option on follow-on investments. This value, calculated in Figure 2, is found to be $3,480,000. The total value of the project is equal to the sum of the call option and the NPV of the initial investment, seen here as $2,900,290.

Linking Quality and Financial Performance

TQM systems do yield cash flow benefits, some of which are not obvious. Valuing such a system must include both a rigorous assessment of improvement opportunities, as compared with benchmarking, and correct application of modern finance theory (NPV and option pricing). Although this process of quantifying (in monetary terms) such a system might offend some quality practitioners, it is still a necessary step for many companies evaluating large capital investments. The model presented here helps to bridge the gap between quality and finance organizations by illuminating and properly valuing the benefits of such a system.

References

1. Richard D. Spitzer. A useful model for assessing a company's progress toward a TQM system is a five-stage quality maturity profile. The five-stage maturity process begins with innocence, then progresses through awareness, understanding, and competence, reaching full maturity in the final stage, excellence. Several elements of the company are assessed in determining its level of quality maturity. A common approach is to use the quantitative scoring of the Baldrige Award to categorize levels of maturity.

2. Quality: Executive Priority or Afterthought? Executives Perceptions on Quality in a Competitive World. ASQC/The Gallup Organization, Inc., 1989.

3. Armand V. Feigenbaum, *Total Quality Control*, third edition (New York, NY: McGraw-Hill Book Company, 1983).

4. David A. Garvin, "Competing on the Eight Dimensions of Quality," *Harvard Business Reviews*, November–December 1987.

5. Frederick F. Reichheld and W. Earl Sasser Jr., "Zero Defections: Quality Comes to Services," *Harvard Business Review*, September–October 1990.

6. *Principles of Quality Costs: Principles, Implementation, and Use*, second edition, ASQC Quality Costs Committee, Jack Campanella, ed., 1990, and SEMATECH's Eight-Volume Series "Partnering for Total Quality." 1991.

7. Richard A. Brealey and Stewart Myers, *Principles of Corporate Finance*, third edition (New York, NY: McGraw-Hill, 1988). Chapter 5.

8. Stewart C. Myers, "Financial Theory and Financial Strategy," *Interfaces*, January–February 1984.

9. Fischer Black and Myron Scholes, "The Pricing of Options and Corporate Liabilities," *Journal of Political Economy*, May–June 1973.

10. Reichheld and Sasser, "Zero Defections: Quality Comes to Services."

Richard D. Spitzer is a senior consultant with Booz Allen & Hamilton in its Dallas, TX, office. He has a master's degree in business administration from Southern Methodist University in Dallas, TX. Spitzer is a member of ASQC and a certified quality engineer.

Total Quality or Performance Appraisal: Choose One

Peter R. Scholtes

This article by the author of The Team Handbook *from Joiner Associates carefully and compellingly makes the case for eliminating performance appraisals as part of any organization that seeks to implement total quality management and what to do instead. It shows why Deming has included performance appraisals among his seven deadly diseases of management.*

While TQM-bashing has recently become fashionable in U.S. business periodicals, the total quality movement is alive and well. Companies like Harley Davidson, Motorola, and Xerox—who understand TQM—aren't bashing total quality. And one doesn't hear of the demise of Japan's total quality control efforts. What we are witnessing is the American appetite for fads. Those who never understood quality in the first place and trivialized it in the second place are now declaring it dead.

Total quality is a compelling and simple approach to management. When intelligently applied, the basic principles of TQM will, however, fundamentally change the way a conventional manager thinks about the nature of work and the purpose of leadership. This fundamental change requires managers to relinquish the old set of premises—the old paradigm—and struggle to understand, internalize and apply a new approach—what Brian Joiner of Joiner

Associates calls fourth-generation management Deming says, "What is required is nothing less than the transformation of Western management." Many managers have learned the rhetoric of total quality and adopted programs to apply TQM to their companies. But relatively few have appreciated the profoundly different approach it requires of those who must lead.

"I believe most of what Deming teaches," is commonly heard from managers. "I agree with ten or twelve of his fourteen points." While adherence to ten or twelve is better than none, these managers fail to see that the fourteen points are an interdependent, integrated whole. If you pull out one row in this tapestry, it unravels. When people reject any of Deming's teachings, it usually is point 12b:

Managers fail to see that the fourteen points are an interdependent, integrated whole.

> Remove barriers that rob people in management and in engineering of their right to pride of workmanship. This means, *inter alia*, abolishment of the annual or merit rating and of management by objective.

Among Deming's Deadly Diseases is listed: ". . . Evaluation of performance, merit rating or annual review." Why is performance appraisal, which often leads to some type of merit pay increase or other reward, on Deming's list of things *not* to do? Why is this time-honored American business practice seen as incompatible with total quality? And if businesses don't conduct performance appraisals, what should they do instead?

Principles at the Heart of Quality

There are principles at the heart of quality that establish a foundation for the new philosophy and, indirectly, the basis for rejecting performance appraisal. These principles are extracted from the teachings of Deming and other originators of total quality:

Principle 1. The Customers and Their Needs Shape Our Organization and Its Work, Not Vice Versa

- We must know what business we are in and who our customers are.
- We must know the needs and concerns of our customers. We must understand what they experience when they apply our products and services.
- Our deep understanding of our customers guides the design of our products and services. Consequent redesign and improvements are also responses to the customer.
- The decisions and plans we make and the improvements we introduce should be mostly defined by the benefits that will flow to our customers.

Principle 2. Quality Products and Services Result from Quality Systems, Processes, and Methods

- The needs of the customers must be understood in terms of the systems, processes, materials, machinery, and methods needed to consistently deliver what customers need, how and when they need it.
- We must build quality so reliably into the system that inspection of the end product is unnecessary.
- Exhortations, threats, pep talks, rewards, and punishments are irrelevant to the production of quality goods and services.
- More than 95 percent of our quality problems are derived from the system. If every worker and manager did his or her best, we would eliminate only a negligible proportion of the current quality problems.
- Improvement efforts should focus on systems, processes, and methods, not on individual workers. Those efforts that focus on improving the attentiveness, carefulness, speed, etc., of individual workers—without changing the systems, processes, and methods—constitute a low-yield strategy with negligible short-term results.
- Leaders must understand their systems, processes and methods in terms of capability and variation. Data gathered on the variation of systems and processes over time will help leaders understand the characteristics of work performance in their organization. When managers don't understand the variation inherent in their systems and processes, they make themselves vulnerable to some serious problems:
  They miss trends where there are trends.
  They see trends where there are none.
  They attribute to employees—individually or collectively—problems that are inherent in the system and that will continue regardless of which employees are doing the work.
  They won't understand past performance or be able to predict future performance.

Principle 3. Quality Is the All-Consuming Focus of the Organization

- In the new competitive era, competitive strategy is based on quality. As described above, this quality is defined by the customer and built into the systems.
- An organization's plans and decisions begin and end with quality. Every aspect of the business is understood through its contribution to quality.

Organizations seek to cut costs, increase productivity, reduce prices, or increase market share. But if they do so without first building customer-defined quality into their product/service designs and their systems, processes, and methods, they are pursuing short-term gains instead of long-term survival and prosperity. This is, indeed, the story of the decline of many American businesses. Quality must become the integrating strategy of the U.S. economy if it is to regain its ascendancy in the world market.

Principle 4. An Organization Achieves Quality by Mastering the Methods of Improvement

- It is not enough to know how to improve. The prize will go to those who have learned to improve faster than their competitors.
- The needs for improvement are so widespread and continuous that everyone in the organization should know the methodology of improvement and be involved in improvement efforts.
- We must learn the difference between improvement and change. We must also learn the difference between improvement and replacement. We must learn to start with what we have and use logic and data to understand and improve it.
- True improvement will ultimately result only when the causes of problems, which usually come from deep within the system, are identified and eliminated. For example, improving Chernobyl involves more than cleanup and damage control at the site. It must involve dealing with policies, practices, and technology in the Russian nuclear power system that caused the Chernobyl accident and could cause other disasters like it. When we are content with culprits, we will never look for systemic causes and the problem will be likely to recur with a new culprit.

> Quality must become the integrating strategy of the U.S. economy if it is to regain its ascendancy in the world market.

Principle 5. An Organization Pursuing Quality Directs and Focuses Its Energies

- The leaders articulate and communicate to the organization its clear and constant purpose, mission, values, and operating philosophy in statements that tell everyone "who we are, what we do, how we do it" and "what legacy we leave to those who follow."
- The operations, tasks, and methods of everyday work are no longer seen as an art form. The single best method for doing any repeated task is established as a standard. It is documented, taught to, and used by everyone doing that work. Attempts to find a better method are pursued "off-line" from the daily work effort.
- We use data to identify the most critical business needs and improvement priorities. From all the worthwhile things to do, we select only a few priorities and pursue them to completion. We seek deep solutions to a few things rather than quick fixes to many.

Principle 6. There Is a New Paradigm of Leadership. Managers Must Reformulate What It Means to Lead

- Leaders must have a customer's point of view.
- Leaders must have a systems' point of view.

- Leaders must have a statistical point of view.
- Leaders must have a worker's point of view.

What Is Meant by Performance Appraisal?

What exactly is this management intervention that undermines total quality?

It has various names: performance appraisal, performance evaluation, performance management, and coaching and counseling, among others. No matter what the name is, several characteristics are common to all such programs:

1. The focus is on an individual's work.
   - Sometimes a team is evaluated instead of or along with the individual. Team evaluation is not a significant improvement over individual evaluation.
2. There are expectations or standards of performance.
   - The standards are usually explicit and specific, a form of performance contract for which the employee is accountable.

Team evaluation is not a significant improvement over individual evaluation.

   - Sometimes the standards are imposed on the employee, sometimes they are negotiated, sometimes the standards are a combination of the two. Having the standards be negotiated does not avoid the problems of performance appraisal.
   - Sometimes the measures are implicit—for example, the employee's job description.
3. There are usually two sessions between the employee and the evaluator: one to establish the standards and another to review performance.
   - The most common unit of reviewed performance is one year (the annual review).
   - A six-month review is the next most common.
   - In sales-dominated jobs, the period of performance is often as short as a month or a week.
   - Some organizations omit the standard-setting conference.
4. The evaluator is usually the person who has line management authority over the one evaluated.
   - Some organizations have peer review and some have a review of supervisors by subordinates. These do not avoid the problems of performance evaluation.
5. The evaluation session usually results in some written conclusion—some paper trail regarding the performance of the person reviewed.
   - Some organizations express a specific or an overall rating with a numbered scale.
   - Some use gradations of rhetoric (from "exceeds standards" to "needs help," for example).
   - Some organizations have forced ranking that requires managers to distribute the rankings of employees to conform to some model, such as a bell-shaped distribution.

6. There are various consequences of appraisal.
    - Some organizations attach merit pay or some other type of pay-for-performance directly to the appraisal. (This includes commissions on sales.)
    - When appraisal affects salary it can indirectly affect pension, if pension is affected by salary.
    - Many companies use appraisals as a basis for determining the promotability of an employee.
    - Some companies use appraisals as a basis for layoffs. IBM, for example, has used performance appraisals as a basis for eliminating 5 percent of its work force.

The suggestion to eliminate performance appraisal often provokes an almost visceral reaction. One manager responded to objections to performance appraisal with, "Boy! You ask people to do a little work and they rise in rebellion!" In his mind, he equated performance appraisal with hard work. For him, the only reason someone would resist performance appraisal would be to avoid work.

Below are some important distinctions to make when sorting out the questions and resistance related to performance appraisal. The left-hand column represents values and methods consistent with TQM. The right-hand column represents values and methods rooted in the old paradigm.

Someone can support . . .	while opposing
- Giving direction to the work force.	- Directing individuals.
- Controlling processes.	- Controlling people.
- Employees receiving systems/processes.	- Employees receiving judgment on themselves.
- Feedback based on the needs of customers and the key process indicators.	- Feedback based on personal characteristics not relevant to the work.
- Feedback from parts of the system that receive one's work (internal customers).	- Feed-down from the next layer up in the hierarchy.
- Feedback useful for improvement.	- Feedback used for ratings, rewards, and sanctions.
- Supporting workers' inherent motivation.	- Motivating or de-motivating workers.

The Case Against Performance Appraisal

Here, then, is what is wrong with performance appraisal. In the era of total quality, performance appraisal supports obsolete values with dysfunctional methods. Specifically, performance appraisal

1. Disregards and, in fact, undermines, teamwork.

2. Disregards the existence of a system. It encourages individuals to squeeze or circumvent the system for personal gain rather than improve it for collective gain.
3. Disregards variability in the system and, indeed, increases variability in the system.
4. Uses a measurement system that is unreliable and inconsistent.
5. Encourages an approach to problem-solving that is superficial and culprit-oriented.
6. Tends to establish an aggregate of safe goals—a ceiling of mediocrity—in an organization.
7. Creates losers, cynics, and wasted human resources.
8. Seeks to provide a means to administer multiple managerial functions (pay, promotion, feedback communications, direction-setting, etc.), yet it is inadequate to accomplish any one of them.

Let us briefly examine each item.

1. Performance Appraisal Disregards and, in Fact, Undermines, Teamwork

Many who seem to be solo performers are actually individual contributors to a group effort, regardless of whether that group is a formally constituted team. When one individual's contribution is evaluated, we must pretend that we can extract from the net outcome that specific value contributed uniquely by that person and not attribute to him or her those contributions for which others deserve credit or discredit.

Some managers want to give recognition to each individual who participates on some successful project team. But true teamwork usually has larger boundaries than this. Chances are each member of that team could participate only by shifting some normal job duties onto others who aren't on the team. Who, then, gets credit?

Performance appraisal undermines teamwork when an employee must choose between attending to his or her individual job standards—on which salary and promotability often depend—or attending to the needs of the team. In such circumstances, the team's needs will suffer. In the spring of 1991, Gallery Furniture in Houston, Texas, eliminated performance appraisal, quotas, and pay for performance (commissions and bonuses). All the measures of business performance improved. But what surprised management most was the teamwork that developed among the salespeople who previously saw each other as competitors. The old system stifled cooperation and teamwork.

> Many who seem to be solo performers are actually individual contributors to a group effort, regardless of whether that group is a formally constituted team.

2. Performance Appraisal Disregards the Existence of a System. It Encourages Individuals to Squeeze or Circumvent the System for Personal Gain Rather than Improve it for Collective Gain

All of us, in doing our jobs, work within a system that consists of

- The organization's policies and procedures that guide and constrain our work.
- Budgets and staffing that provide capability to do work and constraints on what can be done.

- The methods for maintaining and communicating customer awareness and market knowledge.
- Long-, medium-, and short-term plans giving direction, focus, and priority to the organization.
- The facilities, machinery, and equipment we use and the capability and workability of these.
- Maintenance methods and procedures.
- The materials and supplies provided for our use.
- The established methods for doing various tasks and the training provided in those methods.
- The environment of the organization: the unwritten rules of the informal organization that constitute the everyday workplace experience of the mass of employees (the organization's "culture").
- The modes of communication, the accessibility of information, and the receptiveness to feedback and suggestions.
- Every step of work that precedes the point in which we—individually or as a group—get involved.
- The designs of products and services and the designing of the processes to develop and deliver these products and services.

Performance appraisal pretends that the reviewer can discern an individual's contribution apart from all those influences contributed by the system over which no single manager or worker has control.

The parts of the system are interdependent: If I force results here and now, I will pay a price there or later. As Brian Joiner emphatically asserts, there are only three ways to get better numbers: (1) improve the system, (2) distort the numbers, or (3) distort the system.

Improving systems is much too complex a matter to place on an individual's performance standard. Systems improvement often requires a prolonged cross-functional effort involving many people and led by top managers.

Distorting the numbers, a form of creative accounting aimed at looking good rather than doing well, is rampant in American business. Given a standard to reduce employee turnover, one vice president of human resources simply changed the formula for calculating turnover. This change reduced the turnover ratio while improving nothing.

Distorting the system often occurs because performance appraisal encourages individuals to squeeze or circumvent the system for their short-term individual gain, rather than improve it for collective long-term gain. The sales force pulls out all stops to meet one quarter's sales quota and sales sag in the following quarter.

> As Brian Joiner emphatically asserts, there are only three ways to get better numbers: (1) improve the system, (2) distort the numbers, or (3) distort the system.

3. Performance Disregards Variability in the System and, Indeed, Increases Variability in the System

All the elements of a system, such as those listed above, are subject to variation. Sometimes variation is due to special causes. For the most part, these are unusual, infrequent events that are relatively easy to identify and sometimes easy to eliminate. (For example, deliveries were late last Tuesday because the truck had a flat.) This is known as special cause variation. Most variation, however, is due to multiple unidentifiable causes. (Delivery is never at an exactly predictable time because of many varying factors: traffic, weather, sizes of orders, etc.) This latter type of variation is called "common cause variation."

The performance of each employee is variable and each employee works within a variable system. Managers who don't understand variation and don't know how to use statistical methods to plot variation will not see performance within the context of variation and will tend to treat all unsatisfactory things as special causes attributable to individual workers. ("Those truck drivers are always stopping for coffee! That's why deliveries can't be predicted.")

Flight instructors in the Israeli Air Force had learned from experience that reprimanding student pilots when their performance was poor almost always led to improved performance. On the other hand, complimenting good performance led to deterioration of the student's performance. A psychologist who studied this phenomenon for a year eventually discovered that both students and instructors were inadvertently responding to variation. When performance is at the high point in a system of common cause variation, performance cannot help but get worse. Similarly, performance at the low point cannot help but get better. And when does a manager compliment or reprimand? The flight instructors reprimands for poor performance were the equivalent of superstition. Results are attributed to actions that, in fact, have no influence on the outcome. ("Every time there is trouble, I do this and it works.") Having student pilots kiss the fuselage on bad days would have worked as well as the reprimands. Moreover, unnecessary or misguided management intervention will usually result in *increased* variation.

> Managers who don't understand variation will not see performance within the context of variation and will tend to treat all unsatisfactory things as special causes attributable to individual workers.

4. Performance Appraisal Uses a Measurement System that Is Unreliable and Inconsistent

Experts in metrology will tell you that if the scales, calipers, and other devices and tests that measure the key dimensions of products were as unstable as our instruments for measuring employee performance, we would go out of business. There is inconsistency between the various reviewers (different philosophies, different "calibrations"), and the same reviewer is inconsistent from one employee to the next.

A common source of measurement error is the subjective bias of the reviewer. We are not objective in discerning our own subjectivity. Some research in performance evaluation indicates that those who are physically attractive tend to get higher ratings. This is not true, however, for women in management positions, who tend to be rated lower if they are attractive. When seminar participants are asked to identify which of several factors account most for the difference between high-rated and low-rated employees, by far they most often cite "evaluator prejudice."

5. Performance Appraisal Encourages an Approach to Problem-Solving that Is Superficial and Culprit-Oriented

There is a Japanese technique for problem-solving called "Ask 'Why?' Five times." For example, if there is a puddle of oil on the shop floor,

- *Why* is there oil on the floor? Because the machine is dripping oil.
- *Why* is the machine dripping oil? Because the gasket is leaking.
- *Why* is the gasket leaking? Because it is made of inferior material.
- *Why* do we use gaskets of inferior material? Because the purchasing agent got a good deal on them.
- *Why* is it important for the purchasing agent to get a good deal on gaskets? Because his performance is evaluated on how often he can get good deals on things.

Conventional problem-solving would ask such questions as: Whose area is this? Who is supposed to replace worn gaskets? We don't ask "why," we ask "who." We don't look for causes in the system, we look for culprits in the work force. Performance appraisal is a "who-based" approach to problem-solving.

> We don't ask "why," we ask "who." We don't look for causes in the system, we look for culprits in the work force.

6. Performance Appraisal Tends to Establish an Aggregate of Safe Goals— A Ceiling of Mediocrity—in an Organization

This is a corollary to the point made earlier regarding distorting the system. If my appraisal affects my income and career goals, I will seek to be measured against standards that are easy to meet or exceed, standards that are easily within the current capability of the systems within which I work. I will pick goals that will not require me to distort the system, distort the numbers, or improve the system. I will create the illusion of challenge around easy targets seldom perceived by the customers as improvement.

Now imagine everyone choosing easy targets. The net result is a year without challenge. The collective rhetoric describes highly ambitious goals, but the company and its customers don't advance at all. Individual standards risk the twin perils of distorting the system on the one hand or mediocrity on the other. The only legitimate alternative—improving the system—will not result from so simplistic and superficial an approach as performance evaluation.

7. Performance Appraisal Creates Losers, Cynics, and Wasted Human Resources

Most of us believe we deserve to be rated in the top 20 percent of our organization's performers. That means 80 percent of us are in for a shock.

How will people react to the news that they are not in the upper 20 percent? Or top one-third? Or not even above average? Some will accept the news and feel bad about how inferior they are. Some will deny the news and attribute their low rating to a screwed-up rating system. In either case—losers or cynics—what has the company gained? Even those who get high ratings will suspect that they have benefited from a certain amount of luck. Someone dealt a royal flush, however, doesn't question the legitimacy of the deal . . . or the game itself.

Over twenty years ago, researchers began discovering the Pygmalion Effect in management. In his landmark study *Pygmalion in Management*, Dov Eden describes the effect of self-fulfilling prophecy in work situations. Managers' expectations of subordinates can have a powerful effect on the quality and productivity of work.

To what extent do the expectations of a manager affect his or her evaluation of an employee? To what extent does this evaluation communicate a manager's expectations to that employee and, thereby, shape the employee's future performance? To what extent does his or her perception of a subordinate's performance affect the manager's expectations and, thus, trigger the endless cycle of self-fulfilling prophecies? None of these questions has an unequivocal answer, but we do know that positive expectations influence managers' perceptions and evaluations of employee behavior positively, and the negative expectations have adverse effects. Managers engaged in performance appraisal can get trapped in the endless negative spiral.

8. Performance Appraisal Seeks to Provide a Means to Administer Multiple Managerial Functions, Yet It Is Inadequate to Accomplish Any One of Them

We don't do anything unless we expect some benefit from it. If we ask managers to list the various ways performance appraisal serves a useful purpose, the response would be a long list:

Performance appraisal is a fragile cart asked to bear too heavy a load.

- To determine pay.
- To identify candidates for promotion.
- To give employees feedback.
- To provide communications between supervisor and employee.
- To give direction and focus to employees.
- To aid in career development.
- To identify training needs.

The sheer magnitude of this list suggests that the typical four or five hours of conference time per year between supervisor and subordinate is woefully inadequate to the task. If managers spent 400 hours, it would still be insufficient. Performance appraisal is a fragile cart asked to bear too heavy a load.

What to Do Instead?

There are two alternatives to performance appraisal that managers don't like to hear:

1. *Change the way you think.* Until managers let go of their obsession with the individual worker and understand the importance of systems and processes, they will not enter the quality era. Without this change in mindset, managers will continue to look for alternatives that are no different from what they are trying to replace.

2. *Just stop doing it.* When you are doing something that is demonstrably harmful, you can stop doing it without finding an alternative way to harm yourself. Conventional managers are, in effect, beating their heads against the wall and asking, "If we stop

beating our heads against the wall, what will we beat our heads against?"

One way to develop alternatives to performance appraisal is by debundling. If performance appraisal is a fragile cart asked to carry too heavy a load, we can remove each piece of baggage and build for each a separate vehicle designed specifically for that function. Here are some steps to take in debundling:

1. Acknowledge each service and expected benefit as something important for the organization to successfully accomplish.
2. Treat each as a separate function, disconnected from all the others.
3. For each service and expected benefit, ask: What is the best way to successfully accomplish this?
4. Set up separate systems and processes specifically designed to successfully accomplish that service or expected benefit.
5. When identifying the services and expected benefits and designing these systems and processes, keep in mind the principles at the heart of quality.

An Example of a Debundled Function: Giving Each Employee Feedback on His or Her Performance. Why doesn't performance appraisal adequately provide an employee with useful feedback?

- Feedback is, by definition, something derived from one part of the system and given to an antecedent part of the system. Performance appraisal is a feed-down activity that is hierarchical by nature, not systemic. And the hierarchy is not ordinarily the best source of system-focused feedback.

  Performance appraisal is a feed-down activity that is hierarchical by nature, not systemic.

- Performance appraisal, particularly when tied to income and promotability, engenders posing and pretense: easy targets, creative accounting, and evaluation that reflects the preconceptions of the supervisor and the manipulations of the person being evaluated. All of this works against the communication of data needed for improvement.

A better alternative is to have employees, alone or in natural work groups,

- Identify a key work process.
- Identify the customer(s) of that process.
- Learn what characteristics of the product or service—the output of the key process—are most important to the customer.
- Get feedback from the customer(s) on how well these characteristics are met.
- The next step is that managers must refrain from using this data to evaluate an employee and continue to encourage each employee to develop feedback loops such as this for all the key tasks.

The competition in the world market has forced business to re-examine its methods of corporate leadership. We must institute managerial practices that result in improved systems, processes, and methods that produce improved products and services to customers. Performance appraisal is an unnecessary vestige of an out-of-date set of managerial premises. It is irrelevant and detrimental. We can no longer afford it.

Peter R. Scholtes is a senior consultant with Joiner Associates Inc., of Madison, Wisconsin.

Performance Appraisals and Deming: A Misunderstanding?

Jim M. Graber, Roger E. Breisch,
and Walter E. Breisch

Not all practitioners of Deming's approach to quality principles believe that organizations should throw out performance appraisals altogether. This article serves as counterpoint to Peter Scholtes' piece, with the proviso that the process of appraising performance must be substantially revised.

W. Edwards Deming, a tireless apostle of quality, blames performance appraisals for poor quality. In his typically animated fashion, he has denounced them as one of the seven deadly diseases afflicting Western management.[1]

However, organizations will not abandon performance appraisals without a fight, because they have the potential to improve performance, strengthen communication, help reward employees fairly, and provide legal defensibility. There are some appraisal approaches that do not suffer from the afflictions Deming has identified. Some might even support quality efforts.

Deming's lack of enthusiasm is understandable. Why would anyone support a process that typically:

- Doesn't improve performance?
- Angers and alienates many employees?
- Sometimes makes organizations more prone to legal difficulties, rather than validating their approaches and actions?
- Takes a considerable amount of time and requires a lot of paperwork without providing a return on this investment?

Indeed, it is accurate to think of performance appraisals as the pariah of human resource management. Effective methods for compensation, testing and selection, and labor relations have been developed and are widespread in other related disciplines. But when it comes to appraisals, failure is widespread and social scientists and consultants are helpless.

And yet, Deming is shooting at a moving target. The intractability of performance appraisals has spawned a wide variety of approaches. Deming's

---

Reprinted with permission from *Quality Progress*, June 1992, ASQC, Milwaukee, WI.

negative comments about appraisals might apply to some and be invalid about others.

Deming's Charges

Deming identifies many problems with performance appraisals:[2]

- They nourish short-term performance and annihilate long-term planning.
- They are destructive to the individual being reviewed. They leave employees bitter, crushed, battered, desolate, feeling inferior, and unfit for work because they are afraid to present a divergent point of view or ask the boss a question that might appear to bring his or her wisdom into doubt.
- They are detrimental to teamwork because they foster rivalry, politics, and fear. Employees are rewarded for promoting themselves for their own good; the organization is the loser. After all, if employees take time out to help another department, others might receive all the credit, while the helper loses time that could have been spent working on personal goals. Making someone else look good is a dual liability because it takes time away from one's own concerns while strengthening someone else's case for scarce promotions.
- They focus on the end product, not leadership to help people.
- They do not reward attempts to improve the system or take a risk. They reward people who do well under the old system. Taking a risk can result in a lost promotion and finding oneself permanently behind in the race for upper management.
- The measures used to evaluate performances are not meaningful because supervisors and subordinates are pressured to use numbers and count something. Promotions must be defended with numbers.
- The measures discourage quality. People will concentrate on meeting numbers; they won't take time to improve a design if their goals involve quantity or deadlines. An arbitrator who is evaluated on the number of meetings he conducts will take three meetings to accomplish what could have been done in one. A purchasing agent who is evaluated on the number of contracts accomplished will not take time to learn about the losses his purchases caused.
- Despite apparent variation in performance, factors outside an employee's control—an action of the system or expected statistical variance, for example—account for the differences in performance. Even large differences can generally be ascribed to chance.

Analysis of the Charges

If they are true, Deming's charges are a serious indictment of performance appraisals. These charges apply to a number of performance appraisal systems, most notably those derived from the precepts of management by objectives (MBO). In fact, it is possible to specifically identify which aspects of MBO lead to each of the problems mentioned by Deming.

There are four critical design flaws of MBO. Each has significant effects:

1. MBO focuses exclusively on results.
   - Employees are often graded on things that are influenced by factors out of their control, such as co-workers, managers, the steps taken by the competition, and the health of the economy. The result can be an unfair process, cynicism, and employee discontent.
   - Coaching employees is not facilitated. An evaluation only indicates whether the goal was met, but it doesn't help determine why. It does not help people improve.
   - Short-term results are valued over long-term results. MBO preaches loudly against evaluating activities. Presumably, it would be an intrusion to indicate to any executive how to reach a result. Additionally, it is argued, one can do all the right things and still be unsuccessful, or vice versa.

In fact, it is possible to specifically identify which aspects of MBO lead to each of the problems mentioned by Deming.

What happens when a result cannot be accomplished in less than one year? Any result that requires more than one year can be measured only by the activities taken to get there. A refusal to measure and give credit for activities means that short-term goals will predominate.

Finally, a preoccupation with results, without any consideration of methods, often leads to negative side effects. This philosophy is aptly described as the ends justifying the means. The damage caused by this philosophy is legend.

2. MBO is typically quantitative.
   - The goals that are set for performance appraisals are often arbitrary and contrived. For example, how does one know whether a 5% or 10% improvement is justified? Many people end up being unfairly rewarded or penalized.
   - Quality goals have often been overlooked because it often takes more effort to attach a number to quality and is more difficult to gain universal acceptance of the importance of quality. In addition, quality might conflict with quantity and come out the loser.
   - Only a small percentage of employees' performance is evaluated. Since so much of the job is not touched upon, the evaluation is, by definition, unfairly skewed and affects employee morale. An important consequence is that the system is much less defensible should a legal challenge be made.

3. MBO is concerned with a few aspects of the job and special projects for the year to the exclusion of ongoing responsibilities.
   - Little or no attention is given to many important ongoing activities and significant behaviors. MBO focuses employees' at-

tention on results; they tend to ignore everything else. Far more is lost than just attention to teamwork and quality. There are dozens of other significant employee activities that receive no attention: administrative duties such as budget preparation, annual and long-range planning, and equipment and facility management and procurement; human resource management such as staffing, labor relations, training and development, counseling, and performance appraisals; work flow management such as division of labor, communication within the work unit and to higher management, work monitoring and quality control, coordination with other departments, managing and developing subordinates, and change and conflict management; and issues of professionalism such as staying current in one's field, supporting the organization, and professional and equal treatment of others in the organization.

4. MBO discourages setting difficult objectives that involve more work and more risk.
   - Taking risks might be applauded in others, but the savvy players will set goals they are sure they can accomplish.

In sum, all of the ills described by Deming can be explained by these four main design characteristics of MBO.

And yet, among the ruins of performance appraisal failure lie the seeds of success. That is, it is logical to assume that, if performance appraisal systems could be developed without the problematic design flaws, they might circumvent Deming's criticisms.

Successful Performance and Planning Review

Let's look at a different set of performance appraisal design characteristics:

Division, department, and individual goals must be determined by customers' needs..

- Division, department, and individual goals must be determined by customers' needs. Performance planning for individuals begins with setting clear goals and metrics for the entire organization based on customers' needs. These must then be translated into goals and metrics for all subgroups and processes within the organization. Each individual should identify his or her internal and external customers and document their needs in relation to organizational goals. Only then can individuals set priorities, goals, and metrics that fully support the organization and its customers. Performance planning done in isolation, while it might be compatible with work group goals, nearly guarantees that the performance of the organization will fall short.

  Successfully accomplishing many organizational objectives involves the effort of more than one work group. Group objective setting and problem solving, occasionally using task forces, will help define the roles of subgroups and individuals within the context of organization goals.

- Performance appraisals should be devoid of arbitrary or excessive numbers and percentages. Rather than using percentages and numbers in performance appraisals, it is preferable to require that tasks be completed thoroughly and efficiently. Clearly, there is more subjectivity involved in determining whether a task has been done efficiently than in determining, for example, whether 10 cars have been sold. However, frequent coaching and discussions between employees and supervisors, self-reviews, and monitoring the fairness of the review process serve to clearly define subjective standards.

  Getting away from numbers opens up the performance appraisal process to setting expectations in many new and significant job areas. It is also a more credible approach from the employees' standpoint because supervisors lack the time and resources to track quantitative performance measures accurately.

  When numbers are an appropriate means for measuring performance (successful salespeople will tell you their success is directly connected to the quantity of calls they make), statistical methods can help set baselines. Groups and individuals can determine realistic expectations by looking at historical data. They can then set goals that are realistic and meaningful.

- Performance appraisals should be comprehensive. Expectations should be developed for every important aspect of a job. How can someone begin to manage his or her performance when expectations haven't been developed and subsequently evaluated? The philosophy should be "If it's important, we will develop expectations and make evaluations no matter how challenging."

  A distinction should be made between ongoing responsibilities and new or special priorities. Attention should be given to both. Once expectations have been defined for regular parts of the job, however, more time can be spent on emerging priorities.

  Expectations should be developed for teamwork, communication, employee development, job enrichment, employee participation, and other areas that build the organization.

- Performance appraisals should be based on activities and results. Activities are the steps taken to achieve results. People knowledgeable about any given job can identify the activities that tend to lead to success. For example, no matter how tedious the process, it is essential that a chemist thoroughly review previous research findings and current products on the market before trying to develop a new antibiotic. Using activities and results means that employees are being evaluated on elements they truly control. Furthermore, the appraisal form becomes a useful diagnostic and coaching tool that can help determine where an employee might have gone wrong. Finally, the steps required to reach long-

> Getting away from numbers opens up the performance appraisal process to setting expectations in many new and significant job areas.

term results, from organizational focus to cultural change, can be addressed by measuring significant activities.

- Performance appraisals should be criterion-based. People should be evaluated against standards and expectations, not against each other. Forced distributions of ratings are competitive and terribly destructive to morale. All employees should have the opportunity to receive an outstanding rating. It is healthy to adopt the philosophy that the job of every supervisor is to develop and motivate employees so that a high percentage of them will, in fact, be legitimately outstanding.

- Performance appraisals should be participative. Employees should play an active role in developing performance expectations for their jobs. Similarly, they should evaluate themselves on these expectations periodically. Formal performance evaluations should be structured so that the employee leads off the evaluation process, with the supervisor patiently listening and noting remarks and then indicating where he or she agrees or disagrees. A participative approach will improve the quality and relevancy of the whole process while increasing fairness and reducing the devastation that Deming speaks of.

- Performance appraisals should define outstanding performance. Much of the game playing in appraisals stems from a looseness in the way expectations are defined. It is not adequate to evaluate an employee on the trait "teamwork." The meaning of this term within the context of a particular job or even a single responsibility must be defined. Furthermore, an effort must be made to define an outstanding level of teamwork. Misunderstandings occur when an average level is defined and employees are told that they must exceed that standard to achieve an outstanding rating. Too frequently, an employee will guess wrong and define what it means to exceed the standard differently than the supervisor will.

- The development of performance expectations should be facilitated. Developing clear, comprehensive performance standards for most jobs is a difficult and often labor-intensive task. It seems to be most effectively accomplished by a small group of people knowledgeable about the job (typically job incumbents and supervisors) with the help of a third-party facilitator. The facilitator leads the meeting, walks the participants through the process of developing job expectations, and records the responses of the participants. Shortly after the meeting, a rough draft developed by the facilitator is presented to the meeting participants. Using a trained facilitator ensures that the kinds of performance appraisal design criteria identified are met. It results in more positive reactions to the performance appraisal process.

- Supervisors must receive thorough performance management training. Every important aspect of a supervisor's job begins with training; performance management is no exception. The best performance management system can be made ineffective by a few supervisors bent on finding fault rather than leading their employees to improved performance.

Performance planning and review processes based on these design characteristics will provide many benefits:

- Employees will learn about organizational plans and goals. Further, they will feel more positive about their contributions; they will gain a better understanding of the value they bring to the organization.
- Employees will get an opportunity to participate in setting personal, department, and division goals. Participation in this process leads to greater commitment and accomplishment.
- Employees will gain greater insight into what is acceptable performance and what is outstanding performance.
- Employees can help evaluate the variety of activities they perform relative to the organization's needs. Priorities can be set to ensure that critical activities get the attention they require.

Organizational vs. Individual Goals

Suppose your organization wants to reduce the time it takes to process an order from three weeks to two days. Optimizing the performance of individuals will not be enough. Quantum performance gains are achieved through system changes. For example, significantly reducing new product development time will require that the product design, process engineering, and tool development phases occur concurrently, not sequentially as they have in the past.

System changes require organization performance planning. Goals, methods to reach them, milestones, and final measures of success must be worked out with all concerned participants. When group goals are achieved, appropriate recognition for all involved parties should follow. Similarly, accountability is shared, not assigned to one individual. While it is sometimes possible to split a systems change into individual responsibilities with attendant rewards or penalties, it would be ill-advised. There is a risk of creating inappropriate (i.e., competitive) interpersonal dynamics and of treating people unfairly since individuals seldom have the knowledge, authority, and control to carry out a systems change by themselves.

In short, every individual's goal should be linked to the organization's mission, but not every organizational goal can be or should be translated into individual goals.

Every individual's goal should be linked to the organization's mission, but not every organizational goal can be or should be translated into individual goals.

Customer Evaluations

The importance of customer evaluations in the performance review process cannot be overstated. Individuals will devote the majority of their time and effort to satisfying those in the organization who have the most control over their reward systems; in most situations, this means satisfying the supervisor. This is acceptable when the supervisor's goals are 100% in line with those of the work group's internal customers. Usually, however, supervisors' goals are more in line with those of their own supervisors. And so it goes. Employees continually focus upward in the organization rather than peripherally toward their customers. The boss is satisfied first, and if the customer happens to be satisfied, that's nice too.

The solution? Allow customer satisfaction surveys to play a role in performance evaluations. Internal customers can and should be asked whether others in the company support their efforts to meet department and organization goals.

Infusing Quality into Performance Appraisals

Solid, quality-related goals should make up a high percentage of the written performance expectations that direct and evaluate employees. The process for ensuring they do is straightforward. A group knowledgeable about the job should be asked:

- What is the difference between average and outstanding quality for this responsibility?
- What do you have to do to make the quality of your work outstanding?
- If you were training someone to perform this responsibility, what would you emphasize?
- What are the tricks of the trade?
- What are some quality-related events or activities you have witnessed that impressed you?
- Think of a person who is extremely dedicated to quality. What examples can you give to support your argument that he or she is exceptional?

Answers to these and similar questions result in a clear definition of quality. The result is clear targets to shoot at and fair and useful criteria for performance evaluations.

Don't Forgo Performance Planning and Review

Despite Deming's criticisms of performance appraisals, they do perform a number of valuable services when implemented properly. These should be little doubt in anyone's mind that the goal-setting process is powerful. Research during the last 30 years has repeatedly shown that goal setting enhances performance. These findings have been confirmed by experiences in thousands of organizations, although it has also been demonstrated that setting the wrong goals can lead to undesirable effects.

Regardless of whether an organization conducts formal performance appraisals, we have yet to discover one that does not give promotions. Promoting one individual over another is, like it or not, an evaluation. Even worse, it is a ranking. It is better to have formal criteria for promotions rather than an informal, subjective system.

Employees want to know how they are doing. Annual performance appraisals might cause consternation once a year, but a lack of clear goals causes confusion and aimlessness every day. Moreover, performance appraisals are the basis for legal defensibility for any personnel action taken, from promotion to termination.

Deming has strong opinions. His criticism of performance evaluations certainly have merit. There are, however, considerations and design characteristics that can make performance planning and review a valuable practice.

References

1. W. Edwards Deming, *Out of the Crisis* (Cambridge, MA: Massachusetts Institute of Technology, Center for Advanced Engineering Study, 1982), pp. 101–120.

2. Ibid.

Jim M. Graber is an organizational psychologist at Graber Management Consultants in Evanston, IL, and a member of the faculty in the Department of Management at the University of Illinois in Chicago. He has a doctorate in psychology from Claremont Graduate School in CA. Roger E. Breisch is a senior consultant at The Webber Group, Inc. in Wheaton, IL. He has a master's degree in business administration from the Massachusetts Institute of Technology in Cambridge. Breisch is a member of ASQC. Walter E. Breisch is a senior consultant at The Webber Group, Inc. in Wheaton, IL. He has a bachelor's degree in chemical engineering from the Illinois Institute of Technology in Chicago. Breisch is a senior member of ASQC.

The Theory and Practice of Employee Recognition

Brooks Carder and James D. Clark

This article provides a clear description of how to use employee recognition techniques to enhance organizational performance in a quality culture. It includes explanations of what not to do and a complete review of what works and why. It also includes an example of these procedures at work at IBM.

Today, many chief executive officers (CEOs) are faced with the challenge of changing their corporate cultures. The demand for quality improvement is causing more companies, large and small, to begin moving away from a structure dominated by centralized control and a short-term focus on the bottom line toward employee empowerment and process improvement.

CEOs can alter their companies' cultures by recognizing employees. Many companies have recognition programs designed to support the old management system: in other words, the kind of programs that reward the top salespeople with cash, trips, gifts, and public accolades.

These programs are not appropriate for the new culture that many businesses are trying to create. Like many other management systems, the recognition system must be revised in light of what is known about quality.

One could argue that extrinsic motivation in the form of a recognition program could interfere with intrinsic motivation such as pride of workmanship.

Many managers who use recognition systems view them as a source of extrinsic motivation: People who are not working up to their maximum potential in sales, quality, and productivity will do so if they receive some sort of gift or small cash incentive for their work. This view assumes that these incentives provide substantial motivation. Given the other forces at work in most corporations, this is not plausible. In fact, one could argue that extrinsic motivation in the form of a recognition program could interfere with intrinsic motivation such as pride of workmanship.

The reason recognition systems are important is not that they improve work by providing incentives for achievement. Rather, they make a statement about what is important to the company. Analyzing a company's employee recognition system provides a powerful insight into the company's values in action. These are the values that are actually driving employee behavior. They are not necessarily the same as management's stated values. For example, a company that claims to value customer satisfaction but recognizes only sales

Reprinted with permission of the authors. This article originally appeared in *Quality Progress*, December 1992.

achievements probably does not have customer satisfaction as one of its values in action.

Just as the analysis of current recognition practices can give top management insight into values in action, the establishment of new recognition practices can alter the company's values and thereby positively change the company culture.

Theory of Recognition

Recognition is a form of employee motivation in which the company identifies and thanks employees who have made positive contributions to the company's success. In an ideal company, motivation flows from the employees' pride of workmanship. When employees are enabled by management to do their jobs and produce a product or service of excellent quality, they will be motivated.

In this context, recognition can be an important form of feedback on the results of individual or team efforts. Recognition can make a positive contribution to pride of workmanship. Feedback in the form of recognition is especially important in large organizations, where it is often difficult to see the impact of a particular, isolated activity on the overall business.

Recognition can be public or private. Public recognition is often better for two reasons:

1. Some (but not all) people enjoy being recognized in front of their colleagues.
2. Public recognition communicates a message to all employees about the priorities and function of the organization.

The form of recognition can range from a pat on the back to a small gift to a substantial amount of cash. When substantial cash awards become an established pattern, however, it signals two potential problems:

1. It suggests that several top priorities are competing for the employee's attention, so that a large cash award is required to control the employee's choice.
2. Regular, large cash awards tend to be viewed by the recipients as part of the compensation structure, rather than as a mechanism for recognizing support of key corporate values.

There are many facets of recognition that should be addressed:

Recognition is not a method by which management can manipulate employees. If workers are not performing certain kinds of tasks, establishing a recognition program to raise the priority of those tasks might be inappropriate. Recognition should not be used to get workers to do something they are not currently doing because of conflicting messages from management.

For example, consider a manufacturing site in which workers, working under high-production quotas, often cut corners to produce and ship products. This practice results in quality problems. What will happen if management refuses to alter the production quotas but attempts to remedy the situation by recognizing workers who do not cut corners and therefore produce higher quality products? The result will be workers who now have a conflict between quality and quantity. The conflict will be difficult to resolve. The outcome will be difficult to predict, but the workers will certainly be placed under more stress.

A more effective approach is for management to first examine the current system of priorities. Only by working on the system can management help resolve the conflict. If workers can get a plaque or a small cash award for improving quality but will get fired for failing to meet a production quota, the problem cannot be fixed by improving the recognition program.

The workers should understand how to choose between quantity and quality. Only after management resolves the conflict in priorities is it appropriate to establish a recognition program to promote quality.

Recognition is not compensation. In this case, the award must represent a significant portion of the employee's regular compensation to have significant impact. Recognition and compensation differ in a variety of ways:

- Compensation levels should be based on long-term considerations such as the employee's tenure of service, education, skills, and level of responsibility. Recognition is based on the specific accomplishments of individuals or groups.
- Recognition is flexible. It is virtually impossible to reduce pay levels once they are set, and it is difficult and expensive to change compensation plans.
- Recognition is more immediate. It can be given in timely fashion and therefore relate to specific accomplishments.
- Recognition is personal. It represents a direct and personal contact between employee and manager.

Recognition should be personal. Recognition should not be carried out in such a manner that implies that people of more importance (managers) are giving something to people of less importance (workers). This situation can be avoided by making recognition personal rather than bureaucratic and by having employees participate in developing the recognition program and selecting the individuals and teams to be recognized. Recognition should be a joint celebration of the accomplishments that benefit the organization.

Recognition should be a joint celebration of the accomplishments that benefit the organization.

Positive reinforcement is not always a good model for recognition. From the standpoint of fundamental psychological theory, recognition is often viewed as a form of positive reinforcement. The theory says that positive reinforcers (money or gifts) strengthen behaviors that are associated with their presentation. If employees are recognized for doing something, they will do more of it.

One difficulty in the application of reinforcement theory is the employee's perception of the relationship between the behavior and the receipt of reinforcement (recognition). Just because the manager is using a certain behavioral criterion for providing recognition, it doesn't mean that the recipient will perceive the same relationship between behavior and recognition. For example, the manager might feel that he is giving recognition for team participation. The recipient (and his or her peers) might conclude that recognition is given to those whom the manager likes.

In a similar vein, a manager might frequently recognize members of his or her own staff or favorite department. He or she might feel that recognition is based on the achievements of the recipients. Employees might believe, in this case correctly, that recognition depends a great deal on having the right job.

Employees should not believe that recognition is based primarily on luck. One of the worst possible circumstances exists when individuals perceive that obtaining recognition is unrelated to what they do (i.e., it is based on luck). In his work on learned helplessness, Martin E.P. Seligman provided a variety of demonstrations showing that, when people judge that important outcomes (such as recognition) depend on luck rather than on their own efforts, these people will cease to try and can become demoralized or depressed.[1]

Within a corporation, the early sign of this is cynicism. Employees will tell you that management says one thing but does another. For example, consider the company that has a mission statement with four goals: total customer satisfaction, improvement of every business process, respect for employees, and revenue attainment. If recognition is given only for revenue attainment, what is the inevitable conclusion of the employees? It is likely that the employees will decide that the other three goals are less important. What management says (mission statement) is not what management does (recognizes only revenue achievement).

As cynicism develops, employees become lethargic and develop a we/they attitude. Once these conditions are present, they are difficult to eliminate. Each action of management is viewed with a jaundiced eye. Each new program is met with an expectation that management's promises will not be fulfilled. This can be a self-fulfilling prophecy.

Recognition meets a basic human need. An alternative to the view of recognition as a form of positive reinforcement is the theory of Abraham Maslow.[2] Maslow proposes that human needs are organized in a hierarchy. Basic needs such as food, shelter, and safety are at the bottom. Above them, in order, are needs for belonging, self-esteem, and self-actualization. Needs at the higher levels of the hierarchy do not control behavior until the lower needs are met. Thus, the hungry individual does not focus on self-esteem.

Maslow points out that theories of reinforcement are based on the view that the dominant motive is a deficiency in lower-order needs. In this context, using positive reinforcement as a model for recognition assumes that the state of employees in the organization is basically one of deficiency. As long as this deficiency persists, self-actualizing needs, such as pride of workmanship, will have limited control.

Recognition, certainly public recognition, meets the needs for belonging and self-esteem. In this way, recognition can play an important function in the workplace. According to Maslow's theory, until these needs for belonging and self-esteem are satisfied, self-actualizing needs such as pride in work, feelings of accomplishment, personal growth, and learning new skills will not come into play.

Recognition programs should not create winners and losers. Recognition programs should not recognize one group of individuals time after time while never recognizing another group. This creates a static ranking system. The people who get recognized will feel good, and the people who don't get recognized will feel bad. Even worse, however, is the potential influence of this circumstance on the work of those who do not get recognized.

Robert Rosenthal has written extensively about the Pygmalion effect.[3] If, year after year, one group is regularly recognized and another group is not, everyone's evaluations and expectations will begin to change. Not only will the members of the unrecognized group be perceived as worse by themselves and others, but evidence indicates that their actual performance will become worse.

Recognition should be given for efforts, not just for goal attainment. Many companies tend to recognize only what is easy to measure. It is relatively easy to measure sales dollars or revenue. It is often possible (if not misguided) to measure dollars saved. It is more difficult to define and measure behaviors that contribute to customer satisfaction, employee morale, teamwork, and process improvement. However, such activities are essential to the good health of the company and must be recognized if they are to flourish. A story in Masaaki Imai's book, *KAIZEN: The Key to Japan's Competitive Success*, provides an excellent example of recognizing achievements other than increased revenue or significant cost savings.[4] Imai describes the efforts of a group of dining room employees at one Matsushita plant. The employees noticed that, during the lunch period, some people at tables consumed more tea than others. They studied the phenomenon and found that higher consumption was consistently related to the same tables.

> Many companies tend to recognize only what is easy to measure.

The end result of the effort was that they were able to cut the use of tea leaves by 50%. The result was financially insignificant to the company. What was important was the effort that went into the project. This effort led to the award of the Presidential Gold Medal for the year. The obvious effect of this recognition was to provide powerful incentives for everyone to become involved in quality improvement.

According to Imai, a manager who understands that a wide variety of behaviors are essential to the company will be interested in criteria of discipline, time management, skill development, participation, morale, and communication, as well as in direct revenue production. To be able to effectively use recognition to achieve business goals, managers must develop the ability to measure and recognize such process accomplishments.

Employee involvement is essential in planning and executing a recognition program. It is essential to engage in extensive planning before instituting a recognition program or before changing a bad one. The perceptions and expectations of employees must be surveyed. (Often this must be done by someone outside the company to avoid bias.) Extreme care must be taken to ensure that what management wants to recognize is what the employees think is being recognized, that the recognition program fairly represents what management says are its priorities, and that the program is fair to all.

A cross-section of employees should be involved in planning the recognition program. This not only adds valuable information to the planning process, but it also decreases the chance that employees will think management is manipulating them.

Some Findings at IBM

In February 1991, IBM hired The AdGap Group to study the recognition programs at a marketing branch office. The objectives in this study were to obtain the employees' general perception of the recognition program at the branch, including its strengths and weaknesses; their perception of the relationship between what they do and what recognition they receive; and their opinion on how effective the recognition program is in improving the work performance of the branch employees. In addition, there was a need to evaluate how effective the current recognition system was at motivating quality improvement efforts. To obtain the necessary information, several methods were used, including a questionnaire, individual interviews, and group sessions.

A 14-item questionnaire on recognition practices was presented to the entire employee population of the branch. From a population of 130 employees, 80 completed questionnaires were received for analysis. In addition to the questionnaires, 20-minute individual interviews were conducted with eight employees. Two 60-minute group sessions were conducted with groups of about 10 employees each. Finally, an interview with the senior executive was conducted for about 60 minutes.

Results and Discussion

Following are some of the questions from the survey and a discussion of the results. Only the questions that yielded results germane to this discussion have been listed.

1. Do employees feel they receive adequate recognition for their accomplishments?

Sixty percent of the employees surveyed felt they had received adequate recognition for their accomplishments. Sixty-seven percent said they had received some form of recognition in the past year. This ranged from 85% of the systems engineers to 44% of the administrative employees. When asked whether the number of people recognized was too many, about right, or too few, only 3% of all respondents said too many and 45% said about right. Fifty-nine percent of the administrators said that the number of people recognized was too low. A number of people from all departments thought that administrators received too little recognition. Two administrators mentioned that it was difficult to go to meeting after meeting where marketing reps received a great deal of recognition and administrators received little or none. A marketing manager pointed out that, if administrators received more recognition, the marketing reps would treat them better. He said that when a good person makes a mistake it is perceived as a result of the system, and when a bad person makes a mistake it is the fault of the person. Good and bad are perceptions based partly on public recognition.

In the personal and group interviews, marketing reps, systems engineers, and administrators were asked to evaluate the contribution of their three groups to total customer satisfaction. The average contribution of administrators was estimated to be about 21%. Several marketing reps noted that poor administrative performance, especially improper billing, could severely damage customer relations.

It appeared that the allocation of formal recognition to the administrative department was not in proportion to the perceived contribution to customer satisfaction. The system was creating winners (marketing representatives) and losers (administrative personnel).

2. Do employees feel that IBM's recognition program is effective in improving work performance?

Seventy-seven percent of the respondents said that IBM's recognition efforts improved the performance of employees. When asked whether the recognition efforts improved their own performance, however, only 51% said yes. This difference is statistically significant and suggests that people are more willing to admit that others are motivated by recognition than to admit their own responses to the program.

3. Is recognition clearly related to the accomplishments of individuals or groups?

When asked whether recognition was a result of luck or of true accomplishment, a substantial number of employees—more than half—said that luck played more of a role than true accomplishment did. Managers were less likely to feel that luck is involved. This could be predicted because they are the only people involved in the selection process. There is no employee involvement in the development or operation of recognition programs in the branch.

> To the extent that the employees feel luck plays a role in recognition, the recognition is not an effective motivator.

The implications of these findings are important. To the extent that the employees feel luck plays a role in recognition, the recognition is not an effective motivator. In fact, this perception can lead eventually to cynicism and demoralization. Although these were present to a minor extent, the general tone was positive. When asked whether recognition was ever given for team play, 40% of employees surveyed said it frequently was, while 52% said it seldom was. Among systems engineers, however, 63% said recognition was frequently given for team play; only 33% of the other employees agreed. This could be because the systems engineers feel that a great deal of their recognition results from the success of the marketing reps with whom they are teamed.

One systems engineer pointed out that recognition often depends on the sales territory of each rep. He works with three or four marketing reps who have tough accounts. He says that, for this reason, he has been unable to get a significant award in four years. Thus, he perceives that recognition is based not on a lack of accomplishment but on the luck of his assignment.

4. Is recognition timely?

Thirty-four percent of the employees surveyed said recognition was timely, 57% said it was slightly delayed, and 9% said it was very much delayed. When asked if there was too much bureaucracy in the process, 58% of the employees said there was.

5. Is the form of recognition appropriate?

In the group sessions, there was considerable discussion of the effectiveness of certain noncash awards. Many remembered a briefcase stuffed with dollar bills. Others cited merchandise as effective, especially if the item conveyed prestige (such as a special briefcase). The general problem identified was a lack of creativity in the system.

In interviews, it was clear that most recognition for marketing reps was in the form of cash awards tied to the achievement of revenue goals. In fact, they viewed this as part of their compensation. These awards were expected and described as routine.

6. What do employees think they have to do to get recognized?

There was consistent agreement among marketing reps and systems engineers that most recognition was provided for achieving revenue goals. In the administrative area, some recognition was provided for achieving production and cost goals. There was no evidence of any recognition for process improvement or innovation.

Figure 1 lists some of the lessons learned from IBM.

What Was Learned

Based on the results and discussions, the following conclusions were drawn:

1. Allocation of recognition to the administrative function of the branch is not in proportion to its perceived contribution to customer satisfaction.
2. Almost all recognition is in the form of cash and is viewed, particularly by marketing reps, as compensation tied to sales.
3. The current recognition program doesn't give employees an increased sense of dignity, self-worth, belonging, and value to the company. Rather, it fosters a competitive environment in which there are winners and losers. The winners feel good, the losers often feel bad, and the direction of the company is not changed for the better.
4. The current recognition process recognizes only end results, not the processes necessary to achieve them.
5. Employees and customers are not involved in the current recognition process.
6. There is only management-to-employee recognition—there is no peer-to-peer recognition.
7. People like cash, but personalized noncash awards are also appropriate.
8. Employees don't clearly understand what IBM's current recognition program is.

LESSONS IBM LEARNED FROM ITS MIDWESTERN AREA

- It is easy to recognize top performers but difficult to raise—even slightly—the performance of an entire organization.
- Recognition is a process with associated cycle time and defect characteristics.
- Teams of employees must be continuously involved in every facet of a recognition program. Superior performance depends on superior learning.
- Different skills are needed from concept to implementation—ideas vs. detailed tasks.
- Outside assistance is required to evaluate an organization's current environment.
- Recognition is an affair of the heart and the head—both should be used.
- The personal touch is the most important ingredient in a recognition program.
- Recognition must be fun.
- Each functional business unit is unique and requires a general set of directions, personal ingenuity, and creativity to implement a recognition program.
- "Experience teaches nothing unless studied with the aid of theory." (W. Edwards Deming)
- Often, people are slow to learn and quick to forget—organizations struggle to learn from mistakes. Practice common sense.
- Designing a new award requires outside assistance and talent.

Figure 1.

9. Many employees do not clearly understand what they have to do to obtain recognition.
10. Recognition is seldom tied to teamwork or customer satisfaction.
11. Recognition is often not timely. Most recognition comes at the end of the year.
12. Winners in the current program are not documented, and their model behavior is not well-publicized.
13. Managers aren't trained in the theory and practice of recognition.

IBM Action Plan

The findings and conclusions of the IBM committee led to the following four-part plan:

1. The development and circulation of a recognition workbook and video to educate IBM managers and employees

2. A program to make existing cash awards more effective
3. The development of a peer-to-peer award
4. The development of an award for quality improvement teams

Education—the Video and Workbook

To address the committee's concerns about education and skills, an IBM recognition workbook and video were created. The materials describe how a business unit can evaluate and modify its recognition process. The package was made available, on request, to all IBM branches worldwide. The materials were publicized throughout IBM via electronic mail. To date, more than 500 packages have been distributed within IBM, and another 50 workbooks have been shared with IBM customers.

The package was followed by a survey to evaluate its effectiveness. The plan is to revise and improve the package based on the survey results.

How to Make Cash More Powerful

The IBM team concluded that existing cash recognition programs should be continued. Withdrawal would be viewed by employees as a pay cut. Therefore, the team developed a concept entitled "Trifecta" to improve the effectiveness of these cash awards. Borrowed from the trifecta concept in horseracing, it consists of a three-part process to make cash more effective:

1. The employee receives the cash, as before.
2. A gift (flowers, steaks, etc.) is sent to the home to surprise the recipient.
3. The recipient is provided with an experience to remember the award by: show tickets, a dinner, or something else that would be enjoyable for that particular individual. This allows the award to be personal but retains the benefits and flexibility of cash.

One approach to some of the problems in IBM's recognition process was to establish a peer-to-peer award.

Peer-to-Peer Award

One approach to some of the problems in IBM's recognition process was to establish a peer-to-peer award. To quote IBM's internal memo announcing the award:

"In order to drive customer satisfaction with our customers, IBM employees need to be satisfied within the organization and strive to exceed their own internal customer expectations. This award is based upon our goal to exceed the expectations of our customers.

"When someone exceeds your expectations and you want to recognize him/her with an award, you fill out the IBM Midwestern Area form and give it to the process administrator. You receive the envelope and card that contains $20 that you use to purchase a gift for the person who exceeded your expectations. You purchase the gift, personalize it, and present it to the award winner with the envelope and card to say thank you."

The peer-to-peer, or ETHYL (Encourage the Heart with Your Leadership), award addresses several of the observed deficiencies in the recognition process, including:

- Recognition of too few employees due to a process that is too bureaucratic
- Opportunities for awards not extended fairly to all employees
- Desire to have awards other than cash
- The relationship between recognition and customer satisfaction

This form of recognition is tied to the process rather than to end results. It involves employees in the recognition process by increasing the sense of belonging in all employees. This process is not a competition; it does not have winners and losers.

Testing of the ETHYL award in the Midwestern area has given initial indications of success. Based on feedback from the initial testing, a number of business units have adopted the process. Since July 1991, more than 4,000 ETHYL awards have been given. More than 85 business units across the United States and worldwide use the award.

MDQ Professional Process Award

The Market-Driven Quality (MDQ) Professional Process Award has been developed as a response to observations that:

- Only individual efforts are recognized, not team efforts.
- Recognition is given for end results, not for the processes that are necessary to achieve them.
- Employees are not sufficiently involved in the current recognition process.

To quote from the memo describing the award: "Traditionally, business awards have been based on 'most' numbers: most revenue brought in or most profitable new product. IBM, of course, recognizes those individuals who drive bottom-line numbers; profit is a significant reason why IBM is in business. But, since continuous quality improvement is also crucial to long-term success, IBM also singles out those who demonstrate excellence with regard to the processes and behavior of quality.

"The MDQ Process Professional Award is given to IBM teams in recognition of their using quality tools in the work efforts for the Midwestern area. Recipients are selected by a cross-trading area council of MDQ professionals based on nominations by separate process teams. A team can be nominated only by another team. All teams reaching the status of certification are awarded a custom-designed medallion, box, and letter from IBM's vice president and general manager."

Criteria for the award include teamwork, use of quality tools and processes, and use of measurements to capture results.

Tread Carefully

While recognition programs might be an excellent way to promote new values in a business culture, the installation of an appropriate program requires a knowledge of theory, a careful assessment of the current state of the culture, extensive planning, and testing of new ideas. Different cultures will require different actions. However, the stages of learning the theory, assessing the culture, planning, and testing are appropriate and necessary for all businesses.

References

1. Judy Garber and Martin E.P. Seligman, editors, *Human Helplessness: Theory and Application* (New York: NY Academic Press, 1980).

2. Abraham H. Maslow, *Motivation and Personality* (New York, NY: Harper and Row, 1954).

3. Robert Rosenthal and Lenore Jacobsen, *Pygmalion in the Classroom* (New York, NY: Holt, Rinehart, and Winston, 1968).

4. Masaaki Imai, *KAIZEN: The Key to Japan's Competitive Success* (New York, NY: McGraw-Hill Publishing Co., 1986).

Acknowledgment

The authors would like to thank Peter Golombek of The AdGap Group, who was instrumental in assessment and analysis. We would also like to thank Edward M. Baker for his helpful comments on the article, while acknowledging that he has not necessarily endorsed all of our arguments.

Brooks Carder is the chairman of The AdGap Group in San Diego, CA. He has a doctorate in psychology from The University of Pennsylvania in Philadelphia. Carder is a member of ASQC. James D. Clark is the market-driven quality consultant at International Business Machines in Chicago, IL. He has a bachelor's degree in operations management from Bradley University in Peoria, IL.

Standards and Assessments

ISO 9000 Standards
Baseline for Excellence

Asbjørn Aune and Ashok Rao

This article provides a clear, nontechnical explanation of what ISO 9000 is, how companies register to become ISO certified and why, and provides case studies of two companies, Duracell and Foxboro, that went through this process.

As the European Community (EC) lurches toward its January 1993 unification deadline, it is requiring each member country to adopt a single national quality standard, ISO 9000, as a baseline for excellence. In 1987 the European Committee for Standardization (ECS) adopted the ISO 9000 standards, renaming them EN29000 standards.

A truly international organization, ISO (The International Organization for Standardization) is made up of representatives from the standards boards of 91 countries, including the United States.

The ECS objective? The patchwork of each country's multiple technical standards hindered the free flow of goods. Sometimes the intent was to protect the national industry from foreign competition. But requiring each country to consolidate its standards into one national standard would still cause companies wishing to do business in the EC to negotiate 12 sets of standards. The ECS acknowledged a need for a common standard for quality in order to facilitate the flow of goods between the 12 member countries.

John Kirchenstein, a University of Tennessee quality consultant, points out this has happened when mandatory standards related to health, safety, and environmental issues are not satisfied. These standards are in the process of being written for a variety of products. Some of the products for which they have already been written are toys, some pressure vessels, gas appliances, electro-medical devices, and construction products. When toys not meeting these standards were admitted by British Customs, the Local Trading Standards Officers were able to ban distribution.

Reprinted with permission from *Target*, September/October 1992, published by the Association for Manufacturing Excellence, 380 W. Palatine Road, Wheeling, IL 60090.

American companies planning to do business in the EC and those already involved need to understand these standards and the certification process.

Even companies not exporting to the EC will be affected by the ISO 9000 standards if they supply a company that does. AT&T uses ISO 9000 as a tool to evaluate suppliers. The reason stated in the AT&T Quality Manager's Handbook: International customers require conformance to this standard.

Why Pursue Registration?

There are several reasons for a company to become ISO-registered:

- By the end of 1992 the EC will represent a unified market of 350 million people. Potential customers are likely to select suppliers from a registry of companies whose quality level is acceptable for contractual requirements. Failure to obtain registration will result in losing business to companies that are registered.
- European countries are lining up to register. Already more than 10,000 British companies have been registered as meeting ISO 9000 requirements.
- Supplying customers doing business in the EC will be easier. One of the requirements of ISO 9000 is to ensure purchased product conforms to specifications. This is to be done through assessments of the supplier.
- Government organizations, notably the Department of Defense (DoD) are considering replacing MIL-Q-9858A with ISO 9000 plus supplements. Over 50 countries have adopted ISO 9000 standards as national standards and purchasers within those countries are requiring registration.
- Once the certification process is completed, the registering agency has to perform periodic evaluations. The advantage is that the company will have far fewer audits from individual customers and if there is an audit it would be more focused.
- Although ISO-registration does not protect a manufacturer from lawsuits, not being registered in any industry where that practice has been adopted may prejudice the case if a lawsuit is brought against a manufacturer.

The standards were constructed as a generic basic set of requirements for any quality assurance system.

The Status of ISO 9000

The standards were constructed as a generic basic set of requirements for any quality assurance system. They are intended to apply to any industry in any of the 91 countries represented on the ISO, but they do not standardize quality systems implemented by businesses.

Presently, the standards include:

- ISO-9000 Quality management and quality assurance standards guidelines for selection and use.
- ISO-9001 Quality systems model for quality assurance in design/ development, production, installation, and servicing.

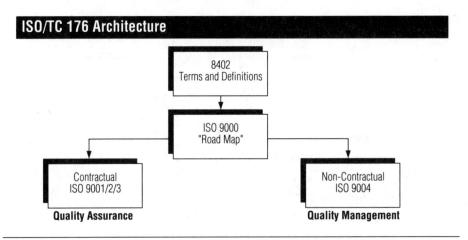

Figure 1.

- ISO-9002 Quality systems model for quality assurance in production and installation.
- ISO-9003 Inspection and test.
- ISO-9004 Quality Management and quality system elements guidelines.

In addition there is:

- ISO-8402 Quality terminology and definitions.

The ISO 9000-series is intended to be used both in contractual and non-contractual situations. Figure 1 provides an overview of the different elements.

ISO 9004 gives guidance to all organizations for establishing a broad-based quality management program. It can be viewed as a short textbook and is considered non-contractual.

ISO 9001/2/3 are intended for external quality assurance purposes in contractual situations between two parties. They reflect the interests of the buyer. While these standards could be adopted as described, frequently they will need to be tailored for specific contractual situations.

ISO-9000 provides guidance on such tailoring. In addition, some industries are developing their own supplements. For example, the Chemical Industry Association provides guidelines for its industry.

Figure 2 shows the relationship between the four elements 9001 through 9004. The table shows that management responsibility is covered in section four of ISO 9004. A company certified to ISO 9001 would meet the most stringent requirements. But to get ISO 9002 certification the requirements would be less demanding. And, for ISO 9003 certification the requirements would be further relaxed.

Regulated Products

Before these standards can be universally respected, a uniform set of certification bodies must be formed in each country. The Global Approach to

Comparing the ISO Standards

Non-Contract	Topic	Contractual		
ISO 9004 Clause		ISO 9001 Clause	ISO 9002 Clause	ISO 9003 Clause
4	Management responsibility	4.1	4.1 *	4.1 **
5	Quality system principles	4.2	4.2	4.2 *
5.4	Auditing the quality system (internal)	4.17	4.16*	—
6	Economics—quality related costs	—	—	—
7	Quality in marketing (contract review)	4.3	4.3	—
8	Quality in spec. and design (design control)	4.4	—	—
9	Quality in procurement (purchasing)	4.6	4.5	—
10	Quality in production (process control)	4.9	4.8	—
11	Control of production	4.9	4.8	—
11.2	Material control and traceability	4.8	4.7	4.4*
11.7	Control of verification status (inspection and test)	4.12	4.11	4.7*
12	Product verification (inspect and test)	4.10	4.9	4.5*
13	Control of measuring and test equipment	4.11	4.10	4.6*
14	Nonconformity (control of nonconformity)	4.13	4.12	4.8*
15	Corrective action	4.14	4.13	—
16	Handling and post-production functions	4.15	4.14	4.9*
16.2	After-sales servicing	4.19	—	—
17	Quality documentation and records	4.5	4.4	4.3*
17.3	Quality records	4.16	4.15	4.10*
18	Personnel (training)	4.18	4.17*	4.11*
19	Product safety and liability	—	—	—
20	Use of statistical methods	4.20	4.18	4.12*
—	Purchaser supplied product	4.7	4.6	—

*Less demanding than ISO 9001
**Less demanding than ISO 9002

Figure 2.

Certification and Testing (adopted in December 1989) established several objectives for fostering confidence in the safety of products and in manufacturers, testing laboratories, and certification bodies. One of the main elements is a modular system of testing and certifying products to assess their conformity to a standard. The system of modules ranges from a manufacturer's declaration of conformity, through the operation of (independently) approved quality systems, to independent testing and certification.

For regulated products, the required method of demonstrating conformity is defined in the applicable directive. Each member state must allow any products so designated (usually by the "CE" mark) to be marketed as being in conformance with the requirements of the directive. The same rules apply regardless of the product's origin.

So, when French customs officials began to stop every shipment of toys for inspection and asked exporters to provide translated documents, the EC Commission took the side of the exporters. The Commission told the French they were in violation of directives. If the French had not complied, formal complaint procedures would have been initiated under Article 169 of the Treaty of Rome.

In conformance with the principles of the GATT Agreement on Technical Barriers to Trade, non-EC products have the same access to the certification systems laid down in EC Directives as EC products.

The Registration Process

First the company will want to compare its existing quality system to the standards, which are available through the American National Standards Institute and through the American Society for Quality Control (ASQC). After documenting the existing system and correcting any deficiencies, the next step is to contact a certification registrar. This body checks the existing quality system against the appropriate ISO 9000 standard. In about three months it delivers a quality system supplement report showing how the standard maps to the existing quality system.

A few European nations have already established third-party registration schemes and government-sponsored accreditation councils. The leader in these initiatives has been Great Britain. There the Department of Trade and Industry has established a National Accreditation Council for Certification Bodies (NACCB). This body has authorized 30 accreditation groups to certify companies as meeting standards. The smaller groups certify companies in specific industries such as electrical equipment. Groups such as Lloyd's Register Quality Assurance Ltd. handle a broader range of companies.

Several U.S. companies are now able to certify companies. Some companies, such as ETL Testing Laboratories, Intertek Services, and Underwriters Laboratory have agreements with other accreditation groups.

ETL and Intertek have an agreement with the Lloyds Register Quality Assurance Ltd. to provide registration services. Underwriters has an agreement with the British Standard Institution. Four organizations have been recently authorized by the Registered Accreditation Board of the ASQC—ABS Quality Evaluators, AT&T Quality Registrar, Quality Systems Registrars, and BBQI.

Several European certification groups have located in the United States. A comprehensive list of quality system registrars is available through the Registration Accreditation Board of the ASQC (phone: 414/272-8575).

An assessment team performs an in-depth examination, documenting their findings as Non-Compliance Notes. This examination typically involves a two- to four-day site visit. Some registrars show two categories of non-compliance: "hold point" deficiencies which must be fixed before a certificate can be issued, and ongoing system improvements which will not delay the issuance of a certificate.

Preparation for registration takes about 16 months. Following registration, system reviews occur twice a year, with some registrars reassessing every three years.

The registration process certifies the company as having a satisfactory quality program. This does not mean the company can place the CE mark on all its products. As described earlier, there are several advantages in affixing the CE mark to a regulated product when marketing it in the European Community.

The registration process certifies the company as having a satisfactory quality program.

Two U.S. Companies' Registration Experiences—Duracell and Foxboro

Both companies recently received ISO 9001 registration, Duracell Inc. at its Worldwide Technology Center (DWTC) and The Foxboro Company.

Duracell

Duracell Inc.'s New Products and Technology Division developed a quality management system to comply with ISO 9001. Other Duracell divisions are now working on similar quality systems to meet ISO requirements.

To Carl Davis, DWTC Management Representative for Quality, being project leader on the ISO 9001 team has been extremely rewarding. ISO is the foundation for DWTC's quality management system.

The DWTC effort started in early 1990 with senior management's decision to implement a corporate quality initiative called "Duracell Xcells." Registering DWTC to ISO 9001 was one part of the Xcells program. ISO registration was championed by senior management, including vice-president Dr. H.F. Gibbard. A European consulting organization experienced in ISO 9000 certification assisted.

A quality team formed of three project leaders—Frank Ciliberti and Ed Sczepanski from the Standards, Performance, and Quality Department in Bethel, CT, and Carl Davis from DWTC in Needham, MA—worked with the consultant and with employees. Due to the magnitude of the project, a top-down commitment was essential.

The team was aware that it had to document quality procedures in order to meet ISO 9000 standards. At the same time, they were concerned that written procedures could create red tape which might alienate some employees and stifle creativity.

The DWTC solution was to create three levels of documentation. Level I is the New Products and Technology Division's Quality Policy Manual, addressing each of the items considered in ISO 9001 (see Figure 2).

Level II, Quality Assurance Procedures for DWTC, provided significantly more detail. Level II formed the bridge between Level I and Level III documents.

The Level III documents controlled methods, specifications, and drawings. Documentation at this level was specific to each department and in several instances was formally written for the first time.

The three levels of documentation were issued on a preliminary basis. Employee training and internal audits were conducted on a weekly basis by the quality team. During the internal audits the auditors checked to verify whether employees were complying with established procedures.

DWTC strategy was to specifically address four major concerns.

1. *Employee commitment* The team and the consultant repeatedly stressed they were as sensitive about red tape as the research scientists and design engineers. They emphasized their intent to document procedures to assure ISO 9001 certification and their commitment to customer needs and to not exceed reasonable limits. However, it took several months for employees to understand this and to actively take part in the development of the new quality system.
2. *Documentation control* The Quality Policy Manual (Level I) and the Quality Assurance Procedures (Level II), were initially written in hardcopy form and distributed to all department managers. However, revision control is an essential requirement of ISO 9001, and it became clear that maintaining photocopies throughout the facility would be difficult.

    The quality team, with help from the Computer Services Department, significantly reduced hard-copies by distributing them electronically to all computers in the facility. Now, DWTC only needs to control revisions to the computer database.
3. *Design control* Specifications, drawings, and methods are critical to the design process. Project leaders and team members were frequently audited to verify the revision currency of product drawings, specifications, and test methods. Today, project teams routinely maintain accurate information and provide traceability to critical documents during the entire design and development process.
4. *Instrument calibration* To support Duracell's worldwide operations, DWTC has hundreds of test and evaluation instruments, all of which were inventoried. Nearly two-thirds were identified as critical and entered into a calibration database. A schedule for recalibration had to be constructed and a process instituted to notify the department manager.

In March of 1991, the team notified Underwriters Lab (UL) they were ready for a Registration Audit. The consultants completed a pre-assessment audit in June. In July, a team of three people from UL conducted a three-day audit. Twenty-one relatively minor action requests required corrective action. Following the resolution of these action requests DWTC received its ISO 9001 registration in September 1991 from UL. DWTC also received dual registration from BSI in December.

Meanwhile, internal audits are conducted monthly by the quality team. UL and BSI will conduct routine surveillance audits every six months.

The Foxboro Company

The Foxboro Company started its push towards certification in January, 1990. An ISO 9000 Steering Committee was formed consisting of senior managers from several functions including manufacturing and marketing. At an operational level a Manufacturing Quality Council was formed under the direction of the corporate director of quality assurance. Concurrently, the senior quality engineer, Richard Anderson, took on the job of rewriting the corporate quality manual to align it with the ISO 9001 standards. The revised manual was distributed to each factory on a floppy.

Next a presentation was made to each of the divisions describing the importance of certification and requiring each to create a manual of procedures. The manuals had to be written by the manufacturing people, not just by the division's quality engineer. Typically, the plant manager and the product line manager would also be involved in the rewrite. Once a plant felt ready, Corporate Quality Assurance would conduct an intense audit followed by informal audits to ensure changes were made to manuals to fit the ISO standards.

Finally, in October of 1990, the company felt it was ready for certification and contacted DnV. The DnV auditors arrived with a checklist of 400–500 items and performed the toughest audit the company had since dealing with the audit by the Nuclear Procurement Issue Committee. The team spent three weeks at the company from mid-February through the first week of March, interviewing people in sales, R&D, service, order entry, marketing, and personnel in addition to manufacturing. Their aim was to see if 100 percent of the procedures were in place, with at least 75 percent implemented.

The auditors targeted these areas for checks:

1. *Implementation of procedures* Implementation of procedures was checked by talking directly to the people working in each function. The auditors made sure the procedures were in the area where the work was being performed. They confirmed that operators were collecting all of the statistics required by procedures.

2. *Special processes* The auditors classified processes such as welding and brazing as special processes, all of which were examined in detail. For example, in welding they looked for a flow chart of the process, written documentation that included the qualifications of the operator, the type of machine, and the type of welding rod.

3. *Documentation* They checked all functional areas for documentation. They checked the marketing plan. They asked how marketing provided input to design and then looked for documentation of these procedures. They checked the design function for documentation. They would pick a job on the factory floor and go back to development to see if the package with it was current.

During this same period, The Foxboro Company was implementing statistical process control (SPC) and a formal Quality Improvement Process

(QIP). This involved 115 teams and 900 people; each team having quality indicators. The DnV auditors used what they observed in SPC and QIP to fulfill the requirements of element 20 of ISO 9000—statistical techniques.

4. *Training* The auditors checked the documentation to establish the required qualifications a person needed for each task. In individual interviews they would check if the person's qualifications matched. They also checked plans for past and future training.

Foxboro Results

Foxboro passed the audit. Each plant had at least 95 percent of the procedures implemented and 100 percent in place. But there still were findings. As the DnV team left each plant they performed an exit interview. One deficiency related to document control.

All people receiving the document had to be listed on the control listing. These people could not circulate copies of the documents to people not on the list. Also, they were responsible for keeping the document and could not throw it out.

The company did obtain certification in April, 1991—16 months after it had started. A follow-up audit took place in July to review the open findings; the first six-month audit took place in September.

At the follow-up audit, DnV told the company they would be examining eight specific elements. The auditors spent a week reviewing these at each plant. The company passed the audit. The next audit on another eight elements took place in March, 1992.

Meanwhile, Shanghai Foxboro Company Ltd. in China also decided to seek ISO certification. They were able to transfer several of the procedures from the American plants. With help from the Corporate Quality group in America and the European quality manager for The Foxboro Company, they achieved certification in December, 1991.

According to Dick Anderson, Foxboro's senior corporate quality assurance engineer, certification has been a help with the multitude of certification forms—"Some customers let us skip the audit because we are ISO certified. We hope someday to have a list of those certified companies—Foxboro might be able to skip their audit. We could cut down on everybody's work."

Mr. Anderson is frequently asked how difficult the process was. He replies that "anyone with a 9858A Milspec quality system, or 10CFR50 Appendix B should have very little trouble with ISO 9000—they're almost there." Foxboro did it with the resources in place; the people doing the job wrote the procedures.

Will ISO 9000 Guidelines Change?

During the next decade we will see revisions of the existing standards and the development of new ones. Several committees are charged with creating new specifications and standardizing the certification activities in each country.

In 1990, an ad hoc task force of TC 176 suggested a new framework of "Generic Product Categories:"

Foxboro did it with the resources in place; the people doing the job wrote the procedures.

- Hardware: Products consisting of manufactured pieces and parts, or assemblies thereof;
- Software: Products, such as computer software, consisting of written, or otherwise recordable information, concepts, transactions, or procedures.
- Processed Materials: Products (final or intermediate) consisting of solids, liquids, gases, or combinations thereof, including particulate materials, ingots, filaments, or sheet structures. (Processed materials typically are delivered [packaged] in containers such as drums, bags, tanks, cans, pipelines, or rolls.)
- Services: Intangible products which may be the entire or principal offering, or incorporated features of the offering, relating to activities such as planning, selling, directing, delivering, improving, evaluating, training, operating, or servicing for tangible product.

The task force's "Vision 2000" was formulated as follows:

- A single QM standard, an updated ISO 9004 for all four categories.
- A single QA standard, an updated ISO 9001 for all four categories.
- A high degree of commonality of architecture and concepts in the updated ISO 9001 and ISO 9004.
- No need for industry-specific standards.

A single Community mark, CE-mark, will be adopted for all future Community legislation. The CE-mark will not indicate that a particular procedure has been followed. However, when a third party is involved in one of the modules of the production phase of a conformity assessment procedure, it should affix its stamp/mark/seal next to the CE-mark.

Other groups—CEN (European Committee for Standardization) and CENELEC (European Committee for Electrotechnical Standardization)—have been charged with determining the basis for regulating and harmonizing certification, accrediting, and testing activities. They developed an extensive series of standards termed EN 45000. The implementation of these standards within the 18 EC and EFTA countries will be the backbone of a system of mutual recognition of ISO certification:

- EN 45001 (the operation of testing laboratories)
- EN 45002 (the assessment of testing laboratories)
- EN 45003 (laboratory accreditation bodies)
- EN 45011 (certification bodies operating product certification)
- EN 45012 (certification bodies operating quality system certification)
- EN 45013 (certification bodies operating certification of personnel)
- EN 45014 (suppliers' declaration of conformity).

Conclusion

Becoming ISO-registered does not imply the company has a world-class quality system in place. *Editor's note: In Europe, being ISO registered means you have a license to drive, but it doesn't mean the bearer is a good driver!*

In order to realize the full benefits of lower costs and productivity improvements, the quality system would have to be developed beyond the requirements laid down by ISO 9000. There is a danger that companies might view getting certified as a destination when it is only a signpost on the road. These standards merely serve to document the status quo. With continuous improvement being a necessity for survival it is imperative that management continue to evolve the quality system.

There is a danger that companies might view getting certified as a destination when it is only a signpost on the road.

The use of ISO 9000 standards and third party certification of products is accelerating in Europe. France, Germany, and the Netherlands have followed Great Britain and organized accreditation councils for certification groups. Non-European countries such as China are also adopting these standards. The momentum will cause the United States to accept the standards. As this happens, it is highly likely the certification bureaucracy will grow and there will be a lack of qualified assessors. This could mean the time required to obtain certification will extend to longer than two years. Companies that move rapidly today and get certified will find they have a significant competitive edge.

References

1. Boehling, W.H. "Europe 1992: Its Effect on International Standards," *Quality Progress*, June 1990.

2. AT&T Quality Steering Committee, *Quality Manager's Handbook*, AT&T Customer Information Center, Indianapolis, IN, 1990.

3. Kendrick, J.J. "Certifying Quality Management Systems", *Quality*, August, 1990.

4. Klock, J.J., "How to Manage 3500 (or Fewer) Suppliers," *Quality Progress*, June, 1990.

5. Ferguson, K.H. "International Quality Standards May Affect Industry's Efforts in Europe." *Pulp & Paper*, March, 1991.

Asbjørn Aune is an associate professor in the Division of Production Engineering, and senior scientist at SINTEF Production Engineering—The Foundation for Scientific and Industrial Research, both at the University of Trondbeim. Ash Rao is a professor of management and quantitative analysis at Babson College in Wellesley, MA.

The 1993 State of U.S. Total Quality Management

A Baldrige Examiner's Perspective

George S. Easton

The author has written this article from his experience "as an Examiner and Senior Examiner for the Baldrige Award over the past four years." It provides a review of the strengths and areas for improvement of firms practicing quality management, using the seven Baldrige categories as areas of analysis. This article gives us an excellent assessment of where quality management is in the United States today.

Quality began to emerge as a key management focus in the U.S. around 1980. This emergence was primarily in manufacturing companies that were suffering severe foreign competitive pressure, most notably from Japan. Since that time, "quality management" has coalesced into a major management movement which has influenced nearly every industry. "Quality management," in this context, means the recognition by senior management that quality is a key strategic issue and therefore an important focus for *all* levels of the organization. Creation of the Malcolm Baldrige National Quality Award by Congress in 1987 contributed to the national visibility of quality management and thus to the momentum of the U.S. quality management movement.

Much of the U.S. quality movement is based on tools and techniques which have been key features in the development of Japanese quality management over the last forty years. Many of these techniques, such as statistical process control, were originally developed in the U.S. Japanese management approaches, such as widespread employee involvement in quality improvement teams, have also been adopted by many U.S. companies. These approaches have often required complete re-development as substantial changes in both methods and emphasis are necessary for successful implementation in U.S. organizations. There have also been many genuine U.S. quality management innovations. In particular prevailing traditional U.S. management approaches have been successfully re-focused to address quality management issues.

> "Quality management," in this context, means the recognition by senior management that quality is a key strategic issue.

The most critical challenge facing the U.S. quality movement is the development and implementation of quality-focused corporate management systems that achieve the coherence, integration, and comprehensiveness of quality management in Japan. Such comprehensive quality-driven approaches to corporate management are becoming known in the U.S. as Total Quality Management (TQM). Much consensus exists about some of the key components of TQM systems, including the necessity of a customer focus, the critical role played by leadership, and the importance of widespread employee involvement. Major differences in opinion remain, however, about both the appropriate components of TQM and the appropriate emphasis among the various components. There is also much disagreement concerning the details of implementation, even in the areas of general consensus.

Few U.S. managers understand the philosophical orientation underlying Japanese management.

One of the factors contributing to the difficulty of developing in the U.S. the same level of unification and integration achieved by Japanese quality management systems is that few U.S. managers understand the philosophical orientation underlying Japanese management. These more subtle aspects of Japanese quality management, however, may be critically important to the success of quality management in any culture. These nuances are difficult for U.S. managers to fully understand because mastering them requires changing unstated assumptions that are intrinsic in U.S. management thought. These misunderstandings contribute greatly to many managers' tendency to trivialize the intellectual content of TQM and to believe they have complete understanding based on superficial experience with a few quality techniques.

As a result of both the consensus and disagreement discussed above, many questions remain concerning both what U.S. TQM currently is and what it ought to be. In this article, I attempt to contribute to the discussion of these questions by providing a critical assessment of the current state of TQM in the U.S. This assessment is primarily based on my experience evaluating companies as a member of the Board of Examiners of the Malcolm Baldrige National Quality Award over the last four years.

The assessment of TQM described in this article is unusual in that it does not focus just on describing the characteristics of winning companies. The focus here is not only on the small number of winners, but on the larger group of very good companies which receive high scores in the evaluation process. Further, the article presents a critical evaluation of the overall state of development of the TQM systems of these companies as a group. Examination of this larger group of companies aids in discerning patterns in the approaches taken and more accurately reflects the overall state of TQM in the U.S. The sample of companies which are the basis for this assessment, and the target group of companies the assessment attempts to characterize, are described in more detail in the next two sections.

The assessment is reported in a format similar to the Feedback Reports that all Baldrige Award applicants receive. For each of the seven major Categories of the Award, strengths and areas of improvement are described. The strengths identify common successful approaches high-scoring companies are taking in their development and implementation of TQM. In most cases, these approaches are quite similar to those taken by companies that actually win. The areas for improvement identify common difficulties, errors in approach, failures, and confusions that limit the potential of these companies' TQM programs. As with the strengths, many of these areas for improvement are also often found in winning companies. It is my hope that specific discussion of the common weakness in approaches will shed some light on, or at least create some discussion of, the factors limiting the continued successful evolution of TQM in the U.S.

Any critical evaluation of the state of U.S. TQM requires comparison to some conceptualization of what TQM should be. The Baldrige Award Criteria attempt to provide such a conceptualization at the level of the issues that must be effectively addressed by a TQM system. The Award Criteria, however, deliberately avoid prescribing specific approaches and allow a great deal of latitude in interpretation. Thus, they give little specific guidance. As a result, the strengths and areas for improvement described in this article inevitably heavily reflect my own conceptualization of TQM. A brief introduction to the Baldrige Award and the Award's scoring process is given in the Appendix.

The Sample

The assessment described in this article is based on my experience as an Examiner and Senior Examiner with the Baldrige Award over the last four years. During this time, I have been involved in the scoring and/or feedback process for 22 companies that have applied for the Award. For three of these companies, I have participated in Site Visits. The 22 companies have been in all categories of applicants for the Award: large manufacturing, large service, and small business (both manufacturing and service). Table 1 shows the number of companies of each type. These 22 companies form the "sample" on which this assessment is based.

Table 1.   **Types of Companies in the Sample**

Size	Manufacturing	Service
Large	5	10
Small	5	2

This "sample" is clearly not random. It is, however, of sufficient scope to develop a very good idea of the characteristics of the population of companies that apply for the Award. It should also be emphasized that the population of companies that apply for the Award is not a representative cross section of U.S. businesses or even of companies that are trying to implement quality management systems. Because of self-selection, companies that do apply are generally far superior to typical companies. Many more companies use the

Baldrige Award Criteria for diagnostic purposes than apply or ever intend to apply for the Award.

Finally, my analysis of this population of companies is largely subjective. Systematic analysis would be difficult because the Award's confidentiality requirements prohibit disclosure of information concerning any applicant. In addition, the applicant's materials can only be used by the Examiner during the actual scoring process. Thus, my "analysis" is based on observation and subjective assessment of common approaches and characteristics—in short, on my experience.

The Target

The assessment which begins in the next section attempts to capture the state of TQM in very good U.S. companies that are committed to quality management and have achieved considerable success. The focus is not only on exceptional companies, such as those that have won the Baldrige Award, but also on the next level of companies which score about 600 or higher out of 1000 in the Award process. While understanding the approaches that winners have used successfully can clearly be beneficial, winning companies are often quite unique in both the approaches they take as well as in their success in deploying TQM and obtaining results. To assess the overall state of the TQM movement and its potential for widespread influence on U.S. management practice requires focusing on the larger number of very good companies that are committed to TQM rather than only on the occasional unique and exceptional company. It is the dissemination of quality management approaches into this larger group that will ultimately determine the success or failure of TQM as a management revolution in the United States. The reason is that these companies are both leaders in management thought and sufficient in number to have widespread influence. In addition, the fact that there are a larger number of companies in this group allows common patterns to be discerned. Baldrige winners are so few in number that even subjective inference is difficult.

While the group of companies targeted by this assessment is broader than just winners of the Award, the strengths and areas for improvement identified are also typical in winning companies. Winning the Baldrige Award is often interpreted as a blanket endorsement of all aspects of the winner's quality management systems. This, however, is not the case. Winning companies are selected to be role models. What role model means in this context is that winning companies do some things exceptionally well and with exceptional results, do most things well, and do not have major flaws or omissions that veto their role-model status. Thus, winning companies generally score above the 600 level in all *key* areas, indicating overall high levels of deployment of their basic approaches. But as the assessment which follows indicates, there are many important areas for improvement in 600-level companies as well as many strengths. These areas for improvement are also often found in winning companies.

Winning the Baldrige Award is often interpreted as a blanket endorsement of all aspects of the winner's quality management systems. This, however, is not the case.

Assessment by Category

In this section, the strengths and areas for improvement that are common among very good TQM companies are described. The assessment is given for each of the seven Categories of the Baldrige Award Criteria. Some important differences between manufacturing and service companies are noted.

Category 1: Leadership
Strengths

- Senior management is committed to quality. Senior managers are actively involved in promoting the importance of quality and customer satisfaction and they devote a substantial fraction of their time to quality-related issues (10% or more). Their involvement includes activities such as speeches, meeting with employees, meeting with customers, giving formal and informal recognition, receiving training, and training others (e.g., new employee orientation).
- Senior management has developed and communicated a set of company quality values. The key values of TQM are emphasized such as the importance of the customer, process orientation, continuous improvement, teamwork, management-by-fact, mutual respect and dignity, and value of individual employees and their contributions.
- The entire organization understands the importance of the external customer. The concept and importance of internal customers is also understood, and most employees feel some connection between what they do and the company's ability to respond to and satisfy the external customers.
- Elements of a quality management structure are in place, such as a senior management TQM council or division and department councils. These councils are involved in the management of the quality improvement teams, suggestion system, and recognition systems.

Senior managers do not apply the concept of processes to their own functions.

Areas for Improvement

- Senior management's *primary* focus is still on "strategy" and strategic business units (SBUs). Management still views the company almost exclusively in terms of financial, not operational, measures. There is only limited awareness of direct quality measures, especially on a month-to-month or day-to-day basis.
- Senior management does not systematically develop or carefully plan its leadership activities. Senior managers do not apply the concept of processes to their own functions. In addition, there is little real management-by-fact. Instead, senior management primarily relies on experience together with financial and cost measures. The measures often have limited effectiveness in guiding management decisions.

RESULTS VS. PROCESS ORIENTATION

In a results-oriented approach, management is still primarily based on setting objectives, feedback, and creating incentives. Behind this orientation is an unspoken belief that the results belong to the individuals, and that management's role is to hire the best people and to create incentives for obtaining the desired results. This presumes that the individuals will be able to figure out how to achieve the goals if left to their own devices.

In a process-oriented approach, the belief is that the results belong to the processes, and the processes belong to the organization. The role of the individuals is process operation and development including improvement of existing processes and development of new ones. The role of results is to guide process development and improvement. Thus, in TQM the emphasis is on developing methods and strategies, and approaches for implementing them, that will generate the best possible results.

At management levels, the development of methods and strategies may be directly tied to achieving particular important goals, but in addition it is focused on providing methods which will enable lower levels of the organization to develop strategies and methods for achieving their goals. The Plan-Do-Check-Act cycle, together with the associated quality tools, is an example. It is not a method for achieving a particular objective, but rather a method for enabling quality-improvement teams to solve problems and generate improvement.

- Overall, senior management's understanding of TQM is quite superficial. While senior management supports TQM in principle, they feel that, other than to promote its importance, it is not a primary activity in their realm. As a result, the scope of senior management's involvement is limited. In addition, senior management does not have a clear conceptualization of the specific roles of lower levels of management in TQM.
- Management still has, almost exclusively, a results, not process, orientation.
- In many cases, senior managers have very little specific knowledge and understanding of the company's processes or of direct customer, operational, employee-related, and supplier data. They do not routinely apply the Pareto principle, either formally or subjectively, and as a result they cannot identify the key problem areas or underlying causes. For example, they are unaware of the key types and causes of customer complaints or the key types and causes of employee injuries. They are also often unaware of adverse trends and have difficulty interpreting the levels and trends in the context of the variation that is generally present in the data.
- While some quality management structure is in place, for the most part the roles of managers and supervision in TQM have not

been developed. As a result, most managers are not clear about what they should do other than promote quality in general terms. They believe that TQM is primarily about attitude and motivation.

■ Management often does not fully appreciate the scope of their business as viewed by the customer, focusing instead on what management perceives the product to be. As a result, the scope of the quality activities, including measurement, is often too narrow.

Category 2: Information and Analysis
Strengths
■ There is excellent advanced technological support of the information systems.

■ The company has identified key quality measures which are tracked and often given high visibility.

■ A lot of data, primarily financial/accounting data, are readily available.

■ Informal benchmarking and other types of information acquisition and sharing are beginning to occur.

■ Competitive comparisons are made against primary competitors.

There is generally no coherent, articulated strategy for ensuring that the information needs of all organizational levels are met.

Areas for Improvement
■ The quality information is not well organized to support quality management. There is generally no coherent, articulated strategy for ensuring that the information needs of all organizational levels are met. Issues of what information is global, what is local, how local information is to be managed and analyzed, how local information is to be aggregated for higher level decision making, how aggregate information is to be analyzed, and how the results of aggregate analysis are to be disseminated, indexed, and otherwise made widely available are generally not adequately addressed.

■ The data that are readily available are often developed to monitor results and assess achievement of goals. These measures tend to be downstream and financially oriented. They are often not well-suited either for managing operations or for maintaining customer focus (i.e., managing customer relationships and tracking satisfaction). In many cases, the cost data do not give an accurate picture of operations because they are based on inaccurate assumptions, such as arbitrary allocation of overhead, or because they merge costs from unrelated causes.

■ The information systems are often inflexible and unable to support the kinds of change that are a part of both continuous improvement and evolving customer expectations.

- Competitive comparisons are often limited to immediate competitors only.
- Benchmarking is often confused with and limited to competitive comparisons. The purpose of benchmarking is to generate process innovation. Benchmarking is often most fruitful when similar processes or process steps are examined in companies in different industries. In addition, non-competitors are usually far more willing to share information.
- Analysis outside of technical functions and production areas is limited. Analysis at management levels is not based on management-by-fact. Rather, it is generally based almost exclusively on informal brainstorming. Effective problem-solving methods are not deployed at all levels.

Category 3: Strategic Quality Planning
Strengths
- Baldrige applicants usually develop some sort of written quality plan. This plan may be separate or part of the overall strategic or business plans.
- Quality-related goals are set in production-related areas of the company. Often quality goals are part of the management-by-objectives process.
- Many companies have adopted stretch goals (e.g., Six Sigma).

Areas for Improvement
- Few companies appear to have a well-developed strategic or corporate quality planning process. When plans do exist, they are seldom derived from systematic analysis of meaningful data and information, including customer, operational, and employee data and information.
- The plans generally stop at setting goals and objectives and developing the budget. They do not realistically address implementation issues or deployment of the plan throughout the organization. Even in companies with a fairly well-developed planning process, failure to realistically consider implementation issues is common and is a key reason the planning process is ineffective.
- The plans are often not effectively communicated to the organization. In many areas of the company, employees are either unaware of the plan or do not understand how the objectives and activities of their area relate to the overall plans. There is often no link between the overall company plans and either approaches to deployment (most commonly individual objective setting through an management-by-objectives process) or individual performance evaluation.
- Senior management believes that creating the right incentives is key to driving change.

> When plans do exist, they are seldom derived from systematic analysis of meaningful data and information.

- In many cases, too many top priorities are set. As a result, overall organizational focus is lost.

Category 4: Human Resource Development and Management
Strengths

- There are a large number of teams focused on quality improvement projects. These teams are concentrated in production and the critical areas that directly support production. There are many examples of team projects that have been successful and have generated substantial improvements.
- There is usually a suggestion system with a required response time. A substantial percent of the employees submit suggestions.
- All employees receive basic quality training. Most employees receive a substantial amount of annual training. In the best companies, employees receive 40 to 80 hours of training per year with training expenditures around 3–5% of payroll.
- There is widespread employee recognition for various types of contributions, including quality.
- Substantial resources are devoted to safety.
- There are a lot of traditional benefits.
- An employee survey is used to assess employee morale.
- Human Resources measures such as turnover, absenteeism, and injuries show identifiable improvement trends and good levels in comparison to industry averages.

In the best companies, employees receive 40 to 80 hours of training per year.

Areas for Improvement

- Most teams do not effectively use team processes such as problem-solving methods or quality tools, relying instead almost entirely on informal brainstorming. As a result, many teams are relatively ineffective. It is difficult to maintain momentum once the easy problems are solved.
- The concept of empowerment is poorly understood by management, even in cases where "empowerment" is an important part of a company's quality initiatives. In some cases, employees or teams are given authority that they are not comfortable exercising because either appropriate decision-making processes have not been developed or the employees have not been adequately trained. In other cases, decisions made by "empowered" teams are routinely reviewed by multiple levels of management prior to authorization. In other companies, empowerment is limited to giving the employee authority to act on behalf of the customer.
- Most employees have only received basic training. The effect of the training is primarily limited to awareness, either because the training is awareness training or because the employees do not successfully integrate the training into their work. In addition,

there is little formal training given in company processes outside of the production area.

- The effectiveness of training is not directly measured. Measurement is limited to course evaluation forms and surveys and does not address how much was learned or how well the training is integrated into the employees' work.
- Much of the employee recognition is superficial and seems to be driven by the feeling that everyone should receive recognition (e.g., employee of the week). In other cases, it is results-oriented and substantially influenced by factors beyond the employee's direct control. In many cases, it is unclear the extent to which the recognition reinforces quality relative to other considerations.
- Recognition of the work of quality improvement teams, such as competitions or presentations to senior management, which focuses on the team's improvement process is not common.
- The performance evaluation system is poorly aligned with the company's quality management system or overall plans and objectives. Performance evaluation emphasizes rewarding results which in many cases are primarily driven by factors beyond the individual employee's control.
- Safety and ergonomics are not part of quality improvement activities. This is often true even when there is substantial organizational focus on safety.

> Much of the employee recognition is superficial and seems to be driven by the feeling that everyone should receive recognition.

Category 5: Management of Process Quality
Strengths
- Many manufacturing companies have vastly improved the design and introduction of new products and services. Approaches taken include increased customer focus, cross-functional teams, joint design with suppliers and customers, design simplification, process capability considerations, simultaneous engineering, experimental design, and Taguchi methods.
- In manufacturing companies, the concepts of variation and control are understood in the context of production. Many production processes are controlled using SPC. The production processes are reasonably in-control. For important processes, they are also demonstrably capable.
- At least one specific approach to quality improvement has been implemented with tremendous improvement resulting. Examples of such improvement approaches include statistical process control just-in-time production, employee involvement, work cells, self-managed teams, suggestion systems, and cycle-time reduction.
- In service companies, some degree of measurement of the service production processes has been developed. In particular, most eas-

ily quantifiable measures are made for key processes and exhibit some degree of stability.

- Production processes are improved by quality improvement teams consisting of either workers or staff employees. The levels of involvement in teams by the production workforce is high. Sometimes the improvement efforts are sophisticated, using tools such as experimental design.
- Some companies have a well-defined quality systems audit function for the production processes.
- Quality improvement teams are also active in repetitive service and business process areas.
- Many companies have extensive programs with their suppliers. These include supplier quality systems audits, supplier rating and qualification systems, training, joint design teams, joint quality improvement teams, and supplier (and supplier employee) recognition programs.

Areas for Improvement

- New product development is still primarily reactive (i.e., responds to rather than anticipates, customer demands) and is driven by generally available technology improvements. Quality assurance of new product development and introduction is not prevention-based, relying instead primarily on inspection and testing. The new product development process is not well defined.
- Many companies, especially service companies, have very limited new product development activity. While they frequently change and augment the characteristics of their products, they do not view these changes as new product development and have no systematic approaches.
- Processes tend not to be very well defined except when they are naturally defined by the production processes, as is the case in many manufacturing and some repetitive service activities. As a result, processes are often not well defined in service companies and job shops, or in most companies outside of repetitive manufacturing and service activities.

> Processes tend not to be very well defined except when they are naturally defined by the production processes.

- In many companies, the approaches taken to quality are limited to one or two approaches such as statistical process control or just-in-time production. Because the company has success with the specific approaches taken, management believes that they have a fully developed quality management system.
- In many cases, there is very little understanding of the idea of driving measurement of processes upstream, the importance of variables measures, or measurement qualification. Rather, management relies exclusively on end-of-process defect rates and customer complaints.
- There is often very little correlation of process measures with customer satisfaction, or of upstream measures with downstream

measures. Identification of these relationships is based on the experience and intuition of management and technical staff.

- While many service companies collect the readily available quantifiable measures of their service processes, these measures are often not direct measures of the key attributes of the service processes. As a result, many service companies have very few direct process measures. Rather, they try to control their processes using customer feedback data. While customer satisfaction is clearly the goal, customer feedback generally cannot be used to effectively control processes because the cycle time for collecting customer feedback is too slow and the relationship between the process parameters and the customer's perceptions is often obscure.

- Many companies do not have a very broad scope of types of improvement teams such as workforce teams, management/technical teams, teams consisting of both management/technical staff and the workforce, and cross-functional teams. Many companies' TQM programs focus entirely on one type of team, usually workforce teams. As a result, the scope of improvement is limited.

- In many cases, improvement efforts are based on informal brainstorming and not on management-by-fact and systematic analysis. This is related to the failure of the quality improvement teams to effectively use a well-developed problem-solving process supported by analysis tools.

- Documentation of the improvement methods and activities and dissemination of the knowledge gained is often limited. Quality improvement teams do not make effective use of devices such as the QC Story.

- The distinction between improvements that result from bringing a process into control and continuous improvement once the process is in-control is often not understood. As a result, while many problems are solved, a state of systematic, on-going refinement is not achieved. Because great improvement often occurs when the processes are brought into control, management believes prematurely that the company has achieved a state of systematic on-going process refinement (i.e., continuous improvement).

The distinction between improvements that result from bringing a process into control and continuous improvement once the process is in-control is often not understood.

- Systematic approaches to improving are less well developed in business processes and support services than in primary production areas. This is associated with the lack of well-defined processes in these areas. Repetitive service activities (e.g., billing) are sometimes an exception.

- Many companies have essentially no quality systems audits. In addition, audits originating from senior management or including senior management involvement are very rare.

- Many companies appear somewhat heavy-handed with their suppliers. A state of cooperation and appropriate integration does not exist.

Category 6: Quality and Operational Results
Strengths
- Very good companies can demonstrate high levels of quality in their products and services for a wide variety of measures relative to similar U.S. companies.
- Sustained improvement trends of at least a several-fold improvement over two to five years can be demonstrated for key product and operational areas. Sustained improvement results, but with weaker trends, can be demonstrated in most areas of the company.
- Quality results for key suppliers also show significant and sustained quality improvement.

Areas for Improvement
- For most companies, the scope of the data used by management to routinely track the results of their quality systems is inadequate. Key measures from all important processes are often not readily available. In addition, management often does not track in-process and upstream measures.
- In many companies, almost no variables-based measures are tracked. Instead the only measures are defect rates and customer complaints. Management is unaware of levels or trends in measures such as process capabilities.
- Linkage between operational measures and key customer requirements is not established.
- In many cases, sufficient data to establish trends are not readily available. Management is only aware of the most recent measures and may be unaware of adverse trends. Sustained improvement trends cannot be established.
- Even winners are not necessarily the best in the world.

Category 7: Customer Focus and Satisfaction
Strengths
- Many companies use a large number of survey-type instruments to assess customer satisfaction and customer needs and expectations. Focus groups are also common.
- There is increasing emphasis on easy access for customers and quick response times.
- Some well-defined customer service standards are developed for such things as time to answer the telephone and response time to queries or complaints. These measures are often tracked.
- There is much motivational training for customer service representatives. There is also often extensive product training.
- Increasing attention is being given to formal complaint resolution. Complaints are aggregated by types and reported to management.

- Customer service representatives are being given increasing authority to satisfy the customer.
- Customer satisfaction levels are high in comparison to similar companies in the United States. Sustained customer satisfaction improvement trends can be established. Market share and repeat customer trends are favorable.

Areas for Improvement

- There is often little understanding of the technical issues relating to the accuracy of surveys (e.g., bias, variability, accuracy).
- There is also often little distinction between determining customer satisfaction and customer needs and expectations. The methods of extracting customer requirements or identifying latent desires from customer information are usually informal.
- There is no formal approach for integrating customer data with the (new) product development process. Product design relies on the designer's intuition and customer data collected primarily for other purposes.
- Often, only the company's current customers are surveyed. Appropriate information about lost customers, new customers, and competitor's customers is not obtained.
- Stratification of customer data is done by attributes important to the company (e.g., account size), not the customer. As a result, the data are of limited use for identifying patterns of satisfaction and dissatisfaction among customers with similar characteristics.
- In many cases, the sales force is used as a primary source of customer information. However, sales usually has no systematic, well-defined approach for gathering and aggregating customer data and no training in these activities. Other types of quality improvement activities in sales are also minimal.
- Customer service standards are not well defined except in cases where there are easy and obvious measures. Much customer service representative training is motivational and not specific. Methods for assessing customer service performance relative to standards are generally poor.
- Customers still have difficulty reaching someone with real authority to resolve their problems. The role of Customer Service is still to "protect" management.
- Companies still seem to think that customers should be completely satisfied with replacement guarantees.
- Usually, formal complaints are the only ones that are tracked. There is no operational definition of what a complaint is. As a result, informal or minor complaints are missed and thus are not aggregated or tracked and cannot be used for assessing customer requirements and satisfaction. In addition, complaint data are not effectively used to drive quality improvement.

> Stratification of customer data is done by attributes important to the company (e.g., account size), not the customer.

- In many cases, customer satisfaction comparisons are left to third parties (e.g., industry associations) that do not use valid and reliable methods.

Discussion: Some Cross-Cutting Themes

As the assessment above indicates, there are many important strengths in the approaches of leading TQM companies. In many cases, these approaches have produced impressive results. But there are also many important areas for improvement. Few, if any, U.S. companies have developed quality management systems with the levels of coherence, comprehensiveness, and integration of quality management in the best Japanese companies. Underlying many of the areas for improvement described above are a number of cross-cutting themes which appear to be limiting realization of TQM's full potential in the United States.

One of the most important cross-cutting themes is that the scope of the concept of "process" in TQM is not fully understood by most U.S. managers, even in companies that are committed to quality management. This is particularly true outside of structured, repetitive manufacturing and service activities where the basic production process is readily apparent and can be defined in specific detail. Thus, for many critical activities, processes are not defined. In fact, the higher-level or more abstract the activity, the less often an appropriately defined process has been developed. As a result, the approaches taken are created on-the-fly by the individuals responsible. Because there is no uniformity in approach, the activities cannot be stabilized or continuously improved.

The scope of the concept of "process" in TQM is not fully understood by most U.S. managers.

This lack of understanding of process is related to the persistent results-oriented perspective of most managers. Because of this perspective, many companies' approach to management focuses on setting goals and objectives, on trying to create the right incentives, and on feedback based on after-the-fact measures. There is little before-the-fact emphasis on strategies, approaches, or methods—the process-oriented notions.

The planning process often exemplifies this problem. First, the planning process itself is often poorly defined. More importantly, planning often stops with the development of goals and budgets with little emphasis on developing strategies and methods for achieving the goals. In addition, there is often insufficient prevention-oriented analysis to anticipate barriers to implementation or to ensure sufficient flexibility to respond to problems as they occur. While an individual's goals may be reviewed by several levels of management, the methods to be used to achieve the goals often receive a cursory review at best. As a result, consensus concerning what strategies and methods to use is not developed in advance and the actual implementation is ad hoc, often developed at quite low levels of the organization. In summary, managers do not view the development and deployment of processes and methods as the fundamental management activities that drive achievement of the goals.

In many companies, the functioning of the quality improvement teams provides another important example of the limited development and deployment of the idea of a process. In the most common case, the improvement teams have been trained in a variation of the Shewart Plan-Do-Check-Act cycle together with a few basic quality tools. These, however, fail to be integrated into an effective team process. One reason is that the team process is not completely developed. This situation is often indicated by management having no clear concept of exactly how the teams are supposed to function. In many cases, there is no structure or method, such as documentation through a QC-story format, to guide deployment of the team process and ensure effective use of methods such as the quality tools. Effective use of the quality tools is difficult. As a result, the teams tend to rely almost exclusively on informal approaches such as brainstorming. The quality tools are seldom used, collection of data is avoided, and root cause analysis is not particularly effective.

A second cross-cutting theme is the lack of effective management-by-fact. In many cases, companies have relatively few direct operational and customer measures that can be stratified for effective root-cause determination. Instead, as was discussed in Category 2, the measures focus on downstream results and after-the-fact assessment of the achievement of goals. The measures used are often indirect financial measures that aggregate effects from a variety of causes. They are difficult to disaggregate or stratify in meaningful ways that directly relate to planning and decision making.

The failure to consistently set clear priorities throughout the organization is another important cross-cutting theme. The principle of consistently developing a small number of key priorities is pervasive throughout TQM. In many companies, however, the key priorities are unclear to middle and front-line managers, and to the workforce. Sometimes this is because of unclear or inconsistent communication. But often a key contributing factor is that far too many top priorities are developed. As a result, departments and individuals pick and choose among the top priorities, and a consistent overall organizational focus is lost.

In many companies, the key priorities are unclear to middle and front-line managers, and to the workforce.

A final cross-cutting theme is that in many companies the primary focus of the quality effort is on the workforce. Consequently, roles for all levels of management and technical staff in TQM are not developed. As a result, management and staff tend to believe that TQM is primarily about attitude and that their role in TQM is to promote the importance of quality and to motivate the workforce. While there is often effort to involve all levels of management in promoting quality, the focus is nevertheless on supporting and encouraging the workforce as the primary generators of quality improvement. The workforce, however, cannot be the primary generators of improvement. While their contribution is very important, the vast majority of quality improvement must come from management and technical staff. Without well-defined roles for direct contribution by all levels, a company's TQM program is unlikely to achieve more than moderate success.

Summary

So, what, then, is the current state of TQM in the U.S.? Overall, the assessment is generally favorable. An increasing number of companies are actively focused on quality as a key approach to improving their competitiveness. And as the assessment above indicates, U.S. companies that are committed to quality have a large number of areas of true strength. In many cases, they also demonstrate some exceptional management innovation. Further, their efforts are yielding clear results in terms of customer satisfaction, operational improvement, and employee involvement.

While the assessment is generally favorable, these companies also have a large number of important areas for improvement. These areas for improvement are not superficial or merely a matter of failure in execution. They are not just blemishes on conceptually well-developed management systems. Rather, they are weaknesses in the fundamental approaches taken to management such as the lack of full understanding of process, the lack of emphasis on planning, the lack of effective systems to implement the plans, the reliance on incentives, failure to apply the principle of management-by-fact, focusing on results to the exclusion of processes or methods, focusing on financial measures to the exclusion of direct operational measures, and inadequate understanding of customer expectations. Senior management is not yet fully aware of the totality of its appropriate role in TQM and is often not even completely comfortable in its present role.

Thus, TQM in the U.S. is far from mature. It is important that TQM approaches continue to be developed, refined, and expanded, even in companies that have already achieved considerable success. Otherwise the competitive advantages that TQM promises will not be realized and many companies will be left struggling against competitive decline without any unified or coherent strategy for revitalization.

George S. Easton is an Associate Professor of Statistics and Quality Management at the Graduate School of Business, University of Chicago. He was a Senior Examiner for the Malcolm Baldrige National Quality Award in 1991 and 1992, and an Examiner in 1989 and 1990.

The Malcolm Baldrige National Quality Award and ISO 9000 Registration
Understanding Their Many Important Differences

Curt W. Reimann and Harry S. Hertz

What's the difference between the Baldrige criteria and ISO 9000 standards? This article, written by the administrators of the Baldrige award, clearly and simply lays out these differences for readers. In doing this, it gives a sense of the value of these two tools that serve as guidelines for implementing quality management.

Introduction

With increasing international trade and opening of markets, customers have wider choices of products and services from around the world. Choice elevates quality requirements, and poses new marketplace challenges as well. For example, single-country regulatory authorities are challenged by global sourcing to ensure safety and quality of products entering their markets. Also, companies faced with increasing quality requirements make greater demands on their suppliers. As a result of these marketplace developments, companies seeking to export and/or those serving many quality-demanding customers may be subject to many separate quality-related requirements and audits. Many believe that there is a need for an independent, consistent, reliable, transportable and economical system to assess conformity of companies' production systems to recognized standards.

In the most competitive markets, high product and service quality are necessary but *not* sufficient to ensure success. Success depends also upon many other important factors—speed, variety, price, and value, for example. Such dynamic and competitive markets place many new pressures on companies, forcing them to become more customer and market focused, to develop high performance work organizations, and to continuously pursue cost reduction. As a high wage nation, the U.S. must succeed in these dynamic

The editors would like to thank Curt W. Reimann and Harry S. Hertz for their courtesy in supplying us with this article, written as part of their responsibility as administrators of the Baldrige Award.

markets. To do so, it must have many successful, globally-competitive companies, backed by an agile, high productivity, high quality supply base.

National competitiveness depends not only upon the vitality of the U.S. manufacturing base. It depends also upon the quality and productivity of the large and growing service sector, public and private, including financial services, hospitality, transportation, education, healthcare and government. Quality and productivity, and in some cases, competitiveness, are key issues in these areas. These organizations, as their manufacturing counterparts, need to become better customer-focused and performance-oriented.

Many of the basic requirements for being competitive are well known but not yet *widely* understood. Of greater concern, few companies in the U.S. have progressed to where these requirements are integrated into their overall system of management. There is, however, a growing consensus that traditional approaches to quality based on inspection are outmoded, and must give way to approaches that are customer-focused, prevention-based, more responsive and directed toward quality and productivity improvement—approaches perhaps better described as pursuit of overall operational excellence. This pursuit requires many management changes, including executive-level leadership and personal involvement, more investment in human resource development and creation of more flexible work organizations. Moreover, competitiveness is a rapidly "moving target". The capabilities for staying competitive must evolve accordingly.

The U.S. and much of the world are in the early stages of a major transition in how work and quality are managed—moving from quality as a narrowly-defined, separate function, managed at lower organizational levels, to quality integrated within all work units and with overall business management. The success of this transition depends upon numerous factors not well addressed within traditional quality—executive-level leadership and involvement, empowerment, rapid deployment of changing requirements, management of innovation, management of diversity, and customer focused planning and operations. The few organizations in the U.S. who are making progress with this transition have much to offer others who are experiencing greater customer and market demands but are unsure how to respond.

> There is a growing consensus that traditional approaches to quality based on inspection are outmoded, and must give way to approaches that are customer-focused, prevention-based, more responsive and directed toward quality and productivity improvement.

Emergence of National and International Quality Thrusts

The globalization of markets, increasing quality requirements, tough competition, and supplier pressures, have led to two parallel and visible "quality" thrusts, nationally and internationally. These thrusts are national/multinational quality awards—the Malcolm Baldrige National Quality Award (Baldrige Award) in the U.S.—and the ISO 9000 series of international standards.

- The focus of the Baldrige Award is enhancing competitiveness. Its central purpose is educational—to encourage sharing of competitiveness learning and to "drive" this learning, creating an evolving body of knowledge, nationally. The content of the Baldrige Award criteria reflects two key competitiveness thrusts:

(1) delivery of ever-improving value to customers; and (2) systematic improvement of company operational performance.

■ The focus of ISO 9000 registration is ensuring conformance quality. Its central purpose is to provide a common basis for an independent and transportable supplier qualification system. It is directed toward reducing audit costs and helping to assure buyers that specified practices are being followed, both important to enhancing and facilitating trade. The content of the ISO 9000 requirements standards reflect key conformity thrusts: consistent practice in specified operations, including proper documentation of such practice.

Overall, the Baldrige Award criteria provide an integrated, results-oriented framework for designing, implementing, and assessing a process for managing all operations. The ISO 9000 are standards used in implementing a compliance system and assessing conformity in company-selected operations.

Despite their numerous, major differences, there is now much confusion regarding the Baldrige Award and ISO 9000. Commentary, surveys, and advertising are often inaccurate or misleading. Two common misimpressions stand out: 1) that the Baldrige Award and ISO 9000 registration are similar—that they cover similar requirements in the same way; and 2) that the Baldrige Award and ISO 9000 registration both address improvement, both rely on high quality results and hence, both are forms of recognition. Based upon these widely-held beliefs, some conclude that the Baldrige Award and ISO 9000 are equivalent, rather than distinctly different instruments that can reinforce one another when properly used.

Despite their numerous, major differences, there is now much confusion regarding the Baldrige Award and ISO 9000.

The misimpressions are cause for concern not merely because they reflect confusion between Award and registration requirements. More importantly, the confusion relates to basic business management issues: quality system definition, operational excellence requirements, and how quality is managed. For example, whereas competitiveness issues tend to marshal executive involvement, compliance and conformity matters more often are delegated, much as inspection and quality control were in the past. If all "quality" is delegated, and focuses primarily on conformity and documentation, there is likely to be a "disconnect" between quality and closely-related competitiveness requirements, reversing a trend toward their better integration. Within companies, this may result in fragmentation of efforts, slow response, and weak productivity growth. Nationally, the focus on improving competitiveness could be diminished.

Strengthening U.S. competitiveness depends upon organizations in all sectors pursuing overall operational excellence. Success depends upon effective integration of all requirements. Conformance quality is one of *many* such requirements. The existence of two visible, partially overlapping, but very different thrusts creates new impediments and costs, frequently confusing efforts to strengthen national competitiveness. The purpose of this paper is to clarify the most important Baldrige Award criteria requirements and how they relate to ISO 9000 registration requirements. This clarification should assist companies which have launched ISO 9000 efforts to integrate these efforts into the Baldrige Award competitiveness improvement initiative.

The Baldrige Award

The Baldrige Award has three central purposes: (1) to promote awareness and understanding of the importance of quality improvement to our nation's economy; (2) to recognize companies for outstanding quality management and achievement; and (3) to share information on successful quality strategies. The Award Program is a public-private partnership. A crucial part of this partnership is the willingness of the Award winners to share information on their successful quality strategies with other U.S. organizations.[1] For purposes of the Award Program, a "successful quality strategy" has three principal features: (1) integration with business strategy; (2) active organizational learning processes tying together all corporate requirements and responsibilities—customer, employee, supplier, productivity, etc; and (3) multidimensional results that contribute to overall business improvement and competitiveness.

The criteria (1994) for the Baldrige Award comprise 28 examination items distributed among seven categories, as follows: (1) Leadership; (2) Information and Analysis; (3) Strategic Quality Planning; (4) Human Resource Development and Management; (5) Management of Process Quality; (6) Quality and Operational Results; and (7) Customer Focus and Satisfaction. An applicant for the Baldrige Award is required to submit a report summarizing its practices and results, responding to requirements in the 28 examination items.

Award applications are reviewed in a four-stage process by a private sector, volunteer Board of Examiners.[2] The first stage consists of multiple, independent, detailed review by at least five Examiners. The top applications are forwarded to the second (consensus) stage to refine the first-stage evaluations. In the third stage, top contenders are site visited (2 to 5 days each) by teams of 6 to 8 Examiners. A Panel of nine Judges reviews the site visit reports and recommends Award recipients. All applicants receive comprehensive feedback reports. Final contenders for the Award each receive about 500 hours of total review.

ISO 9000

While it is not the intent in this paper to give a detailed description of ISO 9000, a brief synopsis is provided. ISO 9001, 9002, and 9003, as stated in the 1987 standards, are "used for external quality assurance purposes." ISO 9004

---

1. In the first five years of the Award, winners have held well upward of 10,000 sharing sessions, reaching hundreds of thousands of organizations in all sectors—business, healthcare, education, government, non-profit, etc. Award winners are not expected to share proprietary information, such as technical or trade secrets, R&D, and some aspects of business strategy.

2. Examiners themselves are selected yearly in a competitive process based upon expertise, peer recognition, experience in various business sectors, and linkages to key organizations in the U.S.

is designed for internal use. The application and use of these standards in third-party registration systems has become their dominant use.

The ISO 9000 standards are used in ensuring a supplier's conformance to specified requirements, which may include design/development, production, installation, and servicing. The quality system requirements specified in these standards are considered complementary to technical product and service requirements. The more detailed standard (9001) includes management responsibility for the quality system, procedures for contract review, and procedures to control and verify product design. Suppliers must establish and maintain procedures to control all documents and data. Purchased products must conform to their specifications. The supplier must plan, identify and document processes affecting product quality, and ensure that these processes are followed. The organization must inspect and test, in accordance with its procedures, incoming product, in-process products and final manufactured products. The supplier must calibrate measuring equipment using its documented procedures. Documented identification and corrective action procedures are required for non-conforming product. The handling, storage, packaging and delivery of product shall be accomplished in accordance with documented procedures. Quality records must be properly maintained, internal audits must be conducted and adequate statistical techniques must be used. All personnel whose duties affect quality must be properly trained to perform their assigned functions and records of training must be maintained. In summary, the standards emphasize documenting conformance of quality systems to the company's quality manual and established quality system requirements.

In summary, the standards emphasize documenting conformance of quality systems to the company's quality manual and established quality system requirements.

Registration to ISO 9001, 9002, and 9003 entails several stages, as follows:

- application to a registrar
- document review—a review by the registrar of the applicant's quality system documents or quality manual
- pre-assessment to identify potential noncompliance (either by the registrar or through self-assessment)
- assessment, typically by 2 or 3 auditors who spend two to four days, leading to registration, or to a period of remediation, followed by a re-audit
- surveillance—periodic re-audits to verify conformity with the practices and systems registered.

Feedback from assessment and surveillance processes includes a record of non-conformance with the specific requirements of the standards.

Key Baldrige Award Competitiveness Characteristics that Differ from ISO 9000

The Baldrige Award criteria address many competitiveness factors not addressed in ISO 9000 or addressed very differently.

Customer Focus

The principal thrust in the Baldrige Award criteria is *customer-driven quality*. Customer-driven quality a strategic concept. It is directed toward customer retention and market share gain. It demands constant sensitivity to emerging customer and market requirements, and measurement of the factors that drive customer satisfaction and retention.

Customer-driven quality is the foundation of the six-item category called Customer Focus and Satisfaction. This category addresses this focus and related results, building upon them as the "front end" of a modern quality process. The criteria probe how organizations address current and future customer requirements, how they listen to customers, how they gather and use customer-related information, how they manage relationships and commitments to customers, and how they determine satisfaction. The category is explicit and detailed in spelling out key requirements, including timeliness and requirements pertaining to customer-contact employees. Numerous results measures are cited, including customer satisfaction, satisfaction relative to competitors, customer retention and company responsiveness. Applicants are expected to present a wide variety of customer-related results (including adverse indicators) and how results are used to improve performance, as viewed by the customers.

Although ISO 9000 registration is frequently a customer requirement, the ISO 9000 registration requirements do not fully address customer focus and satisfaction nor the many dynamic market factors that help ensure a customer-driven and market-driven rationale for internal operations. In not addressing these customer issues and factors, ISO 9000 registration tacitly assumes that customer requirements (stable or changing) are known; conformity in internal operations is then the key requirement.

There are two important observations regarding the Baldrige Award and ISO 9000 registration system definitions of quality: First, the ISO 9000 registration focus on conformity means that it does not fully address either customer-driven quality, described above, or the meaning of quality given in ISO 9000 guidance documents. ISO 9000 registration addresses a narrower meaning of quality, a meaning that includes only one aspect of quality—consistency in the production of a product or service. This distinction is important, particularly for service organizations or for manufacturers which seek service and/or relationship differentiation from their competitors based upon overall *value* delivered.

Second, if the customer's quality requirements can be met by many suppliers, which is often the case, the customer may seek short- and long-term price concessions. This requirement is not addressed within ISO 9000. Also, the approach to cost cutting needs to consider *all* operations. Most ISO 9000 registered organizations involve only their main production units.

> ISO 9000 registration addresses a narrower meaning of quality, a meaning that includes only one aspect of quality—consistency in the production of a product or service.

Continuous Improvement: A Results/Competitiveness Orientation

The Baldrige Award criteria emphasize continuous improvement in overall operations. The approach to improvement needs to be "embedded" in the way the organization functions. There are three basic factors that determine whether or not improvement is embedded: (1) improvement is part of the daily work of all work units; (2) improvement processes seek to eliminate problems at their source; and (3) improvement is driven by *opportunities* to do better as well as by problems that must be corrected. Opportunities for improvement have three major sources: employee ideas; R&D; and benchmarking or other comparative information on processes and performance.

The results orientation means that improvements need to be reflected in all important areas (a composite) which together define what might be called a "competitiveness profile". The key business results areas are:

1. customer indicators—satisfaction, satisfaction relative to competitors, customer retention, response time, complaints and other adverse indicators, etc.
2. market share, profits, ratings by independent organizations, etc.
3. product and service quality
4. productivity and other operational effectiveness measures—cycle time, waste reduction, and energy conservation
5. human resource development indicators—training, employee satisfaction, safety, turnover, absenteeism, etc.
6. supplier performance
7. public responsibility, including environment, health and safety.

Applicants are expected to report all *relevant* and *important* trends and current performance levels in these seven areas. In addition, they are expected to show how these results compare with industry leaders and appropriate benchmarks. A report by the General Accounting Office (1991) summarizes many results reported by some early Baldrige Award winners and site visited companies.

In addition to the composite results described above, Baldrige Award applicants are expected to show how they analyze and use results data to improve in three important areas: (1) customer-related decision making and priorities; (2) operations-related decision making and priorities; and (3) financial performance.

The ISO 9000 assessment does not rely on results. Peach (1990) points out that:

Notably absent in the ISO Standard are specific references to quality results and customer satisfaction. The ISO Standard specifies elements of a quality system, but does not discuss whether products resulting from that system actually meet customer requirements.

Peach notes also that:

The ISO Standard also omits reference to continuous quality improvement.

There are four important observations regarding the ISO 9000 registration exclusion of results: First, ISO 9000 registration does not necessarily mean that registered companies have good product quality. Second, the registration does not mean that all registered companies have similar levels of product quality (the registration process does not deal with comparative factors or benchmarks). Third, a registered company does not necessarily have better product quality than non-registered companies. Fourth, the registration and ongoing audit process do not require registered companies to attempt to continuously improve their product quality.

There is another concern stemming from ISO 9000's exclusion of operational results, such as productivity improvement and waste reduction. ISO 9000 requirements are such that "a traditional, mass-inspection-oriented organization could easily be registered" (Finlay, 1992). Smith (1993) notes: "a conforming supplier could have a very high percentage defective; yet, if non-conforming product were segregated and handled in accordance with procedure, and corrective action process were followed to the letter, the supplier could still be accredited (registered)".

Of course, quality and operational improvement are neither precluded nor discouraged in ISO 9000. Indeed, many ISO 9000 registered companies pursue quality and productivity improvement. An organization's responsibility under ISO 9000 registration is to ensure that practices conform to the organization's registered (and accepted) quality system.

Sensitivity to the Competitive Environment

As a competitiveness instrument, the Baldrige Award criteria and evaluation process rely heavily upon comparative factors in business management. These factors are addressed throughout the criteria in an integrated way. For example: (1) customer needs and customer satisfaction determinations take into account competitors' customers and comparative information; (2) strategic quality planning includes projection of the competitive environment; (3) competitive comparisons and benchmarking are built into the information and analysis "brain center" of the criteria; and (4) results called for in the criteria require applicants to report not only improvement trends but also how actual performance compares to the performance of others. Through this approach, information is obtained regarding *what* to improve, as well as *how effective* the improvement actions actually are.

> The Baldrige Award criteria and evaluation process rely heavily upon comparative factors in business management.

ISO 9000 registration does not address comparative factors and best practices that would signal what should or could be improved to benefit a company's competitive position.

Tie to Business Decisions and Strategy

The Baldrige Award criteria address an organization's overall objectives, including financial performance, through several mechanisms. These mechanisms include integration of quality requirements into overall business strategy development, business decisions and innovation in all aspects of company operations (R&D, business support processes, human resource utilization, etc.). Examples of criteria ties to business decisions and strategy include:

- management of information used in business decisions and strategy—scope, validity, and analysis;
- quality requirements of niches, new businesses, export target markets;
- analysis of factors—societal, regulatory, economic, competitive, and risk—that may bear upon the success or failure of strategy.

The Baldrige Award criteria encourage companies to demonstrate linkages between quality, operational performance improvement and financial performance.

ISO 9000 does not address business strategy.

Integration via Analysis

Integration of quality into business operations, and alignment of activities to support business goals, depends upon understanding the relationships among actions that incur cost and produce revenue. The Baldrige Award criteria call for creating and linking customer satisfaction and operational performance indicators to drive management decisions. Performance indicators represent the "score board" in the Baldrige Award evaluations—the basis for assessing the effectiveness of processes and for feeding back this information to improve the processes. ISO 9000 registration requirements do not address integration and analysis or their connection, except in situations such as correction of product/service non-conformities.

Cycle-Time Reduction

The Baldrige Award criteria emphasize as a "core value" the improvement of cycle time and responsiveness. Applicants are expected to demonstrate cycle-time reduction in key operations, including product and service delivery operations, customer relationship management, business support services, and new product and service introduction. Cycle-time reduction is a powerful management tool as it often drives simultaneous improvements in organization, processes, quality, and productivity.

ISO 9000 does not address cycle-time reduction or relationships of cycle time to productivity and quality.

Public Responsibility

The Baldrige Award addresses how companies include their responsibilities to the public in policies, process management and improvement strategies. Public responsibility includes all basic expectations—business ethics, protection of public health and safety, and the environment. The preventive approach encourages companies to focus on process management factors such as waste reduction at its source. Companies are expected not only to meet legal and regulatory requirements, but also to treat these areas as opportunities for continuous improvement "beyond mere compliance". In other words, issues such as environmental management are addressed in the Baldrige Award criteria as integral with overall business management. Conceptually, this approach builds upon customer focus, addressing the public and the environment as key "customers". Within a company's resource limits, corporate

> Issues such as environmental management are addressed in the Baldrige Award criteria as integral with overall business management.

citizenship is also encouraged. This includes education, community service, improving industry and business practices, and sharing non-proprietary quality-related information.

ISO 9000 registration does not address public responsibility or corporate citizenship issues in its assessment process. Quality plans of regulated industries will include compliance requirements, and therefore these will be assessed. ISO 9004, a quality management guidance document, not used in the registration audit process, states the necessity for consideration of health and safety.

Human Resource Development and Management

The Human Resource Development and Management category in the Baldrige Award criteria is central to the criteria's integrated approach to quality and operational improvement. The category includes five items: (1) Human Resource Planning and Management; (2) Employee Involvement; (3) Employee Education and Training; (4) Employee Performance and Recognition; and (5) Employee Well-Being and Satisfaction. Each item includes a comprehensive set of factors which need to be considered in managing an effective human resource system, directed toward improving quality and operational performance. These factors include *measures of effectiveness* that link human resource practices to overall company results.

In addition to the Human Resource Development and Management category, the Baldrige Award criteria address key human resource issues in service and relationship management. These issues (covered in the category called Customer Focus and Satisfaction) are particularly important to the successful management of customer-contact employees in service organizations.

ISO 9001 addresses human resource issues solely through the training requirement. This requirement deals with procedures for identifying training needs, qualifications of personnel performing specific tasks, and maintenance of appropriate records of training. ISO 9001 does not include consideration of the special factors in services management.

Uses of the Baldrige Award Criteria

Major purposes of the Baldrige Award criteria are to promote education, self-assessment, and sharing.

Despite the importance of award and registration efforts, most of the millions of "business units" in companies, healthcare organizations, schools, government agencies, and non-profit organizations in the U.S. are unlikely to seek either ISO 9000 registration or the Baldrige Award. Nevertheless, these units face the same basic requirements as those who do and may benefit equally from available knowledge and information sharing. Major purposes of the Baldrige Award criteria are to promote education, self-assessment, and sharing. The summary given below is intended to highlight these important uses of the Baldrige Award criteria.

Education

Although the Baldrige Award criteria are the basis for awards, the criteria booklet is designed primarily as an educational instrument[3]. Its principal use

---

3. Each year, about 200,000 booklets are distributed. In addition, a like number of copies are made and distributed by others.

is as a "daily working tool". The criteria define a basic integrated framework spelling out and relating key business requirements. The creation of an integrated framework for all requirements represents an important stage in the evolution of quality—from largely separated from other operational requirements to fully integrated with them. The process-results linkages, coupled with a scoring system, create the basis for a results-based assessment.

There are three important points to note regarding the Baldrige Award criteria as an educational tool:

1. The criteria framework integrates two major thrusts: delivery of ever-improving value to customers; and systematic improvement of company operational performance.
2. The criteria framework addresses generic requirements that are equally applicable to organizations of all types—manufacturing and service businesses and not-for-profit organizations. This is intended to promote and facilitate interest, communication, and sharing among all organizations. Sharing and communication, nationally, are built around *harmonization* of requirements.
3. The framework subordinates tools, techniques, and procedures to key customer and operational requirements.

To support the larger educational purposes of the Baldrige Award Program, the Award criteria booklet includes five interrelated and reinforcing elements:

1. an introduction outlining the core values, concepts, framework, and characteristics of the Award criteria. A key characteristic of the criteria is that they are *nonprescriptive*. The criteria do not prescribe tools, techniques, or organizations, thus fostering innovation. The introduction also addresses three important topics: (1) incremental and breakthrough improvement; (2) financial performance; and (3) invention, innovation, and creativity.
2. the criteria that focus on 28 key requirements (examination items) among the seven categories. These items are detailed, giving the users many ideas on improving practices.
3. item notes—some quite detailed—that illustrate, clarify, and educate regarding the item requirements,
4. the scoring system commentary which gives users a perspective on the factors that are considered in evaluating progress and achievement. The scoring system uses three evaluation dimensions—approach, deployment, and results—which aid in developing *diagnostic* feedback.
5. instructions to applicants which help all users of the criteria to understand how to organize information to facilitate internal and external assessment.

Continuing Education—The Evolution of the Baldrige Award Criteria

To fulfill its educational role, the Award Program must itself be a rapid-cycle-time, learning organization. The primary vehicle to capture and disseminate learning is the annual Award criteria booklet. Since 1988, the booklet has undergone six cycles of revision. With the exception of the seven category framework, all other educational materials are either entirely new or incorporate major learnings. Lessons learned are captured from many sources—from the strengths and weaknesses in U.S. organizations, for example—and from well publicized deficiencies in "TQM" or other management thrusts. The changes from 1988 to 1994, in aggregate, are numerous and significant. They reflect better integration of all business management and competitiveness factors and stronger results orientation. Many other important changes respond to the requirements of service organizations.

Self-Assessment

Few organizations seek either awards or registration, but most wish to have non-costly means to learn how well they are doing and how they could get better. The most cost-effective means to achieve these purposes is through self-assessment. A realistic and thorough self-assessment has three components: (1) understanding of all requirements, what influences them, and how they are changing; (2) how requirements are actually deployed throughout the organization; and (3) how well requirements are actually being met.

An effective self-assessment instrument should have four characteristics: (1) educational value; (2) completeness—addressing all requirements and how they are deployed; (3) an integrated way to collect information so that it may be meaningfully evaluated; and (4) results indicators that address how well requirements are met. Answering "how well?" types of questions depends upon trends (Are we making progress?) and levels (How do our results compare with others?). Together, trend and level information provide a good basis for improvement actions.

The Baldrige Award booklet contains the key elements needed for self-assessment. Case studies prepared for Examiner training, and subsequently available to all organizations, provide information to support the assessment learning process.

The Baldrige Award booklet contains the key elements needed for self-assessment.

Summary of Key Differences Between the Baldrige Award and ISO 9000 Registration

Two visible thrusts, the Baldrige Award and ISO 9000 standards, have emerged—differing significantly in focus, purpose, and content. Despite their major differences, they are often confused and often depicted as equivalent. This occurs largely for two reasons: (1) a misimpression that they cover the same requirements; and (2) a perception that they both recognize high quality. The purpose of this paper is to make understandable their numerous important differences. Particular emphasis is placed on the underlying assessment concepts in the Baldrige Award process which are not part of ISO 9000 registration. This comparison is intended to assist companies which have launched ISO 9000 efforts to integrate these efforts with competitiveness improvement.

In highlighting the differences between the Baldrige Award and ISO 9000 registration, however, the intent is not to portray these instruments as mutually exclusive. To the contrary: the authors wish to encourage U.S. companies which need to, or elect to, pursue ISO 9000 registration to also take part in the national effort to promote improved competitiveness. There are many routes to participation in the Baldrige process, or in related State and local award processes (Bemowski, 1993). An increasing number of excellent companies are using the Baldrige Award and ISO 9000 compatibly, sometimes simultaneously and sometimes sequentially. Either approach requires understanding of their important differences.

Focus

The focus of the Baldrige Award is competitiveness. The criteria reflect two key competitiveness thrusts: (1) delivery of ever-improving value to customers; and (2) improvement of overall company operational performance.

The focus of the ISO 9000 registration is conformity to practices specified in the registrant's own quality system.

Purpose

The Baldrige Award Program's purpose is educational—to encourage sharing of competitiveness learning and to "drive" this learning, nationally. It fulfills this purpose in three major ways: (1) by promoting awareness of quality as an important element in competitiveness; (2) by recognizing companies for successful quality strategies; and (3) by fostering information sharing of lessons learned.

ISO 9000 registration schemes are intended to provide a common basis for assuring buyers that specific practices, including documentation, are in conformance with the providers' stated quality systems. In addition to registration to meet customer requirements, some organizations use the ISO 9000 standards to bring basic process discipline to their operations.

Meaning of Quality

The Baldrige Award defines quality as customer-driven quality—addressing the total purchase, ownership, relationship experience—concerned with all factors that matter to customers. Conformity-related issues are included in the criteria, under process management, which also addresses other key operational requirements.

The ISO 9000 registration's operational meaning of quality is conformity of specified operations to documented requirements.

Improvement Results

The Baldrige Award assessment depends heavily upon results. "Results", however, are a composite of competitiveness factors, including customer-related, employee-related, product and service quality and overall productivity. "Management by fact", tied to results, is a core value in the Award criteria. The concept of results takes into account trends (improvement) and levels (comparisons to competitors and best performance). In the Baldrige Award evaluation process, results play a dual role. First, they represent important business improvement indicators needed to demonstrate a successful quality strategy. Second, they represent indicators that drive further improvement.

ISO 9000 registration does not use outcome-oriented results or improvement trends in the assessment process. Thus, ISO 9000 registration does not require demonstration of high quality, improving quality, efficient operations, or similar levels of quality among registered companies.

Role in the Marketplace

The Baldrige Award is a form of recognition. Despite its heavy reliance on results, it is not intended to be a product endorsement, registration, or certification. Baldrige Award winners may publicize and advertise their recognition and must share their quality strategies with other U.S. organizations. The winners' role is public education and inducement for others to improve. Award winners adhere to a voluntary advertising guideline that prohibits attributing their Awards to their products. Because of the many significant differences in the focus and content of the two types of assessments, it is not meaningful to relate Baldrige Award performance and ISO registration. In other words, an ISO 9000 registration does not translate meaningfully into a Baldrige Award assessment score.

The ISO 9000 registration provides customers with assurances that a registered supplier has a documented quality system and follows it in its operations. In some cases, ISO 9000 registration will reduce the number of independent audits otherwise conducted by customers. While some registrars encourage advertising registration as a market advantage, some also prohibit advertising that registration signifies a product evaluation or high quality.

Nature of the Assessment

The Baldrige Award's focus is the customer and the marketplace.

A Baldrige Award evaluation involves a four-stage review conducted by a volunteer, private sector Board of Examiners. An application may be reviewed by from 5 to 15 Board members, depending upon how far an application progresses in the Award process. Final contenders receive site visits (2 to 5 days) by a team of 6 to 8 Examiners. The Baldrige Award's focus is the customer and the marketplace. Strong evidence of pervasive improvement, backed by results, must be in place. Improvement needs to take into account both customer-related and operations-related factors. It may also include relevant financial indicators provided that they are tied to the other indicators. Conformity and documentation are addressed in the Baldrige Award assessment as part of process management. However, this assessment cannot be described as an audit or a conformity assessment.

The ISO 9000 focus is on the documentation of a quality system and on conformity to that documentation.

The ISO 9000 assessment involves an evaluation of the organization's quality manual and working documents, a detailed site audit to ensure conformance to stated practices and periodic re-audits after registration. The ISO 9000 focus is on the documentation of a quality system and on conformity to that documentation.

Feedback

All applicants for the Baldrige Award receive feedback covering 28 examination items in seven categories. The feedback is diagnostic, highlighting strengths and areas for improvement in an applicant's overall competitiveness management system. Three scoring dimensions—approach, deployment, and results are used in the diagnosis.

ISO 9000 audit feedback covers discrepancies and findings related to practices and documentation. This feedback takes the form of major and minor nonconformities. The organization's documented quality system requirements and deployment of these requirements are used in the assessment.

Criteria Improvement

The Baldrige Award criteria booklet is revised annually to capture lessons learned from each Award cycle. Since 1988, the document has undergone six cycles of improvement, becoming more business-management focused. Major changes over the six years include a greater results orientation, more emphasis on speed, competitiveness, and productivity, improved integration of quality and other business management requirements, greater emphasis on human resource development, and better accommodation to service organizations' requirements.

Revisions of ISO 9001, 9002, and 9003 will be issued in 1994, with a focus on clarification of the 1987 documents, themselves based on the first commercial quality system standard, BS 5750, developed in 1979 (Sawin and Hutchens, 1991). The roots of BS 5750 trace to MIL-Q-9858A, established by the U.S. Department of Defense in 1959. Since 1987, additional ISO 9000 guidance documents have been and are being developed.

Responsibility for Information Sharing

Baldrige Award winners are required to share non-proprietary information on their successful quality strategies with other U.S. organizations.

ISO 9000 registrants have no obligation to share information with others.

Service Quality

About 80% of the U.S. economy, including several large sectors—government, healthcare, and education—are engaged in service. A principal concern in guiding the Baldrige Award criteria evolution has been compatibility with service excellence. Beginning with the customer-driven-quality definition which underlies the criteria, the criteria and supporting information are evaluated to improve compatibility with requirements for service excellence. There is now wide agreement that Baldrige Award criteria are fully relevant to service organizations. In addition, the single most important "process" item in the criteria (Customer Relationship Management) is a principal concern of service organizations, but also a major concern for manufacturers which seek competitive advantage via service.

ISO 9000 standards are directed towards the demonstration of a supplier's capability to control the processes that determine the acceptability of product or service, including design processes in ISO 9001. ISO 9000 standards are more oriented toward repetitive processes, without an equivalent focus on critical service quality issues such as relationship management and human resource development.

A principal concern in guiding the Baldrige Award criteria evolution has been compatibility with service excellence.

Scope of Coverage

The Baldrige Award criteria address all operations and processes of all work units, as the goal is improving overall company productivity, responsiveness, effectiveness, and quality. This approach offers wide latitude in developing customer-focused cost reduction strategies, such as re-engineering of business processes.

ISO 9001 registration covers only design/development, production, installation, and servicing. Registration covers parts of several items in the Baldrige Award criteria (primarily, parts of Management of Process Quality). The ISO 9001 requirements address less than 10% of the scope of the Baldrige criteria, and do not fully address any of the 28 criteria items. All the ISO 9001 requirements are within the scope of the Baldrige Award. Due to the broader nature of the Baldrige criteria and assessment, a rigorous audit of a printed quality manual and compliance with its procedures does not occur during a Baldrige assessment.

Documentation Requirement

The Baldrige Award criteria do not spell out an ongoing documentation requirement for Award applicants. The criteria imply that documentation should be tailored to fit requirements and circumstances, including internal, contractual, or regulatory requirements. Some analysts confuse the Baldrige Award *application* report with an *ongoing* documentation requirement. The Award assessment relies upon evidence and data, but this does not define or prescribe a documentation system.

For ISO 9000 registration, documentation is a central audit requirement. Documentation requirements are ongoing, meaning that documents are a permanent part of the quality system, needed to maintain registration.

The principal use of the Baldrige Award criteria is in self-assessment of improvement practices.

Self-Assessment

The principal use of the Baldrige Award criteria is in self-assessment of improvement practices. The inclusion of a scoring system and evaluation factors allows companies to chart their own progress. Some companies correlate their progress in Baldrige criteria self assessment with changes in financial indicators.

ISO 9000 standards are used primarily in "contractual situations" or other external audits.

ISO 9000 standards are used primarily in "contractual situations" or other external audits. Additional registrar-developed audit check lists define the actual criteria/requirements for registration. Registration by an external assessor is needed to fulfill most contractual requirements (i.e., self-assessment is generally not accepted). Aside from the benefits of self-assessment during the process of pursuing registration, it is not clear that ISO 9000 self-assessment after registration leads to operational improvement. This is because the standards do not address continuous improvement or competitiveness factors.

Acknowledgment

The authors thank the following people for critical reading of the manuscript and for helpful suggestions: Mark Bohannon, Richard Buetow, David Crowell, Sam Kramer, Jim Lynch, Robert Osterhoff, Bill Smith, Fred Smith, Joe Tsiakals, and Craig Walter. The authors particularly appreciate the continuing suggestions received from Maureen Breitenberg and John Donaldson as the manuscript evolved. The opinions and conclusions expressed in the paper are the authors'.

References

1. R. W. Peach, "Creating a Pattern of Excellence", *Target*, Vol. 6, No. 4, Winter 1990, p. 15.

2. *1994 Award Criteria*, Malcolm Baldrige National Quality Award, U.S. Department of Commerce, Technology Administration, National Institute of Standards and Technology, Gaithersburg, MD 20899. The criteria booklet is available, free of charge, phone: 301-975-2036.

3. ISO 9000-1987, Quality Management and Quality Assurance Standards-Guidelines for Selection and Use

> ISO 9001-1987, Quality Systems—Model for Quality Assurance in Design/Development, Production, Installation and Servicing.
> ISO 9002-1987, Quality Systems—Model for Quality Assurance in Production and Installation
> ISO 9003-1987, Quality Systems—Model for Quality Assurance in Final Inspection and Test.
> ISO 9004-1987, Quality Management and Quality System Elements—Guidelines.
> These standards are available in the United States as ANSI/ASQC Q90-1987 through Q94-1987, from the American National Standards Institute, New York, N.Y, and the American Society for Quality Control, Milwaukee, WI.

4. J. S. Finlay, "ISO 9000, Malcolm Baldrige Award Guidelines and Deming/SPC-based TQM—A Comparison", *Quality Systems Update*, August 1992, p. 1.

5. K. Bemowski, "The State of the States", *Quality Progress*, Vol. 26, No. 5 1993, pp. 27-36.

6. W. B. Smith, Jr., "Total Customer Satisfaction as a Business Strategy", *Quality and Reliability Engineering International*, Vol. 9, 1993, pp. 49-53.

7. S. D. Sawin and S. Hutchens, Jr., "ISO-9000 in Operation". *1991 ASQC Quality Congress Transactions*, Milwaukee, WI., pp. 915-916.

8. GAO, "Management Practices—U.S. Companies Improve Performance through Quality Efforts," GAO/NSIAD 91-190, U.S. Government General Accounting Office, Washington, D.C., 1991, 42 pages.

Quality References

We have created *The Quality Yearbook* for your use as an anthology and reference to the quality management movement. Parts One to Three are the anthology part of the book. Part Four is the reference part. Several sections make up this reference, each with its own list of information sources on total quality management. Specifically, you'll find:

- **Comprehensive Annotated Bibliography.** We have ordered this in a similar way to the book's organization. It lists hundreds of articles and books on quality management from a large number of sources. This bibliography is current through the fall of 1993, and should serve as the first place to turn to find more information on any aspect of quality management in which you have interest.
- **Annotated Directory of Organizations.** There are now many U.S. and international organizations that emphasize the study and practice of quality management principles and techniques. This section provides a complete alphabetical listing of all such organizations, both U.S. and international.
- **Directory of Quality Awards.** Many states now have their own quality awards. This section seeks to catalog those awards, with information on the categories for applying, award criteria, and how to get more information. This section also includes brief descriptions of some of the more prominent international awards, with addresses and phone numbers for getting more information.
- **Directory of Magazines and Journals.** This section lists more than 50 different publications that focus on or regularly include articles on quality management. This list rates the magazines according to their usefulness to managers learning about quality.
- **Training in Quality: A Guide to Making Training Decisions for Your Organization.** This section includes a review of the types of training materials now available with advice on making the soundest training decisions for quality management.
- **Quality Quotes.** We have included a selection of quotations from many different people, including writers, philosophers, and practicing managers. These are food for thought and can be helpful when planning a speech or writing a report.

- **Glossary**. We feel especially good about the quality glossary we have included. This is more comprehensive than any other now available. It is almost like a mini-textbook to help you understand the many concepts TQM has promulgated.
- **The 1993 Baldrige Award Winners and the 1994 Baldrige Award Criteria.** Despite the fact that the winners and criteria are announced less than three months prior to the publication of this book, we felt it was vital to be able to provide our readers with this information. By special arrangement with our production staff and the publisher, we are able to include this information for you.
- **Index**. We have prepared a detailed index to supplement the table of contents. This should be very valuable in helping you find more information on many topics covered in our anthology.
- **Feedback Survey**. We have included postage-paid forms with the purpose of finding out what you think of this book. We encourage you to fill these in as appropriate, giving us the direction we need to more effectively meet your quality management information needs. We will report on what you told us in the next edition and use these to continuously improve this book. Our strategy for putting together subsequent editions is to modify and adapt it all the way through the production process, right up until McGraw-Hill says the book is going to the printer. So it is never too late to make suggestions for improvement. Thanks.

Annotated Bibliography of Quality Books and Articles

This bibliography provides you with a quick reference to books, articles, and some video tapes published from late 1992 and through the fall of 1993. We organized the bibliography in a manner similar to the categories in *The Quality Yearbook* itself. The listing of materials is not definitive—that in itself would take a book-length publication to cover everything coming out on quality practices. Rather, we have selected materials with one purpose in mind: to help you review quickly what is being written currently in your industry or functional area.

The best way to use this bibliography is to look at items in your industry and then by topics of interest to you. We strongly suggest that you look through the listings in several catergories when you are searching for a publication on a certain topic since many topics overlap. Note also what journals and magazines are publishing in areas of interest to you because you can expect these to continue offering materials in the years to come.

We would like to have feedback on what you think of this section of the book. Please use the card at the end of the book to give us your reactions and any suggestions for making it more useful to you.

MANUFACTURING SECTOR
General Trends

Carbone, Dominick F. "What's New with Quality Programs," *Management Review* 82, no. 5 (May 1993): 57.

Reports that only a small percentage of U.S. manufacturing firms have fully adopted TQM and that the most fundamental issue being ignored is the empowerment of the workforce.

Ettlie, John E. "Revisiting the 'House of Quality' Foundations," *Production* 105, no. 4 (April 1993): 26.

Survey of QFD deployment in 46 firms suggests what works best. Four critical success factors for these firms are presented.

Manrodt, Karl B.,and Davis, Frank W., Jr. "The Evolution to Service Response Logistics," *International Journal of Physical Distribution and Logistics* 22, no. 9 (1992): 3–10.

This describes the components of an effective logistics process, with suggestions.

Mattsson, Jan. "Quality Blueprints of Internal Producer Services," *International Journal of Service Industry Management* 4, no. 1 (1993): 66–80.

Describes how new industrial services are started, with case studies of two firms.

Pine, B. Joseph, II. *Mass Customization: The New Frontier in Business Competition.* Boston: Harvard Business School Press, 1993.

Probably one of the most important books to appear on manufacturing in a decade, it describes how to organize manufacturing to produce essentially tailored products using mass production methods.

Shipman, Alan. "Quality Defects," *International Management* 48, no. 4 (May 1993): 58–59.

European companies are applying for quality certification in greater numbers as a way to increase the focus of their quality activities while reducing or avoiding costs of major TQM programs.

Suzaki, Kiyoshi. *The New Shop Floor Management: Empowering People for Continuous Improvement.* New York: Free Press, 1993.

This is a comprehensive review of how to manage shop floor activities using quality management principles. It is detailed and significant.

Automotive

Anonymous. "Target Costing Support Systems: Lessons From Leading Japanese Companies," *Management Accounting Research* 4, no. 1 (March 1993): 33–47.

Describes concerns Toyota is having with JIT systems and then describes target costing as a new management control system at the company.

Danjin, Dick. "Making Things Run Well," *Journal For Quality and Participation* (March 1993): 40–44.

The author is with the United Automobile Workers and presents a worker's view of process improvement involving customer satisfaction in his industry.

Ealey, Lance, and Mercer, Glenn. "The Showroom as Assembly Line," *McKinsey Quarterly* no. 3 (1992): 103–120.

Describes trends in the development of automobiles and current activities in this area. Predicts future developments.

Ernst & Young. *International Quality Report: Automotive Industry Report.* Cleveland: American Quality Foundation and Ernst & Young, 1992.

This is an important worldwide survey of quality practices in this industry, covering a wide range of practices and policies.

Green, Norbert, and Reder, Martin. "DFM Boosts U.S. Car Quality," *Machine Design* 65, no. 9 (May 14, 1993): 61–64.

Delco Chassis Division is applying design for manufacturing techniques that are described in this article in detail.

Hall, Robert W. "The Challenges of the Three-Day Car," *Target* 9, no. 2 (March–April 1993): 21–29.

Describes agile manufacturing in the automotive industry and the challenges in achieving it. This is a comprehensive introduction to the issues, topics facing manufacturers in many industries.

Williams, Melanie. "Cottoning on to the Need for Change," *TQM Magazine* 5, no. 1 (February 1993): 35–38.

The author describes how a British automotive company (Cotton) fundamentally changed its culture and its business strategies by implementing quality programs and quality certification.

Wolak, Jerry. "Auto Industry Quality: What Are They Doing?" *Quality* (January 1993): 16–22.

Focusing on the American automotive industry, this is a survey of recent trends in quality practices.

Electronics

Clark, Tom, et al. "Intel's Circuitous Route to Implementing Total Quality," *Quality* (February 1993): 25, 27, 29.

A nice compliment to the Stout article below, it is a case study of how it was done in this computer chip manufacturing firm, which experienced both frustrations and successes with quality programs.

Fishbach, Philip. "Leadership Through Quality Programs Saves Xerox Millions," *Corporate Controller* 5, no. 3 (January–February 1993): 44–46.

With a financial focus to the story, Xerox's experience with quality processes is once again described.

Kirby, John. "Battling with Success," *TQM Magazine* 5, no. 3 (June 1993): 27–30.

Describes the positive experiences of IBM's manufacturing plant in Rochester, Minnesota, which won a Baldrige Award, and the management lessons involved.

Stout, Gail. "Continuous Quality Improvement in the Electronics Industry," *Quality* (February 1993): 16–20, 22.

This is a current overview of trends, identifying common trends in the industry, based primarily on U.S. and Japanese experiences.

Other Manufacturing Industries

Anonymous. "A Team Plant," *Appliance Manufacturer* 41, no. 3 (March 1993): 42–43.

Describes how the Maytag Corporation, a recognized leader in quality practices, created a new plant dominated by empowered employee personnel practices.

Anonymous. "Measure for Measure," *American Printer* 210, no. 4 (January 1993): 59–62.

Describes the use of TQP principles and process improvement and reengineering in a printing company with specific steps taken and quantifiable results achieved.

Anonymous. "TQM Helps You Mind Your Inventory Ps and Qs," *Beverage Industry* (July 1993): 56.

This is a brief overview of a warehouse operation applying TQM. This short report describes the basic steps of the process.

Boaden, Ruth, and Dale, Barrie. "Total Quality Management in the Construction Industry: A Preliminary Analysis," *International Journal of Technology Management* 7, nos. 4–5 (1992): 244–253.

The first major survey of its kind in this industry was done of 28 firms in the United Kingdom. TQM is shown to have made very little progress in the construction industry.

Dennissoff, Basile A. "War with Defects and Peace with Quality," *Quality Progress* 26, no. 9 (September 1993): 97–101.

This is a manufacturing case study, drawing on the experiences of AVX Corporation between 1982 and 1993.

Ernst & Young. *International Quality Study: Computer Industry Report.* Cleveland: American Quality Foundation and Ernst & Young, 1992.

This is an important survey of the quality practices in this industry, based on surveys of companies on several continents. It is the first comprehensive analysis of quality practices in this industry.

Gaynor, Gerard H. *Exploiting Cycle Time in Technology Management.* New York: McGraw-Hill, 1993.

This is a major presentation of quality practices, particularly in a manufacturing environment. It is detailed, technical, yet specific. It is also useful for MIS management.

Gray, James L. "The Total Quality Association," *Association Management* 45, no. 1 (January 1993): 53–58.

Describes how the Manufacturers Association of Central New York (MACNY) applied Baldrige criteria to its own operations similar to what its member companies were doing.

Greenfield, David. "Award Winners Slow Waste Flow to a Trickle," *Modern Paint & Coatings* 83, no. 1 (January 1993): 6–10.

Features efforts at several paint manufacturing companies, detailing waste management processes and successful application of TQM.

Hall, Robert W. *The Soul of The Enterprise: Creating a Dynamic Vision for American Manufacturing.* New York: HarperBusiness, 1993.

Aiming at American businesspeople, the author focuses on best practices evident in companies around the world and includes reviews of such topics as TQM and JIT manufacturing.

Karkada, J. S. "Steeling Itself for Change," *TQM Magazine* 5, no. 3 (June 1993): 43–46.

Describes cultural transformation and TQM practices at the Steel Authority of India, Ltd., world's 10th largest steel firm.

Kelly, A., and Harris, M. J. "Uses and Limits of Total Productive Maintenance," *Professional Engineering* 6, no. 1 (January 1993): 9–11.

Describes a technique for providing shop floor maintenance in a just-in-time manufacturing environment, using cases from Japanese companies. Benefits are also described.

Kendrick, John J. "Whirlpool's World-Class Manufacturing," *Quality* (March 1993): 20–24.

This is a well-written overview of how an appliance manufacturer implemented quality. It is a case study of outstanding success.

Laucis, Peteur K. "1993 to Focus on Quality and the Environment," *Adhesives Age* 36, no. 1 (January 1993): 26–29.

Describes trends and directions in the industry, role of environmental issues and processes, total quality management, and interest in ISO 9000 and Baldrige.

Luciano, Robert. "Packaging by the Numbers 1993: 4 Management Ideas Changing Machinery," *Packaging* 38, no. 1 (January 1993): 45.

Discusses the interrelationship among TQM, environmental issues, and just-in-time manufacturing.

Moody, Patricia E. "Workforce Marketing, Parker Brothers Makes a New Game Plan," *Target* 8, no. 4 (July–August 1992): 22–26.

The manufacturers of Monopoly applied TQM in manufacturing along with new personnel practices. These new methods for manufacturing and personnel management are described.

Parker, Kevin. "Big Blue's Tips on Best Practices," *Manufacturing Systems* 11, no. 6 (June 1993): 14.

Describes IBM's benchmarking services across 20 business processes, designed to improve operations in its manufacturing operations.

Peak, Martha H. "Maquiladoras: Where Quality Is a Way of Life," *Management Review* 82, no. 3 (March 1993): 19–23.

Focusing on Mexico's border factories, the author describes the role of quality circles and TQM programs concentrating on the reduction in the number of manufacturing steps. The problem being addressed is worker productivity since Asian wage rates are now lower than Mexico's.

Sheridan, John H. "Agile Manufacturing: Beyond Lean Production," *Industry Week* 242, no. 8 (April 19, 1993): 30–31, 33, 36–38, 40–41, 44, 46.

This is the latest concept in manufacturing strategies. Using developments in the automotive industry, this article describes this mass customization approach.

Tincher, Michael G. *Top Management's Guide to World Class Manufacturing.* Kansas City, MO.: David W. Buker, Inc., 1993.

This 88-page book briefly introduces the concept of world-class manufacturing practices.

Vickerman, Reed. "Planning for Peace," *Manufacturing Systems* 11, no. 5 (May 1993): 74–76.

Describes how one defense contractor, in need of moving into new markets due to U.S. defense budget cutbacks, is reacting by improving the quality of its operations.

Whittle, Alan, and MacNiven, Sandy. "A Multiple Application," *TQM Magazine* 5, no. 2 (April 1993): 27–30.

This is a case study of the application of TQM within Wavin, a Dutch manufacturer of plastic pipes, over a period of four years.

Witt, Clyde E. "ISO 9000: A Road Map for World Class Manufacturing; How Square D Does It," *Material Handling Engineering* 48, no. 1 (January 1993): 49–54.

The value of this case study is that it moves beyond the ISO 9000 descriptions so common in the literature to an actual case study.

Other Process Industries

Anonymous. "Equipment Users Push for Quality: Chemical Producers Plan to Make Equipment Suppliers and Their Products Part of Total Quality Management," *Chemical Business* (January 1993): 17.

States why chemical producers are expanding TQM out to their suppliers, and describes ISO 9000 certification

as a major reason. Explains what processes are of great concern to the industry.

Anonymous. "Enviro Service Firms are Mixed on Benefits of TQM Techniques," *Environment Today* 4, no. 3 (March 1993): 9.

Presents the results of a survey showing 50 percent of the firms have a TQM program. Offers reasons for success and failure.

Anonymous. "Keeping Total Quality on Track: Perspectives on the Consultant's Fee," *Chemical Week* 3 (September 30, 1992): 48.

Argues that a real challenge is finding employees skilled in TQM and on how to implement quality programs.

Anonymous. "Paper Mill Online Process Control Use and Technology Rises to Aid Total Quality Management Programs in 1990s," *American Papermaker* (March 1993): 19.

Points out how the number of on-line process control systems are rising as a result of TQM practices in pulp and paper mills. They are described along with their benefits.

SERVICES SECTOR
Hotels & Restaurants

Anonymous. "Four Seasons Hotels: Is Tops in Customer Service, According to a 'Business Travel News' Poll," *Fortune* (May 31, 1993): 80.

Key to its success lies in providing business travelers with services they want.

Driben, Louise I. "The Service Edge," *Sales and Marketing Management* 145, no. 6 (June 1993): 80–84.

Describes trends in improved services to hotel customers in the United States.

Dumas, Rene Babich. "Westin Plans Streamlined Room–Service Operations," *Business Travel News* (January 25, 1993): 2.

Describes how this chain introduced new services through process work and piloting. The services are also described along with the results. The effort was to be completed by end of 1993.

Harnett, Michael. "Hyatt Staff Teaches Lesson in Service," *Discount Store News* (May 3, 1993): 105.

Describes a career day program for children held at the hotel as a method of sensitizing employees to customer needs. Seen as a very effective project.

Harnett, Michael. "Marriott Addresses Quality Service By Taking Care of Its Employees," *Discount Store News* (May 3, 1993): 105.

This case study focuses on employees, unlike most articles on quality in the hotel industry. It is specific in what this major hotel chain does in the area of human resources.

Henderson, Cheri. "Putting on the Ritz," *TQM Magazine* 2, no. 5 (November–December 1992): 292–296.

The quality efforts of the Ritz Carlton hotel chain, winner of a 1992 Baldrige Award, are described. The report contains specific statements of cost justification.

Koss, Laura. "A Group Effort," *Hotel & Management Review* 208, no. 14 (August 16, 1993): 38, 42.

Describes special meetings marketing programs at a variety of hotels; describes the process.

Koss, Laura. "Belmonte Sets Ramada Recovery," *Hotel & Motel Management* 208, no. 6 (April 5, 1993): 3, 36.

Describes how this chain is using quality as a strategy to recover its position in the market. It is a turnaround case study.

Macdonald, Julie. "Survival Tied to Quality Management," *Hotel & Motel Management* 208, no. 14 (August 16, 1993): 3, 43.

Reports on a hotel conference in which various CEO's called for application of quality principles and reported hard data on positive results (e.g., personnel turnover down from 100% to 30%).

Sparks, Beverly. "Guest History: Is It Being Utilized?" *International Journal of Contemporary Hospitality Management* 5, no. 1 (1993): 22–27.

The author describes how guest history information can be used to target customer groups and in creating brand loyalty. Reports survey of 114 hotels and how best to go about improving customer service and marketing.

Wagner, Grace. "Checking Out Check In," *Lodging Hospitality* 49, no. 7 (June 1993): 40–42.

This tells the story of the check-in process at the Hyatt, Hilton, and Marriott hotels. It is an introduction to reservation processes.

Watkins, Edward. "Lodging's Summit Meeting IV," *Lodging Hospitality* 49, no. 1 (January 1993): 28–34.

Describes how Westin Hotels & Resorts is using quality strategies to be successful. Comments about the use of TQM by other firms are presented as well.

Zetlin, Minda. "When 99 Percent Isn't Enough," *Managegment Review* 82, no. 3 (March 1993): 49–52.

Reviews the quality program at the Four Seasons Hotels, citing its experiences in Japan.

Banking

Anonymous. "Banc One: Is Said to be the Best in the Banking Industry, in Terms of Customer Service," *Fortune* (May 31, 1993): 76.

Describes the bank's customer satisfaction survey process.

Anonymous. "Building Strong Customer Relations: Co-branding and Affinity Marketing and Service Programs Can Help Banks Build Customer Loyalty," *Bank Marketing Magazine* (June 1993): 16.

How MasterCard does this is the topic of this article. It is a specific "how done" case study.

Anonymous. "Cost Effectiveness Chic," *Institutional Investor* 27, no. 4 (April 1993): 133.

Presents survey results concerning application of TQM by pension plans.

Anonymous. "Putting Technology In Its Place: Huntington Bancshares: Discusses Bank's Use of Technology in Providing Customer Service," *Bank Technology News* (May 1993): 4.

This is a description of customer focus, process work, management attitudes, and the application of computer technology in an effective manner; useful case study.

Anonymous. "Waterhouse Securities: Is Cited for Its Attention to Customer Service, In the Discount Brokerage Industry," *Fortune* (May 31, 1993): 80.

A combination of low rates and full range of financial offerings contributed to this company's high customer satisfaction rating.

Agarwal, Anita, and Bajaj, Mukesh V. "Beyond More Compliance," *Mortgage Banking* 53, no. 7 (April 1993): 57–63.

This is an overview of quality trends across the entire banking industry, from warehouse banks to retail institutions, all driven by customer demands for quality service.

Anonymous. "Want a Baldrige? Make Employees Feel Loved," *ABA Banking Journal* 85, no. 2 (February 1993): 7–9.

This is one of the first articles to appear within the banking industry in the United States to argue the benefits of making employees happy. AT&T Universal Card Service personnel practices are described. This part of AT&T won a Baldrige Award.

Bird, Anat. "One Bank's Approach to Total Quality Management," *Bankers Magazine* 176, no. 3 (May–June 1993): 63–68,

Marquette Bank of Minneapolis presents a positive case study for TQM implementation, with recommendations to other banks.

Boaden, R. J., and Dale, B. G. "Teamwork in Services: Quality Circles by Another Name?" *International Journal of Service Industry Management* 4, no. 1 (1993): 5–24.

Citing the case study of a British bank, the authors studied four branches using quality improvement teams. Results reported were mixed; explains why.

Bogan, Christopher, and Robbins, John. "Steal This Idea," *Mortgage Banking* 53, no. 3 (December 1992): 55–61.

Focus is on the benchmarking activities of a mortgage company, its benefits, specific application, and how the process is managed.

Chebat, Jean C., and Filiatrault, Pierre. "The Impact of Waiting in Line on Consumers," *International Journal of Bank Marketing* 11, no. 2 (1993): 35–40.

Focuses on how to reduce cycle time in doing business with a bank, looking at what banks can do to make it faster for customers to perform transactions. Waiting time is the specific case studied; suggestions on how to improve are offered.

Crawford, Robert. "Service You Can Bank On," *TQM Magazine* 5, no. 1 (February 1993): 53–56.

Describes what the Royal Bank of Scotland did with process improvement techniques to improve customer service. This is a comprehensive look at all their actions as a strategic initiative.

Day, Jacqueline. "Commerce Connection," *Bank Systems and Technology* 30, no. 4 (April 1993): 50–55.

Heralds the arrival of reengineering to banks in the United States. Discusses what processes and business activities are receiving their attention.

Fraser, Bruce W. "24-Carat Banking: Set High Service Standards," *Corporate Cashflow* 14, no. 7 (June 1993): 24–28.

Describes how an increasing number of corporate treasury managers are setting the firm's quality standards and why. More than for just banks, this article is targeted at CFO's.

Furlong, Carla B. "12 Rules for Customer Retention," *Bank Marketing* 25, no. 1 (January 1993): 14–18.

Identifies specific actions that can be taken to curb the serious problems of customer retention faced by this industry.

Hanke, Ed. "The Incredible TQM Journey," *Credit Union Management* 16, no. 6 (June 1993): 40–42.

Presents the values TQM espouses relevant to the credit union movement, such as integrity.

Moore, Herff L., Bounds, William T. Jr., and Bradley, Don B. III. "Employee Involvement in Banks," *Journal for Quality & Participation* 16, no. 3 (June 1993): 34–38.

Describes team programs and the effect they are having on how financial institutions treat their employees; a defense of TQM values in financial institutions.

Hershkowitz, Brian. "TQM in Mortgage Banking," *Mortage Banking* 82, no. 3 (December 1992): 89.

This is a short overview of trends in the use of TQM in mortgage banking, and a call to arms to do more.

Hoke, Gordon E. J. "Gary Wheaton Gives Customer Service," *Bank Automation Quarterly* 18, no. 1 (Spring 1993): 38–40.

Case study of the Gary Wheaton Bank on customer service, describing its centralized customer service information system.

Pittman, Glenis. "Everyday Excellence at Premier Bancorp," *Bank Marketing* 25, no. 4 (April 1993): 10–16.

This is a TQM success story at one bank; interview with senior vice president L. Bliff Motley.

Ernst & Young. *International Quality Study: Banking Industry Report.* Cleveland: American Quality Foundation and Ernst & Young, 1992.

This is a major comprehensive survey of quality practices in the banking industry around the world. It covers all aspects of the subject.

LaPlante, Alice. "Workflow Tool Improves Bank's Customer Service," *Infoworld* 15, no. 14 (April 5, 1993): 62.

Describes the use of software to help answer customer inquiries fast. While the article is primarily about software, the process for handling inquiries is described.

Marshall, Jeffrey. "Smile . . . And Don't Drop the Baton!" *United States Banker* 103, no. 5 (May 1993): 54–57.

Describes a study of why customers leave banks and programs designed to stem the exodus. Its findings are applicable across many industries; this is an important study.

McWhorter, R. P. "Expense Control: Measuring Loan Officers' Productivity," *Commercial Lending Review* 8, no. 2 (Spring 1993): 86–90.

Builds the case for why a measurement is needed and suggests how.

Reynierse, James H. "Building the Quality Service Focused Bank," *Bank Marketing* 25, no. 4 (April 1993): 20–24.

Provides four specific actions one can take to build a service-focused bank.

Richardson, Randall K. "Use Your Data to Improve Your Service Quality," *Bank Marketing* 25, no. 6 (June 1993): 37.

Presents the case for having an accurate profile of customers so as to provide target services.

Rivers, Dale B. "Harnessing the Power of TQM," *Bank Marketing* 25, no. 6 (June 1993): 35–37.

Presents results of a survey of over 50 banks applying TQM; concludes most are implementing only the bottoms up portion of it.

Scott, Miriam Basch. "Employers Implement Total Quality," *Employee Benefit Plan Review* 47, no. 8 (February 1993): 26–28.

Describes how Harris Trust & Savings Bank reengineered personnel policies, focusing on compensation practices.

Seitel, Fraser P. "Do Your Homework!" *United States Banker* 103, no. 8 (August 1993): 57.

Announces that the banking industry has recently started to apply TQM; suggests how other banks can do the same.

Spagnola, Robert G., and Spagnola, Cynthia M. "Total Quality Management in Commercial Lending," *Journal of Commercial Lending* 75, no. 6 (February 1993): 6–17.

A formal statement of what TQM is, followed by how it can be applied in commercial lending institutions.

Sullivan, Michael P. "Marketing to the Mature Woman," *Bankers Magazine* 176, no. 4 (July–August 1993): 68–73.

Argues the case for pinpoint marketing to this group and how it might be done.

Teas, R. Kenneth. "Consumer Expectations and the Measurement of Perceived Service Quality," *Journal of Professional Services Marketing* 8, no. 2 (1993): 33–54.

This very lengthy article is a detailed examination of banking performance against what is today known about customer satisfaction attributes (built on the work of Parasuraman, Zeithaml, and Berry). This is an important study!

Teixeira, Diogo, and Ziskin, Joseph. "Achieving Quality with Customer in Mind," *Bankers Magazine* 176, no. 1 (January–February 1993): 29–35.

Cites the growing trend of banks listening to customers through various methods to understand how to improve services. Results being achieved are described.

Distribution (Wholesale/Retail)

Anonymous. "How To Keep Your Customers," *Hardware Age* (July 19, 1993): 12.

Interviews an executive of the International Hardware Distributors Association who argues the case for increasing customer service by hardware retailers.

Anonymous. "IMRA Study Details Best Customer Service Ideas," *Discount Store News* (June 21, 1993): 26.

Summarizes the contents of the report, called "Best Practices in Retail Customer Service." It contains suggestions for improving services made by customers; some of the ideas in the report are included in this article.

Anonymous. "Service Lifts Thriftway Sales," *Supermarket News* (July 19, 1993): 47.

This case study focuses on West Linn Thriftway in West Linn, Oregon, and includes positive results from its approach.

Anonymous. "Serving Up Quality to Your Customers," *Traffic Management* 32, no. 6 (June 1993): 54–59.

This is the third of a series published on the physical distribution of goods using quality practices. This focuses on how to coordinate activities with carriers to improve delivery times.

Anonymous. "Total Quality Management: A Proven Performer. Total Quality Management Programs Lead to Maximum Effectiveness in Firms of All Sizes," *Automatic Merchandiser* (May 1993): 38.

This article reports on why quality works at ARA, and on the results of a U.S. government study on the effectiveness of quality programs.

Benneyan, James C., and Chute, Alan D. "SPC, Process Improvement, and the Deming PDCA Circle in Freight Administration," *Production & Management Journal* 34, no. 1 (First Quarter 1993): 35–40.

Describes the experience of Digital Equipment Corporation's process for paying freight distributors, the process, and how it was improved; applicable lessons across many industries.

Hammer, Michael. "Reengineering," *Retail Business Review* 61, no. 3 (March–April 1993): 10–19.

This repeats the same message from his previous article and new book on the same subject. It also mentions his work with Taco Bell, an American fast food restaurant.

Halverson, Richard. "Target Empowers Employees To Be Fast, Fun and Friendly," *Discount Store News* (May 3, 1993).

This is an important, trend-setting case study of the application of quality-based employee practices to enhance customer service. It focuses on what the role of employees is on the store floor.

Harnett, Michael. "Disney 'Cast Members' Put 'Guests' In the Spotlight," *Discount Store News* (May 3, 1993): 86.

Like so many other articles on Disney Corporation, this one focuses on the role of employees in dealing with customers, what they do, how, and the positive results obtained.

Lore, Jonathan A. "Which Q Is Right For You?" *Industrial Distribution* 82, no. 6 (June 1993): 73–76.

Describes a four-step quality implementation process applicable to distributors and offers a good overview of various quality-focused strategies.

Matza, Bruce R. "The Science of Value," *Retail Business Review* 61, no. 3 (March–April 1993): 20–27.

Describes how to measure the value of service using five elements. Employees play a critical role in retaining customers; describes how.

Muroff, Cindy. "Zeroing in on Benchmarking," *Distribution* 92, no. 1 (January 1993): 87–88.

Focuses on the use of beanchmarking in improving the order-picking process. Has some suggestions on warehouse layout as well.

Nel, Deon, and Pitt, Leyland. "Service Quality in a Retail Environment: Closing the Gaps," *Journal of General Management* 18, no. 3 (Spring 1993): 37–56.

Reports that quality programs are working in this industry; reports on the reasons for their use.

Peterson, Betsy. "Interviewers: The Vital Link to Consumer Cooperation," *Marketing Research* 5, no. 2 (Spring 1993): 48–49.

A useful introduction to interviewing processes of consumers, and how it is best done.

Richardson, Helen L. "Can You Find Quality by Association?" *Transportation and Distribution* 34, no. 5 (May 1993): 45–48.

Describes how to select a third-party logistics service provider; a process overview, tactical in approach.

Robins, Gary. "Strategic Planning," *Stores* 75, no. 5 (May 1993): 48–52.

Describes how the use of more technology yields more data faster, which is allowing companies to react to their markets quicker.

Tehrani, Nadji. "Customer Service and Inbound Marketing: The New, Powerful Way to Expand Market Share," *Telemarketing Magazine* 11, no. 9 (March 1993): 2, 76.

Takes several case studies of how inbound marketing improves customer service, citing specific, quantifiable results.

Insurance

Anonymous. "Management: Taking Quality to Heart—A Cultural Change at Legal & General," *Financial Times* (August 9, 1993): 8.

Reports on the positive experience with TQM enjoyed by a British insurance company, gaining improved services, lowered costs, and higher levels of client satisfaction.

Britton, Donald. "First Colony Life Insurance Company," *Broker World* 13, no. 1 (January 1993): 52, 60.

Heralds the arrival of quality practices in this industry and uses this company to describe how product development in insurance offerings is done.

Burger, Katharine. "The Ultimate End User?" *Insurance & Technology* 18, no. 2 (February 1993): 26–30.

Compares and contrasts the insurance functions of U.S. government agencies with those in the private sectors, suggesting pressures working on each one are different, thus influencing what they can do to improve operational efficiencies.

Campbell, John D. "The Life Insurance Industry: Getting Back to Basics with Quality Products and Services," *Mid America Insurance* 102, no. 2 (February 1993): 6–8.

In an industry that is only just starting to apply TQM, this short article is a primer on how to get started.

Jackson, Don. "Your Next Choice: Compare Customer Service with Customer Satisfaction," *Life and Health Insurance Sales* 136, no. 2 (February 1993): 26–27.

Argues that insurance companies are being compared to other service-based companies by customers and, therefore, insurance companies have to build processes that are competitive with those of other firms outside their industry. Customer focus and expectations are at the heart of the effort.

Knowles, Robert G. "Quality Service At Life Companies: A Passing Fad?," *National Underwriter's Life & Health* (June 28, 1993): 40ff.

Reports on growing interest in quality practices in the life insurance industry that historically has paid little attention to the quality movement.

O'Hare, Edward. "Reengineering at Aetna," *Life & Health Insurance Sales* 136, no. 6 (June 1993): 25–26.

Aetna Life Insurance and Annuity Co. is the subject of this case study. New products were developed with much input from employees in the field.

Rich, D. Layne. "Quality Service: Who Cares? (And How Much?)," *LIMRA's Marketfacts* 12, no. 3 (May–June 1993): 14–17.

Reports on what three industry organizations found out when they studied the question "what is customer service?" as it applied to their industry. As in other industries, the discussion quickly focused on customer expectations, degrees of this, and industry responses.

Woolsey, Christine. "Outcome Measurements Raise Doubts," *Business Insurance* 27, no. 27 (June 28, 1993): 1, 22.

This is the fastest growing area of interest in health care insurance measurements. Describes current trends and defines the concept.

Transportation

Anonymous. "A Rebuilder Reaches Out. Atelier Montreal Facility: This Rail Rebuilding Business, Once CN Rail Operation Profiled," *Railway Age* (January 1993): 47–49.

Describes the application of quality practices at the Atelier Montreal Facility, a rail rebuilding company once part of the Canadian National. Details its current business plans.

Anonymous. "Total Quality Management in Logistics: Case Study of the Trucking Industry," *Innovator's Digest* (February 2, 1993).

Summarizes a Master's thesis at the U.S. Naval Postgraduate School, looking at logistics and the trucking industry. The case study is of Deming practices in Mason Transporters, Inc., with detailed assessments of approach and results.

Other Services

Anonymous. "Enviro Service Firms Are Mixed on Benefits of TQM Techniques," *Environment Today* 4, no. 3 (March 1993): 9.

The reasons for their reaction are explained, based on a survey of 50 companies of which half were not yet happy with the results of their efforts.

Anonymous. "Hertz: Is Said To Be First in Customer Service, in the Car Rental Industry," *Fortune* (May 31, 1993): 76.

The reason is its #1 Club Gold program, which is described. Long lines at rental counters are thus avoided.

Anonymous. "United Parcel Service: Is Noted for Offering Choice as Well as Value in Its Customer Service," *Fortune* (May 31, 1993): 88.

In the package delivery business, UPS was successful because of the nature of its services, which are described; compared to Federal Express, another firm recognized for its successful implementation of quality-based practices.

Boaden, Ruth, and Dale, Barrie. "Total Quality Management in the Construction Industry: A Preliminary Analysis," *International Journal of*

Technology Management 7, nos. 4–5 (1992): 244–253.

Presents results of a survey of 28 British construction firms and concludes TQM has hardly been introduced in this industry. It is a useful case study of barriers to quality practices.

Bower, Ward. "In Search of Excellence: Applying TQM to a Legal Environment," *Law Practice Management* 19, no. 3 (April 1993): 22–29.

Describes what TQM looks like in a legal practice and how to implement it. It is one of the few articles available on TQM and the legal profession.

Cavaness, Joseph P., and Manoochehri, G. H. "Building Quality Into Services," *SAM Advanced Management Journal* 58, no. 1 (Winter 1993): 4–8ff.

Compares quality programs in services to manufacturing, then how they should appear in service delivery organizations.

Federow, Harold. "Total Quality Management and the Law: A Survey of Legal Issues Relating to Implementation of TQM," *Commercial Law Journal* 98, no. 1 (Spring 1993): 96–116.

Discusses U.S. antitrust law considerations, torts, and insider trading considerations, all potential problem areas created by TQM practices.

House, Robert J. "Charismatic Leadership in Service Producing Organizations," *International Journal of Service Industry Management* 3, no. 2 (1992): 5–16.

Summarizes research of various individuals regarding the role of leadership in service-based organizations. Vision-based leadership has the capability of improving a service organization's performance.

Leuhlfing, Michael S. "Driving Out Inefficiency," *Management Accounting* 74, no. 9 (March 1993): 33–36.

Describes how an accountant can do process work, citing the case of credit card payments at a parking garage. Emphasis is on how to identify and solve problems.

Reid, Douglas. "Wireless Connector," *Canadian Manager* 18, no. 1 (Spring 1993): 20–21 +.

Describes how focus on customer service made it possible for the growth in cellular business to expand dramatically for Bell Mobility in Canada. Emphasis is on customer service-based processes.

Siehl, Caren. "Cultural Leadership in Service Organizations," *International Journal of Service Industry Management* 3, no. 2 (1992): 17–22.

Lists four key leadership challenges in service organizations for the 1990s, then argues how service organizations performance will be influenced by their culture.

Southworth, Miles and Donna. *How to Implement Total Quality Management.* The Graphic Arts Publishing Co., 1993.

This is a 128-page book on how to apply TQM in the world of publishing. It is the definitive industry presentation so far.

Welch, Samuel C. "Total Quality Management in the Performing Arts," *Quality Progress* 26, no. 1 (January 1993): 31–36.

This article illustrates the effective use of TQM strategies in the world of fine arts management with examples of tactics and processes.

PUBLIC SECTOR
Health Care

Anonymous. "Quality Management Targets Health Care," *Nation's Business* (February 1993): 40.

States the case for interest in quality practices in this industry and explains how accreditation in this industry was linked to quality programs; a model for other industries.

Barrett, Mary Jean. "Preventive Systems in a CQI/TQM Environment," *Healthcare Financial Management* 47, no. 8 (August 1993): 22.

Describes the application of preventive systems in a hospital environment, detailing five basic steps.

Benjamin, Marti, and Shaw, James G. "Harnessing the Power of the Pareto Principle," *Quality Progress* 26, no. 9 (September 1993): 103–107.

Describes how the San Jose Medical Group applied the Pareto Principle to improve the process it used to bill insurance companies.

Caldwell, Chip. "What Healthcare Can Learn from TQM's Past," *Healthcare Executive* 8, no. 3 (May–June 1993): 26–28.

Reports on several recent studies suggesting that quality practices are beneficial and what is required of management to achieve such advantages.

Canon, Michael H. "TQM Must Be Based on Data, Analysis to Satisfy Customers," *Modern Healthcare* 23, no. 7 (February 15, 1993): 48.

Describes the kind of data hospitals need in order to improve customer service and what expectations managers should have in seeing results.

Chaufournier, Roger L., and St. Andre, Christine. "Total Quality Management in An Academic Health Center," *Quality Progress* 26, no. 4 (April 1993): 63–66.
This tells the story of how George Washington University Medical Center began applying TQM principles in 1989 with details on strategy, processes, measurements, and results.

Dolan, Thomas C. "Taking TQM Seriously," *Healthcare Executive* 8, no. 3 (May–June 1993): 2.
Describes how the American College of Healthcare Executives is helping expand the use of quality practices in its industry.

Ernst & Young. *International Quality Study: Health Care Industry Report.* Cleveland: American Quality Foundation and Ernst & Young, 1992.
This is a major survey of quality practices across the health industry around the world covering all aspects of the subject.

Gaucher, Ellen M., and Coffey, Richard J. *Total Quality in Health Care: From Theory to Practice.* San Francisco: Jossey-Bass, 1993.
This is a very detailed, large review of how to implement TQM in the health industry; it is part of a series of such volumes being published by Jossey-Bass on TQM by industries.

Hohner, Gregory. "Quality Leadership at Baxter Healthcare Corporation," *Industrial Engineering* 25, no. 1 (January 1993): 31–35.
This case study describes Baxter's TQM strategy and the results achieved. Useful because of the maturity of Baxter's efforts.

Holpp, Lawrence. "Eight Definitions of Quality in Healthcare," *Journal for Quality and Participation* 16, no. 3 (June 1993): 18–26.
These are eight attributes of quality-focused organizations, followed by examples of their application in the health care arena.

Kaluzny, Arnold. "Strategic Alliances Ensure TQM's Full Potential," *Healthcare Executive* 8, no. 3 (May–June 1993): 33–35.
Says that development of strategic business alliances and application of quality practices are major trends in health care management and describes how they are compatible strategies.

Kleeb, Teresa E. "Service Excellence: Unit Based Service Objectives in CQI," *Nursing Management* 24, no. 2 (February 1993): 70–72.
Describes how processes are selected for improvement and what is done by a Care Review Unit, using TQM principles and practices.

Larsen, Gail. "Improving Outpatient Registration with TQM," *Healthcare Financial Management* 47, no. 8 (August 1993): 75–81.
This is a process description for outpatient registration, calling out that cross functional teamwork was the key to successful implementation.

Lopresti, John, and Whetstone, William R. "Total Quality Management: Doing Things Right," *Nursing Management* 24, no. 1 (January 1993): 34–36.
Introduces Deming's ideas to this set of readers.

Lumpason, Kevin. "Hospitals, Suppliers Put TQM to the Test," *Hospitals* 67, no. 6 (March 20, 1993): 58–59.
Describes a conference of 14 vendors of Group Health Cooperative of Puget Sound (Seattle, Washington) to compare notes on the application of TQM. Details of their experiences are offered with an emphasis on doing business with those firms that have a quality-based culture.

MacBridge King, Judith. "Prescription for Change: An Interview On Improving Canada's Health Care System with Donald P. Schurman, President, University of Alberta Hospitals," *Canadian Business Review* 20, no. 2 (Summer 1993): 6–14.
Argues strongly in favor of applying TQM principles in the health care industry, and cites examples from his own organization.

Malone, John. "Creating an Atmosphere of Complete Employee Involvement in TQM," *Healthcare Financial Management* 47, no. 6 (June 1993): 126–127.
Summarizes the Ernst & Young study on the health care industry cited above.

Mozena, James P., and Anderson, Debby L. *Quality Improvement Handbook for Health Care Professionals.* Milwaukee: ASQC Quality Press, 1993.
This short book is a "how to" for practitioners; one of a series of books on the health care industry by this publisher.

Penrod, Phil, and Freeman, Connie. "Memorial Medical Center Takes a Holistic Approach to Organizational Transformation," *National Productivity Review* 12, no. 3 (Summer 1993): 403–416.

This important case study describes how one hospital is transforming its organization, major processes, and employee practices, and improving efficiencies and effectiveness.

Rayworth, J. Fred. "Total Quality Management: Involving Staff in the Search for Perfection," *Health Manpower Management* 19, no. 1 (1993): 25–29.

The health industry is taking considerable interest in TQM. This article reflects that concern by providing an overview of what TQM is and how it is implemented correctly.

Reeves, Carol A., and Bednar, David A. "What Prevents TQM Implementation in Health Care Organizations?" *Quality Progress* 26, no. 4 (April 1993): 41–44.

Relying on the experience of a Veterans Administration medical center, the author describes a survey of 79 managers in the organization about impediments they face to implementing TQM. The results mimic those of other organizations in different industries.

Richards, John D., and Cloutier, Marc G. "TQM, Healthcare Education and Customer Satisfaction," *Journal of Quality and Participation* 16, no. 1 (January–February 1993): 94–96.

Describes how the U.S. Army Medical Department (AMEDD) teaches TQM to its staff and measures the results on customer satisfaction.

Sherer, Jill L. "Crossing Cultures: Hospitals Begin Breaking Down the Barriers to Care," *Hospitals* 67, no. 10 (May 20, 1993): 29–31.

Talks about cultural barriers when non-U.S. patients are admitted into hospitals. This is an example of how an organization can respond to customer service requirements crossing ethnic boundaries.

Steedman, George, and Babbage, Kathleen. "Just What the Doctor Ordered!" *Managing Service Quality* 2, no. 4 (May 1992): 225–26.

Describes specific actions taken by Barnsley District General Hospital to gain certification in the United Kingdom.

Torrey, Eric E. "Why a Focus on Healthcare?" *Industrial Engineering* 25, no. 4 (April 1993): 4.

This editorial comments on why this industry is taking a close look at process reengineering and quality today.

Verespej, Michael A. "Health Care: Cost Controls and Quality Can Coexist," *Industry Week* (January 4, 1993): 18, 22.

Provides examples of cost containment strategies, including the use of wellness programs, with associated processes.

Wachel, Walter. "How TQM May Change Your Job," *Healthcare Executive* 8, no. 3 (May–June 1993): 30–32.

Citing the examples from several hospitals and the experiences of seven health care executives, the author describes what they learned. The lessons relate to the profound changes in the culture, job, and organization of their institutions.

Weinheimer, Christopher F. "Cooperation, Knowledge Are Keys to Controlling Healthcare Costs," *Healthcare Financial Management* 47, no. 7 (July 1993): 10.

Discusses how TQM can help hospitals, particularly in light of the passage of the Healthcare Simplification and Uniformity Act of 1993.

Education—K–12

Bonstingl, John Jay. "The Total Quality Classroom," *Educational Leadership* (March 1992): 66–70.

This is an important article; it describes how to apply Deming's principles in the classroom. Deming is being widely embraced in K–12 education programs today.

Byrnes, Margaret A., Cornesky, Robert A., and Byrnes, Lawrence W. *The Quality Teacher: Implementing Total Quality Management in the Classroom.* Bunnell, Fl.: Cornesky & Associates, 1992.

This is a comprehensive and detailed primer on implementing Deming-like quality programs in school, complete with case studies and examples.

Fields, Joseph C. *Total Quality for Schools: A Suggestion for American Education.* Milwaukee: ASQC Quality Press, 1993.

Describes how to apply Deming-based principles in schools. It is short and to the point.

Goldstein, Leonard J. "Business and Education: The Power of Productive Partnership," *Executive Speeches* 7, no. 5 (April–May 1993): 1–4.

Describes how the Miller Brewing Company is working with schools in Milwaukee, Wisconsin, to improve the quality of education.

Gray, Kenneth. "Why We Will Lose: Taylorism in America's High Schools," *Phi Delta Kappan* (January 1993): 370–387.

This major critique of the U.S. high school system calls for the application of quality-based strategies, with focus on teaching students how to function in teams.

Mazany, Terry. "Putting Service Back Into a School's Central Services," *Journal for Quality and Participation* 16, no. 1 (January–February 1993): 32–36.

The Detroit Public School system applied TQM principles to improve central services to its schools. These are described along with the approach taken.

Moore, Donald R. "Chicago School Reform Meets TQM," *Journal for Quality and Participation* 16, no. 1 (January–February 1993): 6–11.

Describes fundamental changes in the school system since 1989 that involve decentralized decision making (by law) and the application of TQM principles. Critical success factors are reviewed.

Rinehart, Gray. *Quality Education.* Homewood, Ill.:Business One Irwin, 1993.

Describes how W. Edwards Deming's ideas can be applied in schools. This is very much a "how to" and strategic guide, important because so many schools in North America are now looking at Deming's approach.

Schmoker, Mike, and Wilson, Richard B. "Transforming Schools Through Total Quality Education," *Phi Delta Kappan* (January 1993): 389–393.

This is the latest of a long series of articles published in education journals on the benefits of applying Deming's ideas in education. It also includes examples of how this is being done.

Higher Education

Anonymous. "Survey of Business Schools (5): Here the Customers Come First," *Financial Times* (April 20, 1993): 13.

Reports survey results in which the J. L. Kellogg Graduate School of Management at Northwestern University came out as the most "customer" driven and explains what it does.

Artzt, Edwin L. "Advancing TQM," *Executive Excellence* 10, no. 5 (May 1993): 5–6.

Describes TQM activities going on in a forum of higher education in the United States intended to foster application of TQM.

Assar, Kathleen E. "Case Study Number Two: Phoenix Quantum Quality at Maricopa," *Change* 25, no. 3 (May–June 1993): 32–35.

This is a case study of quality practices at a U.S. community college system of 180,000 students.

Ewell, Peter T. "Total Quality Management and Academic Practice: The Idea We've Been Waiting For?" *Change* 25, no. 3 (May–June 1993): 49–55.

This is a defense of the application of TQM in higher education, an industry noted for its lack of application of quality principles. The author lays out the case for its use.

Froiland, Paul. "TQM Invades Business Schools," *Training* 30, no. 7 (July 1993): 52–56.

Positioning TQM as just being introduced into American business schools, the author describes the positive and negative experiences of several universities.

Greenbaum, Stuart I. "TQM at Kellogg," *Journal for Quality and Participation* 16, no. 1 (January–February 1993): 88–92.

TQM at Northwestern University's J.L. Kellogg Graduate School of Management is described. It has one of the best TQM programs in the United States, and its approach is described.

Jacques, March Laree. "National Know-How," *The TQM Magazine* 3, no. 2 (May–June 1993): 41–46.

Based on an interview with Donna Shalala, Chancelor of the University of Wisconsin before joining President Clinton's administration, it details what TQM is about in higher education and how it is being applied at the University of Wisconsin–Madison. Also includes her comments about how she would like to implement TQM as U.S. Secretary of Health and Human Services, the largest department in the U.S. government.

Kendrick, John L. "Universities, Corporations Report Progress in Integrating Total Quality Into Curriculums," *Quality* (January 1993): 13.

Presents results of survey work on the work of five companies and eight universities implementing TQM. Explains the relationships between them and the results of their efforts.

Matthews, William E. "The Missing Element in Higher Education," *Journal of Quality and Participation* 16, no. 1 (January–February 1993): 102–1.

Describes where TQM makes sense in higher education and describes pressure on colleges and universities from business to implement these practices, and how to do so.

Nagy, Joanne, et al. "Case Study Number Three: Madison: How TQM Helped Change An Admissions Process," *Change* 25, no. 3 (May–June 1993): 36–41.
Describes the conversion from a paper-based to a telephone-based admissions process at the University of Wisconsin at Madison.

Schatzberg, D. R. "Total Quality Management for Maintenance Process Improvement," *Journal of Software Maintenance* 5, no. 1 (March 1993): 1–12.
Describes how a major university (University of Wisconsin) applies TQM, and specifically in the area of maintenance. The university has an aggressive TQM program applied in many administrative areas.

Seymour, Daniel. "Quality on Campus: Three Institutions, Three Beginnings," *Change* 25, no. 3 (May–June 1993): 14–27.
This is a substantial review of the efforts at Georgia Institute of Technology, Pennsylvania State University, and the University of Maryland.

Shalala, Donna E. "TQM Applications in Education," *Executive Excellence* 10, no. 5 (May 1993): 6–7.
The then chancellor at the University of Wisconsin–Madison describes how TQM is being applied on her campus in five areas.

Government

Anonymous. "Award Winning Programs: Interviews With the Winners," *Public Personnel Management* 22, no. 1 (Spring 1993): 1–5.
Describes the successes of the Office of Human Resources of the Minnesota Department of Transportation, which received the 1992 International Personnel Management Association (IPMA) Agency Award for Excellence. Focus is on how it decentralized and how it applied TQM.

Anonymous. "Document Management: The Federal Government Develops Document Management Process for Better Customer Service, Save Money, Streamline The Work Flow," *Government Computer News* (March 15, 1993): 53.
Reports on recent TQM initiatives in the U.S. government and on a recent report of the status of these efforts published by the government.

Anthes, Gary H. "State Spurs Process Revamp," *Computerworld* 27, no. 24 (June 14, 1993): 104.
Reports on the State of Washington's Department of Labor and Industries' process reengineering work, which is considered leading-edge in the public sector.

Barrett, Katherine, and Greene, Richard. "Public Sector Wonderland," *Financial World* 162, no. 10 (May 11, 1993): 34–38ff.
Surveys quality efforts in a half dozen U.S. state governments and the issues associated with budget cuts with pressures for increased services. A good review of conditions as of mid–1993.

Barrier, Michael. "Where 'Quality' Is A Language," *Nations Business* (January 1993): 57–59.
This is a case study of how an entire community (Spartanburg, South Carolina) is responding positively to quality practices both in the public and private sector.

Cohen, Steven, and Brand, Ronald. *Total Quality Management in Government: A Practical Guide for the Real World.* San Francisco: Jossey-Bass, 1993.
This is the first practitioner's guide for the application of TQM to appear for the public sector. Earlier books were simply descriptions of what some quality projects were; this is a management guide for governments.

Dopson, Sue. "Are Agencies An Act of Faith? The Experience of HMSO," *Public Money and Management* 13, no. 2 (April–June 1993): 17–23.
Using the case of the British government's printing office (Her Majesty's Stationery Office), the author illustrates how this government agency became more customer focused and reorganized to become more efficient.

General Accounting Office. *U.S. Total Quality Management Utilization and Benefits in the Federal Government.* Washington, D.C.: GPO, 1993.
This is a major survey of practices within the U.S. government. About 68 percent of all agencies are applying quality principles.

Glaser, Mark. "Reconciliation of Total Quality Management and Traditional Performance Improvement Tools," *Public Productivity & Management Review* 16, no. 4 (Summer 1993): 379–386.
Presents discussion of TQM strategies versus more traditional program evaluation and performance measurement and appraisal approaches, a major issue in the public sector.

Gore, Albert, *Creating a Government that Works Better and Costs Less: Report on the National Performance Review.* Washington, D.C.: National Printing Office, 1993.

This is a systematic review of ways to reform the Federal government as an organization based on the principles that underlie TQM.

Hyde, A. C. "Barriers in Implementing Quality Management," *Public Manager* 22, no. 1 (Spring 1993): 33, 36 +.

Aimed at U.S. government managers, the author analyzes why they are not taking TQM seriously enough and real barriers they face in implementing quality programs and reengineering initiatives.

Keehley, Patricia. "Does TQM Spell "Time to Quit Merit'?" *Public Productivity & Management Review* 16, no. 4 (Summer 1993): 387–394.

This is a defense of TQM merit and competitive appointments in the public sector. Should be read by public officials!

Kellough, J. Edward, and Lu, Haoran. "The Paradox of Merit Pay in the Public Sector: Persistence of A Problematic Procedure," *Review of Public Personnel Administration* 13, no. 2 (Spring 1993): 45–64.

Says that pay based on individual performance has failed in the public sector in the U.S. Calls for additional study of the support for merit pay in the face of this failure and defines new ways to compensate people.

Kline, James J. "Quality Tools Are Applicable to Local Government," *Government Finance Review* 9, no. 4 (August 1993): 15–19.

He describes a number of manufacturing tools and techniques being applied successfully in the public sector, such as cause and effect, control charts, and cost of quality concepts.

Kline, James J. "State Governments' Growing Gains from TQM," *National Productivity Review* 12, no. 2 (Spring 1993): 259–271.

This is a good update on what U.S. state governments are doing in the area of quality. The author correctly notes that interest in TQM in the public sector has picked up, and he explains why.

Scully, John. "Can Our Government Watchdogs Support TQM?" *Journal for Quality & Participation* 16, no. 4 (July–August, 1993): 72–75.

Argues that incentives for change in the U.S. government do not exist yet; a call to arms!

Smith A. Keith. "Total Quality Management in the Public Sector," *Quality Progress* 26, no. 6 (June 1993): 45–48, and no. 7 (July 1993): 57–64.

This is a series of two articles on quality efforts in the public sector, focusing on customer focus/support strategies.

Smith, Robert. "Efforts Improve Quality of Life in Viginia Beach," *HR Focus* 70, no. 2 (February 1993): 22.

Describes key TQM-based processes at Virginia Beach, Virginia, including how the city attacks drug problems, provides police protection, and a variety of social services.

Stupak, Ronald J. "Driving Forces for Quality Improvement in the 1990s," *Public Manager* 22, no. 1 (Spring 1993): 32, 34 +.

Describes why public sector managers are being forced to adopt TQM principles (e.g., cost controls, tax payer demands, etc.). It is an introduction to the benefits of quality management.

Zolkos, Rodd. "State Pins Hopes for Better Service on TQM," *City and State* (April 26, 1993): 3.

Describes what the state government of California is doing with quality, and includes comments about what other states are doing both with quality and partnerships with the private sector.

Utilities

Anonymous. "Baltimore Gas & Electric: Is Cited for Customer Service in the Utilities Industries," *Fortune* (May 31, 1993): 88.

Describes its benchmarking with private industry, and its rapid service call process as keys to its success.

Epner, M., and Paramenter, B. "Competitive Utility Environments Require Total Quality Management Techniques," *GIS World* 6, no. 3 (March 1993): 38–41.

Details trends and directions in the industry, its use of quality practices, and the case for specific types of process reengineering in this industry.

Gitlow, H.S., and Loredo, E. N. "Total Quality Management at Florida Power & Light Company: A Case Study," *Quality Engineering* 5, no. 1 (1992–1993): 123–157.

This may be the most thorough case study of FPL done so far and is heavily focused on its work in process reengineering; illustrated with diagrams.

Luthans, Fred, and Kessler, Dan. "Meeting the New Paradigm Challenges Through Total Quality

Management; TQM at Wells REC," *Management Quarterly* 34, no. 1 (Spring 1993): 2–13.

Describes the application of TQM at Wells Rural Electric Company in Nevada in some detail.

Nonprofit Associations

Gray, James L. "The Total Quality Association," *Association Management* 45, no. 1 (January 1993): 53–58.

Argues that TQM is critical to the success of nonprofits, and suggests using the Baldrige Criteria to develop an enterprise-wide strategy.

Katz, Ray, and Greco, JoAnn. "Total Quality Management: Adopting a Customer Oriented Philosophy," *Nonprofit World* 11, no. 2 (March–April 1993): 18–2.

The first of several articles on this theme by these authors. They describe how TQM is being implemented successfully in nonprofits.

Welch, Samuel C. "Total Quality Management in the Performing Arts," *Quality Progress* 26, no. 1 (January 1993): 31–36.

Suggests how a customer-focused, total quality plan can be applied in the performing arts to build customer support and loyalty.

QUALITY TRANSFORMATION

Leadership

Albrecht, Karl. "The Last Days of TQM?" *Quality Digest* 12, no. 11 (November 1992):16–17.

Argues that TQM is beginning to fade as did MBO methods and is being replaced with a return to basic questions about what business to be in and how to satisfy customers. It is a very harsh attack on TQM.

Anderson, Jeffrey W. "Vision Leadership," *Target* 9, no. 2 (March–April 1993): 4–5.

This is a useful summary of what vision-based leadership is, its value, and gives examples of the process at work.

Anonymous. "Staying Off the Scrap Heap and Preparing for the Next Century: Better Management, World Vision Are Sought," *Chemical Week* (May 12, 1993): 54.

This summarizes comments by Frank Popoff, CEO of Dow Chemical, concerning leadership and the role of management. In the process he articulates the value and nature of good vision-based strategic plans.

Aubrey, Charles A. III. "Should the Board of Directors Be Involved in TQM?" *National Productivity Review* 12, no. 3 (Summer 1993): 317–323.

In a fascinating article, the author argues boards today are not involved and, based on a major survey, finds they still feel quality is a function of management. Thinks boards should become involved.

Austin, Nancy K. "The Lowdown on Quality," *Working Woman* 18, no. 3 (March 1993): 22, 26.

Offers the case why senior management must lead the charge in improving quality in an organization and the use of disciplined quality process techniques.

Ballain, Malcolm. "Forging a New Breed of Supervisor," *Personnel Management* 25, no. 4 (April 1993): 34–37.

Describes the role of a supervisor at British Steel, what he does in an environment of total quality management. He presents a model case study.

Barrier, Michael. "Small Firms Put Quality First," *Nations Business* (May 1992): 22ff.

This was one of the first articles to document quality strategies being employed by small American companies and being successful with it. Includes case studies.

Benson, Tracy E. "Quality: If At First You Don't Succeed," *Industry Week* (July 8 1993): 48–59.

The article focuses on presenting a primer to help managers determine which quality strategy to deploy and offers advice on selecting consultants to help in the effort.

Chang, Richard Y. "When TQM Goes Nowhere," *Training and Development* (January 1993): 23–29.

Defines the problem of too much TQM activity with too few results and then provides specific suggestions on how to treat the problem.

Claret, Jake. "In Pursuit of Excellence?" *Management Accounting* 71, no. 1 (January 1993): 12.

A forum of 12 managers with experience in TQM from various industries concluded that top management had to be committed. They define what that commitment is in action.

Cobbe, George B. "Growing Total Quality Into a Management Process," *Business Quarterly* 57, no. 3 (Spring 1993): 96–100.

Describes Hewlett Packard's highly regarded improvement process called Total Quality Control (TQC).

Deming, W. Edwards. *The New Economics for Industry, Government, Education.* Cambridge,

Mass.: MIT Center for Advanced Engineering Study, 1993.

This is a recompilation of Dr. Deming's latest thinking on such issues as his 14 Points, systems, theory of knowledge, and statistical process control. In the world of quality, this is an important publication.

Dennis, Michael C. "Only Superman Didn't Delegate," *Business Credit* 95, no. 2 (February 1993): 41.

Defines what delegation means, targeting credit managers for his comments. His message is applicable to all managers.

Dimitroff, G. R. "Transforming Management," *TQM Magazine* 2, no. 5 (November–December 1992): 280–285.

What makes this article particularly useful is that it recognizes management as a key ingredient in a quality transformation. It also is the only article available that quantifies (as an example of its presentation) that eliminating sales quotas actually improves sales performance!

Dugan, George D. "What the CEO Must Do to Lead the Quality Revolution," *Journal for Quality & Participation* 16, no. 4 (July–August 1993): 20–22.

TQM at Ford Motors and Jabsco Products, Ltd., is presented with specific statements about the role of management.

Ernst & Young. *Best Practices Report: An Analysis of Management Practices That Impact Performance.* Cleveland: American Quality Foundation and Ernst and Young, 1992.

This was one of the first of a series of reports issued by these two organizations presenting the results of a worldwide survey of over 500 organizations active in quality practices. Summarizes current state and practices of these firms; a must-read document.

Fanning, Robert R. "Become a Leader in Collaboration," *Trustee* 46, no. 5 (May 1993): 11.

Suggests that in the health care industry organizations will be successful through collaborative efforts among stakeholders; explains the rationale for his point.

Feigenbaum, Armand V. "A Senior Manager's Quality Mindset: Edge for the 90s," *Journal for Quality and Participation* (March 1993): 36–39.

One of the pioneers of the modern quality movement provides a discussion of what the mindset of senior management does to help or hurt quality. He then describes his keys to quality mastery by management.

Feigenbaum, Armand V. "Creating the Quality Mindset Among Senior Managers," *National Productivity Review* 12, no. 3 (Summer 1993): 313–315.

Suggests that senior management's role in quality implementation is crucial and explains what concepts they must grasp.

Gehani, R. May. "Quality Value Chain: A Meta Synthesis of Frontiers of Quality Movement," *Executive* 7, no. 2 (May 1993): 29–42.

Offers an historical perspective on the evolution of quality and details the role of individuals who made it possible as role models.

Heck, Gary L. "Managing by Example," *Security Management* 37, no. 6 (June 1993): 47–48.

Calls on executives in his industry to lead by example in pursuing quality efforts. Explains why; is applicable to all industries.

Hiam, Alexander. "Strategic Planning Unbound," *Journal of Business Strategy* 14, no. 2 (March–April 1993): 46–52.

Is critical of planners in business not being current with trends in total quality management, participatory management styles, etc., and says they must get contemporary in providing leadership.

Johnson, Richard S. *TQM: Leadership for the Quality Transformation.* Milwaukee: ASQC Quality Press, 1993.

This is a major study on how management leads an organization into and through quality practices.

Kendrick, John J. "New IQS Performance-Based Model for Quality Management Shows What Works Best," *Quality* (November 1992): 11.

This briefly summarizes the Ernst & Young study on best practices in the world of business quality, focusing on process simplification, analysis, and cycle time.

King, Bob. "TQM Can Improve Your Bottom Line," *Executive Excellence* 10, no. 5 (May 1993): 16–17.

Addresses executives on the value of TQM and what its major components are for an organization. Defines what the role of management should be.

Lee, Chris, and Zemke, Ron. "The Search for Spirit in the Workplace," *Training* 30, no. 6 (June 1993): 21–28.

Defines "servant leadership" concepts and why the interest in this approach to management. The main reason is that it makes it possible for managers to take advantage of the collective wisdom of an organization.

Miller, Charles D. "Seeking The Service Grail," *Financial Executive* 9, no. 4 (July–August 1993): 14–16.

The focus is on time-based management strategies for effectively developing a service-oriented company; case study of Avery Dennison Corporation.

Myers, Ken. "A Culture of Value Added Leaders," *Executive Excellence* 10, no. 2 (February 1993): 4.

Describes the characteristics of such leaders, defining four attributes they all display. Targeted primarily at people who are responsible for parts of an organization (e.g., executives and and managers).

Miller, Richard M. "TQM As A Way of Life," *Executive Excellence* 10, no. 5 (May 1993): 13–14.

Argues why managers should learn and apply TQM principles and tools.

Nalore Winter, Concetta R., and Kleiner, Brian H. "Effective Leadership in a Turbulent Environment," *Work Study* 42, no. 2 (March–April 1993): 16–19.

Describes Peter Drucker's most recent ideas concerning the role of leaders and includes such concepts as customer focus, innovation, leadership, and empowered employees.

Picard, Robert. "Reflections on Quality: A New Approach to Managing Business," *OH&S Canada* 9, no.1 (January/February 1993): 38–43.

The author, from Shell Canada Ltd., argues that TQM is a new way to manage business, why, and how; good management overview of the subject.

Smith, Warren, and Dobbs, John. "Beyond the Buzz Words: What It Takes to Make TQM A Reality," *Quality Digest* 13, no. 2 (February 1993): 46–51.

Offers a generalized blue print for management interested in implementing quality improvement programs. Deals with common issues such as objectives, training, leadership, and employee involvement.

Staub, Robert E. "A Culture of Leadership," *Executive Excellence* 10, no. 2 (February 1993): 15.

Defines leadership and the need for it; pleasant, effective.

Sullivan, Rhonda L. "Inside the Baldrige Award Guidelines: Category 1: Leadership," *Quality Progress* (June 1992): 25–28.

This is the best article available on what the Baldrige Award requires of leadership. It explains Category One of the award nomination, the values, and concepts espoused.

Townsend, Patrick, and Gebhardt, Joan E. *Quality in Action: 93 Lessons in Leadership, Participation, and Measurement.* New York: John Wiley & Sons, 1992.

While the title sounds like a gimmick, the book is a useful collection of specific action steps one can take, and is primarily geared toward individuals, and particularly, management.

Weil, Peter A. "Evaluating the CEO in a TQM Environment," *Healthcare Executive* 8, no. 2 (March–April 1993): 30.

This describes what the health industry has developed for measuring performance of CEO's using TQM principles; it is applicable to other industries.

Winston, Michael G. "Battling the Rapids," *Journal of Management Development* 12, no. 1 (1993): 49–54.

This is a good introduction to vision-based leadership for management. Links this description to change, strategic planning, and development of management.

Cultural Transformation

Anonymous. "The Deming Method to Total Quality Management (TQM)," *Innovator's Digest* (February 2, 1993).

This is a detailed report from the ABI/Inform Database describing Deming applications of quality in various industries, including manufacturing, health, and public sector. It offers theory and specific examples of use. This is a major report.

Ashton, Chris. "Employing the Uniqueness Factor," *TQM Magazine* 5, no. 1 (February 1993): 15–18.

Argues that TQM is a strategy many large organizations are using to help overall performance improve following the end of the recession. Cites examples of IBM, Ford, and British Steel.

Bailey, Marvin, et al. "The Semi-Complete Quality Professionals' Cookbook," *Journal of Quality and Participation* (December 1992): 48–60.

Literally presented as a collection of recipes for the successful implementation of quality, it has good practical advice.

Barrow, James W. "Does Total Quality Management Equal Organizational Learning?" *Quality Progress* 26, no. 7 (July 1993): 39–43.

Argues that one needs to understand the relationship between the two issues for employees to be effective, and they must understand the definition of both.

Benson, Tracy E. "TQM: A Child Takes a First Few Faltering Steps," *Industry Week* 242, no. 7 (April 5, 1993): 16, 18.

The author reports on the results of a survey of 536 companies about their use of TQM. Reports important results and high level of acceptance of these practices. Offers information on the 78-page study conducted by *Industry Week*.

Clutterbuck, David, and Dearlove, Dez. "The Basic Lessons of Change," *Managing Service Quality* 3, no. 3 (March 1993): 7–10.

Argues that the existing culture can override the move to a more TQM-based environment. Suggests how "continuous ingenuity" can facilitate the change.

Delsanter, Judith M. "Rewarding Technology," *TQM Magazine* 5, no. 2 (April 1993): 31–33.

This is an interview with Joseph M. Juran, a major figure in the quality movement, on the occasion of his receiving the 1992 U.S. National Medal of Technology. He discusses the importance of technology and quality.

Gray, George R. "Quality Circles: An Update," *SAM Advanced Management Journal* 58, no. 2 (Spring 1993): 41–47.

Reports mixed results for quality circles in the United States and why. Best use is when QC's are folded into an overall TQM program. Presents results from a survey of 46 Fortune 500 companies and their use of QC's.

Harari, Oren. "Ten Reasons Why TQM Doesn't Work," *Management Review* 82, no. 1 (January 1993): 33–36.

Lists ten reasons mostly associated with supposedly making TQM programs too cumbersome to support the business objectives of an enteprise.

Holder, Todd, and Walker, Lorin. "Total Quality Management: Lessons Learned in the USA," *Management Service* 37, no. 7 (July 1993): 16–19.

Describes, through a model of organizational productivity, why people work together and illustrates sources of performance.

Holoviak, Stephen J. *Golden Rule Management: Give Respect, Get Results.* Reading, MA.: Addison-Wesley, 1993.

This short book applies the Golden Rule to business leadership; heavy emphasis on shared leadership (empowerment).

Johnson, H. Thomas. "To achieve Quality, You Must Think Quality," *Financial Executive* 93, no. 3 (May–June 1993): 9–12.

Challenges managers to think of quality as a fundamental paradigm shift in thinking. Documents the shift to ABC-styled cost accounting as a reflection of the change.

Johnson, Richard S. "TQM: Leadership for the Quality Transformation," *Quality Progress*, 26, no. 1 (January 1993): 73–75.

This is the first of a series of five articles published monthly through the first half of 1993 on the topic. Describes in tactical terms how to implement TQM in an organization.

Marion, Larry. "Changing the Culture at Teradyne," *Electronic Business* 19, no. 1 (January 1993): 28–32.

The heart of the change in strategy at Teradyne, Inc., was focusing on customers to make the change in internal processes. How this was done and the benefits achieved are described by an employee.

Peasenell, Dennis A. "Executive Viewpoint: Customizing Quality," *Electronic Engineering Times* (April 12, 1993): 23.

Sees cultural change as at the heart of quality improvement strategies. TQM values work, and this is a case study from one company.

Rinehart, Lawrence. "Total Quality Control: It May Be Right for You," *Signature* 3 (1993): 43–45, 50.

Argues that TQM is relevant for all companies, but cites the publishing industry for examples of application.

Rogers, Robert W., and Ferketish, B. Jean. "Value Driven Change Process," *Executive Excellence* 10, no. 3 (March 1993): 5–6.

This is a useful discussion of the critical success factor analysis now so popular in strategic planning and TQM processes.

Rusling, Patrice. "Ten Ways to Cultivate a Quality Culture," *Executive Excellence* 10, no. 2 (February 1993): 10.

Draws the analogy of gardening to point out 10 principles of agriculture that apply to nurturing organizations.

Saraph, Jayant V., and Sebastian, Richard J. "Developing a Quality Culture," *Quality Progress* 26, no. 9 (September 1993): 73–78.

This is an outstanding article on the subject, with an excellent literature and research summary by two professors.

Sheridan, Bruce M. "Total Quality Management: How to Know When It Will Work?" *Industrial Engineering* 25, no. 5 (May 1993): 18–19.

Argues that management spends too little time with customers and, second, that employee turnover can serve as an indicator of how quality is doing. When turnover declines, quality of processes are improving or are great.

Sherwood, John J., and Hoylman, Florence M. "The Total Quality Paradox," *Journal for Quality and Participation* (March 1993): 98–105.

The authors have their list of why TQM is not always working and represents one of the better analyses available on impediments, and concludes with suggestions for successful implementation.

Smith, Jim. "Japan: Myth or Miracle? Japan and the Battle for Europe," *TQM Magazine* 5, no. 2 (April 1993):47–51.

Argues Japan beat the United States using quality as a strategy and Europe is implementing the U.S. approach, which delights the Japanese. It details how Europe is responding to Japenese competition.

Stoner, James A. F., and Wankel, Charles B. "Putting Total Quality Management into Contemporary Polish Management Development," *Journal of Management Development* 12, no. 3 (1993): 65–72.

The authors cite the fundamental changes underway in Poland's economy to illustrate training methods for TQM. They describe a successful approach taken with management in Eastern Europe to introduce TQM concepts.

Tichy, Noel M., and Sherman, Stratford. "Walking the Talk at GE," *Training and Development* 47, no. 6 (June 1993): 26–35.

This summarizes the ideas that appeared in the authors' 1992 book on GE, one of the more important books on how organizations transform themselves to appear in several years. The GE case study is an important one, and is best studied by these authors.

Tomasko, Robert M. "Intelligent Resizing: View From the Bottom Up," *Management Review* 82, no. 6 (June 1993): 18–23.

Uses the case of General Electric to illustrate working principles of downsizing and the effect on reengineering of processes.

Westbrook, Jerry D. "Taking a Multivariate Approach to Total Quality Management," *Industrial Management* 35, no. 2 (March–April 1993): 2–3.

Offers six facets of TQM implementation of which cultural change is one; describes such other components as teams, customer focus, measurements, continuous improvements, and problem solving.

Zemke, Ron. "Customer Service As a Performing Art," *Training* 30, no. 3 (March 1993): 40–44.

Using the analogy of a theater production and service management, the author describes the role of an organization in a quality world. It is a clever and effective presentation of what organizations and people must do.

Customer Focus

Anonymous. "Customer Satisfaction Roles Grow Crucial," *Electronics Business* (January 1993): 42–43.

This is a case study of focusing on customers as experienced by the Exabyte Corporation, manufactuers of computer tape backup drives.

Anonymous. "Degussa Tracks Improvements: Customer Satisfaction Soars," *Chemical Week* (April 28, 1993): 70.

While this article describes how one company has improved customer satisfaction since 1989, it is a useful model of what has to be done and what one can expect realistically in return for that effort.

Anonymous. "Customer Service Impacts Cash Flow," *American Salesman* 38, no. 5 (May 1993): 13–15.

Presents results of a survey of Fortune 500 firms that indicates high customer service yields faster payments of invoices.

Anonymous. "Dell Computer: Comes Out on Top Among Computer Makers in Terms of Customer Service," *Fortune* (May 31, 1993): 79.

The process most helpful is customer fulfillment; all computer systems are configured to meet customer requirements, along with technical support.

Anonymous. "Letting the Right Hand Know What the Left Hand Is Doing," *Direct Marketing* (July 1993): 18.

This is a specific look at how customer satisfaction can be improved by developing and using a complete fulfillment history in a marketing database.

Anonymous. "MCI Communications: Is Noted for Its Cusomter Service in Its Long–Distance Operation," *Fortune* (May 31, 1993): 84.

Its customer focus is reflected in offering tailor-made services to its customers, such as discounts for most frequently dialed numbers, and discounts on GM automobiles and frequent- flier points on American Airlines.

Anonymous. "TQM: Forging Ahead or Falling Behind?" *HR Focus* 70, no. 7 (July 1993): 24.

Presents results of a survey done in Europe and North America on the critical factors required for successful implementation of TQM. Number one was customer focus.

Arora, Raj. "Consumer Involvement in Service Decisions," *Journal of Professional Services Marketing* 9, no. 1 (1993): 49–58.

This is an overview of the research done on the importance of consumer involvement in product development. The article then introduces ideas on how to involve customers in the development and improvement of services.

Benson, Tracy E. "A Business Strategy Comes of Age," *Industry Week* 242, no. 9 (May 3, 1993): 40–44.

Argues that TQM has come of age, even though executives are still looking for cost justification. Focusing on customer satisfaction leads to such rewards.

Berkin, Michael E. "Breaking New Ground in Service Quality," *Quality* 32, no. 5 (May 1993): 43, 46.

This is an important case study, involving Dun & Bradstreet, in illustrating how to gain small "breakthroughs" in services that are results oriented.

Bielenberg, Christopher. "Service Quality from Administration," *Management Services* 37, no. 4 (April 1993): 20–22.

The author argues that administrative processes must be managed with quality principles in order to insure high customer satisfaction. Defends his position.

Bird, Drayton. "Companies Are Not Listening," *Marketing* (May 20, 1993): 14.

Presents results of research in the United Kingdom suggesting that British firms are not doing a good job in listening to their customers. He compares the effectiveness of advertising to telephone communications with customers.

Boyers, Karla. "Partner's Paradise," *Association Management* 45, no. 1 (January 1993): 141–144.

Describes the growing types of interests of members of the American Society of Association Executives in quality topics.

Casper, Carol. "Customer 5723 in Zip 07652: How to Precisely Target Customers Through Database Marketing," *Restaurant Business* 92, no. 7 (May 1, 1993): 76–82.

This process is clearly described, using the restaurant industry as a successful case study to illustrate what gets done.

Cunningham, Martin E. "Customer Service: The Competitive Advantage," *National Petroleum News* 85, no. 3 (March 1993): 58.

Describes how petroleum companies are focusing on customer service to improve competitiveness in an industry where product quality is about the same from one vendor to another.

Edosomwan, Johnson A. *Customer and Market–Driven Quality Management.* Milwaukee: ASQC Quality Press, 1993.

While yet another book on how to implement TQM, this one has numerous case studies and shows how to link internal activities to market-focused emphasis.

Griffin, Abbie and Hauser, John R. "The Voice of the Customer," *Marketing Science* 12, no. 1 (Winter 1993): 1–27.

This is a formal, thorough statement of the application of quality function deployment (QFD). This article is one of the clearest explanations available on the concept of QFD.

Griffith, Cary. "Mead Data Central: New President, New Focus," *Information Today* 10, no. 5 (May 1993): 1, 16.

More than just a news article, this describes how one service company is changing its customer focus due to a change in its vision of the firm's role.

Halstead, Diane, Droge, Cornelia, and Cooper, M. Bixby. "Product Warranties and Post Purchase Service: A Model of Consumer Satisfaction with Complaint Resolution," *Journal of Services Marketing* 7, no. 1 (1993): 33–40.

Describes how complainers of new carpets and their carpet suppliers reacted to each other. Suggestions based on the results are made concerning the complaint process and warranty fulfillment services.

Hart, Christopher W. L. *Extraordinary Guarantees: A New Way to Build Quality Throughout*

Your Company & *Ensure Satisfaction for Your Customers.* New York: AMACOM, 1993.

This is the first book to appear on the subject of customer guarantees; builds the business case for it, describes the process involved, and advises on issues that must be addressed.

Hayes, Bob E. *Measuring Customer Satisfaction: Development and Use of Questionnaires.* Milwaukee: ASQC Quality Press, 1992.

This short book is a practical guide, complete with examples and case studies; a practitioner's guide.

Klose, Allen J. "Commentary: Customer Service Insurance," *Journal of Services Marketing* 7, no. 1 (1993): 55–58.

Suggests these as strategies to reduce customer perception of buying risks. Examples of how this would work are presented.

Lee Mortimer, Andrew. "Customer Focus Pays Off," *TQM Magazine* 5, no. 3 (June 1993): 37–41.

Describes how a British airport enjoyed successful operations in the late 1980s and early 1990s due to a customer focus in its operations.

Mitchell, V. W. "Handling Consumer Complaint Information: Why and How?" *Management Decision* 31, no. 3 (1993): 21–28.

Explains the value of this very important customer process and how it should be used to advantage by organizations.

Naumann, Earl, and Shannon, Patrick. "What Is Customer–Driven Marketing?" *Business Horizons* 35, no. 6 (November–December 1992): 44–52.

This is a thorough and excellent discussion of the topic. Defines "customer driven" and details what organizations do to implement such an approach. The authors are professors in business administration.

Pollock, E. Kears. "A Vigorous Approach to Customer Service," *Journal of Business Strategy* 14, no. 1 (January–February 1993): 16–20.

Describes how an automotive supply company (PPG) restructured its distribution methods to improve customer service, complete with root cause analysis of issues and customer feedback approaches.

Raphel, Murray, and Raphel, Neil. "An Unhappy Shopper May Be Your Best Friend," *Progressive Grocer* 72, no. 1 (January 1993): 12–13.

Describes a specific process for using customer complaints to improve service; represents a more effective use of complaints applicable to all industries.

Rasmus, Dan. "Learning the Waltz of Synthesis," *Manufacturing Systems* 11, no. 6 (June 1993): 16–23.

Manufacturing and engineering approaches can and are used to satisfy customer needs. The way this is done is described in some detail in this article.

Reid, Robert. "The Five Voices of Quality," *Journal for Quality* & *Participation* 16, no. 3 (June 1993): 76–81.

Argues that the voice of the customer is only one of many that quality-focused organizations listen to and why.

Salter, James N. II, and Sarazan, J. Stephen. *Customer Satisfaction Management Process.* New York: American Management Association, 1993.

One of the best books available on how to assess and manage customer relationships; the focus is on process views. It is an excellent tactical guide by two well-recognized experts.

Sarazan, J. Stephen. *Using Quality Improvement Tools to Build Customer Satisfaction.* New York: American Management Association, 1992.

Deals with the same theme as his publication cited immediately above. Also an outstanding tactical guide on what to do.

Schiemann, William A. "Organizational Change Starts with a Strategic Focus," *Journal of Business Strategy* 14, no. 1 (January–February 1993): 43–48.

Argues that with global competition and a variety of issues complicating management, having a strategic focus is crucial and explains how to achieve that. This is an excellent way to keep focus on customers and their needs.

Schlossberg, Howard. "Good Customer Service Is So Simple It's Often Overlooked," *Marketing News* 27, no. 13 (June 21, 1993): 6–7.

Len Berry, a leading expert on customer service, spoke to the AMA's Customer Satisfaction Congress, describing the basics of providing good customer service and why.

Serafin, Raymond. "Customer Satisfaction Is Key: GM's Losh," *Advertising Age* 64, no. 13 (March 29, 1993): 8.

J. Michael Losh, vice president group executive for North American vehicle sales and marketing, described how GM was using improved customer satisfaction as a way to regain market share.

Voss, Bristol. "Me and My Shadow," *Journal of Business Strategy* 14, no. 3 (May–June 1993): 6ff.

Shows how to identify customer needs by physically following them around as they work.

Wetherell, K. "Mutual Benefits," *TQM Magazine* 3, no. 2 (May–June 1993): 23–27.

The vice president of customer service at the Connecticut Mutual Life Insurance Company describes how to use computers and quality focus to improve customer satisfaction. He is specific in his descriptions of what was done.

Zeithaml, Valarie, Berry, Leonard L., and Parasuraman, A. "The Nature and Determinants of Customer Expectations of Service," *Journal of the Academy of Marketing Science* 21, no. 1 (Winter 1993): 1–12.

Three leading experts on how customers think and react to products and services present their latest findings on customer expectations; an important article for all industries.

Quality Implementation Strategies and Planning

Ackoff, Russell L. "Beyond Total Quality Management," *Journal for Quality and Participation* 16, no. 2 (March 1993): 66–78.

This is a useful, balanced review of why U.S. companies fail to make quality programs work, providing reasons for failure and suggestions for improvements.

Anonymous. "Management By A Thousand Changes," *Engineer* (June 3, 1993): 19.

This is an excellent, short comparison of Japanes and American quality management approaches. Offers a good explanation of KAIZEN.

Ashkenas, Ron. "TQM: Just Do It," *Incentive* 167, no. 4 (April 1993): 52–53.

Presents a three-step process for introducing TQM into companies.

Becker, Selwyn W. "TQM Does Work: Ten Reasons Why Misguided Attempts Fail," *Management Review* 82, no. 5 (May 1993): 30, 32 + .

Responding to recent attacks on TQM, this author presents the case for TQM implementation and what it would take to be successful with it.

Brown, Mark Graham. "Why Does Total Quality Fail in Two Out of Three Tries?" *Journal for Quality and Participation* (March 1993): 80–89.

Offers a list of ten problem areas, with advice by a quality expert on how to avoid them.

Brown, Stanley A. *Total Quality Service.* Englewood Cliffs, N.J.: Prentice-Hall, 1993.

This is a "how to implement" book on quality programs. It also contains more current case studies than available before, including the experiences of the Royal Bank, Four Seasons Hotel, and Northern Telecom.

Cartin, Thomas J. *Principles and Practices of TQM.* Milwaukee: ASQC Quality Press, 1993.

This is a comprehensive overview of TQM and about how to employ its practices.

Chang, Y. S., Labovitz, George, and Rosansky, Victor. *Making Quality Work: A Leadership Guide for the Results–Driven Manager.* New York: Harper, 1993.

Despite its hyped-up title, the book does have many suggestions for management on how to implement, assess, and sustain quality initiatives in business enterprises.

Collins, Brendan, and Huge, Ernest. *Management by Policy: How Companies Focus Their Total Quality Efforts to Achieve Competitive Advantage.* Milwaukee: ASQC Quality Press, 1993.

This is a "how to" book for management, arguing that there is a way to integrate daily running of a business with TQM; shows a way.

Garvin, David A. "Building a Learning Organization," *Harvard Business Review* 71, no. 4 (July–August 1993): 78–91.

Describes the value of organizations learning, defines the process and what organizations can do as part of their overall transformation efforts to quality-based organizations.

Ginnodo, Bill, and Wellins, Richard S. "Research Shows That TQM Is Alive and Well," *Tapping the Network Journal* 3, no. 4 (Winter 1992–1993): 2–5.

Presents results of a survey of 6,429 people about 13 factors, pointing out what works well in TQM practices, and actual results being achieved; a major study justifying TQM.

Hagen, Jack. *Management of Quality: Strategies to Improve Quality and the Bottom Line.* Milwaukee: ASQC Quality Press, 1993.

Lays out a detailed strategy for implementing quality programs in businesses.

Johnson, Richard S. *TQM: Management Process for Quality Operations.* Milwaukee: ASQC Quality Press, 1993.

This is a general overview of how quality is implemented in an organization, and includes a variety of topics ranging from planning through measurements, and other management functions.

Juran, J. M. "Why Quality Initiatives Fail," *Journal of Business Strategy* 14, no. 4 (July–August 1993): 35–38.

A leading quality guru argues that U.S. failures frequently come because CEO's do not know what to do. Offers a five-step process for doing it right; an important article.

Katz, Albert S. "Eight TQM Pitfalls," *Journal for Quality & Participation* 16, no. 4 (July–August 1993): 24–27.

This is an excellent list of very common problems most organizations face when implementing TQM in its early stages.

Katz, Ray. "The Quality Conflict: Choosing Your Approach to Improve Quality," *Manage* 44, no. 4 (April 1993): 30–33.

Describes two conflicting schools of thought about TQM: Crosby's and Deming's.

Kendrick, John J. "Study Looks at TQM: Is It Forging Ahead or Falling Behind?" *Quality* 32, no. 5 (May 1993): 13.

Summarizes a major study of 536 organizations that showed their use of TQM was providing positive results if used for over three years.

Leonard, Allenna, and Bradshaw, William. "Assessing Management Control," *CMA Magazine* 67, no. 3 (April 1993): 25–30.

Argues in favor of a comprehensive model of TQM and a business, and introduces Stafford Beer's Viable System Model (VSM) and is applicable with TQM or ABC strategies.

Long, Kim. "Management by Quality," *American Demographics* 93, *Marketing Tools Supplement* (June 1993): 18.

Documents the transition of TQM from tactical to strategic forms due to such consequences of TQM as the fundamental restructuring of enterprises.

Macdonald, John. "Perspective: Obsolete Absolutes," *TQM Magazine* 5, no. 2 (April 1993): 5–6.

The author says many TQM programs have failed due to blind loyalty to absolute principles when what is needed is a better understanding of what really needs to change. Says organizations must think through their own transformations.

McGee, E. Craig. "The Convergence of Total Quality and Work Design," *Journal for Quality and Participation* 16, no. 2 (March 1993): 90–96.

Identifies the common components of TQM and work design and then suggests how the two can be used together.

Rubinstein, Sidney P. "Democracy and Quality As An Integrated System," *Quality Progress* 26, no. 9 (September 1993): 51–56.

In a very thoughtful article, the author argues that unions and management can improve the chances of TQM being successful if they embrace lifetime employment and invest in their employees.

Soin, Sarv Singh. *Total Quality Control Essentials: Key Elements, Methodologies, and Managing for Success.* New York: McGraw-Hill, 1992.

This is a comprehensive overview of quality practices and how to implement them in an organization. It applies as much to those that have not started as to those that are advanced. It has many customer-focused case studies.

Spenley, Paul. "Perspectives: Step Up to a New Approach," *TQM Magazine* 5, no. 1 (February 1993): 5–6.

Presents a 12-month tactical TQM implementation strategy and defines critical steps for those who require a more short-term approach to continuous improvement.

Squires, Frank H. "Who's Killing TQ?" *Quality* 32, no. 4 (April 1993): 59.

Summarizes an article by Kevin Doyle in *Incentive* in which he argues that TQM, while a major management strategy now, suffers in firms that continue using outmoded short-term accounting practices.

Steele, Jack. "Implementing Total Quality Management for Long and Short Term Bottom Line Results," *National Productivity Review* 12, no. 3 (Summer 1993): 425–441.

In this important survey of how Japanese–American companies are performing, the author concludes that results-oriented TQM programs are the most effective.

Taylor, Glen. "Parallel Processing: A Design Principle for System Wide Total Quality Management," *Management International Review* 33 (Special Issue) (First Quarter 1993): 99–109.

Besides describing the concept of parallel processing, the author presents the case for how it can be applied in organizations, not just within specific processes.

Warwood, Stephen J. *The Role of the Modern Quality Manager.* Hertfordshire, England: Technical Communications, Ltd., 1993.

This 64-page pamphlet is a good introduction to the subject of what a quality manager does, tools available to him/her, and how to select such individuals; only publication on this subject to appear in recent years.

Woudhuysen, James. "Engineers of a Fresh Approach," *Marketing* (June 3, 1993): 10.

Announces that at least 21 of Britain's top 100 firms are doing process reengineering and why.

Communication

Caudron, Shari. "Communicating TQM to Small Groups Improves Understanding," *Personnel Journal* 72, no. 8 (August 1993): 48D.

Describes the use of small meetings to discuss quality issues at Conner Peripherals, Inc.

Coyle, Michael B. "Quality Interpersonal Communications: An Overview," *Manage* 44, no. 4 (April 1993): 4–5.

Describes what individuals can do, and what these skills need to be in a quality-focused environment.

Delfino, Erik. "The Basics on Setting Up An Electronic Bulletin Board System," *Online* 17, no. 2 (March 1993): 90–92.

This is an extraordinarily effective communications tool for organizations to have; how one is set up is briefly described.

Howe, Roger, Gaeddert, Dee, and Howe, Maynard A. "A Failure to Communicate," in their *Quality on Trial* (New York: West Publishing Co., 1992): 25–38.

This may be the single best introduction to communications as a process within an organization and how to manage them well.

Klassen, Cathryn. "Improving Quality Means Improving Communications," *Canadian Business Review* 20, no. 2 (Summer 1993): 15–18.

This is a critical process that continues to receive insufficient attention. This is a useful introduction to the process.

Knorr, Robert O. "A Strategy for Communicating Change," *Journal of Business Strategy* 14, no. 4 (July–August 1993): 18–20.

Builds the case for a corporate vision as part of the change strategy and for the centerpiece of the strategy being good communications. Describes the case of a pharmaceutical company's effective approach.

Toth, S. E. "How We Slashed Response Time," *Management Review* 82, no. 2 (February 1993): 51–54.

This describes a customer-responsive telephone process in one company. The process is one of the most important any organization can have; this is a good introduction to it.

Tunks, Roger. *Fast Track to Quality: A 12–Month Program for Small to Mid–Sized Businesses.* New York: McGraw-Hill, 1992.

While the title makes it look too good to be true, Chapter 18 (pp. 213–223) is a thoughtful and expert chapter on communications as a process.

Training

Anonymous. "EFQM Viewpoint: Assessor Training," *TQM Magazine* 5, no. 2 (April 1993): 7–8.

Says training managers as assessors for the European Quality Award is an excellent way to educate managers about TQM. Describes existing training.

Bragg, Debra D. "Team Basics: How To Develop Teamwork In Training Organizations," *Performance and Instruction* 31, no. 9 (October 1992): 10–14.

Offers a case for teams in training. The article is as much a statement of the value and best practices of teams as it is documentation of why teams are effective in training.

Brown, Alan. "TQM: Implications for Training," *Industrial and Commercial Training* 25, no. 1 (1993): 20–26.

Focuses on six issues critical to any TQM training process; offers a case study of doing training successfully.

Chaston, Ian. "Managing for Total Training Quality," *Journal of European Industrial Training* 17, no. 5 (1993): 6–9.

This article focuses on the application of TQM principles within a training department in a corporation or agency, rather than on training people about quality.

Dawson, Graydon. "The Critical Elements Missing From Most Total Quality Management Training," *Performance and Instruction* 31, no. 9 (October 1992): 15–21.

This is a thorough discussion of TQM training programs and their implications. Also provides suggestions for making them effective.

Gallagan, Patricia A. "How to Get Your TQM Training on Track," *Nation's Business* (October 1992): 24, 26, 28.

Reports on what small businesses in the United States are attempting to learn about quality and how; cases are presented.

Hall, Claire, Bright, David, and Grainer, Bill. "Training and Development Priorities in the North East," *Target Management Development Review* 5, no. 4 (1992): 20–24.

Presents results of survey of training programs in England, finding many problems in these training strategies. Yet nearly half of 191 firms see TQM training as important.

Henkoff, Ronald. "Companies That Train Best," *Fortune* 127, no. 6 (March 22, 1993): 62–75.

Features the employee training programs at Motorola as an excellent set of processes. Compares these programs to those at Federal Express.

Moody, Patricia E. "Workforce Development, Investing in Human Capital," *Target* 9, no. 1 (January–February 1993): 6–18.

Argues the case for employee training/development programs and cites world-class examples. This is one of the more comprehensive and effective publications on training in general.

Muckian, Michael. "Training for TQM," *Credit Union Magazine* 59, no. 5 (May 1993): 38–43.

Calls out that credit unions are beginning to apply TQM principles, presents cases of specific application, and then discusses training commitments.

Nopper, Norman S. "Reinventing the Factory With Lifelong Learning," *Training* 30, no. 5 (May 1993): 55–58.

Discusses what to teach (not just about quality), the benefits of such an investment in employees, and some comments about how to go about this; particularly targeted toward blue collar employees.

Patel, Anoop. "Total Quality Management (TQM): Paving the Way for Future Training?" *Industrial & Commercial Training* 25, no. 2 (1993): 23–32.

Reports that British firms are not taking TQM seriously enough and that their training programs are also not teaching enough about TQM.

Plott, Curtis E. "Train or Tumble," *Executive Excellence* 10, no. 3 (March 1993): 7–8.

Builds the case for why organizations must invest in training, particularly of soft and marketable skills.

Raynor, Michael E. "Quality: Putting the Pieces Together," *Training* 30, no. 2 (February 1993): 90.

Criticizes many corporate training programs as being too narrow when it comes to TQM, teaching tools and techniques and not enough about the holistic approach to performing in a quality-oriented environment. Suggestions for improvements are offered.

Rinholm, Brenda L. "Training For New Product Staff Should Be 'Customer Driven'," *Marketing News* 27, no. 13 (June 21, 1993): 9, 17.

Says product managers rarely do internal training on new products, costing in cycle time reduction and productivity. Suggests steps that can be taken.

Roxburgh, Richard. "A Question of Quality," *Training Tomorrow* (March–April 1993): 25–26.

Reviews why so many firms are having difficulty with TQM, how this problem can be fixed, and concludes with the reasons why training is a critical component of successful programs.

Schaller, Robert C. "The Use of SPC in a Training Environment," *Quality* 32, no. 4 (April 1993): 31–33.

Describes specific application of statistical process control in measuring the effects of training programs on individuals. Presents the results of specific training programs.

Spiess, Michael E. "Four by Four: Finding Time for TQM Training," *Training and Development* (February 1993): 11–15.

Four experts on training discuss how training can be woven into the fabric of everyday corporate life. The suggestions are specific and practical.

Tuttle, Gerald R. "Cascading Quality Through the Training Process," *Quality Progress* 26, no. 4 (April 1993): 75–78.

Describes the well-recognized training programs at Xerox Corporation. TQM and training as converging issues are discussed.

Wick, Calhoun W., and Leon, Lu Stanton. *The Learning Edge: How Smart Managers and Smart*

Companies Stay Ahead. New York: McGraw Hill, 1993.

Describes how individuals and organizations can enhance their personal and organizational skills; directed primarily at mangement, complete with case studies and examples.

Williams, Melanie. "A Measure of Success," *TQM Magazine* 5, no. 3 (June 1993): 47–50.

Discusses the problem of how to evaluate the effectiveness of training and personnel development, and then presents how it is done in some companies (e.g., Motorola).

QUALITY TOOLS AND TECHNIQUES
Benchmarking

Anonymous. "Benchmarking Aids in Benefits Design," *Employee Benefit Plan Review* 47, no. 12 (June 1993): 60–61.

Describes what benchmarking is and then presents examples from the 3M Company.

Anonymous. "Benchmarking at Du Pont," *Business Travel News* (January 1993): 13.

Describes travel processes benchmarked by Du Pont.

Anonymous. "The Benchmarking Boom," *HR Focus* 70, no. 4 (April 1993): 1, 6ff.

Describes Federal Express's experience with benchmarking and the interest other companies have shown in its efforts.

Anonymous. "Logistics Quality Benchmarking: Part 1: How Do You Measure Up?" *Traffic Management* 32, no. 4 (April 1993): 60–67.

More of a statement about the benefits of benchmarking in general and less about logistics of benchmarking. However, the role of quality logistics is discussed.

Anonymous. "Management: A Measure of Success: Companies Are Enthusiastically Embracing the Concept of Benchmarking," *Financial Times* (May 5, 1993): 14.

This reports on the growing trend to use this tool and why companies like it. Offers reasons, case studies, and trends.

Anonymous. "Six Steps to Benchmarking Success," *Traffic Management* 32, no. 4 (April 1993): 64.

Describes benchmarking by Alcoa in the areas of procurement and logistics (warehousing and trucking) since 1987. Details a six-step process for benchmarking in this company.

Barth, Claire. "Office Technology: Software," *Management Accounting* 74, no. 11 (May 1992): 72.

Describes Target, a software benchmarking tool.

Brown, Thomas L. "Capitalizing on Comparisons: Can Benchmarking Actually Slow You Down?" *Industry Week* (March 15, 1993): 46.

He says yes and explains bad benchmarking, especially when it is overdone.

Chung, Ronald K. "TQM: Benchmarking Performance in the Credit Function," *Business Credit* 95, no. 5 (May 1993): 19–21.

He defines benchmarking and then presents guidelines for the use of this tool in the area of credit functions.

Crow, Stephen M., and Van Epps, Pamela D. "Competitive Benchmarking: A New Medium for Enhancing Training and Development Effectiveness," *Training and Management Development Methods* 7, no. 1 (1993): 2.01–2.09.

This is a process for looking at competitors to your organization in an organized and disciplined manner. A case study involving personnel practices is presented to illustrate the technique; excellent!

Davis, Tim R. V., and Patrick, Michael S. "Benchmarking at the Sunhealth Alliance," *Planning Review* 14, no. 1 (January–February 1993): 28–31.

Describes benchmarking activities within an alliance of 250 nonprofit hospitals.

Ettlie, John E. "Benchmarking: Who Are the Leaders in Product Development and Why?" *Production* 105, no. 6 (June 1993): 46.

Discusses benchmarking by Hewlett Packard and offers the results of a survey on benchmarking done with 126 companies.

Ettorre, Barbara. "Benchmarking: The Next Generation," *Management Review* 82, no. 6 (June 1993): 10–16.

Describes very recent trends in benchmarking methodologies and the creation of the Benchmarking Clearinghouse.

Ettorre, Barbara." Ethics, Anti-trust, and Benchmarking," *Management Review* 82, no. 6 (June 1993): 13.

Describes existing codes of protocols being applied by companies in benchmarking.

Gable, Myron, Fairhurst, Ann, and Dickinson, Roger. "The Use of Benchmarking to Enhance Marketing Decision Making," *Journal of Consumer Marketing* 10, no. 1 (1993): 52–60.

This is a brief, effective explanation of what benchmarking is and how to use it.

Gallagher, Peter A. "Quality Means Competitiveness," *Executive Excellence* 10, no. 5 (May 1993): 11–12.

Describes the use of benchmarking at AT&T Universal Card Services, a Baldrige Award winner.

Gamble, Richard H. "Race for the Gold: Benchmarking Credit," *Corporate Cashflow* 14, no. 5 (May 1993): 32–33.

Describes the use of benchmarking to improve operations within a credit department. Significant improvements are described.

Henricks, Mark. "How Do We Measure Up?" *Small Business Reports* 18, no. 6 (June 1993): 29–39.

Presents the case for why companies should conduct benchmarking studies.

Hequet. Marc. "The Limits of Benchmarking," *Training* 30, no. 2 (February 1993): 36–41.

Summarizes the findings of the Ernst & Young studies that indicate poor performing companies do not benefit from benchmarking, but that outstanding ones do.

Hiebeler, Robert. "A Roadmap for Success," *Industry Week* 14, (July 19, 1993): 53.

The author summarizes the criticisms people have of benchmarking and then discusses how to make such a tool effective.

Hitchcock, Nancy A. "Benchmarking Bolsters Quality at Texas Instruments," *Modern Materials Handling* 48, no. 3 (March 1993): 46–48.

This case study is particularly interesting because it is on Texas Instruments, a leader in the use of TQM tools. Also this article is very specific about the dramatic improvements in efficiencies gained by this company.

Johnson, Janet T. "How Benchmarking Works at USAA," *Employment Relations Today* 19, no. 4 (Winter 1992/1993): 433–40.

Describes how process benchmarking is done at one of the best managed insurance companies in the world. It is a step-by-step description.

Julien, Frederick W., and Lampe, James C. "Sharing Best Practices in Internal Audit," *Internal Auditing* 8, no. 4 (Spring 1993): 66–72.

The focus of this article is on comparative analysis of best practices, what it is and how it is done.

Kieley, Thomas. "I.S. Quality: Getting to Know the Neighborhood," *CIO* 6, no. 10 (April 15, 1993): 48–50.

Defines benchmarking, how it is done properly, and what information can be expected from such an exercise.

Krause, Irv, and Liu, John. "Benchmarking R&D Productivity," *Planning Review* 14, no. 1 (January–February 1993): 16–21.

Best practices in 15 R&D organizations are identified; this is a major article for R&D organizations.

Mansconson, Leslie N. "Benchmarking Makes Its Way to Treasury Department," *Healthcare Financial Management* 47, no. 4 (April 1993): 96–97.

Describes AT&T's ongoing benchmarking of its cash management processes. Also details benefits derived.

Micklewright, Michael J. "Competitive Benchmarking: Large Gains for Small Companies," *Quality Progress* 26, no. 6 (June 1993): 67–68.

This is an excellent discussion of competitive benchmarking, how it is done with advice.

Muroff, Cindy. "Zeroing in on Benchmarking," *Distribution* 92, no. 1 (January 1993): 87–88.

Describes benchmarking of the order picking process.

Posson, Mark C., and Barney, Craig A. "Environmental Auditing and Continuous Improvement at Lockheed," *Total Quality Environmental Management* 2, no. 3 (Spring 1993): 267–272.

Describes the environmental audit program at Lockheed Missiles and Space Co., and the effective use of benchmarking as part of the process.

Pouzar, Ed. "Benchmarking Fad Lures Risk Managers' Bosses," *National Underwriter (Property/Casualty/Employee Benefits)* 97, no. 7 (February 15, 1993): 7.

Describes the use of benchmarking in risk management in the insurance industry and how some employees feel its use is a negative reflection on them. Benefits of benchmarking are described.

Prairie, Patti. "An American Express/IBM Consortium Benchmarks Information Technology," *Planning Review* 14, no. 1 (January–February 1993): 22–27.

TQM in MIS organizations remains a little-understood area. This article identifies best practices in 17 MIS organizations, focusing on the benchmarking process and its benefits.

Pryor, Lawrence S., and Katz, Steven J. "How Benchmarking Goes Wrong (And How To Do It Right," *Planning Review* 14, no. 1 (January–February 1993): 6–11.
Describes sales effectiveness as a benchmark target at an industrial firm.

Ransley, Derek L. "Training Managers to Benchmark," *Planning Review* 14, no. 1 (January–February 1993): 32–36.
The author focuses on tips for those who are just starting to use this quality tool, relying on the experiences of a number of benchmarking experts; an important article.

Richardson, Helen L. "Measure Up with Benchmarking," *Transportation & Distribution* 34, no. 6 (June 1993): 32–35.
Describes the work of the International Benchmarking Clearinghouse (IBC), a major resource for companies that wish to benchmark and need a source of "best practices" information.

Rothman, Howard. "You Need Not Be Big to Benchmark," *Nation's Business* (December 1992): 64–65.
This is a short introduction to benchmarking, with cases from small companies, and some advise on how best to execute.

Scheffler, Steve, and Powers, Vicki J. "Ethics in Benchmarking," *Transportation & Distribution* 34, no. 6 (June 1993): 34.
Argues that companies should not share as much information as benchmarking proponents urge for legal and ethical reasons.

Schlossberg, Howard. "Benchmarking Is Hard Process That Offers No Quick Fix," *Marketing News* 13 (June 21, 1993): 14.
A benchmarking expert (Brian Lowenthal) provides his insight on effective benchmarking.

Sheridan, John H. "Where Benchmarkers Go Wrong," *Industry Week* 242, no. 6 (March 15, 1993):28, 30, 32, 34.
This is a useful antidote to the well-intentioned articles that usually appear on benchmarking. This documents cases of malpractice.

Singh, Durgesh K., and Evans, Raymond P. "Effective Benchmarking: Taking the Effective Ap-

proach," *Industrial Engineering* 25, no. 2 (February 1993): 22ff.
This is a general introduction to the tool; argues it is an old technique—competitive analysis—under a new name with more discipline.

Smith, Graham. "Benchmarking Success at Motorola," *CMA Magazine* 67, no. 2 (March 1993): 32–33.
This particular article is interesting because it shows the relationship between measurements and benchmarking and in particular Motorola's use of six sigma.

Spendolini, Michael J. *The Benchmarking Book.* New York: AMACOM, 1992.
This has become a useful, short guide to benchmarking practices. It is very much a "how to" book for practitioners.

Spendolini, Michael J. "Benchmarking Etiquette," *Tapping the Network Journal* 3, no. 3 (Fall 1992): 11–13.
Presents survey results from 23 companies on benchmarking diplomacy and concludes with suggestions on how organizations should interract in benchmarking activities.

Stevenson, Cathy A. "Training for Benchmarking: The Allied Signal Experience," *Total Quality Environmental Management* 2, no. 4 (Summer 1993): 397–403.
At this company, people are taught how to benchmark before they attempt it. The case study documents the experience.

Tomas, Sam. "Benchmarking: A Technique for Improvement," *Hospital Material Management Quarterly* 14, no. 4 (May 1993): 78–82.
Describes a 10-step benchmarking process that can be used by hospitals; applicable to most organizations.

Vaziri, H. Kevin. "Questions to Answer Before Benchmarking," *Planning Review* 14, no. 1 (January–February 1993): 37.
Offers seven questions for managers to ask as they determine how best to employ benchmarking.

Watson, Gregory H. "How Process Benchmarking Supports Corporate Strategy," *Planning Review* 14, no. 1 (January–February 1993): 12–15.
A vice president of Xerox defends benchmarking.

Watson, Gregory H. *Strategic Benchmarking: How to Rate Your Company's Performance*

Against the World's Best. New York: John Wiley & Sons, Inc., 1993.

This is an outstanding book on the subject, a blend of technical "how to" of benchmarking along with linkage to business plans. One of the best books to appear in 1993.

Williams, Fred. "Aiming for the Right Target," *Pensions & Investments* 21, no. 6 (March 22, 1993): 20, 24.

Describes benchmarking as it is applied by money managers.

Young, Steve. "Management: Checking Performance with Competitive Benchmarking," *Professional Engineering* 6, no. 2 (February 1993): 14–15.

Defines benchmarking and explains effective strategies for using this method of finding ways for manufacturing companies to improve.

Yost, Larry. "The Allen-Bradley Story," *Journal of Business Strategy* 14, no. 3 (May–June 1993): 58–60.

Describes the assessment process employed by this electro mechanical product manufacturer, which then was used for designing a major restructuring of manufacturing operations.

Reengineering

Allen, David P., and Nafius, Robert. "Dreaming and Doing: Reengineering GTE Telephone Operations," *Planning Review* 14, no. 2 (March–April 1993): 28–31.

Besides being a successful case on telephone operations, this is the account of one of the largest reengineering projects undertaken so far. Eighty companies, for example, were benchmarked.

Buday, Robert S. "Reengineering One Firm's Product Development and Another's Service Delivery," *Planning Review* 21, no. 2 (March–April 1993): 14–19.

Describes Hallmark Cards, Inc.'s, approach to reengineering a variety of processes, step-by-step, and then the experience of the California State Automobile Association doing the same thing is described.

Dale, Barrie G., and Boaden, Ruth J. "Improvement Framework," *TQM Magazine* 5, no. 1 (February 1993): 23–26.

Offers a framework for planning and control of continuous improvement strategies. Takes a broader view

than most on how processes are changed, for example, includes personnel management and organizational implications.

Davenport, Thomas H. "Need Radical Innovation and Continuous Improvement? Integrate Process Reengineering and TQM," *Planning Review* 21, no. 3 (May/June 1993): 6–12.

A leading expert on process improvement argues that reengineering is increasingly a more important function and that TQM is part of the effort; an important article on strategic uses of process reengineering.

Davenport, Thomas H. *Process Innovation: Reengineering Work Through Information Technology.* Boston: Harvard Business School Press, 1993.

One of the best books out on process reengineering; it is tactical, filled with case studies and a strategy for implementation. Author argues that information technology can be an important part of successful reengineering.

Davidson, W. H. "Beyond Re-engineering: The Three Phases of Business Transformation," *IBM Systems Journal* 32, no. 1 (1993): 65–79.

Argues that business transformation comes in three ways: process reengineering, new organizational structures, and finally creation of new businesses. Davidson is best known for his book *2020 Vision.*

Furey, Timothy R. "A Six–Step Guide to Process Reengineering," *Planning Review* 14, no. 2 (March–April 1993): 20–23.

There are many such articles; they tend to get better over time as more experience is folded into these lists. This is short and effective.

Hammer, Michael, and Champy, James. *Reengineering the Corporation: A Manifesto for Business Revolution.* New York: HarperBusiness, 1993.

One of the "hot" business books of 1993, this is a detailed account of how to redesign processes, it includes a series of case studies. Must reading on the subject of process reengineering.

Harrison, D. Brian, and Pratt, Maurice D. "A Methodology for Reengineering Businesses," *Planning Review* 21, no. 2 (March–April 1993): 6–11.

Describes the basic steps companies find successful in reorganizing work; a good introduction to the topic.

Housel, Thomas J., Morris, Chris J., and Westland, Christopher. "Business Process Reengineering at Pacific Bell," *Planning Review* 14, no. 3 (March–April 1993): 28–33.

This is a description of pioneering work done on cost accounting of processes, as it was done at Pacific Bell; an important article on cost justification.

Hunt, V. Daniel. *Managing for Quality: Integrating Quality and Business Strategy.* Homewood, Ill.: Business One Irwin, 1993.

This is one of the best books available on process reengineering for both the novice and the experienced practitioner. In particular, Chapter 7 (pp. 127–159) summarizes well the most commonly used tools and techniques of process reengineering.

Johnson, Richard S., and Kazense, Lawrence E. *TQM: The Mechanics of Quality Processes.* Milwaukee: ASQC Quality Press, 1993.

This is a current reference book on quality and process improvement techniques and tools. These include SPC, problem solving, process control, and other quality-based activities. Useful for training as well.

Katzenbach, Jon R., and Smith, Douglas K. "The Rules for Managing Cross–Functional Reengineering Teams," *Planning Review* 14, no. 2 (March–April 1993): 12–13.

Essentially calls for teams to meet clear, measurable results.

Levi, Raffaello. "Cautions for Taguchi Lovers," *Manufacturing Engineering* 110, no. 3 (March 1993): 16.

Warns that recent research suggests that Taguchi methods in experimental design are better suited for screening, not for fine tuning designs. Discusses the debate over his use of variation.

Luftman, J. N., Lewis, P. R., and Oldach, S. H. "Transforming the Enterprise: The Alignment of Business and Information Technology Strategies," *IBM Systems Journal* 32, no. 1 (1993): 198–221.

Describes a strategic alignment method by which information technology, business reengineering, and corporate goals are linked together with new methods to transform businesses.

Melon, Eugene H. *Process Management: Methods for Improving Products and Services.* New York: McGraw-Hill, 1993.

More than just another book on how to do process improvement work, it offers a way of looking at all the activities of an organization as a collection of processes. It was co-published with the ASQC Quality Press.

Melvin, Jeremy. "Re-engineering Office Services," *Facilities* 11, no. 3 (March 1993): 22–27.

This is a case study of process reengineering within an office environment as done at Ernst & Young's Central Support Services department.

Morris, Daniel, and Brandon, Joel. *Re-Engineering Your Business.* New York: McGraw-Hill, 1993.

This is a "how to" book on process reengineering with additional material on major areas to work on, such as personnel practices.

Nesbitt, Thomas E. "Flowcharting Business Processes," *Quality* (March 1993): 34–38.

Describes a quality tool that is most frequently used in documenting and analyzing existing processes and in charting out improved ones. This "how to" article also discusses software tools.

Scherr, A. L. "A New Approach to Business Processes," *IBM Systems Journal* 32, no. 1 (1993): 80–98.

This is a presentation of a methodology for analyzing and designing the processes that an enterprise uses to run its business. It is comprehensive and illustrated with examples.

Skinner, Larry. "Change Management Is the Key to Successful Business Process," *Inform* 7, no. 4 (April 1993): 54–56.

Discusses the creation and operation of Texas Instrument's Corporate Business Engineering Center of Excellence as its vehicle for disseminating best practices throughout the corporation.

Spitzer, Richard D. "Valuing TQM Through Rigorous Financial Analysis," *Quality Progress* 26, no. 7 (July 1993): 49–53.

Argues the case for cost justification and then presents an approach for doing that.

Tanswell, Euring Andrew. "Business Restructuring—The Key to Radical Change," *Professional Engineering* 6, no. 1 (January 1993): 24–25.

Explains the theory of business reengineering at a conceptual, introductory level.

Vasilash, Gary S. "Reengineering—Your Job May Depend On It," *Production* 105, no. 6 (June 1993): 9–16.

A call to arms to companies to reengineer appropriate processes. Suggests practical ways on how to get started.

Urges companies to improve processes that add value to customers.

Verity, John W. "Getting Work to Go With the Flow," *Business Week* no. 3324 (June 21, 1993): 156–161.

Describes workflow automation, then urges automation where possible, describes existing software to help.

Vogl, A. J. "The Age of Reengineering," *Across the Board* 30, no. 5 (June 1993): 26–33.

Michael Hammer and James Champy are interviewed regarding their ideas on how firms should reengineer processes.

Werner, Joseph G. *Managing the Process, The People, and Yourself.* Milwaukee: ASQC Quality Press, 1993.

Provides an umbrella strategy for quality that focuses on understanding existing processes within an enterprise, appreciating what you have in your people, and finally understanding yourself (goals, styles, etc.).

Wilson, Paul F., Dell, Larry D., and Anderson, Gaylord F. *Root Cause Analysis: A Tool for Total Quality Management.* Milwaukee: ASQC Press, 1993.

This is a comprehensive view of root cause analysis, a TQM tool considered by most practitioners to be one of the most useful in defining what problems need to be resolved within a process.

Measurement

Colledge, Michael, and March, Mary. "Quality Management: Development of a Framework for a Statistical Agency," *Journal of Business and Economic Statistics* 11, no. 2 (April 1993): 157–165.

Describes a TQM implementation strategy at a firm that specializes in statistical analysis; interesting to see how a numbers-based organization approaches TQM.

Donath, Bob. "Satisfaction Measurement Sometimes Goes Too Far," *Marketing News* 27, no. 6 (March 15, 1993): 9.

Describes the dangers of applying customer satisfaction measurements in employee reward, compensation, and appraisal schemes, detailing important pitfalls.

Evans, Ken. "Measuring: The Route to Credibility," *Facilities* 11, no. 3 (1993): 13–17.

This is a case study of using measurements to track the performance of facility's management of buildings, citing cases in the United Kingdom.

Faloon, Ronald. "Radiographic Inspection Helps Build in Quality," *Quality* (November 1992): 38–39.

Measurement is more than statistics. In this article the author describes how x-ray technology is a key tool used by component and product inspectors.

Ferguson, Jeffrey M., Higgins, Lexis F., and Phillips, Gary R. "How to Evaluate and Upgrade Technical Service," *Industrial Marketing Management* 22, no. 3 (August 1993): 187–193.

The use of data can help improve communications between sales and manufacturing's technical support functions. Presents case study results.

Flanagan, Theresa A., and Fredericks, Joan O. "Improving Company Performance Through Customer–Satisfaction Measurement and Management," *National Productivity Review* 12, no. 3 (Summer 1993): 239–258.

This is an important, well-done article on customer satisfaction measurement. It shows how to do it in detail, with examples.

Flaherty, Richard. "Productivity Is Everybody's Job," *Industrial Distribution* 82, no. 4 (April 1993): 41.

Describes the collection of data in industrial distribution, then the need for sharing it with employees as a way of getting their ideas on how to improve productivity.

Gilbert, Gail. "Customer Satisfaction Measurement Is Core of Firm's Quality Improvement," *Marketing News* 27, no. 1 (January 4, 1993): 18.

Illustrates how a hospital uses a customer satisfaction index as the core of its quality improvement programs.

Hamada, M., MacKay, R. J., and Whitney, J. B. "Continuous Improvement with Observational Studies," *Journal of Quality Technology* 25, no. 2 (April 1993): 77–84.

Describes how to perform observational studies of a process in conjunction with more traditional numerical measurement procedures.

Hiam, Alexander. *Closing the Quality Gap: Lessons From America's Leading Companies.* Englewood Cliffs, N.J.: Prentice-Hall, 1992.

While mainly an overview of the quality subject with case studies, pages 299–318 offer an excellent overview of the how and why of measurements in a quality world, with illustrations.

Hronec, Steven M. *Vital Signs: Using Quality, Time, and Cost Performance Measurement to Chart Your Company's Future.* New York: Amacon, 1993.

Shows how to create a measurement system for a company that is linked to its strategic business plan; intended for senior management.

Hubbard, Gerald M. "How to Gauge Your FM Performance," *Facilities Design & Management* 12, no. 4 (April 1993): 42–43.

This is a brief example of how to measure the performance of one function, in this case facilities management. Applies concepts from Peter Drucker.

Kumar, Sanjoy, and Gupta, Yash P. "Statistical Process Control at Motorola's Austin Assembly Plant," *Interfaces* 23, no. 2 (March–April 1993): 84–92.

This is a useful case study of the use of SPC tool in all aspects of its plant-level TQM program. It is also a useful study of how TQM in general is applied in manufacturing environments.

Levins, Llyssa. "Can Public Relations Actually Move Product?" *Public Relations Quarterly* 38, no. 1 (Spring 1993): 18–19.

Lays out how to measure pre- and post-public relations campaign results; concludes with basic rules on good practices.

Morgan, John. "A Variation in Understanding," *TQM Magazine* 5, no. 1 (February 1993): 39–43.

Illustrates how SPC can be used to understand customers in the service sector companies. This is a discussion of the role of statistical variation in nontechnical terms.

Parsaye, Kamran, and Chignell, Mark H. "The Eighth, Ninth, and 10th Tools of Quality," *Quality Progress* 26, no. 9 (September 1993): 109–113.

Argues that there are three new quality tools available, thanks to computers. They are information discovery, data visualization, and hypermedia. All three are defined and illustrated.

Parker, Kevin. "Advanced Stats for Manufacturing: Beyond SPC," *Manufacturing Systems* 11, no. 6 (June 1993): 32–37.

Argues that Design of Experiments (DOE) techniques are now practical for a variety of listed industries and explains the value of this method, with examples.

Scott, Tim. "Assessing Network Product Reliability: The Reliability Gap Cost," *Telephony* 224, no. 16 (April 19, 1993): 121–126.

This describes GTE's telephone process measurement software and practices, what gets measured and how; excellent and applicable to many organizations.

Sower, Victor E., Motwani, Jaideep, and Savoie, Michael J. "Are Acceptance Sampling and SPC Complementary or Incompatible?" *Quality Progress* 26, no. 9 (September 1993): 85–89.

The authors offer an excellent summary of the debate on this important issue and then offer a model for using both practices, as applied at AT&T.

Thomas, Philip R. "Measuring Quality," *Executive Excellence* 10, no. 5 (May 1993): 18–19.

He describes eight measures of quality that a corporation can use, all customer oriented.

Thompson, James R., and Koronacki, Jacek. *Statistical Process Control for Quality Improvement.* New York: Chapman & Hall, 1993.

This is a textbook on SPC based on teaching done with workers in Europe and in the United States.

White, Robert M. "Competitive Measures," *IEEE Spectrum* 30, no. 4 (April 1993): 29–33.

Discusses the application of metrology, or the science and technology of measurement, as it applies in a variety of organizations within a corporation.

Wilkerson, David, and Kellog, Jefferson. "Quantifying the Soft Stuff: How To Select the Assessment Tool You Need," *Employment Relations Today* 19, no. 4 (Winter 1992/1993): 413–424.

Describes how to measure cultural change, what to worry about, what tools to use, and ways to approach the problem.

Teams and Teamwork

Austin, Nancy K. "Making Teamwork Work," *Working Woman* 18, no. 1 (January 1993): 28, 80.

Describes team-directed work force at the San Diego Zoo; the case study begins with efforts dating back to 1982.

Berlew, David E. "Teams and the Importance of Goals," *Quality Digest* 13, no. 2 (February 1993): 34–39.

Describes how teams can set goals. Also argues that the leader's most important job is to make sure his or her team members understand and endorse a set of goals to improve performance.

Butman, John. *Flying Fox: A Business Adventure in Teams and Teamwork.* Milwaukee: ASQC Quality Press, 1993.

This is a novel that teaches the hows and whys of teams in a business environment.

Clemmer, Jim. "The Coming Teams Crisis: Five Stumbling Blocks or Stepping Stones to Success," *CMA Magazine* 67, no. 4 (May 1993): 30.

Says many teams have been successful, many others are failing. Reviews problems and how to improve teams, with focus on organizational responses to team efficiencies.

Katzenbach, Jon R., and Smith, Douglas K. "The Discipline of Teams," *Harvard Business Review* (March—April 1993): 111–120.

Two leading experts on the use of teams defines them, tells what constitutes good team behavior, and what makes them effective.

Kramer, Mariene, and Schmalenberg, Claudia, "Learning From Success: Autonomy and Empowerment," *Nursing Management* 24, no. 5 (May 1993): 58–64.

This describes the magnet hospital review, a process for assessing hospitals. Says that empowerment and team behavior is a critical component and why. Applicable to all industries.

Pritchett, Price, and Pound, Ron. *Team Reconstruction: Building a High Performance Work Group During Change.* Dallas: Pritchett Publishing Co., 1992.

This booklet is a general introduction to the concepts of teams and about how they should perform.

Zemke, Ron. "In Search of . . . Good Ideas," *Training* 30, no. 1 (January 1993): 46–52.

Describes the use of such team-oriented skills as brainstorming and problem solving to improve effectiveness of team members. A variety of other methods are also described.

Zenger, John H., et al. *Leading Teams.* Homewood, Ill.: Business One Irwin, 1993.

Written by four individuals, it is a "how to" book on creating, leading, and managing teams in the workplace.

FUNCTIONAL PROCESSES
Planning

Baatz, E. B. "Results First, Then Change the Culture," *Electronic Business* 19, no. 1 (January 1993): 19–20.

Advocates management define short-term results required of an organization first then force TQM practices to support these.

Burr, John T. "A New Name for a Not So New Concept," *Quality Progress* 26, no. 3 (March 1993): 87–88.

Defines total quality management in planning terms as a process for change in an organization. This is a clear exposition of how to launch quality programs.

Calfee, David L. "Get Your Mission Statement Working!" *Management Review* 82, no. 1 (January 1993): 54–57.

Defines mission and vision statements, their value, what they should accomplish, and offers advice on how to develop them.

Gill, John, and Whittle, Sue. "Management by Panacea: Accounting for Transience," *Journal of Management Studies* 30, no. 2 (March 1993): 281–295.

Describes three ways to manage: MBO, TQM, and organizational improvement. Compares and contrasts the phases of each.

Greenberg, Richard S., and Unger, Cynthia A. "Plan: The First Step on the Roadmap to Quality," *Total Quality Environmental Management* 2, no. 2 (Winter 1992–1993): 217–219.

Summarizes the classic Plan–Do–Check–Act cycle and describes how it can be applied to planning and quality activities.

Hoskin, Richard, and Wood, Steve. "Overcoming Strategic Planning Disconnects," *Journal for Quality & Participation* 16, no. 4 (July–August 1993): 50–58.

Illustrates modern planning methods as applied at Proctor & Gamble, with specific application to logistics management.

Pan, J. N., and Kolarik, W. J. "Quality Tree: A Systematic Problem–Solving Model Using Total Quality Management Tools and Techniques," *Quality Engineering* 5, no. 1 (1992–93): 1–20.

This is a detailed statement about planning for quality, then the article illustrates the quality tree model, with examples, that can be applied to planning.

Sheridan, Bruce M. *Policy Deployment: The TQM Approach to Long-Range Planning.* Milwaukee: ASQC Quality Press, 1993.

This book is a short introduction to policy deployment and how to implement long-range planning in businesses.

Sales and Marketing

Anonymous. "Quality: A Road to Profits," *Agency Sales Magazine* 23, no. 1 (January 1993): 58–59.

Describes the benefits of TQM and addresses them to an audience in sales.

Carder, Brooks, and Clark, James D. "The Theory and Practice of Employee Recognition," *Quality Progress* 26, no. 12 (December 1992): 25–30.

This is a case study of recognition processes at four sales offices, focusing on sales personnel. It is the only article available on this subject.

Cortada, James W. "Implementing Quality in a Sales Organization," *Quality Progress* 26, no. 9 (September 1993): 67–70.

The article reviews how a sales district of IBM's in Wisconsin implemented Deming-based quality programs and processes.

Cortada, James W. *TQM For Sales and Marketing Management.* New York: McGraw-Hill, 1993.

This is a guide to how to apply quality practices in marketing and sales, complete with justification, action plans, and case studies of process improvements.

Duncan, R. C. III. "The Company With the Most Information Wins," *Industrial Distribution* 82, no. 2 (February 1993): 52.

Describes what measurements might be used in marketing to establish a baseline, benchmark future performance, and apply quality practices.

Griffith, Ian. "Marketable Improvements," *TQM Magazine* 5, no. 2 (April 1993): 39–41.

Offers the case for marketing quality as part of the presentation of products to customers. The process is described along with its benefits.

Kern, Jill Phelps. "Toward Total Quality Marketing," *Quality Progress* 26, no. 1 (January 1993): 39–42.

Describes how Digital Equipment Corporation listens to the "voice of the customer." The process is illustrated and is a good example of hoshin kanri techniques.

Kowalczyk, Philip H. "Death of a Salesman?" *Bobbin* 34, no. 7 (March 1993): 108–116.

Sales people as we have always known them will disappear to be replaced by team leaders providing customer service. The change is described.

Lyle, John F. "Find the 'Superior Need' Before Competitor Does," *Marketing News* 27, no. 4 (February 15, 1993): 16ff.

Builds the case for why customer feedback is an important process, what benefits can be expected from the effort.

Magrath, Allan J. *How to Achieve Zero–Defect Marketing.* New York: American Management Association, 1993.

Describes seven sets of practices in marketing, applying TQM principles.

Mentzer, John T. "Managing Channel Relations in the 21st Century," *Journal of Business Logistics* 14, no. 1 (1993): 27–42.

TQM is fundamentally participating in changing channel strategies. Looks at all channels as part of an overall corporate set of activities and offers advice on how to use channel relations within a strategic planning approach.

Ptashkin, Barry I. "Where Will You Get Your Next Sale?" *Quality Progress* 26, no. 5 (May 1993): 71–74.

Describes a process for growing business with existing customers. It offers an example of a customer service planning model.

Raynor, Michael E. "Fantastic Things Happen When You Talk to Customers," *Marketing News* 27, no. 4 (February 15, 1993): 8.

Describes Diners Card customer feedback program and how it reacted to the data gathered in improving service delivery.

Stovall, Steven Austin. "Keeping Tabs on Customer Service," *Bank Marketing* 25, no. 6 (June 1993): 29–33.

Several methods for understanding what customers think in the banking world are presented.

Suppliers and Purchasing

Anonymous. "Design 2000: Chrysler's LH Story," *Purchasing* 114, no. 2 (February 18, 1993): 48–51, 55–57.

Describes the process by which suppliers of components for this car manufacturer participated in the design of a new product with benefits for both described.

Anonymous. "Equipment Users Push for Quality: Chemical Producers Plan to Make Equipment Suppliers and Their Products Part of Total Quality Management," *Chemical Business* (January 1939): 17.

This article details how suppliers are being integrated into chemical companies' TQM strategies. Also offers evidence of supplier desires to be linked to customers via TQM approaches.

Anonymous. "Materials Traceability," *Work Study* 42, no. 3 (May–June 1993): 29–30.

Describes MT in a TQM program, the source of up to 80% of a factory's hard benefits from quality processes, according to this article.

Anonymous. "Powertex's Quality Saturation Course: Liner Manufacturer Sees a Marketing Tool," *Chemical Week* (April 28, 1993): 54.

Describes Amoco's 'certified supplier' program and the experience of one supplier. Advice on how to implement such a process is given.

Anonymous. "Professional Profile: Allan W. Hall of Sara Lee Intimates," *Purchasing* 114, no. 6 (April 15, 1993): 21.

A pioneer in supplier certification explains the rationale for this process, how it is implemented, and then his own work at Sara Lee as Director of Purchasing and Transportation.

Cali, James F. *TQM For Purchasing Management.* New York: McGraw-Hill, 1993.

This is, at the moment, the only book available on this set of processes. It provides an assortments of processes to work on, but also a discussion of trends in purchasing.

English, Lloyd. "TQM for Purchasing Management," *Cost Engineering* 35, no. 3 (March 1993): 45.

Summarizes the contents of a book by James F. Cali, *TQM For Purchasing Management* (New York: McGraw-Hill, 1992).

Gould, Les. "New Warehouse Payoff: A 200% Jump in Productivity," *Modern Materials Handling* 48, no. 3 (March 1993): 40–42.

This is a case study of warehouse automation, illustrating cycle time reduction in picking and in improving accuracy and effectiveness of operations.

Graham, Jean. "Five Steps to Make Your MRO Buying World Class," *Purchasing* 114, no. 8 (May 1993): 56–57.

Citing the experience of Printpack Inc., the author describes his strategy for excellence in maintenance, repair and operations, with emphasis on buyer processes and relations.

Green, Thomas A. "Pay Attention to Your Partners," *Telephony* 224, no. 19 (May 10, 1993): 26–29.

The Rochester Telephone Company and AT&T worked together to define new products for customers who work at home. He describes how the partnership worked and what was developed.

Howe, Roger J., Gaeddert, Dee, and Howe, Maynard A. "The Supplier Review Process," in their book *Quality on Trial* (West Publishing, 1992): 93–100.

This is a clear description of how supplier processes should work and how to improve them; one of the clearest discussions available on the subject.

Jablonski, Robert. "Quality Supplier Relationships Enhance Performance," *Healthcare Financial Magazine* 47, no. 3 (March 1993): 16.

Defines the relationship between hospitals and suppliers and how they effect the quality performance of the health provider.

Kemezis, Paul. "Powertex's Quality Saturation Course," *Chemical Week* 152, no. 16 (April 28, 1993): 54.

Describes how a supplier to Amoco Chemical participated in a supplier certification program; some discussion also of ISO requirements in the near future.

Lee Mortimer, Andrew. "A Dynamic Collaboration," *TQM Magazine* 5, no. 1 (February 1993): 31–34.

Describes how supplier partnerships were successfully developed between a British aerospace firm and one supplier. Focus is on specific process and management attitudes.

McIntyre, Barry. "Supplier Service Quality: A Necessity in the 90's," *Management International Review* 33 (Special Issue) (First Quarter 1993): 111–120.

Customers are demanding more performance from suppliers, and those who practice TQM are becoming preferred suppliers. Presents research results.

Moody, Patricia E. "Customer Supplier Integration: Why Being an Excellent Customer Counts," *Business Horizons* 35, no. 4 (July–August 1992): 52–57.

This is an important article because most such pieces only focus on how to be a good supplier. This one looks at the other side of the equation and how customers influence suppliers. Offers results of surveys and case studies.

Thryft, Ann R. "Electronic Supply's Quality Push," *Electronic Buyers' News* (April 5, 1993): 31.

Describes how one firm improved dramatically its sales and ability to supply customers through reorganization, process reengineering, and focus on cycle time reduction.

Weber, Richard T., and Johnson, Ross H. *Buying and Supplying Quality.* Milwaukee: ASQC Quality Press, 1993.

This describes how to implement a procurement process. It is targeted mainly at manufacturing and ISO 9000 environments.

Product Development

Anderson, Richard E. "HRD's Role in Concurrent Engineering," *Training and Development* 47, no. 6 (June 1993): 49–54.

Provides a good overview of concurrent engineering and then describes the role that Human Resources can play in the process. It is detailed and specific.

Anonymous. "Another Victory for QFD," *Machine Design* 65, no. 11 (June 11, 1993): 18–19ff.

Describes the success with QFD enjoyed by Dodge Group of Reliance Electric.

Archer, Edward D., Dorawala, Tansukh, and Werner, Thomas J. "Who Says It Can't Work in an R&D Environment?" *Journal for Quality & Participation* 16, no. 3 (June 1993): 40–44.

This is one of a few articles that exist on how to apply quality tools in an R&D environment; describes the nearly ten year effort of one organization.

Bengen, Robert. "Teamwork: It's in The Bag," *Marketing Research* 5, no. 1 (Winter 1993): 30–33.

Details work done at the Samsonite Corporation in using customer feedback in product development. That company's work is very creative and novel; must reading.

Burall, Paul. "Germany: The Missing Link," *Design* (March 1993): 42–43.

Describes how a firm and a university in Germany have linked up to do product design; explains the strategy well.

Carlson, Lloyd. "TQM in the Test Environment," *Quality* 32, no. 4 (April 1993): 25–26.

Describes how to use TQM principles in all aspects of product testing. It is a short, tactical description of what gets done.

Craig, Nick, and Savage, Charles M. "Concurrent Engineering: Hype or Hard Work?" *Target* 8, no. 5 (September–October 1992): 30–34.

Their answer is hard work, but clearly an effective way to develop products. This is a thoughtful discussion of the effects CE has on how organizations work.

Day, Ronald G. *Quality Function Deployment: Linking a Company With Its Customers.* Milwaukee: ASQC Quality Press, 1993.

This is an introduction to QFD, with a step-by-step approach to implementation.

Deming, Stanley, and Morgan, Stephen L. *Experimental Design: A Chenometric Approach.* Amsterdam, Netherlands: Elsevier Science Publishers, 1993.

This is a very detailed look at experimental designs from the experimentor's viewpoint. It is a guide to application; does not take the statistician's view as have previous books on the subject.

Ettlie, John E. "Revisiting the 'House of Quality' Foundations," *Production* 105, no. 4 (April 1993): 26.

Based on the survey of over 40 companies applying QFD, the author presents their observations of what works. It is a useful companion to other publications that tout the bnefits of QFD.

Grady, Jeffrey O. *System Requirements Analysis.* New York: McGraw-Hill, 1993.

This is a practical discussion of the Systems Requirement Analysis (SRA), used in systems analysis and product development. It is intended for product development engineers and is detailed.

Griffin, Abbie, and Hauser, John R. "The Voice of the Customer," *Marketing Science* 12, no. 1 (Winter 1993): 1–27.

This is a detailed explanation of how to involve customer feedback in the use of Quality Function Deployment (QFD) methods. Presents the results of a study of various stages of customer feedback.

Guinta, Lawrence R., and Praizler. *QFD Book: Team Approach to Solving Problems and Satisfying Customers Through Quality Function Deployment.* New York: AMACOM, 1993.

QFD has become a popular way for product designers to incorporate the voice of the customer in their work. This is one of several guides available on the subject.

Hohner, Gregory. "Integrating Product and Process Designs," *Quality Progress* 26, no. 5 (May 1993): 55–61.

A clear overview of how to apply TQM principles in product design. This is a useful strategic outline of the process involved.

Kandebo, Stanley W. "GE Plan Reducing Engine Development Cycles," *Aviation Week and Space Technology* 138, no. 25 (June 21, 1993): 65–67.

Explains the strategy this company has used in product development during the early 1990s to reduce the amount of time it takes to improve performance of existing powerplants.

Karagozoglu, Necmi, and Brown, Warren B. "Time Based Management of the New Product Development Process," *Journal of Product Innovation Management* 10, no. 3 (June 1993): 204–215.

Presents results of a survey of product development in 31 companies, reporting that most were on a strategy of incremental improvements of existing products. How this was done is the heart of the article.

Kelly, A., and Harris, M. J. "Uses and Limits of Total Productive Maintenance," *Professional Engineering* 6, no. 1 (January 1993): 9–11.

This article provides a detailed description of maintenance processes for use in manufacturing environments.

Laugling, Antonio S. "Technical Market Research: Get Customers to Collaborate in Developing Products," *Long Range Planning* 26, no. 2 (April 1993): 78–82.

Describes technical market research processes. TMR is presented as a structured, disciplined approach to understanding what customers want.

Luciano, Robert. "Packaging by the Numbers 1993: 4 Management Ideas Changing Machinery," *Packaging* 38, no. 1 (January 1993): 45.

Packaging machinery is being built using new manufacturing processes that are described, along with benefits. Also describes effects on the product design processes.

Patterson, Marvin L. "Lessons From the Assembly Line," *Journal of Business Strategy* 14, no. 3 (May–June 1993): 42–46.

Provides seven specific suggestions on how to improve the cycle time in product development.

Pease, David A. "Plant Technology Backed by Aggressive Marketing," *Wood Technology* 120, no. 2 (March–April 1993): 20–22.

Boise Cascade Corporation's product development process is described as the process's relationship to other activities, such as marketing.

Rasmus, Dan. "Learning the Waltz of Synthesis," *Manufacturing Systems* 11, no. 6 (June 1993): 16–23.

An excellent overview of modern methods, such as quality, concurrent engineering, and technological change and how they all work together in well-run manufacturing operations.

Regis, Lesley. "Driving Quality Up and Cycle Time Down With Design of Experiment," *Industrial Engineering* (February 1993): 54–58.

The author describes a tool increasingly being used as part of a product design effort. It is detaild and illustrated, giving the reader an understanding of what it is, how it is used, why, and with examples.

Taguchi, Genichi. "Robust Technology Development," *Mechanical Engineering* 115, no. 3 (March 1993): 60–62.

Defines stages of product design and production and how such a view can be used to improve each of the five stages.

Tillery, Kenneth R., Routledge, Arthur L., and Inman, R. Anthony. "Quality Management and POM Textbooks: A Review and Assessment," *International Journal of Quality and Reliability Management* 10, no. 1 (1993): 8–16.

Looks at ten textbooks on production and operations management to see how much discussion they have regarding quality practices. Concludes that it is starting and is not well integrated into the overall topic.

Whiting, Rick. "Designing to the Customer's Order," *Electronic Business* 19, no. 6 (June 1993): 61.

Going beyond quality function deployment, some companies are asking their customers to tell them what products to create.

Zairi, Mohamed. *Quality Function Deployment: A Modern Competitive Tool.* Hertfordshire, England: Technical Communications, 1993.

This is a 68-page pamphlet that describes the use of QFD principles; a useful introduction to the concept.

Information Technology

Anderson, O. "Industrial Applications of Software Measurements," *Information and Software Technology* 34, no. 10 (October 1992): 681–693.

Describes the notion of performance software measurements, and how to exploit such metrics tools.

Anonymous. "TQM in IS: Defining User Expectations," *I/S Analyzer* 31, no. 5 (May 1993): 1–14.

To determine if a process is effective, monitoring user opinions becomes critical. Uses several case studies to illustrate an effective way to define IS user expectations.

Ayers, James B. "TQM and Information Technology: Partners for Profit," *Information Strategy: The Executive's Journal* 9, no. 3 (Spring 1993): 26–31.

Use of TQM in IS declares war on wasteful investment in IT.

Belmonte, Rocco W., and Murray, Richard J. "Getting Ready for Strategic Change: Surviving Business Process Redesign," *Information Systems Management* 10, no. 3 (Summer 1993): 23–29.

Describes business reengineering, including obvious steps for management. Appears to be a wakeup call for MIS.

Champy, James A. "Grand Designs," *CIO* 6, no. 6 (January 1993): 26.

Announces that a CSX/Index survey shows that IS executives are very actively pursuing process reengineering; gives some examples.

Cole, Christopher, Clark, Michael L., and Nemec, Carl. "Reengineering Information Systems at Cincinnati Milacron," *Planning Review* 14, no. 3 (May–June 1993): 22–27.

Describes how MIS functions were aligned with reengineered processes in an $800 million company. This is a pioneering work on MIS and reengineering.

de Ruyter, Ko, and Zuurbier, Joost. "Customer Information Systems: Approaching a New Field in Information Systems From a New Perspective," *Information and Management* 24, no. 5 (May 1993): 247–255.

Describes how designing of applications can be improved through an interplay between systems design and organizational design.

Guha, Subashish, Kettinger, William J., and Teng, James T. C. "Business Process Reengineering: Building A Comprehensive Methodology," *Information Systems Management* 10, no. 3 (Summer 1993): 13–22.

Says business reengineering is replacing information systems development, which only used to focus on automating existing processes. Offers guidelines for the MIS community.

Henderson, J. C., and Venkatraman, N. "Strategic Alignment: Leveraging Information Technology for Transforming Organizations," *IBM Systems Journal* 32, no. 1 (1993): 4–16.

Two leading experts on information technology review a model for linking MIS to strategic business plans, a process that has been well received by American corporations.

James, Philip N. "Cyrus F. Gibson: On IS Reengineering," *Information Systems Management* 10, no. 1 (Winter 1993): 83–87.

This consultant describes recent changes in programming whereby users are doing more of it and integrating their IS work into process reengineering steps.

Jones, David C. "Insurers Slashing Technology Budgets for 1993," *National Underwriter Life and Health* (January 1993): 13.

More than just some news on the insurance industry, it offers information on how IS organizations are operating. There is a shift to process reengineering underway using IT to support the effort.

Koulopoulos, Thomas M. "The Document Factory: Part I," *Inform* 7, no. 6 (June 1993): 42–46.

Talks about the use of TQM principles in office environments and the role of such technologies as EDI to facilitate the transformation.

O'Leary, Meghan. "I.S. Quality Profile: Leading Lights, Carolina Power & Light Co.," *CIO* 6, no. 10 (April 15, 1993): 56–58.

Describes why IS was chosen for the first major process reengineering effort in the company and what was accomplished. The primary concentration was on reengineering customer services while facilitating a more open corporate culture.

Pastore, Richard. "A Virtual Visionary," *CIO* 6, no. 15 (July 1993): 46–49.

Describes the work of Bill Davidow, author of *The Virtual Corporation*, in which he argues that IT links and helps to empower all employees; describes how.

Powers, Jacklyn. "TQM in Software Development Organization," *Quality Progress* 26, no. 7 (July 1993): 79–80.

Software development organizations need to apply TQM. Describes a six-step process to do that.

Rowe, Joyce M., and Neal, Ralph. "TQM in System Development: A Paradigm Without a Sound Foundation," *Journal of Systems Management* 44, no. 5 (May 1993): 12–16.

Argues that IS organizations need to invest in basic building blocks of its own organization before any TQM effort can be implemented.

Shepperd, M. "Products, Processes and Metrics," *Information and Software Technology* 34, no. 10 (October 1992): 674–680.

Reports on recent innovations in the area of software engineering product metrics. Defines strengths and weaknesses of the trend, for example, strong software tools exist but weak processes.

Sullivan Trainor, Michael L. "How Are We Doing?" *Computerworld* 27, no. 20 (May 17, 1993): 81–82.

Argues the case for a thorough end user survey program for the MIS community. Describes what they do and why.

Wetherell, Karen. "Mutual Benefits," *TQM Magazine* 3, no. 2 (May–June 1993): 23–28.

The vice president of customer service at Connecticut Mutual Life Insurance describes how process reengineering and the application of computer technology significantly improved customer service.

Research and Development

May, Colin, and Pearson, Alan W. "Total Quality in R&D," *Journal of General Management* 18, no. 3 (Spring 1993): 1–22.

Surveys R&D use of TQM in British firms over past three years. Shows how it is being done successfully.

Singer, Donald C., and Upton, Ronald P. *Guidelines for Laboratory Quality Auditing.* Milwaukee: ASQC Quality Press, 1993.

The latest methods, best practices, and key government requirements are explained and their application described. All the examples are drawn from health care and microbiological environments.

Accounting

Anderson, Bridget M. "Using Activity Based Costing for Efficiency and Quality," *Government Finance Review* 9, no. 3 (June 1993): 7–9.

Describes the benefits a city can achieve by using ABC accounting to determine value of its services. The article is relevant to all industries.

Anonymous. "In Pursuit of Excellence?" *Management Accounting* 71, no. 1 (January 1993): 12.

A forum of 12 executives concluded that TQM was advantageous and that senior management had to support its implementation for quality to be effective in a business.

Barr, Stephen. "The New Blueprint for Finance," *CFO: The Magazine For Senior Financial Executives* 9, no. 6 (June 1993): 15–33.

Describes process reengineering practices in finance departments. Includes useful and detailed case studies.

Benneyan, James C., and Chute, Alan D. "SPC, Process Improvement, and the Deming PDCA Circle in Freight Administration," *Production and Inventory Management Journal* 34, no. 1 (First Quarter 1993): 35–40.

Illustrates all these tools at work in freight payment at Digital Equipment Corporation; a wonderful case study of how to do it.

Burcke, James M. "Moving Ahead Through Change," *Business Insurance* 27, no. 18 (April 26, 1993): 122–123.

Using as its case study Hallmark Cards Inc.'s risk management services department, the author describes how its functions have been changing over the years and the methods used to achieve them.

Christensen, Linda F., and Sharp, Douglas. "How ABC Can Add Value to Decision Making," *Management Accounting* 74, no. 11 (May 1993): 38–42.

This is a useful explanation of ABC accounting as it applies in the world of quality. Should be read by more than just accountants.

Chung, Ronald K. "TQM: Internal Client Satisfaction," *Business Credit* 85, no. 4 (April 1993): 26–39.

Focuses on credit and accounts receivable processes using TQM principles. It is detailed in its definition of the subject and about suggestions on application.

Dangerfield, Nick. "Just in Time For the Office," *Accountants' Journal* 71, no. 6 (July 1992): 43–44.

This short piece defines JIT as a management philosophy and explains how it could be applied in office environments.

Hamilton Smith, Kaye, and Morris, Ted. "Market Driven Quality," *CMA Magazine* 67, no. 4 (May 1993): 23–25.
Calls on Canadian accountants to support improvements in customer service and refers to surveys on the significance of that focus.

Lowe, Alan, de Wild, Andrea, and Shewan, Carla. "Total Quality Management and the Management Accountant," *Accountant's Journal* 71, no. 6 (July 1992): 25–29.
Explains the role of accountants in defining quality measures for any company. Cost accounting is undergoing significant change as a result of the move to quality practices.

Mackey, James T., and Hughes, Vernon H. "Decision Focused Costing at Kenco," *Management Accounting* 74, no. 11 (May 1993): 22–26.
This case study shows how cost accounting supported one company's efforts to implement both just-in-time manufacturing and total quality management practices.

Masonson, Leslie N. "Benchmarking Makes Its Way to Treasury Management," *Healthcare Financial Management* 47, no. 4 (April 1993): 96–97.
This describes benchmarking of cash management operations at AT&T.

Solovy, Alden T. "Champions of Change," *Hospitals* 67, no. 5 (March 5, 1993): 14–19.
Using the case of hospital CFO's, the author describes how they can employ TQM effectively. The article is applicable to all industries.

Turney, Peter B. B. *Common Cents: The ABC Performance Breakthrough.* Hillsboro, OR.: Cost Technology, 1991.
Still one of the best accounts of activity based accounting available. This is an excellent way of accounting for the costs and benefits of processes and is widely used for that purpose. The book is a clear exposition of this new trend in cost accounting.

Vondra, Albert A., and Schueler, Dennis R. "Can You Innovate Your Internal Audit?" *Financial Executive* 9, no. 2 (March–April 1993): 34–39.
Describes a variety of ways auditing can be more effective, including the use of total quality management principles.

Human Resources

Anonymous. "The Benchmarking Boom," *HR Focus* 70, no. 4 (April 1993): 1, 6ff.

Explains how HR can play a significant role in benchmarking. This includes training people, benchmarking their own HR processes, etc.; includes case studies.

Ashton, Chris. "Investing in People," *TQM Magazine* 5, no. 3 (June 1993): 51–54.
Describes the UK national standard for assessing and recognition of quality in employee training, development, and empowerment.

Bahr, Mort. "Communications Workers of America," *Quality Progress* 26, no. 9 (September 1993):59–60.
Briefly describes this union's role in TQM with a case study of application.

Bieber, Owen. "United Auto Workers," *Quality Progress* 26, no. 9 (September 1993): 61–62.
Describes his union's attitude toward TQM and how it is working with this new management concept.

Blackburn, Richard, and Rosen, Benson. "Total Quality and Human Resources Management: Lessons Learned From Baldrige Award Winning Companies," *Executive* 7, no. 3 (August 1993): 49–66.
Summarizes TQM-focused personnel practices from over a dozen U.S. companies. It catalogs all the usual components of the process as evident in other TQM-focused companies.

Bruner, Jack E., and Jones, Michael B. "Reinventing Benefits," *Journal of Compensation and Benefits* 8, no. 6 (May/June 1993): 59–62.
Describes how to make a benefits program customer oriented with employees being the customers. Introduces concept of a value gap measure of offerings versus what is needed and how to close the gap.

Burns, Frank, and Bull, Owen. "Lighting The Fuse," *TQM Magazine* 5, no. 3 (June 1993): 7–8.
Describes how one British firm has reduced its personnel function, delegating personnel practices to line management.

Caudron, Shari. "How HR Drives TQM," *Personnel Journal* 72, no. 8 (August 1993): 48B–48O.
More than simply a case study of Xerox Corporation, this is a discussion of the role of human resource functions in trnsforming an organization.

Caudron, Shari. "Well Designed HR Policies Improve TQM Initiatives," *Personnel Journal* 72, no. 8 (August 1993): 48N.
Argues the case for individual development performance plans as a way of linking a company's TQM strategies to individual activities.

Charles, Julie. "Reengineering the Workplace," *Benefits Canada* 17, no. 4 (April 1993): 59, 61.

Criticizes personnel communities for not helping employees reconcile work and home pressures, based on a survey of 15,000 Canadian workers. Makes six recommendations for reordering the workplace.

Cleary, Timothy, and Cleary, Michael J. "Designing an Effective Compensation System," *Quality Progress* (April 1993): 69–72 and (May 1993): 97–99.

This is an important presentation of the subject in a two-part article with primary focus on quality-based approaches.

Cohen, Stephen L. "The Art, Science, and Business of Program Development," *Training and Development* 47, no. 5 (May 1993): 49–56.

Describes how to discipline the process of design, development, and marketing of training programs, something many quality-focused companies want to do after they conclude that their own internal effort was effective.

Creelman, James. "An Act of Faith," *TQM Magazine* 5, no. 3 (Jun 1993): 15–18.

Describes the experience of one British company in reducing the number of layers of management, empowering and what had to be done to make the effort effective. An excellent discussion of the role of management in a quality-focused environment.

Drummond, Helga. "Incentive Schemes in a Quality Culture," *Work Study* 42, no. 2 (March–April 1993): 25–27.

Describes the controversy surrounding Deming's desire to see incentive compensation decline and how emperical evidence shows the contrary is the case. Good summary of this major issue.

Gabor, Carol, and Meunier, Greg. "Putting the Power into Empowerment," *Journal for Quality and Participation* 16, no. 1 (January–February 1993): 98–101.

Defines empowerment, shows its use in education, and suggests how to make it effective.

Gilbert, Neal E., and Whiting, Charles E., Jr. "Empowering Professionals," *Management Review* 82, no. 6 (June 1993): 57.

Argues the case for giving more authority to make decisions to professionals who have significant expertise in the areas in which they are being empowered.

Graber, Jim M., Breisch, Roger E., and Breisch, Walter E. "Performance Appraisals and Deming: A Misunderstanding?" *Quality Progress* (June 1992): 59–62.

The author is of the school of thought that appraisals and Deming-based approaches can work together.

Hand, Max. "Freeing the Victims," *TQM Magazine* 5, no. 3 (June 1993): 11–14.

This is a thoughtful discussion of the issues surrounding empowerment and the concerns management sometimes experiences with it.

Harriger, Dan. "Use TQM to Reengineer Human Resources," *HR Focus* 70, no. 4 (April 1993): 17.

Argues the case for weaving TQM and HR together, and how to use software for decision-support activities in implementing new HR processes.

Harris, Beverley. "Music to Their Ears," *TQM Magazine* 5, no. 3 (June 1993): 19–22.

Describes a music company's practices with employee development and empowerment, what was required and how it is working; a positive case study.

Imberman, Woodruff. "Employee Participation: What It Is, How It Works," *Target* 9, no. 1 (January–February 1993): 19–26.

Provides a structured approach to understanding employee participation at its various stages of evolution. Particular emphasis is on the social and organizational dynamics involved.

Kanin Lovers, Jill, and Sheehy, Barry. "Defining the Role of Quality," *Journal of Compensation and Benefits* 9, no. 1 (July–August 1993): 48–51.

Job definition and compensation issues are important in the world of TQM; they are reviewed in this article.

Kennedy, Peter W. "Quality Management Challenges Compensation Professionals," *Journal of Compensation and Benefits* 8, no. 5 (March–April 1993): 29–35.

Attacks traditional compensation methods as being incompatible with empowered and team-based management practices. Offers 10 new principles to guide compensation programs.

Lawler, Edward E. III. "Pay the Person Not the Job," *Industry Week* (December 7, 1992): 19–24.

Argues that job-based pay will not motivate highly involved employees. Argues the case for skill-based pay systems.

Lawler, Edward E. III, Ledford, Gerald E. Jr., and Chang, Lei. "Who Uses Skill Based Pay, and

Why," *Compensation and Benefits Review* 25, no. 2 (March–April 1993): 22–26.

Presents results of a survey indicating skill-based pay practices are becoming increasingly popular.

Lissy, William E. "Currents in Compensation and Benefits," *Compensation and Benefits Review* 25, no. 1 (January–February 1993): 8–10.

Reviews the current debate over compensation and incentive strategies in light of the TQM movement and resultant changes in personnel practices. Presents results of 107 companies surveyed on these issues.

Magjuka, Richard J. "The 10 Dimensions of Employee Involvement," *Training and Development* 47, no. 4 (April 1993): 61–67.

Shows result of 923 companies and how they link employee involvement programs and TQM. The survey identified 10 practices that are effective.

McConalogue, Tom. "Real Delegation: The Art of Hanging On and Letting Go," *Management Decision* 31, no. 1 (1993): 60–64.

Describes specifically what changes must occur in a manager's behavior in order to facilitate effective empowerment of employees.

Miles, Carrie A., and McCloskey, Jean M. "People: The Key to Productivity," 38, no. 2 *HR Magazine* (February 1993): 40–45.

Describes the power of empowerment using the case study of a distribution arm of a high-tech equipment manufacturer.

Oddey, Graham, and Bull, Owen. "Applying Quality in Redundancy," *TQM Magazine* 5, no. 1 (February 1993): 19–21.

The authors describe how quality-based organizations handle job losses, for example, what jobs should go, and how downsizing is done in comparison to more traditional approaches.

Prince, E. Ted. "Human Factors in Quality Assurance," *Information Systems Management* 10, no. 3 (Summer 1993): 78–80.

Responds to the human side of quality implementation by providing four rules for how MIS managers should help people as they implement quality practices.

Raub, Robert R. "Employees' Ideas Yield More Than Just Better Mousetraps," *Personnel Journal* 72, no. 3 (March 1993): 17.

This is a description of one company's product suggestion process. Suggestion programs are some of the most

important innovations organizations can implement to improve quality. This is a good example.

Roberts, Harry, and Sergesketter, Bernard F. *Quality is Personal: Foundation for Total Quality Management.* New York: Free Press, 1993.

This is a fresh introduction to the quality set of values and practices and the role individuals can play.

Roughton, Jim. "Integrating a Total Quality Management System Into Safety and Health Programs," *Professional Safety* 38, no. 6 (June 1993): 31–37.

Describes a health and safety process using TQM principles.

Scherer, Robert F., Brodzinski, James D., and Crable, Elaine A. "The Human Factor," *HR Magazine* 38, no. 4 (April 1993): 92–97.

Focuses on human factor causes of accidents and how TQM programs can be applied to improve prevention efforts.

Scholtes, Peter R. "Total Quality or Performance Appraisal: Choose One," *National Productivity Review* 12, no. 3 (Summer 1993): 349–363.

One of the leading experts of quality-based personnel practices introduces the conflicts that exist between appraisals and TQM, which he argues are mutually exclusive.

Scott, Miriam Basch. "Employers Implement Total Compensation," *Employee Benefit Plan Review* 47, no. 8 (February 1993): 26–28.

Describes how one bank linked its compensation plan to its objective of providing significant levels of customer service.

Schwartz, William J. "Principles of Empowerment," *Executive Excellence* 10, no. 3 (March 1993): 19.

Describes five trends that disempower employees and then a six-step process for empowering them.

Sheinkman, Jack. "Amalgamated Clothing and Textile Workers Union," *Quality Progress* 26, no. 9 (September 1993): 57–58.

Describes his union's response to quality and how it is working with companies applying TQM principles.

Taylor, David L., and Ramsey, Ruth Karin. "Empowering Employees to 'Just Do It'," *Training and Development* 47, no. 5 (May 1993): 71–76.

This particular case study focuses on what is happening at Cummins Engine, where TQM and empowerment have been blended together in an effective approach to personnel deployment.

Thornburg, Linda. "HR Leaders Tell How They Make Their Companies Better," *HR Magazine* 38, no. 5 (May 1993): 49–57.

They are described as facilitators of change and the introduction of total quality management practices. Four case studies of HR executives at work describe the process.

Wilkinson, Adrian, Marchington, Mick, and Dale, Barrie. "Human Resource's Function," *TQM Magazine* 5, no. 3 (June 1993): 31–35.

Presents the results of a survey of 15 British organizations with TQM with a focus on human resources issues and experiences.

Williams, Lynn R. "United Steelworkers of America," *Quality Progress* 26, no. 9 (September 1993): 63–64.

Describes his union's role in the quality movement; interesting case study because the steel producers in the United States are experiencing an economic come-back.

Zingheim, Patricia K., and Schuster, Jay R. "Pay for Performance: Linking Quality and Pay," *HR Magazine* 37, no. 12 (December 1992): 55–59.

Argues that increasingly companies are modifying their pay strategies to align compensation with strategic organizational priorities, such as TQM. Explains how that is happening.

STANDARDS AND ASSESSMENTS
ISO 9000

Anonymous. "ISO 9000 Just Doesn't Qualify with Everybody," *Electronic Engineering Times* (February 22, 1993): 18.

Reports that some electronics manufacturing firms have higher standards than those called for in ISO 9000 and, therefore, are bypassing this certification. Also presents the case for why some firms should not apply for certification.

Anonymous. "Life After Registration: Are We There Yet?; When the Dust Settles, The Real Work Begins," *Chemical Week* (April 28, 1993): 34.

This is one of the few publications that explores what a company does after it achieves certification. Describes various company experiences in living in an ISO 9000 certified environment.

Anttila, Juani. "Standardization of Quality Management and Quality Assurance: A Project Viewpoint," *International Journal of Project Management* 10, no. 4 (November 1992): 208–212.

Offers an overview of how the ISO 9000 certification process can be used to establish quality standards within a company.

Aune, Asbjorn, and Rao, Ashok, "ISO 9000 Standards: A Baseline for Excellence," *Target* 8, no. 5 (September–October 1992): 23–29.

This is a useful introduction to the standard, and offers two case studies of companies registering for certification.

Boyd, Fraser J. "The New Team Builder," *Records Management Quarterly* 27, no. 3 (July 1993): 26–30.

TQM in records management is discussed along with its role within an ISO 9000 series of quality assurance standards.

Chase, Rory L. "Differing Perceptions," *TQM Magazine* 5, no. 2 (April 1993): 19–21.

The significance in 1993 of ISO 9000 certification is documented, summarizing recent trends and management thinking.

Cirulli, Carol. "Adventures in the ISO Jungle," *Journal of European Business* 4, no. 4 (March–April 1993): 22–30.

This is a combination history of the ISO standards, stengths and weaknesses, praise and criticism.

Cottman, Ronald. *A Guidebook to ISO 9000 and ANSI/ASQC 90.* Milwaukee: ASQC Quality Press, 1993.

This is an authoritative introduction to what these standards are presented in a question and answer format in 138 pages.

Girvan, Bob. "Documented Approval," *TQM Magazine* 5, no. 2 (April 1993): 23–25.

Describes the ISO 9000 and TQM experience of BOC Special Gases in the United Kingdom. It is a case study of the application of ISO 9000 standards.

Gorman, Doug. "Beyond ISO 9000 Certification," *Quality Digest* 12, no. 12 (December 1992): 47–50.

Suggests a way of linking employees, action plans, and strategic tools through effective communications to insure an effective implementation of ISO standards.

Kochan, Anna. "Internal Evaluations," *TQM Magazine* 5, no. 2 (April 1993): 15–17.

Describes Shell France's internal auditing process, its ISO 9000 and TQM programs, and how all three effectively tie together.

Leeuwenburgh, Todd. "Quality Standards That Can Open Doors," *Nation's Business* (November 1992): 32–33.

Provides the argument for why a company would want to obtain ISO 9000 certification.

Mullin, Rick, and Kiesche, Elizabeth S. "ISO 9000—Life After Registration: Are We There Yet?" *Chemical Week* 152, no. 16 (April 28, 1993): 34–40.

Describes the experience of companies after certification, noting that not all quality components are in place; reviews their experience.

Peach, Robert. *The ISO 9000 Handbook*. Fairfax, Va.: CEEM Information Services, 1993.

This is a comprehensive overview of the topic with an explanation of the registration process, how to do it, use of consultants, background to the standards, and so forth.

Pinkham, Myra. "ISO 9000 Aids Foundry Controls," *American Metal Market* (April 19, 1993): 4.

This is a case study of ISO 9000 being used to improve quality of operations at the Atlas Foundry & Machine Company. Its lessons are applicable to many firms.

Pirret, Rick. "Automated Calibration For ISO 9000," *Quality* (November 1992): 15–19.

Provides an excellent overview of ISO 9000, then describes the use of software tools to support audit functions concerning ISO 9000 issues.

Schnoll, Les. "One World, One Standard," *Quality Progress* 26, no. 4 (April 1993):35–39.

This is an outstanding overview of what ISO 9000 is, and offers a case study of the Dow Corning Corporation's experience with it. It offers advise on registration and defines the benefits involved.

Baldrige Award and Criteria

Anonymous. "AT&T Universal Card Services: Is Cited for Its High Attention to Customer Service, in the Credit Card Industry," *Fortune* (May 31, 1993): 79.

This Baldrige winner has a telephone-based customer support process that is described and which yields a high customer level of satisfaction.

Appleby, C. "Quality Is Their Calling Card," *Information Week* no. 415 (March 8, 1993): 25.

Explains how AT&T Universal Card won the Baldrige Award by process improvement of its customer services, particularly in solving common customer problems such as card application and billing. Shows how IT was an important part of the successful effort.

Dorio, Martin M. "Total Quality Self–Appraisal: Use of the Malcolm Baldrige National Quality Award Criteria," *Quality Engineering* 5, no. 2 (1992–1993): 225–241.

This is a detailed case study of how one company used the Baldrige criteria to assess its overall performance. It is detailed, specific, and very instructive for companies in various industries.

Doyle, Kevin. "Baldrige Award Applicants Down: Beginning of End for TQM?" *Incentive* 167, no. 6 (June 1993): 9.

Presents reasons why number of applications for the award is down over the past two years.

Fiero, Janet, and Holmes, Gil. "Using Baldrige Assessments at the Department Level," *Journal for Quality and Participation* 16, no. 3 (June 1993): 64–68.

Such an application of the criteria has rapidly become a common practice in TQM-focused organizations. This is an example of how that is done; excellent.

Fisher, Donald C. *The Simplified Baldrige Award Organization Assessment*. New York: Lincoln-Bradley Publishing Group, 1993.

Targeted at small to mid-sized companies, it offers suggestions on how to do assessments and apply for local and state quality awards based on the Baldrige criteria.

Harmon, Marion. "1992 Baldrige Award Winners," *Quality Digest* 13, no. 2 (February 1993): 28–31.

This is a summary of 1992's award winners, who they are, why they won, and what they are doing in the areas of concern vis-a-vis the Baldrige criteria.

Hill, Robert C. "When the Going Gets Rough: A Baldrige Award Winner on the Line," *Executive* 7, no. 3 (August 1993): 75–79.

Describes the case study of the Wallace Company, a Baldrige winner that went into bankruptcy.

Hunt, V. Daniel. *Quality in America: How to Implement a Competitive Quality Program*. Homewood, Ill.: Business One Irwin, 1992.

Besides doing what many other articles and books do—explain how to implement quality programs—Chapter 5 is a collection of case studies of a recent crop of Baldrige Award winners and what they are doing in the world of quality.

Kendrick, John J. "Five Baldrige Awards in Year Five," *Quality* (January 1993): 24–31.

The author provides thumbnail sketches of the 1992 winners, who they are, what their businesses are about, and what their quality accomplishments were to justify the U.S. quality award.

Kendrick, John J. "Small and Midsized Companies Generate Mixed Signals Concerning Baldrige Award," *Quality* (February 1993): 15.

A survey of small to mid-sized U.S. companies indicated that the Baldrige criteria was not as effective as for large companies. The author also reports on another survey of the same type of companies that indicated the opposite.

Knotts, Uly S., Jr., Parrish, Leo G., Jr., and Evans, Cheri R. "What Does the U.S. Business Community Really Think About the Baldrige Award?" *Quality Progress* 26, no. 5 (May 1993): 49–53.

This is one of the most important articles to be published on the award in 1993. It presents survey results of Fortune 500 firms. They conclude that the Baldrige criteria is a relevant model for quality improvement.

Reimann, Curt, and Braden, Pail V. "Two Into One Will Go," *TQM Magazine* 3, no. 2 (May–June 1993): 15–20.

The director of the Baldrige Award and the manager of the National Medal of Technology discuss where their programs intersect and what each one does distinctively. It is an excellent overview of both awards.

Seemer, Robert H. "Winning More than the Malcolm Baldrige National Quality Award at AT&T Transmission Systems," *National Productivity Review* 12, no. 2 (Spring 1993): 143–165.

This detailed article describes how to use TQM stratigically and builds the case for using the Baldrige criteria for measuring the results of a TQM program. AT&T Transmission Systems is featured as the operative case study.

Shetty, Y. K. "The Quest for Quality Excellence: Lessons from the Baldrige Quality Award," *SAM Advanced Management Journal* 58, no. 2 (Spring 1993): 34–40. Reports on the GAO's study of 20 Baldrige Award applicants, first published in 1992.

Other Awards, Standards, and Issues

Ashton, Chris. "Mindset or Mechanism?" *TQM Magazine* 5, no. 2 (April 1993): 43–46.

Reports on the proliferation of certification bodies within the British economy and what subject areas they cover.

Bemowski, Karen. "The State of the States," *Quality Progress* 26, no. 5 (May 1993): 27–37.

This is the most comprehensive survey of quality awards in various states within the United States, complete with addresses of relevant government agencies

Davies, Paul. "Help or Hazard?" *TQM Magazine* 5, no. 2 (April 1993): 35–38.

The author describes the threat to companies of having various quality awards (e.g., Baldrige and the European Quality Award) to pursue when they serve as models for quality implementation. Gives advice on how to deal with these various criteria.

Luther, David B. "How New York Launched a State Quality Award in 15 Months," *Quality Progress* 26, no. 5 (May 1993): 38–43.

This is an excellent case study of how a state and various companies got together to create a quality award.

Mullin, Rick. "OSHA Star: A Fit With Quality Management, Responsible Care," *Chemical Week* 152, no. 14 (April 14, 1993): 27.

Describes this award as the Malcolm Baldrige of safety. Defines the award, how to get it, and its criteria.

Williams, Melanie. "Attaining New Levels," *TQM Magazine* 5, no. 2 (April 1993): 9–14.

Describes the current British Standards Institution (BSI) standards, including the new BS7750 and BS7850.

Annotated Directory of Organizations

A growing number of organizations are dedicated to providing information on quality practices, seminars, and publications. Some have existed for many decades, while others are developing as regional support, either as independent nonprofit enterprises or as attachments to local universities.

The following list is in alphabetical order, with brief descriptions of each organization's offerings. This initial list focuses on organizations in the United States, Europe, and Asia. It includes only organizations that are overwhelmingly concerned with quality process improvement and certification. Many thousands of other organizations are beginning to include quality practices in their programs, but those have not been included in the list.

We intentionally have not broken out the list by country for this edition of *The Quality Yearbook* because we wanted readers to see what organizations exist around the world as they look for local ones. When the list becomes too cumbersome to work with, we will break it out by continent and, later, by country. The list is selective, including only those of national significance within a country. Many hundreds of very small local organizations are not included here, but as they grow in significance or size, they will be added to our list.

AFAQ
Tour Septentrion, Cedex 9
92081 Paris La Defense
France
Tel: 33/1 47 73 49 49
Fax: 33/1 47 73 49 99
This recently established organization conducts certification of quality practices in companies for the EN29000/ISO 9000 series.

AMERICAN CENTER FOR THE QUALITY OF WORK LIFE
37 Tip Top Way
Berkeley Heights, NJ 07922 USA
Tel: (908) 464-4609
This organization has information, training programs, and does consulting in the area of organizational change and renewal.

AMERICAN INSTITUTE FOR TOTAL PRODUCTIVE MAINTENANCE (AITPM)
P.O. Box 5097
Stamford, CT 06904 USA
Tel: (203) 846-3777, (800) 394-5772
Fax: (203) 846-6883
This organization focuses on Total Productive Maintenance (TPM) quality practices. It sponsors a conference in the fall and publishes the TPM Newsletter.

AMERICAN MANAGEMENT ASSOCIATION
135 West 50th Street
New York, NY 10020 USA
Tel: (212) 586-8100
Fax: (212) 903-8168
The AMA has increasingly taken note of quality practices over the past several years, incorporating these new management methods into its sem-

inars. It publishes the *Management Review, Organizational Dynamics*, and *HR Focus.*

AMERICAN PRODUCTION AND INVENTORY CONTROL SOCIETY (APICS)
500 West Annandale Road
Falls Church, VA 22046 USA
Tel: (703) 237-8344, (800) 444-2742
Fax: (703) 237-1071
This has long been an important organization for manufacturing professionals, providing education and certification programs. In recent years its seminars, publications, annual conferences, and local workshops around the United States have focused on just-in-time manufacturing practices, skills development in capacity management, materials requirements, production, and master production planning. Among its publications is *Production Inventory Management Journal.* APICS is organized through a network of local chapters.

AMERICAN PRODUCTIVITY AND QUALITY CENTER (APQC)
123 North Post Oak Lane
Houston, TX 77024 USA
Tel: (713) 681-4020
Fax: (713) 681-5321
APQC is a quality research center that accumulates information on best practices for all processes. It does client research on who has best practices, supplies copies of articles on processes, conducts seminars, and sells publications. It is the leading center for benchmarking activities in North America. It publishes *Continuous Journey* and administers the Texas Quality Award and Benchmarking Awards.

AMERICAN SOCIETY FOR QUALITY CONTROL (ASQC)
P.O. Box 3005
611 East Wisconsin Avenue
Milwaukee, WI 53201-3005 USA
Tel: (414) 272-8575
Fax: (414) 272-1734
This is the most important quality association in the world, with the largest membership. It is also a co-administrator of the Malcolm Baldrige National Quality Award, publisher of several major journals in the field (including *Quality Progress,*

Journal of Quality Technology, Technometrics, Quality Engineering, On Q, and *The Quality Review*), has an extensive series of seminars on quality related issues (primarily focused on manufacturing but rapidly expanding to services), and is a major publisher of books on quality themes. It offers a widely respected certification program for quality assurance and other related quality topics, sells books by mail, has local chapters all over North America, and has a variety of technical divisions and committees. If you could only belong to one quality association, this is it.

AMERICAN SOCIETY FOR TRAINING AND DEVELOPMENT (ASTD)
P.O. Box 1443
1630 Duke Street
Alexandria, VA 22313 USA
Tel: (703) 683-8100
Fax: (703) 683-8103
This the major American association for those developing training programs. Increasingly in the last several years, it has concentrated efforts on quality training. It hosts annual conferences in the spring and fall and publishes *Training & Development, Technical & Skills Training,* and *Info-Line.*

AMERICAN SUPPLIER INSTITUTE
15041 Commerce Drive South, Suite 401
Dearborn, MI 48120-1238 USA
Tel: (313) 336-8877
Fax: (313) 462-4500
This organization has skills in implmenting Taguchi methods, quality function deployment (QFD), and total quality management (TQM). It offers training programs, consulting, conferences, books and videos, and publishes *ASI Journal.*

ASIAN PRODUCTIVITY ORGANIZATION (APO)
8-4-14 Akasaka, Minato-ku
Tokyo 107, Japan
Tel: 81/3 3408 7221
Fax: 81/3 3408 7220
This is an intergovernment organization with representatives from 18 governments from Asia and the Pacific. It surveys on best practices, offers training programs, and publishes on quality topics. Its purpose is to accelerate economic devel-

opment through improved economic productivity; it is a major international quality information clearinghouse.

ASOCIACIÓN ESPAÑOLA PARA LA CALIDAD (AECC)
92 Calle Zurbano, 1-D
28003 Madrid, Spain
Tel: 34/1 441 7777
Fax: 34/1 441 777733
This is a national quality organization that promotes quality practices, offers educational programs, testing, and maintains ties to quality associations in Latin America.

ASSOCIACAO PORTUGUESA PARA LA QUALIDADE
Praca Das Industrias
1300 Lisbon, Portugal
Tel: 351/1 363 6443
Fax: 351/1 364 5081
This association promotes total quality management principles in courses, seminars, conferences and as an information clearinghouse in Portugal. It also administers the Portuguese Quality Award.

ASOCIACIÓN ESPAÑOLA PARA LA CALIDAD (AECC)
92 Calle Zurbano, 1-D
28003 Madrid, Spain
Tel: 34/1 441 7777
Fax: 34/1 441 777733
This is a national quality organization that promotes quality practices, offers educational programs, testing, and maintains ties to quality associations in Latin America.

ASQC QUALITY MANAGEMENT DIVISION
611 East Wisconsin Avenue
Milwaukee, WI 53201 USA
This is an organization with over 30,000 members devoted to promoting quality management as a profession and body of practices and, through a group of committees, to doing research on quality practices. It holds an annual conference in February and publishes the *Quality Management Forum Newsletter.*

ASSOCIATION FOR MANAGEMENT EDUCATION AND DEVELOPMENT (AMED)
21 Catherine Street
Covent Garden
London WC2B 5JS, Great Britain
Tel: 44/71 497-3624
Fax: 44/71 836-0295
This thirty-year old organization concentrates on educational programs for business individuals in Europe. Its focus is on quality; it publishes *AMED Journal* and *AMED News.*

ASSOCIATION FOR MANUFACTURING EXCELLENCE, INC.
380 West Palatine Road
Wheeling, IL 60090 USA
Tel: (312) 520-3282
Member companies use this organization to determine how to excell in manufacturing through the application of education, documentation, research, and sharing experiences.

ASSOCIATION FOR QUALITY AND PARTICIPATION (AQP)
801-B West 8th Street, Suite 501
Cincinnati, OH 45203 USA
Tel: (513) 381-1959
Fax: (513) 381-0070
It focuses on quality improvement through employee involvement, especially of self-managed teams, labor-management cooperation, redesign of work, and other studies on employee involvement. It sponsors conferences, maintains a library and research service on quality and employee issues, publishes a journal called *Quality and Participation,* a newsletter, grants organizational team excellence awards, and sells resource materials. It is organized by local chapters in the United States and Canada. It also administers the Annual National Team Competition.

ASSOCIATION FOR THE PRACTICE OF PARTICIPATIVE MANAGEMENT AND TOTAL QUALITY (PRACQ)
(Association pour la Pratique de la Gestion Participative et la Qualite Totale)
Rue Washington 44, BTe. 5
1050 Brussels 5, Belgium
Tel: 32/2 648 0489
Fax: 32/2 649 3269

It fosters productivity improvements of businesses and other organizations in Belgium, primarily through the application of TQM principles. It consults, offers education, and is active in the major European quality organizations, such as the EFQCA and EFQM.

ASSOCIATION FRANCAISE DE NORMALISATION (AFNOR)
Tour Europe, Cedex 7
92049 Paris La Defense, France
Tel: 33/1 42 91 55 55
Fax: 33/1 91 56 56
AFNOR is the the national ISO member organization representing France. It is responsible for promoting the use of ISO standards by French companies.

ASSOCIATION NATIONALE DES DIRECTEURS ET CADRES DE LA FONCTION PERSONNEL (ANDCP)
29, avenue Hoche
75008 Paris, France
Tel: 33/1 45 63 55 09
Fax: 33/1 42 56 41 15
This is an association of personnel managers in France; it operates regional groups, conducts education, and publishes *Personnel.*

ASSOCIATION QUEBECOIS DE LA QUALITE
455 St. Antoine West, Suite 600
Montreal, PQ H2Z 1J1, Canada
Tel: 1/514 866-6696
Fax: 1/514 866-6724
This local quality association has over 2,000 members, holds an annual conference in June, and publishes *Forum Qualite* and *La Qualite Totale.*

ASSOQUALITY
c/o Assolombarda
Via Pantano 9
20122 Milan, Italy
Tel: 32/2 583 70243
Fax: 32/2 583 04951
This is a small organization of management consultants, and its purpose is to promote the use of Total Quality Management principles in Italy.

AUSTRALIAN INSTITUTE OF MANAGEMENT (AIM)
215 Pacific Highway
North Sydney NSW 2060, Australia
Tel: 61/2 929 7922
Fax: 61/2 922 2210
While a traditional management development association with a large membership, it increasingly has been exposing its membership to quality-oriented management practices. It publishes *AIM News* and *Management Review.*

AUSTRALIAN ORGANIZATION FOR QUALITY
27 Palmerston Crescent
South Melbourne VIC 3205, Australia
Tel: 61/3 699 4144
Fax: 61/3 696 4510
This is the oldest and best recognized quality organization in Australia. It promotes quality practices through education programs and support services.

AUSTRALIAN QUALITY COUNCIL
P.O. Box 298
St. Leonards NSW 2065, Australia
Tel: 02-439-8200
Fax: 02-906-3286
This umbrella organization comprises the Enterprise Australia, Ltd., Australian Quality Awards Foundation, Total Quality Management Institute, and the Quality Society of Australia. It hosts seminars and courses on quality, does evaluation consulting, and publishes various resources including *The Quality Magazine* and the guidelines for the Australian Quality Awards.

BRITISH DEMING ASSOCIATION
2 Castle Street
Salisbury, Wiltshire SP1 1BB, Great Britain
Tel: 44/722-412-138
Fax: 44/722-331-313
Its purpose is to promote Dr. Deming's view of quality practices. It has both individual and corporate members and holds an annual conference each April.

BRITISH QUALITY ASSOCIATION (BQA)
P.O. Box 712
61 Southwark Street

London SE1 1SB, Great Britain
Tel: 44/71 401-2844
Fax: 44/71 401-2715
This large organization is the administrator of the
British Quality Award. BQA promotes TQM prin-
ciples, consults, holds seminars, training pro-
grams and seminars. It is one of the major Euro-
pean quality organizations.

BRITISH STANDARDS INSTITUTION (BSI)
2 Park Street
London W1A 2BS, Great Britain
Tel: 44/71 629-9000
Fax: 44/71 629-0506
The primary purpose of this organization is to ad-
minister the ISO 9000 certification process in the
United Kingdom.

BUNDESVERBAND DEUTSCHER
UNTERNEMENSBERATOR (BDU) EV
Friedrich Wilhelm Strasse 2
5300 Bonn 1, Germany
Tel: 49/2282 38055
BDU is composed of institutional members, with
a particular emphasis on management and re-
cruiting consultants, and software companies.

CANADIAN NETWORK FOR TOTAL
QUALITY
c/o Conference Board of Canada
255 Smyth Road
Ottawa, ON K1H 8M7, Canada
Tel: (613) 526-3280
Fax: (613) 526-4857
This is a newly established organization of quality
associations. Like similar structures already in existence in the United States, it promotes coordinated activities to foster the use of total quality
management practices.

CANADIAN SUPPLIER INSTITUTE
Skyline Complex
644 Dixon Rd.
Rexdale, Ontario M9W 1J4, Canada
Tel: 1/416 235-1777
This organization has skills in the application of
Taguchi techniques, quality function deploy-
ment, total quality management, and other pro-
ductivity tools in the area of manufacturing and
production. It has training programs, does some

consulting, offers an assortment of books and videos, and hosts conferences.

CENELEC ELECTRONIC COMPONENTS
COMMITTEE (CECC)
Gartenstrasse 179
6000 Frankfurt 70, Germany
Tel: 49/6963 9171
Fax: 49/6963 9427
It develops the European Standards (ENS) for elec-
tronic components and advises on ISO certifica-
tion in Germany.

CENTER FOR QUALITY AND APPLIED
STATISTICS (CQAS)
Rochester Institute of Technology
98 Lomb Memorial Drive
Rochester, NY 14623-5604 USA
Tel: (716) 475-6990
Fax: (716) 475-5959
It offers seminars on quality engineering, quality
management and quality standards, applied mathematical statistics, quality and productivity, and
custom training programs, using RIT professors
who have practical experience. CQAS advises and
consults in these areas around the world. It also
offers a master's degree in applied and mathematical statistics.

CENTER SATELLITE DEVELOPMENT—
INDUSTRIAL COORDINATION CENTER
(CSD)
No. 8 Tun-Hwa N Road, 7th Floor
Taipei, Taiwan ROC
Tel: 886/2 751 3468
Fax: 886/2 781 7790
CSD coordinates activities for 25 companies for
the purpose of improving the quality of their op-
erations and products. It also offers seminars, pub-
lishes on quality, and administers the National
Quality Award. It also publishes *CSD Monthly
Magazine*.

CENTRUM VOOR KWALITEITSZORG
WEST-VLAANDEREN VZW.
Doorniksesteenweg
8500 Kortrijk, Belgium
Tel: 32/2 5620 4723
Fax: 32/2 5625 9684

This organization offers hundreds of courses on quality topics and publishes *Kwaliteit Nu.*

CHINESE MANAGEMENT ASSOCIATION
13th Floor, 4 Roosevelt Road, Section 1
Taipei 0757
Taiwan ROC
Tel: 886/2 396 5207
Fax: 886/2 396 9143
As part of its effort to promote quality management, it offers seminars, consulting, and conferences on the subject, and organizes teams to work on quality-related projects. It publishes *Journal of Management Science* and *CMA Newsletter,* and administers a quality management award program.

COMMUNITY QUALITY COALITION
c/o Transformation of America Industry Project
Jackson Community College
2111 Emmons Road
Jackson, MI 49201 USA
Tel: (517) 789-1627
This organization promotes quality practices in Mississppi targeted largely at businesses.

CONFERENCE BOARD, INC.
P.O. Box 4026, Church Street Station
New York, NY 10261-4026 USA
Tel: (212) 759-0900
Fax: (212) 980-7014
This nationally recognized council of American businesses is best known for its research on business trends. It also hosts an annual quality conference covering various tools and techniques in the general management of business. It also publishes its research, some of which is related to quality practices.

DANISH SOCIETY FOR QUALITY CONTROL (DFK)
(Dansk Forening for Kvalitetsstyring)
P.O. Box 52
2950 Vedbaek, Denmark
Tel: 45/42 89 13 05
Fax: 45/42 89 08 12
Its purpose is to promote awareness and use of quality practices in Denmark. It holds from four to six conferences annually and administers the

Danish Quality Award. It also published *Quality News.*

DANSK STANDARDISERINGSRAD (DS)
P.O. Box 77
Aurejojvej 12
2900 Hellerup, Denmark
This is the ISO 9000 standards association organization for Denmark.

DEUTSCHE GESSELLSCHAFT FUR PERSONALFUHRUNG MBH (DGP)
Niederkasseler Lohweg 16
4000 Dusseldorf 11, Germany
Tel: 49/2115 978
Fax: 49/2115 978 505
It focuses on helping personnel and education functions in German organizations through training programs, consulting, and seminars. It publishes *Personalfuhrung.*

DEUTSCHE GESELLSCHAFT FUR QUALITAT
August-Schanz Strasse 21A
P.O. Box 50 07 63
6000 Frankfurt am Main 50, Germany
Tel: 49/6995 4240
Fax: 49/6995 424133
This is the major German society for quality, has both corporate and individual members, and provides quality programs nationally.

DEUTSCHES INSTITUT FUR NORMUNG (DIN)
Burggrafenstrasse 6
Postfach 1107
1000 Berlin 30, Germany
Tel: 49/3026 011
Fax: 49/3026 01231
This is Germany's national ISO member institution, responsible for the implementation of ISO 9000 certification programs in the country.

DIMENSION CLIENTELE
Quebec Customer Service Association
7339 rue Baldwin
Montreal, PQ H1K 3C9, Canada
Tel: (514) 353-4612
Fax: (514) 353-4612
This organization assists members improve customer services, concentrating on companies in

Quebec. It hosts conferences, an annual convention in May, and publishes *Client*.

EUROPEAN FOUNDATION FOR QUALITY MANAGEMENT (EFQM)
Avenue des Pleiades 19
B-1200 Brussels, Belgium
Tel: +323-775-3511
Fax: +322-779-1237
The EFQM supports the use of quality practices by Western European companies. Membership is by company. It manages the European Quality Award program, begun in 1992; hosts conferences and education programs; and publishes *Quality Link Newsletter*.

FEDERAL QUALITY INSTITUTE (FQI)
441 F Street, NW, Room 333
Washington, D.C. 20001 USA
Tel: (202) 376-3747 or 376-3753
Fax: (202) 376-3765
FQI is the most important U.S. government organization involved in fostering the use of quality practices. It is responsible for helping all U.S. government agencies implement start-up activities in the area of total quality management. It is a government-wide source for information on quality, using the FQI Information Network, which offers to agencies materials such as books, articles, videos, and case studies, all at no cost on-line. It publishes *Federal Quality News* and administers the QIP Award and the Presidential Quality Award.

FINNISH SOCIETY FOR QUALITY
(Suomen Laatuyhdistys ry)
Laaksolahdentie 11A
02731 Espoo, Finland
Tel: 358/0 597 348
Fax: 358/0 509 1807
It promotes all facets of quality applications in Finland, from TQM to quality assurance. It holds an annual conference in April and publishes *Laatuviesti*.

FOX VALLEY QUALITY/PRODUCTIVITY RESOURCE CENTER (Q/PRC)
Fox Valley Technical College
5 Systems Lane (Bordini Center)
P.O. Box 2277

Appleton, WI 54913-2277 USA
Tel: (414) 735-2277
Probably the best-known center for quality practices and education among all community colleges in North America, this is a center for quality education, consulting, and research. Its library on quality management practices is extensive. Its mission is to help local business and nonprofit organizations improve their quality practices through speakers, training, and library resources.

GERMAN ASSOCIATION FOR QUALITY CIRCLES (DQCG)
Am. Puttkamp 27
4000 Dusseldorf 12, Germany
Tel: 49/2112 84969
Fax: 49/2116 800168
This organization promotes the use of all kinds of quality practices, runs seminars and conferences for German companies, administers the German Quality Circle Award, and publishes *QC-intern*.

HELLENIC INSTITUTE OF QUALITY
Ipirou 6
104 33 Athens, Greece
Tel: 30/1 822 7430
Fax: 30/1 823 8301
This is a national Greek organization that promotes quality practices among Greek businesses.

HELLENIC MANAGEMENT ASSOCIATION
36, Amalias Avenue
105 58 Athens, Greece
Tel: 30/1 323 2792
Fax: 30/1 322 7048
This organization promotes quality practices, primarily through an extensive TQM education program. It hosts an annual conference in March and publishes *Manager* and *Marketing Review*.

HONG KONG QUALITY MANAGEMENT ASSOCIATION (HKQMA)
P.O. Box 90952
Tsimshatsui Post Office
Kowloon, Hong Kong
Fax: 852/719-3064
It promotes better management through seminars, conferences, and by managing ten specialist clubs. It offers quality certification programs, ad-

ministers the HKMA Quality Award and publishes *Hong Kong Manager*.

HONG KONG Q-MARK COUNCIL
Federation of HK Industries
4/F Hankow Centre
5-15 Hankow Rd., Tsimshatsui
Kowloon, Hong Kong
Tel: 852/723 0818
Fax: 852/721 3494
The Q-Mark Council, within the Federation of Hong Kong Industries, is a council of prominent business, government, and academic leaders. They offer ISO 9000 education, publications and courses, and manage The Hong Kong Q-Mark Quality Award.

HONG KONG QUALITY ASSURANCE AGENCY
1/F, HKPC Building
78 Tat Chee Avenue
Kowloon, Hong Kong
Tel: 852/788 5333
Fax: 852/788 5322
This government agency administers the local ISO 9000 certification process.

HONG KONG SOCIETY FOR QUALITY CONTROL
c/o Manufacturing Engineering Dept.
Hong Kong Polytechnic
Hong Kong, Kowloon
Hong Kong
Tel: 852/766 6591
Fax: 852/362 4741
This ASQC-affiliated society promotes awareness and use of quality practices by local businesses and government agencies. It offers a variety of educational opportunities for business and government, administers ASQC certification programs locally, and publishes a quarterly newsletter.

HUMAN RESOURCES DEVELOPMENT ASSOCIATION OF R.O.C.
No. 51 Chung-Ching S. Road, 17th Floor
Taipei, Taiwan ROC
Tel: 886/2 396 4605
Fax: 886/2 341 7971

This organization promotes quality practices in human resource management. It publishes *Human Resources Development Monthly*.

INSTITUTE OF ADMINISTRATIVE MANAGEMENT (IAM)
40 Chatsworth Parada, Petts Wood
Orphington, Kent BR5 1RW, Great Britain
Tel: 44/689 875 555
Fax: 44/689 870 891
This is one of the oldest professional associations in Europe; its members are administrative managers. It administers a certification program, offers courses, releases publications, and administers the ATQ Award.

INSTITUTE OF MANAGEMENT SPECIALISTS
58 Clarendon Avenue
Leamington Spa, Warswickshire CV32 4SA, Great Britain
Tel: 44/71 401-7227
Fax: 44/71 401-2725
It focuses on training in the area of quality assurance, with particular emphasis on TQM, QA, and quality control. It consults on ISO and publishes books, magazines, and videos on quality.

INSTITUTE OF PERSONNEL MANAGEMENT, NEW ZEALAND, INC. (IPMNZ)
P.O. Box 34-620
Birkenhead, Auckland, New Zealand
Tel: 64/9 480 1349
Fax: 64/9 480 0423
This is a personnel management support organization that, in particular, promotes the use of TQM principles in personnel practices. It hosts a national conference in September and publishes *IPM News*.

INSTITUTE OF QUALITY ASSURANCE
P.O. Box 712
61 Southwark Street
London, SE1 1SB, Great Britain
Tel: 071-401-7227
Fax: 071-401-2725
One of the oldest quality organizations (founded 1919), it certifies various grades of quality practitioners in a variety of subject areas and provides education on a broad range of quality-related topics. It publishes the monthly *Quality News* and

quarterly the *Quality Forum*. It also has a bookstore and training center located at 10 Grosvenor Gardens, London SW1W ODQ.

INSTITUTO PORTUGUES DE QUALIDAD (IPQ)
Rua Jose Estevao, 83A
1199 Lisbon Codex, Portugal
Tel: 351/1 523 978
Fax: 351/1 530 033
IPQ is part of the Ministry of Industry and Energy, and is responsible for implementing national quality programs. It hosts an annual conference in May and publishes *Qualirama* and *Opcao Q*.

INTERNATIONAL ACADEMY FOR QUALITY (IAQ)
P.O. Box 50 07 63
50 Frankfurt am Main W6, Germany
Tel: 49/6954 80010
Fax: 49/6954 800133
To be a member, one must be sponsored by three or more scholars operating on at least two continents. Members encourage international understanding of quality issues, promoting research on the philosophy and practice of quality. It also administers the IAQ Award.

INTERNATIONAL ASSOCIATION FOR CONTINUOUS EDUCATION AND TRAINING (IACET)
1101 Connecticut Avenue, NW, No. 700
Washington, D.C. 20036 USA
Its purpose is to provide help in the development and implementation of continuous training programs.

ITALIAN ASSOCIATION FOR QUALITY (AICQ)
Piazza A. Diaz 2
20121 Milan, Italy
Tel: 39/2 720 03460
Fax: 39/2 720 23085
The Associazione per le Qualita promotes the use of quality practices in Italy, its members are corporate enterprises, and it publishes *Qualita*.

JAPAN MANAGEMENT ASSOCIATION (JMA)
Nihon-Nohritsu Kyokai Building
3-1-22 Shiba-koen, Minato-ku
Tokyo 105, Japan
Tel: 81/3 3434 6211
Fax: 81/3 3434 1087
JMA offers courses, seminars, and conferences on all aspects of business; conducts trade shows,and international visits; publishes extensively on all manner of management topics; publishes *JMA Management News, JMA Journal*, and *Human Resource Development;* and administers awards of excellence. Membership consists of over 2,500 corporations.

JAPANESE STANDARDS ASSOCIATION (JSA)
1-24 Akasaka 4-chome
Minato-ku
Tokyo 107, Japan
Tel: 81/3 3583 8008
Fax: 81/3 3583 0698
JSA promotes standardization on quality issues and offers education, all as an organization under the control of the Ministry of International Trade & Industry. It also manages many of the ISO functions in Japan, sponsors a national conference in May, publishes *Standardization & Quality Control* and *Standardization Journal*, and administers the JSA Excellent Standardization Document Award.

JOINT ACCREDITATION SYSTEM OF AUSTRALIA AND NEW ZEALAND
JAS-ANZ Secretariat
P.O. Box 164
Civic Square ACT 2608, Australia
Tel: 61/6 276 1999
Fax: 61/6 276 2117
Formed in 1991, this organization has the mission of developing a unified quality accreditation process for both Australia and New Zealand, while strengthening trade bonds.

JUSE—UNION OF JAPANESE SCIENTISTS AND ENGINEERS
5-10-11, Sendagaya, Shibuya-ku
Tokyo, 151 Japan
Tel: 03-5379-1227 or 1231
Fax: 03-3225-1813
This organization is best known as the administrators of the Deming Prize, Japan's highest quality award. It is Japan's leading quality organization and provides training, hosts symposia,

consults, maintains a library and publishes a variety of magazines and journals, including the monthly *Total Quality Control* and *Engineers,* and every two months, *Societas Qualitatis,* which describes activities of JUSE.

KOREAN SOCIETY FOR QUALITY CONTROL
5-2 Soonhwa-dong, Chung-ku
Seoul, South Korea
Conducts research on quality practices, offers educational programs, publishes and distributes materials on quality, and provides channels of communication between local businesses and academia.

KOREAN STANDARDS ASSOCIATION (KSA)
5-2 Soonhwa-dong, Chung-ku
Seoul 100-130, South Korea
Tel: 82/2 772 3417
Fax: 82/2 754 0346
This is the national industrial standardization organization for South Korea. It offers a full compliment of courses and seminars, along with consulting, to organizations seeking quality certifications. It hosts a national conference held in either October or November each year, and publishes *Quality and Management, Standardization,* and *Factory Management.*

MADISON AREA QUALITY IMPROVEMENT NETWORK (MAQIN)
1010 Mound Street
Madison, WI 53715 USA
Tel: (608) 256-5300
Fax: (608) 256-5222
This very active quality organization is best known for hosting the annual Hunter Conference on Quality, beginning in 1988. Usually held in June, it runs several days, covers all aspects of quality implementation programs, (both in the private and public sector), and is considered one of the more important national quality conferences. Local seminars are also held throughout the year.

MICHIGAN STATE UNIVERSITY INSTITUTE FOR QUALITY AND PRODUCTIVITY
Michigan State University
7 Olds Hall
East Lansing, MI 488824-1047 USA

Tel: (517) 353-0796 or (800) 356-5705
Fax: (517) 353-0796
Typical of many such organizations available in the United States, it offers educational programs in services, business administration, and quality.

MILWAUKEE FIRST IN QUALITY
Metropolitan Milwaukee Association of Commerce
756 North Milwaukee Street
Milwaukee, WI 53202 USA
Tel: (414) 287-4100
This is one of the largest and most active local quality organizations in the United States. It offers a variety of quality skill-building seminars and hosts a major annual convention in the area of quality. Particular focus has been in the area of implementing quality in manufacturing environments, although its offerings are expanding into the service sector.

MINNESOTA COUNCIL FOR QUALITY (MCQ)
2850 Metro Drive, Suite 300
Bloomington, MN 55425 USA
Tel: (612) 851-3181
Fax: (612) 851-3183
This is a very active state council that promotes quality in Minnesota through conferences, seminars, other educational programs and administers the Minnesota Quality Award and the Quality Service Award; it is a model regional quality council.

MOUVEMENT FRANCAIS POUR LA QUALITE (MFQ)
5, esplanade Charles de Gaulle
92733 Nanterre cedex, France
Tel: 33/1 40 97 06 40
Fax: 33/1 47 25 32 21
This is an important French quality association with the mission of promoting exchange and application of information on quality practices by French organizations and companies. It offers training and conferences, runs regional quality circles, administers the Prix Nationale de la Qualite, and publishes *Qualite en Mouvement* and *Regard sur la Qualite.*

NATIONAL ASSOCIATION OF SERVICE MANAGERS (NASM)
1030 West Higgins Road, No. 206
Hoffman Estates, IL 60195 USA
Tel: (708) 310-9930
Fax: (708) 310-9934
This is the oldest association of product service managers in North America. It promotes service quality by businesses, improved practices by service industry organizations, and provides educational programs. It hosts an annual conference in September and publishes *Service Management.*

NATIONAL INSTITUTE OF STANDARDS AND TECHNOLOGY
Rt. 270 and Quince Orchard Road
Administration Bldg, Room A537
Gaithersburg, MD 20899 USA
Tel: (301) 975-2036
Fax: (301) 948-3716
This organization, along with the ASQC, manages the Malcolm Baldrige National Quality Award. It is responsible for defining the criteria and point values for the award and also for the judging process.

NATIONAL PRODUCTIVITY BOARD
2 Bukit Merah Central
NPB Building
0315 Singapore
Tel: 65/278 6666 or 279 3721
Fax: 65/278 6665
NPB is part of the Ministry of Trade and Industry with the purpose of creating an outstanding workforce, focusing on quality and productivity in the workplace and in life. Provides training, management guidance, measures of productivity and quality, and publishes *Productivity Digest.*

NATIONAL QUALITY INFORMATION CENTRE
P.O. Box 712
61 Southwark Street
London SE1 1SB, Great Britain
Tel: 44/71 401-7227
Fax: 44/71 401-2725
This very large British quality organization promotes the use of quality assurance practices in British industry through education programs, consulting, publications, and research done jointly with universities. It publishes *Quality News* and the *Quality Forum.*

NATIONAL SOCIETY FOR PERFORMANCE AND INSTRUCTION (NSPI)
1300 L Street, NW, Suite 1250
Washington, D.C. 20005 USA
Tel: (202) 408-7969
Fax: (202) 408-7972
This is a large organization, with members from many countries, dedicated to improving productivity and effectiveness in the workplace. Over 600 chapters meet monthly where one of the more important topics is the science of performance technology, an organized process for solving problems concerning performance. It holds an annual conference in April and publishes *Performance & Instruction* and *Performance Improvement Quarterly.*

NATIONAL SOCIETY FOR QUALITY THROUGH TEAMWORK (NQST)
2 Castle Street
Salisbury SP1 1BB, Great Britain
Tel: 44/722 326 667
Fax: 44/722 331 313
This organization promotes the application of quality principles with particular emphasis on teamwork strategies. It hosts regional member meetings, training programs, annual conferences, and publishes *Executives Brief* and *TeamTalk.* It also administers the Annual Team Excellence Award, Michelin Award, and the Perkins Award.

NEDERLANDS NORMALISATIE-INSTITUT (NNI)
Kalfjeslaan 2
Postbus 5059
2600 GB Delft, Netherlands
Tel: 31/15 690 390
Fax: 31/15 690 190
This is the Netherlands' standardization institute, responsible for promoting the certification of companies by such international standards as ISO; it offers training in industrial quality standards.

NEW ZEALAND ORGANIZATION FOR QUALITY (NZOQ)
P.O. Box 622
Palmerston North, New Zealand

Tel: 64/6 3569 0099
Fax: 64/6 350 5604
This organization is the major quality organization for New Zealand, promoting quality practices as a means of improving New Zealand's competitive posture in the world economy. It hosts a national conference in May, and publishes *Quality New Zealand*, *Q-NewZ*, and *Software Q-NewZ*.

NORGES STANDARDISERINGSFORBUND (NSF)
P.O. Box 7020
Homansbyen
0306 Oslo 3, Norway
Tel: 47/2 466 094
Fax: 47/2 464 457
This is the national ISO 9000 association member for Norway.

NORWEGIAN SOCIETY FOR QUALITY
Brynsveien 96
1352 Kolsas, Norway
Tel: 47/2 137 775
Fax: 47/2 133 518
This is Norway's primary national quality organization, supporting the quality efforts of businesses within the nation; it administers the Norwegian Quality Award.

PENN STATE MANAGEMENT DEVELOPMENT PROGRAMS AND SERVICES
2790 West College Avenue
University Park, PA 16801-2605 USA
Tel: (814) 865-6341
Fax: (814) 865-7837
Created in 1915 to provide education programs to assist state industries, the bulk of its current programs focus on a broad range of TQM topics for business managers and are delivered around the state. It also offers quality diagnostic services to assess the effectivness of organizations.

PHILADELPHIA AREA COUNCIL FOR EXCELLENCE (PACE)
1234 Narket Street, Suite 1800
Philadelphia, PA 19107-3718 USA
Tel: (215) 972-3977
Fax: (215) 972-3900

PACE promotes the application of Total Quality Management and Deming approaches. It offer educational programs and hosts a four-day Deming seminar. PACE distributes publications on quality and administers the Pennsylvania State Quality Award.

QCI INTERNATIONAL
P.O. Box 1503
Red Bluff, CA 96080 USA
Tel: (916) 527-8875
Fax: (916) 527-6983
QCI fosters employee involvement, application of total quality management, and statistical process control techniques. It offers seminars, in-house training, books and viedeos for sale, and publishes a monthly magazine called *Quality Digest*.

QUALITY & PRODUCTIVITY MANAGEMENT ASSOCIATION (QPMA)
300 North Martingale Road, No. 230
Schaumburg, IL 60173 USA
Tel: (708) 619-2909
Fax: (708) 619-3383
This network of business professionals focuses on continuous improvement strategies that can be applied in the workplace. It conducts educational programs and workshops, distributes publications, and administers the Annual QPMA Leadership Award.

QUALITY COUNCIL OF ALBERTA
c/o Industry Development Board
Alberta Economic Development & Trade
10th Floor, Sterling Place
9940-106th Street
Edmonton, AB T5K 2P6, Canada
Tel: (403) 427-2005
Fax: (403) 427-5924
This is a newly established organization with the purpose of providing regional support for the application of quality practices in the Alberta region.

QUALITY MANAGEMENT INSTITUTE
5-2 Soonhwa-dong, Chung-ku
Seoul, South Korea
Performs research on successful quality improvement projects, and promotes uses of quality practices. Collects information on worldwide quality

activities and serves as an information clearinghouse.

QUALITY SOCIETY OF AUSTRALIA (QSA)
P.O. Box 298
St. Leonards NSW 2096, Australia
Tel: 61/2 906 5788
Fax: 61/2 901 4677
This newly established organization offers networking and recognition of quality activities for its members. It is beginning to offer information on quality practices as well.

SINGAPORE QUALITY INSTITUTE (SQI)
Blk. 18, Ngee Ann Polytechnic
No. 03-08 Clementi Road
2159 Singapore
tel: 65/467 4225
Fax: 65/467 4226
Like the American ASQC, it promotes quality practices, particularly in business, through seminars, conferences, and publications; it is a clearinghouse for local information on quality. It publishes *QC Focus* and the *SQI Yearbook*.

SIS QUALITY FORUM
Box 3295
103 66 Stockholm, Sweden
Tel: 46/8 613 5320
Fax: 46/8 241 331
It promotes quality practices and, in particular, those of the ISO 9000 standards. It publishes *Nytt om Niotusen*.

STANDARDISERINGKOMMISSIONEN I SVERIGE (SIS)
Box 3295
103 66 Stockholm, Sweden
Tel: 46/8 613 52000
Fax: 46/8 117 035
This is Sweden's national standards organization. Its certification programs are based on ISO 9000, supports training efforts, and publishes the *SIS Quality Forum Newsletter*.

STANDARDS ASSOCIATION OF NEW ZEALAND
181-187 Victoria Street
Private Bag
Wellington, New Zealand

Tel: 64/4 384 2108
Fax: 64/4 384 3938
This is the national standards body for New Zealand with responsibility for promoting quality standards, product certification (S Mark award), and for accreditation under the ISO 9000 banner.

STANDARDS AUSTRALIA
(Standards Association of Australia)
P.O. Box 1055
Strathfield NSW 2135, Australia
Tel: 02-746-4700
Fax: 02-746-8450
This is Australia's major supplier of independent quality systems accreditation and product certification services. Certification includes AS3900/ ISO 9000, and local and regional certifications. It also offers a variety of courses on implementing quality programs.

STANDARDS COUNCIL OF CANADA
45 O'Connor Street, Suite 1200
Ottawa, ON K1P 6N7, Canada
Tel: (613) 238-3222
Fax: (613) 995-4564
This organization acredits quality certification associations and companies. It coordinates the activities of Canada's ISO Technical Committee responsible for ISO certification activities.

SUOMEN STANDARDISOIMISLIITTO (SFS)
P.O. Box 205
00121 Helsinki, Finland
This is Finland's national ISO member association and is responsible for promoting ISO standards within the country.

SWEDISH INSTITUTE FOR QUALITY (SIQ)
Box 5178
Gardatorget 1
402 26 Goteborg, Sweden
Tel: 46/31 773 0875
Fax: 46/31 773 0645
SIQ promotes the study and application of quality principles in business and in other organizations. It does teaching, research, and development, and is the administrator of the Swedish National Quality Award.

TMI FINLAND
Heikkilantie 6
00210 Helsinki, Finland
Tel: 358/0 692 7788
Fax: 358/0 692 7388
This is an association devoted to training and development of human resources, relying on continuous improvement strategies. It also has affiliations and operations in most other European countries. TMI is a defined human improvement process.

TOTAL QUALITY MANAGEMENT INSTITUTE
1st Floor (Fernz Corp)
81 Carlton Gore Road
Box 90-455, Auckland, New Zealand
Tel: 0-9-302-0062
Fax: 0-9-307-3831
Membership is targeted at senior management in the belief that all quality efforts must begin with them. The Institute offers education on TQM, forums, distribution of papers on TQM, and attendance at national conferences. Through the NZ National Quality Awards Foundation, it administers the NZ National Quality Awards, patterned after the Baldrige Award and to which government agencies can also apply.

U-MAN FINLAND OY
Tuusuutarintie 3
00620 Helsinki, Finland
Tel: 358/0 799 266
Fax: 358/0 757 3564
This organization promotes the application of total quality management principles in human resources.

UNI—ENTE NAZIONALE ITALIANO DI UNIFICAZIONE
Via Battistotti Sassi 11
20133 Milan, Italy
Tel: 39/2 700 241
Fax: 39/2 701 06106

UNI establishes and promotes the use of technical standards by Italian manufacturing companies and is associated with ISO. This seventy-two-year-old organization publishes *U&C* and *UNI Notizie*.

UNIVERSITY CONSORTIUM IN QUALITY ENGINEERING
Piazza del Pozzetto 9
56127 Pisa, Italy
This is a recently established group for the purpose of promoting research, teaching and application of quality practices in Italian economic and social actions; members are university and industrial representatives.

WAUKESHA AREA QUALITY/PRODUCTIVITY NETWORK
Waukesha County Technical College
800 Main Street
Pewaukee, WI 53072 USA
Tel: (414) 691-5543
This is an organization of local companies who meet to share experiences in quality practices. It serves as a resource center and organizes local presentations, tours, training, roundtables, and study groups in the Waukesha, Wisconsin, area.

WORK IN AMERICA INSTITUTE
700 White Plains Road
Scarsdale, NY 10583 USA
Tel: (914) 472-9600
Fax: (914) 472-9606
Like other quality associations, it conducts research and member advisory services on productivity (with a special emphasis on employee involvement) and has expertise on labor-management relations and working conditions. It conducts forums, seminars, and site visits; studies company policies; publishes a newsletter called *WORK IN AMERICA*; maintains a library; does research on demand; issues a variety of publications; and has a speaker's bureau and a list of quality consultants.

Directory of
Quality Awards

This section of *The Quality Yearbook* profiles quality awards with an emphasis on award programs established by various states. For each state, we have listed award categories, criteria, and where to get more information. Several states use Baldrige criteria, but with various modifications and different weighting. For this reason, we have summarized these criteria for each state when they were available to allow readers in each state to have as much information as possible. This also allows comparison from state to state. The amount of information available varies, as the level of organization from state to state varies.

This awards section also provides a *directory of selected international and country awards*, with information on where to get information on the award.

State Awards Directory

ALABAMA

Award: Alabama U.S. Senate Productivity and Quality Award

Categories: There are four categories in which prizes are given:
Small Business. Less than 100 full-time employees.
Manufacturing Sector. Companies or subsidiaries that produce and sell manufactured products or manufacturing processes, including agricultural, mining, or contruction products.
Service Sector (includes government agencies and education). Organizations, companies, or subsidiaries that sell or provide a service.
Special Category. Called *Award of Excellence in Continuous Productivity and Quality Improvement* that previous winners may apply for.

Award Criteria: There are seven areas in which applicants are judged, similar to the Baldrige criteria (820 points):
1. *Leadership.* Examines senior management personal leadership and involvement in creating and sustaining productivity and quality improvement efforts, including how productivity and quality values are integrated into the company's management system. (90 points, 11%)
2. *Strategic Planning for Productivity and Quality.* Examines the company's planning process and how all key quality and productivity requirements are integrated into the overall business plan. (80 points, 10%)
3. *Measurement of Performance.* Examines the scope, validity, analysis, management, and use of data and information to drive productivity and quality excellence and improve competitive performance. (80 points, 10%)

4. *Human Resources Management.* Examines the key elements of how the company develops and realizes the full potential of the work force to pursue the company's productivity and quality improvement efforts, including the company's efforts to build and maintain an environment for excellence in productivity and quality. (150 points, 18%)

5. *Management Improvement of the Productivity and Quality Process.* Examines the company's systematic process used to pursue ever-higher productivity, quality, and company performance, including design, management or process quality for all work units and suppliers, systematic quality improvement, and productivity and quality assessment. (140 points, 17%)

6. *Customer Focus and Satisfaction.* Examines the company's relationships with customers and its knowledge of customer requirements. It also examines the company's methods to determine customer satisfaction, current trends, and levels of satisfaction. (210 points, 25%)

7. *Improvement Tactics.* Asks applicants to describe the specific productivity and quality improvement techniques in place beyond those described in previous categories. (70 points, 8%)

How to Apply: For information and application forms, contact:
Linda Vincent
Award Coordinator
The Alabama Productivity Center
P.O. Box 870318
Tuscaloosa, AL 35487-0318
Phone: (205) 348-8956
Fax: (205) 348-9391

ARIZONA

Award: The Arizona Governor's Award for Quality (Called "The Pioneer Award")

Categories: Any organization, public or private, may apply for the award, awarded in three categories:
Small (less than 100 employees)
Medium (100–499 employees)
Large (500 or more employees)

Award Criteria: Similar to the Baldrige criteria, applicants are judged on:
1. *Leadership.* Examines senior executives' success in creating and sustaining a customer focus and clear and visible quality values, including how those values are integrated into the organization's management system and reflected in the manner in which the organization addresses its public responsibilities. (90 points, 9%)

2. *Information and Analysis.* Examines the scope, validity, analysis, management, and use of data collection to drive excellence and improve competitive performance, including the adequacy of the organization's data, information, and analysis system to support improvement in all activitie. (75 points, 7.5%)

3. *Strategic Quality Planning.* Examines the organization's planning process and how all key quality requirements are integrated into overall organization planning. (60 points, 6%)

4. *Human Resources Development and Management.* Examines the key elements of how the organization develops and realizes the full potential of work force to pursue the organization's quality and performance objectives. (150 points, 15%)

5. *Management of Process Quality.* Examines the systematic processes used to pursue ever-higher quality and operational performance, including key elements of process management. (140 points, 14%)
6. *Quality and Operational Results.* Examines the organization quality levels and improvement trends in quality operational performance, and supplier quality. (180 points, 18%)
7. *Customer Focus and Satisfaction.* Examines the organization's relationships with customers and its knowledge of customer requirements and of key factors that determine marketplace competitiveness. (300 points, 30%)

How to Apply: Applicants must submit a written application and must agree to a CEO interview if a finalist. A free copy of the award application is available by contacting:
Dennis Sowards
Arizona Quality Alliance
1221 East Osborn, Suite 100
Phoenix, AZ 85014
Phone: (602) 265-6141
Fax: (602) 265-1262

CALIFORNIA

Award: Governor's Golden State Quality Award

Categories: There are five categories of awards:
Quality in Management Award. Companies that excel in managing their core activity, be it manufacturing, services, or a combination.
Quality in the Marketplace Award. Companies that excel in translating an approach to quality into improved levels of customer satisfaction and business results.
Quality in the Workplace Award. Companies that excel in creating a workplace that realizes the full potential of their people to achieve the company's performance objectives.
Quality in the Community Award. Companies that excel in their interaction with their communities; local, state, and national.
The Governor's Golden State Quality Award. Companies that achieve excellence in all the above areas.

Award Criteria: For each award area, an organization must provide information sufficient to allow examiners to evaluate:
1. *Approach*: This has to do with the methods or process the organization uses to carry out each task.
2. *Deployment*: This looks at the application of the approach to all relevant areas and activities in the organization.
3. *Results Assessment*: This looks at the outcomes and effects of the deployed approach, including performance and quality levels relative to benchmarks and the rate of performance improvement.
4. *Continuous Improvement*: This refers to both incremental and breakthrough improvements of all types, including enhancing value to customers, reducing errors and defects, reducing cycle time, and improving productivity.
For these general criteria, the state provides specific information on what is evaluated for each award category.

How to Apply: To get more information and to apply for the California Governor's Golden State Quality Awards, contact:

Peter Brightbill
Department of Commerce, Executive Office
801 K Street, Suite 1700
Sacramento, CA 95814
Phone: (916) 322-3406
Fax: (916) 322-3524

CONNECTICUT

Award: Connecticut Quality Improvement Award

Categories: There are six categories in which awards are given:
Small (1–100 employees) in *service* and *manufacturing.*
Medium (101–500 employees) in *service* and *manufacturing.*
Large (over 500 employees) in *service* and *manufacturing.*

Award Criteria: The Connecticut award is based on the Baldrige award criteria:
1. *Leadership.* The senior executives' success in creating and sustaining a quality culture.
2. *Information and Analysis.* The effectiveness of information collection and analysis for quality improvement and planning.
3. *Strategic Quality Planning.* The effectiveness of integrating quality requirements into business plans.
4. *Human Resource Development and Management.* The success of efforts to develop and realize the full potential of the work force for quality.
5. *Management of Process Quality.* The effectiveness of systems and processes for assuring the quality of all operations.
6. *Quality and Operational Results.* The results in quality achievement and quality improvement, demonstrated through quantitative measures.
7. *Customer Focus and Satisfaction.* The effectiveness of systems to determine customer requirements and demonstrated success in meeting them.

How to Apply: To get additional information and to apply for this award, contact:
Sheila Carmine, Director
Connecticut Quality Improvement Award, Inc.
P.O. Box 1396
Stamford, CT 06904-1396
Phone: (203) 322-9534
Fax: (203) 329-2465

DELAWARE

Award: Delaware Quality Award

Eligibility: An organization must be in operation within the state for at least three years. For concerns that have other locations nationally or internationally, only Delaware operations are eligible.

Categories: There are five categories of organizations available for this prize:
Large Manufacturing. Companies with 100 or more employees.
Small Manufacturing. Companies with fewer than 100 employees
Large Non-Manufacturing. Companies with 100 or more employees.
Small Non-Manufacturing. Companies with fewer than 100 employees.
Non-Profit Organizations. Organizations of any size.

Award Criteria: As with most state programs, applicants are judged in seven areas, based on the Baldrige criteria:

1. *Customer Satisfaction.* Examines what product or service improvements a company is making that directly result to customer benefit, including changes made to improve the efficiency and effectiveness of the business. (30% weight)
2. *Leadership.* Examines how the principal leader of the organization is involved in the establishment of quality objectives, planning for the implementation of those objectives, establishing measurements, reviewing progress, and initiating adjustments that may be necessary. (15% weight)
3. *Valuing People.* Examines how much time organizations have their employees spend in formal training to learn new skills and techniques. (15% weight)
4. *Operational Processes.* Examines exactly what organizations have done to analyze and improve processes to increase the effectiveness and productivity of the company's operation. (14% weight)
5. *Supplier Enhancement.* Examines if the organization's assessment of suppliers is based on fact versus intuition and the measurement systems used to determine needs. Also examined are the ways organizations interact with suppliers. (10% weight)
6. *Results.* Examines the results of organizations, using such measurements as defect rate reduction, cycle time reduction, and "key success indicators." (11% weight)
7. *Community Impact.* Examines how the entire organization shares quality knowledge and plays a responsible role within the community. (5% weight)

How to Apply: To get additional information and to apply for this award, contact:
Delaware Quality Consortium, Inc.
Delaware Development Office
99 King's Highway
P.O. Box 1401
Dover, DE 19903

FLORIDA

Award: The Governor's Sterling Award

Categories: There are five categories in which awards are given:
Manufacturing
Service
Public Sector
Education Sector
Health Care Sector

Award Criteria: Florida uses the seven Baldrige criteria as a basis for its award, but with special modifications for public and nonprofit organizations:

1. *Leadership.* Includes: Senior executive leadership, management for quality, public responsibility, and corporate citizenship.
2. *Information and Analysis.* Includes: Scope and management of quality and performance data and information, competitive comparisons and benchmarking, and analysis and uses of company-level data.
3. *Strategic Quality Planning.* Includes: Strategic quality and organization performance planning process, and quality and performance plans.
4. *Human Resource Development and Management.* Includes: Human resource planning and management, employee involvement, employee education and train-

ing, employee performance and recognition, and employee well-being and satisfaction.

5. *Management of Process Quality.* Includes: Design and introduction of quality products and services, process management, including product and service production and delivery processes, and business processes and support services, and supplier and quality assessment.

6. *Quality and Operational Results.* Includes: Product and service quality results, organization operational results, business process and support service results, and supplier quality results.

7. *Customer Focus and Satisfaction.* Includes: Meeting current and future customer expectations, customer relationship management, commitment to customers, customer satisfaction determination, customer satisfaction results, and customer satisfaction comparison.

How to Apply: To get additonal information and to apply for this award, contact:
John A. Pieno, Jr.
Chairman, Florida Sterling Council
P.O. Box 13907
Tallahassee, FL 32317-3907
Phone: (904) 922-5316
Fax: (904) 922-6405

ILLINOIS

Award: The Illinois Quality Award

Categories: Currently in the planning stage, with several categories under consideration, including manufacturing and service enterprises, plus health care, legal, public sector, and education.

Award Criteria: Still to be determined, but with the Baldrige criteria as a base.

For information: contact:
Mary Wright Kohlmeier
Executive Director, Illinois Quality Award
658 Pine Court
Lake Bluff, IL 60044
Phone: (708) 234-4924
Fax: (708) 234-8782

LOUISIANA

Award: U.S. Senate Productivity Award and U.S. Senate Innovation Award

Categories: Private organizations of all types are eligible to apply.

Award Criteria:
For the Productivity Award, judges review:
1. The specific productivity and quality improvement program put in place.
2. The driving force behind the program.
3. The nature and extent of senior management's commitment to productivity and quality improvement.
4. The involvement of the company's work force in the program.
5. The impact of the program on owners, managers, employees, customers, and vendors.

6. The transferability of the productivity- and quality-improvement program to other private-sector business, particularly in the state of Louisiana.

For the Innovation Award, judges review:
1   The specific innovation activity undertaken
2.   The driving force behind this activity
3.   The nature and extent of the senior management's commitment to activity
4.   The involvement of the company's work force in this activity
5.   The risks taken in developing this activity
6.   The impact of this activity on owners, managers, employees, customers, vendors, and competition
7.   The transferability of this specific innovation to other private sector businesses, particularly in the state of Louisiana

How to Apply: For information and to apply, contact:
Edward J. O'Boyle
Selection Board
U.S. Senate Productivity Award
Louisiana Tech University
P.O. Box 10318
Ruston, LA 71272
Phone: (318) 257-3701
Fax: (318) 257-4253

MARYLAND

Award: United States Senate Productivity Award for Maryland

Eligibility: All organizations, public and private, are eligible for this award.

Categories: There are three categories in which organizations may apply for this award:
   Manufacturing
   Services
   Small Business

Award Criteria: There are five areas in which applicants are judged for this award:
1.   *Productivity and Quality Leadership.* Examines senior executives' personal leadership and involvement in creating and sustaining a customer focus and clear, visible quality values. (20% weight)
2.   *Human Resource Excellence.* Examines the ways an organization develops and realizes the full potential of the work force to pursue its quality and performance objectives. (20% weight)
3.   *Productivity/Quality Results.* Examines the organization's quality and productivity trends in quality, both operational and supplier quality, including current quality and productivity levels relative to competitors. (25% weight)
4.   *Customer Orientation and Results.* Examines the organization's relationships with customers and its knowledge of customer requirements and of key quality factors that determine marketplace competitiveness. (25% weight)
5.   *Impact on State and Local Community.* Examines the economic and environmental impact of the organization's quality values on the state and local community. (10% weight)

How to Apply: This award is sponsored by the two Maryland U.S. Senators. For more information or applications, contact:
   Nellie Freeman

The Office of the Honorable Paul S. Sarbanes
United States Senate
Washington, DC 20510
Phone: (202) 224-4524
or
Amit Gupta
The Maryland Center for Quality and Productivity
College of Business and Management
University of Maryland
College Park, MD 20742-7215
Phone: (301) 403-4535
Fax: (301) 403-8152

MASSACHUSETTS

Award: Massachusetts Quality Award—up to two awards per category will be given in each eligible category.

Eligibility: Any business or appropriate subsidiary located in Massachusetts may apply.

Categories: There are four categories in which organizations may apply for this award:
Manufacturing. Companies that produce and market manufactured products or manufacturing processes and those companies that produce agricultural, mining, or construction processes.
Service. Companies that market services.
Small Business. Complete businesses (not business subsidiaries) with not more than 200 full-time employees. Business activities may include manufacturing and/or service.
Nonprofit. All governmental, educational, health care, social service, and other nonprofit organizations.

Award Criteria: Based on the Baldrige criteria, applicants are judged on the following areas:
1. *Leadership.* Examines how senior executives leadership and personal involvement creates and maintains clear and visible values and management systems focused on the customer and sustains an environment for quality excellence. (9% weight)
2. *Information and Analysis.* Examines the scope, validity, analysis, management, and use of data and information to drive quality excellence and competitive performance. (8% weight)
3. *Strategic Quality Planning.* Examines the planning process with particular emphasis placed on the integration of the key quality and overall performance planning requirements in both the short (1 to 2 years) and long term (more than 3 years). (6% weight)
4. *Human Resource Development.* Examines the efforts to develop and realize the full potential of all employees while achieving quality and performance objectives. (15% weight)
5. *Management of Process Quality.* Examines key systemic processes used to pursue every higher quality and organizational performance. (14% weight)
6. *Quality and Operational Results.* Examines the current levels and improvement trends in operations and supplier quality performance, including current quality and performance levels relative to competitors. (18% weight)

7. *Customer Focus and Satisfaction.* Examines the relationships with customers, with an emphasis on the knowledge of customer requirements and key quality factors that determine marketplace competitiveness. (30% weight)

How to Apply: For more information on the Massachusetts Quality Award, contact:
Dave Cohen
Massachusetts Council for Quality, Inc.
University of Massachusetts, Lowell
Continuing Education
One University Avenue
Lowell, MA 01854
Phone: (508) 934-2405

MINNESOTA

Award: Minnesota Quality Award—up to two awards are given in each of three categories.

Eligibility: Any FOR-PROFIT business or appropriate subsidiary located in the State of Minnesota may apply for an award.

Categories: There are three categories in which companies may apply for this award:

Manufacturing. Companies that produce or sell manufactured products or manufacturing processes and those companies that produce agricultural, mining, or construction products (SIC Codes 01–39).

Service. Companies that sell services (SIC Codes 07, 40–89).

Small Business. Complete businesses (not business subsidiaries) with not more than 200 full-time employees. Business activities may include manufacturing and/or services.

Note: An additional category for education is planned for 1994 and additional awards for government and other nonprofit organizations in subsequent years.

Award Criteria: The Minnesota Quality Award criteria mirror the Baldrige criteria, and applicants are judged on:

1. *Executive Leadership.* Examines senior executives' personal leadership and involvement in creating and sustaining a customer focus and clear and visible quality values. (10% weight)
2. *Information and Analysis.* Examines the scope, validity, analysis, management, and use of data and information to drive quality excellence and improve competitive performance. Also examines the adequacy of the organization's data, information, and analysis system to support continuous improvement of the organization's customer focus, products, services, and internal operations. (6% weight)
3. *Strategic Quality Planning.* Examines the organization's planning and how all key quality requirements are integrated into the organization's overall planning, its short-term (one to two years) and long-term (three or more years) priorities for quality and performance. (9% weight)
4. *Human Resources Development and Management.* Examines the extent of the organization's efforts to develop and realize the full potential of all its employees in pursuing the organization's quality and performance objectives, including the organization's efforts to build and maintain an environment for quality excellence conducive to full participation and personal growth. (15% weight)
5. *Management of Process Quality.* Examines the key systematic processes the organization uses to pursue every higher quality and organizational performance. (15% weight)

6. *Quality and Operational Results.* Examines the organization's quality levels and improvement trends in quality, organizational operational performance, and supplier quality, including current quality and performance levels relative to competitors. (15% weight)

7. *Customer Focus and Satisfaction.* Examines the organization's relationship with its customers and its knowledge of customer requirements and key quality factors that determine marketplace competitiveness, including the organization's methods to determine customer satisfaction, current trends and levels of satisfaction, and these results relative to competitors.

How to Apply: For more information on the Minnesota Quality Award and information on the Minnesota Council for Quality, contact:
Jim Buckman, President
Minnesota Council for Quality
2850 Metro Drive, Suite 300
Bloomington, MN 55425
Phone: (612) 851–3181
Fax: (612) 851–3183

MISSOURI

Award: Missouri Quality Award, awarded by the Excellence in Missouri Foundation.

Eligibility: Any business or subsidiary of a business that has employees in Missouri and has existed in Missouri for at least one year. Additional eligibility information is available in the award booklet.

Categories: There are two business categories and three size categories in which organizations may apply for this award:

Manufacturing. Includes companies or subsidiaries that produce and sell manufacturing processes, and those companies that produce agricultural, mining, or construction products. (SIC codes 01–39)

Services. Includes companies or subsidiaries that sell services. (SIC codes 40–89)

Size. Organizations are judged in three sizes: Small—less than 100 employees, Medium—100–499 employees, and Large—500 employees or more.

Award Criteria: The Baldrige criteria form the basis for seven areas of the Missouri Quality Award:

1. *Leadership.* Examines senior executives personal leadership and involvement in creating and sustaining a customer focus and visible quality values, including how the quality values are integrated into the company's management system and reflected in how the company addresses the public responsibilities and corporate citizenship. (9.5% weight)

2. *Information and Analysis.* Examines the scope, validity, analysis, management, and use of data and information to drive quality excellence and improve operational and competitive performance. (7.5% weight)

3. *Strategic Quality Planning.* Examines the company's planning process and how all key quality requirements are integrated into overall business planning. (6% weight)

4. *Human Resource Development and Management.* Examines the key elements of how the workforce is enabled to develop its full potential to purse the company's quality and operational performance objectives. (15% weight)

5. *Management of Process Quality.* Examines the systematic processes the company uses the pursue ever-higher quality and company operational performance. (14% weight)
6. *Quality and Operational Results.* Examines the company's quality levels and improvement trends in quality, company operational performance, and supplier quality, including current quality and performance levels relative to those of competitors. (18% weight)
7. *Customer Focus and Satisfaction.* Examines the company's relationships with customers and its knowledge of customer requirements and of the key quality factors that drive marketplace competitiveness. (30% weight)

How to Apply: For detailed information about the Missouri Quality Award, contact:
John Politi, Executive Director
Excellence in Missouri Foundation
P.O. Box 1709
Jefferson City, MO 65102
Phone: (314) 634-2246
Fax: (314) 634-4406

NEVADA

Award: The U.S. Senate Productivity Award

Categories: There are seven categories for different types of organizations. Awards are non-competitive and small businesses will not be judged against larger organizations:
Education
Government
Health and Medical Services
Manufacturing and Mining
Non-Profit
Resort and Travel
Service and Retail

Award Criteria: Matches the Baldrige criteria:
Leadership
Information and Analysis
Strategic Quality Planning
Human Resource Planning
Quality and Operational Results
Management of Process Quality
Customer Focus and Quality

How to Apply: For more information, contact:
Ted Atencio/Bob Grant
Co-Chairmen
U.S. Senate Productivity Award
c/o Quality and Productivity Center
P.O. Box 93416
Las Vegas, NV 89193-3416
Phone: (702) 798-7292
Fax: (702) 798-8653

NEW MEXICO

Award: New Mexico Quality Award

Eligibility: Any for-profit or not-for-profit or nonprofit New Mexico organization may apply.

Categories: Three sectors at three levels:

Sectors: Manufacturing, Services, and Government

Size Levels: Small (less than 25 employees), Medium (26–150 employees), and Large (over 150 employees).

Award Criteria: The criteria for the New Mexico Quality Award are modeled after the Baldrige Award and use the present year's Baldrige criteria and training material.

How to Apply: For more information or to apply for this award, contact:
Karen P. Martin, Award Administrator
Economic Development Department
1155 South Telshore, Suite 201
Las Cruces, NM 88001
Phone: (505) 521–3699
Fax: (505) 521–4099

NEW YORK

Award: The Governor's Excelsior Award. This award includes special emphasis on the workforce and labor-management relations.

Eligibility: Public and private organizations operating in New York State.

Categories: There are awards in three categories:

Private Sector. For applicants from manufacturing and service organizations, including for-profit health care organizations.

Public Sector. For applicants from state and local governmental entities.

Education Sector. For applicants from public and private schools, colleges, and universities.

Award Criteria: As with many other state awards, this one is similar to the Baldrige award:

1. *Leadership.* Examines senior executives' personal leadership and involvement in creating and sustaining a focus on customers, developing clear and visible quality values, and fostering a management system to guide the company toward quality excellence. (17% weight)

2. *Information and Analysis.* Examines the scope, validity, use, and management of data and information to drive excellence and improve competitive performance. (5% weight)

3. *Strategic Quality Planning.* Examines the company's planning process and how all key quality requirements are integrated into overall business planning, including the company's short-term and longer-term plans and how quality and performance requirements are deployed in work units. (5% weight)

4. *Human Resource Excellence.* Examines the effectiveness of the company's efforts to develop and realize the full potential of the workforce, including management, and to maintain a work environment conducive to full participation, empowerment, quality leadership, and personal organizational growth, and cooperative interaction between management and labor. (24% weight)

5. *Management of Process Quality.* Examines the systematic processes used by the company to pursue ever-higher quality and company performance, including the

key elements of process management, the design of products and services, management of process quality for all work units and suppliers, systematic and continuous quality improvement, and quality assessment. (10% weight)

6. *Quality and Operational Results.* Examines the company's quality levels and improvement trends in quality, company operational performance, and supplier quality, including current quality and performance relative to competitors. (15% weight)

7. *Customer Focus and Satisfaction.* Examines the company's relationships with customers and its knowledge of the key factors that determine marketplace competitiveness, including the company's methods to determine customer satisfaction, current levels and trends in customer satisfaction, and these results relative to the competition. (24% weight)

How to Apply: To find out more information and to apply for these awards, contact:
The Governor's Excelsior Award
NOOSE Department of Labor
Averell Harriman State Office Campus
Building 12, Room 540A
Albany, NY 12240
Phone: (518) 457-6747
Fax: (518) 457-0620

NORTH CAROLINA

Award: North Carolina Quality Leadership Award

Categories: The award is given in two sectors and three levels:
Sectors. Manufacturing and Services, for both profit and not-for-profit organizations
Levels. Small (less than 100 employees and less than $5 million in annual sales).
Medium (between 100 and 500 emplyees and between $5 and $40 million is annual sales).
Large (More than 500 employees and more than $40 million in annual sales).

Award Criteria: North Carolina models its award after the Baldrige Award and uses the previous year's Baldrige criteria and training material.

How to Apply: For more information and to apply, contact:
Carla Visser
Director of Recognition Programs
North Carolina Quality Leadership Foundation
4904 Professional Court, Suite 100
Raleigh, NC 27609
Phone: (919) 872-8198
Fax: (919) 872-8199

OREGON

Award: The Oregon Quality Award (first award to be give in 1994)

Categories: Manufacturing, with an emphasis on small business in 1994; Service and Health Care to be added in 1995, and public sector to be added in 1996.

Award Criteria: Oregon will base its award on Baldrige criteria, but to be rescaled to take into account that 96 percent of Oregon businesses have 50 or fewer employees. To encourage participation, awards will be given to all Oregon applicants that meet the standards.

How to Apply: For information on the award and applications, contact:
Tami Lohman
Executive Director
Oregon Quality Initiative
7528 SE 29th Avenue
Portland, OR 97202
Phone: (503) 777-6057
Fax: (503) 639-5453

TENNESSEE

Award: The Tennessee Quality Award

Eligibility: Any public or privately held organization of any size located in the state of Tennessee.

Categories: Awards are given for four levels of quality, based on where an organization is in its quality transformation:

Level 1, Quality Interest. This is for organizations just starting to express interest in adopting and applying quality principles.

Level 2, Quality Commitment. This is for organizations that have progressed to a point of demonstrating serious commitment to the use of total quality principles.

Level 3, Quality Achievement. This is for organizations who have demonstrated, through their commitment and practice of quality principles, significant progress to building sound and notable processes.

Level 4, Governor's Quality Award. This is for organizations that have demonstrated, through their practices and achievements, the highest level of quality excellence.

Award Criteria: The criteria for the Tennessee Quality Award mirror the Baldrige criteria:

1. *Leadership.* Examines senior executives' personal leadership and involvement in creating and sustaining a customer focus and clear and visible values. (10% weight)
2. *Information and Analysis.* Examines the scope, validity, analysis, management, and use of data and information to drive quality and excellence and improve competitive performance. (7% weight)
3. *Strategic Quality Planning.* Examines the company's planning process and how all key quality requirements are integrated into overall business planning, including the company's short-term and longer-term plans and how quality and performance requirements are deployed in work units. (6% weight)
4. *Human Resource Excellence.* Examines the effectiveness of the company's efforts to develop and realize the full potential of the workforce, including management, and to maintain a work environment conducive to full participation, empowerment, quality leadership, and personal organizational growth, and cooperative interaction between management and labor. (15% weight)
5. *Management of Process Quality.* Examines the systematic processes used by the company to pursue ever-higher quality and company performance, including the key elements of process management, the design of products and services, management of process quality for all work units and suppliers, systematic and continuous quality improvement, and quality assessment. (14% weight)
6. *Quality and Operational Results.* Examines the company's quality levels and improvement trends in quality, company operational performance, and supplier quality, including current quality and performance relative to competitors. (18% weight)

7. *Customer Focus and Satisfaction.* Examines the company's relationships with customers and its knowledge of the key factors that determine marketplace competitiveness, including the company's methods to determine customer satisfaction, current levels and trends in customer satisfaction, and these results relative to the competition. (30% weight)

How to Apply: For more information and to apply for this award, write or call

Marie B. Williams, Director
Tennessee Quality Award
National Center for Quality
500 James Robertson Parkway, Suite 660
Nashville, TN 37243-0406
Phone: (615) 323-0224
Fax: (615) 477-5760

TEXAS

Award: The Texas Quality Award

Categories: There are four categories for this award:

Industrial Organizations. Small and Large Industrial.

Service Organizations. Small and Large Service.

Governmental Agencies and Non-Profit Organizations. Small and Large Agenices/ Non-Profits.

Educational Organizations. Small and Large Educational Organizations.

Criteria: This is based on Baldrige criteria:

Leadership. The senior executives' success in creating and sustaining a quality culture.

Information and Analysis. The effectiveness of the company's collection and analysis of information for quality improvement and planning.

Strategic Quality Planning. The effectiveness of the integration of quality requirements into the organization's business plan.

Human Resource Development and Management. The success of the organization's efforts to realize the full potential of the work force for quality.

Management of Process Quality. The effectiveness of the system for assuring quality control of all operations.

Quality and Operational Results. The organization's results in quality achievement and quality improvement, demonstrated through quantitative measures.

Customer Focus and Satisfaction. The effectiveness of the organization's systems to determine customer requirements and their demonstrated success in meeting those requirements.

How to Apply: For information and application forms, contact:

Administrator
Texas Quality Award
American Productivity and Quality Center
123 North Post Oak Lane
Houston, TX 77024
Phone: (800) 776-9676 or (713) 681-4020
Fax: (713) 681-8578

VIRGINIA

Award: The U.S. Senate Productivity Award for Virginia. This award originated to recognize productivity but has now evolved into an award for quality management.

Eligibility: Any organization, regardless of size or profit status, practicing continuous improvement of quality and productivity in the Commonwealth of Virginia.

Categories: The are four categories of awards:
Private Sector Manufacturing
Private Sector Service
Public Sector State and Federal Agencies
Public Sector Local Agencies

Criteria: The overall criteria are derived from the Baldrige Award but have been modified. Applicants are asked to supply information in response to questions in eight areas:

1. *Maturity of Effort.* When was the organization's improvement effort initiated? How was the effort conceived? Is the organization's approach original, or was an existing approach tailored to fit the organization's needs? How extensive is the effort within the company?

2. *Top Management Commitment and Involvement (Leadership).* Describe resource commitments/allocation. How are the quality values of the organization epitomized by the leaders? What are specific examples of the level of commitment and involvement by top management?

3. *Employee Involvement and Training, Development and Management of Participation.* How is employee involvement encouraged by top management? What types of quality and productivity training opportunities are provided to employees? How are teams used? To what degree are teams empowered? Are employee training and development plans derived from quality and company performance plans?

4. *Recognition/Rewards Systems.* How are contributors to and participants in the quality/productivity improvement effort recognized? Is there an established method for sharing gains?

5. *Plan for Continuous Improvement.* How do the quality and productivity efforts integrate with the organization's vision, long-range plans, business plans, and human resources programs? Are the individuals responsible for implementing these plans involved in developing them? Are targets for long-term goals established? Are self-evaluations made or conducted against other successful efforts? Does the process link plans to action? And how are plans implemented?

6. *Performance Measurement Process (Use of Information).* What types of measures are in place? How are they linked to the overall improvement effort? How do you determine what to measure? What categories of information do you collect? Is the quality of the product or service measured at the customer's and supplier's location? Is quality measured internally from a customer perspective? Is there evidence of statistical thinking? Is competitive benchmarking evident?

7. *Customer/Supplier Involvement.* How do you assess supplier quality? How are customers and suppliers involved in your organization's ongoing efforts to improve quality and productivity? Are customers and suppliers recognized for their efforts? Is customer satisfaction measured? How? What use is made of this information?

8. *Results Over Time.* What are the specific results from the organization's quality and productivity improvement efforts?

How to Apply: For more information and application forms, contact;
Elizabeth Holmes
U.S. Senate Productivity Award for Virginia
567 Whittemore Hall
Virginia Tech

Blacksburg, VA 24061-0118
Phone: (703) 231-6100
Fax: (703) 231-6925

WYOMING

Award: The Wyoming Governor's Quality Award

Categories: No formal categories—the award is open to all Wyoming businesses with not less than five full-time employees and not less than $250,000 annual sales.

Criteria: Not formally specified, but applicants are judged on the Baldrige-type elements.

How to Apply: For more information and application form, contact:
Ann Redman
Division of Economic and Community Development
Barrett Building
2301 Central Avenue
Cheyenne, WY 82002
Phone: (307) 777-7284
Fax: (307) 777-5840

INTERNATIONAL AWARDS DIRECTORY

The Deming Prize

This is sponsored by the Union of Japanese Scientists and Engineers (JUSE) and named for W. Edwards Deming. The prestigious award was established in 1951, with categories for *individuals, small companies, factories,* and for *application of Company-Wide Quality Control statistical methods.* Organizatons and individuals from any nation may apply. Most winners come from Japan. For detailed information, contact:
Junji Noguchi, Executive Director
The Union of Japanese Scientists and Engineers (JUSE)
5-10-11 Sendagaya Shibuyaku
Tokyo 151, JAPAN
Phone: 81 3 5379 1227
Fax: 81 3 3225 1813

The European Quality Award

Sponsored by the European Foundation for Quality Management. Criteria have overlap with the Baldrige Award, but with some modifications. For detailed information, contact:
The European Foundation for Quality Management
Building Reaal, Fellenoord 47a
5612 AA Eindhoven
The Netherlands
Phone: 31 40 461075
Fax: 31 40 432005

International Benchmarking Award

This award is designed to recognize benchmarking excellence by organizations in a variety of specialities, with specific criteria tied to the benchmarking task. For more information, contact:
International Benchmarking Clearinghouse

American Productivity and Quality Center
123 North Post Oak Lane, Suite 300
Houston, TX 77024-7797
Phone: (800) 336-9606 or (713) 681-4020
Fax: (713) 681-8578

Canada Awards for Business Excellence

The Services to Business Branch of the Canadian government sponsors these awards in several categories including an award for Total Quality. For information, contact:

Services to Business Branch
Industry, Science, and Technology Canada
235 Queen Street
Ottawa, Ontario K1A OH5
Phone: (613) 954-4079
Fax: (613) 954-4074

Prix Nationale de la Qualite

The French National Quality Award is designed to encourage and recognize French companies who practice quality mangement. The criteria for this award is similar to the Baldrige Award. For more information, contact:

Mouvement Francaise pour la Qualite-MFQ
5, esplanade Charles de Gaulle
92733 Nanterre cedex
FRANCE
Phone: 33 1 47 29 09 29
Fax: 33 1 47 25 32 21

Quality Circle Award

This is the national quality award for Germany. Designed to recognize companies that excel in the application of quality control. For information, contact:

Dr. H. J. Dorr
Rationalisierungs-Kuratorium des Deutsche Wirkschaft
Sohnstrasse 70
4000 Dusseldorf 1
GERMANY
Phone: 49 211 6800
Fax: 49 211 6800 168

British Quality Award

This national award of Great Britain includes criteria similar to that for the Baldrige. Detailed information is available from:

The Award Secretary
The British Quality Association
PO Box 712, 61 Southwark Street
London SE1 1SB
Phone: 44 71 401 2844
Fax: 44 71 401 2725

Directory of
Magazines and Journals

This section includes a comprehensive (though not exhaustive) listing of publications that regularly cover issues on quality. Some of them are dedicated to quality issues, and some of them cover quality as part of their regular editorial policy. Many quality organizations, such as the American Society for Quality Control, and others include a variety of newsletters of interest to members, depending on area of specialization. Most local quality organizations also publish their own newsletters. Those publications are not listed here as they are available only to members. You can find out more about these organizations in the state awards section and the quality organizations section of *The Quality Yearbook*.

We have organized this listing into three categories:

1. Magazines, journals, and newsletters dedicated to quality
2. General business magazines, journals, and newsletters that often include articles on quality
3. Industry and special interest magazines, journals, and newsletters that often cover quality issues

All magazines, journals, and newsletters included have something of value to anyone interested in TQM, depending on background and specialty. However, to help you sort through these in terms of their value in learning about and implementing quality, we have developed the following ratings:

★★★ = Highest recommendation, regularly includes very useful information on quality management
★★ = Highly recommended, frequently includes useful articles
★ = Recommended, includes some useful articles

Note: In establishing these ratings, they do not apply to the overall "quality" of the magazines, but to their coverage of quality management topics.

Magazines, Journals, and Newsletters Dedicated to Quality
Journal for Quality and Participation
Published seven times a year (January/February, March, June, July/August, September, October/November, and December) by the Association for Quality and Participation, 801-B West 8th Street, Suite 501, Cincinnati, OH 45203, (513) 381-1959.

Subscriptions: Available as part of membership in AQP. Nonmembers: $52 per year in the United States and $75 for international orders.

Includes a variety of practical, detailed articles on implementing quality in different industries and organizations. Articles are nearly always intriguing, useful, and well-written. One of the best magazines available on quality for managers. Rating: ★★★

Journal of Quality Technology

Published quarterly by the American Society for Quality Control, 611 East Wisconsin Avenue, P.O. Box 3005, Milwaukee, WI 53201-3005, (414) 272-8575.

Subscriptions: For ASQC members, annual subscription is $20 in the United States, $38.50 in Canada, and $36 for other international; for nonmembers, $30 annually in the United States, $40 for other international subscriptions.

A technically oriented journal, with heavy use of statistics, emphasizing the practical applicability of new techniques, instructive examples of the operation of existing techniques, and results of historical researches. Useful only to those involved in quality control technology. Rating: ★★

National Productivity Review

Published quarterly by Executive Enterprises Publications Co., Inc., 22 West 21st Street, New York, NY 10010-6990, (800) 332-8804.

Subscriptions: United States and Canada, 1 year $168, 2 years $309. International, 1 year $218. Discounts available on multiple copy subscriptions.

A journal that includes practical articles focusing on the implementation of quality in all types of organizations. Divided into three sections: Ideas and Opinions, Features, and Reviews. Rating: ★★★

Quality

Published monthly by Hitchcock Publishing Company, One Chilton Way, Radnor, PA 19089.

Subscriptions: United States, 1 year $70. Canada and Mexico, 1 year $85. International, 1 year $160.

Includes articles that focus mainly on the technical aspects of implementing total quality management in production and manufacturing environments. Includes reviews and event calendar. Specially of interest to engineers and quality technicians. Rating: ★★★

Quality Abstracts

Published bimonthly by Advanced Personnel Systems, P.O. Box 1438, Roseville, CA 95678, (916) 781-2900.

Subscriptions: 1 year $95; add $12 for all non-U.S. subscriptions.

Each issue is 28 to 36 pages and includes abstracts of articles gleaned from a review of about 250 different magazines, journals, and newsletters on quality. For those who must keep up with the latest on quality or are doing research in this area, this is a valuable resource. Rating: ★★

Quality Digest

Published monthly by QCI International, 1350 Vista Way, P.O. Box 882, Red Bluff, CA 96080, (916) 527-6070.

Subscriptions: Official rate $75 per year but discounted to $45 for United States and $69 for international orders.

Includes a variety of how-to articles and pieces on how various organizations implement quality, especially in people management. Also includes monthly columnists such as Tom Peters, Karl Albrecht, and Ken Blanchard, plus book reviews and other information.

Rating: ★★

Quality Engineering

Published quarterly by the American Society for Quality Control and Marcel Dekker, Inc. Subscriptions available through Marcel Dekker Journals, P.O. Box 5017, Monticello, NY 12701-5176.

Subscriptions: 1 year $35; add $14 for surface mail and $22 for airmail to Europe and $26 for airmail to Asia.

Dedicated to quality management articles that deal with this message: "What the problem was, how we solved it, and what the results were." Articles tend to be detailed and moderately technical, but quite relevant to quality professionals. Rating: ★

Quality in Manufacturing

Published bimonthly by Huebcore Communications, Inc., 29100 Aurora Road, Suite 200, (216) 248-1125.

Subscriptions: 1 year $75; Canada and Mexico 1 year $95; international 1 year $155. Available free to qualified people in manufacturing (call for sample copy).

A closed circulation large format four-color magazine devoted to reviews and articles about quality technology in manufacturing. Rating: ★

Quality Management Journal

Published quarterly by the American Society for Quality Control, 611 East Wisconsin Avenue, P.O. Box 3005, Milwaukee, WI 53201-3005, (414) 272-8575.

Subscriptions: Available to members of ASQC in the United States at $50 annually, to nonmembers at $60; Canada: $74 to members and $84 to nonmembers; international: $74 to members and $84 to nonmembers.

A new peer-reviewed journal designed to present academic research on quality management in a style that makes it accessible to managers in all fields. Rating: ★★★

Quality Progress

Published monthly by the American Society for Quality Control, Inc., 611 East Wisconsin Avenue, P.O. Box 3005, Milwaukee, WI 53201-3005, (414) 272-8575.

Subscriptions: Available as part of membership in the ASQC. $50 per year for nonmembers in the United States and $85 for first class to Canada and international airmail.

This is the foremost magazine on quality management available. It includes a wide variety of general and technical articles plus event calendars, reviews, and many other features. Rating: ★★★

Target
Published bimonthly by the Association for Manufacturing Excellence, 380 West Palatine Road, Wheeling, IL 60090, (708) 520-3282.

Subscriptions: Available to members of AME as part of membership. Cost of annual membership: $125.

Includes many practical articles on how various industries and companies are implementing TQM in manufacturing and management. Also includes reports from regional chapters, book reviews, and event calendar. Practical, accessible, and well-done. Rating: ★★★

The Center for Quality Management Journal
Published quarterly by the Center for Quality Management, 70 Fawcett Street, MS 15/4B, Cambridge, MA 02138, (617) 873-2152.

Subscriptions: $70 per year.

This is a new journal, started in 1992, and it includes a selection of practical articles focusing on the implementation of TQM in different organizations. Rating: ★

The Quality Observer
Published monthly by The Quality Observer Corporation, 3505 Old Lee Highway, P.O. Box 1111, Fairfax, VA 22030, (703) 691-9295.

Subscriptions: 1 year $53, 2 years $90, and 3 years $130; overseas, 1 year $68, 2 years $120, and 3 years $175; libraries, 1 year $90 (2 copies each issues sent to same address); corporations, 1 year $180 (5 copies each issue sent to same address).

Billed as the "International News Magazine of Quality," this is a three-color tabloid-sized publication, with case studies, international news, interviews, and regular columns on quality topics. Rating: ★★★

The TQM Magazine
Published bimonthly by MCB University Press, Ltd. Write to TQM Magazine, P.O. Box 26007, Alexandria, VA 22313-9864, (800) 945-4551 for subscriptions.

Subscriptions: Officially $156 per year, discounted to $123.

Organized around different themes each month, it includes a variety of how-to articles and descriptions of what is going on in various organizations. Rating: ★★

Total Quality in Hospitality
Published monthly by Magna Publications Inc., 2718 Dryden Drive, Madison, WI 53704-3086, (608) 246-3580 or (800) 433-0499.

Subscriptions: $198 per year, with additional subscriptions to the same organization available at a discount.

A monthly eight-page two-color newsletter covering specific ideas for implementing quality, case studies, and company profiles for the hospitality industry. Rating: ★★

Total Quality Management
Published three times a year by Carfax Publishing Company, P.O. Box 25, Abington, Oxfordshire OX14 3UE, United Kingdom or P.O. Box 2025, Dunnellon, FL 32630.

Subscriptions: Information available by writing to either of these addresses.

An academic journal with a practical bent, it includes articles of practical interest to managers and academics. It covers all aspects of quality management. Rating: ★★

Total Quality Newsletter
Published monthly by Lakewood Publications, 50 Ninth Street, Minneapolis, MN 55402, (800) 328-4329.

Subscriptions: Available at $128 per year; add $10 for Canada and $20 for other international locations.

An eight-page two-color newsletter covering one major topic per issue plus reviews of training materials and short practical articles on what various companies are doing in quality. Rating: ★★

TQM in Higher Education
Published monthly by Magna Publications Inc., 2718 Dryden Drive, Madison, WI 53704-3086, (608) 246-3580 or (800) 433-0499.

Subscriptions: $129 per year with discounts available for additional subscriptions to the same location.

A monthly eight-page, two-color newsletter covering ideas on applying TQM principles, case studies, information on TQM tools, and other practical articles on quality management in colleges and universities. Rating: ★★

General Business Magazines, Journals, and Newsletters That Include Coverage of Quality

Across the Board
Published ten times annually (January/February and July/August combined issues) by The Conference Board, Inc., 845 Third Avenue, New York, NY 10022, (212) 759-0900.

Subscriptions: $20 annually for Conference Board Associates and $40 annually for nonassociates.

A thoughtfully edited magazine on issues of interest to all managers. Includes columns, commentaries, how-to and company profiles, and issue-related articles. Articles occasionally directly related to quality, but nearly all are indirectly related. Rating: ★★★

Business Ethics
Published bimonthly by Mavis Publications, Inc., 52 South 10th Street, #110, Minneapolis, MN 55403-4700, (612) 962-4700.

Subscriptions: $49 per year in the United States and $59 for international subscriptions.

Includes articles on topics of ethical and social concern to business, all of which are arguably related to quality in one way or another. Occasionally includes articles specifically on quality management and its implementation in socially responsible organizations.

Rating: ★★

Business Horizons

Published bimonthly by JAI Press, Inc., 55 Old Post Road, No. 2, P.O. Box 1678, Greenwich, CT 06836-1678, (203) 661-7602.

Subscriptions: $60 per year in the United States; outside the United States add $20 for surface mail and $30 for airmail.

Published out of the Indiana University Graduate School of Business, there is a diversity of articles of interest to managers, often shorter than found in the *Harvard Business Review*. Rating: ★ (because it only occasionally includes articles on quality)

Business Week

Published weekly by McGraw-Hill, Inc., 1221 Avenue of the Americas, New York, NY 10020, (212) 512-2000.

Subscriptions: Official subscription rate: 1 year $44.95, 2 years $74.95, and 3 years $99.95. Widely available at discounted subscription rates.

The leading business newsweekly in the United States. Gives special attention to quality in one or two issues per year and includes articles on quality management as appropriate during the year. Rating: ★★

California Management Review

Published quarterly by the University of California, Walter A. Haas School of Business, 350 Barrows Hall, University of California, Berkeley, CA 94720, (510) 642-7159.

Subscriptions: 1 year $45, 2 years $80, and 3 years $115; international subscriptions 1 year $68, 2 years $126, and 3 years $184.

A serious journal, but with a practical orientation, often including in-depth articles on quality management theory and implementation. Rating: ★★

Fortune

Published biweekly by Time Warner, Inc., Time & Life Building, Rockefeller Center, New York, NY 10020, (800) 621-8000.

Subscriptions: Official subscription rate: $52.95 1 year, United States and $53.75 1 year, Canada. Widely available at discounted subscription rates.

Provides in-depth reviews of management and other business topics and profiles of executives. Articles do not often focus on quality per se, but they are useful as benchmarks for understanding quality management practices in relation to traditional perspectives on managing. Rating: ★★

Harvard Business Review

Published bimonthly by the Harvard Business School, Boston, MA 02163, (617) 495-6800.

Subscriptions: $75 per year, United States, $95 per year in Canada and Mexico, and $145 in all other countries.

Includes in-depth articles on management techniques in all functional areas by highly regarded researchers and executives. Often includes articles of direct or indirect relevance to those interested in quality. Rating: ★★★

Inc.

Published monthly by *Inc.*, 38 Commercial Wharf, Boston, MA 02110, (617) 248-8000 or (800) 234-0999 for subscription information.

Subscriptions: Available at various rates, often discounted. Currently being offered at $19 for 1 year or $38 for 3 years.

The premier magazine covering issues of interest to small- and medium-sized businesses. Loaded with practical how-to techniques and articles and company and executive profiles. Often covers issues directly related to quality management issues, though it only occasionally uses the word quality to describe this approach. Rating: ★★★

Industry Week

Published biweekly by Penton Publishing Company, 1100 Superior Avenue, Cleveland, OH 44114-2543, (216) 696-7000.

Subscriptions: Distributed as a closed circulation magazine to qualified executives in administration, finance, production, engineering, purchasing, marketing, and sales. To those who do not qualify, it is available by subscription at $60 per year or $100 for two years; Canada $90 per year or $150 for two years; international $110 per year or $195 for two years.

Includes articles, columns, and reviews of timely interest to managers on a wide range of business and management topics, with frequent articles on quality management.
Rating: ★★★

Journal of Business Strategy

Published bimonthly by Faulkner Group, Inc., 11 Penn Plaza, New York, NY 10001, (212) 967-7000.

Subscriptions: $98 per year in the United States and Canada and $128 per year in all other countries.

Each edition includes a Special Focus section that provides an in-depth look at one topic of interest in strategic planning and thinking, plus additional articles, columns, and features. Often covers topics on quality management.
Rating: ★★

Management Review

Published monthly by the American Management Association Publications Division, Box 408, Saranac, NY 12983-0408.

Subscriptions: $45 per year in the United States; Non-U.S. subscriptions $60 per year.

The official magazine of the American Management Association, it includes a variety of articles of interest to managers and often includes items on quality issues. Rating: ★★

Nation's Business
Published by the U.S. Chamber of Commerce, 1615 H Street NW, Washington, DC 20062-2000, (202) 463-5650.

Subscriptions: 1 year $22, 2 years $35, and 3 years $46; Canadian and international subscriptions add $20 to each rate.

Includes articles of interest to small- and medium-sized business, with frequent coverage of quality management issues. Rating: ★★

Sloan Management Review
Published quarterly by the MIT Sloan School of Management, 292 Main Street, E38-120, Cambridge, MA 02139, (617) 253-7170.

Subscriptions: $59 per year; $79 for Canada and Mexico, and $89 for all other international subscriptions.

Includes practical, yet thoughtful articles on a variety of issues of direct interest to managers. Articles often directly or indirectly related to quality issues. Easier to read than the *Harvard Business Review*. Rating: ★★★

Tom Peters On Achieving Excellence
Newsletter published monthly by TPG Communications, P.O. Box 2189, Berkeley, CA 94702-0189, (800) 959-1059.

Subscriptions: United States: 1 year $197 and 2 years $244. Call for international rates.

A slick, readable, and practical 12-page two-color newsletter in the Peters style. Each issue has a theme with lots of short pieces on what different companies and people are doing to solve various business problems. Rating: ★★

Industry and Special Interest Magazines, Journals, and Newsletters that Cover Quality
APICS-The Performance Advantage
Published quarterly by the American Production and Inventory Control Society, Inc., 500 West Annandale Road, Falls Church, VA 22046-4274, (800) 444-2742.

Subscriptions: Included as part of membership package. Nonmembers subscriptions available at $30 per year; $40 in Mexico and Canada, and $50 for all other international subscriptions.

Covers the latest manufacturing principles and practices, case studies, columns, and news. Often includes articles on quality management in its field. Rating: ★★

Change
Published bimonthly by Heldref Publications, 1319 Eighteenth Street NW, Washington, DC 20036-1802, (212) 296-6267 or (800) 365-9753 for subscriptions.

Subscriptions: United States: $31 per year; outside the United States, add $12 per year.

Billed as the magazine of higher learning, it addresses issues of interest to the administration of colleges and universities, and occasionally carries articles on quality management topics. The May/June 1993 devoted an entire issue to this topic. Rating: ★

Hospitals
Published the 5th and 20th of each month by American Hospital Publishing, Inc., part of the American Hospital Association, 840 North Lake Shore Drive, Chicago, IL 60611, (312) 280-6000.

Subscriptions: Included as part of membership or by nonmembers at $60 per year; add $30 per year for outside the United States.

Focuses mainly on management issues for health care executives. Occasionally includes articles on quality management. Rating: ★

HR Focus
Published by the American Management Association, 135 West 50th Street, New York, NY 10020, (212) 903-8389.

Subscriptions: 1 year $51.75, 2 years $88, and 3 years $132. Add $10 per year for outside the United States.

Newsletter-like publication, but longer than the average newsletter. Covers a variety of issues and news items of interest to HR managers. Sometimes includes articles on quality subjects. Rating: ★

HRMagazine
Published monthly by the Society for Human Resource Management, 606 North Washington Street, Alexandria, VA 22314, (703) 548-3440.

Subscriptions: Members of SHRM receive magazine as part of their membership. Nonmember subscriptions available in the United States, Canada, and Mexico at 1 year $49, 2 years $79, and 3 years $119. Write for information on international subscription rates.

Dedicated to human resource issues, with occasional articles on quality issues related to HR. Rating: ★

Industrial Engineering
Published monthly by the Institute of Industrial Engineers, 25 Technology Park, Norcross, GA 30092, (404) 449-0461.

Subscriptions: Included as part of membership. Subscriptions available in the United States to nonmembers for 1 year $49, 2 years $82, and 3 years $110; Canada and international subscriptions 1 year $61, 2 years $104, and 3 years $146.

Regularly includes articles on quality management and techniques related to industrial engineering, though that is not its entire focus. Includes a regular monthly column on quality. Rating: ★★

Manufacturing Engineering

Published monthly by the Society of Manufacturing Engineers, P.O. Box 930, Dearborn, MI 48121, (313) 271-1500.

Subscriptions: Closed circulation magazine sent free to members of the society and others involved with manufacturing. Personal subscription information available by contacting SME.

Covers articles on manufacturing, with some coverage of quality issues, including a monthly column, "The Quality Adviser." Rating: ★

Industrial Management

Published bimonthly by the Institute of Industrial Engineers, 25 Technology Park/Atlanta, Norcross, GA 30092, (404) 449-0460.

Subscriptions: 1 year $32, 2 years $54, and 3 years $80; international subscriptions 1 year $40, 2 years $68, and 3 years $94.

A serious journal with an academic bent that includes quality-oriented articles that are accessible to practitioners. Rating: ★

Modern Healthcare

Published weekly by Crain Communications Inc., 965 East Jefferson, Detroit, MI 48207-3185, (800) 678-9595.

Subscriptions: 1 year $110 and 2 years $200; add $48 for all non-U.S. subscriptions.

A health care industry weekly magazine including news articles plus a variety of articles on managing health care facilities. Occasionally includes articles on quality management. Rating: ★

Performance and Instruction

Published monthly except for combined May/June and November/December issues by the National Society for Performance and Instruction, NSPI Publications, 1300 L Street NW, Suite 1250, Washington, DC 20005, (202) 408-7969.

Subscriptions: Available as part of membership; annual subscriptions available to nonmembers for $50.

Includes detailed articles on practical training techniques that will be of direct use to TQM trainers, though the orientation of the journal is not directed to TQM. Rating: ★★

The School Administrator

Published monthly by the American Association of School Administrators, 1801 North Moore Street, Arlington, VA 22209, (703) 875-7905.

Subscriptions: Included as part of membership.

Dedicated to the problems and opportunities of school administrators, occasionally including articles on quality in schools. Rating: ★

Training

Published monthly by Lakewood Publications, Inc., 50 South Ninth Street, Minneapolis, MN 55402, (612) 333-0471.

Subscriptions: U.S.: 1 year $64, 2 years $108, and 3 years $138; Canada and Mexico: 1 year $74; international: 1 year $85.

Includes articles on issues of interest to corporate trainers, with frequent articles on quality management and training. Articles are practical, well-written, and of interest to all involved in quality management. Often includes articles on quality management.
Rating: ★★★

Training & Development

Published monthly by the American Society for Training and Development, Inc., 1640 King Street, Box 1443, Alexandria, VA 22313-2043, (703) 683-8100.

Subscriptions: Members of ASTD receive this magazine as part of their membership. Nonmember subscriptions available in the United States at $75 per year. Write for information on international subscription rates.

Includes articles on training, human resources, and management issues, with frequent coverage of quality management topics in these areas.
Rating: ★★

Training in Quality
A Guide to Making Training Decisions for Your Organization

Introduction

The biggest challenge we experienced in the creation of the 1993 version of *The Quality Yearbook* was sorting through a vast amount of materials on courses in quality. In the mid to late 1980s, there were a few consultants providing training and, of course, the major quality organizations around the world did the same. They also hosted annual conferences. Then came an explosion in offerings from many sources, including:

- Quality organizations
- Consultants
- Graduate schools of engineering and business
- Private training companies
- Professional societies
- Authors
- Businesses selling their techniques
- Military and government agencies
- Training departments of companies

We have now reached the point where an individual—even just mildly interested in quality issues—can expect to receive from three to five pieces of mail each week on quality training. Everyone, it seems, is selling quality training.

Trends in Quality Training

Over the past two years, educational offerings have expanded substantially from the long-offered seminars on the general principles of quality, statistical process control, and quality assurance to a much longer, more specific list. The most dramatic new trends in offerings seen in the last two years include:

- Industry-focused training (e.g., in health care and education)
- Function-oriented training (e.g., sales)
- Quality tools (e.g., benchmarking)
- Certification (e.g., ISO 9000)
- Schools of quality (e.g., Deming)
- Strategy focused (e.g., Crosby)

Major increases in offerings have appeared most on such topics as bench-marking, reengineering, ISO 9000, and human resource practices (including teamwork).

The trend of offering two-to-three-day seminars, evident first in the early 1980s, has continued unabated in North America, as well as in Asia and Europe, and appears to be the most popular delivery method for training. However, the source of this training has changed. Up to about two years ago, the major sources for seminars were graduate schools and professional associations, such as the ASQC. In fact, the most comprehensive set of classes available in North America still comes from the ASQC.

New Sources of Quality Training

Two new sources of training have appeared. The first comes from companies recognized as having excellent training programs and quality implementation strategies, such as IBM and Xerox. Others with specific skills are also offering courses, such as the Disney Corporation in the area of human resources.

A second important source of training are major consultants either in the field of quality (e.g., Joiner Associates) or "boutique" consultants, who specialize in some aspect of quality implementation. The value delivered in the seminars from associations long in the quality movement continues to be consistently excellent and cost effective. The same applies to courses offered by quality-focused major corporations. The rest varies in value from outstanding to bordering on the grossly incompetent to evangelical proselytizing of quality's benefits.

Conferences are now a third important source of quality training. These typically offer a combination of case studies on specific quality-oriented issues presented by those involved (e.g., how a particular company implemented TQM) and workshops by consultants, practitioners, or professors on specific skills (e.g., benchmarking, statistical process control, etc.). These are numerous and a very important type of education because they represent current real-world experiences with case studies of efforts underway.

Sources of Information About Quality Training

There are several simple ways to learn about what is available in training today:

■ **Conferences** For conferences, look at the magazines or newsletters of quality organizations or those publications devoted to quality. These invariably publish lists of conventions and conferences, often a year-out in advance. For example, *Quality Progress*, published by the ASQC, has a standard section called "Calendar" in each issue that chronologically lists conferences in North America, with addresses and phone numbers for finding out more. The same applies to European and Asian quality publications. Major industry and professional societies do the same. Conferences are valuable for training for three reasons: (1) they hold sessions designed to present the latest theory and applications in a particular area; (2) they are a way to become exposed to the people and companies that put on training seminars; and (3) the exhibitors often are training organizations. Besides national conferences, there are also many regional and local conferences that you can find out about once you become involved in a quality-related organization.

■ **Quality Organizations** By joining an organization, you will trigger much direct mail announcing various conferences, seminars, and workshops without having to exert any effort to get this information.

■ **Professional Association Training** Almost every professional society today offers training programs ranging from one-day seminars to workshops lasting several days. Many also offer videos, books, and other training materials for use in company training programs. For example, a large part of the mission of the American Management Association (AMA) is training, and they make available a large number of videos, audio tapes, and books, some of which cover quality practices. Such materials are also available from various book publishers, such as McGraw-Hill, for example.

■ **Local Quality Associations** There are now local quality associations throughout North America, Asia, and Europe, many of which serve as clearinghouses of information. Many have libraries of books, videos, and other materials, which allow you to preview materials before investing. You can also network with members of such organizations to find out their experiences with various training companies and programs. See the Quality Organizations and Quality Awards sections of *The Quality Yearbook* for information on several of these local organizations.

■ **Books and Other Literature** Quality practices now has its own body of literature made up of books, magazines, journals, and newsletters, many of which are listed elsewhere in this book. The Magazines, Journals, and Newsletters section includes reviews of these publications with ratings of those with the best information on quality management. In the business section of bookstores, you will also find a variety of books on quality management (though the usefulness of these books varies greatly). Our bibliography can be a place to start.

How to Get Started with Your Training

If you personally or your organization are just starting to learn about quality practices, this discussion is for you. Otherwise, skip this section and read the following section on training tactics for Advanced Organizations.

There have been heated debates over the past few years about what are the best training curricula, methods, and practices for learning about quality. The bibliography includes a section on training publications, a review of which can give you some ideas about what might be appropriate for you. A number of practical steps are emerging that have proven by experience to be useful ways to learn about quality management and its techniques and practices. These include:

1. *Begin by training top management,* then move down through the organization, with top managers being involved in hosting, kicking off, and some of the teaching for the rest of the company. This is vital because quality management requires a change in culture and behaviors that top management has primary responsibility for shaping and perpetuating.
2. *Try to teach quality's tools as close to the time when someone can apply them as possible.* Teaching SPC methods to a team that can use them the next day, for example, is ideal. In this way, the value of these methods is quickly reinforced. Otherwise, these ideas can remain classroom ideas with no application on the job.
3. *Adults need to know several things at the same time:*
   - The philosophy and rationale behind quality
   - How to implement quality management
   - Case studies that demonstrate the successes of implementing quality
4. *Minimize lectures and maximize hands-on workshops.* Adults learn best by doing, not just by listening.
5. *Avoid the now-disproven strategies of sending everyone in the corporation off to a 10-day class in which they are baptized in quality.* Instead, give your people several doses of education in 2- to 3-day increments or less over a period of several years, designed to increasingly enhance the quality skills they are using on the job.
6. *Encourage self-study of those aspects of quality practices that employees find relevant to their immediate work.* This includes starting and maintaining a small company library of books and videos, paying for employee purchases of such materials, and providing time to study. More advanced quality practitioners find it useful to bring in speakers for departmental meetings to discuss specific quality issues in a timely manner.
7. *Alter performance expectations and compensation and award plans to encourage and support the development of skills.* In other words, make continuous learning and improvement of quality skills part of everyone's job. A move toward skills-based compensation is now underway. The bibliography includes a number of citations on this area under the human resources section.

The initial introduction and institution of quality practices usually takes an organization two to three years to accomplish. This first phase makes employees aware of the concepts, teaches them basic techniques, and gets them experience with some results.

Remember: Avoid the problems surrounding the running of all your employees through quality education without some specific expectation of results. Too often experts on training report that the only measure of success is that a certain percentage of employees have been trained. That is unacceptable; training for the sake of training is not a good use of an organization's resources or its employees' time. The expected results should emerge from changed activities that require the application of the skills taught in seminars or workshops.

Formal Processes

By the end of your second or third year of being exposed to quality, your organization should have moved from casual or even program-oriented quality training to a formal process for training employees. Like all critical processes, training should be woven into the fabric of the organization's culture and employees' job descriptions. Thus, there will be a documented set of skills that all new employees must learn. There also will be expectations that they will continuously upgrade their skills.

Certification

All major quality award programs and certification processes in Asia, Europe, and North America require the existence of such a process for training. In the Baldrige framework, for example, one of the seven criteria is devoted to human resources, and within that criteria, training is a significant element. ISO 9000 certification has a similar requirement for a training process. Many companies are moving toward certifying skill levels of employees, much like universities granting diplomas in recognition of certain academic achievements. Professional associations in the world of quality are now routinely offering formal certification programs. Some, like those of the ASQC, have been around for many years and are being broadened to accommodate new areas of interest, such as outside of manufacturing processes.

There was a large increase in skills certification in Europe and North America during 1992–93, and we can expect this trend to continue unabated in 1994.

Training Tactics for Advanced Organizations

An advanced organization, as defined by the quality management movement, is one in which quality tools and techniques are routinely used across the entire enterprise. Proof of being advanced might include having won a regional or national quality award, having many plant locations ISO certified, or the company on the verge of applying for such certification or for a state or national quality awards. Such enterprises have a variety of internal training programs on the basics for new and experienced employees. The challenge for these advanced companies is to develop new bodies of skills and practices, rather than simply learning already widely understood skills.

Benchmarking

Such organizations shift to *learning* more about how other enterprises carry out various processes and compare results. Thus, *benchmarking* becomes an important tactic for improving. Benchmarking initially becomes a process for finding out who is doing something well that the organization can quickly adapt to its own purposes once the new processes are in place. A second phase of benchmarking is comparing performance of one process or company to those of others either in one's industry or, as is most frequently the case, to another.

A third phase, which has become prominent in 1993, is *consortium-based benchmarking*. Here, a group of companies agrees to compare specific processes to each other for a period of time and share the costs of doing the study and the findings of such benchmarking among themselves. Organizations did much work in 1993 to define the best way to perform such benchmarking, in areas such as how to handle sensitive information.

Typically, a management consulting firm handles the project. It is not uncommon to find between a dozen and 50 organizations participating. We are finding that the initial application of such benchmarking tactics is by functional area, for example, IBM's benchmarking project to identify and measure best practices in MIS organizations. Various industry associations also are starting their own benchmarking activities. Finally, reports on the Ernst & Young industry surveys (a form of benchmarking) began to appear in late 1992 and in 1993, several of which are industry-focused reports (automotive, health, computer, and banking industries). In 1994 we can expect another raft of benchmarking studies by various industry-focused organizations.

Quality Meetings

Benchmarking is only one manifestation of an advanced organization's actions. A second behavior pattern, more evident in Japan, but now increasingly in the United States, is the department meeting devoted to quality. Instead of someone coming in to present how to do root cause analysis, for example, groups of employees gather to discuss the results of such analysis themselves and what they will do with the findings. At this advanced stage, you can also expect employees to ponder the question of how to do root cause analysis more effectively (or whatever problem-solving, improvement approach they are using).

When a group of employees requires training, they typically request it for a specialized area in which they need to improve their knowledge and skills. For example, a group of employees in a department might need to understand a specific aspect of some statistical tool. Thus they would call in an expert for two hours one afternoon and be prepared to use the tool the next morning, and review it the following week. These employees also will want to network with peers in other companies and spend more time looking at how others do similar functions. In advanced organizations, management supports this kind of learning activity.

Learning Organizations

Finally, advanced enterprises are reporting a cultural change to what is now being called a "learning organization" (see Cultural Transformation articles for more on this idea.) While the first major books documenting this phenomenon appeared in 1991–92, articles on all aspects of this approach to organizational culture came out during 1993. Many are referenced in the bibliography under Organizational Culture.

Advanced organizations crossed international borders more frequently in 1993 than in previous years to do benchmarking, but not formal training. Large companies are prepared to go anywhere in the industrialized world to find benchmarks, but so far they are finding adequate training resources within their own countries. There are some exceptions, however. For example, IBM trains its consultants in quality skills both in the United States and in Belgium with Americans sometimes going to Europe for training and Europeans coming to the United States.

Globalization of Quality Literature

Major publishers of quality literature, including John Wiley & Sons, McGraw-Hill, and the ASQC Quality Press, report that sales of their quality products had become global in 1993. Major growth markets, particularly for English-language publications included Western Europe, Canada, the United States, and Australia/New Zealand. French publications grew in number as well, indicating growing demand for information. In Japan, the market for such publications in English and Japanese remained large as it had been for several years, despite recessionary conditions.

Growth in sales of publications are indicators of interest in quality topics. So too are memberships in quality organizations. While preparing the list of organizations for *The Quality Yearbook*, we learned that memberships in most such organizations were increasing in 1993 and were expected to continue to do so in 1994. Subscriptions to quality magazines and journals increased in a similar fashion. Indeed, the existence of this book is one more indication of the interest and need for up-to-date information on quality management implementation.

The Role of Universities in Working with Advanced Organizations

We found some evidence of universities attempting to support government and private sector organizations in their implementation of quality during 1993. However, the fact remains that higher education institutions have yet to take the changes in management seriously enough to make a major contribution. In 1993 some universities, particularly in the United States, began to implement TQM, but this is not yet a trend. There have been some pioneers, though, who have been at it a decade or more (See article "TQM Invades Higher Education" in the Public Sector section).

Major grants by corporations such as IBM and Procter & Gamble to seed research and curriculum development have encouraged a few universities to get more into quality management. Most business and engineering schools throughout the industrialized world (except for Japan) are only just now deciding if they should implement quality practices in their own operations, let alone teach it to students.

Nevertheless, some interesting partnerships have formed over the past two years between businesses and universities to study best practices, and the expectation is that this trend will continue in 1994 and 1995. This strategy allows a company to rapidly develop new intellectual capital for improving quality and productivity while providing additional funding sources to universities, particularly schools of business and centers of manufacturing excellence.

Quality Quotes

The purpose of these quotes is to provide inspirational insight into the new management paradigms, offer material useful in speeches and presentations, and to capture essential quality management concepts. The material below is organized loosely by topic. We recommend that you glance as various categories for suitable quotes.

If you have any quality quotes that you would like to share with others, send them to the editors c/o McGraw-Hill and we will include them in next year's edition with your name as the source.

Philosophy

Includes definitions of quality, attitudes, principles, and customer focus.

"Excellence is not an act, but a habit."

—Aristotle

"The problem is not to increase quality; increasing quality is the answer to the problem."

—Myron Tribus

"Quality is not any single thing but an aura, an atmosphere, an overpowering feeling that a company is doing everything with excellence."

—John F. Welch, GE CEO

"This is the way the world ends. Not with a bang but a whimper."

—T.S. Eliot

"I don't worry whether something is cheap or inexpensive, I only worry if it is good. If it is good enough, the public will pay you back for it."

—Walt Disney

"It does not matter how slowly you go as long as you do not stop."

—Confucius

"I define quality as conformance to requirements. Period. We should perform the job or produce the product as we agreed to do it."

—Philip B. Crosby

"The truly market driven company knows that the best product it can produce is a delighted customer."

—John Akers, Former IBM CEO

"Quality, a particular and essential character: nature, degree of excellence . . ."

—Webster's Dictionary

"Quality is not what happens when what you do matches your intentions. It's what happens when what you do matches your customers' expectations."

—John Guaspari

"Most of our so-called reason consists of finding reasons to go on thinking as we already do."

—J. H. Robinson

"The customer generates nothing. No customer asked for electric lights."

—W. Edwards Deming

"Good quality does not necessarily mean high quality. It means a predictable degree of uniformity and dependability at low cost with a quality suited to the market."

—W. Edwards Deming

Management

Includes management issues, leadership, attitudes of quality gurus, and personnel involvement and commitment.

"Management is like sex or politics or religion; all of us do it, most of us are convinced that our way is the best, few of us bother to ask if we have met the other's needs and expectations."

—R. J. Moriboys

"You do not have to do this; survival is not compulsory!"

—W. Edwards Deming

"Quality does not happen by accident; it has to be planned."

—Joseph M. Juran

"The determined executive has to have a brain transplant where quality is concerned."

—Philip B. Crosby

"Improve constantly and forever the system of production and service."

—W. Edwards Deming

"Nothing concentrates a man's mind so wonderfully as the prospect of being hanged in the morning."

—Samuel Johnson

"Set high standards."

—Norman Schwartzkopf

"Make no little plans; they have no magic to stir men's blood."

—Daniel Hudson Burnham

"Indecision is nearly always the worst mistake you can make."

—Unknown

"There is nothing more difficult to take in hand, more perilous to conduct, or more uncertain in its success than to take the lead in the introduction of a new order of things."

—Nicolo Machiavelli

"If you can't come, send nobody."

—William E. Conway

"Adopt and institute leadership."

—W. Edwards Deming

"In times of crisis or high turbulence people expect, indeed demand, great change."

—Joel Barker

"There is dignity in work only when it is work freely accepted."

—Albert Camus

"There is no such thing as a free lunch."

—Milton Friedman

"The genius of good leadership is to leave behind a situation which common sense, even without the grace of genius, can deal with successfully."

—Walter Lippmann

"If you want your people to do it right the first time, you've got to tell them simply and clearly what 'it' is."

—Philip B. Crosby

"Talent without motivation is inert and of little use to the world."

—John W. Gardner

"If we are to get the reflexes and speed we need, we've got to simplify and delegate more . . . simply trust more."

—John F. Welch, GE CEO

"We have to undo a 100-year-old concept and convince our managers that their role is not to control people and stay on top of things, but rather to guide, energize, and excite."

—John F. Welch, GE CEO

"The great leader is he who the people say, 'We did it ourselves.' "

—Lao Tsu

"Quality is determined by top management. It cannot be delegated."

—W. Edwards Deming

"The first thing you as an executive have to find out is what your customers want. Those become your requirements. Then you have to translate those requirements into things your employees and suppliers can understand and do."

—Philip B. Crosby

"The damn thing won't fly at all until top management people are 100% behind it. . . . Where is the bottle neck? Just look at the top of the bottle and you will find it."

—Bill Conway

"We are all born with intrinsic motivation, self-esteem, dignity, and eagerness to learn. Our present system of management crushes that all out."

—W. Edwards Deming

"Some managers believe that the main quality problem is the carelessness and lack of motivation of the workers. These managers are simply mistaken. When the facts are studied it is typical to find that over 80% of the defects are management controllable."

—Joseph M. Juran

"The best executive is the one who has sense enough to pick good men to do what he wants done, and self-restraint enough to keep from meddling with them while they do it."

—Teddy Roosevelt

"Good management consists in showing average people how to do the work of superior people."

—John D. Rockefeller

"Never tell people how to do things. Tell them what to do and they will surprise you with their ingenuity."

—George S. Patton

"To fight and conquer in all your battles is not supreme excellence; supreme excellence consists in breaking the enemy's resistance without fighting."

—Sun Tzu

Measurements

Includes statistics and results.

"Statistical thinking will one day be as necessary for efficient citizenship as the ability to read and write."

—H. G. Wells

"I know of scarcely anything so apt to impress the imagination, as the wonderful form of cosmic order expressed by the Law of Frequency of Error. The law would have been personified by the Greeks and deified, if they had known it."

—Sir Francis Galton

"Nothing is good or bad but by comparison."

—Thomas Fuller

"A state of Statistical Control is not a natural state for a process; it is an achievement."

—W. Edwards Deming

"You have to be able to mathematically compute quality."

—Frederick W. Smith, Jr. Federal Express CEO

"The great thing about History is that it is adaptable."

—Peter Ustinov

"However certain our expectations, the moment foreseen may be unexpected when it arrives."

—T. S. Eliot

"There are worse things which he stretched, but mainly he told the truth."

—Mark Twain

"I recommend you to take care of the minutes; for hours will take care of themselves."

—Earl of Chesterfield

"A state without the means of some change is without the means of its conservation."

—Edmund Burke

"The wider you spread it, the thinner it gets."

—Gerald M. Weinberg

"Measures of productivity do not lead to improvement in productivity."

—W. Edwards Deming

"You have to keep score."

—Jack Fooks, Westinghouse VP

"No institution which does not continually test its ideals, techniques, and measure of accomplishment can claim real vitality."

—John Milton

"Count what is countable, measure what is measurable, and what is not measurable, make measurable."

—Galileo Galilei

"In physical science a first essential step in the direction of learning any subject is to find principles of numerical reckoning and methods for practicably measuring some quality connected with it."

—Lord Kelvin

"You can't manage what you can't measure."

—Tom DeMarco

"A system cannot understand itself."

—W. Edwards Deming

"It is better to aim at perfection and miss than it is to aim at imperfection and hit it."

—Thomas J. Watson, Sr.

Process Improvement

Includes continuous improvement and reengineering.

"It is not uncommon to find an MIS department with no formal quality program, whose quality costs are 30 percent or even 50 percent of the annual MIS budget. This is a very expensive and slow way to build software."

—Richard Zulner

"Stop paving the cow paths."

—Michael Hammer

"We shall build good ships here; at a profit if we can, at a loss if we must, but always good ships."

—Collis P. Huntington

"Defects are not free. Somebody makes them, and gets paid for making them."

—W. Edwards Deming

"There is no silver bullet."

—Fred Brooks

"Don't patch bad code, rewrite it."

—Kerningham and Plauger

"Do it badly, do it quickly, make it better, and then say you planned it."

—Tom Peters

"We should focus on solutions that will bear fruit quickly, within a manager's 12-month planning horizon."

—Brad Cox

"The increase in productivity has been caused primarily by the replacement of labor by planning, brawn by brain, sweat by knowledge."

—Peter Drucker

"We realize that we are in a race without a finish line. As we improve, so does our competition. Five years ago, we would have found that disheartening. Today we find it invigorating."

—David Kearns, Former Xerox CEO

"I am the world's worst salesman, therefore, I must make it easy for people to buy."

—F. W. Woolworth

"You have to recognize that every 'out front' maneuver you make is going to be lonely, but if you feel entirely comfortable, then you're not far enough ahead to do any good. That warm sense of everything going well is usually the body temperature at the center of the herd."

—John Masters

"The moral is that it is necessary to innovate, to predict needs of the customer, give him more. He that innovates and is lucky will take the market."

—W. Edwards Deming

"Instead of setting numerical quotas, management should work on improvement of the process."

—W. Edwards Deming

"No amount of care or skill in workmanship can overcome fundamental faults of the system."

—W. Edwards Deming

"Doing things right the first time adds nothing to your costs, but plenty to your profits."

—Philip B. Crosby

"If our factories could, through care, impose the superior quality of our products, foreigners would see the advantage of purchasing French goods and money would flow to our kingdom."

—Jean-Baptiste Colbert

"Good merchandise, even when hidden, soon finds buyers."

— Plautius

"Anybody can cut prices, but it takes brains to make a better article."

—Alice Hubbard

"Quality is not only right, it is free. And it is not only free, it is the most profitable product line we have."

—Harold S. Geneen

"Quality is free."

—Philip B. Crosby

Quality Tools

Includes such quality techniques as benchmarking, problem analysis, root cause, and other quality-oriented methods.

"Life is the art of drawing sufficient conclusions from insufficient premises."

—Samuel Butler

"There is only one thing worse than being talked about, and that is not being talked about."

—Oscar Wilde

"The truth is rarely pure and never simple."

— Oscar Wilde

"If one assumes a linear model (i.e., no interactions), thinking it correct, then one is a man removed from natural science or reality, and commits the mistake of standing just upon mathematics which is nothing but idealism."

—G. Taguchi

"Deal with the difficult,
While it is still easy.
Solve large problems
When they are still small.
Preventing large problems
By taking small steps
Is easier than solving them.
By small actions
Great things are accomplished."

—Lao Tzu

"No problem can stand the assault of sustained thinking."

—Voltaire

"I keep six honest serving men
(They taught me all I knew)
Their names are What and Why and When
And How and Where and Who."

—Rudyard Kipling

"For every thousand hacking at the leaves of evil, there is one striking at the root."

—Henry Thoreau

"Take away the cause and the effect ceases."

—Miguel de Cervantes

"Wise people seek solutions
The ignorant only cast blame."

—Lao Tzu

"A defect is an instance in which a requirement is not satisfied."

—Michael Fagan

"Cease dependence on inspections to achieve quality."

—W. Edwards Deming

"The 'objective' is to nudge forward the process of discovering goals along the way to induce the largest number of people possible to quickly change, to try something; to maximize the odds of serendipity."

—Tom Peters

"Man is a tool-using animal . . . Without tools he is nothing, with tools he is all."

—Thomas Carlyle

"The winners of the Nineties will be those who can develop a culture that allows them to move faster, communicate more clearly, and involve everyone in a focused effort to serve ever more demanding customers."

—John F. Welch, GE CEO

"Lost time is never found again."

—Benjamin Franklin

Human Resources

Includes skills, training, and teamwork.

"Leave my factories but take away my people and soon grass will grow on my factory floors. Take my factories, but leave my people, and soon we will have new and better plants."

—Andrew Carnegie

"Most people have spent their lives reinventing the wheel, then refusing to concede that it's out of round."

—George Leonard

"Total Quality Control starts with training and ends with training. To implement TQC, we need to carry out continuous education for everyone, from the president down to line workers."

—Kaoru Ishikawa

"Competent [people] in every position, if they are doing their best, know all that there is to know about their work except how to improve it."

—W. Edwards Deming

"The half-life of the knowledge of a new engineer is about five years."
—Gary Tooker, Motorola President

"No matter how hard Western nations try to engage in QC education, they may not catch up with Japan until the 1990s, since it requires ten years for the QC education to take effect."

—Joseph M. Juran

"In one of our concert grand pianos, 243 taut strings exert a pull of 40,000 pounds on an iron frame. It is proof that out of great tension may come great harmony."

—Theodore E. Steinway

"Coming together is a beginning.
Keeping together is progress.
Working together is success."

—Henry Ford

"There is no substitute for knowledge."

—W. Edwards Deming

"Ranking is a farce."

—W. Edwards Deming

"Reward for good performance may be the same as reward to the weather man for a pleasant day."

—W. Edwards Deming

"Without theory, there is nothing to revise. Without theory, experience has no meaning. Without theory, one has no questions to ask. Hence without theory, there is no learning."

—W. Edwards Deming

Glossary

Over the past decade, the world of quality management has accumulated a growing vocabulary of its own, much like other fields have done. Many of these phrases are common English words, but with slightly new meanings. Phrases used in various fields have crossed over into business and management language. For example, many terms originally found only in engineering or in statistical analysis are now the working vocabulary of managers in human resources, sales, and so forth. Terms from science, psychology, and mathematics have also made this transition. During the early 1990s, the pace of penetration picked up to all corners of business language. By 1993—1994, many of these terms were commonly used in business, not just in science or manufacturing. For that reason, we feel there needs to be a consolidated glossary. It is a vocabulary that is increasing in size each year, reflecting a process of codification underway within quality practices as they become the mainstream of a renewed body of management practices.

Acceptable quality level A level of quality acceptable for a lot or group. These are levels set for purposes of establishing the acceptable quality of inspected samples.

Acceptance sampling Where decisions are made to accept or reject products or services. The term also refers to an approach consisting of procedures or processes by which managers make decisions to accept or reject relying on the results of inspections of samples. Acceptance sampling is designed to avoid having to inspect, for example, all raw material.

Acceptance sampling plan A plan that includes criteria for accepting and rejecting samples. Plans may involve single, double, sequential, chain, multiple, or skip-lot sampling strategies. These also are used in attribute sampling strategy. With variables samples, single, double, and sequential sampling strategies are deployed.

Accreditation Same as certification, it is a formal process that validates the skills of an individual by a recognized organization. This is done, for example, by the Registrar Accreditation Board for ISO 9000 standards, the ASQC for quality experts, and APICS for manufacturing specialists.

Action team (AT) A group of people management has authorized to implement improvement changes to an existing process.

Activities Steps (also tasks) in a process.

Affinity diagramming A technique for organizing a variety of subjective data (such as opinions) into logical topics based on the relationships among individual pieces of information.

Agenda A plan for conducting a meeting. In the quality world, meeting disciplines become a process integral to the operations of an organization. Agendas also include discussion of outcomes expected from a meeting.

American Quality Foundation An independent organization established under the auspices of the American Society for Quality Control for the purpose of fostering the application of quality practices by business and public officials. It also has a research and development mission, responsible for programs to foster U.S. business competitiveness.

American Society for Quality Control (ASQC) One of the world's leading nonprofit professional associations dedicated to the promotion and application of quality-related practices in both public and private sectors. It has over 96,000 individual members and over 700 corporate members in 64 countries.

Analysis of Means (ANOM) A statistical technique used to identify problems in an industrial process and that involves the analysis of experimental designs with factors at fixed levels. This technique was created to help nonstatisticians apply variance analysis techniques.

Analysis of Variance (ANOVA) Used to analyze experimental data, one subdivides the total variation of a set of data into relevant groups that are associated with sources of variation so as to test a hypothesis or to estimate types of variances. Three models are recognized in this process: fixed, random, and mixed when studying hypothesis.

Analytic Hierarchy Process (AHP) A method for making decisions regarding complicated issues through simplifying a natural decision-making approach. You break down a circumstance into its logical components, rank them with numeric values assigned to otherwise subjective data, and then summarize the variables in a prioritized fashion.

ANOM Analysis of means.

ANOVA Analysis of variance.

AOQ Average outgoing quality.

AOQL Average outgoing quality limit.

Appraisal costs Costs incurred in inspecting products to insure they meet customer or your specifications or needs.

ASQC American Society for Quality Control.

Attribute data Also called "go/no-go information," it is a collection of data represented on control charts reflecting attribute data such as a percent, number of affected units, counts, counts-per-unit, quality scores, and demerits.

Augmented product Any product that provides more than a customer expects or normally receives.

Availability A state of being of a machine, product, process, or person to perform a function under predetermined conditions. In a formal definition, it is the ratio of uptime divided by the total of uptime and downtime. Uptime is when something is in active use (such as a machine), while downtime is when it is not active (such as when a machine is being repaired, or retooled).

Average chart Refers to a control chart in which a subgroup average (X-bar) is employed to evaluate the stability of a process's level. This is frequently employed in manufacturing situations.

Average outgoing quality (AOQ) The anticipated quality of output or products that normally occurs.

Average outgoing quality limit (AOQL) The maximum amount of quality of outgoing quality over all possible levels of incoming quality. It is determined by using an acceptance sampling approach that establishes a value for incoming quality of products.

Bar chart A widely used form of a chart that displays events or items in wide horizontal or vertical lines (bars).

Baseline Information that answers the questions, what is the level of our quality now and where are we today? Baselines are created in measurable terms from which future progress on improvements are measured.

Baseline cycle time The amount of time it takes a process to perform the first time it is measured. All future improvements in the speed with which the process is performed is measured against this original cycle time.

Benchmark A quality target that answers the question, where should we be? It can be based on a number of targets: customer requirements, best performing comparable process, or some other goal. It is also a formal process for comparing the performance of a process against that of another process.

Benchmarking The act of continually comparing the performance of one process against that of another, usually of comparable or greater performance. Thus, for example, comparing your billing process to that of a "world class" or "best-of-breed" process, such as that of American Express. Benchmarking is done to determine the effectiveness of existing processes and to find ways to improve those quickly.

Best-of-breed The best example of a process or measurement available usually within an industry, but could be worldwide. Quality is determined by efficiency, effectiveness, value, or defect elimination.

Best-of-class Another way of saying best-of-breed, superior to all comparable goods or services.

Big Q, little q The phrase is used to contrast differences between managing quality in business products and processes (implying many and major) from managing quality in a more narrowly defined scope, such as for one product or process.

Blemish As with a stain on cloth or an imperfection in our skin's complexion, the word refers to a deviation in quality, but not of such a severe type as to constrict the performance of the process or, more frequently, a product.

Blind survey A survey of customers or other individuals in which they do not know who is sponsoring the survey or who are chosen from a pool of candidates. This is a technique often used to compare the performance of one company or process against another.

Block diagram Blocks on a piece of paper each representing a function, process, or task, illustrating interdependencies and operational relationships. These are used to illustrate the flow of work or processes and where things or tasks interface. Functional block diagrams illustrate the flow of a system's subsystems and outputs, and how all relate to each other. Reliability block diagrams are similar except that they emphasize factors that influence reliability of systems, processes, or items.

Brainstorming A widely used technique for generating ideas about how to improve a process or solve a problem. It results in a large number of ideas being created from which a group can pick the best to implement.

Breakthrough Often also referred to as breakthrough thinking, this is the idea of searching for a significant improvement in how a process is designed, implemented, and performs. Emphasis is on a radically new, or revolutionary approach as opposed to the evolutionary improvement in an existing process.

C chart A count chart of any type.

Calibration In the world of quality, it is a comparison of one measurement system or instrument of an unverified accuracy to one that is accurate.

This is done to identify variations from a required specification for performance.

Capability index A technique for measuring the odds of failures or defects. It is calculated by dividing current performance by anticipated performance to measure the ability of a process to meet expectations (results) and which has a significant effect on the quality of a process.

Causal analysis This technique concentrates on identifying failures or defects, followed by an analysis of the root causes of those failures, and concludes with recommendations on how to eliminate those defects. It is a popular component of defect prevention activities within a process.

Cause A reason for a specific condition or action.

Cause-and-effect analysis A method used by a group of individuals to study underlying causes. It is often also called fishboning since the output is a fishbone chart.

Cause-and-effect diagram This type of graph illustrates the relationship between one problem and its possible various causes. It is best known as a fishbone diagram because it looks like the skeleton of a fish with each "bone" being the answer to the question Why? It is one of the most widely used and effective quality tools.

Chart A graphical representation of data indicating significant trends and relationships. As a hammer and saw are to a carpenter, a chart is to anyone working with data.

Check sheet This simple recording document is a widely used method for keeping track of data. It is considered one of the formal quality tools. Since the data is tailored to the requirements of the user, it should not be confused with normal checklists or data sheets.

Checklist Refers to a list of steps or actions in a process that are tracked (checked off) as done.

Closed-loop process The notion that activities go through a series of steps in a never-ending, continuous fashion with no beginning or end.

Coach Any individual who serves as a guide leading people through process improvement, usually through the application of Total Quality Management principles. The term is also used to describe a manager who counsels and advises employees instead of telling them what to do.

Commitment Often used in an organization that has developed a vision-based strategic plan or that is embarking on the application of fact-based quality management principles, it refers to the personal resolve to apply TQM-like values and practices.

Common cause Refers to one or more sources of variation in the output of a process that affects all individual results or values of output.

Communication Simply the process for exchanging information. It is also considered a critical process in quality-based organizations.

Competition More than rivalry among vendors, it is also the act of competing among individuals and groups for total customer satisfaction. In the Deming-like view of the world, competition is also considered inefficient and contrary to customer benefit, calling instead for cooperation among vendors to provide best quality goods and services.

Concurrent engineering (CE) A systematic approach to the design of products and their related processes that is integrated and concurrent. That is to say, multiple steps in the process take place at the same time, including manufacturing and product support. The intent of this kind of approach is to lead developers to weigh all elements of a product life cycle from the initial conception of an idea to the final disposition of a product, taking into account such factors as quality, cost, and customer requirements and expectations.

Conformance Refers to a judgment that a product or service has conformed to a predetermined set of requirements, usually drawn from desires of customers.

Consensus A form of agreement reached by a group of people working on a plan or development of a process. It is not a majority vote to adopt a position but rather the state of mind that each individual can live with the decisions of the group and will support and implement them.

Continuous improvement (CI) An important value statement that endorses the notion that all processes and activities can be improved on a regular basis through the application of systematic techniques. It also embraces the idea that there should be a relentless, ongoing hunt for sources of defects

to be eliminated. The Japanese call CI "KAIZEN." Another definition calls CI a disciplined process for achieving, first, commitment to excellence and, second, the actual efforts to accomplish ongoing improvements in quality of processes, services, and products.

Control In the world of quality, this word refers to those activities that are performed to maintain a desired state of performance or to correct deviation from standards. It looks at past activity to call out what needs to be changed to return to a predetermined level of performance.

Control chart A graph, a statistical process control method used to track the performance of a process over time expressed in numerical terms. Statistical upper and lower control limits are set within which variance is tolerated. It is one of the most widely used process improvement tools.

Correction Any and all actions taken to reduce or eliminate variations in performance. It is also used to describe similar activities designed to eliminate causes of variation in performance.

Corrective action Refers to actions taken to eliminate problems in products, services, and processes.

Cost of poor quality (COPQ) Expenses generated by providing poor quality goods or services. These are sourced from internal failure costs (from defects before customers get the product), external failure costs (costs after a customer receives the poor product or service), appraisal costs (expenses generated to determine the degree of conformance to quality of a product or service), and prevention costs (expenses to reduce or avoid failures and appraisal costs).

Cost of quality (COQ) More than the cost of quality programs, this refers to all costs for the prevention of defects, assessments of process performance, and measurement of financial consequences. It is used to document variations against expectations and as a measure of efficiency and productivity.

Count chart This type of control chart is used to evaluate the stability of a process by counting events of a particular type that occur in a sample.

Count-per-unit chart This type of control chart tracks the stability of a process by looking at the average count of events within a precise classification per unit occurring in a sample.

Cp Stands for a process capability index. It is calculated by taking the difference between upper and lower control limits and dividing that answer by 6.

Cpk Another popular process capability index.

Criterion A standard by which to base a decision.

Critical path Process owners use this term to describe the shortest distance between the beginning and end of a process or activity. Activities within a process are customarily documented along a critical path.

Critical success factors Activities that absolutely have to go right in order for a process, program, or a team to make its objectives. Traditionally a part of strategic planning, it is frequently a catalog of process elements that must be managed with extra care to insure the overall success of the process.

Cross-functional team A process team made up of people from various departments or organizations affected by their process. This kind of a team works on a specific problem or process that affects multiple departments or organizations, often with the mandate to develop a new or improved process.

Cross plot Another way of saying scatter diagram, used to study the relationship between two variables.

Culture A term used often in the quality world, it defines patterns of shared activities, values, beliefs, and attitudes within an organization. In enterprises introducing quality practices, defining the nature of existing and desired institutional culture becomes an important activity.

Cumulative sum control chart This type of control chart plots a value that is the cumulative sum of deviations of successive samples taken from some target value. Ordinate of each point represents the algebraic sum of the previous ordinates and most recent deviations from a preset target.

Customer Increasingly this word is being used to describe anybody who is the recipient of work that you do, or the next person in a process who receives the output of your work. Often divided

into Big C (paying customers) and Little c (fellow employees), it is the concept that everyone should be treated as respectfully and enthusiastically as a paying customer.

Customer delight A phrase to describe the delivery of a product or service that exceeds a customer's requirement. For many organizations, it is a shorthand description of a corporate quality goal.

Customer requirements The things Big C and Little c customers want from a product, service, or process. It is a central concept of quality that all processes and organizations should understand very thoroughly what are the requirements of their customers. Whole processes are implemented to insure that customer requirements are sought and factored into the development and implementation of an organization's processes.

Customer satisfaction Refers to either the delivery of a product or service that meets or exceeds customer expectations or requirements.

Customer/supplier analysis A collection of methods for providing insight into the needs and expectations of customers seen through the relationship between an organization and its suppliers. It is intended to cause the activities between suppliers and vendors to conform to customer requirements.

Customer-supplier partnership Shorthand for a long-term relationship between a buyer and supplier in which mutual trust, teamwork, and dependence are typical. Vendors are considered an extension of a buyer's operations. Buyers use fewer suppliers and commit to long-term contracts and relationships. Suppliers meet quality standards of their customers. This strategy is employed to reduce operating and inspection costs, while improving overall quality of goods and services.

Cycle time The time from beginning to end of a process. It is an important measure of the quality of a process. Many organizations also have found that the reduction in cycle time to get things done represents a significant cost justified benefit of applying quality techniques and values.

D chart Stands for demerit chart (see below).

Data Facts or information presented in descriptive or graphic forms. Information is either measured data (also called variable data) or counted data (also called attribute data).

Data/statistical analysis A collection of techniques and tools for collecting, sorting, analyzing, and presenting information that leads to decisions and process management.

Decision matrix Teams will use such a matrix to analyze problems and possible solutions. Solutions or problems are listed along one vertical column, while criteria are posted along the horizontal. Solutions are ranked 1 to 5, 1 to 8, or 1 to 10 in terms of positive impact and are entered on the grid. Total scores are accumulated vertically to determine which solution is the most attractive.

Defect Any action, error, or circumstance that either does not meet a customer's requirement or fails to make a measurable goal. Examples of defects can be service-oriented (e.g., number of unanswered phone calls) or faulty products (e.g., poorly designed). Defects are usually catalogued into four types (classes) by degree, from 1 to 4: very serious (e.g., can cause injury or major financial problems), serious (significant injury possible or major financial loss), major (in the ability of a product or service to do as designed), and minor (some problem but still capable of performing).

Defect elimination The act of identifying and then eliminating defects in products, services, and processes. It is also a group of techniques for reduction of failures or defects in processes.

Defect prevention process (DPP) A collection of techniques used to understand the causes of existing errors or defects. DPP also includes a method for determining how to prevent these errors in the future. Often the process includes actual implementation of defect prevention actions as an on-going round of error elimination.

Defects per million (DPM) The number of defects (errors) that occurs in one million opportunities. This could be the number of faulty items out of a million or the number of defects (malperformance) in a million times. This measure is widely used and is applicable across all actions of a process, product, or service, hence its popularity.

Demerit chart This type of control chart tracks failures or weaknesses in a process by deducting quality points, which cumulatively is a score of nonconformance.

Deming cycle Another way of saying "plan-do-check-act" cycle in which you plan what is to be done (e.g., in a process, you do it, check to see how it went, and act to improve it). It was developed as a concept by W. Edwards Deming.

Deming Prize Established in 1951 by the Union of Japanese Scientists and Engineers (JUSE), it recognizes companies that have made outstanding progress in improving the quality of their operations. This very important quality prize is named after W. Edwards Deming who, in 1950, first introduced the Japanese to many industrial quality control practices.

Dependability The degree to which a product or service functions and remains capable of doing as required by specifications. Dependability is determined by a judgment of random samples of the process or product and for the time it is supposed to be available. To express it as a ratio, take time available and divide it by the total of time available plus time required.

Deployment Occasionally used in quality circles, the terms refers to the actions taken to implement a consistent or process approach, usually across an entire organization or over multiple departments.

Design of experiments A formal branch of applied statistics that focuses on planning, conducting, studying, and interpreting controlled tests. This is done to evaluate those factors that control values of one or more parameters.

Design phases Three specific phases in the design of a process or product: systems design, parameter design, and tolerance design. The three were designated by Taguchi, a leading Japanese quality expert.

Designing in quality vs. inspecting in quality The notion of prevention vs. detection, in which one improves the quality of a product beginning at the design phase so as to avoid either inspecting the end product or allowing conditions early in a product manufacturing cycle from creating quality concerns further down the process cycle.

Detailed process diagram A flowchart documenting each step in a process.

Detection The act of identifying any nonconformance to some standard after the fact.

Deviation Refers to any departure from a set of desired or anticipated value or pattern of performance. Standard deviation is the measure of the spread for most frequent distributions; used primarily in monitoring process performance.

Diagnostic journey and remedial journey Used together, this is a two-part investigatory process employed by teams to solve chronic quality problems. In the diagnostic phase, a team will go from identification of a symptom to its cause. In the second, it moves from cause to remedy.

Directed survey The opposite of a blind survey, participants know who the sponsor of the survey is. It is an effective approach when asking customers to define how a company or agency can improve its services and products.

Disciplined continuous improvement methodology Another way of saying continuous improvement approaches.

Dodge-Romig sampling plans Developed by Harold F. Dodge and Harry G. Romig, these are four sets of tables: single-sampling lot tolerance, double-sampling lot tolerance, single-sampling average outgoing quality limits, and double-sampling average outgoing quality limit tables.

DOE Short for design of experiments.

Downstream value chain Value chains within consumer and channel organizations and outside of your enterprise.

Driving forces Those circumstances that cause actions leading toward achieving some goal.

Efficient process This phrase refers to a process that generates the results or output desired at the lowest or minimum cost, or in the least amount of time, or with the lowest use of resources (people or ingredients), or other assets. Efficiency is measured by a ratio of required output to cost to produce that result. Cost is defined in a variety of units of resources, such as hours, money, energy, and raw materials.

Efficiency Often this word is used to characterize performance of a process, usually in terms of minimum cost of effort, resources, or money. It is often measured by a ratio of quantity of resources planned for consumption in the execution of the process to resources actually used.

Effect Often applied to a problem or defect that exists within a process or activity.

Effective process A process that generates results that conform to customer requirements or those of the process owner. Lack of effectiveness is the delta between actual and required performance, usually expressed in numeric terms. The delta is always the degree to which results (output) differ from requirements.

Effectiveness Refers to how much the output of a process meets or exceeds expectations or goals. Expectations can be defined by customers or process owners.

80-20 rule Also known as the Pareto Principle, it was rescued from history by J. M. Juran in 1950 to suggest that most effects come from few causes; in other words, 80 percent of all effects come from only 20 percent of possible causes.

Employee involvement A code term for a body of personnel practices in which employees routinely play a critical role in making decisions about operations, priorities, suggestions for improvements, planning, setting of goals and targets, and monitoring performance. It is a major component of modern quality practices.

Empowerment The act of delegating responsibility and authority to employees to make decisions and take actions. In the world of quality, this is a code word for delegation. It embraces the assumption that employees, when properly trained, can often make the best decisions on how to manage and improve a process.

Enterprise processes The major processes of an organization. For example, for a manufacturing company, they could be design, product manufacture, sales, and customer satisfaction. These are typically "mega-processes" that catalog the major activities that support the mission of an organization and become the basis of significant process identification and improvement. Each has many sub-processes, but when added together they constitute the major quality focus items of an organization.

Entitlement Every process, because it exists, has the potential for additional improvement. That potential is called entitlement; additional effectiveness or efficiency if a process is optimized.

Expected product Often a way of explaining a customer's minimum requirements for a product, service, or process.

Experimental design Always a formal (well-documented) plan describing how to conduct a specific experiment.

Extended enterprise An organization that sees its links to members of its value chain in multidimensional ways. Processes and value chains are seen as extending beyond the enterprise into suppliers, customers, or other stakeholders.

External customer Someone or some organization that pays for your goods and services and who is not a formal or legal part of your enterprise.

External failure costs. Costs generated when a defective product or service is delivered to a customer. The expenses to an automobile manufacturer for a recalled vehicle is an example.

External linkages Refers to those linkages that exist between an organization and its suppliers and its customers. Upstream linkages are with suppliers and downstream linkages are with channels of distribution or consumers.

Extrinsic reward Any award or recognition given by other people. This can include recognition of the performance of a process team by another process team.

Facilitator Anyone who helps a process team apply TQM tools and methods. Sometimes the word is used interchangeably with coach.

Fail-safe technique Application of automatic checking devices to capture common problems or errors either in the design or production process. The Japanese call such fail-safe production methods poka-yoke.

Failure mode analysis (FMA) A process for determining which symptoms of a malfunction appear before or after a failure of a critical element or parameter in a process or system. Possible causes are listed and then the product is designed to eliminate the problem.

Failure mode effects analysis (FMEA) A way of taking each potential failure mode in each sub-item of an item to analyze to identify its effect on other sub-items and upon the function required of the process or product.

Failure mode effects and criticality analysis (FMECA) A procedure done after a failure mode effects analysis has been conducted to classify all potential failure effect ranked by severity and probability of occurrence again.

Fishbone diagram This cause and effect diagram is a graphic that illustrates the series of causes of a problem and gets its name from the fact that the lines (representing causes of problems) looks like the skeleton of a fish.

Fitness for use A phrase used to indicate that a service or product is "fit" for customer use, that is to say, meets a customer's requirements.

Flow diagram This kind of drawing defines the steps of a process. It is used to identify areas of problems in a process, redundant and unnecessary steps that complicate a process, non-value-add activities, and where simplification is possible. It is usually a combination of flowcharts and text.

Flowchart A graphical presentation of all the steps in a process. Relying on a technique used in software design, inputs, process, outputs, and decisions are represented in blocks and other symbols. This is one of the most widely used quality tools because it allows one to document easily the flow of activities in a process.

FMA Failure mode analysis.

FMEA Failure mode effects analysis.

FMECA Failure mode effects and criticality analysis.

Focus group A group of customers or users of a process who are brought together in a meeting (or a series of meetings) for the purpose of understanding how they feel about a service, product, or process. Focus groups are also used to generate ideas on how to improve continuously those goods and services.

Focus setting A method employed to concentrate attention on a specific outcome.

Force field analysis A technique used to identify forces that for or against a particular action. Variables for or against might include probability of occurrence or magnitude. Such an analysis can lead to preventitive measures to minimize occurrence of a negative circumstance.

Form-fit-function A phrase used in conjunction with the control of a configuration in which Engineering Change Notices (ECNs) support drawing or component changes that do not affect the "form, fit, or function" of the component or item in the relationship it has to the system in which it is used.

14 Points W. Edwards Deming's management practices designed to improve quality and productivity. They are: (1) create constancy of purpose to improve products and services; (2) adopt the new philosophy of quality improvement; (3) cease dependence on inspection as the way to achieve quality; (4) stop making purchase decisions just on price alone, work instead with fewer suppliers; (5) improve constantly and forever processes for planning, manufacture, and service; (6) have training on the job; (7) practice leadership; (8) drive fear out of the workplace; (9) break down barriers between staffs; (10) eliminate slogans, targets, and exhortations for workers; (11) get rid of numerical quotas for workers and numerical goals for managers; (12) remove obstacles that rob workers of pride of work and eliminate annual merit or rating systems; (13) educate employees and implement self-improvement for all; (14) put everyone to work on transforming the enterprise.

Frequency distribution Used to describe the distribution of a discrete variable and refers to the number of occurrences of individual values over a defined range. When applied to the distribution of a continuous variable, then we have a count of cases that lie between predetermined limits over a range of values that the variable being measured may assume.

Functional administrative control technique Refers to a technique for improving performance by employing a method that combines time management and value engineering. You break down activities into functions and then create teams to solve problems within each function.

Functional organization Refers to an organization responsible for a major part of an enterprise, such as accounting, distribution, legal, marketing, or manufacturing.

Functional team A team made up of representatives from only one functional organization (e.g., only salespeople or accountants).

Funnel experiment This kind of experiment is used to demonstrate effects of tampering. In this one, marbles are dropped through a funnel for the purpose of hitting a flat surfaced target below. This activity is done to illustrate that adjusting a stable process to compensate for an undesirable result or a lucky result will generate a result worse than if no adjustment had been made.

Gainsharing A reward process by which the gains in productivity within a functional organization or company are shared between owners (e.g., stockholders) and employees. In other words, it is a variant of profit sharing and is used to incent employees to improve productivity within an organization.

Gantt chart A type of bar chart often used to display planned and completed activities in specific time periods (e.g., planned sales next to actual sales by quarter).

Gap The delta between how things or processes are today (baseline) and how they should be (your vision or customer requirements).

Gauge repeatability and reproducibility (GR&R) The process of evaluating the accuracy of a gauging instrument by establishing whether measurements taken with the device can be repeated and are reproducible (i.e., roughly the same answer over and over again).

GDT Geometric dimensioning and tolerancing.

Generic product Any basic item or product without any variance or enhancements in features.

Geometric dimensioning and tolerancing (GDT) A method used to minimize costs of production by illustrating dimension and tolerancing on a drawing while taking into account functions or relationships of part features.

George M. Low Trophy This prestigeous award is given annually by NASA to those contracts, subcontractors, and suppliers to this space agency who consistenty mantained and improved their quality performance. Large and small businesses compete in one or the other size category. Previously called the NASA Excellence Award for Quality and Productivity, the award is named after NASA's administrator for almost three decades.

Goal There are many definitions, however, they all generally involve a statement of an achievement or attainment that is desired and leads to actions directed toward its achievement. Goals increasingly are expressed as measurable targets.

Go/no-go This describes the condition of a unit or product in which one of two circumstances prevail: go (conforms to requirements or specifications) and no-go (does not conform).

GR&R Gauge repeatability and reproducibility.

Group Another word for team.

Guideline Increasingly refers to a set of specific suggested practices to encourage conformance to predetermined standards but that are not mandatory.

Hierarchical nature of a process Various levels of any process. It is often depicted as a high level flowchart of the major parts of a process followed by other charts illustrating the sub-parts of the high level phases.

Histogram A graphical representation of a distributed set of measurement data. Typically this is a bar graph.

Hoshin planning This Japanese method of planning calls for senior management of an organization, working with various teams of process or unit employees, to establish strategic goals and work on their implementation. It calls for focus on customer satisfaction goals, effectiveness, and efficiency of process work. Goals are set and communicated within an organization and woven into the fabric of employee performance plans, process objectives, and goals for organizations, all of which are measured and improved upon in a disciplined manner. Also often called breakthrough planning of where a company should be in five years.

House of Quality This graphical depiction, widely used by quality experts to illustrate the components of a quality strategy or process, grew out of a formal and rigorous process for identifying customer requirements called Quality Function Deployment (QFD).

Human resources Employees or members of any organization.

Hypothesis Traditionally thought of as an assertion made about some parameter or circumstance in science. Increasingly, the use of hypothesis in the study of business problems and circumstances is becoming popular as a way to focus analysis.

Imperfection A quality departure from requirements or standards. Another word for defect, blemish, or nonconformity.

Improvement methodology Refers to a way of implementing improvements in an organization or process.

In-control process Refers to any process in which variations, by statistical measurements, are within control limits.

Individual involvement The personal role played by individuals in the output of a company, agency, or organization.

Information processing component The component of a value activity that includes recording, use, and distribution of information necessary to perform that activity.

Information system Usually refers to automated (computer-based) systems. Increasingly, this also is becoming a description of the flow of information that allows one to review, analyze, and then take corrective actions within a process.

In-plant Quality Evaluation program (IQUE) The method by which a firm judges the controls over product quality, especially that of a contractor.

Input The injection of energy, information, data, or materials into a process or conversation required to complete an activity to produce an output or work product. The term was borrowed from information processing in which pieces of information (data) were input into a computer.

Input/output analysis A technique used to identify interdependency problems.

Inspection The act of measuring, testing, examining, or gauging one or more characteristics of a product or service and then comparing results to specified requirements. The objective is to determine if conformance by each feature has been achieved.

Instant pudding A slang term employed to illustrate an obstacle to quality. It assumes that quality and productivity improvement can be realized quickly through affirming faith rather than by education and work. Coined originally by James

Bakken of Ford Motor Company, it was more widely used by W. Edwards Deming to criticize an approach.

Institutionalize The act of making something (usually a cultural value or a process) an integral aspect of an organization's way of life.

Internal customer Also known as little c customer, this is a person in an organization who receives the output of another fellow-employee's process work; the opposite of external customer.

Internal failure costs The costs caused by defects found in products and services before they reached a customer outside the enterprise. These are often distinguished from failure or defect costs that are generated by failures once they have reached a customer.

Internal linkages Linkages within a value chain. The effect of an order entry process on delivery costs, for instance, is an internal linkage between a primary activity and a support function.

Intrinsic reward Usually refers to a feeling of accomplishment or satisfaction within an individual caused by doing something satisfactory to a person. The reward is, in effect, given to oneself by mental recognition of achievement. Deming would link this notion to his concept of the "joy of work" in which doing well is something satisfactory and pleasing to all people.

Ishikara diagram A cause-and-effect diagram.

ISO 9000 series standards Constitutes a set of five standards for quality management and assurance documentation to support quality standards. Developed in 1987 by the International Organization for Standardization (ISO), it is intended for organizations in all industries. The ISO standards, however, come to be associated with specific standards for manufacturing companies wishing to market goods and services in 91 countries. For many manufacturing organizations, it is a specialized set of quality criteria.

Just-in-time (JIT) Refers to a body of practices, primarily in manufacturing, that calls for production of goods to be as close as possible to the time when they are sold. Implied is the availability of raw materials within hours of consumption or provision of a service as needed.

Just-in-time manufacturing In pure manufacturing terms, it is a material requirement planning approach used in production in which hardly any inventory of parts or raw materials are kept at the factory and in which little to no incoming inspection of parts or raw material occurs.

KAIZEN This Japanese word is the equivalent of the English phrase "continuous improvement" in which processes are incrementally enhanced to improve overall performance of a process or organization.

Lagging measure A measure issued after the fact it is measuring.

Leadership In the world of quality, it calls for guiding an organization to accomplish its objectives through the application of total quality principles and valuing quality principles. The leadership embraces such values and practices them personally.

Lead team The team that guides or supervises other process teams. Frequently the term is used to describe the senior managers of an organization and their role in guiding other teams.

Leading measure A measure upstream in a process.

Life cycle cost The total cost of a system or product, but may include a process, over its useful life. Costs include acquisition, ownership, and final disposal.

Line chart This kind of chart displays and compares quantifiable data. Often the data presented is amount over time.

Linkage analysis A formal process (tool) for identifying internal and external linkages to identify those activities of value that have a high information processing component or that identify organizations highly dependent on others in delivering or buying services.

Linkages Relationships between interdependent activities within a value chain or between more than one interdependent organization. Linkages are often identified as existing if the effects of the performance of a task on the costs and performance of other actions depend on linkages.

Listening The act of receiving, understanding, and reacting to information, such as customer interests and concerns. In customer feedback processes, the term "listening posts" is often applied.

Loss function Those operations of an organization that study costs related to any variation from the assigned values of any quality characteristic.

Lot A specific quantity of products brought together within conditions considered uniform and for the purpose of sampling.

Lower Control Limit (LCL). The control limit for points below the mid-point horizontal line on a control chart.

Maintainability An old manufacturing term widely used to refer to the characteristics of the design or installation of a piece of equipment that make it possible to repair it later either easily or efficiently. Often replacement products for an earlier generation are designed to improve maintainability to lower costs of support.

Maintenance Always defined as the repair or preservation at a predetermined level of quality of something. In quality, it is usually of a process or body of information.

Malcolm Baldrige National Quality Award The award established by the U.S. Government in 1987 to recognize quality achievements of American companies. It is awarded by the U.S. Department of Commerce and is today the most prestigious quality award in the United States.

Management The collective leadership of an enterprise.

Manufacturing Resource Planning (MRP) Historically, an important system for planning and controlling manufacturing operations. Today, this is seen as a major collection of manufacturing processes.

Margin In the world of quality, this means the difference between total value and combined costs of executing the value activities.

Market-Driven Quality (MDQ) IBM's term for Total Quality Management (TQM). It is the idea that quality is driven by market needs, that a company achieves complete customer satisfaction by delivering defect-free and timely goods and services that effectively meet their needs.

Materials Review Board (MRB) A quality control organization or team, usually employed in manufacturing or process installations, for the purpose of determining how to deal with materials that do not conform to predetermined standards of quality. Members typically are process-control engineers, designers, purchasers of materials, and quality inspectors who are all trying to cause their organization to use materials that meet specific standards of quality.

Mean Any average of a group of data.

Mean time between failures (MTBF) A measure of the average time between successive failures in the performance or quality of a product. For example, it can refer to the number of months between the times when a computer goes down (fails to function). Improvements in design are intended to extend MTBF's from one generation of product to another.

Measurement More than just a major philosophical component of the quality practice's value system, it is an act or process of measuring to compare actual results with intended requirements. Measurements of performance are always expressed in quantitative terms.

Mentor An individual whose responsibility is to advise and guide a process team while serving as an interface between management and teams. Often a mentor is seen as a coach or advisor.

Military standards The specific, documented standards of performance or quality issued by the U.S. Government for any product employed by the military branches (MIL-Q-9858A). Such standards encompass quality measures, performance criteria, statistical sampling reporting (MIL-STD-105E and MIL-STD-45662A), and specifications of components. Since the U.S. military buys almost every kind of product made, their standards often influence design characteristics of commercially available goods.

Mission Usually defined as the intended result of a process. For an organization, it is a statement of its current purpose for existence, what it does.

Mistake proofing A form of quality inspection, it is a technique to avoid human errors from passing through a process; poka-yoke is another name for proofing.

Modeling More than simply a representation of a process, it is a mindset that groups of activities can be described (process), tested, and finally, articulated as approaches.

Moment of truth The moment when someone is face-to-face with a customer providing a product or service. The phrase was originally coined at Scandinavian Airlines (SAS) to describe what happens when an employee sold a ticket to a customer. Now it refers to any customer contact: a telephone call, meeting, letter, and so forth. It embodies the idea that the quality of an organization's performance occurs and is measured at the moment when you deal with a customer.

Multifunctional team This kind of a team has members from various functions, usually to work on a process that crosses more than two organizational functions.

Multivariate control chart This kind of control chart is used to evaluate the stability of a process by looking at the levels of two or more variables, such as a process's characteristics.

n Sample size, such as the quantity of units in a sample.

Need A requirement, often generated from what customers want, desire or is essential. It is also used in design and manufacturing to define a lack of something that must be fulfilled in order for a process to function or a product to be completed.

Noise A slang term for any disruption of a process, system, or function.

Nominal group technique (NGT). An increasingly popular tool or technique for generating ideas in groups. It is used to define business problems and their solution, and to articulate quality measures, goals, and objectives. Ideas are gathered from a group and clustered together by theme or subject, leading to possible definitions and solutions.

Nonconformity The lack of conformity to a prespecified set of standards or customer requirements. Often used as a synonym for defect, imperfection, or blemish.

Nondestructive testing and evaluation (NDE or NDT) Refers to the testing and evaluation techniques that do not damage or destroy what is being tested, such as products or parts.

Non-value-added A descriptive for an activity, process, or task that fails to add any value to a product or service. In process improvement activities, these are sought out for elimination.

Normative performance measurement technique Another quality-oriented group technique, it is a structured workshop method that leads teams through the design of measurement systems that are relevant to their needs. This approach factors in behavioral consequences of a measurement in order to encourage acceptance of a particular measurement.

Number of affected units chart (np chart) This kind of control chart is used to evaluate the stability of a process by looking at the total number of units in a sample in which a certain type or class of event happens.

Objective A desired end result to be achieved within a specified period of time. In practice an objective should always have a schedule for achievement. It is often confused with goals, even used interchangeably.

Operating characteristic curve (OC curve) This kind of graph is employed for determining the probability of accepting lots as a function of the lots' or process's level of quality when deploying a variety of sampling plans. Type A curves show probabilities of the acceptance for a specific lot from finite production; Type B curves measure the probability of acceptance of a lot from some continuous process; Type C curves track the long-run percentage of product accepted during some sampling phase and is applied when using a continuous sampling plan.

Opportunity for error (OFE) This is the number of times any event could possibly have an error. Better known as Total OFE, you calculate this by multiplying the number of units times the OFE per unit.

Out-of-control process A process which, when measured, is performing outside the bounds of acceptable variation. The results of any sample are seen to be caused by chance and not by a controllable circumstance.

Out of spec This slang phrase means something is not conforming to specifications, such as the quality of a product.

Output A term borrowed from information processing and the world of computers; it is a specific result or end work product that emerges from a task or a process. In the world of quality, the nature of that output is defined by the customer (recipient).

Outputs Usually refers to information, but can also be any end result that comes out of a process to customers or users.

Owner That individual who has sufficient authority to change a process without requiring further approval. The term "process owner" is often used to say the same thing.

Ownership The power or ability to control actions and processes. Also used to describe one's personal commitment to actions or values. As employees take on more responsibility for the consequences of actions (empowerment), the concept and use of the word is more frequent.

Parameter design The design of a process or product that results in the performance impervious to variation by moving toward a quality target for quality characteristics or features. Often called robust design. In such a design, performance is considered output of a process.

Parametric design Refers to the design phase during which sensitivity to disruption of a function is reduced or eliminated.

Pareto Diagram or Chart Named after Vilfredo Pareto (1848–1923), who we know because of his 80/20 rule. However, in the world of quality, it is a breakdown of defects, or causes of defects, which are ranked (classified) by their frequency of occurrence or by priority. Problems are classified by cause or phenomenon; the chart looks like the New York skyline with the tallest building being the most frequent occurrence. It answers the question: Which are the most important?

Pareto's Principle The widely known concept that a large percentage of results are caused by a small percentage of causes. Often called the 80/20 rule, approximately 80 percent of all problems are created by 20 percent of the possible causes.

Participation The involvement of employees in decisions or actions that involve both processes they implement or their own work.

People involvement The act of individuals or groups participating in an activity, process improvement, or in making decisions within a process or organization. Another variation of the concept of empowerment.

Percent chart (p chart) A chart in which all data is represented by percentages. Used to measure the stability of a process by the number of samples that conform to expectations.

Performance This widely used word refers to description of an attribute of a task, process, or product. The criteria most commonly associated with performance concern cost or efficiency, quality or effectiveness, and availability or schedule.

Physical component A value component that includes all the actions required to perform one activity.

Pie chart A chart that appears as a circle divided into near triangular shapes to reflect relationships between items and the whole.

Plan Increasingly, this is a detailed list of actions that have a specific, anticipated objective. In the world of quality, plans are increasingly documented, actions measured for effectiveness and efficiency, and results measured as outcomes of performance.

Plan-Do-Check-Act cycle (PDCA cycle) A basic tenet of quality in which you plan an action, do it, check to see how it conformed to plan, make improvements to the process, and do it again. Often this is called either a Shewhart cycle or a Deming cycle, after two quality gurus who advocated this approach.

Poka-yoke A slang term for mistake proofing.

Policy Often a documented statement of principles, values, or beliefs, they represent guides to the management of processes and actions. They increasingly are linked to the attainment of specific goals and have performance objectives. Policies are often used today to facilitate use of quality-based practices and values.

Population In quality and statistics, refers to a collection of data, items, or observations from which findings can be identified and then conclusions reached, leading to decisions. In fact-based decision making, the use of data populations is critical.

Potential product Any product or service that has not yet been developed that could be used to replace an existing product or service that attracts and retains customers beyond what existing products can do. Also known as "follow-on" or "replacement" products once created, they should always exceed performance of predecessor products or services.

Presentation The vehicle for providing data and obtaining approval for action, it is considered a formal way of dealing with important issues. Many of the charts defined in this glossary are used to present data in visually pleasing forms.

Prevention In process management, it is an act taken to avoid a future defect or error in order to improve quality of goods or performance.

Prevention costs Costs incurred in implementing actions to avoid future defects or errors in goods and services.

Prevention vs. detection The contrast between two types of quality-oriented actions. Prevention refers to actions taken to avoid defects, while detection focuses on actions to already existing problems in goods and services. These two approaches are sometimes also called "designing in quality vs. inspecting in quality."

Primary activities Those tasks required to create a product or perform a service, transfer either to a customer, or is a service provided to a consumer after the transfer of a product or performance of a service.

Problem A circumstance or question that is a candidate for resolution. It is also the consequence of not conforming to a quality standard. The word is also used to describe a defect or error that needs to be resolved.

Process A collection of actions or activities that are definable, repeatable, predictable, and measurable. A process is the grouping of actions that lead to a specific result (e.g., billing, customer surveys). All actions are components of processes. Processes are the sum total of an organization's organized activities.

Process Analysis Techniques (PAT) A methodology for defining customer needs, analyzes effectiveness of existing processes, and leads to their improvement. It was most widely defined by IBM and reflects common process improvement techniques.

Process average A measure of a primary tendency, it is calculated by dividing the sum of the values of a collection of readings by the number of readings.

Process capability A measure of the performance of any process as compared to its requirements. Also is seen as a measure of long-term performance after a process has stabilized. Sometimes also called process capability index.

Process control This speaks to a collection of actions used to identify and then eliminate special causes of variation. The intent is to restore stability to an existing process.

Process design Refers to the development of any process.

Process diagram A flowchart or other graphic representation of the various steps in a process.

Process efficiency measurement A ratio of value-add time to total cycle time, it is an attempt to measure the relationship of time in process work.

Process flow analysis This technique is used to identify and analyze important processes. It is particularly useful in identifying specific actions, steps, or roadblocks within processes that can be improved or eliminated.

Process improvement Those activities used to identify and then remove common causes of variation so as to improve the overall performance or capacity of a process. This is not to be confused with process reengineering, which is a total reconstruction or new construction of a process to replace a previous one.

Process improvement and Problem-solving teams Teams brought together for the purpose of either improving a specific process or solving a problem. It is a temporary group that disbands after the problem is solved or becomes permanent if it comes to own the process.

Process logistics All aspects of logistics within an enterprise.

Process management A collection of practices used by management to implement and improve quality management and process effectiveness within an enterprise.

Process map A graphical representation of all the steps in a process. It looks like a flowchart of boxes of steps following one after the other. It may also be a graphical representation of a group of related processes.

Process optimization The act of improving both the efficiency and productivity of a process. Focus is typically on economic issues and more broadly on productivity.

Process owner The person responsible for the implementation of a process and held accountable for its results. Process owners typically are required to establish a set of measurements of success for a process, use continuous improvement techniques to eliminate defects and improve cycle time, while delivering results.

Process performance Refers generally to the effectiveness of a process but, when properly done, is a measure of a process's performance against standards, a benchmark, or customer requirements.

Process reengineering Often used interchangeably with process improvement, in the past several years it has become a distinctive term to describe a body of activities that lead to the creation of a new process radically different from its predecessor. It rapidly is acquiring its own set of tools and techniques, but retains the same criteria for performance sought after in process improvement, only on a more dramatic scale, often by at least one factor of magnitude.

Process review A formal, objective assessment of how well a process has been developed and managed, not necessarily on the output of a process. The intent is to improve both the process being reviewed and the methods used to improve and manage it.

Process simplification The act of reducing the complexity of a process, usually done by eliminating steps, such as redundant activities, multiple signoffs and audits. Removal of non-value-add activities is often the most effective way to improve the quality of a process.

Product More than an item, it is also the output of a process delivered to internal or external customers. This may include systems, equipment, data, services, parts or items for sale.

Product design The activities involved in the development of a product; usually a design process with the voice of the customer very prominent.

Product genealogy Simply an historical record of the components and configuration of a product; it may include data about its manufacture, testing, inspections, and maintenance. The record of quality audits of both components and products is also part of a product genealogy.

Product or service liability The moral or legal obligation of a firm to make restitution to a customer for damage or personal injury caused by that company's products or services. This is often a source of cost justification for quality of products, especially for the cost of safety features.

Production process The collection of activities required to make a product. It often is seen as a collection or family of related manufacturing processes.

Productivity Used widely with various meanings, it generally refers to the ratio of outputs produced, or services rendered, to inputs required for these goods and services. It is also used to explain the desired results or outcomes in terms of quality.

Proportion chart Same thing as a percent chart.

Q chart A quality score chart that may come in various forms.

Q90 series Shorthand for ANSI/ASQC Q90 series of standards, the U.S. version of ISO 9000 standards, adopted in 1987.

Quality While there are many definitions of the term, they all boil down to descriptions of excellence in goods and services and especially to what degree they conform to customer requirements or satisfy customers. Equally important is the notion that all activities and things can be improved upon continuously, and that meeting requirements the first time is a necessary objective.

Quality assurance/quality control Used interchangeably, the terms refer to those activities executed to ensure a high level of quality for a product or service.

Quality audit A systematic inspection by an outside body to determine if quality activities conform to quality plans and expectations. Often the effectiveness of plans and activities is included in the audit.

Quality circle First made popular in the 1970s, this is a small group of employees and their managers who came together voluntarily to identify and solve work-related problems employing structured methodologies. For many American and European firms, this was the first vehicle used to apply quality techniques.

Quality control Just another way of saying quality assurance.

Quality costs Another way of saying cost of poor quality.

Quality engineering The analysis of a manufacturing process or system done to maximize the quality of work done (process) and the output of that work (products).

Quality Function Deployment (QFD) A highly structured methodology for identifying customer requirements, then linking them to the design specifications of goods and services. The primary objective of this disciplined methodology is to solve quality problems before a product is designed. Design engineers and marketing and manufacturing personnel work together to create a product design that most closely meets customer requirements. Survey work on what features customers want (are important) is followed by ranking of features by significance, then by identification of possible problems, and concluding with well-defined engineering specifications. QFD is a widely used approach in manufacturing.

Quality improvement team That team of people responsible for planning and implementing improvements in the quality of processes or organizations.

Quality loss function A parabolic representation of quality loss that happens when a quality feature deviates from its standard or value. The measure is always in monetary terms. The greater the deviation from standard, the more the cost of lost quality increases.

Quality score chart A control chart used to measure the stability of a process. Quality score is the weighted sum of a count of the sums of various classes of events in which each classification is assigned a weight.

Quality team Quality improvement or performance action teams of employees all working on various aspects of a process. Such teams are used for process improvement projects.

Quality trilogy A three-part approach to managing for quality results through planning, control, and improvement. The first focuses on the development of processes and products that meet customer requirements; the second to meet the objectives of products and processes; and the third to continue improving even greater levels of performance.

QUINCUNX This tool creates frequency distributions, often used to simulate manufacturing processes.

Quantitative methods The application of measurements.

R chart Shorthand for range chart.

RAM or R&M. Shorthand for reliability/availability/maintainability. It is a process applied by the U.S. Department of Defense to insure combat readiness of products through reliability and maintenance. This process includes reduction of costs through defined practices.

Random sampling A widely used sampling method by which random samples of units (e.g., products) are chosen such that all combination of these units have an equal chance of being chosen as the sample. This technique is used frequently for selecting products to be inspected for quality.

Range The gap between high and low values of a set of data. Ranges are defined statistically and activities within the gap are variables that are tolerated. Incidents that are recorded beyond the ranges are considered exceptions. It is also more classically defined as the difference between the maximum or minimum values of data in any sample.

Range chart This type of control chart uses R as the subgroup for the purposes of evaluating the stability of variability within a process.

Recognition The attention paid to either an individual or group for outstanding accomplishments. In the world of quality, this is often tendered to teams and in itself is a process designed to reward individuals for embracing and applying effectively quality tools and values.

Red bead experiment This famous experiment was devised by quality guru W. Edwards Deming to show that it was impossible to rank employees by performance for the following year based on last year's performance because differences in performance have to be attributed to a system, not to employees. To perform the experiment, take 4,000 red and white beads of which 20 percent are red, all in a jar, and find six people. They have to produce white beads since their customer does not want red. The first individual starts by stirring the beads and then, after being blindfolded, selects 50 beads. That person next hands the bead jar to the second individual, who repeats the process, then passes the jar on. After all six have selected their 50 sample beads, the number of red beads is counted for each person. Then the limits of variation among them (i.e., employees) attributed to the experiment is calculated. These calculations show that no evidence exists that one person will outperform another in the future. Rather, the experiment demonstrates that management wastes its time trying to determine why a particular employee could gather 10 beads while another could find 20. The lesson is that management should focus on the system for performance (e.g., for selecting the red beads), thus making it possible for everyone to select more white beads. (Deming's own description of this experiment is included in the Classics section of this book.)

Registrar Accreditation Board (RAB) This board evaluates the reliability and competence of organizations that assess and register companies to appropriate ISO 9000 series standards. This board was formed by the ASQC and is governed by members from industry, higher education, and management consulting.

Registration to standards A defined process by which an accredited, independent third-party organization performs on-site audits of a company's operations measuring them against a set of independent standards. Used in certification for ISO 9000 standards, successful audits are rewarded with a certification of compliance to standards.

Regression analysis A statistical technique for calculating the best mathematical expression that describes the functional relationship between a response and one or more independent variables. It is a widely used SPC calculation.

Reliability Often it is defined as the probability of a product or service performing its role under predetermined conditions without failure or problem for a specific period of time. Such a specified statement of performance is frequently made a design requirement for the product or process. First measured in products, it is now increasingly applied to processes and services.

Requirements This is always stated as the needs or wants of customers. Requirements is a profoundly influencing factor in determining the content and output of any process. In addition to this being a statement of what needs to be, it is increasingly also stated as a measurable outcome.

Restraining forces Those realities that prevent a situation from improving. They can be intrinsic to a process or be caused by some circumstance outside of the organization (e.g., economic reality).

Reward A recompense or recognition for something well done. In the world of quality, a distinction is made between external and internal rewards. External rewards are given to individuals or teams by management or peers for quality results. Internal rewards are the personal satisfaction of meeting a challenge, doing a job well, or accomplishing a personal goal.

Right the first time The phrase is used to suggest that it is less expensive and more beneficial to make a product or deliver a service correctly the first time. Taking steps to insure that products and services perform as required is seen as more cost beneficial than having to "do it over again." It is another way of suggesting that defect prevention strategies are more beneficial than defect identification.

Roadblock identification analysis This technique is used to identify circumstances or other obstacles that do or could prevent improvements in performance or that block existing products or services from achieving specified levels of quality. Applying nominal group technique, users identify issues and prioritize them by the degree to which they represent roadblocks to success. Then teams can perform analysis of key barriers and propose ways to remove them.

Robust design Refers to the design of a product or service with minimal losses of quality due to variation from quality expectations.

Robustness One of the most recent entrants into the quality vocabulary, it refers to the condition or quality of a product, service, or process in which performance is relatively stable, with a minimum of variability, despite changes in the environment or operating conditions.

Root cause Refers to the underlying reason why a process does not conform to specifications. The removal of a root cause brings the process back to conformance.

Root cause analysis An important quality process for identifying the source of defects or problems, it is a structured approach that focuses on the ultimate or original cause of a condition. The approach discounts judgment or symptoms about the cause of a problem and relies instead on the collection of possible sources of a problem. It is one of the most widely used and effective approaches in process work.

Rules of conduct A body of guidelines usually established by a team at the start of its process work to govern the behavior and performance of its members. Efficient teams always establish rules of conduct at the beginning of their work.

Run chart A graph that plots performance information over time for processes or defects, for example.

Sample A specific (finite) number of items of a similar type taken from a population or lot for the purpose of examination to determine if all members of the population or lot are conforming to quality requirements.

Sample size A specific number of items of data from a larger body of information.

Sample standard deviation chart (s chart) This kind of control chart takes a subgroup standard deviation, s, and uses it to evaluate the stability of variation within a process.

Sampling The process of collecting a sample of data about the quality of a lot or population of goods, actions, or information as reflective of the patterns of the entire population or lot.

Scanlon committee Refers to a committee made up of various levels of an organization who come together to implement a philosophy of management/labor relations with the intention of improving the productivity of the organization. Specific principles and methods are employed by such committees to facilitate the process. Like many other team-like activities, it relies heavily on employee involvement and responsibility.

Scatter diagram A widely used graphic, it is a technique employed to analyze relationships between two variables. Two sets of data are plotted graphically, with the x axis representing a variable to make a prediction and the y axis to display the variable to be predicted. The illustration shows possible relationships.

Selection grid A tool used to compare each problem, alternative, or opportunity against each other.

Selection matrix This technique is used to rank in importance or effect problems, opportunities, or options based on predefined criteria.

Self-directed teams Teams that work on processes or within functions with little or no management control. They tend to do self-appraisals of each member and have enormous authority over how to use their time and on how to perform their duties.

Seven tools of quality Techniques widely used by enterprises to understand the performance of their processes for the purpose of improving them. They are cause-and-effect diagram, check sheet, control chart, flowchart, histogram, Pareto chart, and scatter diagram.

Shewhart cycle Another name for Plan-Do-Check-Act cycle.

Sharing rallies Meetings in which individuals, but usually teams, are recognized for their contributions and successes with processes. Often these are run like recognition events with awards, motivational speakers, and trips, and are celebrations of progress. Those honored typically have to explain to their audiences what they did and what they learned from the effort.

Signal-to-noise ratio (S/N ratio) This mathematical equation illustrates the extent of an experimental effect above the effect of experimental error caused by chance fluctuations.

Sigma A measure of statistical variability of distributions. In statistical process language, it is a Standard Deviation. In practice, it is a measure of the number of defects per million.

Sigma Capability This sigma measure is of defects per million opportunities.

Simulation The observation of a model or other artificial representation that mirrors a realistic situation and is employed instead of actual direct experimentation for either economic or technical reasons. Often it is a fast way to study the possible performance of an as yet unbuilt product.

Six Sigma One of the most popular forms of measuring performance in manufacturing and also in large corporations. Six Sigma means 3.4 defects, errors, or failures per million occurrences or performances. Such events can be errors in lines of programming, telephone calls missed, or billing mistakes. It is a statistical measure that focuses on virtually no defects as the acceptable level of quality. Popularized by Motorola Corporation, it has proven to be an effective way to translate many types of activities into a measure of defects needing improvements at a very stringent level.

Skills The word today is widely used to refer to someone's experiences, competencies, values, attitudes, and patterns of behavior. Often formally catalogued, they provide an organization with an inventory of capabilities and also for people, a list of possible areas for further training and practice.

Sorting The act of arranging data in some useful order. These may include placing data in classes or categories to provide insight into actions or process performance.

Special cause A source of variation in the performance or output of a process that is unpredictable, intermittent, random, or sometimes unstable. Engineers will often also use the phrase "assignable cause" to mean the same thing; the cause of an exception.

Specification A specific, often documented, description of a product or process, focusing on its features and the results it should produce.

Stakeholder An individual or organization that has an investment (stake) in your success and judges your performance. They are customers, employees, stockholders, the nation, or whoever. They are people or organizations who you have to serve and are interested in your achievements. Another set of examples using schools and universities: students, faculty, employers, alumni, and funding organizations.

Standard deviation The spread of a process, denoted by the Greek letter sigma. In mathematics it is defined as the positive square root of a variance. In quality it is the spread in the variety of output from a process.

Statistic A parameter that can be defined based on quantitative features of a sample, a measure of value. A varient, called inferential statistics, suggests the level of confidence placed on a statement regarding the probability of its accuracy or truth, or about its applicability. The intent is to provide a decision-maker with confidence about a decision to be made after reviewing specific pieces of data.

Statistical control Typically it is used to describe the status of a process from which all special causes of variation have been eliminated, leaving only common causes. When a process is said to be under statistical control, that is another way of suggesting it is stable.

Statistical elimination This analysis of a sample parameter is performed to predict values of a corresponding population parameter.

Statistical estimation This kind of analysis of a sample parameter is done to predict values of its corresponding population parameter.

Statistical methods Refers to the application of the theory of probability to variations or problems. Basic statistical methods are tools and techniques widely used in process work and include such popular items as control charts, capability analysis, and statistical inference. A more sophisticated set of tools, less widely used in normal process work, involves statistical analysis and design of experiments, regression analysis, correlation analysis, and variance analysis. Both sets of tools, however, are evident today in all types of processes and organizations.

Statistical process control (SPC) A body of statistical techniques used to measure the performance of processes. The reason for applying these is to identify specifically areas for improvement in processes and to measure outputs of processes, all leading to actions that will result in continuous improvements and results. Objectives include getting processes to a stable state and to improve their capability or output. Another way of describing SPC is to see it as a management philosophy that seeks out to reduce variation around a predetermined target value and as a disciplined approach to the identification and resolution of problems. Popular SPC tools include fishbone diagrams, graphical representations, Pareto charts, and control charts. All are used to track numerically what a process is doing, analyzing that performance, and suggesting improvements.

Statistical quality control (SQC) Used both in manufacturing and services, it is a methodology for tracking current conditions against a target for quality performance.

Statistics A branch of applied mathematics whose purpose is to describe and analyze observations so as to predict events, leading to decisions that are made in a circumstance of uncertainty. The techniques of statistics rely on the theory of probability, making possible the mathematical study of a problem. Statistics were first introduced into manufacturing processes in the 1920s and after World War II began to appear in office processes. Today the use of statistics is an integral part of any total quality management effort.

Steering committee or group A committee, usually made up of senior management, to oversee and guide a cross-functional or focus activity. It is a widely used mechanism for coordinating the quality improvement activities of an organization at large.

Strategic Total Quality Management Plan (STQMP) The overall plan for introducing, sustaining, and improving the application of TQM tools in an organization.

Strategic Total Quality Management planning cycle A plan for implementing TQM. It includes definition of an enterprise-wide vision, identification of strategic improvement opportunities, their selection, development and maintenance of a TQM plan of action, evaluation of results, and renewal of the plan to reflect changing realities.

Strategy Any broad set of activities to achieve specific goals. Processes, and how they are structured, are often employed to implement strategies.

Structural variation A variation caused by regular, systematic changes in output. These can be, for example, in response to seasonal patterns or to long-term trends.

Subprocess A part of a larger process that can be seen as almost a small process in itself. For example, in a process for renewing a driver's license, a subprocess might be those activities surrounding the written examination or the eye test.

Supplier Anyone or organization who provides input into a process. This can be a high school supplying students to a college, a company delivering raw materials to a factory, or another department, providing you data that you need to do your work. Suppliers are measured on effectiveness and are brought into your processes as a participant rather than simply as a vendor. They may be others within your own enterprise or vendors from other firms.

Supplier/customer analysis This technique is used to gather and exchange data on the needs and requirements of an organization to its key suppliers. It also involves both agreeing to a common definition of what the buying organization's customers needs and expectations are to be fulfilled by both.

Supplier quality assurance A very obvious concept today, it is the expression of confidence that a supplier's quality will match a customer's requirements. This is brought about by a relationship between supplier and customer defined by processes that insure a standard, routine high-level of quality of supplies meeting a customer's needs. This allows a manufacturer, for example, to work with fewer suppliers. J. M. Juran defines nine essential activities to insure supplier quality assurance: (1) definition of product and service quality requirements, (2) evaluation of alternative suppliers, (3) selection of suppliers, (4) conduct of joint quality planning exercises, (5) cooperations with supplier during the execution of a contract, (6) gathering of proof of conformance to requirements, (7) certification of approved (qualified) suppliers, (8) implementation of quality improvement programs as needed, and (9) creation and use of supplier quality ratings.

Support system Refers to a process within an organization for the purpose of guiding the enterprise through the application of TQM principles.

System Used to describe a collection or interdependent processes for the purpose of accomplishing a specific function or goal.

System improvement This method focuses on the improvement or change of any system (often a collection of processes).

Systems (parts) or concept design A design phase whose purpose is the design architecture (materials, size, shape, number of components, etc.). It does this by examining the best available components or technology. Often the phrase used for this kind of activity is "parts design phase."

Taguchi methods Named after Genichi Taguchi, a leading Japanese expert on quality improvement, they comprise a body of techniques for evaluating quality and how to improve it. He pioneered the concept that quality improvements should be measured in terms of cost savings (loss function), arguing that all quality improvements are cost savings.

Tampering In the world of quality, this is an action initiated to compensate for some variation within the control limits of a process. Experimentation has shown that tampering does increase the variability in performance of a process or stable system.

Task A specific action done to complete a task; it is always a component of a process.

Team Much as in sports, this is a group of employees who work together to achieve a common objective. They are typically working on a process or within a department and rely heavily on personal skills applied in a collaborative environment that fosters teamwork and concensus decision-making practices.

Team building Activities for creating, developing, and maintaining a team of individuals who work on a common goal or process. Activities include definition of roles, obligations, and objectives of a team; improvement of relations among team members; enhancing techniques in problem solving, decision making, planning, and resource utilization; reduction of conflict and tension among members; and enhancing the organizational environment in which the team works. Team building is a major activity in a quality-driven organization.

Teamwork The shared responsibility and actions for the completion of any task or process with a common objective by a group of individuals working together.

Timeliness More than just the completion of services or delivery of goods when expected, it is the notion that completion is determined by customer expectations.

Tool In the world of quality, a tool is usually a technique (such as Pareto charts), a discipline (such as SPC), or actually a physical tool (such as software or a device to measure performance of a machine).

Tolerance design A stage in any design process that defines the tolerances of variation in performance that will be acceptable in a final product or service. At this critical phase, where costs of end products can be increased dramatically, designers focus on producing robust designs and products in earlier parameter design phases to contain possible expenses.

Top-down process diagram A kind of chart that defines the major and minor steps in a process.

Top-level process diagram A kind of diagram that displays a complete process.

Top-management commitment The commitment and personal involvement of senior management in the implementation of quality programs. Their roles can include personal participation in quality committees; creation of quality processes, goals, measures, and policies; providing training on quality; and allocation of appropriate resources. Other activities include participation in process teams, inspection of quality progress, rewarding those who have contributed to quality improvements and who are "champions" of quality.

Total More than just another word for complete or everything, it describes the absolute commitment or involvement of everything or everyone in a continuous improvement program.

Total customer service A widely used term, it encompasses all the acts, features, and data that enhance a customer's ability to enjoy the potential capabilities and benefits of a service or product.

Total integrated logistics The integration of all logistics concerning inputs into an enterprise, even all processes within the organization, and the outputs of the enterprise. The purpose of looking at all the inflows and outflows of an organization is to ensure a comprehensive customer support strategy that is optimized for cost and quality.

Total product concept An approach to offer insight into the wide range of possibilities for a product. Such a concept includes a generic product, the anticipated product, an augmented product, and a potential product.

Total production maintenance Refers to a system for all of an organization's maintenance activities.

Total quality control (TQC) Originally conceived by quality guru Armand V. Feigenbaum, it is a system used to integrate quality development, maintenance, and improvement of all parts of an organization so that the manufacture of goods and the execution of services are done most economically while providing excellent customer service.

Total Quality Management (TQM) A body of management and process practices designed to improve the performance of any organization to satisfy customers. TQM calls for the integration of quality activities of organizations and people, applying scientific and disciplined approaches to continuous improvement while fostering customer or market-driven values, and blending the most economical performance while satisfying totally customer needs. It seeks to impose standards, achieve efficiencies, define roles of all individuals within a process and organization, specify controls, reduce errors and defects, apply statistical process control, and employ teams effectively.

Total Quality Management action planning The detailed plan for implementing and managing TQM within an organization.

Total Quality Management philosophy That body of beliefs and general concepts that embraces practices of continuously improving organizations.

Total Quality Management principles The key fundamental rules and practices of TQM necessary to achieve effective implementation of continuous improvement.

Total Quality Management process The process by which all inputs into an organization are transformed into products and services that meet the requirements of internal and external customers; generating a quality output.

Total Quality Management umbrella The integration of all the basic management tools and techniques, and existing efforts at improvement, to create a coordinated, disciplined approach to continuous improvement throughout an organization.

Trainers Individuals who teach TQM principles within an enterprise. Often they are also quality coaches and mentors.

Transactional analysis A series of activities to identify how people and organizations are performing; in other words, what psychological or political games people are playing. The intent is to change people's performance and attitudes so that they may become more effective on their jobs .while facilitating cultural transformation in an organization.

Trend control chart A type of control chart that illustrates the deviation of a subgroup average (X-bar) from some expected trend in a process level. The purpose of such a chart is to assess the stability of a process.

Type I error An incorrect decision to reject such items as a statistical hypothesis or a lot of goods when they were acceptable.

Type II error Another type of incorrect decision to accept something, but in this case when it was unacceptable.

U chart A count per unit chart.

Upper control limit (UCL) The control limit for points above the central horizontal line on a control chart.

Upstream value chain The value chains within suppliers to an organization.

Value Considered the amount consumers will pay for a product or service.

Value-adding process Simply put, these are activities that convert an input into a customer-usable output.

Value chain A phrase made famous by Michael Porter, it consists of all the activities performed by an organization that have effects on costs of products or services. Value chain models are used to divide all processes or activities into discrete components that can be identified so as to establish their individual costs (value). Primary value activities might include, for instance, sales or manufacture. Support activities could include personnel management.

Value engineering This kind of organized effort has as its purpose to analyze functions of a system, equipment, services, supplies, and facilities to achieve critical functions at the lowest life cycle cost consistent with defined criteria for performance, reliability, maintainability, manufacturability, quality and safety, and all consistent with requirements of the market (customers).

Value system The total of all actions within all value chains encompassing an organization's suppliers, channels of distribution, and customers.

Variable A variable is a piece of data that has a value when it is within a range exhibiting a specific frequency or pattern. Discrete variables are data limited in value to quantities, such as the number of invoices generated by a billing process, and always relate to attribute data. Continuous variables are measured to a degree of accuracy, such as width of a component, and always relate to variables data. This measurable information is sometimes also called variable data.

Variance Nonconformance to expectations or specifications. In the world of statistics, variance is the square of the standard deviation. But in quality, it is simply how far off the mark something is in meeting customer expectations.

Variation Always a change in data, characteristic, or function caused by one of four possible factors: special causes, common causes, tampering, or structural variations.

Victory-C TQM model A systematic model encompassing an entire organization, and consisting of all the elements necessary for victory (success). It is always focused on total costumer satisfaction.

Vision A concept of an ideal state that an organization would like to achieve at some point in the future (e.g., three to five years out). Vision-based strategic planning is then focused less on today's problems and more on what strategies are required to make the vision come true.

Vital few, useful many J. M. Juran coined this phrase to describe use of the Pareto concept in which most effects come from a few causes, that is, 80 percent of effects from 20 percent of possible causes. The 20 percent of possible causes are the "vital few," the other causes are the "useful many."

World-class This descriptive is often used with such expressions as world-class quality, world-class company, world-class process. It means the best in the world. In the case of world-class company, using the Malcolm Baldrige Criteria, it is a firm that achieves at least 876 points out of 1,000 in its quality appraisal.

World-class quality A standard of excellence that is the best in the world.

X-bar chart Another way of saying average chart.

Zero defects In the world of quality, it is an aspiration but also a way of explaining to employees the notion that everything should be done right the first time, that there should be no failures or defects in work outputs. Developed by Philip B. Crosby, it is the notion that by observing details and avoiding errors, people can avoid almost all errors. It promotes the concept that "close enough" is unacceptable.

1993 Malcolm Baldrige National Quality Award Winners

In 1993, there were two companies that won the Baldrige Award. In the small company category, the winner was the **Ames Rubber Corporation** of Hamburg, New Jersey. This company manufactures the rubber rollers and other components used in printers, copy machines, and other devices that require precision rubber products.

In the manufacturing category, the winner was the **Eastman Chemical Company**, a subsidiary of Eastman Kodak, located in Kingsport, Tennessee. This company manufactures and markets more than 400 chemicals, fibers, and plastics throughout the world.

In 1993, there was a total of 76 applicants for the Baldrige Award. Thirteen companies received site visits. In commenting on the fact that there were just two winners this year, compared to previous years with four to five winners, Baldrige officials noted that the bar is being set up higher and higher. The award recognizes especially outstanding efforts and results in an environment where the competition is much tougher than in the past. An especially important consideration in choosing the winning companies is their position as role models for others to emulate. Given the stiff competition and the judges' desire to select those companies that they view as the best role models, these two companies stood out above all other applicants in 1993.

The Real Value of the Baldrige Award

While winning the Baldrige is a visible and public payoff for companies actively implementing total quality management as a philosophy and mode of operating, this is only the frosting on the cake for those firms involved in the process. The real value of the Baldrige Award is its use as a set of guidelines for transforming a company. Thousands of organizations of all types use the Baldrige criteria to help them proceed down the road to a more realistic, customer-oriented, efficient, and effective management process. Further, the award helps publicize the importance of doing this, and the winners become benchmarks to help others in their quality journey. Finally, the Baldrige Award has fostered the majority of states to start quality award programs as well. The criteria for many of these awards mirror the Baldrige Award. (See the awards section of *The Quality Yearbook* for a review of these state programs.)

As Baldrige winners become benchmarks, we present the following overviews of 1993's winners to give you a sense of what the Baldrige committee determined were outstanding examples of companies that practice total quality management. In doing this we first reproduce the announcement from the National Institute of Standards and Technology citing their reasons for selecting each winner. We then include edited versions of the winning companies' descriptions of their approaches to quality. While we could write our own descriptions of these companies, we feel there is more value in allowing you to read what they say they are doing in their own words. This should help you start to see the similarities between your organization and these winning companies and perhaps how you can develop or forward your own program.

1993 Baldrige Award Winner, Small Business Category: Ames Rubber Corporation

The following is the press release from the National Institute of Standards and Technology announcing that Ames Rubber Corporation had won a Baldrige Award for 1993.

Based in Hamburg, New Jersey, Ames Rubber Corporation's primary products are rubber rollers used in office machines such as copiers, printers, and typewriters to feed paper, transfer toner, and fuse toner to paper. The company is the largest manufacturer in the world of rollers for mid- and large-sized copiers. The company also produces highly specialized parts to protect the transaxle of front-wheel-drive vehicles. Founded in 1949, Ames Rubber Corporation employs 445 "Teammates" at four New Jersey sites.

The following briefly summarizes their quality improvement efforts:

- Every Teammate at Ames is a member of at least one "Involvement Group" dedicated to quality improvement. The company currently has 40 of these groups.
- The percentage of defective parts reaching customers is among the lowest in the industry. For Ames' largest customer, the defect rate has been reduced since 1989 from over 30,000 parts per million to 11.
- Productivity, as measured by sales per employee, increased by 48 percent from 1989 to 1992.
- Ames is the "benchmark" producer of fuser rollers for the very highest speed copiers.
- Over the past five years, Teammate ideas have saved the company and its customers more than $3 million and will average over $2,700 per Teammate in 1993.
- Ames product warranties are among the best in the industry and include a comprehensive warranty for prototypes, which refunds development costs if specifications are not achieved.

- Ames has developed a consolidated supplier base by selecting suppliers who share the company's quality values and are responsive to its established "Continuous Improvement" goals. Down from 42 key suppliers in 1989, Ames now relies on 19 suppliers whose quality performance is about 99 percent.

*   *   *

On their selection as a 1993 winner, the managers of Ames Rubber Corporation issued a background report that describes the total quality process at their company. In the spirit of the Baldrige award as one way of recognizing companies that can serve as role models, we present here an edited version of that background report.

History

Ames Rubber Corporation was founded in 1949 to manufacture high quality elastomeric parts primarily for the office machine industry. The company grew and produced excellent profits for more than three decades.

In the mid-1980s, the company found itself facing fundamental changes in the international marketplace. These included more competition and demand from their customers for higher quality. Ames adopted a total quality management philosophy as a way to respond to this customer demand and to achieve its goals for productivity and profitability. It became a "Total Quality" company. Total quality to Ames meant much more than making defect-free products to exact specifications. The company understood that making a part exactly the right size is important, but it is only a small part of what managers called their *Total Quality* process.

For Ames, Total Quality refers to an ongoing team effort involving everyone in building a culture that encourages responsibility with authority, communication, creativity, and innovation. The company sought to create an environment where everyone minimizes waste and rework, where measurement is a way of life, and where new ideas are encouraged and tested. Management wanted a company that rewards accomplishments, where morale is high, turnover is low, and customers seek out its goods and services.

As a mature manufacturing company, where procedures, policies, and personal attitudes were well established, the principles of Total Quality appeared revolutionary. The successful implementation has required the full support and leadership of the company's top executives.

The Quality Revolution Starts at the Top

Ames managers knew that management behavior is the single most important factor in communicating the Total Quality process. The company's senior executives had to make an uncompromising commitment to implement Total Quality and personally involve themselves in the effort. The process began in 1987 when President Joel Marvil and six members of the Executive Committee met and began their Total Quality strategy development. As a Xerox supplier, they used Xerox Corporation as their role model.

The formulation of a Vision Statement was an important early step. Ames' Vision of the Future still serves as a guide for action today. It calls for " . . . a customer and people-centered culture which encourages participation, creativity, openness, balanced risk-taking, recognition, and accomplishment of specific objectives as a way of life."

After adopting Total Quality as the basis for defining and implementing company strategy, top management faced the major task of introducing the Total Quality process to the rest of the people in the organization. They did this with a series of small group presentations. Each member of the Executive Committee took personal responsibility for explaining one key element of the Total Quality process as part of a two-hour presentation. They scheduled meetings with groups of 50 people, and in one week they presented the program to the entire company.

Training

They understood the importance of training, and their goal was for an active, participatory learning experience. This involves classrooms and scheduled training sessions during which they introduced Total Quality concepts and basic, step-by-step procedures that will allow anyone to analyze a problem and find a solution. The Quality Improvement process is a nine-step path to improving a process or procedure. The Problem Solving Process is a six-step plan that can be used to tackle any specific problem. They also provide classroom training in special manufacturing-related quality concepts, communications skills, and analytic tools that Teammates can use in their daily assignments.

Every new Teammate participates in 24 hours of Total Quality training after their first 90 days with the company. This training ensures that everyone understands the same concepts and quality improvement procedures. They see it as an essential step in the process.

Top management knew that the corporate hierarchy can be one of the biggest obstacles to change and innovation in a mature company. As part of their commitment to becoming a Total Quality company, they created a new corporate structure. One of the key concepts of Total Quality for Ames was to relinquish authority and decision-making to functional levels. The Executive Committee identified a group of their best managers and assigned them responsibility for reorganizing the company around functional processes. They asked those managers to use the Quality Improvement Process and other skills they had learned to create the plan.

This group of managers represented some of the best and brightest people in the company, though in some ways in the past they had been rivals. The Total Quality process forced them to work together to reach consensus. The members of the group created the reorganization and made it work, in part because they authored it. They had a major stake in its success and it gives them an opportunity to show the Executive Committee that they can do it.

Besides the Vision Statement and Total Quality training, three other examples of important ways they improved communication are:

- **Interactive Skills Training**. They provide direct training in communication skills. Consensus building, an essential part of their Total Quality process, is easier if everyone understands the "rules" for participating in a discussion. The elements of any conversation can be divided into three categories — Initiating, Clarifying, and Reacting. The training focuses on verbal behaviors used by effective groups in their day-to-day meetings and discussions.

- **"Dear Teammate" Letters**. Every quarter the president sends a letter to all Ames Teammates at their homes, telling them how their company is doing. He tells them about plans for the future, what he thinks about the current economy, about new contracts and new customers. Instead of hearing about developments "through the grapevine," they get the news from "the boss."

- **MBWA**. They don't underestimate the value of Management by Walking Around (MBWA). Seeing top management reminds Teammates that they are committed to the Total Quality process, and that they're ready to talk and to listen. To help remind their top executives of the need to be available, the company mandates that they keep a record of their visits to various plants and departments on a Management Visibility Matrix. This is a simple form that allows these executives to chart their travels and report their activity back to the president.

Teamwork

The company does not have employees, they have Teammates, as has been noted. The company knows that words don't guarantee teamwork. They see Total Quality training and communication skills training as key steps to establishing effective communications, the foundation for teamwork.

In addition, every Ames Teammate is assigned to an Involvement Group. These groups were created to replace formal departmental meetings. Involvement Group meetings are designed to solicit opinions and ideas from everyone, to be open and non-threatening, and to be a place where information is exchanged in an informal give-and-take session.

They define teamwork as a synthesis of four elements: discipline, roles, goals, and relationships. *Discipline* refers to their quality improvement procedures that they teach in their quality training sessions. They use these procedures in all their team efforts. *Roles* are decided on interests and involvement, not job titles or seniority. Teammates rotate roles at team meetings. Everyone who wants to be the leader gets an opportunity to lead. *Goals* spring from their Mission Statement, but they're also expressed in clear and specific objectives for daily activities, too. For example, they require written goals for every meeting. Finally, when they understand the process, the roles, and the goals, this creates the foundation on which to build successful relationships, where members of the teams subordinate their personal glory to the good of the group.

Consensus

Communication is the foundation, and teamwork is the essential condition required for consensus decision-making. The decision that Ames would become a Total Quality company was by consensus of the Executive Committee. To implement Total Quality throughout the company, they decided it was best to have as many people participate as possible in the decision-making process. They're more likely to support decisions that way.

The old authoritarian way of making decisions lingers, sometimes out of necessity, but more often it's a matter of breaking old habits. To help their Teammates break this habit, the company provides training for supervisors to help them enhance their skills in building teams and consensus decisions. Equally important, they measure Teammates' attitudes and feelings in response to their supervisors.

Like many companies, they conduct assessments in which Teammates evaluate their supervisors anonymously. Supervisors then compare the results with their own self-evaluations. This provides them with invaluable feedback. Additionally, they conduct an annual Cultural Changes Survey. In this survey, Teammates rank the company's "Total Quality attitude" in areas such as management style, teamwork, and decision-making. To some degree, the scores represent a company-wide consensus on how they are doing in these areas. It's a measure of whether they're practicing what they're preaching.

Getting Quality via SPC, PCs, and Fail-Safing

The company realizes that it is impossible to reduce defects if you don't count them and that you have to have a way of measuring progress. Their actions in the quality area include implementation of extensive, computer-based statistical process control. They can generate real-time statistics on the processes they monitor. This gives their operators real-time access to the information they need to stop a process if the data warrants this action.

When they talk about "the customer," they're not talking about the end-user of their product. They're referring to the *next person* in the production process. The use of this *internal customer* concept is a key element in reducing the number of defects, simply by not producing them. If the computerized readouts show the manufacturing process is moving off course, operators stop the machine and adjust it, rather than waiting for an inspector somewhere down the line to catch the problem.

Computers and sophisticated analytic programs represent the high-tech end of the quality improvement spectrum. Fail-safing is the other extreme. They're training Teammates to be innovative and look for simple, no-cost or low-cost ways to improve quality. Fail-safing encourages their people to use human ingenuity to develop simple devices to prevent defects from occurring. These types of improvements can range from something as simple as attaching a Post-it note to a form (to be sure copier adjustments are set correctly before reprinting) to the redesign of a part to make it impossible to install it incorrectly.

Their goal, in the framework of a Total Quality environment, is to put these quality enhancement tools in the hands of all our Teammates so they can use them to help satisfy customers.

Recognition and Rewards

Recognition is an important part of their Total Quality process. They believe in it, encourage it, and put an $80,000 budget behind it. Their rewards range from "Attaboys"—printed certificates posted all around Ames to thank Teammates for satisfying internal customers—to the President's Award, an annual $5,000 prize. The Recognition Plan that spells out criteria for various awards is a 70-page document written by Teammates. To encourage supervisors to look for successful performance, they ask them to fill out a Manager's Recognition Report that summarizes their recognition activities.

Empowerment and Innovation

Ultimately, the innovation and creativity of any company is the sum of the contributions of the individuals who run it. That's everyone. Empowerment is a popular term used for giving employees the authority, the enthusiasm, and the tools to do their jobs better. Total Quality, as a company philosophy, requires commitment at the top to a management style that empowers people. This gives everyone real power to make a difference.

The Total Quality process assumes that everything is changing. The principle of continuous improvement concentrates on managing the dynamics of change. This involves teaching and implementing a decision-making process that allows all participants to feel they've played a role in determining the course of action so they'll be committed to its successful outcome. This emphasizes skill development in listening and consensus building. It encourages risk-taking and driving out fear.

Total quality at Ames Rubber Corporation is a process—not a goal in itself. It's a process that can reinvigorate a mature company, stimulate invention, innovation, and creativity, and make it a world-class competitor.

* * *

For more information on the Ames Rubber Corporation and their Total Quality program, contact Charles L. Roberts, Vice President, Total Quality, Ames Rubber Corporation, Ames Boulevard, Hamburg, NJ 07419, Phone: (201) 209-3200, Fax: (201) 827-8893.

1993 Baldrige Award Winner, Manufacturing Category: Eastman Chemical Company

The following is the press release from the National Institute of Standards and Technology announcing that Eastman Chemical Company had won a Baldrige award for 1993.

Founded in 1920, Eastman Chemical Company is a $4 billion company that manufactures and markets over 400 chemicals, fibers, and plastics for 7,000 customers around the world. A division of Eastman Kodak Company, Eastman ranks as the 10th largest chemical company in sales in the United States and 34th in the world. Employing 17,750, the company operates manufacturing plants at its headquarters in Kingsport, Tennessee, as well as in Arkansas, New York, South Carolina, Texas, Canada, and the United Kingdom.

The following briefly summarizes their quality improvement efforts:

- Eastman is well accepted by its surrounding communities and has a strong environmental record. Safety serves as a driving force. The company earned inclusion in OSHA's voluntary Protection Program.
- Eastman averaged 22 percent of sales from new products commercialized within the last five years, compared to an average of 11 percent for 13 leading chemical companies, twice the average in a recent study.
- Eastman has adopted a no-fault return policy on its plastic products that states a customer may return any product for any reason. This policy is believed to be the only one of its kind in the chemical industry.
- Over the past four years, over 70 percent of Eastman's worldwide customers rated Eastman their number one supplier. For the last seven years, Eastman has been rated outstanding in five important customer factors—product quality, product uniformity, supplier integrity, correct delivery, and reliability. Shipping reliability consistently has been near 100 percent for the last four years.
- Eastman's new product development practices are ranked second among a group of 13 leading chemical companies.
- Eastman uses multiple approaches to drive continuous process improvement through an "interlocking team" structure that involves virtually every employee in the teaming and quality improvement process.
- Data use is deployed widely with virtually all employees using data to track their individual and/or their team's performance.

- Eastman has a fully integrated planning process that systematically deploys the key business priorities to all employees and all work groups throughout Eastman's innovative four-dimensional organizational structure.

* * *

As with the Ames Rubber Corporation, Eastman Chemical Company also issued a report describing their "quality journey." Again, in the spirit of the Baldrige Award that requires that winners share their techniques and serve as role models, we present here Eastman's story, as reported by them after selection for the 1993 award.

In its over 70 year history, Eastman Chemical Company has always had a dedication to supplying its customers with high quality products and services. In the 1970s, new competition came into its markets, and Eastman began to lose market share for one of its major product lines. This led executives to reexamine the company's approach to delivering value to its customers and continually improving its offerings. The company updated its technology and processing equipment and implemented new systems and processes to assure the quality of its products. The success of these efforts made a substantial impact on Eastman's management philosophy, and the company made continual improvement a part of every employee's job.

Quality in Manufacturing

In 1980, Eastman set a goal to be *First in Quality*. Manufacturing employees began working much more closely with marketing employees to understand customer needs. The company established statistical process control systems to assure that product specifications met customer needs. There were process improvement breakthroughs which resulted in dramatic quality improvements.

All these steps to improve the quality of the company's major product lines yielded solid results. Managers saw complaints decrease to less than one-tenth their original levels in the product line. At the same time, they substantially reduced manufacturing costs while increasing productivity and market share.

These results made believers of management and led the company to expand its quality efforts throughout the company. In 1982, a *Customer Emphasis Program* brought about a company-wide awareness of customers—both internal and external. Employees identified the customers of their products or services and developed plans to better serve these customers.

Establishing a Quality Policy

In 1983, to bring a sharper focus to Eastman's quality efforts, management developed the company's first stated *Quality Policy*. This policy communicated the vision of quality excellence and formally acknowledged that quality was the company's top priority. An important part of the Quality Policy was the *Quality Goal*: To be the leader in quality and value of products and services.

To implement this policy, the company began training its employees in quality management tools and techniques in the mid-1980s. They trained employees in statistical process control, problem-solving skills, and performance management. This training emphasized using quality tools to improve processes to assure product quality. Performance management taught employees and management the value of reinforcement.

As the quality training progressed, Eastman formed teams to address specific areas where improvements were needed. There were two different kinds of teams: Natural Unit Teams, which included employees in a common work area, and Quality Improvement Teams, which included employees from different work groups to address specific problems. The formation of these teams allowed increasing numbers of employees to participate directly in the company's quality improvement efforts.

A major shift in policy dealing with how Eastman worked with customers occurred in 1984. Prior to this time, Eastman rarely invited customers into the processing areas. However, in 1984, the company began inviting customers to visit its plants and to be a part of its improvement efforts. This change in policy has resulted in tremendous progress toward high-quality products and services. Today, customers visiting Eastman's plants contribute toward process improvements that help them use Eastman's products better in their own processes.

Corporate Culture and Quality

Recognizing the strong linkage between corporate culture and quality excellence, Eastman initiated an in-depth study of the company's principles, values, beliefs, and norms. The goal of this study was to emphasize the people elements of the Quality Policy. From this study, the company developed a document called *The Eastman Way*, which describes how the company would conduct its business and how it wants employees to view the company. This document deals with values such as honesty, integrity, trust, creativity, innovation, and teamwork. The Eastman Way enables employees to address important issues and removes barriers to reaching quality excellence in all areas of the company's life. The Eastman Way has become a companion document to the Quality Policy.

At this point in the company's quality journey, it had directed most of its efforts toward manufacturing. Then the company began to expand beyond manufacturing and developed what it called the *Quality Management Process*, a company-wide process for facilitating improvement in all its activities. All employees, from operators to senior management, use this process to design, implement, and continually improve their processes. The Quality Management Process begins and ends with a focus on customers.

In 1986, Eastman's senior management used the Quality Management Process to define the company's Mission and Vision and to establish what they call Key Result Areas for performance and for measuring how well they are doing. By personally using the Quality Management Process, senior management signaled to all employees their commitment to the concepts and tools of quality. At the same time, senior management also identified three areas that every employee was to work on to improve overall company performance. These *Major Improvement Opportunities* provide the company with unified focus of effort.

In 1987, the company committed to a major change in the workplace environment. Empowerment at Eastman means that employees have the knowledge, skills, and authority to decide and act, and take responsibility for their actions. Eastman's empowerment fosters a commitment to and ownership of business success.

In the late 1980s, the company recognized standardization as a key step in the improvement process and added ISO 9000 registration to its quality efforts. At this same time, the company updated its Quality Policy to reflect its expanded understanding of quality, including even stronger emphasis on customer and supplier relationships.

Continually Improving

In 1988, Eastman began using the Baldrige Award criteria for annual internal assessments. These assessments have provided further guidance to the company in its quality improvement efforts and have reinforced employees' accomplishments.

Eastman introduced its *Pay for Applied Skills and Knowledge* effort to recognize the increasing value of employees' skills and knowledge to the company. This effort, a result of Eastman's emphasis on quality processes, is an integral part of the company's empowered work system. The company also abandoned its traditional performance appraisal system and instituted an *Employee Development System* in its place. This system encourages each employee to achieve his or her full potential through feedback and coaching by supervisors. It focuses on employee strengths and opportunities for development and gives each employee primary responsibility for his or her development.

In 1991, the company established its *Strategic Intent* with a vision to be the world's preferred chemical company. The company's Quality Policy and The Eastman Way drive the vision and the company's updated mission to create superior value for customers.

At the same time, to give itself a sharper customer and market focus, the company reorganized itself into 12 market-focused business units. This was a more effective structure than the company's previous product-oriented structure. Finally in 1991, the company also initiated a regularly scheduled *Quality Management Forum* to share the company's quality experiences with customers, suppliers, and other publics. The "Quality First" Supplier Relations Program is the vehicle the company uses to build and strengthen long-term relationships with suppliers.

In the spirit of continual improvement, in 1992 the company once again reviewed its Quality Policy, The Eastman Way, and Strategic Intent documents. Management modified these three statements to reflect increased understanding of quality, corporate culture, and organizational change. They also added a fourth foundation document, the *Responsible Care Policy*, to demonstrate Eastman's commitment to managing its operations according to the highest environmental standards.

All these efforts have led to the company applying for and receiving the 1993 Baldrige Award as recognition of the success of their efforts. Through the years, Eastman has increasingly understood that quality is an ongoing journey. Its quest for excellence grows stronger with each milestone achieved. It has dedicated itself to creating superior value for all stakeholders—customers, employees, investors, suppliers, and the public. And it is committed to be the world's preferred chemical company.

*   *   *

For more information on Eastman Chemical Company's quality programs, you can contact Nancy Ledford, Eastman Chemical Company, Stone East Building, Kingsport, TN 37662, Phone: (615) 229-5264, Fax: (615) 229-1525.

1994 Malcolm Baldrige National Quality Award Criteria

This section provides you with a summary of the 1994 Baldrige Award criteria, including changes from the 1993 criteria, with points given in each category. You can receive a complete copy of the criteria and the 1994 Application Forms and Instructions (criteria and application are two separate documents) by writing to:

Malcolm Baldrige National Quality Award
National Institute of Standards and Technology
Route 270 and Quince Orchard Road
Administration Building, Room A537
Gaithersburg, MD 20899-0001
Phone: (301) 975-2036
Fax: (301) 948-3716

Description of the 1994 Award Criteria

Award Criteria Purposes

The Malcolm Baldrige National Quality Award Criteria are the basis for making Awards and for giving feedback to applicants. In addition, the Criteria have three important roles in strengthening U.S. competitiveness:

- to help raise quality performance practices and expectations;
- to facilitate communication and sharing among and within organizations of all types based upon a common understanding of key quality and operational performance requirements; and
- to serve as a working tool for planning, training, assessment, and other uses.

Award Criteria Goals

The Criteria are designed to help companies enhance their competitiveness through focus on dual, results-oriented goals:

- delivery of ever-improving value to customers, resulting in improved marketplace performance; and
- improvement of overall company operational performance.

Core Values and Concepts

The Award Criteria are built upon a set of core values and concepts. These values and concepts are the foundation for integrating the overall customer and company operational performance requirements.

These core values and concepts are:

Customer-Driven Quality

Quality is judged by customers. All product and service characteristics that contribute value to the customer and lead to customer satisfaction and preference must be the focus of a company's management system. Value, satisfaction, and preference may be influenced by many factors throughout the customer's overall purchase, ownership, and service experiences. These factors include the company's relationship with customers that helps build trust, confidence, and loyalty. This concept of quality includes not only the product and service characteristics that meet basic customer requirements, but it also includes those characteristics that enhance them and differentiate them from competing offerings. Such enhancement and differentiation may be based upon new offerings, combinations of product and service offerings, rapid response, or special relationships.

Customer-driven quality is thus a strategic concept. It is directed toward customer retention and market share gain. It demands constant sensitivity to emerging customer and market requirements, and measurement of the factors that drive customer satisfaction and retention. It also demands awareness of developments in technology and of competitors' offerings, and rapid and flexible response to customer and market requirements.

Success requires more than defect and error reduction, merely meeting specifications, and reducing complaints. Nevertheless, defect and error reduction and elimination of causes of dissatisfaction contribute significantly to the customers' view of quality and are thus also important parts of customer-driven quality. In addition, the company's success in recovering from defects and errors ("making things right for the customer") is crucial to building customer relationships and to customer retention.

A company's customer-driven focus needs to address all stakeholders— customers, employees, suppliers, stockholders, the public, and the community.

Leadership

A company's senior leaders must create a customer orientation, clear and visible quality values, and high expectations. Reinforcement of the values and expectations requires substantial personal commitment and involvement. The leaders' basic values and commitment need to include areas of public responsibility and corporate citizenship. The leaders must take part in the creation of strategies, systems, and methods for achieving excellence. The systems and methods need to guide all activities and decisions of the company. The senior leaders must commit to the growth and development of the entire work force and should encourage participation and creativity by all employees. Through their regular personal involvement in visible activities, such as planning, communications, review of company performance, and recognizing employees for quality achievement, the senior leaders serve as role models, reinforcing the values and encouraging leadership in all levels of management.

Continuous Improvement

Achieving the highest levels of quality and competitiveness requires a well-defined and well-executed approach to continuous improvement. The term "continuous improvement" refers to both incremental and "breakthrough" improvement. The approach to improvement needs to be "embedded" in the way the company functions. Embedded means that: (1) improvement is part of the daily work of all work units; (2) improvement processes seek to eliminate problems at their source; and (3) improvement is driven by opportunities to do better, as well as by problems that must be corrected. Opportunities for improvement have four major sources: employee ideas; R&D; customer input; and benchmarking or other comparative information on processes and performance.

Improvements may be of several types: (1) enhancing value to customers through new and improved products and services; (2) reducing errors, defects, and waste; (3) improving responsiveness and cycle time performance; (4) improving productivity and effectiveness in the use of all resources; and (5) improving the company's performance and leadership position in fulfilling its public responsibilities and serving as a role model in corporate citizenship. Thus improvement is driven not only by the objective to provide better product and service quality, but also by the need to be responsive and efficient—both conferring additional marketplace advantages. To meet all of these objectives, the process of continuous improvement must contain regular cycles of planning, execution, and evaluation. This requires a basis—preferably a quantitative basis—for assessing progress, and for deriving information for future cycles of improvement. Such information should provide direct links between desired performance and internal operations.

Employee Participation and Development

A company's success in improving performance depends increasingly on the skills and motivation of its work force. Employee success depends increasingly on having meaningful opportunities to learn and to practice new skills. Companies need to invest in the development of the work force through education, training, and creating opportunities for continuing growth. Such opportunities might include classroom and on-the-job training, job rotation, and pay for demonstrated skills. Structured on-the-job training offers a cost effective way to train and to better link training to work processes. Increasingly, training, development, and work organizations need to be tailored to a more diverse work force and to more flexible, high performance work environments.

Major challenges in the area of work force development include: (1) integration of human resource management—selection, performance, recognition, training, and career advancement, and; (2) aligning human resource management with business plans and strategic change processes. Addressing these challenges requires acquisition and use of employee-related data on skills, satisfaction, motivation, safety and well-being. Such data need to be tied to indicators of company or unit performance, such as customer satisfaction, customer retention, and productivity. Through this approach, human resource management may be better integrated and aligned with business directions, using continuous improvement processes to refine integration and alignment.

Fast Response

Success in competitive markets increasingly demands ever-shorter cycles for new or improved product and service introduction. Also, faster and more flexible response to customers is now a more critical requirement. Major improvement in response time often requires simplification of work organizations and work processes. To accomplish such improvement, the time performance of work processes should be measured. There are other important benefits derived from this focus: response time improvements often drive simultaneous improvements in organization, quality, and productivity. Hence it is beneficial to consider response time, quality, and productivity objectives together.

Design Quality and Prevention

Business management should place strong emphasis on design quality—problem and waste prevention achieved through building quality into products and services and into production processes. In general, costs of preventing problems at the design stage are much lower than costs of correcting problems which occur "downstream." Design quality includes the creation of fault-tolerant (robust) or error resistant processes and products.

A major issue in the competitive environment is the design-to-introduction ("product generation") cycle time. Meeting the demands of ever-more rapidly changing markets requires that companies carry out stage-to-stage coordination and integration ("concurrent engineering") of functions and activities from basic research to commercialization.

From the point of view of public responsibility, the design stage involves decisions regarding resource use and manufacturing processes. Such decisions affect process waste streams and the composition of municipal and industrial wastes. The growing demand by consumers and others for a cleaner environment means that companies will need to develop design strategies that place greater weight on environmental factors.

Consistent with the theme of design quality and prevention, continuous improvement and corrective action need to emphasize interventions "upstream"—at early stages in processes. This approach yields the maximum overall benefits of improvements and corrections. Such upstream intervention also needs to take into account the company's suppliers.

Long-Range Outlook

Achieving quality and market leadership requires a company to have a strong future orientation and a willingness to make long-term commitments to all stakeholders—customers, employees, suppliers, stockholders, the public, and the community. Planning needs to determine or anticipate many types of changes including those that may affect customers' expectations of products and services, technological developments, changing customer segments, evolving regulatory requirements and community/societal expectations, or thrusts by competitors. Plans, strategies, and resource allocations need to reflect these commitments and changes. A major part of the long-term commitment is development of employees and suppliers, fulfilling public responsibilities, and serving as a corporate citizenship role model.

Management by Fact

A modern business management system needs to be built upon a framework of measurement, data and analysis. Measurements must derive from the company's strategy and encompass all key processes and the outputs of those processes. Facts and data needed for quality improvement and quality assessment are of many types, including: customer, product and service performance, operations, market, competitive comparisons, supplier, employee-related, and cost and financial. Analysis refers to the process of extracting larger meaning from data to support evaluation and decision making at various levels within the company. Such analysis may entail using data to reveal information—such as trends, projections, and cause and effect—that might not be evident without analysis. Facts, data, and analysis support a variety of company purposes, such as planning, reviewing company performance, improving operations, and comparing company quality performance with competitors' or with "best practices" benchmarks.

A major consideration relating to use of data and analysis to improve performance involves the creation and use of performance measures or indicators. Performance measures or indicators are measurable characteristics of products, services, processes, and operations the company uses to track and improve performance. The measures or indicators should be selected to best represent the factors that lead to improved customer satisfaction and operational performance. A system of measures or indicators tied to customer and/ or company performance requirements represents a clear and objective basis for aligning all activities with the company's strategy and goals. Through the analysis of data from the tracking processes, the measures or indicators themselves may be evaluated and changed. For example, measures or indicators selected to track product and service quality may be judged by how well improvement relative to the quality measures or indicators correlates with improvement in customer satisfaction.

Partnership Development

Companies should seek to build internal and external partnerships to better accomplish their overall goals.

Internal partnerships might include those that promote labor-management cooperation, such as agreements with unions. Agreements might entail employee development, cross-training, or new work organizations, such as high performance work teams. Internal partnerships might also involve creating network relationships among company units to improve flexibility and responsiveness.

Examples of external partnerships include those with customers, suppliers, and education organizations. An increasingly important kind of external partnership is the strategic partnership or alliance. Such partnerships might offer a company entry into new markets or a basis for new products or services. A partnership might also permit the blending of a company's core competencies or leadership capabilities with complementary strengths and capabilities of partners, thereby enhancing overall capability, including speed and flexibility.

Partnerships should seek to develop longer-term objectives, thereby creating a basis for mutual investments. Partners should address the key requirements for success of the partnership, means of regular communication, approaches to evaluating progress, and means for adapting to changing conditions.

Corporate Responsibility and Citizenship

A company's management objectives should stress corporate responsibility and citizenship. Corporate responsibility refers to basic expectations of the company—business ethics and protection of public health, public safety, and the environment. Health, safety and environmental considerations need to take into account the company's operations as well as the life cycles of products and services. Companies need to address factors such as resource conservation and waste reduction at their source. Planning related to public health, safety, and environment should anticipate adverse impacts that may arise in facilities management, production, distribution, transportation, use and disposal of products. Plans should seek to prevent problems, to provide a forthright company response if problems occur, and to make available information needed to maintain public awareness, safety, trust, and confidence. Inclusion of public responsibility areas within a quality system means meeting all local, state, and federal laws and regulatory requirements. It also means treating these and related requirements as areas for continuous improvement "beyond mere compliance."

Corporate citizenship refers to leadership and support—within reasonable limits of a company's resources—of publicly important purposes, including the above-mentioned areas of corporate responsibility. Such purposes might include education, environmental excellence, resource conservation, community services, improving industry and business practices, and sharing of nonproprietary quality-related information. Leadership as a corporate citizen entails influencing other organizations, private and public, to partner for these purposes.

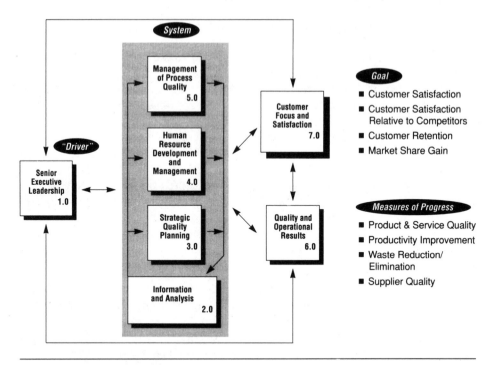

Baldrige Award Criteria Framework
Dynamic relationships.

Award Criteria Framework

The core values and concepts are embodied in seven categories, as follows:

    1.0 Leadership
    2.0 Information and Analysis
    3.0 Strategic Quality Planning
    4.0 Human Resource Development and Management
    5.0 Management of Process Quality
    6.0 Quality and Operational Results
    7.0 Customer Focus and Satisfaction

The framework connecting and integrating the categories is given in the figure above.

The framework has four basic elements:

Driver

Senior executive leadership creates the values, goals, and systems, and guides the sustained pursuit of customer value and company performance improvement.

Goal

The basic aim of the quality process is the delivery of ever-improving value to customers.

System
The System comprises the set of well-defined and well-designed processes for meeting the company's customer, quality, and performance requirements.

Measures of Progress
Measures of progress provide a results-oriented basis for channeling actions to delivering ever-improving customer value and company performance.

The seven Criteria Categories shown in the figure are subdivided into Examination Items and Areas to Address:

Examination Items
There are 28 Examination Items, each focusing on a major management requirement. Item titles and point values are given on page 13, and the Examination Item Format is shown on page 35 of the official criteria booklet.

Areas to Address
Examination Items consist of sets of Areas to Address (Areas). Information submitted by applicants is in response to specific requirements of these Areas.

Changes from the 1993 Award Criteria
The 1994 Award Criteria are built upon the seven-category framework used in previous years. However, a number of changes have been made in the Criteria booklet to strengthen key themes and to clarify requirements. Changes are:

- The number of Areas to Address has been reduced from 92 to 91. (The number of Examination Items remains at 28.)
- More Item Notes have been added to improve clarity.
- The Examination Response Guidelines have been rewritten and integrated with the Business Overview to help applicants and other users of the Criteria focus better on key business requirements. These Guidelines stress the importance of including information of the type that permits assessment and feedback.
- The Description of the Award Criteria has been revised and expanded. The major addition is: The Strategic Quality Planning Category—Integrating Quality and Operational Performance Requirements with Business Strategy.
- The description of the Scoring System has been expanded and clarified. Sections added are: Item Classification and Scoring Dimensions; and "Relevance and Importance" as a Scoring Factor. The latter section is intended to help applicants and other users of the Criteria to focus better on key business factors given in the Business Overview.

Key Themes Strengthened in the 1994 Criteria
The principal theme strengthened in 1994 is integration/linkage, with particular focus on the integration of quality and operational performance issues

with overall business planning. This integration is reinforced throughout the Criteria booklet, including the booklet's four major sections: Description of the 1994 Award Criteria; 1994 Award Examination Criteria; Scoring System and Guidelines; and the 1994 Examination Response Guidelines.

A summary of the relationships between 1994 and 1993 requirements, by Category, follows:

Leadership
- The basic requirements in this Category are unchanged. Notes have been added and/or clarified.

Information and Analysis
- The basic requirements in this Category are unchanged. Notes have been added and/or clarified. Descriptions of the items in this Category are given on pages 7–8 of the criteria booklet.

Strategic Quality Planning
- The basic requirements in this Category are unchanged. Notes have been added and/or clarified. The importance of the Category is stressed in the expanded Description of the 1994 Award Criteria. The intent is to emphasize the need to fully integrate quality and operational requirements with business planning. Descriptions of the Items in this Category are given on pages 6–7 of the criteria booklet.

Human Resource Development and Management
- The basic requirements in this Category are unchanged. Notes have been added and/or clarified. All changes respond to two concerns: (1) the need for greater alignment between business plans and human resource plans and practices; and (2) the need to improve integration of the individual elements of human resource practices—selection, performance, recognition, and training, for example.

Management of Process Quality
- The basic requirements in this Category are unchanged. Notes have been added and/or clarified.
- One Area has been eliminated from Item 5.2, leaving two Areas—one addressing process maintenance, and the other, process improvement. The design of the processes addressed in Item 5.2 is part of Item 5.1. Item 5.3 retains three Areas—those addressing process design, process maintenance, and process improvement.
- The title of Item 5.3 has been changed to Process Management: Business and Support Service Processes.
- The intent of Item 5.4 has been clarified to include other units of the applicant's company in its supplier relationships, if appropriate.

Quality and Operational Results

- The basic requirements in this Category are unchanged. Notes have been added and/or clarified. Descriptions of the Items in this Category are given on page 8.
- The title of Item 6.3 has been changed to Business and Support Service Results. This is parallel to the title change of the closely-related Item, 5.3.

Customer Focus and Satisfaction

- The basic requirements in this Category are unchanged. Notes have been added and/or clarified.
- Item 7.2 (Customer Relationship Management) has been focused better on the requirements of the customer relationship. The overlap with Item 2.3 (Analysis of Company-Level Data) has been clarified through the requirement that *complaint aggregation and analysis* be part of Item 2.3. The complaint management process, including complaint resolution, remains part of Item 7.2. Also in Item 7.2, 7.2f addresses customer-contact employee requirements for all the customer relationship issues addressed in 7.2a, b, c, d, and e.
- Items 7.5 and 7.6 now include the requirement for trends and *current levels* of satisfaction.

On the next page you will find the 1994 Award Examination Criteria— Item Listing with the points assigned to each item.

1994 Award Examination Criteria—Item Listing

1994 Examination Categories/Items	Point Values

1.0 Leadership — 95
1.1 Senior Executive Leadership ... 45
1.2 Management for Quality ... 25
1.3 Public Responsibility and Corporate Citizenship ... 25

2.0 Information and Analysis — 75
2.1 Scope and Management of Quality and Performance Data and Information ... 15
2.2 Competitive Comparisons and Benchmarking ... 20
2.3 Analysis and Uses of Company-Level Data ... 40

3.0 Strategic Quality Planning — 60
3.1 Strategic Quality and Company Performance Planning Process ... 35
3.2 Quality and Performance Plans ... 25

4.0 Human Resource Development and Management — 150
4.1 Human Resource Planning and Management ... 20
4.2 Employee Involvement ... 40
4.3 Employee Education and Training ... 40
4.4 Employee Performance and Recognition ... 25
4.5 Employee Well-Being and Satisfaction ... 25

5.0 Management of Process Quality — 140
5.1 Design and Introduction of Quality Products and Services ... 40
5.2 Process Management: Product and Service Production and Delivery Processes ... 35
5.3 Process Management: Business and Support Service Processes ... 30
5.4 Supplier Quality ... 20
5.5 Quality Assessment ... 15

6.0 Quality and Operational Results — 180
6.1 Product and Service Quality Results ... 70
6.2 Company Operational Results ... 50
6.3 Business and Support Service Results ... 25
6.4 Supplier Quality Results ... 35

7.0 Customer Focus and Satisfaction — 300
7.1 Customer Expectations: Current and Future ... 35
7.2 Customer Relationship Management ... 65
7.3 Commitment to Customers ... 15
7.4 Customer Satisfaction Determination ... 30
7.5 Customer Satisfaction Results ... 85
7.6 Customer Satisfaction Comparison ... 70

TOTAL POINTS   **1000**

Index

1994 *Quality Yearbook* Feedback Survey

Please cut this form out, fill it in, and mail it to us. We need your feedback. On a scale of 1 to 5 (1 = poor, 5 = outstanding), please respond to the following questions:

1. Overall, how would you assess the value of this book to you? ____ (Rate 1–5)

   Please describe how it has been valuable or not valuable to you. _____

   _____

   _____

   Why? _____

   _____

2. How would you assess the value of Part One to you? ____ (Rate 1–5)

   What did you find valuable about this part and why? _____

   _____

   _____

3. How would you assess the value of Part Two to you? ____ (Rate 1–5)

   What did you find valuable about this part and why? _____

   _____

   _____

4. How would you assess the value of Part Three to you? ____ (Rate 1–5)

   What did you find valuable about this part and why? _____

   _____

   _____

5. How would you assess the value of Part Four to you? ____ (Rate 1–5)

   What did you find valuable about this part and why? _____

   _____

   _____

6. What changes and improvements would you like to see in the 1995 yearbook?

   _____

   _____

1994 *Quality Yearbook* Feedback Survey

Please cut this form out, fill it in, and mail it to us. We need your feedback. On a scale of 1 to 5 (1 = poor, 5 = outstanding), please respond to the following questions:

1. Overall, how would you assess the value of this book to you? ____ (Rate 1–5)

   Please describe how it has been valuable or not valuable to you. _____

   _____

   _____

   Why? _____

   _____

2. How would you assess the value of Part One to you? ____ (Rate 1–5)

   What did you find valuable about this part and why? _____

   _____

   _____

3. How would you assess the value of Part Two to you? ____ (Rate 1–5)

   What did you find valuable about this part and why? _____

   _____

   _____

4. How would you assess the value of Part Three to you? ____ (Rate 1–5)

   What did you find valuable about this part and why? _____

   _____

   _____

5. How would you assess the value of Part Four to you? ____ (Rate 1–5)

   What did you find valuable about this part and why? _____

   _____

   _____

6. What changes and improvements would you like to see in the 1995 yearbook?

   _____

   _____

▲ Tape Here

▼ Fold on line

NO POSTAGE
NECESSARY
IF MAILED
IN THE
UNITED STATES

BUSINESS REPLY MAIL

FIRST CLASS MAIL   PERMIT NO. 9   BLUE RIDGE SUMMIT, PA

POSTAGE WILL BE PAID BY ADDRESSEE

McGraw-Hill, Inc.
Blue Ridge Summit, PA 17214-9984

▲ Fold on line

The Quality Yearbook Order Form

Use this form to order additional copies of *The Quality Yearbook*.
Please send me ____ copies of *The Quality Yearbook 1994 Edition* for
$69.95 each, plus $4.50 each for local tax, postage, and handling. I
understand I'll also receive *automatic priority updates* of future
editions as soon as they come off press, which I can return with no
obligation at all.

Name _____

Firm/Organization _____

Daytime Phone _____
(for verifying orders only)

Address _____

City _____ State _____ ZIP _____

You may also call 1-800-262-4729 24 hours a day to order, or fax this
order form to 1-717-794-5291.

(Cut this form out, fold on dotted lines, tape, and mail. The postage is paid.)

Method of payment

☐ Check enclosed (Payable to McGraw-Hill, please)

☐ Visa

☐ American Express

☐ Mastercard

Account No. _____

Expiration date _____

Signature _____

▲ Tape Here

▼ Fold on line

	NO POSTAGE
	NECESSARY
	IF MAILED
	IN THE
	UNITED STATES

BUSINESS REPLY MAIL

FIRST CLASS MAIL   PERMIT NO. 9   BLUE RIDGE SUMMIT, PA

POSTAGE WILL BE PAID BY ADDRESSEE

McGraw-Hill, Inc.
Blue Ridge Summit, PA 17214-9984

▲ Fold on line

The Quality Yearbook Order Form

Use this form to order additional copies of *The Quality Yearbook*.
Please send me ____ copies of *The Quality Yearbook 1994 Edition* for $69.95 each, plus $4.50 each for local tax, postage, and handling. I understand I'll also receive *automatic priority updates* of future editions as soon as they come off press, which I can return with no obligation at all.

Name _____

Firm/Organization _____

Daytime Phone _____
(for verifying orders only)

Address _____

City _____ State _____ ZIP _____

You may also call 1-800-262-4729 24 hours a day to order, or fax this order form to 1-717-794-5291.

(Cut this form out, fold on dotted lines, tape, and mail. The postage is paid.)

Method of payment

☐ Check enclosed (Payable to McGraw-Hill, please)

☐ Visa

☐ American Express

☐ Mastercard

Account No. _____

Expiration date _____

Signature _____